Independent
Careers

Independent Careers

Be Your Own Boss

Editors
**Klaus Boehm and
Jenny Lees-Spalding**

Assistant Editor
Maurice Geller

B L O O M S B U R Y

First published as
The Alternative Careers Book in 1988

Fifth edition published in 1992 by
Bloomsbury Publishing Limited
2 Soho Square, London W1V 5DE

Copyright © 1988, 1989, 1990, 1991, 1992
Klaus Boehm Publications Limited,
Klaus Boehm, Jenny Lees-Spalding

A CIP record for this book is available from
the British Library

ISBN 0 7475 1306 6

Typeset by Florencetype Ltd, Kewstoke, Avon
Printed by Clays Ltd., St Ives PLC

About the Editors

Klaus Boehm specialises in reference books and publishing sponsorship. He works with a number of publishing houses, developing a broad range of titles including the *Dictionary of the History of Science, British Archives. The Royal and Ancient Golfer's Handbook*, the *Macmillan and Silk Cut Nautical Almanac* and two with a clear European focus: *The European Community* ('the best single source on Europe') and *Business Europe*, published in 1992 by the Macmillan Press.

Jenny Lees-Spalding was academic registrar at the City Poly, dealing with the students on first degree courses and the related academic administration. She left to develop reference books with Klaus Boehm. They work together as Klaus Boehm Publications, often in association with Maurice Geller, the assistant editor of this edition.

Their titles include two annuals published by Bloomsbury and one with Pan Macmillan – *The Student Book* – which is widely acknowledged to be the leading consumer guide for would-be undergraduates. The two Bloomsbury reference books are *The Equitable Schools Book* ('the Wisden of the fee-paying circuit') and *Independent Careers*, which has a very simple message: do not let yourself be bureaucratised just because careers advice and information is stacked in favour of bureaucracy – become your own boss.

Klaus Boehm and Jenny Lees-Spalding are keenly interested in the European Community. Recently the European dimension to their work led to Klaus Boehm Publications being included as one of two commended publishers in the 1991 European Information Association's Awards for European Sources.

Contents

Foreword

Lifelines for 1993

To make any kind of sense, personal career strategies must take account of prevailing economic circumstances, and for those unlucky enough to graduate in 1991, when the sum total of government labour market policies amounted to whistling for a wind, those circumstances were dire.

The labour market has shown little interest in those who graduated in 1991 or 1992 – and will not now, not tomorrow, probably never, as Mr John Major forgot to say in his General Election campaign. Little can be expected to change in the short term: prospects for those graduating in 1993 look equally unpromising.

For very many aspiring bureaucrats intent on climbing a career ladder the message is simple: there ain't no bottom rung of the ladder for you this year.

For those planning to become their own boss – the message is rather different: stick to your strategy but review your tactics. Look for lifelines and lower your sights. Start work in your chosen job in any sort of position you can get – teaperson, receptionist, porter, gofer, but get in so that you begin to acquire job know-how. And mix and match, especially with lifelines.

In some jobs like the Bar, politics, land use, publishing, journalism and so on there is a long and honourable tradition of mixing and matching jobs. In the arts there has been an age-old necessity to mix the main job with lifelines – actors working in bars, composers earning their living through journalism, etc. In many others it's new for the nineties. So keep your eyes open for lifelines as you plan your career in 1993.

Lifelines are what you do to earn money while you are trying to do what you really want to do. In this edition we spotlight some of them, ranging from bookkeeper, tutor, typist and market research interviewer to motorcycle messenger, bartender, garden gnome maker and painter/decorator. There are of course many more, there's no magic in our selection – they're jobs where we know real people actually mix and match with their mainline jobs. To find them, see our **Independent Job Spotter**.

Klaus Boehm
Jenny Lees-Spalding
April 1992

How To Use This Book

This book is designed to help you work out your own personal strategy. We cannot do it for you. Once you have a strategy and a shortlist, follow it up with further reading and interrogate your careers adviser. Then, most important, find out about the jobs and their difficulties. Find people doing those jobs and *talk to them*.

We would like to have suggestions for information you would like to see in the next edition of this book. Please write to the editors at the publisher's address.

Part 1 – Jobs

This is divided into three sections so that you can get a strategy and start your short-listing from different starting points.

Independent Job Spotter A quick way of finding which jobs might interest you in the Jobs A–Z. Taking yourself as the starting point, you may know, for example, you want to work in the country, or work using your writing skills or your musical ability, or simply want to work in an area like tourism, wine and food or the law. If that's so you could start with the Job Spotter.

Independent Jobs A–Z More than 250 profiles of jobs where you can be your own boss, based on real people. Browse through and see what interests you. Beware of comparing one job profile with another. Sources and contributors were asked to provide insights, not measurable data; in particular the financial and training information is often personal and impressionistic. The book makes no attempt to cover jobs in employment – thus the piece on Solicitor does not cover work in the Crown Prosecution Service or local authorities; the profile on Publican does not cover pub managers, employed by the brewery.

Each profile starts with a panel summarising the key information:

Qualifications/Training This tells you if you need to do a course, leading to a certificate, to do the job.

Licence For some jobs (eg Publican) you are legally required to hold a licence; for others (eg Architect) it is a professional requirement; for a few (eg Actor), it is necessary to have a union card. This section is only concerned with personal licences; it is not concerned with any need to register your activities with any local or government department, seek planning permission, or get permission for the change of use of land or buildings.

Experience/Springboard For many jobs, you need to have worked in the business before becoming your own boss in order to gain experience or contacts or both. This section tells you whether this is required or recommended. Some training courses include some work experience, eg barristers must serve as a pupil before qualifying, and this is not included here. If the answer is 'no' it means you can (or must) go straight into the job as a freelance, self employed or as a professional partner.

Mid-career entry Some jobs are really only for starting when you are older (consultants, Psychoanalyst); others are almost exclusively young people's jobs; others are particularly suitable for mid-career job changes.

Entry costs How much you need to start. This always excludes the cost of your own home; also of living expenses. The costs may be lower than we've indicated if you have some of the start-up kit already, eg it need cost you nothing to become a jazz singer if you already have a telephone and a record player.

Income bracket Low means up to £12,000 per annum; medium is broadly £12,000–£30,000; and high, more than £30,000. The bracket given is the norm, eg actor is given as low because that is the case for the majority. But even as an actor, you can strike lucky and be a tax exile. Good luck!

Town/Country Where you usually need to locate the business.

Travel Whether you need to travel as part of the job.

Exit sale If the answer is 'yes', it means you may be able to sell the business for more money than you put in.

Work at home This means you can

work in your own home: you can in some cases – but it is hopeless in others. The answer is no if you only happen to live above the shop.

Mix and match Almost all jobs can be combined with others to a greater or lesser extent. The list given under each job is to give you ideas, not a blueprint for your life. You obviously can't do a job requiring travel with another where total accessibility is important; you can't run a shop with another job which requires 18-hour working days; you probably won't want to do more than one three-year training course. But there is still plenty of scope – and if you have a partner or you are large enough to have employees, the scope is greater still. The mix and match lists are of different sorts: jobs you can sensibly do at the same time, eg MP and novelist; jobs to keep you going while you start up a business or are between jobs (Actor); lines into which you can diversify when you are successful (Racehorse Owner, landlord etc).

Enquiries Where you can get more information about the job.

★★★ European Community Notes
These are our gleanings on the current position for British citizens wanting to work in other member states. The information is therefore job-specific.

Independent Job Search Index The key information on all the jobs in the book is here, in compact form so you can glance down eg the column on entry costs and see what jobs to look up with the fortune you have amassed or money you think you could con out of the bank. For explanations of the headings, see explanations of the 'At A Glance' box under **Independent Jobs A–Z** above.

Part 2 – How To Go About It A–Z
This gives some information you may consider before choosing which career best suits you, and on starting up in business (and any job when you work for yourself is a business, whether you are an accountant or actor).

Part 3 – Reference
Abbreviations This gives the meanings of some of the more common of the thousands of ghastly abbreviations you may meet.

Addresses Addresses of those organisations mentioned in the text in small capitals, eg EQUITY.

Bibliography This gives details of the books and trade mags given in the text in italics, eg *Farmers Weekly*.

Index Use it!

Part 1

Jobs

CONTENTS

Independent
Job Spotter

A quick way of finding jobs that might interest you.

Accommodation
Animals
Art
Books and Magazines
Business Services
Cars, Bikes and Driving
Children
Clothes
Construction
Cottage Industries
Country
Crafts
Design
Finance
Grooming
Health
House and Garden
Investments (Possible)

Land Use
Law
Lifelines
Marketing, Advertising,
   Sales and Promotion
Music
Outdoors
People
Performing
Photography and Film
Plants
Shops
Sport
Tourism
TV, Radio and Press
Wine and Food
Writing

Accommodation

How about looking up:
bed and breakfast; caravan park owner; holiday accommodation owner; hotelier; Italian property finder; landlord; property manager; publican; timeshare developer?

Animals

How about looking up:
beekeeper; farmer; farrier/blacksmith; greyhound trainer; kennel/cattery owner; oyster farmer; racehorse owner; riding school owner; salmon farmer; shepherd/shepherdess; snail farmer; taxidermist; trout farmer; vet; zoo keeper?

Art

How about looking up:
art historian/critic; artist; artist's agent; calligrapher; china restorer; contemporary art gallery owner; illustrator; picture agent; picture framer; picture researcher; print maker; sculptor; tattooist; textile designer?

Books and Magazines

How about looking up:
book designer; book packager; book publisher; bookseller; desk-top publisher; editorial photographer; graphic designer; illustrator; indexer; literary agent; magazine designer; magazine publisher; music publisher; newsletter publisher; novelist; picture agent; picture researcher; proofreader/copy editor; space sales agent; sub-editor; typesetter; UK correspondent (overseas media)?

Business Services

How about looking up:
accountant; actuary; advertising agent; book-keeper; caterer; cleaning contractor; company doctor; computer consultant; computer hardware engineer; computer software author; conference organiser; courier service; desk-top publisher; direct marketing consultant; employment agent; events organiser; graphic designer; graphologist; haulier; headhunter; hire shop owner; import/export broker; in-company trainer; insurance broker; interior designer; interpreter; list broker; man with a van; market research interviewer; marketing consultant; media trainer; motorcycle messenger; office cleaner; office services bureau; para-legal; patent agent; picture agent; printer; proofreader/copy editor; public relations consultant; sales agent; shipbroker; solicitor; space sales agent; telesales person; typesetter; typist; word processor?

Cars, Bikes and Driving

How about looking up:
courier service; driver (car hire); driving instructor; garage owner; haulier; man with a van; mini-cab driver; motorcycle messenger; motorcycle racer; taxi driver?

Children

How about looking up:
careers adviser; childminder; child/educational psychologist; dance teacher; English language school owner; English language teacher; guardian ad litem; music teacher; nanny/babysitting agent; prep school owner; puppeteer; social worker; swimming teacher; teacher; tutor?

Clothes

How about looking up:
costume designer; dress agent; fashion designer; fashion retailer; shoe designer/maker; tailor; wedding shop owner?

Construction

How about looking up:
architect; builder; carpenter; hire shop owner; house converter; Italian property finder; landscape designer; painter/decorator; property developer; surveyor; thatcher?

Cottage Industries

How about looking up:
antique dealer; antique furniture restorer; bed and breakfast; beekeeper; caterer; childminder; china restorer; desk-top publisher; English language teacher; fish curer and smoker; garden gnome maker; graphologist; inventor; kennel/cattery owner; network marketing; newsletter publisher; novelist; proofreader/copy editor; taxidermist; tourist attraction; toymaker; tutor; typist; upholsterer; word processor?

Country

How about looking up:
bed and breakfast; beekeeper; caravan park owner; farmer; farrier/blacksmith; fish curer and smoker; garage owner; garden centre; greyhound trainer; haulier; holiday accommodation owner; kennel/cattery owner; landscape designer; oyster farmer; publican; racehorse owner; riding school owner; sailing school owner; salmon farmer; shepherd/shepherdess;

smallholder; snail farmer; sub postmaster; thatcher; tourist attraction; tourist guide; trout farmer; vet; village shopkeeper; windsurfing school owner; wine grower?

Crafts

How about looking up:
antique furniture restorer; calligrapher; carpenter; china restorer; dental technician; farrier/blacksmith; furniture designer/maker; garden gnome maker; glass designer/maker; musical instrument maker; musical instrument repairer; piano tuner; picture maker; potter; print maker; puppeteer; saddler/leatherworker; shoe designer/maker; silversmith/jeweller; stage technician carpenter; tailor; taxidermist; textile designer; thatcher; toymaker; upholsterer; wood carver?

Design

How about looking up:
architect; book designer; contemporary art gallery owner; costume designer; desk-top publisher; editorial photographer; exhibition designer; fashion designer; furniture designer/maker; gardener/garden designer; graphic designer; interior designer; inventor; landscape designer; magazine designer; patent agent; stage designer; stylist; textile designer; wedding shop owner?

Finance

How about looking up:
accountant; actuary; book-keeper; company doctor; futures broker; independent financial adviser; insurance broker; investment manager; shipbroker; stockbroker?

Grooming

How about looking up:
beauty consultant; chiropodist; dental technician; embalmer; hairdresser; makeup artist; stylist; tattooist?

Health

How about looking up:
acupuncturist; Alexander technique teacher; child/educational psychologist; chiropodist; chiropractor; counsellor; dentist; dietary therapist; doctor; healer; healthfood shopkeeper; homeopath; hypnotherapist; music therapist; naturopath; night carer; nurse; nursing home owner/manager; optician; osteopath; pharmacist; physiotherapist; psychoanalyst; psychologist; psychotherapist; reflexologist; sex therapist; vet?

House and Garden

How about looking up:
antique dealer; antique furniture restorer; builder; caterer; childminder; china restorer; cleaning contractor; coal merchant; gardener/garden designer; garden centre; garden gnome maker; hire shop owner; interior designer; nanny/babysitting agent; painter/decorator; piano tuner; property manager; tree surgeon; upholsterer; window cleaner?

Investments (Possible)

How about looking up:
brewer; caravan park owner; English language school owner; farmer; franchisee; garage owner; garden centre; holiday accommodation owner; hotelier; house converter; impresario; landlord; nursing home owner; office services bureau; oyster farmer; picture agent; prep school owner; property developer; publican; racehorse owner; record company owner; recording studio owner; restaurateur; riding school owner; sailing school owner; salmon farmer; smallholder; timeshare developer; tourist attraction; trout farmer; windsurfing school owner; wine bar owner; wine grower; zoo keeper?

Land Use

How about looking up:
beekeeper; caravan park owner; farmer; garden centre; gardener/garden designer; landscape designer; oyster farmer; riding school owner; sailing school owner; salmon farmer; smallholder; snail farmer; tourist attraction; trout farmer; windsurfing school owner; wine grower; zoo keeper?

Law

How about looking up:
accountant; barrister/advocate; conveyancer; guardian ad litem; para-legal; patent agent; private investigator; solicitor?

Lifelines

How about looking up:
bartender; bed and breakfast; book-keeper; cabaret performer; caterer; driver (hire cars); English language teacher; film extra; garden gnome maker; indexer; interpreter; market research interviewer; mini-cab driver; motorcycle messenger; music copyist; network marketing; night carer; office cleaner; painter/decorator; photographic assistant; proofreader/copy

editor; street entertainer; sub-editor; swimming teacher; telesales person; tourist guide; tutor; typist; window cleaner; word processor?

Marketing, Advertising, Sales and Promotion

How about looking up:
advertising agent; advertising photographer; conference organiser; desk-top publisher; direct marketing consultant; events organiser; exhibition designer; graphic designer; list broker; market research interviewer; marketing consultant; media trainer; network marketing; public relations consultant; sales agent; sales promoter; space sales agent; telesales person?

Music

How about looking up:
cabaret performer; chamber group musician/manager; classical composer; classical singer; concert agent; conductor; disco owner/DJ; festival director; impresario; instrumental soloist; jazz musician/singer; keyboard hire; music copyist; music critic; music/instrument retailer; music publisher; music teacher; music therapist; musical instrument maker; musical instrument repairer; musician; musicians' answering and booking service; opera director; orchestral fixer; orchestral musician; piano tuner; pop group sound engineer; record company owner; recording studio owner; repetiteur/accompanist/coach; street entertainer; TV and film music composer?

Outdoors

How about looking up:
beekeeper; farmer; farrier/blacksmith; football commentator; garden centre; gardener/garden designer; greyhound trainer; kennel/cattery owner; landscape designer; market stall holder; motorcycle messenger; motorcycle racer; oyster farmer; riding school owner; sailing school owner; salmon farmer; shepherd/shepherdess; smallholder; snail farmer; street entertainer; surveyor; thatcher; tourist guide; tree surgeon; trout farmer; window cleaner; windsurfing school owner; wine grower; zoo keeper?

People

How about looking up:
artists' agent; bed and breakfast; careers adviser; child/educational psychologist; childminder; cleaning contractor; conductor; counsellor; dietary therapist; doctor; employment agent; English language teacher; events organiser; film director; guardian ad litem; headhunter; healer; homeopath; hotelier; hypnotherapist; in-company trainer; independent financial adviser; Italian property finder; literary agent; media trainer; MEP; MP; music therapist; nanny/babysitting agent; network marketing; night carer; nurse; nursing home owner/manager; opera director; para-legal; prep school owner; private investigator; psychoanalyst; psychologist; psychotherapist; publican; restaurateur; sex therapist; social worker; swimming teacher; teacher; telesales person; theatrical agent; toastmaster; tourist guide; tutor; wine bar owner; yoga teacher?

Performing

How about looking up:
actor; cabaret performer; chamber group musician/manager; classical singer; conductor; dancer; disco owner/DJ; film extra; instrumental soloist; jazz musician/

singer; motorcycle racer; musician; orchestral musician; puppeteer; repetiteur/accompanist/coach; street entertainer; toastmaster; tourist guide?

Photography and Film

How about looking up:
advertising photographer; assistant film director; camera crew; continuity person; editorial photographer; film director; film extra; film production person; high street photographer; photographer; photographic assistant; photojournalist; stylist; TV and film music composer?

Plants

How about looking up:
farmer; food manufacturer; garden centre; gardener/garden designer; market stall holder; smallholder; thatcher; tree surgeon; wine grower?

Shops

How about looking up:
antique dealer; bookseller; butcher; coal merchant; contemporary art gallery owner; dress agent; estate agent; fashion retailer; franchisee; garden centre; healthfood shopkeeper; hi-fi shop owner; high street photographer; hire shop owner; market stall holder; motorcycle dealer; music/instrument retailer; pharmacist; picture framer; shopkeeper; sports retailer; sub postmaster; village shopkeeper; wedding shop owner?

Sport

How about looking up:
bookie; events organiser; football commentator; greyhound trainer; motorcycle racer; physiotherapist; racehorse owner; riding school owner; sailing school owner; sports retailer; swimming teacher; windsurfing school owner?

Tourism

How about looking up:
bed and breakfast; caravan park owner; contemporary art gallery owner; English language school owner; English language teacher; festival director; holiday accommodation owner; hotelier; interpreter; Italian property finder; kennel/cattery owner; property manager; publican; restaurateur; riding school owner; sailing school owner; sports retailer; timeshare developer; tourist attraction; tourist guide; travel agent; windsurfing school owner; wine bar owner?

TV, Radio and Press

How about looking up:
advertising photographer; assistant film director; camera person; continuity person; desk-top publisher; editorial photographer; film production person; football commentator; foreign correspondent; graphic designer; journalist; magazine designer; magazine publisher; media trainer; newsletter publisher; photographer; photojournalist; picture agent; picture researcher; printer; radio reporter/presenter; recording studio owner; scriptwriter; space sales agent;

stylist; sub-editor; telesales person; theatrical agent; TV and film music composer; typesetter; UK correspondent (overseas media); word processor?

Wine and Food

How about looking up:
bartender; bed and breakfast; brewer; caterer; fish curer and smoker; food manufacturer; franchisee; healthfood shopkeeper; hotelier; publican; restaurateur; wine bar owner; wine grower; wine merchant?

Writing

How about looking up:
art historian; book packager; classical composer; desk-top publisher; foreign correspondent; indexer; journalist; music critic; newsletter publisher; novelist; scriptwriter; sub-editor; UK correspondent (overseas media); word processor?

Independent Jobs A–Z

Aa

Accountant

Qualifications/Training	Yes
Income bracket	Medium–High
Licence	Yes, to audit
Town/Country	Town
Experience/Springboard	Necessary
Travel	Yes, including international
Mid-career entry	Possible
Exit sale	Yes
Entry costs	£20,000
Work at home	Possible
Mix and match	Possible.

You could think about: *Company doctor, Journalist, MP, Holiday accommodation owner, Cabaret performer*

Enquiries
Institute of Chartered Accountants, Chartered Association of Certified Accountants

If you are happy doing people's book-keeping, you often need no other qualification than a way with figures. However, if you want to do more, you will need to become a qualified accountant. By law, only those accountants who are registered auditors can audit the accounts of public limited companies.

To become a chartered accountant you will need to take out a training contract usually with a firm of chartered accountants or with an authorised commercial organisation, under the TOPP (Training Outside Public Practice) Scheme, eg certain organisations in industry, commerce and the public sector. The training period usually lasts three years for graduates and four years for non-graduates. During this time you have to pass two sets of professional examinations – students with a degree in a relevant subject are exempt from the foundation stage exams. Training as a certified accountant is similar, except you do not have to sign a training contract with a firm.

Two years after qualification, and subject to meeting certain practising regulations, it may be possible to set up in your own practising firm of accountants, or become a partner in a chartered or certified practice (dependent on the examinations you have studied). To become a partner in an existing firm normally involves working for the firm and proving your ability first. You usually contribute towards the firm's working capital when you are made a partner, and may be asked to pay towards its goodwill. But it is usually a worthy investment, as your profit share will normally increase to a parity with other partners over a period of years.

Most small firms provide general accounting services, but a few are more specialised and other firms may refer specialist problems over to them. Mixed practices (ie containing both qualified chartered and certified accountants) are now becoming more common as firms diversify their business interests to cover all aspects of business, rather than just accountancy.

In addition to those listed above, there are two other professional accountancy bodies: the CHARTERED INSTITUTE OF MANAGEMENT ACCOUNTANTS (CIMA), and the CHARTERED INSTITUTE OF PUBLIC FINANCE AND ACCOUNTANCY (CIPFA). With the former, you would work in industry, commerce or the public utilities acting as an interpreter of financial information to managers of the company. In the latter, you would work in the public utilities (eg local government, NHS, or civil service), and be responsible for the use of public money.

On qualification with CIMA – though not CIPFA which is public sector based – or having attained certified or chartered accountancy status, you would have the option to move into general management, or become a financial director/controller of a company.

As a sole practitioner, either start on your own or buy an established practice – through practice brokers or adverts in *Accountancy Age*, *Accountancy* or the *Certified Accountant*. If you are working on your own from home you should aim to turn over at least £35,000 in the first year and will need at least £20,000 to get going, apart from buying the practice. You may, in due course, want to hire staff and buy a computer. It is recommended that not more than 15 per cent of your fee income is from one client.

The job gives you good insight into other industries and working practices. To succeed you will need to be a good communicator as you will often be required to explain financial statements to non-accountants. Certainly, you'll have to be numerate and accurate, but it helps if you are literate too – you will have to write reports and interpret data on a daily basis.

It is hard work to qualify as an accountant so you need to be determined. Don't expect to enjoy the training – though your responsibility and work satisfaction increases with your experience. But, certainly from a financial angle, your efforts will be rewarded.

European Community Notes

Qualifications: To a certain point, UK qualifications are recognised throughout the EC and are well-respected but qualified accountants may need to sit 'top-up' tests before being allowed to practise in other EC member states. EC qualifications recognised in UK.

Languages: To succeed, local language necessary.

Earnings: UK income generally higher than or same as elsewhere in the EC, depending on the country in question.

Setting up: You will find it difficult to succeed in Denmark, Greece, Italy; possible in France and Germany; easier in Belgium, Eire, Luxembourg, Spain.

Advice/Training: Advice, information and training available for those wishing to work in Europe.

Enquiry point for those wishing to work in the EC: Overseas Relations Dept., CHARTERED ASSOCIATION OF CERTIFIED ACCOUNTANCY

International Affairs Dept., INSTITUTE OF CHARTERED ACCOUNTANTS

Recommended reading: ACCA Basic Fact Sheets on EC member states (available free) *Accountancy*; *Financial Times*.

Notes: Accountants would be ill-advised to set up on their own in another EC country until they have considerable experience of its tax and legislative systems – not to mention a high degree of fluency in its language. Different regulations on the practice of accounting apply to each member state; get up-to-date advice and information.

Working in a multinational company or firm of accountants provides a secure way of gaining experience in Europe before going independent.

Chartered accountant students may spend all or part of their training in a authorised office in another EC state.

Actor

Qualifications/Training	Recommended
Income bracket	Low–Medium
Licence	Union card essential
Town/Country	Town
Experience/Springboard	No
Travel	Yes

Mid-career entry	Unlikely
Exit sale	No
Entry costs	£100
Work at home	No

Mix and match Often essential.
You could think about: *Puppeteer, Cabaret performer, Street entertainer, Scriptwriter, Novelist, Illustrator, Theatrical agent, Mini-cab driver, Bartender, Market research interviewer, Window cleaner, Toastmaster*

Enquiries
Equity, National Council for Drama Training

According to the UK actors' union EQUITY, at any one time 70–80 per cent of its 46,000 members will be without work. And that's after going through the whole business of getting an Equity Card, which is pretty much essential unless you can offer professional skills other than acting (perhaps a show needs a professional boxer). Most branches of the profession operate a quota system; so a provincial repertory company might have an annual allotment for two new actors and two stage management staff, who are employed with provisional membership. It's because these allotments are so limited that people are moved to take up anything from fire-eating to striptease as a means of getting into the profession.

To get provisional membership in the field of 'variety', whether you're a pub-theatre group, comedian or exotic dancer you have basically to show a number of contracts at professional rates. Once you've got your provisional card you need 30 weeks' Equity-recognised work (mercifully, not consecutive) to qualify for full membership. Not everything counts – check with Equity.

In certain specialised areas like opera or ballet you can get membership as soon as you are accepted for a company and a similar system is planned for the theatre. This means a company can hire graduates of accredited drama schools (get a list from the NATIONAL COUNCIL FOR DRAMA TRAINING) – and it won't eat into their allowance of provisional cards.

The whole question of drama school is a moot one. It's generally regarded as an important process – even if you reject a lot of what you learn – and it gives you a chance to perform. It's a lengthy and an expensive business – it will cost you over £1,000 a term, though scholarships or LEA grants may be available (but grants for drama students are discretionary, except for degree courses). While drama school doesn't automatically lead to an Equity card, it is a great help in finding an agent, another essential ingredient. Having an agent certainly doesn't guarantee you work, but it's difficult even to get auditions without someone to represent you – open auditions are very much the exception, especially in film and TV. But don't undervalue 'work training' if drama school is not your scene.

Acting is not a career that lends itself to precise planning – there's so much luck and chance involved. At the start of your career, aim for as much and as diverse experience as possible. Setting up a pub group or some profit-sharing production at the further reaches of the Fringe will hardly make your fortune but it will keep you working, practising your art, and it can provide you with some very worthwhile exposure.

The financial side is no more predictable. You could work for years on £5,000 pa – and count yourself lucky – then hit a smash soap and earn twenty times that. To give some idea of the range of rewards, the Equity minimum rates for theatre work hover around the £150–£180-a-week mark, depending on size, location and so on. Big success could lead to a percentage of the gross, so that a handful of stars might take a few thousand pounds a week on the West End stage (by contrast with the National Theatre and the RSC where, almost without exception, nobody gets more than £400). The BBC television minimum rate, for anything more than a walk-on role, is £304; the independent companies generally pay more. The star of an average ITV sitcom would probably get £4,000–£5,000 an episode, while the star of big hourly TV drama might earn three times that. The real money of course is in films, but you could be a long time in the wilderness before anyone offers you a million dollars a movie plus a share of the gross. Women might also want to take on board the recent revelation that on average actresses earn half the pay of actors. Equity showed that annual average earnings for men in TV are around £26,500 against £13,200 for women; the gap is even more pronounced in commercials – £18,000 compared to £6,650. Even working side by side men may be on more. One household name recently learned that a production in which she had top billing also included two male actors being paid 30 per cent more than her. Add to that the fact that, on the whole, women work less often and find work progressively more difficult to get once they are in their 30s and 40s – no such difficulty afflicts men . . .

Apart from the fundamental problems of survival on no guaranteed income, you'll have some essential expenses. You'll need some publicity shots done, photos for agents and so on, which could run to about £150; travel expenses; clothes for auditions (if you're auditioning for the part of a glamour puss, say, you'll make a better impression turning up in something chic). Most expenses can be written off against tax – should you ever earn enough to pay any. But if you appear regularly, you now have to pay tax through PAYE, rather than Schedule D, which makes it more difficult to claim for expenses.

Whether or not you're drama-school trained, a voice coach is definitely advisable – you have to learn to use your voice properly or you can lose it, especially if you're going to work in the theatre. Singing lessons are a worthwhile investment, even if you're not planning to follow a musical route; they are a big help with general technique – breathing, projection and so on. By the same token, dance classes won't hurt either, especially when you're starting out – it will all make you more employable, as well as helping you keep in shape. You won't be able to afford all these; but if you're in London (or Birmingham) you'll find lessons available cheap at the ACTORS CENTRE.

An actor's life can be peculiarly demand-ing. That is not to say it can't be fun, but it can certainly take a toll on your personal life and it is not conducive to lasting relationships. The hours can be preposterous. Filming always starts at some unearthly hour in the morning; the theatre ends late at night. In words of one thespian: 'When you're out of work you're miserable, when you're working you're exhausted, when you finish a job you're sure you'll never work again – but if you can't take a joke you shouldn't have joined the profession.'

Contacts is a vital publication with the names and numbers of agents, management, studios etc – everything you need to know. From the same stable comes the casting directory, *Spotlight*, which serves the same function for actors, so you must be in it – everybody is. It costs you around £60 for a year, for a photograph and a half page entry. The *Stage* is not the greatest read but it is very useful, particularly for jobs, auditions and so on; and get *The Actor's Handbook*.

European Community Notes
Fundamentally an itinerant profession. There are obvious problems of language although several countries have their own English language theatres. EQUITY checks your contract for you before you sign and arranges local union representation if necessary.

Actuary

Qualifications/Training	Essential
Income bracket	High
Licence	Yes
Town/Country	Town
Experience/Springboard	Essential
Travel	Yes
Mid-career entry	Possible
Exit sale	Possible
Entry costs	£2,000+

Work at home	Yes
Mix and match	Possible.

You could think about: ***Journalist, Newsletter publisher, Oyster farmer***

Enquiries
Institute of Actuaries, Faculty of Actuaries

Actuaries are problem solvers concerned with forecasting and with assessing future effects of (usually) financial decisions. It's a small profession (there are about 2,000 qualified actuaries in the UK). Some 60 per cent are employed in the insurance industry where actuaries use their special knowledge and training to formulate and implement pension, life assurance and insurance policies and schemes. A few actuaries are employed by the government, as watchdogs for life assurance companies or as advisers on DSS benefits and pensions. Deregulation and expansion of the financial services industry have increased the demand for actuaries and the opportunities for small actuarial companies to act as consultants on a wide range of financial matters are expanding. Many companies who do not employ an actuary on their staff, seek advice on company pensions, employee benefits, investment and business consultancy; those with in-house actuaries need second opinions and the specialist advice an independent can give them.

To satisfy the statutory definition of actuary, you must be a Fellow of the INSTITUTE OF ACTUARIES (IA) or, in Scotland, the FACULTY OF ACTUARIES (FA), before you can practise. This requires at least three years' practical training with an approved employer (usually, but not always, an insurance company or firm of actuaries); your careers services can help you to find one. During this time you are a student member of the IA or FA and you'll have to pass the eight subjects of the qualifying exam – exemptions from some papers are possible. Teaching is done by correspondence course and tutorial, and you are only allowed to sit each subject a maximum of four times (it's rare to pass them all in less than four–five years). Most recent entrants to the profession are gradu-

ates and you're recommended to get a degree in maths, economics or statistics. You need to be numerate (good maths A-level), attentive to detail and be good at explaining what you're doing, and why, to people who don't understand. Assessing the best policies to adopt needs flair. There are no hard and fast rules or procedures to follow and this isn't a job for anyone who wants only to crunch figures all day. Set up costs aren't great; you don't need an office because you can visit clients at theirs. You'll need a telephone, a word processor/ computer, a desk and some stationery. Most actuaries are in the South-east, Edinburgh or Glasgow. You don't need to follow them but you must be close to the institutions that use actuaries, i.e. close to a commercial centre.

Actuaries are well paid – in employment in London you can expect £35,000 pa on qualifying rising to £40,000+; as an independent, with the experience you need before you set up alone, you'll be able to get a lot more.

The usual way of setting up is to springboard from a large company once you've had some experience and have collected enough clients to live on. You can operate as a sole proprietor, in partnership or as a limited company. Seek out the owners of small businesses with their own self-administered pension schemes; larger firms will want help as their needs change through growth and restructuring; insurance companies also need independent actuaries and some work is available through sub-contracting (bear this in mind when you're springboarding and keep your employer on your side). Remember that pension scheme valuations are only needed once every three years (unlike company audits) so make sure you've got enough clients to keep you going. Advertise in accountancy and personnel management magazines and in the *Financial Times*; good editorial in any of these is better than a paid ad. Useful organisations (as well as the Institute/Faculty of Actuaries) are the ASSOCIATION OF PENSION TRUSTEES, the ASSOCIATION OF CONSULTING ACTUARIES, the SOCIETY OF PENSION CONSULTANTS and the PENSIONS MANAGEMENT INSTITUTE.

The people you're likely to see are finance directors and chief executives; accountants for some of your smaller clients. About a third of your time will be spent in management and administration; correspondence, reports and discussions with colleagues. The rest of the time you'll be with clients or working on their cases; setting contributory rates for pensions, advising on how to respond to new financial legislation, evaluating life assurance schemes, acting as consultants on investments etc. To a degree the work is seasonal – life assurance valuations after a December 31 year-end must be in by the end of June (Department of Trade and Industry rule); pension scheme work tends to bunch around April 5. Other factors are new accounting standards regulations, financial legislation and company takeovers, all of which increase the demand for actuaries. The IA and FA publish useful leaflets.

✴ European Community Notes

Qualifications: UK qualifications recognised throughout EC and EC qualifications in UK.

Languages: To succeed, local language necessary although English is understood perfectly well at the professional level.

Earnings: UK income generally same as elsewhere in the EC.

Setting up: You will find it difficult to succeed in Denmark, Greece, Italy, Spain. You will find it easier in Belgium, Eire, France, Germany.

Advice/Training: Advice, information and training available within companies for those wishing to work in Europe.

Exchanges: Formal job exchanges exist, office to office, within companies.

Enquiry point for those wishing to work in the EC: INSTITUTE OF ACTUARIES

Note: Within the EC, it is a small profession where the individuals generally know and respect each other; the position is improving day by day.

Acupuncturist

Qualifications/Training	Yes
Income bracket	Low–Medium
Licence	Recommended
Town/Country	Town
Experience/Springboard	Yes
Travel	No
Mid-career entry	Possible
Exit sale	No
Entry costs	£100+
Work at home	Yes
Mix and match	Yes.

You could think about: ***Doctor, Artist, Journalist, Physiotherapist***

Enquiries
Acupuncture Association

Acupuncturists treat the cause and symptoms of illness by inserting special needles into specific locations of the patient's body. These needles alter the flow of energy within the body causing chemical changes and so facilitating the healing process. To practise you must study this form of medicine. You can do this at a number of colleges e.g. the BRITISH COLLEGE OF ACUPUNCTURE or at the COLLEGE OF TRADITIONAL CHINESE ACUPUNCTURE. Each has an association or register.

You need a compassionate, sensitive personality, to be dedicated and to possess some counselling skills. The career prospects vary across the country. Increasingly, other medical professionals, e.g. doctors, physiotherapists, are training in acupuncture and offering it as an alternative to conventional treatment.

Once you're trained, it's a good idea to start by working in a mixed clinic, with other kinds of complementary medical practitioners. This makes referrals easy and helps in setting up a network of useful contacts such as physiotherapists and those doing therapeutic massage. Make sure your name is on a Register of Acupuncturists, join the ACUPUNCTURE ASSOCIATION and take out the good insurance they provide. After three–four years it is safe to start a practice of your own. This can be in your own home if you live near public transport and have parking facilities. You can treat two or three patients at the same time, in separate cubicles, if you have enough space.

You will need hot and cold running water, separate loo, needles, telephone, answerphone, filing cabinet and stationery, say £1,000 in all. But to start, you need very little – disposable needles are about £10 per hundred. You can buy yourself an autoclave (£200) but, with AIDS or Hepatitis B to consider, disposable needles remain attractive. Your premises must be inspected and licensed by your local authority. You can charge £20–£30 an hour.

This is a satisfying job as you are independent, can organise your own hours, see your patients improve and continually learn something new. Patients tend to disappear during the summer holiday season.

As translations of more Chinese medical books become available in this country, the practice of acupuncture is widening.

Advertising Agent

Qualifications/Training	Useful
Income bracket	Medium–High
Licence	No
Town/Country	Town
Experience/Springboard	Essential
Travel	Possible
Mid-career entry	Unlikely
Exit sale	Yes
Entry costs	£7,000
Work at home	Unlikely
Mix and match	Yes.

You could think about: *Marketing consultant, Public relations consultant, Direct marketing agent, Illustrator*

Enquiries
Communications, Advertising and Marketing Foundation

Advertising agents promote their clients' products and increase their sales by telling people about them. They do this by launching advertising campaigns, in which they play two key roles: creating advertisements; and buying media space or time in which to display them. Campaigns are of varying intensity, depending on how much clients want to spend and how desperate they are for coverage. Regular clients are called accounts; account handling is the third, and one of the most important, aspects of advertising. Advertising on TV, radio, the press and cinema is called above the line advertising. Agents also arrange advertising outside the media (brochures, mail shots, giveaways etc) which is called below the line advertising. Below the line tends to be one-off jobs and clients don't always have agency accounts as they usually do for above the line. To run a successful agency you have to exploit any opportunities of extending the client's market and find gaps in their current supply of advertising above or below the line.

You don't need any formal qualifications but you can take the COMMUNICATIONS, ADVERTISING AND MARKETING FOUNDATION (CAMF) exams by post or at some local colleges (further details from CAMF). This will give you a certificate and a good grounding in advertising but is of little practical use when you're finding work. Experience is essential and a small agency is particularly good for this because it gives an overview of the whole business rather than limiting you to one department as you may be in a larger one. Advertisers need to be good at self-presentation and promotion. You'll have to build up your clients' confidence in your ability and trustworthiness: self-confidence is a great help because clients tend to know very little about advertising. Anything that *you* don't know you can soon find out. You need to be able to write and to have ideas for the creative side of advertising; understanding and manipulating people will make it easier to create successful adverts and to handle accounts.

You'll need an office to operate from with a telephone and a typewriter/word processor. Thereafter, your only expenses are running the office. Even though most agencies sub-contract a lot of work to freelances, cash flow doesn't cause problems because suppliers' bills are sent directly to the client. Occasionally (especially for below the line) you may have to pay up front (eg for a brochure) and it's worth having credit insurance in case any of your clients go bust before they've paid their bills. Most media space and time buying is done by special companies – you'll need to lodge bonds of about £50,000 if you want to do this yourself. You charge commission (usually about 17 per cent) on everything that your clients spend on a campaign. For producing one-off below the line services you can charge a fixed fee. Obviously the more advertising you create the more money you'll make. Some campaigns cost millions of pounds.

Clients come through personal contact and knowing something about a specific business. You can't advertise, although, during your early days, you can approach potential clients with your ideas. You may be able to poach some from wherever you're getting experience, especially if you've been account handling. Other useful people to know are possible subcontractors eg writers, artists, designers, planners, printers and radio, TV and video production companies. It's a good idea to set up with somebody else whose skills and specialisation complement yours eg somebody creative if you're good at handling accounts. On the whole, there is a wider range of advertising opportunity in large cities and the South-east but some small local agencies survive on accounts from local businesses who have little interest in advertising and who are willing to pay for it to be handled by somebody else.

Read *Ogilvy on Advertising* and subscribe to all or some of *Campaign, Marketing Week* and *Media Week*.

Advertising Photographer

Qualifications/Training	Recommended
Income bracket	Medium–High
Licence	No
Town/Country	Town
Experience/ Springboard	Recommended
Travel	Yes
Mid-career entry	Possible
Exit sale	Yes
Entry costs	£6,000
Work at home	Yes
Mix and match	Yes.

You could think about: **Photojournalist, Picture researcher, Editorial photographer, Wood carver**

Enquiries
British Institute of Professional Photography, Association of Fashion Advertising and Editorial Photographers

This is where the real money is in the photographic field. A top photographer, shooting say a Benson and Hedges ad, can charge £1,500–£4,500 per day – and will charge for the days spent setting up the shoot as well as the actual studio work. The professional association, the ASSOCIATION OF FASHION, ADVERTISING AND EDITORIAL PHOTOGRAPHERS (AFAEP) can advise its membership on usual rates, etc.

As with all photographic jobs, you must be meticulous, and have top technical skills. Commissions come from advertising agencies and most work is in central London. In most cases you will work closely with the creative director from the agency, and if you're working for a top agency, no expense will be spared in getting things right down to the last detail. You may find yourself constantly bowing to their wishes, but some creative directors appreciate your comments on the shoot. Sometimes, you may even be able to create work for yourself by coming up with new ideas for ads in a current series – then you can charge extra fees for the concept, as well as the actual shooting involved.

Most advertising photographers have an art school training, but generally learn more about the business through assisting experienced photographers. Vocational courses at art school are recognised by the BRITISH INSTITUTE OF PROFESSIONAL PHOTOGRAPHY. Cultivate contacts working in advertising agencies, get to know other photographers and get your name known as widely as possible. You will have to do a lot of legwork, showing your folio to creative directors.

Creative Review will keep you up to date with design developments in the advertising field; *Marketing and Campaign* will keep you informed about which agencies are handling which products. The *Creative Handbook* is a useful annually revised handbook. Get your name in it.

You can start out by hiring studios and equipment, but most successful advertising photographers will have their own studios or share facilities with other photographers. You will certainly want to buy your own cameras and a range of lights as soon as you can afford to. The total bill for equipment when setting up will be several thousand pounds. Overheads include studio facilities, repairs, processing, motorbike messengers, a well-stocked drinks cupboard and an allowance for entertaining clients at lunch.

European Community Notes

Qualifications: No qualifications needed to work in EC on freelance basis.
Languages: To succeed, local language necessary.
Earnings: UK income generally same as elsewhere in the EC.
Setting up: You will find it difficult to succeed in Belgium, France, Germany, Luxembourg. You will find it easier in Denmark, Eire, Greece, Italy, Netherlands, Portugal, Spain. This depends on individual talents but Belgium, France, Germany and Luxembourg have a large indigenous threshold to break through. Languages are essential, as is intense market research to establish needs, trends and fashions.

Advice/Training: Advice, information and training not available for those wishing to work in Europe.
Exchanges: Formal job exchanges do not exist.

Alexander Technique Teacher

Qualifications/Training	Yes
Income bracket	Low–Medium
Licence	No
Town/Country	Town
Experience/ Springboard	Recommended
Travel	Local
Mid-career entry	Yes
Exit sale	No
Entry costs	£500
Work at home	Yes
Mix and match	Possible.

You could think about: ***Antique furniture restorer, Newsletter publisher, Book-keeper***

Enquiries
Society of Teachers of Alexander Technique

Teachers of this technique advise their clients on how to use themselves more effectively through better balance and co-ordination to give greater efficiency, release more energy and thus improve their physical and emotional well being.

You need to have a good all-round education and be between 20 and 40 to enter a school recognised by the SOCIETY OF TEACHERS OF ALEXANDER TECHNIQUE. You can take one lesson a week for a year to make sure that this is what you want to do before doing a three-year full-time course, which costs £8,500. You need to be interested in people, be a good communicator, dextrous and sensitive and are trained to sense what is going on inside a pupil's body.

It is best to go it alone after a period of supervised probation following qualification. Many parts of the country have no Alexander teachers so you should be able to succeed. It is useful to join the SOCIETY OF TEACHERS OF ALEXANDER TECHNIQUE. You can advertise discreetly; you can let GPs know of your existence as they can send you many referrals; also any local art and music colleges. You need a ground floor room, possibly in your own home, and a work table costing £250. You also need a phone, answerphone, filing cabinet and chair. You can charge from £12–£20 per half-hour.

You tend to work outside normal working hours to fit in with clients. The advantage of his job is that you have the freedom to plan your own day and the pleasure of seeing clients get better. The disadvantages are that your income fluctuates, clients disappear in the summer and after Christmas, and you must be careful if working at home that the job is kept separate from family life. You can do another job at the same time if you organise yourself so as not to get over-tired: teaching can be very demanding, both physically and mentally.

Useful books are *Alexander Technique*, *Body Learning*, *Alexander Principle* and *The Use of the Self*.

Antique Dealer (Large Antiques)

Qualifications/Training	Not formal
Income bracket	Low–High
Licence	No
Town/Country	Town/Village
Experience/Springboard	Recommended
Travel	Essential
Mid-career entry	Excellent
Exit sale	Yes

Entry costs	£50,000++
Work at home	Possible
Mix and match	Yes.

You could think about: **Antique dealer (small antiques and collectibles), Man with a van, Art historian/critic, Antique furniture restorer, Book packager, Beekeeper, MP**

Enquiries
London and Provincial Antique Dealers' Association

Large antiques dealing includes furniture, statuary and masonry like fireplaces. Antiques dealing runs the gamut from bijou Bond Street showrooms to dank junk shops or aircraft-hangar-style 'antiques warehouses'. Antique dealing is ostensibly a very attractive pursuit. No obstacles exist to anyone becoming a dealer – you can build it up from part-time or collecting as long as you've got enough specialist knowledge – and, of course, cash – to buy and sell. To trade independently on any serious level you need knowledge of current prices and adequate capital as well as historical and artistic know-how.

To be a dealer, you have to study the market; the best way to learn is by working in the trade with a dealer or in auction rooms, coping with prices, pieces and punters. Ideally you should also get involved in selling for the complete picture. Local antique markets are a cheap way of testing whether you really want to get into the business. You can learn buying and selling and make good contacts. A good visual memory is a valuable asset, as is an eye for shape and colour – a good eye or informed observation connected with your visual memory, which has a great deal to do with taste. You can cultivate it to an extent and it grows with experience. This has always been a most international trade. Knowledge of foreign languages is a great boon: Spanish is currently the favourite tongue while French, German or Italian are always useful. A few words of Japanese can also have a rather startling effect. The important American market has taken a major hammering but this means it is in fact a good place to buy – a lot of English antiques are coming back to the UK from the US now, so fret not heritage-lovers. The opening-up of eastern Europe is also rather intriguing – if there's anything left.

Fine/decorative arts courses are available but they are expensive and often over-subscribed; you can read and go to lectures or evening classes. But there's no substitute for going around, looking at antiques in museums and country houses, then visiting antique shops and auction rooms where the sheer volume of things passing through gives you an idea of price and how to handle antiques. Auction room experience also helps you to build up contacts and a track record. Getting on with other dealers is important. Anonymous faces are viewed with suspicion in this business – where has your stock come from? – so make sure that people know who you are and don't be secretive about your address and phone number. Likewise, you should be wary of anyone you don't know. Don't buy any-thing that's been stolen – if you do, you have to hand it back to the owner and risk being done for handling stolen property. You also have to contend with being robbed yourself; nicking large antiques may not be easy, but a lot of people manage it. You may regard the insurance premiums as too prohibitive to make comprehensive theft cover feasible but it should be given some thought and there are specialist brokers for art and antiques.

Your real concern must be to ensure adequate finance – first, to get the right premises (the appropriate location is vital), then to purchase, maintain and keep pur-chasing stock even if weeks go by without any business.

You may need to pay somebody else to man the shop while you go buying or use a trucking company to transport your stock (they aren't cheap). Useful contacts (as well as other dealers) include truckers, restorers and runners who scour the country for pieces that you may not be able to find yourself. Runners will also be look-ing to 'borrow' pieces from you that they think they can place somewhere. If you know them, and it's practical, and you don't mind the piece being off the prem-ises for a while, and they don't keep bring-ing things back unsold . . . then you'll let them now and then. A period as a runner incidentally is very worthwhile apprentice-ship for later dealing. Get to know the tastes of dealers and customers yourself so that you know where to try and place a specific piece.

You will buy at auction – whether it's a smart St James's salesroom or a cow-shed in the middle of the Fens, say, with a ring of local dealers or fabulously rich farmers to contend with. Get to know the auctio-neer – and the porters (very important people, salesroom porters). You will also buy privately and from runners and from other shops. It may also be worth using the *Yellow Pages*, preferably getting your-self listed in the 'A's. Those bequeathed entire houses plus contents tend to look there for house clearance.

You have to know your place in the antiques chain. This means other people may make more money from some of your finds than you made but there's nothing wrong with that. While you shouldn't undersell something special, it's important to keep your stock moving. The average antique dealer will be looking for a gross profit of 25–33 per cent over the year. Most of the time (about 70 per cent), your business is going to be with other dealers who will be – vocally – concerned about their own margins and try and beat your prices down. Interestingly, in recession 70 per cent of trade in London is with private buyers. You have to be good at *trading* – at buying, selling and haggling. If it irritates you, you might just as well run a shoe shop. Read the *Antiques Trade Gazette* every week. Once you are established you may want to join a trade organisation such as the LONDON AND PROVINCIAL ANTIQUE DEALERS' ASSOCIATION; membership cri-teria include three years' trading experi-ence and references.

European Community Notes

Trade with Europe has always been im-portant and vigorous – sometimes more so than at others. The opening-up of the Single Market – easier border controls, less paperwork, tax harmonisation, fewer re-strictions on hauliers (which might reduce transport costs) – can only boost that trade. Off you go!

Antique Dealer (Small Antiques and Collectibles)

Qualifications/Training	Not formal
Income bracket	Low–High
Licence	No
Town/Country	Town/Village
Experience/ Springboard	Recommended
Travel	Yes
Mid-career entry	Excellent
Exit sale	Possible
Entry costs	£5,000++
Work at home	Possible
Mix and match	Yes.

You could think about: *Antique dealer (large antiques), Art historian/critic, Picture restorer, Interior designer, Illustrator, Italian property finder, Proofreader/copy editor*

Enquiries
London and Provincial Antique Dealers' Association

You can drift into dealing if you are wealthy or as a part-time pursuit or from a hobby habit. Depending on what you want to make of it, it can be as large or small a business as you like. Opportunities for selling and buying range from car boot sales to big London auction houses. If you've got a lot of energy and enthusiasm you should be able to find a niche somewhere.

Assuming you've made the commitment – and intend to make a living from it – what do you need to know? There are no formal qualifications. You'll need to know your stuff, whatever that is; it helps to have some basic abilities such as telling silver from plate, recognising different woods and gemstones. A lot of this comes from experience, talking to customers and colleagues, browsing in museums, fairs and auction rooms. You can deal generally in small antiques and bric-a-brac; or you can specialise in almost anything – clocks,

Victorian jewellery, boxes, 1920s clothes, stamps, oriental ceramics. . . .

As well as liking old things, antique dealers should enjoy bargain hunting – success depends on getting more than you paid for things. You can't be clumsy – breakages do happen and can be financially disastrous because it's seldom worth shouldering the massive costs of insurance.

Car boot sales are an inexpensive way of starting up (a pitch costs about £5 per day) and you don't need much stock. In large towns there are regular outdoor antiques markets. These cost £5–£12 per day and you can book a regular pitch there through the local authority. Antique fairs (in hotels etc.) cost about £20–£30 per day. Details of these from the trade press, in particular the *Antiques Trade Gazette*. Otherwise you can rent a space in a permanent covered market (especially common in London and tourist areas). This is cheaper than a shop, and also means that advertising costs can be shared and the concentration of a group of traders in the market makes it more of an attraction. Rent for these varies depending on size and location – (perhaps £40 a week including heating, lighting etc rising to three figures for pitch in one of the senior antique markets.

Unlike some other small retailers, antique dealers flourish by being close to competition because this creates an increased antique-buying traffic. Many customers buy things they like the look of rather than being serious collectors. There are exceptions especially at annual antique fairs which attract a lot of trade business. Stock comes from other dealers, auctions and people bringing things in. There is a chain of antique dealing: pieces being bought for a fiver in a flea market, going through several dealers and ending up at auction. As long as you don't mislead your customers, by selling old china as Ming dynasty, you can charge what you like. But anything that appears in a price guide will be difficult to sell for any more. Auctions provide pricing guidelines. Your mark-up will depend on how well you've bought and what you think you can get away with – plus how badly you need to sell something at that time. As a general rule though, the average antique dealer would be looking for a gross profit of between 25–33 per cent pa.

If you get your hands on pieces that are worth more than you could get from your usual market, sell them through an auction room. The value of an antique is equal to what you can sell it for; you'll learn how to tell how much that is through experience.

Keeping abreast of the trade is essential. The date-line of what is defined as an antique moves forward. Collections become more modern. You must be conscious of the cyclical and faddish nature of the trade. Those who spotted Clarice Cliff china, say, before it hit the colour supps, go to the top of the class. But those who failed to unload their repro Tiffany lamps . . . Visit other shops and dealers to get an idea of how prices and fashions are fluctuating. Small antiques tend not to be things that people buy because they're useful, and unfashionable ones are difficult to move. Read the *Antiques Trade Gazette* weekly. Of the masses of other publications around, the most useful include *The Antique Dealer and Collectors' Guide* and *Miller's Professional Antique Price Guide*. But price guides are dangerous and can be misleading – especially if you don't know the difference between 'right' and 'wrong' items or between original pieces and, perfectly legit, copies. When you've been trading seriously for a while you may find it useful to join a trade body such as the LONDON AND PROVINCIAL ANTIQUE DEALERS' ASSOCIATION – they require a minimum of three years' experience and references for membership.

European Community Notes

After 1992 and the opening of the Channel Tunnel, the EC Member States should be very good places to sell antiques and you'll need to keep your eye on Europe both as a seller and buyer.

Antique Furniture Restorer

Qualifications/Training	Recommended
Income bracket	Low–Medium
Licence	No
Town/Country	Either
Experience/Springboard	Essential
Travel	Possible
Mid-career entry	Yes
Exit sale	No
Entry costs	£5,000
Work at home	Possible
Mix and match	Yes.

You could think about: *Antique dealer, Wood carver, Furniture designer/maker, Man with a van*

Enquiries
British Antique Furniture Restorers Association, UK Institute for Conservation

This has become highly scientific – techniques are being updated constantly – and requires an aptitude for woodwork and a love of antiques. It is extremely labour intensive – you may have to work for weeks on the same piece. There will always be a demand for your skills, but you need total commitment and self-discipline to succeed. It can be a very rewarding but solitary and frustrating occupation.

You will need to take a suitable course – the Conservation Department at the VICTORIA AND ALBERT MUSEUM has information, as does the BRITISH ANTIQUE FURNITURE RESTORERS ASSOCIATION, or local education authorities. The Mecca is WEST DEAN COLLEGE. Some experienced restorers will take on apprentices. You can specialise (eg gilding, french polishing). A good understanding of cabinet making prior to a restoration course is certainly desirable.

Tools cost approximately £1,500 (vice £80; bandsaw £500 – though, as most work is by hand, a small one is ok, at much lower cost; kit for polishing, colouring, staining £100+). You also need access to a van to transport pieces between client and workshop. Some commissions incur a high outlay on materials, eg veneering (£500). Repairs may involve buying 'breakers' (eg a mahogany wardrobe) for suitable material (up to £1,000). Find suppliers through *Woodworker*.

Many restorers prefer to share a workshop for financial reasons and general working methods – better discipline, shared expertise, new techniques. Initially you may be better off taking smaller commissions. Frequently a seemingly uncomplicated job can involve far more detailed restoration once taken to pieces – take this into account when giving estimates. It may be better to complete at a break-even price but near the estimate. Likewise if the job takes less time, reduce the price and gain goodwill.

You will need to advertise – local papers, *Antiques Trade Gazette*. Approach local antique dealers – a useful source of steady work – but be aware that they will not give you any credit, so unless you are prepared to work for just the trade, do your own promotion. The ideal is to find, restore and sell your own pieces, but it's risky unless you're experienced in all these fields.

Architect

Qualifications/Training	Essential
Income bracket	Medium–High
Licence	Yes
Town/Country	Either
Experience/Springboard	Yes
Travel	Yes
Mid-career entry	Possible
Exit sale	Yes
Entry costs	£2,000+
Work at home	Possible

Mix and match   Possible.
You could think about: *Property developer, Furniture designer/maker, Inventor, Builder, Film extra*

Enquiries
Royal Institute of British Architects

Architects design buildings and supervise their erection; on a smaller scale, they also handle conversions, extensions, conservatories etc, that are beyond the scope of a builder. This involves producing plans that are aesthetically acceptable and technically feasible; obtaining planning permission; contracting builders; working with surveyors and engineers and keeping an eye on building in progress by visiting the site regularly. Most of the work done by architects in private practice is for houses and offices; there are some opportunities for private sector hospitals and schools but they are mostly in the public sector, designed by local authority/government employees. The demand for architects fluctuates. Recently big clients have included property developers who are converting old buildings. Some firms become specialists – often in the type of building for which they were first commissioned – while others prefer to keep their options open.

An architect, like a doctor, is a member of a registered profession and must be a member of the ARCHITECTS' REGISTRATION COUNCIL OF THE UK (ARCUK). This means passing the ROYAL INSTITUTE OF BRITISH ARCHITECTS (RIBA) exams (usually done over a five-year course at an RIBA-recognised school of architecture), and having two years of practical training with an ARCUK registered firm followed by the professional exams. Most newly qualified architects first join an established practice. Unless you've got some capital and win a competition, or have a friend/relative to commission you, it is difficult to start up alone immediately after training: dangerous too, without some experience in an established office. Alternatively you may choose to stay with an existing firm and hope to graduate as a partner (probably after several years as an associate); in many cases this will bring a more interesting range of work than could be expected in the earlier years of a new firm. You need to be creative and practical in order to design good buildings that suit their function and surroundings; but you also need to be good at presenting yourself and your ideas – this is a competitive profession.

Set-up and running costs depend largely on your ambitions and location. You could operate from home or a very small office with a telephone and that minimum of equipment you would have had as a student. Read *Starting up in Practice*. Early commissions are likely to be small: designing extensions and inserting new kitchens. Once you've broken into the market for bigger projects, you'll need a proper office and a staff of assistants and secretaries (a bank loan may be available if you can prove the validity of the commission). Architects are paid in stages and, as some projects can take several years to complete, you may have cash flow problems, especially when the project necessitates a team of assistants. For a large finished building design there may be thousands of drawings, completed by a team of many architects. They must be paid – perhaps before your own fees arrive.

Some commissions come through competitions, often for showpiece buildings, banks, parts of large developments etc. This will bring publicity and can help get your own practice started, as long as you make the most of the publicity and get further commissions to follow. If you don't win, you won't be paid for the work you've done or had done by employees. Fees are negotiable – sometimes in competition with other architects; you usually get about 6 per cent of the costs of new buildings and a higher percentage for alterations. In your early days the traditional sources of work include friends and relations and anyone else you can interest in your work. Architects depend on establishing a reputation because the majority of clients don't need their services regularly and go to someone they've heard something about. This also means that architects who do well as associates for another firm may have difficulty when they set up alone. On the other hand, the firm you've left may well pass on small jobs.

It is hard and taxing work but worth the inevitable struggle to ensure your original ideas are carried out and buildings of merit added to the environment.

⁂ European Community Notes

Qualifications: UK qualifications recognised throughout EC and EC qualifications in UK.

Languages: To succeed, local language necessary.

Setting up: You will find it difficult to succeed in Greece, Italy. You will find it easier in Eire, France, Spain.

Advice/Training: Advice, information and training available for those wishing to work in Europe.

Exchanges: Formal job exchanges do not exist.

Enquiry point for those wishing to work in the EC: Overseas Affairs Dept., ROYAL INSTITUTE OF BRITISH ARCHITECTS

Recommended reading: RIBA Country profiles; *Euronews Construction* from the DOE.

Notes: The DOE and the DTI can provide a wealth of information for anyone in this sector who is casting an eye Europe-wards, whether reviewing legislation or assessing markets and pointing to commercial opportunities.

Art Historian/ Critic

Qualifications/Training	Recommended
Income bracket	Low–Medium
Licence	No
Town/Country	Either
Experience/Springboard	Essential
Travel	Yes
Mid-career entry	Yes
Exit sale	No
Entry costs	Nil
Work at home	Yes

Mix and match   Yes.
You could think about: *Journalist, Antique dealer, Artist, Picture restorer, Contemporary art gallery owner*

Enquiries
Art Colleges or auction houses

As well as writing art books, self-employed art historians can be reviewers, journalists, authors, cataloguers, researchers, lecturers or exhibition organisers who have proved themselves especially knowledgeable in some field. This may be Rembrandt etchings or Andy Warhol. Your expertise will become known and required but it may take years to build up and, to succeed, you must be 100 per cent immersed in your job. The going is tough at the bottom, hawking your knowledge around the art journals, newspapers, local radio; once successful, however, you will be fêted. The usual way in is through a good History of Art degree. You will need languages – German, French and Italian but also Latin and Greek for medieval studies. The COURTAULD INSTITUTE has a reputation that will take you one step closer to success; short courses are offered by specialists like Sotheby's and Christie's. Once you've got a degree, you'll need experience in the field to build both your knowledge and contacts. This can be through working for a public or private gallery, teaching, working at an auction house – anywhere you'll be in touch with works of art and art experts. While you're doing this, you can start submitting your work to likely publications. The *essential* qualifications are talent and a good eye. You must enjoy forming and defending opinions; for this you need to know what you're talking about; one loudly voiced argument from you that proves to be wrong could blow your career. Starting-up costs are minimal and you work from home (which needs to be near a cultural centre). You should have a second source of income for at least 10 years. Finding a toe-hold can be luck, but you will not become known unless you are prepared to sell yourself. Very few art journals (*Arts Review, The Artist, Burlington, Apollo, Antique Collector*), or newspapers, have large budgets for sending their reviewers around the country. Offer to cover an exhibition in Manchester/Liverpool/Cardiff (or better still abroad while on holiday). Try reviewing books; they may pay very little (sometimes just the book) but keep at it as the articles will follow (you shouldn't really take less than £100 per 1,000 words but, certainly to begin with, you *will*, and it's the readership you're out to impress. Museums, galleries, academics all read these magazines and once your name is known you can get involved in exhibitions or lecturing. Try local radio stations which need experts on exhibitions or paintings that need saving for the nation. Very often you will be required at short notice, so make sure it's your telephone number that they can find. It can be a stressful life, you're staking your career every time you open your mouth but, as long as you've got the necessary knowledge and interest, it's a rewarding and enjoyable way of living.

Artist

Qualifications/Training	Recommended
Income bracket	Low
Licence	No
Town/Country	Either
Experience/Springboard	No
Travel	Possible
Mid-career entry	Yes
Exit sale	No
Entry costs	£50
Work at home	Yes
Mix and match	Yes.

You could think about: *Illustrator, Art historian, Picture restorer, Artists' agent, Mini-cab driver, Telesales person*

Enquiries
Royal Watercolour Society, Royal Society of Painter-Printmakers, Art colleges

Artists make money from creating and selling works of art. You'll need a lot of talent and drive to succeed and, in the early days at least, will almost certainly have to mix and match with other work. For anyone with artistic flair, it's a wonderful way of making money while surrounding yourself with whatever pleases you most – plants, Mediterranean landscapes, nudes, animals. . . . You don't need any formal qualifications but a degree course at a good art school is an excellent way of learning some basic techniques, choosing your favourite media, practising and developing your own style and building up contracts. You may want to study further abroad, eg at the BRITISH SCHOOL AT ROME or in the USA through the BRITISH COUNCIL. Most artists concentrate on one or two media – water colours, etchings, lithographs, oils, murals . . . Few, however, work exclusively in one without experimenting in others at some point in their career. There are specialist societies like the ROYAL WATERCOLOUR SOCIETY and the ROYAL SOCIETY OF PAINTER-PRINTMAKERS. You may find the Regional Arts Associations easier to get into and maybe more useful.

Set up costs depend on the media you're going to use. Brushes can cost about £35 each though you can get away with £10; you will need at least 5–10 brushes and may need up to 30–40; an easel costs £200. You may need carrying cases for your paints, portfolios for your work, paper, pencils, canvas. You can buy second-hand equipment through the *Artist*; *Artists Newsletter* and *Artscribe* give information on courses, studio workshop space, exhibitions, etc. Other expenses may include having plates cut for etchings or transporting yourself and equipment to places you want to paint. It may be difficult to make much money. In the early days, you'll probably have to do something else to keep the wolf from the door. Ideally you want something you can fit around your art rather than something that demands your presence in an office for eight hours a day.

You'll have to create things that people will buy; this doesn't necessarily mean prostituting your art but it does mean working hard to find your particular market and being prepared to accept that this market may be very small. To find buyers, your work must be seen; art college graduation exhibitions are a good first step. Try to get local libraries, theatres and restaurants to show some of your work and tramp around art galleries with your portfolio. Some galleries specialise in the work of young artists; look out for galleries where your work would fit in particularly well with what they usually sell. Galleries take up to 50 per cent commission and most want framed pictures, but they have excellent contacts amongst art buyers and critics. In addition to selling and showing completed works you may be able to get some commissions eg for portraits. There are several ways of supplementing your income, most of these are easier to get into once you've started to establish your reputation – the ARTS COUNCIL gives advice and sponsorship on exhibitions. You can lecture, teach, become an artist in residence or an art therapist. There are opportunities in commercial art, painting murals for interior designers or illustrating books, a good way of getting wide coverage for your work. There are also competitions. As long as you're not too worried about owing a Porsche by the time you're 25, you can have a wonderful life as an artist; there are plenty of biographies that tell you what's entailed.

Artists' Agent

Qualifications/Training	No
Income bracket	Low–Medium
Licence	No
Town/Country	Town
Experience/Springboard	Helpful
Travel	Local
Mid-career entry	Yes
Exit sale	Possible
Entry costs	£5,000
Work at home	Not recommended

Mix and match Yes.
You could think about: *Contemporary art gallery owner, Illustrator, Printer, Bed and breakfast*

Enquiries
Artists' Agents

Commercial artists – whether they are illustrators for books and magazines, advertising or marketing – often need an agent to do the donkey work.

If you've got a good background in design (you needn't have technical skills), and an understanding of printing techniques (so that you can talk to the art editors and advertising agents intelligently) you can start up your own business. Agents usually work for another agency to start with, and build up a close relationship with several artists, then 'encourage' the illustrators they like to work with them – some call this poaching – and build up their own stable of artists.

Most agents specialise in a particular field, such as illustrating practical step-by-step features, or producing illustrations for romantic fiction. Or you may be an agent for a range of illustrators, so that whatever the commission, you have the contacts to fulfil it. The technical knowledge can be picked up at art school, if you do an option in printing or book design. The selling skills come naturally to some people, or you can pick them up while working for another agent.

As well as a fair knowledge of printing, you must be outgoing and get on easily with people. You will have to be clued up about accounting and be able to cope with 'cold calling' (plenty of small talk when you are showing folios to people whom you have had no previous contact with).

The *Creative Handbook* is revised annually, and lists agencies, artists, photographers and so on. You must get yourself (and your artists) listed in it. You may even find it worth taking a full colour page ad to promote yourself.

Your income comes from the commissions: art editors and directors will commission you and pay you once the finished artwork has been accepted – you will have to pay the artists, taking your own cut on the way.

For a professional image, you will need an office (or at least an office address) in the centre of town (preferably London), complete with telephone line and receptionist (or answering machine). You will also need to employ an accountant to deal with finances and the Revenue (not to mention the bank manager).

Junior jobs in the field are advertised in the design magazine of the moment (*Creative Review*, *Design* or *Blueprint*). Artists' agents will also recruit assistants and illustrators direct from art college – the finals show can be all-important.

Assistant Film Director

Qualifications/Training	No
Income bracket	Low–Medium
Licence	No
Town/Country	Town
Experience/Springboard	Yes
Travel	Yes
Mid-career entry	No
Exit sale	No
Entry costs	£500
Work at home	No

Mix and match Limited.
You could think about: *Mini-cab driver, Market research interviewer, Bartender, Film extra*

Enquiries
BECTU (Broadcasting, Entertainment, Cinematograph and Theatre Union)

The assistant director handles the director's practical needs, including planning the schedule for the day's shooting on set or location, drawing up call-sheets and working with the production manager on the equipment required for the shoot. They are also go-betweens for the producer and director. Depending on the scale of the film, there may be more than one assistant director (called 1st, 2nd and 3rd etc. in decreasing order of seniority). The 2nd and 3rd assistants have more to do with the nitty-gritty of getting equipment and cast on set on time, as well as general organisation while filming.

Film, television and video are all difficult to get into. There are no formal qualifications yet, although some NVQS are on the way. BECTU membership is recommended but not essential. A qualification from a BECTU accredited school is useful for background experience, credibility and contacts. The best way in is via a production company as receptionist/secretary/runner so that you can get an inside view of filming and build up some contacts before you start to freelance. Get to as many shoots as possible so that you're seen and can be on site should any extra help be needed. Offer your services to anyone likely to use them. Ultimately it's a case of pushing; nag producers, they may hate you but at least they'll remember you and may pass you on to somebody else who can use you. Investigate the JOBFIT scheme, which gives you on-the-job training and experience through temporary junior positions with various production companies (CYFLE for Welsh-speakers or SCOTTISH FILM TRAINING TRUST if you're in Scotland).

When you set up you'll need a telephone and an answering machine; better still register with a booking service who will handle all your calls while you're away. As you become better known, it's worth getting an agent who can hustle and negotiate for you. The BECTU sets minimum rates of pay although you can earn more; you may find yourself offered less during recessions, so it is worth knowing the agreement between your union and employers' associations. Commercials and promos usually pay a higher rate because the bookings you get for them are for shorter lengths of time than for feature or documentary films.

Assistant directors have to be indefatigable and are at the heart of the film making process, liaising between the production office and the director. They are usually the first to know when something goes wrong. Their responsibility is to ensure that no shooting time is wasted. This is a close knit world where good reputations are hard-earned but easy to lose.

Money into Light gives an account of what goes into making a film.

Bb

Barrister/Advocate

Qualifications/Training	Essential
Income bracket	Medium–High
Licence	Yes
Town/Country	Town
Experience/Springboard	No
Travel	Yes
Mid-career entry	Unlikely
Exit sale	No
Entry costs	£2,000+
Work at home	No
Mix and match	Possible.

You could think about: *MP, Novelist, Property developer, Journalist, Puppeteer, Toastmaster*

Enquiries
Council of Legal Education, General Council of the Bar

Barristers in England, Ireland and Wales, and advocates in Scotland present cases in court, dressed in wigs and gowns. They also provide legal advice. Barristers cannot be directly contacted by lay clients but are engaged by solicitors on their behalf. Superior court cases must be presented by barristers although this monopoly is under threat. They tend to have specialised knowledge of legislation and precedent in an area of the low, and are consulted for their opinion and advice by solicitors whose knowledge is far more general. The work can be broadly divided into criminal and civil law; civil then divides broadly into commercial and general common law.

Roughly speaking, criminal barristers spend more time in court than commercial ones whose main role is as consultants. Advocates do not specialise. Greater amounts of money can be made in commercial work but it takes longer to assimilate the specialist knowledge involved. After 15–20 years of successful practice barristers may apply to the Lord Chancellor as prospective Queen's Counsel. Only the very best (judged on earnings and ability) will make this grade and they handle only the most important cases.

Whatever area they go into, barristers have to have a good short-term memory, be able to grasp situations and information quickly and to remain emotionally detached. In addition they need flair, the ability to think logically and excellent communication skills in order to present cases in court convincingly and in such a way as to be comprehensible to the judge and, in criminal cases, the jury. The Bar is steeped in tradition; women are beginning to make their presence felt, and in fact now account for 40 per cent of the intake though this has yet to be reflected at a senior level. Ethnic minorities are pretty thin on the ground, too, though initiatives have been launched to swell numbers. The first black woman QC was recently appointed.

Qualifying as a barrister requires a law degree or another degree and a law diploma, a year's study leading up to the Bar exam, eating 24 dinners at your inn, being called to the Bar (if you pass the exam) and serving pupillage for a year. Pupils are attached to barrister pupil masters and cannot earn money from practice for the first six months. Many get scholarships from their inn or chambers – more scholarships are now offered, but not much money. You may earn some money in the second six months. One problem for the future is overcrowding: 1992 sees 1,000-plus students on the Bar course chasing some 600 pupillages. Tougher criteria for admission to CLE is being introduced to limit numbers – including a suitability test. Successful completion of your pupillage does not guarantee tenancy. In Scotland you do 21 months with a solicitor after your LLB degree and diploma, then 'devil' for nine months with a member of the Bar.

Barristers are self-employed but are obliged by the Bar council to work from a set of chambers (rented from the Inns of Court in London and Scotland) and have a clerk to administer their work. Sets, usually of between 15 and 30 barristers, share a clerk and junior clerks and may pass work to one another but are in no sense partnerships. On finishing pupillage you must find a tenancy at a set of chambers (either criminal or commercial depending on the field you're in). There are far fewer of these than of pupillages; about 200–300 as against 700, they tend to go to pupils of the set or through contacts. While you're looking for a tenancy you may be able to stay on with your pupil master and take on work from these; this helps to build up useful contacts for when you move to your own chambers. Although new sets of chambers can be set up with the consent of the circuit leader outside London, the Bar Committee in London, it is extremely unlikely that a group of young barristers will be allowed to do so because they will lack the necessary experience to operate chambers successfully.

It's financially difficult at first. The £200–£300 or so you'll need for a wig and gown (essential for court appearances) is minimal compared to the cash flow problems caused by being paid only on completion of a brief and having to pay rent (based on income), travel and other expenses in the meantime. Initially you'll spend a lot of time handling parts of cases for other barristers; solicitors brief a barrister but are not usually averse to the case being handled by another barrister from the same set of chambers. There can be a lot of paperwork, too – lots of drafting of pleadings etc. You may also get some research and consultancy work. By appearing in court for others you will be noticed and solicitors will start to bring work to you. It takes roughly three–five years to become established (commercial takes longer than criminal). There are limits to how selective you can be about which cases you take, in theory at least. A lot of work comes on the taxi rank system: if it's your turn you have to take the case unless you are too busy or it's outside your field.

Legal Aid fees are set nationally; when work is paid for by Legal Aid, you have to resign yourself to low rates and long delays before being paid. Private fees are negotiated between the clerk of the chambers and the solicitor. On average you could be earning upwards of £25,000–£30,000 a year (sometimes a lot more) but this depends on a lot of factors. Some barristers choose to represent only the defence, fewer the prosecution, most represent either – clerks encourage this because the more flexible the chambers, the more work they will get.

Even criminal barristers will usually spend far more time in the preparation of cases than on their presentation. Court work is unpredictable, cases can go on for far longer than predicted or be cancelled at very short notice. You may find yourself under great pressure to prepare for a case in a short time and you must expect to work long and irregular hours. Sometimes you may have very little to do, on other occasions you'll be scheduled to appear in two different courts at the same time (pass on one to someone else in chambers). Court work is physically and mentally demanding. Most of the time you will deal with other members of the legal profession, but you'll meet your clients, often in prison if you're a criminal specialist, and have to be able to overcome any aversion or sympathy that you may feel – or any moral principle at all, some say, but it's ok if the price is right . . . they are of course only joking.

Further information from the COUNCIL OF LEGAL EDUCATION and the SENATE OF THE INNS OF COURT AND THE BAR. Read

Counsel, the magazine of the Senate of the Inns of Court and the Bar.

⁎⁎⁎ European Community Notes

Qualifications: UK qualifications recognised throughout EC and EC qualifications in UK though probably subject to an aptitude test of 'top-up' exam – job experience also counts.

Languages: To succeed, local language necessary.

Setting up: You will find it possible to succeed throughout most of Europe. You will find it easier in Eire.

Advice/Training: Advice available for those wishing to work in Europe.

Exchanges: Formal job exchanges do not exist.

Financial help: May exist for study, training or travel in the EC, specific to this job.

Enquiry point for those wishing to work in the EC: COUNCIL OF LEGAL EDUCATION, GENERAL COUNCIL OF THE BAR.

Notes: The whole position of the legal profession throughout the EC is *very* complex and diverse. As with other professions, such as accountancy, barristers/advocates would be ill-advised to attempt setting-up 'on their own' in another EC country until they have considerable experience of its legislative systems and practices – not to mention a high degree of fluency in its language.

Bartender

Qualifications/Training	No
Income bracket	Low
Licence	No
Town/Country	Either
Experience/Springboard	No
Travel	No
Mid-career entry	Yes
Exit sale	No
Entry costs	Nil
Work at home	No
Mix and match	Yes.

You could think about: *Actor, Musician, Novelist, Mini-cab driver, Painter/decorator, Gardener*

Enquiries
Pubs, wine bars, hotels

Bartenders work in pubs, wine bars or cocktail bars, mixing and serving drinks. Most establishments employ part-time, casual labour as well as full-time employees. Rates set by breweries are pitifully low – around £2 per hour. A session (say 5.30–11.30) pays as little as £12–£15; but it you work in a cocktail bar you can make a healthy living as you will pick up tips as well as an inflated hourly wage reflecting unsocial hours. Most establishments will also provide meals.

Being a bartender is often thought as an easy number. It isn't. It can be hard work, on your feet non-stop for long hours with smoke, noise and garrulous bores – or worse – for company. The hours mean you may have to be prepared to make the job the centre of your social life or get your friends to drink in the place (though you won't get a chance to talk until after the session). For all these reasons, if you can, choose a place where the atmosphere suits you – but remember that things can look very different from the other side of the bar.

If you want to run your own business, then you could set yourself up as a bartender or a freelance cocktail mixer, providing drinks at private parties. The main problem is getting round the licensing laws: you cannot actually sell drinks without a licence, but you can arrange for the hosts to buy drink on a sale or return basis through your wholesaler – you deliver and serve the drink. You will need some basic equipment – tables, cloths and glasses – you provide the garnish – lemon, cherries, ice, paper parasols and so on. You will need transport, and to promote yourself you should have a cocktail menu printed, and business cards. The best promotion is by word of mouth, and you can also advertise your services in local papers, society magazines and so on. It may also be worth going into partnership with someone who does food for parties, so you can give a complete party service.

One of the great advantages of working as a bartender is that you meet people all the time. If you are aiming to get into a particular career, you can use your hours behind the bar to great advantage, if you choose the right drinking hole. If you want to get into advertising, choose the right bar, close to the advertising agencies. If theatre is your area, go for jobs in pubs and clubs in theatreland. You'll need a sense of humour and be able to keep cool under pressure. You'll also need mental arithmetic – though itemised tills have removed some of the strain – and a memory doesn't hurt so you can organise a round in one go. It is not a job for the clumsy.

The bartenders' bible is the *Savoy Cocktail Book* with recipes for all the traditional mixes. There are several other cocktail books on the market.

Beauty Consultant

Qualifications/Training	Recommended
Income bracket	Low–Medium
Licence	No
Town/Country	Town
Experience/ Springboard	Recommended
Travel	Local
Mid-career entry	Possible
Exit sale	No
Entry costs	£2,000
Work at home	Possible

Mix and match	Possible.

You could think about: *Makeup artist, Hairdresser, Fashion designer, Yoga teacher*

Enquiries	

Beauty houses or beauty parlours

A beauty consultant normally starts by working for one of the beauty houses. Their job is to offer advice and instruction on that company's products, normally for a salary plus commission. This is quite distinct from beauty therapists who usually complete Diploma courses at recognised schools not just in the make-up and beauty courses the consultants take, but in the intricacies of waxing, electrolysis, hair removal, etc. Such training is then usually followed by entry to a beauty parlour specialising in beauty 'problems', rather than the speculative buying indulged in by Ms Average who just wants 'to look like Madonna or Kelly Emberg'.

Anyone branching out on their own will normally have followed one of these routes. Freelance opportunities exist, generally for beauty advisers who are prepared to visit clients in their own homes.

Good reputations travel fast, and you need to be patient, informative, instructive – as well as ready to make up people who need a facelift or a paper bag over the head. For the impatient, or anyone too inexperienced to gain entry directly to a beauty house or beauty parlour, one option could be to try one of the agencies which supply the beauty houses with temporary staff to give extra cover for promotions, Christmas, etc. These will give two–three day cramming courses on several houses' products and then hire out staff for short periods, thus providing minimal experience.

Most good companies will not employ people under 21, which fixes the lowest point of entry, unless you have something special to offer such as languages or training at a recognised beauty therapy school. Race and, perhaps surprisingly, sex, offer no barrier, as many female customers find it appealing to have a man giving them time and attention. Nevertheless, most men would find it intimidating to work in such an unquestionably female environment.

There is no world so bitchy as that of the beauty consultant, few others where one's appearance is analysed every hour by customers and fellow consultants, and where one is open to such personal criticism. You'll need patience to compromise between what the customer actually needs and what she says she needs, and strong legs, as you need to stand for long hours, sometimes virtually all day. Delicate flowers tend to wilt very quickly in this over-heated atmosphere.

The main requirements are an obvious desire to enter the beauty world, plus willingnes or proven ability to deal with the public. Good grooming, self assurance and an interesting personality will cross almost all bridges. Driving licences and similar extra strings to one's bow are useful but not essential.

A consultant starting work in London might expect to earn £130 a week, less for the provinces, although this will depend upon how many customers you can pack into a working day.

Any magazines on beauty and health care are useful.

Bed and Breakfast

Qualifications/Training	None
Income bracket	Low
Licence	No
Town/Country	Either
Experience/Springboard	No
Travel	No
Mid-career entry	Excellent
Exit sale	Minimal
Entry costs	£200
Work at home	Yes

Mix and match	Excellent.

You could think about: ***Publican, Artist, Windsurfing school owner, Antique dealer***

Enquiries
Bed & Breakfasts

If you're lucky enough to have the space and you need to supplement your income, look no further. Running B & B can be combined with almost any other job (or none), so long as someone is around to cook the breakfast and change the sheets and no-one in your house practises their drums at three in the morning. Staying in a B & B appeals to many people who prefer the more homely touch to staying in a hotel and, in the experience of someone with years in the business, if you treat your guests right, you don't get problems from them. But you shouldn't be squeamish about cleaning dirty lavatories.

First step, clear out the old hat boxes, goldfish bowls, seeding potatoes or whatever you keep in your spare room(s) – for serious business you'll require three or four, at least, otherwise it's just an income supplement. Add instead whatever you feel should be in the room and will suit the type of customers you propose to aim for and expect: nylon sheets or linen; chintz, lace or candlewick bedspreads; plastic flowers, the real things or bowls or pot pourri; Hockneys, family portraits or flying china ducks on the walls; kettle, television, magazines.

You don't need a licence if you are only doing B & B but you do need to register with the council to serve food, for which you need a Food Hygiene Certificate. It does not affect your poll/council tax position. If you are busy, you will need three pairs of sheets and towels for each bed and a washing machine; if you've no reliable drying facilities, or you are not able to wash every day, you may need more. It's worth making sure you have spare blankets/duvets in case of accidents and you should anyway expect to replace all the bedding, including the matresses, every six–eight years or so. A couple of spare front door keys and you are equipped. All you need is customers.

How you get these will depend on where you are. Some insist the key to success is advertising. It may be worth putting a notice in your front window (**Accommodation** or **Bed and Breakfast** are the traditional ones). Unless you are very central to your customers, this is unlikely to be enough. Make sure you are on the list provided by your local council. If you are in a holiday area, the tourist board will also have lists and there are specialist lists, for example for travelling businessmen, American tourists etc. Busy in summer, you'll aim to make enough to carry you over winter.

They will pay different rates, of course: as a rough guide, you might expect a minimum of £10 a night at the bottom of the market in a holiday area: £17–£25 for something a little ritzier and £25–£40 at the top of the market. You can, of course, charge more for a room with an en suite bathroom (increasingly expected; you should at least provide a basin), if there is a television in the bedroom or if you are prepared to offer dinner as well. If you do offer dinner you'll need a licence to serve drinks. You'll be subject to inspection by environmental health officers under the Food Safety Act. Food is heavily – and increasingly – regulated; check *everything* with the local authority. If you are at the really pukka end, you may need to be able to take credit cards, otherwise people will happily pay by cheque or cash.

Whatever you expect, you will find your customers a curious cross section – garrulous salesmen, harrassed mothers with horrible children, walkers with smelly feet, as well as model guests who are quiet and tidy and pay in cash. What they will expect is personal contact and being made to feel at home. A friendly atmosphere will bring people back or encourage recommendations.

Beekeeper

Qualifications/Training	Available
Income bracket	Low
Licence	No
Town/Country	Country
Experience/Springboard	Useful
Travel	Local
Mid-career entry	Yes
Exit sale	Yes
Entry costs	£5,000
Work at home	Yes
Mix and match	Yes.

You could think about: *Farmer, Gardener/garden designer, Smallholder, Book publisher, Inventor, Stockbroker*

Enquiries
Bee Farmers Association

Successful beekeeping needs complete dedication. The active season starts slowly in March, faster in April, with May to August being the busiest months, dealing with swarming and harvest. Bees should be fed with winter stores by mid-September, when they hibernate. You must check bees for swarming about every nine days from mid-May to mid-July when the main honey flow ends.

The site of your apiary is vital. You need good nectar-producing flora like white clover, limes, sycamore, apples, oil seed rape, rosebay willow herb, blackberries etc. The site should be sunny; have protection from the weather particularly from the north and east; be snug, warm and airy; be easily accessible to transport and not too close to other people. If you are close to heather moors, it is possible to get another crop of honey from mid-August to mid-September; it will also provide the bees with two-thirds of their winter stores, so making the transport cost and site rental worthwhile.

Very few people have succeeded in making a living by bees alone. The average yearly yield per commercial hive for flower honey (as opposed to heather) is about

30 lb. But in 1985 and 1986 it was only 20 lb and 50 per cent of bees perished in the cold winter of 1985–86. By contrast, 1989 was a bumper year, with average commercial hives yielding 63 lb of flower honey (and 14 lb for heather honey).

There are no legal requirements for setting up a bee farm. A tiny piece of ground is needed to accommodate 10–15 hives; don't put too many in one location or you reach saturation point and get nothing. Equipment is expensive but it is frequently possible to buy bees and hives advertised locally for £50–£60 from someone giving up. You can sometimes pick up a swarm for nothing. Some can be easy and some suicidal. You need a bee-proof shed for storing equipment and extracting; also a veil, gloves, smoker, hive tools, overalls, feeders, riperer and extractor (sometimes you can borrow one from an association). Your main expenses are sugar, transport and honey jars (in the event of your having honey to sell).

You can join your local county beekeeper's association which exist in most parts of the country. These have regular meetings and practical demonstrations during the summer. Many counties have beekeeping instructors who run courses. These are also courses at agricultural colleges at SPARSHOLT and WRITTLE for those intent on commercial beekeeping. Once you are commercial, you can join the BEE FARMERS ASSOCIATION. There are two journals – *Beecraft* and the *British Bee Journal*. The *Beekeeper's Quarterly* is also worthwhile.

You can sell honey in grocers' shops; but it is less likely to get lost among the jars of marmalade and chutney in cafés, pubs and garden centres.

It is useful to have an assistant (who won't bolt) who can use the smoker while you examine a hive and who can help you lift supers (honey boxes) on and off hives, as they can become very heavy. It is sometimes possible to obtain a pollination fee for, say, taking your bees to the fruit orchards of Kent or fields of beans.

Beekeepers work in any weather during the season and all hours of the day – the bees won't wait. The job can be very rewarding at times and heartbreaking at others and sometimes very painful. You must: be in an area with suitable flora; keep diseases under control; not let your bees swarm out; rid yourself of any useless queen heading your hive; and be sure not to let your bees starve – if you fail on any of these counts, you will get nothing and there will be some more cheap bees for sale.

No one who wants to become prosperous would become a professional beekeeper. There are a few who make a good living. But for many it's a rewarding second job, or seasonal pursuit – in the UK there is very little year-round work. But it is congenial and can be very fulfilling, for example, for those with early retirement.

European Community Notes
Beekeeping in the UK is very inward looking. There is little involvement in EC – Eire is probably the most promising prospect.

Book Designer

Qualifications/Training	Recommended
Income bracket	Medium
Licence	No
Town/Country	Town preferably
Experience/Springboard	Recommended
Travel	Local
Mid-career entry	Doubtful
Exit sale	No
Entry costs	£1,000–£5,000+
Work at home	Yes
Mix and match	Yes.

You could think about: *Book packager, Magazine designer, Book publisher, Greyhound trainer, Potter, Illustrator*

Enquiries
National Union of Journalists, Art Colleges, Publishers

Increasingly book publishing companies are using freelancers, both to edit and design books. So there are plenty of openings for working freelance if you have the experience and the contacts. Illustrated book design is by far the most interesting to most people.

On the old model, for most freelance book designers, the job starts with a book manuscript being sent by an editor. The style of the book may have been set by an in-house designer or it may be up to you. Then you fit copy, tables and illustrations into the set number of pages. After producing a rough mini-plan of the book, you 'mark up' the copy. This involves indicating on each page of the typescript what typeface, type size and column width the typesetter should use. The next stage is usually galley proofs, which are read by an editor, laid out on the appropriate pages with the appropriate pictures traced in by the designer.

This is followed by page proofs and colour proofs as appropriate; if you've got it right they all fit together. Certainly, the designer must be able to visualise how his rough layouts will look when the book is finally printed, as there is usually no budget for major alterations once the colour proofs have been produced. The fact is though that with the advances in desk-top publishing technology of the last few years, you are just as likely now to be carrying out the entire operation on screen using page make-up and graphics software then supplying the publisher with anything from disks for them to output to finished camera-ready copy and artwork. And your ability to do this is part of your attraction as a freelance.

Book designers, like magazine designers, usually start with art school training or specialist courses at, eg, LONDON COLLEGE OF PRINTING, then work for a book publisher to gain experience and contacts before going freelance – your old firm is a good source of work. Jobs are advertised in the creative and media pages of the quality national press, the *Bookseller*, and sometimes *Campaign*. There are also openings for design consultants who will advise publishing companies on, eg, choosing the right typefaces and other ways of making their books more attractive.

To set up on your own, you can start in a room of your own house, equipped with drawing board, Grant projector (for blowing up pictures), and light box (for examining transparencies etc. If you are going the full DTP route you'll need a computer – probably a Mac – and decent printer. The quality of the hardware will depend on what you are handing over, eg disks, CRC – if it's finished artwork you'll need a *good* printer. You should keep abreast of new technology. That can be harder to do on your own than in a big company but so many publishers are still in the dark ages, anyway. A fax is almost essential too. Some designers find it better to work from an office near the centre of London, either on their own or in partnership with other designers and editors. This makes communication with the publishers easier, and means that you are easily available for the inevitable rush jobs. If you do this, you may find that you actually form a packaging company with other designers and editors, producing final film or camera-ready copy, even printed books to sell to publishing houses.

As a freelance you're going to have to *sell* yourself. Ask why publishers want you. It could be because you're cheap – at least, cheaper than keeping someone on wages to do special jobs, say. And publishers *are* cheap, some of them, with interesting notions of accounting; in-house design costs can be buried but you will be charged against a project so subject to greater scrutiny. *Or*, you can be very, very good – certainly better than they could afford to keep on wages. They will want both – cheap and good – but don't sell yourself short. You should be looking for, say, £25 an hour pro rata and then up, up, up.

Book designers may diversify into magazine design, although this is more often an in-house job. Traditionally, book designers belong to the NATIONAL UNION OF JOURNALISTS and the GRAPHICAL PAPER AND MEDIA UNION. You will find *Editing and Design*, *Creative Review* and *Direction* useful.

✺ European Community Notes

Qualifications: UK qualifications (NVQs) are being developed. EC qualifications in UK would be welcomed by the UK industry but nobody would know what to do about it. In Germany, France and the Netherlands there is formal training, with bits of paper on graduation and then on a formal requirement.

Languages: To succeed, local language absolutely necessary.

Earnings: UK income generally lower than elsewhere in the EC.

Setting up: You will find it possible to succeed throughout Europe.

Advice/Training: Advice, information and training not available for those wishing to work in Europe.

Exchanges: Formal job exchanges do not exist, but *ad hoc* arrangements between companies which have a real commercial interest in their partners are known to exist.

Financial help: Exists for study, training or travel in Germany (Bertelsmann Foundation).

Enquiry point for those wishing to work in the EC: BOOK HOUSE TRAINING CENTRE.

Recommended reading: The equivalent to the *Bookseller* in each country. The *European*.

Notes: Local languages are a pre-requisite. Do not try without thorough preliminary research in the UK and a period of work experience in a local publishing house where you can access the gaps in the market. The golden rule is to visit the member state's embassy in London and find out what you can from them and in particular whether there is a UK cultural institute from that country in London. France, Italy and Germany do have them. You'll need to do the most thorough and painstaking cultural research, including an examination of the books published/distributed locally.

Bookie

Qualifications/Training	Available
Income bracket	Highly variable
Licence	Yes
Town/Country	Town or on-course
Experience/Springboard	Essential
Travel	Yes (on-course)
Mid-career entry	Yes
Exit sale	Possible
Entry costs	£1,000 (on-course)
Work at home	No
Mix and match	Possible.

You could think about: ***Mini-cab driver, Market research interviewer, Painter/ decorator, Smallholder***

Enquiries
National Association of Bookmakers

Turf accountants offer odds and accept bets on the results of sporting or other events. They usually work in a shop, supervising cashiers who take money and record the time of the bet and are responsible for settling winning bets, balancing cash and keeping records. Some fix odds and travel to race courses. Betting and gambling are a small but significant part of the leisure industry – which is strictly regulated, generally with a view to limiting gambling rather than encouraging it (although long overdue legislation finally made betting shops slightly more pleasurable places). There is a living to be made from betting and gaming – despite the intention to limit gaming there will always be people who wish to place bets and the industry is there to cater for them.

Start by working for someone else (no formal qualifications required). The big three betting chains give on-job training and have training schools. You can also contact the NATIONAL ASSOCIATION OF BOOKMAKERS. The calculations involved can be quite complex viz in the case of multiple bets with doubles, trebles and accumulators. You have to know the rules, be good with figures (lightning settling centring on percentage), fractions and anything to do with bet calculation; happy with, or used to handling money, and sure you don't infringe any regulations. You yourself will need honesty, a careful calm nature, attention to detail, numerical ability, the ability to manage people, quick thinking, good organising ability; and most important you will need to know how to handle people who are trying to cheat you.

On-course you need to hold a permit (renewable each year) and operate under national rules. There's a lot of driving, courses being scattered all over the country and you're out there in all weathers (usually dreadful). You live by pitting your judgment against that of others, which is exciting. You can lose a lot of money but make it as well. You don't need a lot of money to set up (if you're on-course all you need is an umbrella, a blackboard and a carrying voice). You do need to know a lot about 'form' – how horses or dogs are likely to perform – as this is how you make your living.

Anyone considering working in this industry must be prepared for unsocial hours – betting shops are open six days a week with Saturday being the busiest day (and who knows what will happen with Sundays). Betting shops are regulated by law – though not as strictly as casinos or other gaming establishments and are not quite the Godforsaken places they used to be – now allowed to sell light refreshments and to install TV (offering live televised coverage). The opening hours are around 10–6 every day except Sunday (currently) and Christmas – Boxing Day is a busy racing day. Also some evenings (summer for horses; dogs, especially on-course). Work is pressurised at times and can involve people who are being awkward or aggressive. Conditions are noisy and crowded (not for people who can't bear cigarette smoke). You might also read *Law of Betting, Gaming and Lotteries*.

European Community Notes
One can only say, on current form your chances must be limited. In most of Europe off-course bookies simply don't exist in any legitimate form – nor, often,

on-course either: witness pari-mutuel – like the Tote – on French tracks. And if you ever did find a niche, it's likely that local competition would be 'intense'.

Book keeper

Qualifications/Training	Available
Income bracket	Low–Medium
Licence	No
Town/Country	Either
Experience/ Springboard	Recommended
Travel	Some
Mid-career entry	Yes
Exit sale	No
Entry costs	£2,000
Work at home	Yes
Mix and match	Excellent.

You could think about: ***Word processor, Musician, Snail farmer, Office services bureau***

Enquiries
Local accountants and book-keepers

If you're good with figures and enjoy keeping accounts, you'll find plenty of people and businesses who will pay you to prepare their accounts for bank managers and auditors, leaving them free to concentrate on other things. You can operate from anywhere near shops and offices and can work as much and when you like. This makes bookkeeping a good option for people who want to mix and match with something else. You don't need any formal qualifications to be a bookkeeper but you'll have to know what you're doing. You should know about VAT (if you need any help with a particular case contact the CUSTOMS AND EXCISE – contrary to popular belief, they can be helpful and would far rather you got it right first time than left them with a muddle to sort out later on). You'll also need an accounting system you can use; to know how to present accounts, draw up graphs and make reasonably accurate forecasts. It's inadvisable to set up on your own without having had some experience; say in an insurance office, sales or accounts department or in some position (eg sales rep) where you're accountable for money. There's a useful basic book called *Teach Yourself Bookkeeping* which will fill in any small gaps in your information. From experience you'll learn to see certain patterns in your clients' cashflows. Book-keepers have to be logical, accurate, honest and patient, so that they can cope with other people's lack of these qualities.

Essential equipment is a computer with appropriate software, a telephone and an answering machine. You may also need a car to get to your clients and to transport bags and boxes of their bills and receipts. Book-keepers provide the stationery for the accounts they make, so get supplies of files, account ledgers and graph paper from stationery wholesalers. Learn how to judge the amount of time a job is going to take, charge by the hour and give an indication of how long you think the job is going to take. The number of clients you need depends on the workloads that each generates, six or seven can make you a living. Approach small local businesses and one man bands. The best way of doing this is through a mail shot; the Post Office offers one of 1,000 free to new businesses so use this and the *Yellow Pages*. Put up adverts in shop windows; advertising in the local press may bring you nothing but offers from rival publications to place further adverts. Once you're established, you'll get more clients by word of mouth and clients tend to stick with you once you've established a system with them.

Clients are liable to call on you at the last minute, when the VAT man is breathing down their necks and they're in danger of being liable for non-payment surcharges. They'll hand you carrier bags full of receipts and bills which you have to put in order. Most clients need your services once a month or once a quarter, they may also want help with cashflow forecasts to present to their bank managers or building societies. Do these cautiously; don't be too specific in forecasting or you risk being sued and always put in a disclaimer.

Clients may want to see you at a specific time but once you've picked up their stuff the hours you work are up to you. Allow yourself more time to do a job than you expect to need – it's better to hang on to finished work for a day or two than to be late with a job. You can easily build holidays into your schedule as long as you take into account clients' VAT deadlines and arrange to get the work done at a different time.

If you're happy doing book-keeping you need no other qualification than a way with figures. But of course the scope is limited. If you want to do more – especially in Europe – you should look at becoming an accountant.

Book Packager

Qualifications/Training	Available
Income bracket	Medium
Licence	No
Town/Country	Either
Experience/Springboard	Essential
Travel	Possible
Mid-career entry	Likely
Exit sale	Yes
Entry costs	£5,000–£10,000++
Work at home	Possible
Mix and match	Yes.

You could think about: ***Book designer, Book publisher, Desk-top publisher, Football commentator, Jazz Musician, Trout farmer***

Enquiries
Book House Training Centre

Book packaging involves conceiving, writing (or commissioning), illustrating and designing a book (known in the trade as the pre-production costs) so that the publisher has only to manage the production and sales. Increasingly, however there is a trend to take on much of the production work too so that you are delivering the publisher camera-ready copy and artwork or film, even finished books so all they have to do is sell it. Obviously, your outlay is greater but so is your income. Packagers as a breed concentrate on supplying packages that reflect their own strengths, expertise and interests rather than supplying goods to publishers' precise specifications.

Book packaging companies are usually set up by groups of experienced publishing people – perhaps an editor and a designer working together. The minimum premises needed are an office with a couple of desks and a drawing board, plus the usual filing cabinets and light box, phones, fax and photocopier. Increasingly, you'll need computer hardware for processing copy, design and page make-up, artwork and graphics, and so on. How much – and how good – kit you need depends on the work you're doing and how far along the production road you go, but the more you can handle – and quickly – the more attractive you can be to publishers.

Direct costs are dependent on the type of book you are producing – whether highly illustrated, technically complex with lots of tables and graphs or a relatively simple narrative. Plenty of contacts in the publishing world are vital. The market is becoming somewhat overloaded, so there is more risk involved than, say, five years ago, and some book packagers have gone under. A couple of good signed contracts with reputable publishing houses to show the bank manager are more important than vast amounts of investment capital.

Packagers are paid partly in advance, partly on completion and, more rarely, partly on sales performance. But there are very many different packaging arrangements and packagers' contracts usually contain tailor-made clauses, within a standard package contract, for each specific title under contract.

The trick to packaging is pricing – costing is your key problem. You'll inevitably want 5–10 per cent more than the publisher wants to pay, so you'll be cutting margins all the time. But *do not underprice* – many is the packager who took the long walk down Carey Street because he thought £5,000 a week to produce a part-work, say, was a lot of money. Well it is, but is it enough? You are *not* gong to be cheaper than a publisher producing work in-house – although of course, they are saving the overhead. But you are offering a creative service, and a high quality one. And if you can always take on a job at short notice – which is where the new technology is such an advantage – so much the better.

The *Bookseller* is a useful publication; full of information on what books are being launched, which publishers are doing well, what other packagers are doing and news about promotions/appointments within the industry, to keep your contacts book up to date. The BOOK HOUSE TRAINING CENTRE has useful information.

⁕⁕⁕ European Community Notes

Qualifications: UK qualifications (NVQs) are being developed. EC qualifications in UK would be welcomed by the UK industry but nobody would know what to do about it. In Germany, France and the Netherlands there is formal training, with bits of paper on graduation and then on a formal requirement.

Languages: To succeed, local language absolutely necessary.

Earnings: UK income generally lower than elsewhere in the EC.

Setting up: You will find it possible to succeed throughout Europe.

Advice/Training: Advice, information and training not available for those wishing to work in Europe.

Exchanges: Formal job exchanges do not exist, but *ad hoc* arrangements between companies which have a real commercial interest in their partners are known to exist.

Financial help: exists for study, training or travel in Germany (Bertelsmann Foundation).

Enquiry point for those wishing to work in the EC: BOOK HOUSE TRAINING CENTRE.

Recommended reading: The equivalent to the *Bookseller* in each country. The *European*.

Notes: Local languages are a pre-requisite. Do not try without thorough preliminary research in the UK and a period of work experience in a local publishing house where you can access the gaps in the market. The golden rule is to visit the member state's embassy in London and find out what you can from them and in particular whether there is a UK cultural institute from that country in London. France, Italy and Germany do have them. You'll need to do the most thorough and painstaking cultural research, including an examination of the books published/distributed locally.

Book Publisher

Qualifications/Training	Available
Income bracket	Low–High
Licence	No
Town/Country	Town
Experience/Springboard	Essential
Travel	Yes
Mid-career entry	Possible
Exit sale	Yes
Entry costs	£20,000
Work at home	Yes
Mix and match	Possible.

You could think about: *Desk-top publisher, Novelist, Beekeeper, Jazz musician*

Enquiries
Book House Training Centre

Book publishers are in business, trading in books and in rights – paperback rights, film rights, serial rights, electronic publishing rights, foreign language rights. In the past, many book publishers only published hardcover editions and sold the paperback rights to specialist houses such as Pan or Penguin. This is now less common as, with a flurry of takeovers/mergers, the industry is now full of mega-publishers with both hard- and paper-back divisions. The same mega-publishers are predators on established authors but their sheer size leaves openings for the small operator. While there is a worldwide English language book market, many publishers begin by publishing their own editions in the UK only, selling the right to publish in key overseas markets (such as Australia, Canada or the US) to local publishers whose distribution and sales arrangements are already in place. It is possible, technically, to enter the world market by publishing only one title.

The job falls neatly into two unequal components. First, investment – 10 per cent of the job at the most. It requires flair, the ability to make specific choices on the basis of little experience and much intuition: what books to publish; what niche to occupy in the worldwide English language market; what parts of your business are best run hands-on and what you can safely delegate to suppliers (eg printers). Secondly, managing that investment – 90 per cent of the work is managing authors, data, sources, manuscripts, typesetters, paper buyers, printers and binders, rights, sales, advertising sales, relationships with booksellers, book promotion, reviews, distribution, cash and currency (pound v dollar) etc. Without flair, do not attempt to set up on your own. The giant publishers are littered with managers masquerading as publishers who command sufficient resources to beat you at your own game. You can acquire the management skills inside or outside the industry. Some obviously successful publishers have moved into the industry, but within publishing specific technical skills can be acquired from courses run by BOOK HOUSE TRAINING CENTRE or you can take postgraduate courses at for instance the LONDON COLLEGE OF PRINTING, OXFORD POLYTECHNIC or WATFORD COLLEGE. It is almost certainly worth working for an established publisher for a few years, to acquire some know-how. Get in at any level – secretary, VDU operator, sales rep, editor – and then look around for further openings. Once in, you can begin to assess whether you are likely to have the necessary flair. By visiting the warehouse, you will also discover the only fact of publishing life worth committing to memory: it's easy to publish books but enormously difficult to sell them. Indeed, you could do worse than work in bookselling for a while.

All you need to set up as a publisher is notepaper, a telephone, a typewriter (or preferably word processor) and the finance to carry one or two projects through to profitability. Later you may require more sophisticated finance, for instance the injection of venture capital, plus whatever you need to live on until your cash flow becomes positive, together with a good bank manager who understands your business plan and a printer and typesetter willing to extend generous credit terms (as they often are to small new publishers). Keep overheads to a minimum. Successful new publishing houses often began in a spare room. Use good quality restaurants to do business with those who need to be impressed. Avoid employing staff as long as you can. One reason why it is relatively easy to set up as a publisher is that the industry boasts a host of sophisticated suppliers eager to sell their services to you. They do their job excellently and to time – writers, book designers, illustrators, editors, printers, warehouses, advertising and PR agencies, direct mail specialists and freelance sales forces. Many can be located through the *Creative Directory*, the *Writers' and Artists' Yearbook* or *The Writer's Handbook*. Make sure you read the intensely narcissistic trade press (the *Bookseller*, *Publishing News*) but do not let it put you off. The definitive text on the business is still Sir Stanley Unwin's the *Truth about Publishing*; the authoritative careers guide is *Inside Book Publishing*; the most entertaining and informative bedside companion is *Bluff Your Way in Publishing*.

Dealing with a very wide variety of busy suppliers will leave little time in your life for anything but your business. Do not set up as a publisher if you want to segment your life into work and play.

✶✶✶ European Community Notes

Qualifications: UK qualifications do not yet exist but NVQs are on their way. EC qualifications in UK would be welcomed by the UK industry but nobody would know what to do about it. In Germany, France and the Netherlands there is formal training, with bits of paper on graduation and then on a formal requirement.
Languages: To succeed, local language absolutely necessary.
Earnings: UK income generally lower than elsewhere in the EC.

Setting up: You will find it possible to succeed throughout Europe.
Advice/Training: Advice, information and training not available for those wishing to work in Europe.
Exchanges: Formal job exchanges do not exist, but *ad hoc* arrangements between companies which have a real commercial interest in their partners are known to exist.
Financial help: exists for study, training or travel in Germany (Bertelsmann Foundation).
Enquiry point for those wishing to work in the EC: BOOK HOUSE TRAINING CENTRE.
Recommended reading: The equivalent to the *Bookseller* in each country.
Notes: Local languages are a pre-requisite. Do not try without thorough preliminary research in the UK and a period of work experience in a local publishing house where you can access the gaps in the market. The golden rule is to visit the member state's embassy in London and find out what you can from them and in particular whether there is a UK cultural institute from that country in London. France, Italy and Germany do have them. You'll need to do the most thorough and painstaking cultural research, including an examination of the books published/distributed locally.

Bookseller

Qualifications/Training	Available
Income bracket	Medium
Licence	No
Town/Country	Town
Experience/ Springboard	Recommended
Travel	None
Mid-career entry	Yes
Exit sale	Yes
Entry costs	£20,000
Work at home	No

Mix and match   Possible.
You could think about: *Novelist, Artist, Word processor*

Enquiries
Booksellers Association

Many small booksellers have to compete more and more against the large chains, but local shops in the right areas can still survive and increased spending on books is predicted. Do bear in mind though that slightly under half the adult population is reading a book at any point in time; choose a fairly middle-class area to set up in. To sell books you will need to know a lot about them (both classics and new titles) so that you can advise customers. Bookshop owners need a lot of enthusiasm to put up with long hours and bookkeeping. Also patience and the ability to think laterally in order to cope with vague or difficult customers. Hard retailing skills are just as necessary as a great love of books.

The BOOKSELLERS ASSOCIATION has a whole range of training courses and publishes a guide to starting and running a bookshop. But certainly you should also work in a bookshop for a while. This gives an idea of pitfalls and problems and of how the business is run as well as helping to broaden your knowledge of books. It is also worth reading the economic survey published by the Booksellers Association, which gives an idea as to the likely costs involved. To set up you need premises, freehold or leasehold, with shelving, some sort of cash register and, preferably, a microfiche of British Books in Print (£500). The Booksellers Association recommends that you start off with somewhere between £25,000 and £80,000's worth of stock (although other sources suggest that you can get away with about half as much). You get this from a wholesaler who will send you a general selection to begin with until you get a better idea of what books to concentrate on and may offer extended credit (six weeks). Once you've advertised in the trade press you may also get stock from publishers' reps.

It's important to establish a good credit rating so that you can open accounts with suppliers (two trade references and a banker). The Net Book Agreement (currently under some threat) sets the retail price of most books. This means that you aren't free to make special offers to your customers on net books; however, you're less likely to lose out to larger booksellers who can buy in bulk. Publishers usually give 35 per cent trade discount and pay for the carriage. In addition publishers' credit terms (they demand very quick settling of accounts) mean that some of your stock will remain unsold long after you have paid for it.

The Booksellers Association suggests that you should try and achieve a complete turnover of stock four or five times a year. It takes about three years to become established and you are very unlikely to get rich; the trade as a whole suffers from low profits and subsequent lack of funds for developing, marketing etc. Bear in mind that about 40 per cent of annual book sales are made in the six–eight weeks before Christmas.

Booksellers have to sell what their public wants, which may mean stocking books that you hate (although some booksellers refuse to stock war books, however profitable). There are obvious risks in being overtly political or specialised unless you choose your area very carefully, and you are bound to face criticism at some time for the books you do or don't stock.

Brewer

Qualifications/Training	Available
Income bracket	Low–High
Licence	Yes
Town/Country	Either
Experience/Springboard	Essential
Travel	No
Mid-career entry	Likely
Exit sale	Excellent
Entry costs	£60,000+++
Work at home	Yes

Mix and match   Possible.
You could think about: *Publican,*
Farmer, Wine merchant, Property
developer

Enquiries
Small Independent Brewers' Association

Brewing's rather more complicated than
the rubric on the side of a can of home
brew material would have you believe.
First step is to work out what you want to
brew – ale, strong or weak, lager, stout,
etc. It's relatively easy to brew traditional
ale but it requires more complicated equipment (filters and refrigeration) to brew
lager. Ten years ago lager represented
under 30 per cent of the beer market;
today it's 50 per cent and rising, inexorably
squeezing out ale and the ale brewer. This
is not a business for bucolic amateurs. The
second step is to work out who will buy
what you're going to produce. It's easier if
you have your own pub – preferably in a
populated area or by a main road.

The beer must be good, healthy and
palatable – and you'll have to be a good,
hygienic brewer. Some experience,
apprenticeship or education in brewing is
essential. Good quality materials must be
bought, recipes created and adapted to suit
your drinkers' palates. Care must be taken
in the brewing process to avoid any spoil-
age and, hence, off-flavour. You're subject
to all the usual hygiene, safety and other
regulations covering food factories – ie
white coats, no smoking – and getting
stricter. Brewing hygiene and sterility are
vital – it is very costly if they are less than
perfect, rendering your product undrink-
able. The fact that you're brewing for sale
rather than personal consumption, makes
you eligible for excise tax, calculated on the
potential strength of the beer before it
starts fermenting. The strength is calculated on the original gravity (or OG) of the
liquid before fermentation starts. From
this point onwards, the liquid becomes
valuable, every drop wasted effectively increases the tax rate on the rest of the brew
and it's difficult to get the excise tax back
on any beer which subsequently becomes
unsellable. Depending on the strength,
excise tax can be between £50 and £70 per

barrel of 36 gallons (288 pints). On top of
this, you have to keep detailed records for
frequent visits from the Excise (sometimes
at unlikely hours to make sure you aren't
cheating). Many pubs have large out-
houses which can be used as breweries. If
you could build a brew-pub, you would
save on transport because you don't need a
lorry to cart all those barrels about. In this
case, you should think of spending some
£650,000 – a good pub (not the best)
£600,000+; and a mini-brewery £50,000.

If you aren't going to get your own pub
or want to sell your beer to other pubs,
you'll have to buy barrels (no, you can't
nick anyone else's). An 18-gallon beer
barrel costs almost £70 – for a 10-barrel-a-
week brewery, you might need about 100
casks. You'll also need to buy the raw
materials. You can use traditional malt and
hops, in which case you'll need a mill
and associated equipment for extracting
the fermentable sugars. Alternatively, you
can use syrups and concentrates which are
made from the same raw materials, require
less kit to use, but cost more. Malt comes
from maltsters, hops from hop merchants
(most are based in the south-east) and
syrups from corn merchants.

About 60–70 per cent of pubs are tied
to a particular brewery: either because they
are owned by one, or they are so-called free
houses, which have been loaned money in
exchange for their agreement to sell the
brewer's beer. This makes 60 per cent of
the market in effect closed to you. Not
surprisingly this 60 per cent represents the
bigger, high volume pubs leaving you with
the smaller ones.

The cat has been put among the pigeons
by the Monopolies and Mergers Commission's report which recommended substantially lessening the breweries' hold on
pubs. The DTI's watered-down Beer
Orders insist on a far less radical break
between brewers and outlets. There *has*
been a shake-up of sorts, but the dust has
yet to settle either on ownership of pubs
by breweries or on tied houses stocking
'guest beers' – which *could* provide a useful
outlet for the independent.

Recommended reading includes *Brewers'*
Guardian and *Brewing & Distilling Inter-*
national and there are a host of technical

books. Further information on the industry from the SMALL INDEPENDENT BREWERS' ASSOCIATION and on suppliers from the ALLIED BREWERY TRADERS' ASSOCIATION.

✱✱ European Community Notes

Qualifications: UK qualifications recognised throughout EC except in Germany and EC qualifications in UK.

Languages: To succeed, local language necessary.

Advice/Training: Advice, information and training not available.

Exchanges: Formal job exchanges do not exist.

Enquiry point for those wishing to work in the EC: SMALL INDEPENDENT BREWERS' ASSOCIATION.

Builder

Qualifications/Training	Yes
Income bracket	Medium
Licence	No
Town/Country	Either
Experience/ Springboard	Recommended
Travel	Local
Mid-career entry	Unlikely
Exit sale	Possible
Entry costs	£1,500+++
Work at home	No
Mix and match	Possible.

You could think about: *Mini-cab driver, Man with a van, Greyhound trainer, Stage technician carpenter, Thatcher, Property developer, House converter*

Enquiries
Federation of Master Builders,
Construction Industry Training Board

Maintenance builders do small and medium-sized building jobs such as shelving, putting up gates and garden walls, underpinning, roof repairs, building garages and extensions and conversions. Their clients tend to be householders or small businesses. As a self-employed builder you're going to have to spend quite a lot of time managing others because, for all but the smallest jobs, you'll need to employ or subcontract other people as, for example, plumbers, plasterers and electricians. Your income is at the mercy of the economy: when interest rates are low and the house market is active, builders do very well; when interest rates go up, people have less ready money to spend on their houses. To start with you should learn as much of the trade as possible. Local colleges run night classes and day-release courses in aspects such as bricklaying, plumbing, plastering and decorating. Although you may not be doing all of these yourself, it's helpful to know something about each of them so that you can estimate your clients' jobs properly. You should also gain awareness of building regulations, health and safety legislation, etc. The best experience is by working for another builder, especially if you spend part of your time working in a builders' office. This will give you an idea of how to run your own business, which needs a combination of building and business know-how. Successful builders are also good with people; you need to communicate well with clients to build up trust; to be a good manager/employer and to be businesslike and organised. You also need selling skills and the ability to price work accurately

Initially you can set up with a car, a ladder, a phone and public liability insurance. You can start off by hiring any plant that you need although, rapidly, it becomes worth buying most of this yourself. You'll also have to pay for any advertising you want to do. As you become established you'll need some stationery, a van (plus insurance) and somewhere to store tools and equipment. Invest in a yard for this as soon as you can, it can also be a useful investment to sell in the future. Realistically you're also going to have to employ a team of craftsmen so that you can be ready to take on a wide range of jobs as they come up. This involves you in employer's liability insurance as well as wages which can be as much as

£20,000 pa for a good craftsman and which you'll be paying regularly whether you're making any money yourself or not. This all demands good cash flow especially as you'll have to find the money for equipment and materials while you're doing a job (for instance, bricks costing 50p each and skip hire about £65–£75). It's common to ask for part payment in advance, the rest of the client's bill being payable on completion. On the whole you can expect to charge a mark-up of about 20 per cent on your own expenses for each job; this rises to about 25–33 per cent for roofing jobs which require special equipment, scaffolders and extra insurance.

Word of mouth is the best source of work. Start off by advertising locally (try *Thomson's Directory* or card drops through letter boxes) and develop contacts in the trade who may recommend you to their clients. This means that you have to be consistently good; develop habits that clients will appreciate, always clean up after each job, make sure that the people you employ and sub-contract are trustworthy and efficient and get jobs done as quickly as possible (no one likes having half-completed building jobs in their house). It's also helpful to visit each site as often as possible so that you can be aware of any potential problems and respond quickly to them. Local estate agents and property managers are excellent sources of regular work so it's worth getting in with some of them. As well as a five-day week you'll probably have to be available at weekends and in the evenings. Prospective and existing clients are likely to ring at any time and many won't talk to an answering machine so you could lose work if your phone isn't manned. Once a client has told you what they want done you'll have to visit to see the site and discuss the job in greater detail – it's helpful to be able to do this at weekends when people are more likely to be at home. After this you put in an estimate for the job and wait to be accepted; when business is buoyant it's likely that a higher percentage of your estimates will be accepted than when people are feeling poor. Make sure that your client knows exactly what they're getting for the estimate: if you quote for the best quality

wood you're going to look a lot more expensive than someone who plans to do the job in plywood. Problems do arise and clients may blame you for them, so make it obvious that you're doing your best.

There is a FEDERATION OF MASTER BUILDERS and the BUILDING EMPLOYER'S CONFEDERATION, membership of either may boost your credibility with new clients. The CONSTRUCTION INDUSTRY TRAINING BOARD can also be a big help, as, especially regarding legislation etc. and larger business opportunities, can the DEPARTMENT OF THE ENVIRONMENT and THE DEPARTMENT OF TRADE AND INDUSTRY.

European Community Notes

Qualifications: There is mutual recognition of some qualifications though many professionals may require an 'aptitude test', 'supervised practice' or similar. There are also Certificates of Experience available for a wide range of construction industry trades and occupations. These confer EC-wide recognition of experience and qualifications.

Languages: To succeed, some knowledge of local language necessary.

Setting up: You will find it difficult to succeed in Eire, Greece, Portugal, Spain.

Advice/Training: Advice, information and training available for those wishing to work in Europe.

Exchanges: Few formal job exchanges exist at apprentice level.

Enquiry point for those wishing to work in the EC: CONSTRUCTION INDUSTRY TRAINING BOARD.

Recommended reading: Euronews Construction, Gateway to Europe.

Notes: The EC provides a lot of scope for independent builders. Wherever you settle there is building work going on – or not, according to the climate; frankly, with the effects of the recession on the UK building sector, anywhere on earth starts to look attractive. Under the EC Supplies and Works Directives a large body of contracts to be let by central, regional and local government are put out for tender Europe-wide; generally of interest to larger concerns, it provides a means to dip a toe in the Euro-pool. But, just as wide and diverse as the trades and occupations that come under the 'building' umbrella is the vast body of relevant legislation – from health and safety standards to recognition of qualifications, public procurement to insurance and liability. Cue the DTI and the DoE, which can provide a huge amount of advice and information not just on regulation but on markets and commercial opportunities.

Butcher

Qualifications/Training	Available
Income bracket	Medium
Licence	No
Town/Country	Town/Village
Experience/Springboard	Essential
Travel	Local
Mid-career entry	Possible
Exit sale	Yes
Entry costs	£20,000
Work at home	No
Mix and match	Limited.

You could think about: *Caterer, Journalist, Network marketing, Potter*

Enquiries
Local butchers

Not a glamorous job and one that is very male dominated. Butchers have to know a lot about meat and perhaps more about their public ('often patronising, demanding or irritatingly vague about what they want'). Fierce competition with supermarkets has meant small butchers are experimenting with specialist meats eg free range produce, game etc. You need to know your market well and be prepared to provide extra services such as delivery; and to help educate your public.

You must be strong enough to carry bits of meat around. Otherwise there are no qualifications necessary (although courses are available at many local colleges). You do need some experience of working in a butcher's to get an idea of what it's like and to learn some of the techniques of meat chopping, preparing and storing. Go for a small butcher, not a large chain or a supermarket.

Establishing a new shop will mean getting compliance from the local public health authority which may stipulate the type of display, flooring, and refrigeration and they're getting more stringent. You should expect to spend over £25,000 equipping your shop (block is £500, commercial mincer £3,500, cold room, refrigerators, etc) as well as the cost of the shop itself. You need a good high street site – corner sites are best. If you set up in a rustic village, allow for deliveries over a wide area. Credit is difficult to get at the start and many people find that banks do not understand food retailing.

Join any local traders' association (eg, the LONDON RETAIL MEAT TRADERS ASSOCIATION) which will provide ladies' nights and public liability insurance in case you cause an outbreak of salmonella.

You should aim to turnover your stock completely at least every 10–14 days. Meat keeps for a long time but its looks deteriorate and it becomes difficult to sell. Surplus stock can be turned into sausages, pies etc. There is no sale or return and you should expect to sell less in summer when people eat less meat (particularly red meat). You will need to turn over some £4,000 a week; £8,000 a week to do well.

Many butchers prefer to go to the market (at least until they have found a supplier they can trust); in the country, you can buy meat on the hoof. Once you have found a wholesaler (or farmer) you trust completely, you can order by telephone but you must then wait for delivery. Once the meat is in the shop, you need to hang it and chop it, as well as serve customers. A good assistant is essential, but difficult to find since the pay and image of the job are both poor. It is your responsibility to maintain your standards; the British reserve makes customers reluctant to complain, they just shop elsewhere.

The EC may bring even more regulations (eg, prohibition on gutting chickens where you sell them which means goodbye to giblets) but time will tell. As people's expectations on food hygiene increase, so also does their expectation that their food will taste of something.

Cc

Cabaret Performer

Qualifications/Training	Recommended
Income bracket	Low–High
Licence	No
Town/Country	Town
Experience/Springboard	No
Travel	Yes
Mid-career entry	Possible
Exit sale	No
Entry costs	£2,000
Work at home	No

Mix and match   Probably essential.
You could think about: *Actor,
Puppeteer, Jazz musician, Dancer,
Stockbroker, Typesetter, Office
cleaner, Swimming teacher*

Enquiries
Equity, Cabaret bookers, Theatrical
agents

Cabaret performers entertain people in clubs, pubs and theatres. There's a massive range of ways of doing this: telling jokes, doing magic tricks, singing, stripping, dancing, juggling. There are two main types of cabaret venue (called circuits). The mainline circuit is nationwide and includes working men's and political clubs and holiday resorts. Alternative cabaret circuits are more local; London's the best place for these but there are opportunities in other towns especially during festivals and carnivals (eg the EDINBURGH FRINGE FESTIVAL). Alternative cabaret venues include pubs and alternative theatres such as

the COMEDY STORE in Leicester Square. You can work both circuits as long as you have material that suits both traditional mainline cabaret and the experimental alternative. You can work as many nights as you want, making this a good job to mix and match with others. You should be prepared to do a lot of travelling between venues and some low or even unpaid work when you're starting out.

There are no essential formal qualifications but you'll need a skill that people will enjoy watching. You could do a short (one–two year) course in various basic stage skills; contact your local adult or further education college for details. This might help you to stand up in front of an audience and perform but it won't give you any material for the show; for that you need your own ideas. Creating an act which works is largely a matter of trial and error; you won't be given many opportunities for experimenting on the cabaret circuit so get some experience of live audiences in children's theatre, at parties or doing street entertainment – children's parties and the like also mean income, never to be sniffed at. Cabaret performers have to be sensitive to audience response and quick witted enough to develop their show to suit each audience (there's a certain amount of patronising in this). You mustn't mind being heckled as long as you can usually get the better of the hecklers. You'll have to be good at late nights, energetic and dedicated enough to go on with the show no matter how ill you feel – missing a booking is breaking an unwritten law of cabaret. It's hard work and tiring but very rewarding.

Apart from any equipment you need for

the show, you also need a telephone and answering machine; a car is useful when you're touring. As a group, entertainers have to pay more for things like pensions and insurance (house insurance premiums can be up to 50 per cent more expensive than for other people). On the mainline circuit you can expect to get from £45–£50 for 25 minutes, up to about £5,000 if you're very famous; many bookers want a free trial unless they've seen you at one of the top places. Cabaret bookers (usually the managers of clubs or pubs or the organisers of special events) have budgets which don't allow much leeway; it's up to you to decide whether or not a job's worth taking. Always ask for expenses; most will pay. Alternative cabaret varies even more than this but generally pays less. New performers have a chance to perform for nothing; sometimes the night's takings are shared amongst performers – not lucrative if the audience was small.

You get work by being seen: start off with talent shows and open (unbooked) spots in alternative cabaret. You can sometimes get work from bookers who haven't seen you if you're good at selling yourself. Get some agents; there's no limit to the number you can have and each has a slightly different speciality. They charge commission but should provide work for you. Establish a personality – your own will do unless you find it easier to pretend you're someone else when you're performing. Never accept work that doesn't suit you; bookers often don't know exactly that they want so you should be able to tell them. Alternative cabaret is expected to be socially and politically correct (ie no racism or sexism); mainline isn't always.

Wednesday–Sunday are the busiest days of the week and in the early days when you want to accept any booking that comes, taking time off to suit you can be a problem. Cabaret bookings are often made up to a year in advance. There's plenty to do when you aren't performing or rehearsing; letters and confirmations to write, researching new material from books or by working out ways of getting the final result you want, writing and experimenting with new material. Keep in touch with cabaret contacts. It's a close-knit world and there

are opportunities for travel; work on cruise liners, at holiday camps and resorts. Don't publicise your new idea too widely though unless you want to see someone else perform them first.

✦✧ European Community Notes
Fundamentally an itinerant profession. There are obvious problems of language although less with cabaret than 'straight' theatre. Equity can check your contract for you before you sign and will arrange local union representation if necessary.

Calligrapher

Qualifications/Training	Necessary
Income bracket	Low
Licence	No
Town/Country	Town preferably
Experience/Springboard	Good idea
Travel	No
Mid-career entry	Possible
Exit sale	No
Entry costs	£200
Work at home	Yes
Mix and match	Yes.

You could think about: *Illustrator, Graphic designer, Artist, Book designer, Interior designer*

Enquiries
Crafts Council, Society of Scribes and Illuminators

Traditionally, calligraphy is the art of beautiful writing combined with illustration techniques, mainly in connection with books. More modern calligraphers, particularly in America, use calligraphy as an art form in its own right, sometimes marrying calligraphy and typography. Calligraphy is now used commercially in advertising, packaging and posters. Classic techniques are still needed eg illumination, heraldic art, gilding, burnishing, and work related to manuscripts and books.

Specialist maps, family trees and botanical illustration are commissioned. The bread-and-butter side of the business is writing certificates, cards, invitations and place names: some commissions are for very traditional work with rule-bound formation of letters; others are for something modern/artistic.

You need to do a calligraphy course for at least two years (although there are hopes of a degree course soon). You can apply for a CRAFTS COUNCIL grant. You can attach yourself to a master calligrapher as an apprentice for a couple of months. A spell in America often opens up your ideas. The CRAFTS COUNCIL may give you a workshop grant so you have a base to work from; in which case it will promote your work to prove that you are a good investment. You do not need a lot of space, just enough for a leaning drawing board, pens and inks. But beware of your posture while you spend hours writing in one position and take plenty of exercise to off-set physical problems.

Survival is hard until you have made enough contacts and gained a reputation. You can do certificates, place names, or invitations, or perhaps teach in the local art college, to keep you ticking over, while taking your portfolio to design groups or advertisers or commercial groups to persuade them of your ideas. Your first orders may come from friends and it snowballs as your work is seen. You can then move on to business cards, letter-headings, packaging, book jackets, logos, shop signs, record sleeves if you are good. To appeal to the fashion or record industries your work should be in the modern idiom. Try entering competitions and get your work into exhibitions. Advertise your services in magazines, but only in those relevant to your own specialism.

The *Scribe* is the journal of the SOCIETY OF SCRIBES AND ILLUMINATORS and is full of information about forthcoming exihibitions, lectures and articles.

European Community Notes
Qualifications: There are no *calligraphy* courses in UK which are valid internationally at present. There is nothing in Europe either; the qualification would have to be a graphic design one.
Languages: To succeed, local language necessary.
Advice/Training: Advice, information and training not available for those wishing to work in Europe.
Exchanges: Formal job exchanges do not exist.
Enquiry point for those wishing to work in the EC: SOCIETY OF SCRIBES AND ILLUMINATORS (send SAE).
Notes: In all EC countries 'calligraphy' is 'lettering' and as such is taught as part of graphic design courses. Our correspondent knows of *one* professional calligrapher in Spain, *two* in Italy (who are graphic designers) and none at all in Luxembourg, Portugal and Greece. In Germany and the Netherlands there are some, but they're really graphic designers too. There is one practising calligrapher in Paris, who says calligraphy is not appreciated at all in France and that life is extremely difficult for a calligrapher – which is why he comes to England and America to show his work.

Camera Crew

Qualifications/Training	Recommended
Income bracket	Low–Medium
Licence	No
Town/Country	Town
Experience/Springboard	No
Travel	Lots
Mid-career entry	Unlikely
Exit sale	No
Entry costs	£500+
Work at home	No
Mix and match	Limited.

You could think about: ***Photographer, Mini-cab driver, Film director***

Enquiries
BECTU (Broadcasting, Entertainment, Cinematograph and Theatre Union)

The camera crew shoot the film so that it recreates the director's artistic intentions on the screen – be it film, video or television. The top job here is the lighting camera person, sometimes called the cinematographer or director of photography. Unless the crew is very small, the lighting camera person does not usually handle the camera but is concerned with creating the lighting, camera angles, close ups and other techniques that will achieve the effect the director wants. Years of experience on the job are required to gain necessary creative expertise. Camera operators control the camera and ensure that the shot is exactly what is wanted. They are assisted by layers of assistants with various different responsibilities for focussing the lens, loading the film, moving the camera on its rigging, building rig for special shots etc.

The best way of getting the initial know-how to operate the camera is through a BECTU recognised course although NVQs are on their way. After that it's a case of getting a foot in the door at whatever level you can; building up a portfolio of stills or a show reel helps here. Establish contact with as many film people as possible, and try to get onto film shoots – you can do this initially by working for a production company as a general assistant or runner. Alternatively some of the big equipment companies run training schemes or need general helpers from time to time. Also find out about the JOBFIT Scheme (CYFLE for Welsh speakers'; SCOTTISH FILM TRAINING TRUST for Scots). Once you've got the contacts you can hustle for work by offering your services to other camera people as extra assistants, grip, etc. You'll need technical know-how and talent tempered with the ability to work to other people's ideas rather than being free to exercise your own creativity. To actually get into this field in the first place you'll need great persistence and determination. Nowadays you must be able to work in film, video and television in order to survive.

Because of the vast range of sophisticated and expensive equipment available, film production companies usually rent rather than own camera equipment. You'll need a telephone and an answering machine, better still, register with a booking service who will handle all your calls while you're away. As you become better known, it's worth getting an agent who can hustle for you and negotiate rates. BECTU and the employers negotiate minimum wages – which are normally below the market rate. Because bookings for commercials and promos are for far shorter lengths of time you usually get paid more per week for them than for longer feature film bookings.

The director/producer will appoint a lighting camera person and usually leaves it to them to appoint operators and assistants. This leads to the establishment of freelance teams and you may find yourself doing quite a lot of work with the same people. Work snowballs: every shoot you go to will remind someone about you and may lead to more. The film world is a very close-knit industry, word travels fast and reputations are easily ruined if you make a mistake. Life can be unpredictable and you may find yourself with a broken camera or dealing with a thunderstorm in the middle of a crucial take.

Read *Money into Light* for further information.

Caravan Park Owner

Qualifications/Training	No
Income bracket	Medium
Licence	No
Town/Country	Country
Experience/Springboard	No
Travel	No
Mid-career entry	Good
Exit sale	Yes
Entry costs	£125,000
Work at home	Yes
Mix and match	Excellent.

You could think about: *Trout farmer, Publican, Farmer, Holiday accommodation owner, Tourist attraction, Import/export broker*

Enquiries
British Holidays and Home Parks Association

Running a caravan park is a convenient way of combining home and work in a country setting, but no one entering the holiday parks industry should be looking for a 'quiet life'. Most operators of fairly small parks will do all the work themselves. Larger parks will have managers, cleaning staff and groundsmen.

The first thing to do is to find a site. It is generally better to buy an existing park than to consider buying land and hoping to get planning permission for a new site; most local authorities in beauty spots seem to think there are enough sites in their area already.

It is worth joining the BRITISH HOLIDAYS AND HOME PARKS ASSOCIATION (formerly the National Federation of Site Operators) as a prospective operator. Their journal carries advertisments for sites which are on the market as well as advice on park operations. You can also try estate agents in the area you are interested in.

A small viable park, including a house, would cost in the region of £300,000. On this you can expect to earn about £20,000 per annum. This may not sound like a particularly good return though if the house alone is worth £75,000 this is actually a return of £20,000 on a slightly more modest capital outlay of £225,000. On a small site there is no need to employ much extra labour: on a park of up to about 60 pitches, a couple, plus a part-timer in the high season, can cope quite adequately. But, there are opportunities for expansion in setting up a shop on the site and providing extra facilities for the campers.

Caravan park operators usually start by advertising in one of the guides produced by their local tourist information office, and guides produced by various camping and caravanning clubs. On a larger scale, they can advertise in one of the 20 or so magazines which specialise in the field.

Besides the administration involved in taking bookings and collecting fees, the main work is dealing with customers. There is also the business of cleaning and maintaining the site. Larger sites will have part- or full-time cleaning staff and groundsmen. During the winter months there will be long-term maintenance, such as repairing or rebuilding toilet blocks and other facilities, or laying on power and water to different parts of the site.

Each site has planning permission for a set number of touring caravans (and tents in some cases) and a set number of caravan holiday-homes (statics). To increase the size you will need to apply for planning permission.

Careers Adviser

Qualifications/Training	Recommended
Income bracket	Medium–High
Licence	No
Town/Country	Town
Experience/Springboard	Usual
Travel	Local
Mid-career entry	Yes
Exit sale	Possible
Entry costs	£2,000
Work at home	Possible
Mix and match	Yes.

You could think about: *Counsellor, Conference organiser, Headhunter, Picture restorer, Office services bureau*

Enquiries
AGCAS, Careers Advisers

There is a considerable (largely unrecognised) need for independent careers advisers to help new graduates, school leavers, the recently redundant or people who are stuck in a rut. While careers advisers are found at virtually all schools, universities and polytechnics, they are usually only able to see their immediate client group, though most higher education institutions will see graduates for between three months and three years after leaving. This service is therefore closed to many people who would benefit from advice and counselling aimed specifically at them and they form a strong market for the independent careers adviser to exploit.

You need a lot of determination to succeed as an independent. Many people still regard it as a sign of failure to seek careers advice and resent paying for it. Half the battle lies in convincing people that is *is* worth paying for help in making one of the most important decisions of their lives.

To provide this sort of analytical counselling you need a wide range of knowledge and know-how. Not only do you need to know a lot about careers and the practicalities of job hunting (CV-writing for example), you also need to know a lot about people. Springboarding from employment in eg a school/university or a management consultancy is a good way of building up a network of contacts and information sources to keep you in touch with developments in the careers market. To become a careers adviser in schools you'll need to do a year's postgraduate course in career guidance (not necessary for work in universities, often required in polytechnics or colleges of higher education).

For those wanting to set up on their own and provide more analytical advice, a useful short course is run by the UNIVERSITY OF LONDON, DEPARTMENT OF EXTRA-MURAL STUDIES. You should also have a background in psychology or counselling; you need to be able to recognise the difficulties your clients have in certain areas and to help them overcome these. Careers advisers need to be interested in and good with people, analytical and imaginative enough to suggest suitable careers.

To set up you need an office, a telephone, a filing system, a typewriter or computer as well as a basic library of careers books. Having ready access to current job vacancies isn't necessarily worth the expense as long as you can point clients in the direction of likely sources of work: recruitment consultants, the relevant sections of the daily press and employment agencies. Ideally you should charge an hourly counselling fee of about £35. However, many clients are used to the idea of careers advice coming in the form of a tangible package with written assessments and advice. Charges for this range from £300 to £3,000 but you'll have to supply a lot of backup support at the upper end of this range – some of the larger consultancies, for example, provide clients with a temporary office and secretarial backup for several months of job hunting.

You need a steady flow of clients; this is an area where people expect quick results and aren't going to go on paying for your service if they don't get them. Advertise in the educational and careers press (*Executive Post, Graduate Post*), other publications aimed at job hunters (*DOG* and *ROGET* for example) and the job pages of the national press. Other clients come through referral; you may be able to convince school/university careers officers to recommend you to anyone they can't help themselves. Clients are likely to be pretty desperate when they seek your advice and it's important that you find out as much as you can about them and follow up your analysis and counselling with practical advice on self-presentation, how to go about finding a job, interview technique etc. Helping people to overcome the blockers that prevent them from succeeding is immensely rewarding.

European Community Notes

Qualifications: Mutual recognition of qualifications varies, depending on particular qualification.

Languages: To succeed, local language necessary.

Earnings: UK income generally lower than elsewhere in the EC.

Setting up: You will find it difficult to succeed in France, Germany, Greece, Luxembourg, Portugal. You will find it easier in Belgium, Denmark, Eire, Italy, Netherlands, Spain. Legal obligations/regulations and contacts are different for each country and need careful consideration.

Advice/Training: Advice, information and training not available for those wishing to work in Europe.

Exchanges: Formal job exchanges do not exist.

Financial help: exists for study, training or travel in the EC, special to this job.

Recommended reading: Working in the European Communities.

Carpenter

Qualifications/Training	Recommended
Income bracket	Low
Licence	No
Town/Country	Either
Experience/ Springboard	Recommended
Travel	Local
Mid-career entry	Possible
Exit sale	No
Entry costs	£2,000
Work at home	No
Mix and match	Possible.

You could think about: *Wood carver, Furniture designer/maker, Man with a van, Stage technician carpenter, Physiotherapist*

Enquiries
Carpenters, Construction Industry Training Board, Guild of Master Craftsmen

Carpenters do woodwork on buildings – either constructing new buildings or maintaining old ones. That means constructing door and window frames, putting in floor and skirting boards and building shelves and cupboards. On the whole you'll do more varied and interesting work by working for yourself. There is almost always a demand for carpenters to do smaller jobs for private customers or larger ones under sub-contract to building and construction companies. Formal qualifications aren't essential; you should start by working for someone else as a way of learning the trade. For the best training work as an apprentice, but it's not always easy to get an apprenticeship. It will take between three and five years to become competent. Use this time to learn as much as possible,

never be afraid to ask for advice or help from experienced colleagues and build up a network of other people in the construction industry which will be useful in the future. It helps if you've got a working knowledge of other areas of construction. You'll also need to be good with people, patient with their lack of knowledge of what's possible and as reliable as possible at timing and pricing jobs.

To set up you need the tools you'll already have collected while you were learning: hammers, saws, chisels, planes etc. You also need a van and some ladders. An answering machine helps to ensure that you don't lose new work while you're out. Additional expenses are advertising, dropping cards through letter boxes and putting ads in the local press; stationery, letterheads for quotes, invoice books, business cards. You may need money/credit for materials which you might have to buy in advance before the client pays you. Make sure that you've got a good supplier of wood, screws and nails. Charges are based on materials plus time (allow for unforeseen problems and consider things like awkward sites and difficult access). The better you are and the more experience you have the more you can charge; remember you also have to pay for insurance and public liability insurance. You give potential clients an estimate and some indication of when the job will be completed. They'll expect these to be pretty accurate if they give you the job, but most are reasonable if you've had to do more work to take longer because of unforeseen contingencies.

First jobs may come through friends or relations while you're still in employment. Once you're confident enough to work for yourself other work comes through advertisements and word of mouth. Respond to potential clients quickly. Always view a job and, when you're calculating how long the job will take, take into account anything you think could possibly go wrong. Giving verbal quotes is a very bad idea; take measurements and notes and calculate your estimate at home. For some jobs you may want to employ an assistant who'll need to be paid. It's important to establish a reputation for being prompt and reliable and tidying up after every job is a good way of keeping clients happy and ready to recommend you.

Although you may have some lean times in the early days, you stand to make more by working for yourself in the long run. Make sure that you book some time off and that all your jobs are finished before you go away.

⁂ European Community Notes

There is always scope for skilled craftsmen, and the Single Market should mean wide opportunities in the EC. Contact the DoE and the DTI, both of which are mustard-keen on Europe, and see *Builder* entry for more information on all construction industry trades and occupations.

Caterer

Qualifications/Training	Useful
Income bracket	Low–Medium
Licence	No
Town/Country	Town or nearby
Experience/Springboard	Useful
Travel	Local
Mid-career entry	Yes
Exit sale	Possible
Entry costs	£2,500+
Work at home	Yes
Mix and match	Yes

You could think about: *Publican, Restaurateur, Wine bar owner, Food manufacturer*

Enquiries
Local caterers

There are many areas that caterers can opt for such as directors' lunches, providing a fairly regular service to offices, or party food and perhaps equipment hire (crockery, cutlery etc) and service (waitresses etc). What you decide to do will depend largely on experience and opportunities. On the whole cooking for a handful of offices provides more regular, secure work than parties which are far more subject to seasonal demands and many people combine the two. Whatever you do there is a lot of competition so perseverance is essential.

There are no hard and fast rules about experience and qualifications but both are obviously very useful. You may find a formal qualification such as cordon bleu a useful way into directors' lunches and everyone working in your kitchen must have taken a hygiene course (check with your enviromental health officer). Some business knowledge is essential especially when you're setting up and need to decide on menus and pricing and to make cash flow predictions. You'll need cooking flair (to turn out large quantities of consistently saleable food; mistakes cost a lot) and enough enthusiasm to carry you through shopping and paperwork. Expect to spend at least 25 per cent of your time on this.

You can share the responsibilities by setting up with a partner whose skills or interests complement yours but you need to ensure there will be enough profit to support both of you. Image is important – develop one that suits your speciality and clientele; you may meet clients before you cook for them and first impressions count for a lot.

To set up you need a good-sized kitchen, typewriter (useful but not essential), telephone, answering machine, freezer, cooking utensils and stationery, including business cards. A car or van is necessary but can be hired until you feel secure enough to make the necessary financial outlay. You must inform the local environmental health officer before you start; they will inspect your kitchens and tell you about the necessary stringent regulations in food handling. Most clients will provide a kitchen to do some of the work in but you'll do a lot of cooking at home particularly for parties. You are required by law to take out insurance against accidentally poisoning your clients or damaging their property (through fire for instance).

Cash flow problems are rife. Supplies have to be bought well in advance of receiving payment. Insisting on a deposit and payment of invoices within 15 days helps but the accounts departments of large companies aren't geared to cope with this. Payment for supplies can be delayed by opening accounts with wholesalers (eg meat and veg). You'll also have to pay casual serving staff; pay them slightly more than the usual rate to build up a willing workforce (one caterer reports paying more for a night's serving than he pays himself in a week). Don't expect to reach more than subsistence level in less than two years so ensure you have enough savings or another source of income to tide you over. Base your charges on the competition. Most caterers offer menus at a price per head (between about £6 for cocktail party food, to about £25 for dinner) and charge extra for corkage if the client provides the wine. Offer to supply the drink as you can add a reasonable mark-up. You can also offer service and hire of cutlery, plates etc – provide these through a hire company, many of which open accounts for established companies.

Good clients are businesses (financial firms and maybe publishers, galleries, promoters etc) and established (often middle aged or overseas) business people. There is also a market in wedding and christening party catering. When you start it is essential to enlist the help of friends and contacts to get business – don't be afraid to ask as people are usually happy to help. Choosing a specialist or unusual cuisine will get you noticed and give you an edge in an overcrowded market. This is seasonal work with surprises – January is not always quiet. You can use quiet times to drum up more customers through advertising and visiting potential clients. Catering involves hours of cooking alone and lots of washing-up! You have to make a lot of effort to retain customers and gain new ones. *Caterer and Hotelkeeper* is background reading but not specifically aimed at small catering companies. Get hold of *Running Your Own Catering Business*.

Chamber Group Musician/Manager

Qualifications/Training	Essential
Income bracket	Low
Licence	No
Town/Country	Town
Experience/Springboard	Vital
Travel	Lots
Mid-career entry	Yes
Exit sale	No
Entry costs	£6,000
Work at home	No
Mix and match	Yes

You could think about: *Orchestral musician, Orchestral fixer, Music teacher, Classical composer, Counseller, Man with a van*

Enquiries
Incorporated Society of Musicians

A group's director recruits the musicians, organises, promotes and finds engagements for them. Chamber music work is part-time with little financial reward unless your group is outstanding, has won an international competition or has been taken on as, say, quartet-in-residence at a university.

You can train (and meet other musicians) at music college; or you can do a postgraduate year at music college after university to reach the necessary technical standard. Most chamber musicians teach, coach and work as freelance orchestral players.

Before setting up, you will need a room where the group can rehearse without disturbing the neighbours, £2,500 for publicity brochures, stationery and postage. Get lists of promotors and write to them and to the diminishing number of members of the NATIONAL FEDERATION OF MUSIC SOCIETIES large or rich enough to employ you. Use the NFMS labelling service. Get a good accountant; keep receipts of everything.

You will need a typewriter (or preferably a word processor), telephone, answering machine and diary service. Canvass the musical grapevine and consult the INCORPORATED SOCIETY OF MUSICIANS before fixing your group's rates. Allow for a management fee for yourself and sufficient for overheads as well as musicians' fees. If you join the ISM, their legal service can provide a contract with protection from cancellation, ruthless and dishonest promoters. It can also chase up unpaid fees. Music, music stands, dresses for female musicians, bags/suitcases will cost a further £1,500. A car is useful; if you hire a van, include the cost in your fee.

Good national press notices are important so invest £1,500 in a concert preferably in London, eg the Wigmore Hall. Aim to fill the hall with friends and relations to cover its hire and advertising costs. A concert manager will charge £300 and should persuade the critics to attend. Use every bit of influence to persuade the Arts editors to send someone; avoid a Friday night or weekend booking when they are out of town.

Having received good reviews, print brochures with the group's photograph. Send these with sample programmes and press notices to anyone who might engage you. Approach BBC Radio 3 for an audition, although they like proof of a number of concerts to show you are a permanent ensemble.

Agents prefer full-time string quartets which are more economic, but try and get a recommendation to others on the Continent. You must believe in your group, overflow with enthusiasm and energy. You should also be a good communicator and be able to cope with rejection. There should be a clear understanding with members of your group that, having agreed to work with the group, they do not disappear to do another gig. You need to be calm, patient, logical, resilient and diplomatic with them – you will be at the mercy of their private lives and moods. An owner/administrator of a chamber orchestra deals direct with impresarios and borough entertainment/arts officers. Chamber music improves your standard of playing but is demanding. The job is stressful, artistically creative and satisfying; it provides greater freedom of expression than other musical work. The future is gloomy unless you have a really good original idea or approach; if you do, you will be successful only if you can become a workaholic for three years. Read *The First 10 Years* and *Musicians Handbook*. A free booklet *Careers in Music* is available from the ISM.

European Community Notes

Qualifications: Generally, UK qualifications recognised throughout EC and EC qualifications in UK.

Languages: To succeed, local language not necessary.

Earnings: UK income generally same as elsewhere in the EC.

Setting up: Is not 'easy' anywhere. You will find it difficult to succeed in Denmark, Eire, France, Greece, Italy, Luxembourg, Portugal, Spain. You will find it easier in Belgium, Germany, Netherlands.

Advice/Training: Advice, information and training available for those wishing to work in Europe.

Exchanges: No formal job exchanges.

Financial help: exists for study, training or travel in the EC, specific to this job.

Enquiry point for those wishing to work in the EC: INCORPORATED SOCIETY OF MUSICIANS.

Chemical Engineering Consultant

Qualifications/Training	Essential
Income bracket	Medium–High
Licence	No
Town/Country	Either
Experience/Springboard	Essential
Travel	Yes
Mid-career entry	Yes
Exit sale	Possible

Entry costs	£12,000+
Work at home	Possible
Mix and match	Yes.

You could think about: **Newsletter publisher, Landlord, Musical instrument repairer**

Enquiries
Institution of Chemical Engineers

Chemical engineers are concerned with processing and handling solids, liquids and gases in bulk. Approximately 5 per cent of practising chemical engineers are self-employed or work as consultants in the chemical, food, pharmaceutical, steel, energy and related industries. As a consultant you act as an adviser or help in formulating projects. Much of the work concerns improving productivity of existing plant, rather than starting from scratch.

A degree in chemical engineering is essential and you should be a Chartered Engineer. You will also need experience in a large company, working as part of a team, before going solo. Verbal and written communication skills are important for explaining your plans to the uninitiated; also imagination, salesmanship and the ability to solve problems. Your time in employment should be used to develop a range of contacts so personal recommendations will result in consultancy contracts from large companies. Write technical articles, attend trade fairs and conferences to be seen and become known.

To set up on your own, you will need capital to acquire or rent premises and purchase drawing equipment, microcomputer, a vehicle, telephone, answering machine or service and secretarial help; also, most importantly, sufficient funds to tide-over the first four to six months in business.

You will spend a lot of time visiting sites and selling your services; three-quarters of your time might be spent on real chemical engineering and the remainder on administration and sales. You will need to read the *Chemical Engineer*, published by the INSTITUTION OF CHEMICAL ENGINEERS, which also provides information. You will also find useful *Inside the Technical Consultancy Business* and the *Standard Handbook of Consulting Engineering Practice*.

This is a 'feast and famine' occupation: a balance between work flow and income is not easy to achieve. Contracts can last several months, ranging from local farms to multi-million pound schemes. You may be searching for your next contract, or working a 50-hour week to meet a deadline.

Any advance you make must involve increasingly lucrative contracts. Expansion will be difficult because highly skilled professionals are highly paid and may earn more in large firms. Opportunities for working abroad, particularly in developing countries are good, and increasing. At home, there are more opportunities as large firms cut back on their own engineering and training staff.

European Community Notes

Qualifications: UK qualifications recognised throughout EC and EC qualifications in UK.

Languages: To succeed, local language necessary.

Earnings: UK income generally comparible to other major EC states.

Advice/Training: Advice, information and training available for those wishing to work in Europe. See Institution of Chemical Engineers publication on consultancy.

Enquiry point for those wishing to work in the EC: INSTITUTION OF CHEMICAL ENGINEERS.

Child/Educational Psychologist

Qualifications/Training	Essential
Income bracket	Medium
Licence	Recommended
Town/Country	Town
Experience/Springboard	Essential
Travel	Local
Mid-career entry	Possible

Exit sale	Possible
Entry costs	£1,500
Work at home	Yes
Mix and match	Possible.

You could think about: **Psychologist, Careers adviser, Counsellor, Musician**

Enquiries
Association of Educational Psychologists, British Psychological Society

Child and educational psychologists help children to overcome social, emotional and learning problems. Clients are families – child psychologists work with both children and parents, assessing and providing follow up counselling and advice. The Warnock Report suggested that about 20 per cent of children up to the age of 19 would benefit from access to a psychologist; currently only a very small proportion of this 20 per cent are given any help and those that are have usually been referred by their local authority education or health departments. Most child psychologists work for local authorities, operating within tight budgets. This means that a lot of children slip through the net unless their problems are making them a nuisance to others. Many children who are regarded as passing through difficult or unhappy phases could be helped but aren't, not least because of parents' and schools' reluctance to admit that the child has the sort of problem a psychologist could alleviate. But this seems to be changing gradually.

Although there is a clear need for independent child and educational psychologists to work with children in both the independent and maintained sectors, the move to independence from employment is slow. Gaining professional recognition almost certainly necessitates springboarding from local authority employment both to acquire sufficient experience and an essential network of contacts.

In the public sector of education, legislation requires that recommendations concerning provision for special needs of a child (perhaps extra tuition or placement in a special school) may be accepted only from an educational psychologist employed by a local education authority. As much of the work of educational psychologists involves working within schools with the teachers, independents experience limitations on the services they can offer children being educated in the public sector.

The BRITISH PSYCHOLOGICAL SOCIETY has recently introduced the registration of psychologists and, although this isn't yet a legal requirement, you're advised to register as a chartered psychologist before attempting to set up on your own. To become a chartered educational psychologist you need a degree in psychology, a post-graduate educational psychology qualification, a teaching qualification, at least two–three years of teaching experience and at least a further year as a psychologist working under supervision. As an independent you'll need a lot more experience; you've got to have the courage of your convictions. In addition, the longer you've been at the job, the easier it is not to become too emotionally involved in cases and, even more important, you need good networks. Networks work in two ways, firstly, professional referrals from psychiatrists, teachers, children's organisations and GPs from whom you obtain your clients. It's useful having colleagues who have regular contact with schools and local authorities or to remain partially involved yourself in an employed position. Child psychologists work with children and parents and they themselves must be well rounded people, lively, agile and fit.

You can work from home as long as you're accessible to clients and have an amenable consulting room. You also need a typewriter and a phone (answering machines should be used as little as possible). As soon as you can afford it, employ a secretary to type reports, answer the phone and receive clients; suitable secretaries aren't easy to find but make a great difference, you shouldn't be interrupted in the middle of a consultation. Compared to other professions which have similar lengths of training, psychology is undervalued; this is reflected in the rates that you can charge, currently about £50 an hour in London – remember that's for the consultation only and you'll have to do some follow-up work on each meeting as well as the writing of a detailed and often lengthy report.

New clients do not only come from referrals, but from satisfied clients: people are only likely to talk to you about their problems if they can see that you are being professional about your work. As an independent you need an additional commitment to break into a completely new market, starting off by educating parents and teachers to accept your services as valuable rather than a sign of failure on their part. Visit schools and tell teachers what you do and how you can help a wide range of children; design and teach training courses for teachers which will help them to recognise and deal with some of the minor problems they are most likely to come across.

Child psychologists see children from a wide range of ages and backgrounds and with very various problems. As an independent you're freer to expand the help you can give and aren't restricted to dealing with only those few cases a local authority regards as being severe enough to warrant psychological help. You're as likely to be working with children who are gifted as with children who seem to be slow learners. As well as children were severe and deep rooted emotional problems, you'll see children who only need some encouragement to overcome what's bothering them.

Read *Careers in Psychology* for further information. As well as the British Psychological Society investigate the ASSOCIATION OF EDUCATIONAL PSYCHOLOGISTS although they tend to be of more use to those in employment than to the self-employed.

⁑ **European Community Notes**
Qualifications: UK qualifications recognised throughout EC and EC qualifications in UK (as per EC Directive 89/48).
Languages: To succeed, local language necessary.
Advice/Training: Advice, information and training for those wishing to work in Europe is produced by individual countries.

Exchanges: Formal exchanges do not exist.
Notes: The problem of assessing prospects and conditions for UK psychologists working in Europe is that there is so little evidence or experience of UK citizens setting up in private practice in the EC and the primary reason must be the language barrier. To be effective as a psychologist in another country one would have to be completely fluent in the language of the local people, including slang, dialect and so on. The problems presented by trying to handle a person's difficulties in a foreign language can be readily imagined.

Childminder

Qualifications/Training	No
Income bracket	Low
Licence	Yes
Town/Country	Town/Village
Experience/Springboard	Yes
Travel	None
Mid-career entry	Yes
Exit sale	No
Entry costs	Nil
Work at home	Yes
Mix and match	Limited.

You could think about: *Typist, Unholsterer, Novelist, Artist, Naturopath*

Enquiries
National Childminding Association;
Local authority social service department

This is an ideal job for someone who loves children, probably has some of their own, and wants to spend as much time at home as possible. However, it is not lucrative; it's difficult to take time off; and you have to keep cheerful even when you don't feel it.

Most childminders look after other people's children while their parents are at work. Hours can be long (perhaps 8.00–

6.30) if the child's parents do a full working day and have to travel a long way. However, you can fit in your own household chores around the children you look after. It can also be very enjoyable, taking children to local parks, and watching their development day by day.

Childminders have to be registered with the local council. You cannot take on children unless you are registered, and registration can take some time. You don't need any special equipment or any capital, but your life will be easier if you have an automatic washing machine, suitable (ie washable) flooring in the rooms where the children will be, and space to store toys. Assistance from the local authority varies, but it is often possible to borrow high chairs and double buggies when necessary. The local authority will want to check your premises for adequate safety provision (stair guards, safety glass, window locks) before issuing a licence. In some areas, you may be asked to have a chest X-ray.

The number of children you are allowed to look after, so the amount you can earn, is strictly controlled by law and supervised by the local authority. Usually you are not allowed more than one child under the age of one, and not more than three children under five. You may look after six children between the age of five and seven, and six children up to the age of seven where no more than three are aged under five. In London you can earn £60–£80 a week per child but in other parts of the country the weekly figure can be as low as £25. You will not be paid if you take a holiday, although the children's parents should continue to pay you if they are away (it helps if you can all take holidays at the same time). It is essential to agree on terms and draw up a contract before taking on a child.

Local authorities will supply your name to people who come to them looking for a childminder, but you can also advertise in local newsagents. If you build up a good reputation word will soon spread and, since most children stay for three or four years, you should not have difficulty finding children to look after.

The NATIONAL CHILDMINDING ASSOCIATION produces advisory leaflets and draft contracts for childminders and parents. There is a chapter on childminding in *Working Mother – a Practical Handbook* and you may find *Nursery World* helpful.

China Restorer

Qualifications/Training	Recommended
Income bracket	Low
Licence	No
Town/Country	Town preferably
Experience/ Springboard	Recommended
Travel	Local
Mid-career entry	Possible
Exit sale	No
Entry costs	£1,000
Work at home	Yes
Mix and match	Good.

You could think about: *Picture restorer, Potter, Art historian/critic, Beekeeper, Bed and breakfast, Caterer*

Enquiries
West Dean College

There's more to this than shoving some superglue on to detached cup handles or tea pot spouts. The pieces that are sent to a professional china (and porcelain) restorer are likely to be old and fairly valuable; the work they will need ranges from re-joining a simple break to rebuilding bits that have been broken off and lost. Restored antiques are less valuable than perfect originals but look better and are worth more than obviously broken ones so, as long as you can do a good job and are in an area where there are enough antiques (in both shops and houses), you can make a living from restoring china. You can work at this when it suits you, which makes it something that can be combined with another job.

You'll have to be able to mend broken china; mix clay to the right consistency for replacing missing parts; model and paint missing bits so that they fit in as well as possible with the rest of the piece. There aren't many places where you can learn all of this on the job but you can do a course in ceramic conservation and restoration at WEST DEAN COLLEGE. This lasts one–three years and you'll get a diploma at the end. As well as being artistic enough to be able to recreate broken china, you have to be incredibly dextrous for this job. Not only is the work you're doing extremely fiddly, anyone who's remotely clumsy stands a pretty good chance of destroying whatever it is they're meant to be mending. You'll have to be diplomatic with clients, many of whom will have little idea of what's involved in the job they're asking you to do.

You'll need a studio to work in. This can be a room in your house but, while you're deciding which one, remember it'll soon start to smell strongly of glue. You'll need a table to work at and some sort of kiln. Kilns can be bought second-hand from a variety of sources from about £300. You need access to some very expensive books (eg the *Royal Doulton figures*) which will show you what a broken piece of china ought to look like. You'll also need a supply of ceramic paints, glue and clays. Take out all-risks insurance to cover your clients' pieces while they're in your charge. Charges are based on the amount of time you expect to take on a job; get good at judging this accurately and don't undervalue. Agree the price with the client before you start a job. Allow plenty of time to get a job done, it's better to be early than late; this also allows you to take on emergency jobs at short notice without messing up your schedule (you can charge a higher rate for rush jobs). Most china restorers are in London so, if you aren't, local antique dealers will be delighted to find you and will have plenty of work. Some may want to make a piece look more valuable than it really is; it's up to you what you do but if you forge a manufacturer's mark you're breaking the law. It's worth advertising in antique shops and the antique press (trade and collectors') as some people may want a damaged antique restored straight away, especially if they're shipping it overseas. British china restorers have a good reputation worldwide. Other clients are anyone who has some china they value. Some jobs are far more troublesome than others. You may have to do a lot of research to find how to restore something to as close to its original as possible. Others need long hours to get something mended before its owner gets back from holiday, for example. Your own holidays needn't be a problem once you've established a good enough reputation to have people prepared to wait longer than usual for jobs to be done.

Chiropodist/ Podiatrist

Qualifications/Training	Vital
Income bracket	Medium–High
Licence	No
Town/Country	Town
Experience/ Springboard	Recommended
Travel	Local, possibly
Mid-career entry	Yes
Exit sale	No
Entry costs	£5,000
Work at home	Possible
Mix and match	Possible. You could think about: ***Journalist, Wood carver***
Enquiries	Society of Chiropodists

Chiropodists specialise in illness or discomfort of the lower leg and foot. They can give medical aid ranging from cutting the toe nails of the elderly to minor surgery. To be State Registered you need to study at one of the 14 recognised chiropody schools. These are in polytechnics, higher education colleges or universities – you can get a list from the SOCIETY OF CHIROPODISTS.

You need manual dexterity, as you handle a knife a lot of the time; a liking for people; a sense of humour and excellent communicating skills. You will be dealing with all kinds of people – children, geriatrics, and the physically and mentally handicapped.

There is a shortage of state registered chiropodists. Join the SOCIETY OF CHIROPODISTS an affiliated trade union and the negotiating body at all levels. The society holds lectures and meetings; has its own magazine, the *Journal of British Podiatric Medicine*; and has its own malpractice insurance. Have a good accountant.

Once qualified, it's best to do some regular part-time sessions in an NHS hospital or industry until you have built up enough clients for your practice. Circularise your local doctors and have a block insertion in the local *Yellow Pages* and *Thomsons*.

You can use a room in your home but it should be on the ground floor and near public transport. You can share premises with other professionals, such as dentists, so saving on overheads. You need hot and cold running water, a separate loo, an operator's chair (£100), a patient's chair (£2,000), an autoclave (£1,200) – essential to avoid the risk of Hepatitis B, *et al*. Apart from the premises, this will cost a total of £4,000–£5,000.

Your patients will probably be private if you do not go into the NHS. (OAPs will be treated free but only at their own local health centre.) NHS treatments are usually given in clinics/centres/hospitals, by state registered chiropodists. A few authorities still offer NHS treatment (per capita) in SRChs' surgeries. About half the Society of Chiropodists' members are in the NHS and half are self-employed. It's easy to mix your employment, ie pro rata NHS and private practice. Education, too, is fun. You can expect to start in the NHS at £12,500. Unless you purchase an established practice, initial income will be nil but, depending on the area, you can build up to as much as £50,000 if it's somewhere bijou. The average is £25,000–£30,000 per annum.

You can vary your hours of work to suit yourself and take a holiday when you feel like it. You can do home visits if you wish. However, you can develop a bad back or chest from bending over all day. Useful information is found at the Society of Chiropodists.

✲✲✲ European Community Notes

Qualifications: UK qualifications recognised throughout EC; EC qualifications need to be acceptable to the State Registration Board and unless the training is on a par with the Society of Chiropodists' three-year course they probably won't be.

Languages: To succeed, local language necessary.

Setting up: You will find it difficult to succeed in Italy, Portugal, Spain.

Advice/Training: Advice, information and training not available for those wishing to work in Europe.

Exchanges: Formal job exchanges do not exist.

Enquiry point for those wishing to work in the EC: SOCIETY OF CHIROPODISTS – the leading member in the Federation International Podologie, which is the European body. The Society has members in about three dozen countries and a usefully international outlook.

Chiropractor

Qualifications/Training	Essential
Income bracket	Medium–High
Licence	No
Town/Country	Town
Experience/Springboard	Yes
Travel	No
Mid-career entry	Unlikely
Exit sale	No
Entry costs	£9,000
Work at home	Possible
Mix and match	Limited.

You could think about: ***Antique dealer, Musician***

Enquiries
British Chiropractic Association

A chiropractor is a specialist in the treatment of spinal pain syndrome by using manipulation rather than drugs.

You need three A-levels, including science subjects, to gain admission to the ANGLO EUROPEAN COLLEGE OF CHIROPRACTIC. The four-year course now leads to a BSc (Chiropractic) which will be recognised in the USA, Australia, New Zealand, Canada and Europe. It has yet to be officially recognised by the NHS in the UK. Soon you will need to have worked as an assistant to another experienced chiropractor to qualify. For the time being, you would be wise to anticipate this. There is no union but the professional body to join is the BRITISH CHIROPRACTIC ASSOCIATION, which has its own malpractice insurance scheme which is vital.

You need an open personality, good communication skills, energy, sensitivity and a strong belief in your particular calling – very important when at present it lacks the recognition of the establishment.

You need £9,000-plus capital, in addition to premises, to set up in a ground floor consulting room near public transport and a car park if possible. This can be in your own house but you must have planning permission to use it as a clinic. You need, for example, a treatment table, phone, answerphone, filing cabinet, typewriter and X-ray and developing equipment, or access to such equipment. A receptionist may cost £8,000 or more per annum.

You can work any hours but usually 9.00am to 7.00pm with a movable lunch hour so patients can come out of normal working hours. Your income to start with is usually between £12,000 and £15,000 per annum rising to £25,000 upwards. There is a shortage of chiropractors, but you must be situated where people can or will pay for treatment as it is not yet available on the NHS.

If you enjoy helping people you will get a big buzz from this job but you must be prepared to see patients after hours, or at the weekends in an emergency, which can interfere with your family/social life. If you do sessions at a clinic with other kinds of primary care medical practitioners, it is possible to work part time.

You can get more information from the BRITISH CHIROPRACTIC ASSOCIATION.

European Community Notes

Qualifications: UK qualifications recognised throughout EC.

Languages: To succeed, local language necessary.

Earnings: UK income generally same as elsewhere in the EC.

Advice/Training: Advice, information and training not available for those wishing to work in Europe.

Exchanges: Formal job exchanges do not exist.

Enquiry point for those wishing to work in the EC: BRITISH CHIROPRACTIC ASSOCIATION.

Classical Composer

Qualifications/Training	Recommended
Income bracket	Low
Licence	No
Town/Country	Either
Experience/Springboard Recommended	
Travel	Possible
Mid-career entry	Possible
Exit sale	Yes
Entry costs	£1,000
Work at home	Yes
Mix and match	Essential.

You could think about: *Music copyist, Music teacher, TV and film music composer, Conductor, Musician, Festival director, Music critic, Journalist*

Enquiries
Association of Professional Composers, Composers Guild

A classical composer writes serious music to be performed by 'straight' musicians in concert halls and opera houses. You must be born with the unusual ability to hear music going on inside your head and want to write it down. To do this and to understand the problems of performing, study other people's compositions and learn to play an instrument, preferably piano. It is not necessary to attend music college or university; but this will put you in touch with other musicians and composers and provide mutual support when you want your works to be performed. Serving an apprenticeship with a composer you admire will encourage you to overcome practical difficulties and gain inspiration. You need this, along with talent, persistence, optimism, courage and luck. If you have all these and become accustomed to rejection, eventually you will succeed. You must believe in your talent.

Few composers can live on performing rights. You will probably always need another job such as teaching, copying, arranging, freelance editing or journalism (like Berlioz). Some thrive on links with a particular orchestra. Writing for films full time is lucrative but dangerous to the composer trying to write music which will stand the test of time.

You need a small piano or synthesiser, a quiet room where you will not disturb the neighbours, manuscript paper, pencils and a rubber.

Join the SOCIETY FOR THE PROMOTION OF NEW MUSIC and hope that they will accept one of your works and give it a performance. If this attracts good notices in the national press you may be approached by a publisher. Send scores to BBC Radio 3. Be sociable and get to know as many performing musicians as possible. They may commission a work from you and the more performances they give, the better for your reputation. You are paid a rate suggested by the COMPOSERS GUILD and the ASSOCIATION OF PROFESSIONAL COMPOSERS, based on the minute and number of instruments. Composers making £100,000 pa exclusively from serious composing are likely to be dead.

It is marvellous to write music enjoyed by performers and audience but also nerve-racking and exciting; it's depressing to have a work refused or experience a bad performance. You can set your own working hours; a daily routine suits most com-

posers. The one-time bias against female composers is changing. Travel will come once you are successful and are asked to attend premiers. You are vulnerable to cuts in government grants to the ARTS COUNCIL unless you have other good commercial connections.

Read a good book on orchestration such as *Instrumental Orchestration* or *The Anatomy of The Orchestra* and the *British Music Year Book*. The APC has produced a valuable booklet on concert music and a new version of its book *The Composer's Guide to Music Publishing*.

Classical Singer

Qualifications/Training	Recommended
Income bracket	Low
Licence	No
Town/Country	Mostly town
Experience/Springboard	No
Travel	Yes
Mid-career entry	Unlikely
Exit sale	No
Entry costs	£500+
Work at home	No
Mix and match	Essential.
You could think about: *Music teacher, Word processor, Photographer, Market research interviewer, Bartender, Mini-cab driver, Indexer*	
Enquiries	
Incorporated Society of Musicians	

This is someone who sings a classical repertoire in concerts/recitals groups, oratorios and in opera companies. To be successful you need an exceptional voice, accurate ear, sense of rhythm, pleasant appearance (weight for a man, good figure for a woman), firm build, stamina (for the long hours and travelling), self-discipline (for the training) and persistence. A solid family background which produces good self-esteem is important as the voice reflects personality, and an extrovert one helps. Above all you must have the rare ability to communicate emotion to an audience. A good singing teacher is vital. GCSE and A-levels are not necessary but a knowledge of French, German and Italian is useful, and how to pronounce them correctly is very important. Going to music college is not essential, but the advantages include good contacts and the opportunity to give free performances to agents and opera companies.

To satisfy your bank manager, get a job which is not too physically tiring. When you and your teacher feel you have the necessary technical grounding, enter a music festival or vocal competition to gain experience of public exposure. Approach the YOUNG CONCERT ARTISTS' TRUST or apply to an opera company or the conductor(s) of amateur choral societies for an audition. If you are lucky enough to join the chorus of a main opera company, or take a main role in one of the small touring operas, your contract may be short or long, depending on the company, and earnings will be about £170 a week. With this experience you can cover for the principal singers' understudies, and possibly have the opportunity of going on one night unexpectedly.

Get a fixed address where you can practise without disturbing the neighbours, a telephone and answering machine or service. You will need about £600 to cover singing lessons, coaching, publicity and postage. You do not need an agent to start with.

There is no sex or race bias and the number of black and Asian singers in the UK is increasing. The hours are long, lonely and unsocial and you will need to fill in the time spent hanging around whether by learning music or relaxing with knitting, crossword puzzles etc. Family life will be disrupted by the travelling, often abroad and sometimes for weeks at a time. Air travel can cause dehydration of the voice. Rehearsals, costume fittings and work with repetiteurs are demanding. In spite of the exhaustion of constantly working with new people in strange places you still have to give a first-class performance, and there's often a party afterwards.

The job is marvellous if you enjoy communicating with others and cannot bear to do anything else. Losing your voice is a hazard and you should have alternative work to call on.

Consider joining the INCORPORATED SOCIETY OF MUSICIANS or other professional body. Consult *Careers in Music*, *British Music Year Book* and *The First Ten Years*. Find out about competitions from the *British Music Yearbook* and *Music Journal*. The ISM produces a free booklet, *Careers with Music*.

European Community Notes

Qualifications: Generally, UK qualifications recognised throughout EC and EC qualifications in UK.

Languages: To succeed, local language not necessary.

Earnings: UK income generally same as elsewhere in the EC.

Setting up: Is not 'easy' anywhere. You will find it difficult to succeed in Denmark, Eire, France, Greece, Italy, Luxembourg, Portugal, Spain. You will find it easier in Belgium, Germany, Netherlands.

Advice/Training: Advice, information and training available for those wishing to work in Europe.

Exchanges: Formal job exchanges do not exist.

Financial help: exists for study, training or travel in the EC, specific to this job.

Enquiry point for those wishing to work in the EC: INCORPORATED SOCIETY OF MUSICIANS.

Cleaning Contractor

Qualifications/Training	No
Income bracket	Medium
Licence	No
Town/Country	Town
Experience/Springboard	No
Travel	Local
Mid-career entry	Yes
Exit sale	Possible

Entry costs	£3,000+
Work at home	Not recommended

Mix and match   Possible.
You could think about: *Nanny and babysitting agent, Magazine publisher, Property manager, Interior designer*

Enquiries
Local cleaning contractors

Cleaning contractors provide cleaning services for their clients. Much of their time is spent recruiting cleaning staff and scheduling staff and jobs. In some parts of the country (eg the South-east) there is a high demand for domestic help. The service of cleaning contractors is especially useful for busy people who do not have time to find their own reliable cleaners. There are opportunities in office cleaning but, on the whole, this is highly competitive and tends to operate in different areas.

There are no formal qualifications. It's essential that you're good with people; you'll have to discuss, with interest, the cleaning needs of your clients and to cope with staff. You should also have some idea yourself of how to clean so that you can provide reasonable quotations to prospective clients. (You may prefer to sub-contract jobs like upholstery cleaning to specialist firms – see *Cleaning* and *Cleaning Business News* for addresses.) Cleaning staff can't always work outside their regular, set hours so you may have problems juggling the work force around to fulfil these needs and should be prepared to do a spot of cleaning yourself from time to time. Image is important both for you and the staff. Clients may have preconceived ideas and prejudices which you'll have to indulge if you want their business.

Recruit staff initially via ads in local papers and shop windows. Your accountant will insist that your staff is on the books and you may find that many cleaners, used to working in the black economy, are reluctant to commit themselves to this. Once you've got some staff they may introduce their friends to you but even then you'll spend a lot of time inter-

viewing and recruiting. Cleaners don't want to spend a lot of time and money getting to work so operate in a mixed area where staff can walk to work. Other problems here are in reliability (many cleaners have commitments to family etc. and will not always be available). Employ people you can trust (they will have access to your clients' houses), and who will maintain high standards of cleaning. Ensure this by getting references and employing them for a supervised trial clean before taking them on. Employing staff means paperwork, so be prepared for that.

Business comes from ads and articles in local papers, *Yellow Pages*, leaflet drop and word of mouth. As well as private clients who want regular cleaning, a lot of work comes from letting agencies and one-off jobs (spring cleans etc). There is more money to be made from these, and a one-off may lead to a contract, but they are often at very short notice.

You'll need an office to operate from and to store some equipment in, a phone and an answering machine; also a car or van for ferrying staff to distant, lucrative one-offs. Have cards printed. On the whole clients will supply their own materials and equipment but having backups is useful. As well as employer's liability insurance you'll have to be insured against damage to clients' property (depending on the area this could mean up to £1 million worth of cover); broken ornaments may cost a lot and lost keys mean having to replace the locks. Expect to pay your staff slightly above the normal rate to ensure a reliable workforce (about £3.50 per hour in London). You can charge about £6 and upwards per hour for regular contracts but profits on spring cleans etc are a lot higher. Clients will expect excellent service for this.

Although the cleaning gets done during the day you may have to see new clients in the evening. You'll also have to cope with crises such as cleaners refusing to work in filthy houses and clients who have managed to live in squalor noticing any speck of dust left by a cleaner. As well as operating to a strict schedule for much of the time, you'll have to deal with last-minute extra jobs.

Coal Merchant

Qualifications/Training	Recommended
Income bracket	Low–Medium
Licence	Yes, if new
Town/Country	Either
Experience/ Springboard	Recommended
Travel	Local
Mid-career entry	Possible
Exit sale	Yes
Entry costs	£5,000
Work at home	Possible
Mix and match	Possible.

You could think about: *Haulier, Man with a van, Tree surgeon, Jazz musician/singer*

Enquiries
Coal Merchants' Federation, Solid Fuel Advisory Service

Coal merchants can operate from coal yards, buying supplies and storing them until they're sold. Otherwise they can act as a sort of delivery service between large suppliers and customers – charging more for the coal than they paid for it.

To set up a new coal merchant's business, you need to be a member of the APPROVED COAL MERCHANTS' SCHEME before suppliers will deal with you. This involves demonstrating a knowledge of fuel (there are about 15 different sorts) and the trade. You will also need to know suppliers who are willing to supply you once you've joined. One way of learning is through apprenticing yourself to a good coal merchant, preferably not too close to where you hope to set up in business. You'll need an HGV licence (course and exam cost about £500) and an operator's licence from the MOT if you propose to operate a lorry over 7.5 tons. Another useful organisation is the COAL MERCHANTS' FEDERATION who run courses through the SOLID FUEL ADVISORY SERVICE. You need to be au fait with accounts, VAT etc or hire someone who is and who could perhaps take orders as well.

To set up in business you need premises, a yard and some arrangement for taking orders while you're out delivering. To convert your garden into a coal yard, you need planning permission and the neighbours are unlikely to be enthusiastic. You also need sacks, gloves, aprons and a good weighing machine (£200) and a lorry or two (handy when one is undergoing its annual MOT). Second-hand lorries cost about £2,000 rising to about £17,000 new. You collect the coal from Concentration Depots or in bulk from wholesalers near the pits (cheaper but reluctant to give credit). Besides insuring against the normal things, you need public liability insurance and professional indemnity insurance in case somebody's stove explodes because you've supplied the wrong coal.

It is very hard and dirty work and not recommended for those with bad backs or *folie de grandeur*.

Company Doctor

Qualifications/Training	No
Income bracket	Medium–High
Licence	No
Town/Country	Town
Experience/Springboard	Essential
Travel	Yes
Mid-career entry	Essential
Exit sale	No
Entry costs	Nil
Work at home	No
Mix and match	Yes.

You could think about: *Accountant, Marketing consultant, Timeshare developer, Racehorse owner, Novelist*

Enquiries
Management Consultants Association, Large accountancy firms

Failing companies may call in outside help to try to save themselves from imminent collapse. The people who are called upon, company doctors, are expected to diagnose the problems, come up with a remedy and implement it. They are at the top end of management consultancy and their expertise is such that they are usually called upon only by quoted companies and often when drastic action is needed. Demand for company doctors has increased over the past 20 years; while long established companies find that their old ways are no longer successful, there has been a rash of new companies who find that they are unable to maintain their, often quickly won, success. Even in the face of the 1986 Insolvency Act which combines the role of receiver with that of company doctor, company doctors are unlikely to disappear; there will always be companies prepared to call on expert help to avoid collapse rather than waiting for collapse before being doctored.

Essential qualifications are credibility and connections. Success depends to a large extent on restoring internal and external faith in an ailing company. This means raising money from sources which may have been pouring money into the company for years and introducing changes that won't always be popular with those they affect. You'll need to be so highly thought of that the right people are prepared to listen to you even when you're backing something they think is a loser. Contacts are also essential when you're saving a company and need to call on more expertise either as a second opinion or to take on an executive role in the client company to put your suggestions into effect. Most company doctors are over 50 with a lifetime in industry or business behind them and an impressive track record as managing directors. They have to know virtually all there is to know about how companies operate – management, accounting systems, marketing. Most will continue to hold directorships but will be free enough of other commitments to be able to throw themselves into full-time rescue when needed.

Company doctors need to be analytical and to combine some of the generalities learned through experience with the specifics observed about a particular company before focusing on the problems. You must be entrepreneurial enough to see

the potential for success even in a company that's floundering and willing to accept the formidable challenge this presents. The work often involves making sweeping changes to the structure of a company or redirecting its main activities (leading a company whose turnover was principally in eg chemicals, on to other areas). At other times companies need to be shown how to make the best of assets they already have; to build up previously underdeveloped areas. It can take years to lead a company on to success and needs patience and determination coupled with the ability to cope with only partial success or even failure. Company doctors often find that the root of the problems faced by client companies lies in the management. The first job is often to appoint new executive and financial management and weed out some of the old; so in spite of the great things your presence may herald, don't expect to be greeted with cries of welcome by everyone at client companies.

There are no set-up costs but you shouldn't depend on a regular income from company doctoring; companies don't get into financial trouble to order. On the other hand, you don't have to pay for advertising, because all the people who are interested in company doctors will know who to call on. The fees you charge can be enormous; you're charging for expertise, experience and connections, and the work you do, in the long run, could be worth millions to clients. Client companies are likely to have reached the limits of their credit and to have no more bank support. Sometimes the bank will have called the doctor in advance; other times it may be management consultants who realise a problem is extremely serious before it has exploded. Once called in, you can expect to be working full-time for several months. You start with a period of intense activity, liaising with the present management, finding out what's gone wrong and what can be made to go right; working out how to alleviate the immediate problem (this usually means getting hold of some more money and investors, working out a new finance system and, often, appointing a new finance director. Then you move on to the more positive role of establishing conditions that will prevent the same thing from happening again as soon as you've gone. There will be times when you have to drop everything and put in some long hours but most of the time your role is that of expert consultant. Company doctors and their assistants tend to have direct day-to-day contact with the company they're saving for at least 3–12 months, followed by a watchdog period during which they are on call should they be needed. Although there are failures, there are great rewards when the company you have rescued from the brink of disaster goes on to great things. There is a MANAGEMENT CONSULTANTS ASSOCIATION; many accountancy firms have corporate rescue teams; banks, eg HAMBROS, have intensive care units and INVESTORS IN INDUSTRY has a special management unit.

Computer Consultant

Qualifications/Training	Available
Income bracket	Medium–High
Licence	No
Town/Country	Town
Experience/Springboard	Vital
Travel	Local
Mid-career entry	Usual
Exit sale	No
Entry costs	£8,000+
Work at home	Yes
Mix and match	Yes.

You could think about: *Computer hardware engineer, Computer software author, Desk-top publisher, Fish curer and smoker, Timeshare developer*

Enquiries
British Computer Society

This job provides the bridge between computer hardware and software dealers who sell standard products, and their customers whose needs are anything but standard. Business computing is a growth area and consultancy provides an essential service at its current stage of development. Consultants specialise in particular systems, but the current boom area is in business microcomputers – IBM PCs and compatible computers.

Most customers are business or professional people who need someone to interpret their computer needs and set up a working system. Normally, you can expect to spend some time getting to know clients' business and discussing their needs prior to recommending the purchase of a suitable system and overseeing its installation. To be a good consultant – there are plenty of bad ones – you need a sound practical knowledge of business computer hardware and software plus an all-round understanding of how a variety of businesses operate.

Some consultants specialise and work as part of a team, but if you go it alone you need many skills. At minimum you should be familiar with a wide range of software and have practical programming experience in the main industry-standard databases, spreadsheets, word processors, accounts and integrated packages. You should also be familiar with a range of computers, printers and other peripherals, and on top of this you'll need a working knowledge of accountancy and business practice, plus good communication skills. Contacts with computer dealers are useful but not essential and tend to develop naturally.

Having said all that, there are no formal qualifications and people set up consultancy practices from many different backgrounds. Some start by working in a dealership and gain experience by providing a service linked to the dealer's sales. Others work from within the computer department of a larger company until branching out on their own.

You won't need much in the way of space – a small office, a telephone and answering machine is enough to get started – but you will need computers, peripherals and a wide range of software. If you work in the industry for a while you should be able to acquire much of what you need cheaply. But if you buy at retail prices, budget a minimum of £3,000 for hardware, and probably as much again for software. Fees vary widely, depending on the type of client as well as the quality of your work, but expect to receive from £100 to £300 per day, and to have the possibility of long slack periods.

You can advertise your services in the specialist press, but the most worthwhile jobs come by word of mouth and personal recommendation. It helps to be listened to if you are personable and look convincing in a business suit (or female equivalent).

There are many consumer computer magazines but the more serious are: *MicroScope*; *Computing*; *PC User*; *PC Week* and *Systems International*. Most of these are controlled circulation and free to legitimate business readers. Also read the *Computer Users' Year Book*. The BRITISH COMPUTER SOCIETY runs courses and has useful information.

European Community Notes
Qualifications: UK qualifications recognised throughout EC and EC qualifications in UK.
Languages: To succeed, local language necessary.
Earnings: UK income in some fields generally lower than elsewhere in the EC.
Setting up: You will find it difficult to succeed in France, Greece, Italy. You will find it easier in Belgium, Denmark, Eire, Luxembourg, Netherlands, Portugal, Spain.
Exchanges: Formal job exchanges exist (Youth Exchange Programme).
Enquiry point for those wishing to work in the EC: BRITISH COMPUTER SOCIETY, which is a member of the Council of European Professional Information Societies.

Computer Hardware Engineer

Qualifications/Training	Necessary
Income bracket	Medium
Licence	No
Town/Country	Town
Experience/Springboard	Recommended
Travel	Local
Mid-career entry	Yes
Exit sale	No
Entry costs	£5,000+
Work at home	Possible
Mix and match	Possible.

You could think about: **Computer consultant, Motorcycle racer, Disco owner/DJ, Import/export broker**

Enquiries
British Computer Society

Most computer engineers' jobs involve repairing or modifying the basic machine. Although computers are inherently reliable, they and their printers or other peripherals do break down and need mending. And some users need special modifications to suit their own requirements – anything from a simple job like making a special head, through to constructing a special interface. The other main opening for hardware engineers is development of new hardware add-ons, which can still be done on a small scale and a manageable budget. Manufacture and marketing on any scale takes substantial resources, however, and if you have perfected a new expansion card for a PC, say, you may be better off taking it to a company who has established manufacturing and distribution chains – rather than setting yourself up as a cottage industry manufacturing and selling direct. If the idea and the product are good enough, you can reasonably ask for an advance on setting up the deal, and a royalty on sales of the product – although if it is unlikely to sell in large numbers, you may prefer a cash sum.

Repairs may seem to offer more regular work, but many repair jobs – particularly on new business machines – are handled through service contracts. These usually guarantee the owner a quick response and fixed terms in return for an annual fee, usually linked into their dealership. The service company employ their own service agents and demand standard qualifications. But openings exist for private enterprise to fill the gaps left by service contracts. Generally, these comprise the cheaper machines, ones which don't have a large enough dealer network to have negotiated service arrangements, and second-hand equipment.

There are two ways to approach such business. One is to establish friendly links with local dealers. If they are small, they may themselves need the occasional bit of wiring modification done or special circuit made up that they cannot do themselves. They may also be prepared to refer business to you from customers who need this kind of work. The alternative is to advertise, but this may prove expensive compared to the amount of business you can expect to handle as a single operator. You need practical qualifications for the job and a relevant course in computer or electronic engineering is desirable. As a sole operator, you don't need a particularly large workshop, but you'll need to be able to store bits and pieces and customers' equipment. Transport capable of moving you and machines around is desirable, although ways can be found around this if it is a problem. You need standard electronic test and repair equipment, plus a range of components or spares for the type of machines you intend to work on. You should also think about the consequences of failing to fix, worse still, damaging someone's equipment: it may be worth obtaining professional indemnity insurance against this contingency. Get information from the BRITISH COMPUTER SOCIETY; there are many computer magazines eg *MicroScope*, *Computing*, *PC User*, *PC Week* and *Systems International*. Also read the *PC Year Book* and the *Computer Users' Year Book*.

European Community Notes

Qualifications: UK qualifications recognised throughout EC and EC qualifications in UK.

Languages: To succeed, local language necessary.

Earnings: UK income in some fields generally lower than elsewhere in the EC.

Setting up: You will find it difficult to succeed in France, Greece, Italy. You will find it easier in Belgium, Denmark, Eire, Germany, Luxembourg, Netherlands, Portugal, Spain.

Exchanges: Formal job exchanges exist (Youth Exchange Programme).

Enquiry point for those wishing to work in the EC: BRITISH COMPUTER SOCIETY, which is a member of the Council of European Professional Information Societies.

Computer Software Author

Qualifications/Training	Usual
Income bracket	Medium
Licence	No
Town/Country	Town or nearby
Experience/ Springboard	Recommended
Travel	Local
Mid-career entry	Possible
Exit sale	No
Entry costs	£2,000+
Work at home	Possible
Mix and match	Possible.

You could think about: *Computer consultant, Word processor, Kennel/ cattery owner, Teacher, Desk-top publisher*

Enquiries
British Computer Society

Software isn't what it used to be in the days when teenage millionaire whizzkids seemed to make the headlines every week for writing a best-selling game. Things have quietened down since then, and generally programs don't sell in such epic numbers nor are they so often the work of one inspired enthusiast. Software publishing has settled down to become perhaps closer to book publishing than record publishing.

The market splits into two – entertainment and business software. Major business packages nowadays are almost invariably the work of a team who each contribute different skills, and involve a lengthy development period. And selling such a program successfully generally calls for massive production, documentation and use support. Having said that, there are still some examples of programs written by small independent groups that have found a niche.

Perhaps the most rewarding field (though not necessarily financially so) is in specialist, so-called 'vertical market' applications. If you have specialist knowledge of the needs of a particular business and can write a program to meet them, your market is easily defined. Such software is often written using a standard applications package (dBase III, for example), or it may use a programming language (a surprising number use BASIC).

Typically, such software costs a substantial amount – £1,000 or more is not uncommon, in addition to any basic software required to run it. In some cases the software was developed for a single user who will have helped to meet the costs, and if it can then be sold on, there may well be potential for profit. Because it sells to a small specialist market, it is unnecessary to provide extensive packaging and so on, since sales will be very much on a personal, consultative basis. But it will be difficult to find a field which is not already well tapped, and many programs fail to sell in substantial numbers. For examples of the kind of things on offer, see the back pages of *Micro Decision* (which lists the numbers sold against each package) or the listings in the *PC Year Book*. Advertising such software tends to have easy avenues through the trade press, exhibitions, etc.

Entertainment software – games, music and graphics packages etc – is possibly less demanding than the business market. But the field is flooded with many competing products and success still tends to mean professional attention to marketing. Software houses are much more hard-bitten than they once were, and although they are always on the look-out for a new product, it will have to offer something special.

In either business or entertainment software, if you do succeed in interesting a software house, expect your royalty to reflect the size of the program – whether it needs heavy investment in packaging, documentation etc – in other words how much work they will have to put into it.

Of the host of computer magazines, the more serious are *MicroScope*, *Computing*, *PC User*, *PC Week* and *Systems International*. Contact the BRITISH COMPUTER SOCIETY.

European Community Notes
Qualifications: UK qualifications recognised throughout EC and EC qualifications in UK.
Languages: To succeed, local language necessary.
Earnings: UK income in some fields generally lower than elsewhere in the EC.
Setting up: You will find it difficult to succeed in France, Greece, Italy. You will find it easier in Belgium, Denmark, Eire, Germany, Luxembourg, Netherlands, Portugal, Spain.
Exchanges: Formal job exchanges exist (Youth Exchange Programme).
Enquiry point for those wishing to work in the EC: BRITISH COMPUTER SOCIETY, which is a member of the Council of European Professional Information Societies.

Concert Agent

Qualifications/Training	Recommended
Income bracket	Low–Medium
Licence	Yes
Town/Country	Mostly Town
Experience/Springboard	Essential
Travel	Yes
Mid-career entry	Possible
Exit sale	Possible
Entry costs	£5,000
Work at home	Yes
Mix and match	Possible.

You could think about: *Impresario, Orchestral fixer, Festival director, Musician, Music publisher, Word processor*

Enquiries
British Association of Concert Agents

The agent, or manager, procures engagements for a few chosen performing musicians/singers and also organises individual concerts, usually recitals. Ideally you should have musical interests and secretarial skills and have completed either a business studies or arts administration course (eg City University). You need to be able to recognise talent and predict what promoters will like; you must possess patience, persistence, iron determination and diplomacy when dealing with artists and promoters.

Five years' experience of working in different fields of arts administration is essential for contacts and making mistakes in a safe environment. In order to go it alone, you will then need at least £5,000 capital. You can work from one room at home with a supply of stationery, a typewriter (or perferably a word processor), telephone, answering machine or service and, as soon as possible, a computer and fax. You will also need a good accountant.

It's a good idea to join the BRITISH ASSOCIATION OF CONCERT AGENTS and you will need a DEPARTMENT OF EMPLOYMENT licence to act as an employ-ment agent. You can charge 15–20 per cent commission fee on an artist's concert fee and £400–£600 for organising a Wigmore Hall recital. This will involve arranging publicity and encouraging critics to attend. You cannot expect to make a decent living for three–five years so it is necessary to have other employment as well or an earning partner; but the sky's the limit for a successful international agent. You will attend your artists' concerts, in addition to working office hours. If you want to chat up promoters you will have to travel. Female agents feel they are not taken as seriously as their male counterparts.

The disadvantages of the job are that it disrupts social life and, unless you strike lucky with a genius of a client, you will find it difficult to become rich: artists' fees are low; concert organisation in the UK is badly funded; the music agent is the victim of Arts Council and government arts policies, or lack of them. The advantages are the interesting people you meet, the flexible hours and the satisfaction of making concerts happen.

Useful books are *British Music Year Book*, the *British Association of Concert Agents' List of Artists*, the *Musicians' Handbook*, the *National Federation of Music Societies Handbook* and the *Incorporated Society of Musicians' Arts Festival Book*.

European Community Notes

Qualifications: UK qualifications recognised throughout EC and EC qualifications in UK.

Languages: To succeed, local language necessary.

Earnings: UK income generally lower than or same as elsewhere in the EC.

Advice/Training: Advice, information and training not available for those wishing to work in Europe.

Exchanges: Formal job exchanges do not exist.

Conductor

Qualifications/Training	Recommended
Income bracket	Low–High
Licence	No
Town/Country	Town
Experience/Springboard	Yes
Travel	Endless
Mid-career entry	Possible
Exit sale	No
Entry costs	£2,000
Work at home	No
Mix and match	Yes.

You could think about: *Musician, Classical/TV and film music composer, Music teacher, Instrumental soloist, Music copyist, Music critic, Repetiteur/accompanist/coach, Book-keeper*

Enquiries
Music colleges

To become a conductor you need an excellent sense of rhythm, a quick intelligence, confidence, courage and determination. Going to music college or university is useful for skills – keyboard ones are very helpful – and for contacts. It is not necessary to have a degree in music but being able to play an instrument and/or sing is a distinct advantage.

Most important, apart from being able to hear music from a score before it is played and to memorise it, is the ability to communicate with other people – musicians, directors, designers, concert promoters and sponsors. To speak several languages is an advantage, as is diplomacy and the imagination to inspire other artists, and to sell yourself and your ideas. Career prospects are grim unless you have personality, talent, luck or money.

To get started, try to join a number of good quality amateur musical organisations. Conduct local choirs/orchestras and, if at college, form your own orchestra/choir/opera group. Persuade well-established musicians to come and hear your work so that it becomes known. Then you need to either win an international competition, get appointed assistant conductor or repetiteur in an opera house, or be given the opportunity to conduct a professional orchestra. It helps to have a private income or a sponsor in order to make a recording, which is aural proof of your prowess and the best tool with which to promote yourself. If you can persuade the critics of the national press to attend one of your concerts and their judgement is encouraging you may begin to get more engagements.

There is no union you need to join, but it is helpful to know as many influential people as possible. It is a good plan to have a job either playing, teaching or editing music as you may have no income for several years. You will require a room with a piano, telephone and answering machine or service, and a working partner to help with income for the first 10 years. You can become successful either under 30 or over 45 – in between it is necessary just to keep struggling.

Income will start at £15 an hour as a repetiteur. At the top, income can be £100,000 per annum plus royalties on recordings etc (up to a further £100,000).

The disadvantages are the lack of security and depression at having to work with poor orchestras so being unable to express oneself. The hours are very long: often starting early in the morning learning or studying scores; travelling to a rehearsal anywhere in the UK; rehearsing all day; followed by an evening concert or meetings with organisers and artistes.

You will need to consult *Grove's Dictionary of Music*, the *BBC Index* and a book on orchestral timings; also read *Music and Musicians*.

European Community Notes
A famously itinerant profession. Germany is the most receptive host to UK conductors. Few language barriers.

Conference Organiser

Qualifications/Training	No
Income bracket	Medium–High
Licence	No
Town/Country	Town
Experience/Springboard	Essential
Travel	Yes
Mid-career entry	Yes
Exit sale	Possible
Entry costs	£5,000+
Work at home	Yes
Mix and match	Yes.

You could think about: *Public relations consultant, Events organiser, List broker, Tourist attraction, Hotelier*

Enquiries
Conference organisers, PR agencies

Business and professional conferences and seminars are thriving – it's an industry in which professional conference organisers can flourish.

Conference organisers act either as principals (taking the financial risk and managing the entire event) or as suppliers of an administrative conference service – running the event directly on behalf of the client or indirectly on contract to the client's PR agency. At the same time, hotels, local authorities, schools, universities, polytechnics and colleges are clamouring for people who will buy their services and hire their amenities. If you have an idea for a conference which people will pay for and the wherewithal to make it worthwhile for them to do so, you can organise your own conference and make money.

Usually, the people you book conference accommodation from provide food, refreshments and often hire of equipment. It's up to you to do everything else: organise travel, decide who will speak when, choose a suitable centre and, above all, publicise the conference.

You must have some idea of what's involved before you launch; you need contacts among the people who are likely to attend or contribute towards your conference. Go to a few conferences yourself (see the *Conference Blue Book*) to get an idea of the sort of scheduling you'll have to do; what you can lay on by way of spin-offs (eg books and videos) and as entertainment; ways of encouraging sponsorship from businesses and organisations. Hotel and catering experience (especially if it includes working at large conference hotels and centres) is useful for this especially if you're going to specialise in internal company conferences for clients who can lay on their own speakers and who aren't dependent on external publicity for attendance.

People go to conferences to listen to speakers rather than for free pens and the chance to see London or Cannes by night. That means knowing people who are prominent in major interest groups. Likely areas for this are in higher education or within professional bodies; if you're involved in either of these they may be enthusiastic about your organising a conference under their auspices. Anyone with PR, journalism or marketing experience may have built up a network of suitable speakers and interested participants. You need phenomenal organisational skills coupled with the flair to come up with interesting ideas and the imagination and attention to detail necessary to turn those ideas into successful and enjoyable conferences.

You're going to need some money to start out with. As well as publicising your conference in suitable trade, professional and consumer press or by mailings (lists for which have to be bought, if you don't have your own), you need to book a centre and pay a deposit. Although you can make a provisional booking well in advance without paying a deposit, it's unlikely that you'll be able to whip up enough interest in time to avoid having to finalise the booking (usually about nine months in advance) before you're sure you've got a full contingent. During very quiet times, you can sometimes negotiate with a centre willing to take a provisional booking rather than nothing at all. Students' halls of residence are a lot cheaper (but a lot less comfortable) than hotels and you'll probably get free use of projectors and videos as well (hotels often charge £100+ for this). Conference rates are usually less than normal hotel rates but rooms can cost up to £150 per night with an additional minimum charge of £35 per person per day for food and drinks. The food supplied by hotels at conferences isn't usually the best the kitchens can offer. On top of accommodation costs are the costs of speakers and extras like buses from the station/airport to the centre. You may be able to raise some sponsorship from professional institutions or companies which will use the conference for their own publicity (eg giving commemorative presents). You must be sure you'll be able to charge enough to cover your expenses and make a profit. Don't forget the months of work you've put in when you're calculating how much you want for each day of the conference. Conferences aimed at business may draw a lot of participants whose employers pay the fees; people are more aware of how much a conference costs to attend when they have to pay it themselves. A day's conference including food but no accommodation raises about £75 per participant. It can take two–three years of liaising to get speakers and participants to be at the same place at the same time. If you're short of a speaker, PR consultants may be able to provide one from their clients. Schedule everything (including time to cope with the shortage of lavatories in halls of residence; conferences cause constipation). You must meet deadlines. That means having contingency plans for virtually everything: speakers may be ill at the last minute so have reserves on hand; coaches break down or fail to turn up; crises are normal.

Contemporary Art Gallery Owner

Qualifications/Training	No
Income bracket	Medium
Licence	No
Town/Country	Town
Experience/ Springboard	Recommended
Travel	No
Mid-career entry	Yes
Exit sale	Yes
Entry costs	£20,000+
Work at home	No
Mix and match	Yes.

You could think about: *Art historian/ critic, Journalist, Public relations consultant, Artist, Picture framer*

Enquiries
Local galleries

Contemporary art galleries are market places for the works of living artists. Gallery owners sometimes buy works of art outright from artists but the majority sell on behalf of artists for a commission. Selling affordable art (anything under about £2,000) is much like many other kinds of specialist retailing; you've got to know both your market and your supplier, to be flexible enough to move with both and inspired enough to develop them. A lot of people are eager to buy the works of living undiscovered artists either in the hope that they may be making an investment or because they like the pictures. You may not stand to make millions on the sale of one painting but neither do you have to make massive capital outlays in order to get your stock in the first place.

You don't need any formal qualifications but a knowledge of the art world is essential; you have to know which artists to use and to have an idea of how much they should be charging for their work. You should also be able to talk about art authoritatively to customers and so you need some idea of the different techniques used as well as some knowledge of art history. Working in someone else's gallery is a good way of finding out what you're taking on. Other useful experience (and a good source of contacts) is working on an art magazine or journal. Keep up with what's going on by visiting galleries and reading *Galleries*, *Arts Review*, the *Burlington Magazine* etc. You'll need to know how to organise, promote and put up exhibitions; to have excellent organisational skills, to keep punctilious records and to be good at dealing with people, whether they are artists unhappy with the way you're displaying their work or demanding customers. Some of your artists may be registered for VAT so make sure you know about this. Unlike a shop, where stock is displayed until it is sold and deliveries are made whenever they're needed, art galleries operate by mounting exhibitions of the work of one or more artists and releasing the pictures to clients at the end of an exhibition. Shows last about three–six weeks and are planned up to two years in advance to give the artist time to build up a collection. You have a complete change of stock at the end of every exhibition. Draw up a contract with each artist, stipulating the number of works to be shown and their agreement not to mount any other one-man exhibitions in local galleries in the meantime. Keep a careful log of what the artist brings in and takes out of the gallery.

You need to have the right sort of premises for an art gallery. It helps to be in an area with other galleries and you need enough wall space to hang pictures. The right premises tend to be in expensive areas – surrounded by buyers or somewhere they'll travel to. On top of this you need security and alarms (art galleries aren't popular with everyone and can be the victims of attack) and insurance to cover the art that's in your gallery. If you don't have a partner, you'll have to employ someone to look after the gallery while you're talking to artists, going to exhibitions, etc. Then you need to consider fixtures and fittings and promotion: press releases, invitations, food and wine for exhibition openings (ultimately, however, you may be able to get some of this

through sponsorship from food and wine companies). Although many artists frame their own work you might have to pay for framing of some pictures – make sure you know some good reliable framers. When you're organising an exhibition, make sure that you've got enough art of value to make it worth while. Although it's obviously dependent on what you're exhibiting and on how experimental you want to be – some exhibitions sell nothing. If in doubt, price works moderately; you can always increase the artist's prices next time if you sell out. At the end of the day, only good art sells. An 80 per cent sell out is extremely good; it's safer to reckon on about 50 per cent. You can augment your own income by selling prints and cards.

You need to find suppliers. Most established artists already have galleries which they use but there are plenty of lesser known ones desperate to show their work. You can find suitable ones through contacts and through the endless stream of artists who will drop in to the gallery in the hope you may like their work. You may need to advise the artists on how much to charge for their work; this will increase as the artist becomes better known. You'll have to know your own price bracket and may find that you've helped to price an artist out of your market. You should be able to build up a regular clientele; keep a mailing list so you can let them know when you're mounting a new exhibition. Days are long, and there's a lot of paper work keeping tabs on whose work you've got and who wants to buy what (selling the same picture twice isn't impossible if you don't keep careful records). You'll have to change exhibitions regularly, arranging for art to be collected and delivered. This is a very personal business, it's important that the artists you work with trust you (that may mean having to shell out yourself if anything gets stolen) and that customers know that you're likely to have something they like. Busy seasons are at Christmas and in early summer.

Continuity Person

Qualifications/Training	No
Income bracket	Medium
Licence	No
Town/Country	Town
Experience/Springboard	Yes
Travel	Yes
Mid-career entry	Yes
Exit sale	No
Entry costs	£100
Work at home	No
Mix and match	Limited.

You could think about: *Typist, Market research interviewer, Wood carver, Film extra*

Enquiries
BECTU (Broadcasting, Entertainment Cinematograph and Theatre union)

In film making the continuity person is responsible for seeing that costumes, hairstyles and set designs remain consistent, especially when scenes that are to be only seconds apart on the finished film have been shot out of sequence over several days. Continuity people also keep a log of each day's work, details of each shot, dialogue timing, lenses and any other important information the film crews and editor will need.

There are no formal qualifications (although NVQs are on their way) but you'll need to have a wide general knowledge of filming and film equipment; how using different lenses affects the shots and how to record camera and set positions. Continuity people do not usually come from film school. The most likely route in is by starting as a secretary in a production company or as a personal assistant to a producer, production manager or director. You'll probably learn more in a small company where there is overlap between different departments and roles and where there are fewer general assistants around to help out at shoots. You need to pick up as much as possible from as many areas of film production as you can. Try and get to shoots where you'll see what happens and pick up contacts who may be useful in future. Continuity people need to be observant and efficient with good eyesight and hearing and the stamina to concentrate all the time. Although they're freelance, they have to be able to work as part of a team.

Your first continuity job will probably come from knowing the right person at the right time. Set-up costs are therefore virtually nil but you'll need a telephone and some business cards as work increases and your network of contacts grows. Consider registering with a booking service who will manage your diary for you while you're on the set all day. Contact BECTU for minimum rates.

Continuity people are hired for the duration of a shoot and spend the day on the set keeping an eye on what's going on and making sure that actors limp on the right leg, don't change their accents, etc and that furniture doesn't move. At the end of the day you have to record the duration of each shot, the number of shots filmed and any problems.

Continuity is responsible and exacting but it is not likely to help you on your way to being a producer; the experience and knowledge that you need as a continuity person takes a long time to accumulate and is far more general and broadbased than the sort of experience that you need for other areas of film production.

Conveyancer

Qualifications/Training	Essential
Income bracket	Medium
Licence	Yes
Town/Country	Town
Experience/Springboard	Essential
Travel	Local
Mid-career entry	Yes
Exit sale	Possible

Entry costs	£5,000
Work at home	Possible
Mix and match	Yes.

You could think about: *Surveyor, Estate agent, House converter, Music teacher, Reflexologist*

Enquiries
Council for Licensed Conveyancers, Society of Licensed Conveyancers

Conveyancing is the transfer of land or property rights from one person to another. Licensed conveyancers form a separate branch of the legal profession and are qualified to advise buyers and sellers and to transact the conveyance. It's a relatively new profession created in 1985 by the Administration of Justice Act; before that conveyancing could only be done by solicitors and 'certain others' (mainly barristers and public authorities). Currently there aren't many independent licensed conveyancers around (most are employed by solicitors) and there's room for more; especially with the introduction of one-stop house buying, which has encouraged close working contact between estate agents, financial advisers and conveyancers.

All conveyancers must, by law, be licensed by the COUNCIL FOR LICENSED CONVEYANCERS (CLC). This is the profession's regulatory body, established to set standards and protect consumers. To get a licence you must be at least 21, have passed the CLC's three-part exam, have two years' practical training in employment with a supervising conveyancer or solicitor and be deemed fit and proper as a licence holder by the CLC. Register as a student with the CLC; this costs £50 and you'll need at least four GCSEs or (if you're over 25) some appropriate work experience. Six months later you're allowed to sit the exams if you're ready; at least one year of training must be done after passing.

To set up your own firm you need to have been licensed for at least three years and, if you want to practise as a limited company, your firm must be a recognised body with the Council. Conveyancing is a legal profession, you'll need to have a general knowledge of the law (tested in the preliminary exam) to be able to advise clients on the legal aspects of property ownership. You must pay attention to detail and be patient with clients. House buying is considered one of the most stressful acitivities people indulge in and you'll probably see some very worried clients. You must also be quick and efficient – when the house market is buoyant, speedy conveyancing can make the difference between buying or losing a house. You'll need an office with a phone and an efficient filing system – a computer/word processor helps but is not essential. A photocopier is useful and a fax will speed up communications when you're in a hurry. Expect to charge an average of about £250 per job. The average charge made by solicitors is more – at least £350.

There's an increase in the number of house buyers with no experience of employing solicitors who are, therefore, more willing to call on licensed conveyancers. Many clients come through referral; develop contacts at estate agents or busy solicitors. You won't just be needed when someone is buying a house or flat; conveyancers can advise and act in cases of change of use of premises, mortgages, property development, and so on. Although it's possible to mix and match this with other jobs, the Council for Licensed Conveyancers lays down the conditions under which you can, for example, practise as both a conveyancer and an estate agent. They are looking into ways of including some estate agency in the profession of licensed conveyancer; in the meantime, unless you or one of your partners is a member of the RICS (ROYAL INSTITUTION OF CHARTERED SURVEYORS) or ISVA (INCORPORATED SOCIETY OF VALUERS AND AUCTIONEERS) you can only work alongside estate agents.

The SOCIETY OF LICENSED CONVEYANCERS represents the professions in England and Wales and aims to increase public awareness of the profession. Contact them and the CLC for further information, and read *The Licensed Conveyancer*.

Corporate Video Producer

Qualifications/Training	Recommended
Income bracket	Low–High
Licence	No
Town/Country	Town
Experience/ Springboard	Recommended
Travel	Essential
Mid-career entry	Possible
Exit sale	Possible
Entry costs	£2,000
Work at home	No
Mix and match	Yes.

You could think about: *In-company trainer, Media trainer, Film director, Public relations consultant, Landlord, Private investigator*

Enquiries
Independent Film, Video and Photography Association

Corporate video is the general term used for videotape or film productions made for businesses, government, or other groups, notably training bodies. They tend to be short but can be of any length and are usually made to sell a corporate image, product or service or simply to inform.

The corporate video producer's job is to co-ordinate all aspects of production from the original idea right through to delivery of the video to the client, on time and within the client's budget. Making videos is primarily a creative process but alsof a money-making operation, so sympathy for creative ideas, creative people and an aptitude for managerial and business matters is important.

As video producer, you'll obviously be liaising closely with your client; also with the directors, editors, cameramen, all of whom you hire. Members of the video team will look to you for decisions regarding budget, pay, as well as quite trivial matters like where to park their car on the location shoot.

There are no formal qualifications, but obviously a good understanding of video production techniques is necessary. Short introductory production courses are available (look in the *Guardian* or industry press such as *Broadcast*). Working in the industry for a while is another good way to get the necessary experience – joining one of the many corporate production companies as a runner, production assistant, researcher or secretary will teach you the basics. The corporate video market is expanding rapidly with smaller companies increasingly using video for promotions and training. It is easier to get into than film – there are no unions – and more work is available.

If you have the confidence and plenty of ideas about ways of presenting information in words and pictures, all you will need to start with is a phone and the usual business cards etc. Start by approaching local small businesses that you think would benefit from their own video; try community groups and especially local authorities which are increasingly using video.

Having completed a few low budget and simple videos you will have a show reel with which you can tout for more work. Remember that working in any creative field is notoriously difficult as people are often very unclear what it is they want until you produce it and then it may be too late. Be prepared for disappointments; you can avoid them through meticulous planning and good communication with your clients.

Producers' earnings are directly related to the budget which for a corporate video can range from a little under £1,000 to several hundred thousand pounds. How well you do will depend on your ability to find work and the type of work it is. Some videos, eg training films, can be very lucrative if there is a market for copies of the original; anywhere between £10,000 and £20,000 is reasonable.

You will have to work hard for your rewards. Days, especially shoot days, can be very long and you will experience slack periods followed by intense activity. Be prepared to bid for plenty of jobs with the probability of only a fraction coming to you.

Costume Designer

Qualifications/Training	Yes
Income bracket	Low–Medium
Licence	No
Town/Country	Town
Experience/ Springboard	Recommended
Travel	Yes
Mid-career entry	Difficult
Exit sale	No
Entry costs	£100
Work at home	No
Mix and match	Limited.

You could think about: *Fashion designer, Stage designer, Artist, Network marketing*

Enquiries
BECTU

A costume designer can work in repertory theatre, television or film. It is a tough world and you have to have a vocation and a love of the business to give you the determination to succeed. This is not the job for the home lover or those with family commitments. It is hard work, with long hours, late nights, overtime and last-minute crises to sort out. You might have to work through the night to meet deadlines. Your social life will revolve round the others in the production. If you are filming, you may be away from home for weeks, possibly in bad hotels.

Costume designers in repertory are very busy; they usually work out the costume requirements for two plays ahead, while sorting out the daily problems of the current play. In a small company they will probably have to act as dresser and wardrobe mistress as well. For a new production costume details have to be got right with the scenery and lighting in only two days (and probably nights).

In television there may be 12-hour recording days, plus an hour to check all the costumes before the cameras start rolling and an hour to clear up at the end. If, for example, a large ball scene is being shot, there might be hundreds of period costumes to check. You will have the help of a wardrobe staff, an assistant designer, and dressers (who also press and hang clothes up, mend, etc) and the job is to oversee the whole operation. Filming on location brings its own problems, eg small hotel space to prepare costumes and distance from suppliers. While shooting, the designer shares responsibility for continuity; keeping a continuity book and recording what each actor is wearing in every scene, down to the watch and how many buttons are undone. Then if an adjoining scene is shot days later there are no discrepancies between the scenes. A polaroid camera is essential.

Part of the costume designer's function is to be able to manage people and delegate. There is a lot of tension, it's a long day, everyone gets fraught, and tempers can get frayed. The designer is always working under pressure and has to remain calm while ironing out the perpetual small problems.

In addition there is research. You need artistic flair as well as historical knowledge to be able to interpret the scripts and the characters, working closely with the director. You need to work out the costume requirements; how many outfits are needed, cost, and the accurate clothes for a particular character in relation to class, background, and period. For a big show both costume designer and assistant will be working for several weeks before it opens, researching, ordering costumes (hiring, buying or having made), hiring wigs, buying rights and safety pins, taking the measurements of actors, and working out eg whether to double up on costumes that might get damaged in a fight scene.

You should be a member of BECTU (Broadcasting, Entertainment Cinematograph and Theatre union) which works out the rates of pay and conditions.

Most designers have a diploma in theatre design from an art college. After that you might get a start in repertory (usually means getting involved in all aspects of production, lighting, props, wardrobe, scene painting, stage management as well as costume design). Or you could become an assistant to a costume designer in television or films. Some people come from a fashion background.

Further reading: The *Stage* is invaluable as a source of information. Also read *Contacts* (publication listing all the theatre companies etc) available from *Spotlight* offices.

Counsellor

Qualifications/Training	Essential
Income bracket	Medium
Licence	No
Town/Country	Either
Experience/Springboard	No
Travel	None
Mid-career entry	Essential
Exit sale	No
Entry costs	£600+
Work at home	Yes
Mix and match	Excellent.

You could think about: *Orchestral musician, Furniture designer, Gardener/garden designer, Night care, Telesales person*

Enquiries
British Association for Counselling (BAC)

Counsellors give their clients regular periods of time when, in complete confidence, they support and help the clients work through their personal or emotional problems and discover more satisfactory ways of living and relating to others. They give their clients uncritical regard, empathy and insight and, through their psychological training and awareness, help the client to fulfil their potential as a human being.

To enter one of the many training courses (full- or part-time) you need to be mature and have broad life experience. Some counsellor training courses (diploma or equivalent) are recognised by the BRITISH ASSOCIATION FOR COUNSELLING but there are also many with university validation which are very good. Educa-

tional qualifications don't matter so much as a good natural intelligence, emotional stability, intuition, common sense, sense of humour and a fascination with other people. Most important is an ability to be unjudgmental and to communicate with others. Counsellors work in educational, medical, industrial and pastoral settings. As well as learning psychological theory on your course, you have to be prepared to grow and develop emotionally which can at times be quite painful. You need to be well motivated and, on some courses, receive counselling or psychotherapy (which can cost £25 or more a session). The number of good counsellors is increasing throughout the country. The BAC insist that counsellors should always be supervised by an experienced counsellor or psychotherapist at least once a month to retain a healthy, balanced view of themselves and their job.

You can start your practice in a quiet room in your home as soon as you are qualified. Let local GPs know you exist. You need a phone which you can turn off, and an answerphone and lockable filing cabinet. Make sure that you are properly insured. A session lasts 50 minutes and rates vary from £15–£25. You can mix this with another job and it's possible to fix clients' appointments at a mutually satisfactory time, often outside working hours. It's important to balance counselling with a rich personal life. The good part of this job is that it is never boring if you are interested in and enjoy helping people to help themselves. The bad points are that it needs enormous energy and concentration so it's quite exhausting and if you work within your home, be careful to keep your work separate from the family. There is a heavy bias towards people who are mature with plenty of life experience.

Get more information from the BRITISH ASSOCIATION FOR COUNSELLING. Also read *On Being A Counsellor* and *Individual Therapy in Britain*.

European Community Notes
Qualifications: UK qualifications recognised throughout EC and EC qualifications in UK.

Languages: To succeed, local language necessary.

Advice/Training: Advice, information and training not available for those wishing to work in Europe.

Exchanges: Formal job exchanges do not exist.

Notes: BAC is working with others in the UK and Europe to establish acceptable common standards throughout the EC. If you want to know more contact BAC.

Courier Service

Qualifications/Training	No
Income bracket	Medium–High
Licence	No
Town/Country	Town
Experience/ Springboard	Recommended
Travel	No
Mid-career entry	Excellent
Exit sale	Yes
Entry costs	£10,000
Work at home	No
Mix and match	Limited.

You could think about: *Novelist, Inventor, Employment agent, Motorcycle racer*

Enquiries
Courier companies

Couriers on foot or horseback were used to carry messages for thousands of years. Much of this job has changed with quicker transport, telephones and radios, fax, telex and computers. But couriers are still much in demand, especially in town centres where they are used to carry a variety of documents and parcels for distances of a few hundred yards to thousands of miles. Courier service companies liaise between customers and couriers who may be motorcycle messengers, bicycle messengers, van drivers, and aeroplace passengers.

Their job is to get couriers to where they're needed. People use couriers either because the alternatives (eg postal service or railway) are too slow, or because they are sending something of value. This means that couriers have to be fast, reliable and trustworthy.

You don't need any formal qualifications to set up a courier service but a knowledge of accounting is essential, as are management skills. You will need to know your area of operation extremely well, not just the street names and lengths, but normal traffic conditions, one way systems and anything else that may affect journey times for your couriers. Couriers use various forms of transport – usually motorbikes, with vans for larger commissions. Even though you won't necessarily be doing much of the couriering yourself, it helps if you can drive these. In places with very heavy traffic, or for very short distances, you may also want to use bicycles. For couriering overseas, you'll use air transport. You may get business collecting parcels and documents from your nearest airport for delivery but, if you're going to offer a full courier service overseas, you'll have to get hold of air tickets at short notice. Most of this business is done by large companies for whom it's easier to get the necessary airline co-operation. You'll have to cope with people who are probably under pressure and in a hurry; this means being calm and organised.

To set up you'll need a telephone (which has to be manned all day) and some couriers: use contacts or advertise. Couriers sometimes provide their own bikes or vans (but need extra insurance cover for couriering). Increasingly the companies rent their own bikes/vans to the couriers, which helps with reliability, a corporate image and ensures adequate insurance cover. You'll need radio phones so you don't have to be based centrally. Join the DESPATCH ASSOCIATION. Base your charges on local competition; couriers are paid on commission so, if you undercut too much, you won't be able to pay them properly – it's better to compete with good service. Payment is made either when the courier collects the parcel, or on account for regular customers. Most of your customers will be local businesses; you get them by advertising and coming up with the goods. Think up a name for your company that implies speed and efficiency and use your couriers as mobile bill boards. Use the *Yellow Pages* and leaflet drops. Read *Motorcycle News*; check what the competition is up to in *London Biker* and *Despatch Rider* magazine.

Dd

Dance Teacher

Qualifications/Training	Essential
Income bracket	Low
Licence	No
Town/Country	Town
Experience/ Springboard	Recommended
Travel	Local
Mid-career entry	Possible
Exit sale	No
Entry costs	£200
Work at home	No
Mix and match	Yes.

You could think about: *Dancer, Swimming teacher, Caterer, Typist, Market research interviewer*

Enquiries
Council for Dance Education and Training

If you're thinking of becoming a dance teacher it's probably because you're in love with dancing or because you're a professional dancer who isn't trained to do anything else. Whatever your standard as a dancer you'll certainly need some formal training to teach, as well as a thorough grounding in music notation, anatomy, etc. Whether you plan to teach spring points to tiny tots or kicksteps to troopers, to make any real headway you'll need a decent qualification. Otherwise some options could be closed to you altogether – teaching ballet to schools, for example; and if you're setting out on your own, you won't find the right openings or attract the pupils – the competition is too great.

The full works probably means a three-year, full-time course (contact the COUNCIL FOR DANCE EDUCATION AND TRAINING for accredited courses), though shorter-term alternatives are available such as a one-year teaching certificate for professional dancers. Good courses are not by any means restricted to classical ballet but also include modern theatre dance, jazz, contemporary and other disciplines.

Many people's first move on qualifying is to join a school staff (in the UK or overseas) for a year or two to build up some form and teaching practice. If and when you're ready to go you own way, you can start by hunting around the dance centres looking for empty slots in their timetables – the better the centre, of course, the harder it will be to get in and to begin with you'll probably be offered all the worst hours.

Typically, you'll be offered a medium size room, to hold around 15 dancers, with some music facilities such as a piano and a tape player; the dance centre may offer to supply or refer you to a pianist, if you don't know one. You can use tapes but many teachers find while they're hunting for the appropriate track, the class will lose concentration completely. Some teachers think even a mediocre pianist is far better than none; others find records and tapes they know well are a better (and cheaper) solution – but you must be aware of current copyright laws regarding the use of recorded material.

The hours in this job are not too unnatural, though early evening and Saturdays tend to be busy. It can be quite tiring physically, but as a dancer you're trained for that. Brilliant dancers are not necessarily good teachers; the most important qualities are probably enthusiasm and temperament, especially working with children. You need dedication because the rewards are not great and can be a long time in coming. You could aspire eventually to work with a good school or be attached to a ballet or theatre company. If you're *very* successful you could make £15,000 pa but this is unusual.

Read *Dancing times*, *Dance and Dancers* and *Dance Theatre Journal*. There are also good mags produced by the recognised trading associations such as RAD, ISTD etc.

✷ European Community Notes

Qualifications: Some UK qualifications recognised throughout EC.
Languages: To succeed, local language necessary.
Earnings: UK income generally lower than elsewhere in the EC.
Setting up: France, Greece and Italy have posed problems in the past, not wanting to recognise UK qualifications initially.
Advice/Training: Advice, information and training available for those wishing to work in Europe.
Exchanges: Formal job exchanges exist, but more along the lines of student exchanges. Individual dance schools may have their own arrangements.
Financial help: exists for study, training or travel in the EC, specific to this job.

Dancer

Qualifications/Training	Necessary
Income bracket	Low
Licence	No
Town/Country	Town
Experience/Springboard	No
Travel	Lots
Mid-career entry	No
Exit sale	No
Entry costs	£200
Work at home	Limited
Mix and match	Yes.

You could think about: *Dance teacher, Film extra, Bartender, Typist, Book editor, Office cleaner*

Enquiries
Council for Dance Education and Training, Equity, Dance UK

Most dancers are self-employed and work under contract for companies – some accept only very short-term contracts and move around a lot. Dancers tend to specialise in one field of dance (ballet, contemporary, modern, jazz etc) and different disciplines are required for each of these. Competition for jobs is stiff; most dance in the corps or chorus with few opportunities to be a principal or soloist. Not many make it to the top and the drop-out rate is high. Most dancers stop performing in their late 30s or early 40s and move into choreography, teaching, administration or into something completely different. Many dancers are prone to accident and injury partly due to limited awareness of practice and training techniques especially when compared to athletes.

You'll need to train, preferably on an accredited course in your chosen field of dance – see *Dance Theatre Journal* and THE COUNCIL FOR DANCE EDUCATION AND TRAINING for a list of accredited courses. Ballet dancers normally start at six or seven (although boys can start later – at 12 or 14). Jazz, contemporary and modern dancers usually start by the time they are 18, although some decide to train as performers later eg after taking a degree course in dance. Training is expensive and you will have to take classes even when you are unemployed just to keep in shape for auditions.

You'll need to provide your own practice clothes and shoes, which wear out quickly and are sometimes difficult to find; some companies subsidise these while you're working. Earnings are paltry: a corps member in a major company gets about £130 a week, £100 in smaller companies. Soloists get more, £160–£180 per week – up to about £100,000 per annum plus the perks that come with megastardom. You'll need an accountant and also an agent.

A lot of work comes via agents who are told of auditions when they come up. Other auditions are listed in the *Stage* or on dance studio notice boards. Contracts may be for a year, a season or for the run of a production. They are somewhat one-sided, you'll have great difficulty getting out of your commitment but companies tend to pay only their top performers for broken contracts; so, if a show flops, you could be out of work very quickly. If you trained with a good school or one which is attached to a dance company, it's easier to find work, also if you can sing or have other talents that may be useful on stage.

Dancing is an international area and you may be able to work abroad for a foreign company. In some countries, though, you'll have to be pretty exceptional to justify getting a work permit. Otherwise you can tour with a British company – not as glamorous as it may sound; this usually involves a lot of bus travel, living in cramped, grotty hotels and dancing in run-down theatres. You may get time to explore if you're lucky.

It is an arduous way of life requiring complete dedication and constant training and practice. Be prepared for periods of unemployment and to have to travel to find work sometimes. Injuries may prevent you from dancing but there are stories of dancers failing to recover properly from injuries and going on with broken toes and painkillers. Rheumatism and arthritis are rife among ex-dancers. Hours are long, with classes, rehearsals and performances; there is little free time and little social life outside the company. Being under contract to a company means fitting in with their requirements and whims, and it may take a long time to get the sort of role you find interesting. For some the commitment required is limiting and the sense of being a piece of company property dispiriting; in general this is harder for people who come late to dancing. There is some encouragement in the thrill dancers get from performing to an appreciative audience and from the close friendships that build up in the company.

Contact DANCE UK and the COUNCIL FOR DANCE AND EDUCATION AND TRAINING for advice and information on courses and resources for dancers.

European Community Notes
Fundamentally an itinerant profession. Few language barriers. Equity will check your contract for you before you sign and arrange local union representation if necessary.

Dental Practice Broker

Qualifications/Training	Recommended
Income bracket	Medium
Licence	No
Town/Country	Town, preferably
Experience/Springboard	Useful
Travel	Yes
Mid-career entry	Yes
Exit sale	Possible
Entry costs	£5,000
Work at home	Possible
Mix and match	Yes.

You could think about: *Surveyor, Estate agent, Conveyancer, Antique dealer, Beekeeper*

Enquiries
Dental practice brokers

Dental practice brokers organise the sale or leasing of dental practices, premises (including attached living areas) and equipment. They also help and advise dentists who are looking for partners or partnerships to join. The work is a mixture of selling and offering specialist advice. There are opportunities for firms to deal exclusively with dental practices but most are attached to estate agents, chartered surveyors or insurance brokers.

There are no formal qualifications for dental practice brokers but to make anything of it you'll need to qualify as a surveyor through the ROYAL INSTITUTION OF CHARTERED SURVEYORS. Estate agency experience is useful – you'll have to know how to advertise and sell property. Developing the more specialist ability required to evaluate dental practices comes with time, helped by keeping an eye on dental exhibitions and catalogues. You'll need the selling ability for the property market – perseverance and persistence coupled with a convincing appearance, knowledge of values and potential problems with areas and types of building.

Actual set-up costs needn't be great. You can operate from home. You'll need a telephone, business cards, office stationery and a car (your area of operation may be quite extensive and clients may want you to find a practice for them in a distant part of the country). You'll spend a lot of time on the phone. You're likely to have cash-flow problems as you're paid on commission once you've sold a practice and completion make take six months; you're not paid at all if you fail. That means you'll have to shoulder the costs for advertising the practice, circulating particulars, showing potential buyers around etc. Valuations and other services are charged for separately. There's a lot of work involved and returns aren't massive. Set up with enough money to keep yourself for a year.

A lot of business comes via word of mouth. Dentists are useful contacts, not only as clients but to keep you in touch with the needs of dentists and the running of dental practices. A lot of your clients will know all about mouths but not have much idea of what's involved in running a business. Keep in touch with your network by circulating them with particulars of properties you have on your books. The wider the geographical area you cover the more business you should be able to drum up but broking practices abroad can lead to problems with currency regulations. Add to this network by advertising in the *British Dental Journal*.

You have to value the property and also the equipment and the practice. The practice is valued according to its goodwill, based on patients' records, NHS schedules and accounts. It gives only an approximation because it's affected by the reputation and popularity of the dentist. Dental practice brokers, with relevant RICS qualifications can be called on to arbitrate in disputes between dentists, to review rents and leases of practices and, rarely, as expert witnesses in court. It is vital that you operate professionally and build up a reputation for honesty and fairness.

Dental Technician

Qualifications/Training	Recommended
Income bracket	Medium
Licence	Not yet
Town/Country	Town
Experience/Springboard	Essential
Travel	Local
Mid-career entry	Unlikely
Exit sale	Yes
Entry costs	£65,000
Work at home	Unlikely
Mix and match	Limited.

You could think about: *Silversmith/ jeweller, Illustrator, Makeup-artist*

Enquiries
National Joint Council for the Craft of Dental Technicians

Dental technicians are contracted by dentists to make false teeth, bridges, plates, braces and other dental appliances for their patients. Technicians also repair broken appliances. Most of their work is done in small laboratories usually run by themselves or in partnership with one or two other technicians.

There is no official register although the NATIONAL JOINT COUNCIL FOR THE CRAFT OF DENTAL TECHNICIANS is working on one in conjunction with the Dental Technicians Education and Training Advisory Board. Most technicians take a BTEC diploma following a four-year course and then a year's experience working in a dental laboratory. Alternatively, the traditional way in is through serving a five-year apprenticeship. In either case, some experience of working for a lab is essential before you set up on your own.

This is a delicate craft, no two commissions will be alike and all have to be made by hand. You'll have to be painstaking and accurate with a good eye for colour (mistakes are bad for business). You'll also need technical knowledge of how to operate specialist equipment and how to work with a wide range of material: gold, porcelain, plastics etc.

Set up costs are massive. As well as premises, telephone etc., you need up to £50,000 worth of equipment, furnaces (about £3,000), ultrasonic cleaner, polishing lathes, casting machine etc. Materials can be bought as required from dental suppliers. The dentist is your client and will pay you for each job you do. You set the fees for private work; the NHS sets it for anything you do for them and although you can undercut their rates you can't charge any more.

Build up your clientele through contact with dentists – try an initial mailing to start. Your business will build up by word of mouth and you can advertise in the *British Dental Journal* and others if you want to expand. About 10–12 dentists should produce enough work to support a two-technician partnership. You get a completion date with each job giving you about 10 working days. Most of the time you can work to a fairly regular schedule, some times are busier than others (for some reason the lead-up to Christmas is one), and you may have to deal with some emergency repairs when teeth are required by the following day. Small labs serve predominantly private patients who, having opted to pay for treatment, expect particularly reliable and prompt service.

Dentist

Qualifications/Training	Essential
Income bracket	Medium–High
Licence	Yes
Town/Country	Town
Experience/Springboard	No
Travel	None
Mid-career entry	Highly unlikely
Exit sale	Yes
Entry costs	Highly variable
Work at home	Possible
Mix and match	Yes.

You could think about: *Inventor, Jazz musician/singer, Landlord, Antique dealer, Network marketing*

Enquiries
General Dental Council

The dental profession has become much more oriented towards prevention rather than cures or artistic reconstructions.

To practise as a dentist, you must by law be registered with the GENERAL DENTAL COUNCIL. This means taking a five-year degree course at a dental school. You will need respectable A-levels to get in, as well as having the necessary aptitude for the job, which includes manual dexterity, precision, good general health, reasonable eyesight and an understanding of the human race – which will certainly be increased by pursuing this profession! One-year post-qualification vocational trainee schemes in general practice have been introduced into both general dental practice and the community dental services.

Most dentists work in general practice and there is the choice of joining an existing practice or setting up on your own – although only the foolhardy would set up on their own the day after graduation. Most general practitioners are self-employed – even in the NHS. A few practices are wholly private; many are within the National Health Service, or a mixture of the two. However, the profession was shaken-up somewhat by the new dental contract introduced in 1990, which, among other things, considerably increased the administration work. The new system has led to a number of practices, mainly in the South-east, either going totally private or treating certain groups under the NHS. Many dentists who go independent are continuing to treat the old, and people on low income who are entitled to free treatment, but only if they are already on their list. Also, a number of practices, while withdrawing from the NHS, charge fees which are comparable with NHS scales. Private practitioners fix the fees which they charge the patient; the NHS sets out a scale of fees, part of which are recoverable by the dentist from the patient and part from the NHS. This is time-consuming and there are rules and regulations covering the materials and the treatment available under the NHS. Some forms of treatment require prior approval. The recommended target NHS income for general practitioners is over £33,000. Those in private practice may be able to earn substantially more depending on the local population's wealth – and interest in their teeth.

Unlike doctors, dentists can open up shop anywhere. It's up to you to make sure you'll have some customers. To start up a practice involves finding and equipping a surgery. The cost of premises will depend on local prices (you will need planning permission unless you take over an existing practice). Equipment will cost anywhere between £15,000–£40,000. Second-hand equipment is possible.

To join an existing practice, read the *British Dental Journal* (the journal of the BRITISH DENTAL ASSOCIATION), or go through dental practice brokers. There are a variety of financial arrangements: associates pay a percentage of their income to the practice owner; those in expense-sharing arrangements pay their share of the practice costs; or dentists may buy a share of the practice to become full partners.

Each practice will need access to a source of materials and a range of staff (dental surgery assistants, hygienists) and facilities such as laboratories and X-ray equipment but these may be shared by even the most respectable West End practices. You should assume the annual overheads for a one-man practice are between £30,000–£50,000. NHS practices are subject to inspection of the premises and scrutiny of proposed treatment plans. You are also allowed to advertise.

Your hours are under your own control but practitioners are responsible for providing emergency cover for registered partners. You must enjoy people, although you will effectively gag most of your patients.

Also worth reading may be the *Dentist* and *Dental Practice*.

European Community Notes

Qualifications: UK primary qualifications are recognised throughout EC and EC primary qualifications in UK.

Languages: To succeed, local language necessary.

Earnings: Earnings vary according to country.

Setting up: You may find it difficult to succeed in Denmark, Greece, Italy, Netherlands, Portugal, Spain. You will find it easier in Belgium, Eire, France, Germany, Luxembourg.

Advice/Training: Advice, information and training available for those wishing to work in Europe.

Exchanges: Formal job exchanges do not exist.

Financial help: exists for study in the EC, specific to this job.

Enquiry point for those wishing to work in the EC: BRITISH DENTAL ASSOCIATION.

Recommended reading: 'Practising dentistry in the EC', BDA Advice Sheet E1.

Notes: Addresses of registration bodies and dental associations all available from BDA.

Desk top Publisher

Qualifications/Training	Recommended
Income bracket	Low–High
Licence	No
Town/Country	Either
Experience/Springboard	Essential
Travel	No
Mid-career entry	Yes
Exit sale	Yes
Entry costs	£10,000+
Work at home	Yes
Mix and match	Excellent.

You could think about: *Magazine publisher, Newsletter publisher, List broker, Book designer, Typesetter, Book packager*

Enquiries
Periodical Publishers' Association

Desk-top publishers use computers to produce printed material which can be anything from a menu for a local restaurant, to a fully colour-illustrated coffee-table book. As well as books, magazines and directories, desk-top publishing is often used to produce in-house magazines, advertising and promotional material and specialist publications for small markets. Normally, desk-top publishers hand material over to publisher/packager clients to distribute, market and sell. This could mean supplying clients with computer disks from which they arrange for printing and binding or it could mean supplying copies of the publication ready-printed and bound for sale. It's a new development and has revolutionised publishing by making it possible to package, and in some cases publish, on your own or as part of a very small team. Although some publishing houses are still wary of desk-top publishing, it is developing so quickly that even they will soon have to accept it as an efficient alternative to traditional methods.

Desk-top publishing is a complex skill to learn. There are a plethora of courses on offer from both computer companies and art colleges. These are not legally required but you'll almost certainly have to enrol on one and are well advised to do this at an art college whose approach tends to be less technical than that of computer companies. Although there are several different desk-top publishing packages around, once you've mastered one, converting to any of the others is relatively straightforward. Even more important is to have some relevant publishing experience to learn the editing, design and setting skills which are essential. You can get this through working for a publishing company; even more relevantly working in the publications department of one of the big financial or professional organisations which produce their own information leaflets, books and directories in-house. The wider the range of publishing experience the better because, as well as know-how, it will give you contacts who will commission work from you or to whom you can subcontract jobs such as printing and binding. Desk-top publishing demands a rare combination of computer and technical expertise with creative skills such as design, page-layout, editing and writing. You'll need to pay attention to detail, be a good self-promoter and capable of planning and sticking to your own budgets and schedules.

Set-up costs include about £4,000–£5,000 for the necessary computer and good quality printer. This will allow you to produce artwork of 90 per cent definition, good enough for many jobs although some will need to be re-done from your disks, eg for magazines. You'll also need a phone and a fax but you don't necessarily need a separate office and can work from home. For most jobs you'll be commissioned to produce a contracted number of copies by a certain time and will be paid per copy on delivery. This means finding the money to finance each project you do.

The amount needed varies tremendously, from less than £100 to tens of thousands of pounds. This depends on whether you're supplying disks (when all you'll have to pay for are the costs of the software and any editorial expenses); supplying bound copies (which means you also have to finance the printing and binding); or publishing the product yourself. Printing and binding can cost thousands of pounds if the print run is large or the printing procedures complicated; but you're guaranteed to get it all back when you are working to a client's commission. There's no such guarantee if you publish your own product yourself when you'll also be responsible for its distribution and sales. This involves an element of risk that can easily amount to tends of thousand of pounds, depending on the job. There's potential to make a very good living from a few lucrative commissions or to make a fortune from a few well-taken publishing risks. But remember, whether you plan to supply disks, bound copies or publish your product yourself, your business running costs will inevitably include equipment maintenance and upgrading.

To begin with, at least, you'll have to generate your own work. This could mean going around local businesses offering to produce advertising material, menus or price lists; approaching larger companies and institutions (whether they have their own in-house publishing department or not) and offering to produce in-house magazines or relevant books and leaflets for their area of interest. Packagers and book and magazine publishers may also be interested in your service but for these you'll almost certainly need to have contacts or some very good sellable ideas which they are willing to risk buying from you. For magazines and high-quality books you'll need to have sophisticated hardware and printer. If you're publishing on your own you'll have to make sure that you can sell the product at the end. For some things, like directories, it may be possible to take orders in advance before you even start work on the project; for others, people will want to see what they're paying for which means a financial risk for you and an organised marketing and distribution system through book shops.

It's a flexible job and is compatible with other commitments such as a young family because you're free to do your own scheduling and work your own hours although some jobs may be needed more quickly than others – advertisements for example.

A fax is especially useful because it speeds up production time by allowing you to discuss design, layout and content with clients over the phone. The future of desktop publishing looks good as technological developments (such as improved printers) make it able to produce a wider range of material and as it is increasingly accepted throughout the publishing industry.

Useful reading from magazines such as *Desk Top Publishing Today* and further information from the PERIODICAL PUBLISHERS ASSOCIATION.

European Community Notes

Qualifications: UK qualifications do not yet exist athough towards the end of 1992 the new Institute of Publishing should have produced NVQs. EC qualifications in UK would be welcomed by the UK industry but nobody would know what to do about it. In Germany, France and the Netherlands there is formal training, with bits of paper on graduation and then as a formal requirement.

Languages: To succeed, local language absolutely necessary.

Earnings: UK income generally lower than elsewhere in the EC.

Setting up: You will find it possible to succeed throughout Europe.

Advice/Training: Advice, information and training not available for those wishing to work in Europe.

Exchanges: Formal job exchanges do not exist, but *ad hoc* arrangements between companies which have a real commercial interest in their partners are known to exist.

Financial help: exists for study, training or travel in Germany (Bertelsmann Foundation).

Enquiry point for those wishing to work in the EC: BOOK HOUSE TRAINING CENTRE.

Recommended reading: The equivalent to the *Bookseller* in each country.

Note: Local languages are a pre-requisite. Do not try without thorough preliminary research in the UK and a period of work experience in a local publishing house where you can access the gaps in the market. The golden rule is to visit the member state's embassy in London and find out what you can from them and in particular whether there is a UK cultural institute from that country in London. France, Italy and Germany do have them. You'll need to do the most thorough and painstaking cultural research, including an examination of the books published/distributed locally.

Dietary Therapist

Qualifications/Training	Essential
Income bracket	Low–Medium
Licence	Yes
Town/Country	Town
Experience/Springboard	No
Travel	Local
Mid-career entry	Good
Exit sale	No
Entry costs	£1,000
Work at home	Yes
Mix and match	Yes.

You could think about: *Yoga teacher, Journalist, Potter, Caterer*

Enquiries
Dietary Therapy Society

Dietary therapists prescribe diets and dietary supplements to treat and prevent illness. They may also use naturopathic techniques such as enemas and water treatments and are complementary to many other areas of alternative medicine. Dietary therapy is an holistic therapy (it aims to treat the whole person rather than merely suppressing the symptoms of disease), and may be successful in patients where years of conventional medicine has failed. It can be used to treat all sorts of health problems: mental or physical; chronic or degenerative. With the increasing number of cases of illness that conventional medicine can't yet treat (for example ME), more and more people are investigating alternative medicines.

Dietary therapists need to be registered from 1992 as part of the opening up of Europe to professionals; you're strongly advised to join the DIETARY THERAPY SOCIETY. For this you need a diploma (which can be taken by correspondence with the addition of some clinical experience). You can start straight after A-levels so long as you have some science background but very young therapists may have problems establishing credibility without the sort of worldliness people expect of someone who's telling them how to lead their lives. For this reason, lots of people take up dietary therapy after they've worked at other things. Dietary therapists must like and be interested in other people. They have to be good listeners and able to read between the lines of what people are saying. Many therapists have been through some health or emotional trauma themselves and so are able to understand and empathise with patients. You'll find it easier not to become too emotionally involved with your patients as time goes on. The success of dietary therapy depends on patients persevering and taking responsibility for their own health, and so you'll have to be very enthusiastic and committed about it even if it means never eating another hamburger.

You can practise from home but this may be too isolated – you want as high a profile as possible to keep up a good supply of patients. Renting a room at an alternative or natural health centre is probably the best way of doing this though it can be expensive. You'll need a telephone and answering machine, some sort of filing system and a couple of chairs. Much diagnosis can be done by iridology (the examination of the iris) and if you use this method, you'll need some eye examining equipment. It's a good idea to get some cards and leaflets printed to explain some of the basics of dietary therapy to your patients. You can get insurance (essential in case one of your patients has a very bad reaction to your prescriptions) via the DIETARY THERAPY SOCIETY.

Your first meeting with a new patient will probably last about 1½ hours because you need to get a complete history (medical, family and personal) before you're able to prescribe a diet. After that patients come back every six to eight weeks for about 45 minutes consultation. When you're working out a scale of charges, allow for some free time between consultations – this is demanding work and you've got to give patients your full attention. You can charge up to £25 for the first and £15 for subsequent consultations. You may be able to earn some money from running or working on short residential courses; cookery demonstrations; lecturing or consultancy for restaurants wanting to offer healthier options on their menus. Many patients come through referral from other patients and alternative practitioners (rarely from GPs), which is why being in a centre with others is useful. A natural health centre can advertise itself which the Dietary Therapy Society code forbids you from doing. Your patients will be of all ages and conditions. Some will continue to consult you for ages, others will drop out quickly when they find it impossible to keep to the diet that you prescribe – many people have difficulty accepting responsibility for their own health and expect you to make them better on your own. It can be immensely satisfying to see a chronically ill patient recover and improvements are often noticeable very quickly. During the early stages of the cleansing process that dietary therapy causes, it is possible for patients to have violent reactions while their bodies adjust so you should be on call for any emergencies. Evenings after office hours are busy times of day and spring can be a slightly busier time of year (everyone goes on self-improvement binges). Holidays need forward planning; make sure your patients know in advance. You may want to find a locum who can give a few consultations although this isn't ideal. It's useful to know about other therapies which may help your patients; the *Journal of Alternative and Complementary Medicine* and *Here's Health* are useful sources for this and also for keeping you in touch with developments in your own field.

Direct Marketing Consultant

Qualifications/Training	Useful
Income bracket	Medium–High
Licence	No
Town/Country	Town
Experience/Springboard	Essential
Travel	Yes
Mid-career entry	Yes
Exit sale	Possible
Entry costs	£1,000+
Work at home	Possible
Mix and match	Yes.

You could think about: *List broker, Sales agent, Marketing consultant, Exhibition designer, Photojournalist, Employment agent*

Enquiries
Direct Marketing Association, Direct Marketing Centre

Direct marketing involves selling products and services directly to the final customer, rather than selling through wholesalers and retailers. Direct marketing agencies act as specialists for suppliers of a wide range of industrial and consumer goods and services. This is done through advertisements in the press, radio, television and specialist press and by direct mail shots or telephone sales. Direct marketing agencies often do the work of a marketing department for client companies which are too small to have their own: planning, designing and writing projects, advising on whom to contact and how, chasing up material etc. For larger companies they act as consultants, on specific products or problems. Success depends on having good ideas and the confidence to put them forward. This is an expanding industry, having doubled in size during the last five years (approximately £500 million spent on it per annum). Direct sales now make up 10 per cent of Britain's retail spending and there are many opportunites for small companies or partnerships particular if they specialise.

There are no formal qualifications necessary but a marketing diploma is useful. The Post Office runs short introductory courses on direct marketing, as do the DIRECT MARKETING ASSOCIATION and the DIRECT MARKETING CENTRE and various companies like Ferrari. Marketing experience is essential. At least a year spent in a fairly small marketing department gives an overview of the business (better than working for a large agency where jobs are specialised and you won't get experience of certain areas). Set-up costs aren't great. You need a telephone, a fax machine, an answering machine, and a word processor. You don't need an office if you're prepared to visit clients or take them out. Have enough money to live on for at least six months – even if you start with a lot of work, there may be cash-flow problems. Large companies are often slow to pay up and you may have to pay your suppliers before you've been paid yourself.

What you charge is based on the time and costs you expect to spend on the agreed project. Clients will use you for a specific job (rather than running accounts, as with an advertising agency) so you need to establish a reputation to ensure a sufficient supply of work. If you do good work, you will find yourself recommended to new clients by existing ones.

Contacts are all-important. Sources of work are everywhere, so carry business cards with you all the time ('You're never off duty in this business'). Useful contacts are designers, printers, mailing houses, list-brokers, telephone sales bureaux and anyone else you can sub-contract to. Using freelances rather than full-time staff gives greater flexibility and a choice of different styles as well as cutting down on overheads. Build up a portfolio for use in the early days to encourage new clients. Once you are better known, touting for custom must be more subtle. Get onto as many mailing lists as possible (AA, Reader's Digest) to keep you in touch with developments ('Change in style of one of the big mailing companies indicates something!').

It's helpful to be able to bounce ideas off at least one partner. Your area of specialisation will extend when clients return to you with work in different fields. Life revolves around your diary. Some projects are planned months in advance; others must be completed in days. An average day is a mixture of working to your schedule and fitting in any ad hoc developments. You'll spend a lot of time liaising with clients.

Direct marketers need to understand both their clients and their clients' customers; so they can come up with ideas that the clients will like and which have the desired effect on customers. Good communication skills are essential; you need to establish trust. You have to be able to work to deadlines and prepared to work overnight and weekends if necessary. Realism is essential, as is the ability to mix creativity with a business-like approach.

Useful further reading, *Precision Marketing*, *Marketing Week* and *Marketing*; a basic source of reference, published in association with the Royal Mail, is the *Direct Mail Handbook*.

European Community Notes

Languages: To succeed, local language necessary.

Advice/Training: Advice, information and training not available for those wishing to work in Europe.

Exchanges: Formal job exchanges do not exist.

Notes: Local knowledge – from legislation to markets – and first-class local contacts are essential.

Disco Owner/DJ

Qualifications/Training	No
Income bracket	Medium–High
Licence	No
Town/Country	Town
Experience/Springboard	No

Travel	Lots
Mid-career entry	Highly unlikely
Exit sale	Possible
Entry costs	£5,000
Work at home	No
Mix and match	Yes.

You could think about: ***Piano tuner, Hi-fi shop owner, Light music composer, Venue manager, Man with a van, Mini-cab driver, Accountant***

Enquiries
Dealers, eg Young Disco Centre, DJs, Club owners

These provide, set up and organise discos. They are responsible for amplification and lighting as well as acting as disc jockey and playing the records.

A business studies course or degree will give you an enormous advantage in this highly competitive field. Good organisational and sales skills will enable you to sell your product down the phone and deal with the public, drunk or sober (if they're 'modern' all they're drinking is Evian and guarana milkshakes – but why are they smiling so much?). A clean driving licence is essential. Get advice on insurance, and from an accountant. Be able to present your records in a relaxed, chatty and confident manner. You will need to be diplomatic and able to prevent fights when your customers become tired and emotional.

A profound knowledge of music is not necessary, but you must keep vaguely in touch with radio as well as clubs, dances, etc. to learn what people like, eg 'golden oldies' as well as recent hits.

Peak working hours are Friday through Sunday, though people do groove every night – even lunchtimes too. You could earn about £100–£200 per night at a bijou spot like the Hippodrome, while MECCA clubs pay £70 or £80 per night. Arab countries might offer £400 tax-free but things are a little quiet of late . . .

Most DJs start at £20 a night in pubs or clubs, or work as a roadie for a disco owner. This is good experience before starting on your own. Jobs are advertised in *Disco International, Jocks* magazine, local shops, pubs and newspapers.

The cost of recording equipment, records, transport and lights is high. For your own disco you will need to invest at least £1,750 in hi-fi equipment, turntable, speakers etc (cheap electronics break down) and a large car or van. Records are obviously going to be a substantial and continuing expense; if you have to provide all your own, getting some sort of tie-in with a local record store in return for plugging it (if it's specialist you've a better chance) is invaluable. You will need a telephone, answering phone or service, and a typewriter/word processor. Get business cards printed and advertise your services in the local press and shops. If you have a large room or garage you can keep a mobile disco at home – if you can stand the smell of smoke which emanates from it.

Long drives on motorways, loading and unloading before and after a gig are exhausting, so you need physical strength and stamina. Most gigs last at least four hours; if you leave home in the late afternoon or early evening, you cannot expect to get home until the early hours of the morning. You will then have to get up at a reasonable hour to answer the telephone, take messages, and prepare for the next job. You may feel like death but must always be charming and enthusiastic towards your customer, the party giver.

The work is irregular and the long hours can limit one's social life and disrupt sleep patterns. Expect to earn a maximum of £300 per night before tax, ie £600 to £900 per week, so you will never become rich though you may get addicted to the excitement of it. You can also run a separate business, eg selling or hiring equipment to other DJs. It is worth taking advice from dealers, eg Young Disco Centre.

The House, Acid House and Rave waves of recent years, not to mention all that scratching and rapping and speciality spinning, have taken the focus off performers and put the DJ right in the spotlight. You could be a star!

Doctor
(GP in the NHS)

Qualifications/Training	Essential
Income bracket	High
Licence	Yes
Town/Country	Town/Village
Experience/ Springboard	Recommended
Travel	Local
Mid-career entry	Limited
Exit sale	Possible
Entry costs	Highly variable
Work at home	Possible
Mix and match	Yes.

You could think about: *Homeopath, Doctor (private GP), Bookseller, Restaurateur*

Enquiries
Royal College of General Practitioners, British Medical Association

There are some 30,000 general practitioners in the National Health Service (NHS) who work either in partnerships or in single-handed practices. There are conditions of service to which they must comply, and they can only set up where it is deemed there is a need. But they are not employed by the NHS and have considerable independence in running their own clinical practices, which are businesses in their own right with balance sheets and profit and loss accounts.

It is less the case now that doctors breed doctors – instead it is highly competitive. The long training and the difficulty of earning money during the course, because the vacations are shorter, mean that medicine generally draws heavily from the middle, professional classes.

First you must qualify – usually five years after being accepted for medical school. London medical schools still have much of the prestige but you may not see a live patient for some time – less common in the provinces. Then you must do at least one year in a hospital job (house job) to get on the Medical Register. The training for general practice takes three years. It involves you being attached to a practice and doing 24 months' relevant hospital jobs eg paediatrics or geriatrics; if you're lucky, it will include topics such as management and budgeting to help you run your practice. You will need to pick up communications skills although they are still not normally taught explicitly. Take the course in the area where you will want to work so you get known. You can apply for membership of the ROYAL COLLEGE OF GENERAL PRACTITIONERS (means another exam), though this is not necessary to practise. You can then look for a job as an assistant or junior partner in a practice or do any locums that come up in the area you want to settle in. Vacancies are normally advertised in the *British Medical Journal*. You will however need to obtain a Certificate of Prescribed/Equivalent Experience from the Joint Committee on Postgraduate Training for General Practice in order to work as a principal in the NHS.

Single-handed vacancies must be advertised and you are chosen by the local Family Health Services Authority (FHSA), subject to approval by the Medical Practices Committee. You may find yourself in competition from local partnerships, seeking to incorporate the practice and its list. There is no obligation on partnerships to advertise vacancies; the partners choose (and it may be their son/ daughter or the current assistant) so long as it meets with the approval of the FHSA. You may have to buy your way into a partnership, ie contribute to the capital value of property and equipment ('hidden sale of goodwill' is illegal). NHS may make loans at favourable rates for the capital needed but as they are agreed nationally, they may not be much use in areas of very high property prices. Some health centres are owned by the health authority.

Unlike the private doctor, you are under an obligation to provide cover 24 hours a day, 365 days a year. Partners usually cover for each other so there is no cost. Single-handed doctors use a locum/answering service when they aren't available. Locums (mostly doctors between jobs or waiting to find a first job) are found through commercial agencies or a bureau such as that run by the BRITISH MEDICAL ASSOCIATION (BMA). There are also deputising services, which provide locums and deputies to see patients when the doctor can't; these are run by groups of doctors or commercially, on the basis of a monthly retainer plus a fee per visit. The FHSA must approve the arrangements you make and the amount you use them. Most doctors have something over 2,000 patients; the maximum is 3,500. How you define your area is up to you, within guidelines laid down by your FHSA. You can also decide your style of operation.

The funding arrangements are changing with the introduction of the internal market; a practice can now hold its own budget and negotiate its own contracts with hospitals. The target income of a GP after expenses is more than £37,000; the turnover of a practice of four partners might be some £200,000. It is worth finding both an accountant and solicitor who specialise in general practice. Medical schools teach you little or nothing about the business side of the practice at present.

In rural communities, the local family doctor has a distinct role in the local community – more anonymous in a city practice. The setting-up of the ROYAL COLLEGE OF GENERAL PRACTITIONERs has helped to make general practice more respectable; most medical schools have opened academic departments of general practice and it is now the favoured option for medical students. It is rewarding, stimulating work and highly unpredictable. You must be able to get on with all sort of people and be able to live with your inevitable mistakes. The difficulties include differentiating the ill from the not so ill; maintaining standards all the time; and knowing your own limitations. Many value the fact that there is no direct link between the amount of work you do for the patient and the amount the patient pays into the system. Others combine work in the NHS with some private work. You can also combine general practice with work in hospital clinics, work for industry (eg, stress clinics) or life insurance examinations. Some GPs run book shops or restaurants. No matter, so long as you maintain your obligations to your patients.

☆☆ European Community Notes (not NHS)

Qualifications: UK qualifications recognised throughout EC and EC qualifications in UK
Languages: To succeed, local language necessary.
Advice/Training: Advice, information and training available for those wishing to work in Europe.
Exchanges: Formal job exchanges do not exist.
Enquiry point for those wishing to work in the EC: BRITISH MEDICAL ASSOCIATION
Recommended reading: European Communities: General Guidance for Doctors

Doctor (Private GP)

Qualifications/Training	Essential
Income bracket	High
Licence	Yes
Town/Country	Town
Experience/ Springboard	Recommended
Travel	Local
Mid-career entry	Highly unlikely
Exit sale	Yes
Entry costs	Highly variable
Work at home	Possible
Mix and match	Yes.

You could think about: *Doctor (GP in the NHS), Homeopath, MP, Novelist, Farmer*

Enquiries
Royal College of General Practitioners, British Medical Association

Private family doctors in general practice are paid directly by their patients. The basic medical training takes five or six years. It is advisable to follow the NHS vocational training scheme that lasts a further three years, including a year as a trainee in general practice and several junior appointments in hospitals giving a broad range of clinical experience.

In private practice, you must not mind being available 24 hours a day. You also need patience and the ability to compromise between what your patients want and what you think they need. There is more to medicine than just prescribing: you will need to understand your patients' viewpoints. They are paying for your time and expertise and as a private practitioner you take full responsibility.

Big cities are generally best for private practice and the prospects for private practice in London are reasonable; those in business and the professions prefer to pay for quick service, when and where it is convenient to them.

It is advisable to work as an assistant in a practice for five–ten years to gain experience and make useful contacts before going alone. It takes about five years to build up a practice, and can cost two years' income or more to buy into an existing one. If you haven't the ready cash, it is possible to be paid half salary for the first few years.

It is not necessary to join the BRITISH MEDICAL ASSOCIATION (BMA) nor the ROYAL COLLEGE OF GENERAL PRACTITIONERS but, as with all doctors, it is vital to arrange a protective insurance. Your income to start with may be £20,000 plus per annum and it's possible for this to rise to £50,000 or more. Your surgery should preferably not be in your home, but close by. The costs of the practice will include a medical secretary (about £13,000 per annum), rent of premises (this varies according to area), telephone and answering service (vital) with a bleeper so you can be contacted at all times. A car phone ensures you can make calls when stuck in traffic while making domiciliary visits. You may wish to take on the cost of providing and running such diagnostic equipment (and the staff to run it) as you feel makes professional life more interesting. Arrange a joint rota with three other doctors for emergency duty, say one night a week and one weekend in four.

The job's advantage is the freedom to practise good medicine, with the best referral system and technical equipment readily available. Private medicine is generally satisfying to patients, making them feel more important than the system. There's little red tape but it is hard work.

Read the *British Medical Journal*, the *Handbook* of the Royal College of General Practitioners, and use the libraries of the ROYAL SOCIETY OF MEDICINE or the ROYAL COLLEGE OF GENERAL PRACTITIONERS.

✪ European Community Notes

Qualifications: UK qualifications recognised throughout EC and EC qualifications in UK.

Languages: To succeed, local language necessary.

Advice/Training: Advice, information and training available for those wishing to work in Europe.

Exchanges: Formal job exchanges do not exist.

Enquiry point for those wishing to work in the EC: BRITISH MEDICAL ASSOCIATION

Recommended reading: European Communities: General Guidance for Doctors (BMA).

Dress Agent

Qualifications/Training	No
Income bracket	Medium
Licence	No
Town/Country	Town
Experience/Springboard	Useful
Travel	None
Mid-career entry	Ideal
Exit sale	Yes
Entry costs	£2,000
Work at home	No
Mix and match	Yes.

You could think about: ***Antique dealer (small antiques), Sub postmaster, Potter, Hairdresser, Fashion designer***

Enquiries
Local dress agents

Dress agents have shops from which they sell their clients' old clothes for a proportion of the proceeds. Although there is a market for most second-hand clothes their selling price means that it is usually only worthwhile dealing in good quality clothes in good condition. Most dress agents specialise to a degree (men or women or children's); some choose to specialise further, with, say, wedding outfits or evening dress. It helps if you have a strong sense of style yourself.

There are no formal qualifications but you'll have to have some idea of how to sell things, how to deal with awkward customers, how to display the stock etc. You also have to be numerate and methodical to cope with all of the paper work involved. Stock has to be labelled with the supplier's name so that you know who to pay when you've sold it. Records have to include names and addresses, date when stock was brought in and when it goes out; you'll get through a lot of cheques and will probably want to establish a system for returning/disposing of unsold clothes after a few weeks. Even more important is knowing how to price second-hand clothes so they'll sell – you'll need several years of second-hand clothes buying and browsing behind you.

You need suitable shop premises with good storage space because any 'new' stock has to be checked before going on sale. Nearby parking is useful; you don't necessarily want to be on a high street because customers are prepared to travel to get to you. You may attract passing trade by being close to complementary shops and businesses (eg nursery schools if you're selling children's clothes). On top of rent or mortgage, set up costs are about £2,000 to equip the shop and fund printing and initial advertising (in local shops and newspapers and by posting leaflets).

Most second-hand clothes are worth about a quarter of their original value but this varies according to the condition and demand; if you're too greedy, you won't sell. Clients sometimes grumble at how little you expect to get for their nearly new

designer clothes but aim for a fast turnover rather than a big mark-up, this attracts both buyers and sellers. Decide what proportion of the sale price you'll take and make sure this is clear to clients – usually 50:50. Some dress agents experiment with manufacturers' end of line mark-downs – this may work but equally the price range may be wrong compared to your usual stock.

It will take a few months before you can see how business is going; after that you may find that you want and can afford to hire help to look after the shop from time to time. It may take a long time before you feel like delegating pricing, which is largely a matter of judgement. Clients must trust you and it helps if you spend some time in the shop meeting them, certainly to begin with. You'll build up a regular clientele which grows by word of mouth. The busy times for most dress agents are at the beginning of new seasons (March–May and September–November) when clients and customers replace the contents of their wardrobes.

Driver (Hire Cars)

Qualifications/Training	No
Income bracket	Low
Licence	Yes
Town/Country	Both
Experience/Springboard	Yes
Travel	Yes
Mid-career entry	Yes
Exit sale	No
Entry costs	Nil
Work at home	No
Mix and match	Excellent.

You could think about: *Actor, Indexer, Musician, Illustrator, Swimming teacher, Mini-cab driver*

Enquiries: Car hire companies

People who rent cars leave them in all sorts of places – ranging from the double yellow lines in front of the Park Lane Hilton to the screws' car park at Wormwood Scrubs. Hire contracts don't necessarily oblige them to return their cars to their starting point anyway and even if they have undertaken to do so, they don't always make it. Conversely, most people who hire out cars – often but not always huge international companies – want them back. This creates a job for drivers – collecting cars from where the punter left them and returning them to where the hire company specifies.

It's a good job if you want the chance to burn out all the latest models and like driving. It also helps to like travelling – you are never in one place for more than a couple hours. Although the entire UK is your field of operation, you always operate from a depot in, say, the Midlands or Scotland or South-east.

You can alleviate the boredom of long motorway hauls by taking your linguaphone tapes on the trip. What's more difficult is to avoid being caught speeding or picking up points on your licence.

To find a job, phone hire firms direct and offer your services. To get the job in the first place, you'll probably have to demonstrate that you hold a clean licence and have been driving (legally) for two–three years. Normally you should be over 21 under the terms of the company's insurance policy – hire companies always arrange insurance themselves.

It's worth getting hold of one or two hire companies' in-house magazines – all the large companies have them.

Driving Instructor

Qualifications/Training	Essential
Income bracket	Medium
Licence	Yes
Town/Country	Town
Experience/ Springboard	Recommended
Travel	Local
Mid-career entry	Good
Exit sale	Possible
Entry costs	£12,000
Work at home	Yes
Mix and match	Yes.

You could think about: *Garage owner, Courier service, Mini-cab driver, Motorcycle messenger, Disco owner*

Enquiries
Driving Instructors' Association,
Approved Driving Instructors National Joint Council

Almost all driving instructors are self-employed. Probably 95 per cent of them work either directly for themselves, or on a 'franchise' from larger schools such as BSM. A franchise may be a total package of car, uniform, office facilities and advertising; or simply some form of group practice where the instructor pays a weekly fee to belong. The exceptions are heavy goods and public service vehicle instructors, who tend to work for small schools of 10–40 vehicles.

Every year some 20,000 people take the exams to become professional instructors of whom some 3,000 are successful; 2,000 leave the industry every year but this still adds 1,000 extra instructors each year. In the early 1980s there were 20,000 instructors coping with 1m new drivers every year; now there are 33,000 catering for a smaller intake.

Although the traditional way of learning to drive, taking practical lessons in the instructor's car, will continue to be predominant, more use is being made of video tapes and printed learning material. This results from the publication of the first Department of Transport 'recommended syllabus' for all learner drivers, intended to prepare British drivers for a harmonised European Driving Test in the 1990s.

The legal requirements to be an instructor are that you must have held a clean, full British car driving licence for four years; must pass three stringent examinations; and must expect your instruction to be check-tested at regular intervals in order to remain on the Government Register of

Approved Driving Instructors. While there is no requirement to take professional training, the examinations have been so designed that you are unlikely to pass without good professional preparation.

Training is best taken with a specialist training establishment, although some schools do train their own future instructors. Fees will vary between £1,000 to £2,000 for training; government fees for examination, registration and licences total £405. Beware of anyone who offers to train for less than £500 (usually for a week's training; this usually means a further three or four weeks' training to take each examination). The three examinations are: a multiple choice written examination; a practical driving test; a practical test of your ability to teach while in a car on the move.

Once you have passed the first two exams, you can apply to take a trainee licence to get practical experience of teaching for money, or money's worth. This licence lasts for only six months. You are normally only allowed three attempts at each of the practical tests; failure to pass after three attempts means you cannot reapply to become an instructor for two years.

Bad driving habits acquired over 10 or 20 years cannot be eradicated in a month or two's intensive training. So you should start with excellent driving abilities and be a natural at communicating with others.

Apart from driving and teaching skills, every good driving instructor needs to have a fairly dominant personality. You need the ability to listen and care, patience, tact, alertness and a good sense of humour. Perhaps most obviously, you should be one of those people who do not panic when everyone around you is. You need to be able to plan well ahead, both in your driving and in your lessons, and able to judge when pupils are finding it tough going.

Becoming established takes quite a long time, even though it is estimated that 92 per cent of Britain's million new drivers each year take some professional driver training (this still only works out at 30 pupils per instructor). You can expect to take a minimum of six months to qualify as an ADI (Approved Driving Instructor); but it will take a further 18 months or so before your 'name' and school become sufficiently well known to attract enough business to keep you solvent. Advertising helps, but not a great deal; the only successful advertising is word of mouth from satisfied clients. In that 18 months, two things happen. You will have taught sufficient pupils to gain a good reputation; and your car will be in urgent need of replacement. If you have earned enough in that time to cover the costs you can reasonably expect to make a success. If not, you may join the other 2,000 who fail each year.

Costs are fairly standard around the country except insurance rates, which are fixed according to area. But prices of driving lessons vary; in general you should expect to charge £15 per hour, which is too low but about all that can be achieved in present market conditions. This will cover £5 for vehicle costs and £5 per hour for administration etc, leaving £5 gross income – or less if you charge less than £15 per hour. It is worth noting that the driving test fee (for which no car is supplied) is currently £21.50 for 50 minutes.

Driving instructors must expect to work unsocial hours as those who can afford lessons are invariably in work. The bulk of those wanting lessons are the 17–24 age group, followed by a smaller group in their mid-20s who can now afford a car – or a second car for spouses, etc. As elsewhere, recession has made its mark on the driver trading industry. The number of people learning to drive has dropped from a peak of 1.2m in 1990 to an estimated 600,000 in 1992. In addition, because of some kink in the birth rate 17 years ago – at least, in part – more than 80 per cent of those learning to drive are now under 22: unfortunately for you, they take fewer lessons than older learners do!

Further information from the DRIVING INSTRUCTORS' ASSOCIATION who have a Hotline to answer any question. See also *Driving, Running Your Own Driving School* and the *Driving Instructor's Manual*.

European Community Notes

As far as can be established, entry into Europe for UK driving instructors is not currently something which can be achieved with consummate ease, though the introduction of the harmonised European driving test will help pave the way.

Enquiry point for those wishing to work in the EC: The Driving Standards Agency.

Ee

Editorial Photographer

Qualifications/Training	Recommended
Income bracket	Medium–High
Licence	No
Town/Country	Town
Experience/ Springboard	Recommended
Travel	Yes
Mid-career entry	Possible
Exit sale	Yes
Entry costs	£5,000+
Work at home	Possible
Mix and match	Yes.

You could think about: *Advertising photographer, Photojournalist, Photographer, Artist, Picture researcher, Tourist guide*

Enquiries
National Union of Journalists, British Institute of Professional Photography, Association of Fashion, Advertising and Editorial Photographers

For many photographers, editorial photography offers the best balance between commercial and artistic photography. Within the field, you can specialise in fashion, home interiors, still life, travel, cookery portraits or even narrower fields such as underwater or aerial photography. The copyright laws have changed in favour of the artist – the law now states that the copyright remains the property of the photographer. Each client is negotiating with the individual photographer. What that also means is you get paid every time one of your pictures is reproduced so that over the years, if you're good you are building up a goldmine of a library either as a source of income or to sell outright to a picture library or agency – figures as high as half-a-million pounds are not unkown for exceptional photographers.

The best training is at colleges, such as Newport or London College of Printing in editorial photography. Another route is through art school, completing a course recognised by the BRITISH INSTITUTE OF PROFESSIONAL PHOTOGRAPHY.

As with so many other freelance jobs, the main problem is getting yourself known to start with. You will need top class, reliable photographic equipment (cameras, lenses, lights) and most editorial photographers work from their own studios. However, to start with, and if you find you are doing a lot of work on location, you can hire studio space – perhaps from other photographers you know in studio complexes. You can also hire the equipment you need while you are starting out – though if you do hire everything you need (including a photographic assistant) you will soon find that your fees have all been swallowed up.

Fees vary according to the type of work you are doing, but top magazines and national newspapers would probably pay in the region of £400 per day in combined commission and reproduction fees, though many titles pay much less than this: the cost of film and processing is also met, but usually few other extras. The NATIONAL UNION OF JOURNALISTS can advise on minimum rates and contracts etc. ASSOCIATION OF FASHION, ADVERTISING AND EDITORIAL PHOTOGRAPHERS (AFAEP) provides help in finding studios, assistants, stylists, lighting and so on for its membership.

The work is varied and usually interesting: most photographers build up a working relationship with a dozen or so popular publications. A typical day's work for a top magazine will involve liaising with the client (fashion editor, home or cookery editor, art editor or picture editor) to discuss the shoot, arriving at the studio to get cameras and backgrounds set up. The stylist (or appropriate editor) usually arranges for props to be delivered and books any models that are needed. Together, you will work out a programme for the day, and then the shooting begins. Sometimes there is a tight brief, and you have little opportunity for creative work: your skill is needed to create the right lighting and atmosphere for the shot. On the other hand, you may be given a free hand in deciding what props to use and what angles to shoot at. At the end of the day you will have to straighten up the studio and arrange for the processing of the film, ready for delivery the next day. And if anything goes wrong you may have to re-shoot at your own expense.

You may also work on books: for example you may find yourself booked for a two-week period, working with a free-lance home economist and stylist to photograph a hundred or so dishes for a cookery book.

Top fashion photographers may find themselves in demand for foreign trips: colour magazines have to go into production well ahead of publication, so to shoot summer fashions in February you have to go abroad to find the sun. The client will arrange for travel, and a party of half a dozen or so (fashion editor, assistant, two models, yourself and your assistant) will spend a week shooting several spreads for publication later in the year.

As well as faultless technical skill and an ability to work under pressure, it helps if you are outgoing and adaptable. There is a lot of lugging around of equipment and props, and although this could be considered the assistant's job, it helps to speed up and keep relations good if everyone mucks in.

Many editorial photographers will take on a certain amount of advertising work as well: usually pay is better, but the brief is tighter.

European Community Notes

Qualifications: No qualifications are required to work in EC on freelance basis.

Languages: To succeed, local languages necessary.

Earnings: UK income generally same as elsewhere in the EC.

Setting up: You will find it difficult to succeed in Belgium, France, Germany and Luxembourg. You will find it easier in Denmark, Eire, Greece, Italy, Netherlands, Portugal and Spain. This depends on individual talents, but Belgium, France, Germany and Luxembourg have a large indigenous threshold to break through. Languages are essential and intense market research to establish needs, trends and fashions.

Advice/Training: Advice, information and training not available for those wishing to work in Europe.

Exchanges: Formal job exchanges do not exist.

Embalmer

Qualifications/Training	Essential
Income bracket	Low–Medium
Licence	No
Town/Country	Either
Experience/ Springboard	Recommended
Travel	Local

Mid-career entry	Yes
Exit sale	No
Entry costs	£500+
Work at home	No
Mix and match	Yes.

You could think about: *Funeral director, Kennel/cattery owner, Driving instructor, Taxidermist, English language teacher*

Enquiries
British Institute of Embalmers

Embalmers treat dead bodies to preserve them, disinfect them and present them in a viewable state for funerals. Most self-employed embalmers own undertaking companies; there are still some opportunities to work freelance by taking up contracts from funeral directors although the trend is for them to offer their own embalming service in-house. It is a predominantly male profession – only about 12 per cent are female.

Embalming is not legally required but is advisable in most cases, eg many airlines will not transport dead bodies without some sort of assurance that they are not infectious and funeral directors usually insist on a body being embalmed before being transported from one undertaker to another (see the *Law of Burial, Cremation and Exhumation*). Formally, you don't need any qualifications but membership of the BRITISH INSTITUTE OF EMBALMERS (BIE) is recommended. This involves a course (with an accredited teacher or school) and passing qualifying exams. It gives professional recognition and support, as well as the professional journal, *The Embalmer*.

To set up you will need at least £500+ worth of equipment. You'll also need access to a mortuary because, although some people, especially in rural areas, like you to work from their houses, most embalming is done at the undertaker's and the body returned to the mourners if requested. You are paid through the funeral director.

Embalming involves draining out all the body fluids and injecting sterilising agents into the circulatory system (this takes about an hour), followed by any cosmetic work necessary to repair the effects of violent or unpleasant death. (See the *Principles and Practice of Embalming*.) It is not a job with universal appeal and requires knowledge of anatomy and bacteriology. Although you'll have to take a fairly scientific approach in dealing with the dead, your clients, the bereaved, will require tactful and sympathetic handling if you come into contact with them.

Your job is easier if you work as soon after death as possible; you will only know a few days in advance about a job (funerals are usually arranged to take place within a week of death). There are slight seasonal variations, the death rate is slightly higher in winter (December–March) and after a flu epidemic. You usually work alone, occasionally with an assistant.

You'll encounter mixed reactions to your profession. Taken far more seriously in America and Canada, embalming tends to provoke mirth or distaste in the UK although the BIE reports that this is gradually changing.

European Community Notes
Qualifications: UK qualifications recognised in some EC countries.
Languages: To succeed, local language necessary.
Earnings: UK income generally lower than elsewhere in the EC.
Setting up: You will find it difficult to succeed in Denmark, Germany, Greece, Italy, Luxembourg, Netherlands, Portugal and Spain. You will find it easier in Belgium, Eire and France. Emblaming is not carried out in all EC countries.
Advice/Training: Advice, information and training not available for those wishing to work in Europe.
Exchanges: Formal job exchanges do not exist.
Enquiry point for those wishing to work in the EC: EUROPEAN COUNCIL OF THANATOPRACTIC ASSOCIATIONS.

Employment Agent

Qualifications/Training	Possible
Income bracket	Medium
Licence	Yes
Town/Country	Town
Experience/ Springboard	Recommended
Travel	No
Mid-career entry	Yes
Exit sale	Yes
Entry costs	£2,000+
Work at home	Possible
Mix and match	Yes.

You could think about: *Musician's answering service, Property manager, Careers adviser, List broker, Travel agent*

Enquiries
Federation of Recruitment and Employment Services, Institute of Employment Consultants

Employment agents match applicants to job vacancies. Their clients are people who are looking for employees and their product is the applicants who are looking for jobs. Employment agents can be asked to find staff for virtually any job; some specialise in, for instance, computer, accounting or medical personnel, while others serve a variety of local businesses and industries, by supplying applicants for marketing, sales, secretarial, administrative and technical vacancies. This broadness of range helps to make the employment agency a good option for people who want to change career after gaining experience in another area. 1992 will affect employment agencies by broadening the job market into the rest of Europe for both applicants and employers – although much still depends on relaxation of European legislation, in relation to skilled and professional jobs.

You must be licensed by the DEPART-MENT OF EMPLOYMENT. If you are supplying permanent staff you must register as an employment agency; for temporary staff you're an employment business. The DoE will check out your personal and professional references before granting you a licence. You can be licensed for different categories of employment. Then you'll need relevant experience. Although a spell of working in someone else's employment agency is essential to give you the know-how, credibility and confidence to set up on your own, you can also get helpful experience in, for instance, sales (especially tele-sales – employment agents do a lot of work over the phone), management, estate agency, training or active personnel (ie recruiting rather than administrative).

The INSTITUTE OF EMPLOYMENT CONSULTANTS runs correspondence and other courses in employment consultancy. They offer training programmes with recognised qualifications as well as advice and other benefits such as insurance. Any specialist knowledge you have can be useful, especially in areas like computing where clients will want to be sure you are aware of the sort of skills they are looking for in their staff. Go into markets that you know about to start with so you can intelligently discuss requirements and know which qualities to look for. You'll need commitment and energy to succeed as an employment agent. You're working with people all the time so you need good communication skills, perception and sensitivity combined with an organised business-like approach (there's a lot of paperwork) and good selling skills. You'll also have to be diplomatic and unemotional, there's no point sending an obviously inappropriate candidate off to a job interview just because you feel sorry for them. You will have to be capable of remaining patient under pressure however.

You should have at least £2,000 to set up with. You need at least one telephone line, typewriters or word processors, stationery (including information forms for applicants and clients) and filing cabinets – the law requires you to keep files on all clients and applicants for at least one year. A fax and a photocopier are also extremely useful. You can work from home but a shop or office front is a good bait for passing job-hunters as well as creating a heavyweight impression; equally, applicants may be reluctant to visit your home for interviews and you will need planning permission. In addition you'll need to finance your own advertising as well as advertising the jobs that your clients want you to fill. If you're going to supply temporary staff you'll need a lot more money to tide you over while you pay your temps their weekly salary before you are paid by the client; this can take up to six weeks. You will also be responsible for deducting PAYE and NI for temporary workers which could make at least a part-time bookkeeper necessary. As you expand you'll have your own staff of interviewers to pay, staff in employment agencies are paid a basic salary usually with commission payable on placements made. You are paid by clients whose vacancies you fill. The amount you get is usually worked out as a percentage of the new employee's starting salary, this is usually on a sliding scale and is about 12–20 per cent. For other clients you may make an arrangement to supply staff for, say, £500 a head. As a rough guideline, an agency with 50–60 vacancies and about 250 applicants on its books can hope to make 10, or perhaps 15, placements a month. It's a competitive business, clients will often be dealing with more than one agency and if you don't find the right applicant you don't get paid.

You get clients by going round all local businesses and advertising your services. Start in markets you know well so that you can discuss requirements knowing the background and the necessary qualities for the job. Keep an eye open for any new businesses in your area and once you've satisfied them once they'll probably use you again. Applicants come from recommendation and advertisements for specific jobs. The service that you provide to both clients and applicants has to be consistently good or you'll lose both. Employment agents' days are seldom plannable or dull. Much of the work is unscheduled, people drop in to look for a new job and you've got to interview them there and then; this should take 30 minutes and lunchtimes are likely to be the busiest times. Some employment agencies interview only on an appointment basis. Clients will also expect instant action; once you've got the details of the vacancy you need to find suitable candidates and then send the clients either a selection of CVs or those candidates you think are most suitable. This is usually done on the phone but you'll have to visit clients from time to time. All of this generates a lot of form-filling and filing. Some agencies offer a CV service, helping applicants to present themselves in the best way; this may stretch to helping them to change career by suggesting what options they have. You'll have to know your stuff to do this properly. At the same time you'll be dealing with people whom you know you can't help, and this requires diplomacy. You should also always be abreast of all changes in the employment laws, including discrimination, employment protection, etc.

Once you are established it is worth joining the self-regulating FEDERATION OF RECRUITMENT AND EMPLOYMENT SERVICES; you can do some basic reading on the requirements for employment agents from DoE information booklets and leaflets.

European Community Notes

Business differs greatly throughout Europe. All that can be said for sure is that you will need to speak the local language – and that, in many cases, UK job earnings are lower than other EC countries. The rest depends on the state of the market – and you. As stated above, the Single Market should broaden the scope for both applicants and employers with, it is hoped, a positive result for agents but much depends on relaxation of existing legislation. Even with '1992' opportunities in Europe are limited because many countries will accept only temp placements. Even if a temp then became permanent a foreign agency will only be entitled to three months' temp fees and no permanent fee can be charged.

English Language School Owner

Qualifications/Training	Recommended
Income bracket	Medium
Licence	Recommended
Town/Country	Town
Experience/ Springboard	Recommended
Travel	No
Mid-career entry	Yes
Exit sale	Yes
Entry costs	£8,000
Work at home	No
Mix and match	Yes.

You could think about: ***Tourist guide, Book packager, Landlord, Travel agent, Wine grower, Interpreter, Employment agent***

Enquiries
British Council, Arels-Felco Ltd

There are two basic types of private English Language Schools teaching English as a foreign language (EFL): language schools set up in this country to teach English to foreign visitors, and schools set up in foreign countries to teach English to the local population. This is a thriving business these days.

Whichever type of school you want to set up, it is useful to start by getting some qualifications: the Royal Society of Arts sets examinations in teaching English as a foreign (or second) language (TEFL and TESL). Courses are run by some FE colleges, and may be taken on a part-time basis (you usually have to be a mature student, or have some previous academic qualification). There are also courses sponsored by the BRITISH COUNCIL which are usually short, intensive courses, and quite difficult to get on.

Once you've got the teaching qualifications, you can start to get experience: there is plenty of demand for private tutoring in English: put notices on boards in colleges or universities. Hospitals are another area where there is some demand for tutorial English classes: qualified doctors from, say, the Indian sub-continent may have perfect knowledge of English as far as technical terms are concerned, but often need extra coaching in 'bedside manner' (discussing tummy aches with patients, and so on). It might be more constructive to get a job in an English Language School to learn the ropes.

Language schools in Britain are often set up to run during the summer period only: you can hire premises (private educational establishments during the school holidays), you will need to hire teachers, and you will have to put a lot of publicity material – advertisements in foreign press are a good start. Other schools own their own premises – large houses, redundant school buildings and so on. The best way to attract students is to offer a complete package: lessons, assessment, examination courses (Cambridge Certificate), extra curricular activities (visits to historic sites and cultural entertainments), accommodation and travel. Accommodation is usually offered with private families on a half or full board basis. Up-market schools may provide hotel or self-catering accommodation. You may need to appoint someone to take care of these arrangements. For travel facilities, you will probably have to make special deals with travel agents. To make the most of the costs, students are usually split into two groups, each getting three hours of teaching a day, giving them time to sightsee, travel or relax the rest of the day. Teachers work two three-hour shifts a day, teaching two different groups.

Language schools should be inspected and 'recognised' by the British Council. Once you have been recognised you can join ARELS-FELCO LTD – the association of schools recognised by the British Council (Association of Recognised English Language Schools and The Federation of English Language Course Organisers – the two organisations merged). They can offer you advice and publish information leaflets. If you are setting up a school abroad, controls will depend on the legislation in the country you work in. Budgets for promotion and accommodation will be low or non-existent.

Whichever type of school you set up, word of mouth is the best form of advertising. Offer good courses and make the students feel they have achieved something and you will be assured of a good name, and will be able to inflate your prices. Read the *Guardian* Education Supplement.

⁂ European Community Notes

Qualifications: UK qualifications recognised throughout EC and EC qualifications sometimes in UK.

Languages: To succeed, local language not necessary.

Earnings: UK income generally same as elsewhere in the EC.

Advice/Training: Advice, information and training available for those wishing to work in Europe.

Exchanges: Formal job exchanges do not exist.

Enquiry point for those wishing to work in the EC: ARELS-FELCO LTD

English Language Teacher

Qualifications/Training	Recommended
Income bracket	Low–Medium
Licence	No
Town/Country	Town
Experience/Springboard	No
Travel	Yes
Mid-career entry	Yes
Exit sale	No
Entry costs	Nil
Work at home	Yes

Mix and match Excellent. You could think about: **Musician, Magazine designer, Novelist, Tutor**

Enquiries: English Language Schools

With 1992 a reality, more and more people want to learn English. Teaching it to them is as much of a career as you want it to be. You can spend only a few hours earning spending-money or build a full-time business. The two-day and one-week 'Introductions to TEFL' are not especially recommended. A qualification like the four-week RSA Certificate is a big help, not simply beause students use qualifications as a barometer of who to go to as a teacher, but because the added confidence the certificate and/or experience gives you makes the teaching a whole lot more enjoyable. The courses are not cheap (from £500 up), but are intensive. You can earn back the outlay in a matter of weeks. Many schools provide the RSA course. The best-known is run at *International House* in London, but there is bound to be one near you. For an impartial view, ask to speak to someone who has done the course before you.

The easiest teaching to organise is 1:1 from home. It requires only a few cards in a newsagent's window and a few reliable books. You can find out the price per hour charged in your local area by ringing other local teachers. Try to work out a system whereby students either pay one lesson in advance or by block booking. It is inevitable that some students fail to turn up. Make sure they lose out from this and not you (attendance improves with this method too). Only the number of chairs and your own inclinations determine how many students you teach at one time. Whether you work out a class rate or charge the students individually is up to you (although the former method allows for natural wastage).

There are two main problems in teaching entirely from home: producing a regular flow of students; and the never-ending task of inventing new and exciting lessons. Both these hiccups are easily cured by working a few hours a week in an established language school. You have vastly increased resources and contact with other teachers. Some schools take over all the organisation and send students to your house. They take a sizeable cut for this service, but all you have to worry about is the actual teaching. Many schools are happy to recommend students needing extra tuition. The more contacts you have in the TEFL world, the more students you will get. Word of mouth can be more effective than any advertising.

When teaching from home you are relying entirely on your own skills to produce interesting and workable lessons. Keep copies of every lesson you teach in an organised filing system. Although this is more time consuming in the beginning, once the system is up and running you will save hours (this does not mean you cannot update material as the whim takes you). Many of your students will be students in the UK solely to learn English. You hit the big time if you cash in on the expanding (and lucrative) market for teaching English to business people – travel to their offices and take tutorials and classes of employees who are on company time and paid for by the company. And don't forget, people don't always come to Britain to learn English. You can teach English in almost any country in the world. So if you are an itinerant soul, it is a great way to earn money as you go.

For more information, read *EFL Gazette*, the *Guardian* on Tuesdays or, for a light-hearted look, the *Education of Hyman Kaplan*.

Estate Agent

Qualifications/Training	No
Income bracket	Low–High
Licence	No
Town/Country	Town
Experience/Springboard	Essential
Travel	Local
Mid-career entry	Yes
Exit sale	Yes
Entry costs	£10,000+
Work at home	No

Mix and match	Yes.

You could think about: *Surveyor, Independent financial adviser, Property manager, Property developer, Italian property finder, Conveyancer, Solicitor, Magazine publisher*

Enquiries
National Association of Estate Agents

Estate agents find buyers for property on behalf of their clients (called vendors). This means agreeing an asking price with the vendor, taking measurements and details of the property, preparing particulars (with photographs if appropriate) and circulating them around applicants. Then arranging for potential buyers to view properties, showing them round yourself if necessary, and liaising between vendor, buyer, solicitors and financial sources while a property is being sold.

A lot of estate agent chains were bought by banks and building societies in the boom years and a lot of branches of those chains have been closed down in the process. Indeed the financial institutions have set about rationalising the agency field in a becalmed market. This leaves the way for new businesses to open up, especially in places like the South-east even when the property market is not buoyant.

You don't need any formal qualifications to become an estate agent unless you want to do professional, structural surveys and valuations (in which case you must be a qualified member of the ROYAL INSTITUTION OF CHARTERED SURVEYORS). Under the Financial Services Act you need to be registered and therefore properly qualified if you want to give any financial advice (with mortgages, insurance etc). In any case, however, you will have to be able to judge accurately the market value of a property. This depends on how well it suits the market and the sort of people who buy in that area; a structurally sound house can lose value because it's decorated in the wrong taste. You will certainly need some experience of the business before setting up alone and may find it useful to join the NATIONAL ASSOCIATION OF ESTATE AGENTS, a mildly self-regulating body, membership of which sometimes inspires public confidence. Property selling is often by negotiation, so you'll need to be diplomatic and sometimes quick thinking to keep everyone happy; also good at convincing people that what you say is true.

Finding good, central premises is important. High street sites are best or somewhere where you are easily visible so that both sellers and buyers know you're there. You'll need a telephone and somebody to answer it when you're out who can talk intelligently about the properties on your books (answering machines don't sell houses). A computer makes life easier and a typewriter and photocopier are essential for particulars. A fax is also useful if you're involved in a contract race with other agents when getting documents delivered quickly is essential. The vendor pays you commission on the sale, which will depend on your area and the amount of nearby competition. It's normally about 2–3 per cent or even more if you're sole agent, and if you're one of many you can expect to charge more than that, although some estate agents (not generally respected in the business) work for less. You are paid when, and if, you sell the property; in the meantime you'll have had to pay for advertising etc. Sometimes buyers pay agents a retainer for finding a suitable property.

You get clients by advertising. Straightforward mail drops aren't very satisfactory (people ignore them), but try local newspapers (and freebies) until word of mouth and reputation take over. Some properties are sold at auctions especially if they're ready for development when property speculators step in. Others that are difficult to sell, you can share with another agent and split the commission. Useful contacts are financial sources (for help with buyers' mortgages), solicitors; also reliable damp proofers, woodworm killers etc; this is because almost always a buyer will get an independent survey done which sometimes finds a problem with the property and you will have to negotiate with the vendor to try to get it put right. Business is affected by the market (it slows down after Stock Market crashes) and by the season. January to June are busy with a drop off in

July until October. December is usually quiet. That means that some days you are very busy and on others you have to look for things to do to make business. Trade press includes the *Estates Gazette*, the *Negotiator* and the *Estate Agent*.

European Community Notes

Many up-market UK estate agents are now selling properties in other EC member states. You can specialise in finding properties for UK buyers.

Events Organiser

Qualifications/Training	No
Income bracket	Medium–High
Licence	No
Town/Country	Town
Experience/Springboard	Recommended
Travel	Yes
Mid-career entry	Likely
Exit sale	Possible
Entry costs	£3,000
Work at home	Partly
Mix and match	Possible.

You could think about: **Caterer, Public relations consultant, Artists' agent, Toastmaster**

Enquiries
Events organisers, public relations consultants

No jobs, or few, are entirely recession-proof. But just as those such as baliffs, servers of distress warrants, debt-collectors and the like, are thriving compared to the go-go eighties, so providers of treats, especially big, expensive, *conspicuous* treats are finding the early nineties somewhat sticky. None the less, there has been and doubtless always will be a lot of demand for organisers who will help corporate and private clients arrange special events to impress customers, the media or their friends. Events organisers are particularly useful to clients who need to put on spectacular promotional or social events which they are too busy to organise themselves. You can make a living by undertaking all the organisation for anything from getting a birthday cake to the launch of a major new consumer product with a multi-million advertising and promotional budget. In addition, you can offer a wide range of personal services (secretarial, ticket finding, weddings, party decorations); the core of the work will mainly involve organising some sort of party or event. Potential private and corporate clients are, by definition, people with a lot of cash; you need to be based near them, in London, Edinburgh, Bristol or anywhere else where corporate money is freely spent on ostentatious consumption.

You don't need any formal qualifications but you need experience and contacts. You need a proven track record as a good organiser, secretarial skills and have financial experience. You also need to be good with people and have real personal flair to make people interested in using you rather than your competition. A few years in PR or sales-promotion is the most useful springboard; it'll give you a chance to learn how to organise some complex, large-scale events and will also let you get to know reliable suppliers, eg caterers, the owners and managers of venues, entertainers, equipment hire companies, graphic artists and designers, secretarial services agencies. Before you start up you need to have built up a network of suppliers you can trust: if the food you supply is disgusting or the clown too drunk, it reflects badly on you.

Success depends largely on your personality: as well as being a good organiser and liaiser, you should be outgoing and friendly; good at making things happen without being too grim about it. It's a good idea to set up with a partner who has complementary skills and contacts, who will help come up with new ideas and who can share the work. Essential set up equipment is a telephone and answering machine, a photocopier, files, a word processor and stationery – presentation is important so be prepared to spend on this and your own promotional material. A fax is also useful for rushing last minute details to clients but doesn't provide good enough quality reproduction for main communications like quotes. Once you're established you may want to employ an assistant to help with the administration while you spend more time dealing directly with clients. You are paid at an hourly rate (say about £25 per hour but don't undercharge) and also charge commission on anything supplied by other people and agencies. You yourself pay suppliers with your own cash before you charge your client, for the supplies plus commission. Cash flow can be a problem. Make sure your client pays you in advance for at least 50 per cent of the estimated final cost of the event (including your fees and what you pay to suppliers). Invoice for the rest the day after the event, chase after 15 days (clients are usually good at paying quickly but one client in financial troubles before you've been paid the balance of your account for a massive event could be serious financial trouble for you). Pay your own suppliers' invoices as late as is decently possible but remember that many of the people you use are small businesses equally dependent on prompt settlement. It's a business that badly needs a good accountant and understanding bank manager and it's probably worth investing in a short business course for yourself.

Every event you organise should be a source of more work from the satisfied client and the impressed guests. Yet more will come by word of mouth and good write-ups in magazines and newspapers. You can start off in a small way, perhaps mixing and matching meanwhile, by organising events for friends and business contacts.

Although each job will be vastly different in scale and detail the basics are similar. Meet the client and find out what's wanted and whether it's possible to provide it within their budget, put in your quote, get it accepted and go ahead. Select a shortlist of suitable venues and take the client around two or three of these before deciding, then contact suppliers and make sure that they can provide what you want on the night. You'll almost certainly be expected to attend the event itself in order to make sure everything runs smoothly, while the guests must be allowed to think that your clients have organised the whole thing themselves. Make sure you stay sober. A lot of your work will overlap with your own social life because many clients will want to see you outside office hours. At Christmas you could find yourself attending at least one of your own parties every night. Make sure you book a holiday.

Exhibition Designer

Qualifications/Training	Yes
Income bracket	Medium
Licence	No
Town/Country	Town
Experience/Springboard	No
Travel	Yes
Mid-career entry	Unlikely
Exit sale	No
Entry costs	£2,000
Work at home	No
Mix and match	Yes.

You could think about: *Graphic designer, Advertising photographer, Sales promoter, Stage technician carpenter, English language teacher, Garden gnome maker*

Enquiries
Art colleges and design agencies

Exhibition design involves making displays for exhibitions or shops; making film or theatre sets; setting up museum and educational displays; industrial model making. Exhibition designers are responsible for the appearance of the various stands in an exhibition, for ensuring that all fire and safety regulations are adhered to and for planning the directional flow of visitors to the exhibition. It's a good area for freelances because few companies need full-time exhibition designers.

Routes into the business are via an interior design course, or a special exhibition design course – see *Design Courses in Britain*. Good colleges have close contacts with industry and teachers tend to be practising designers. Exhibition design interrelates with a lot of other disciplines like graphics (for the notices at exhibitions or museums), crafts, photography, advertising and promotions. There are side lines for the freelance.

To set up you'll need a telephone and design equipment. You'll also need somewhere to work but not necessarily a studio that clients will visit because most meetings are on site.

A lot of exhibition design is done under contracts which last for from six months to two years. It can be difficult finding work to begin with because of the Catch 22 of having to have experience before you're taken on; the work you've done at college may help here but is unlikely to be on the large scale of many of the jobs you'll be going for. There are design agencies (usually specialist), where you can place your work when you first start.

Ff

Farmer

Qualifications/Training	Recommended
Income bracket	Low–High
Licence	No
Town/Country	Country
Experience/Springboard	Useful
Travel	Local
Mid-career entry	Yes
Exit sale	Yes
Entry costs	£100,000+++
Work at home	Essential
Mix and match	Excellent.

You could think about: *Holiday accommodation owner, Caravan park owner, Butcher, Tourist attraction, MP, Accountant, Antique dealer, Racehorse owner*

Enquiries
National Farmers' Union

If you can afford to start farming in the south of England, you can afford to retire, with prices in excess of £3,500 an acre. If you choose to start on a small scale in, say, the hills of Scotland or Wales the land is cheaper, under £1,000 an acre, but you must be foolhardy and tough. The government is currently trying to reduce production generally, while keeping people living in the countryside – so there is enthusiasm for farmers to turn their hands to other things, eg turning the cowshed into holiday flats.

You can start farming part-time, as a millionaire looking for investment or if your parent(s) are farmers who are conveniently elderly and about to retire (most modern farms cannot support two families). Starting part-time can be a good way so you can keep another source of income – eg use farm buildings for tourism, keep your existing job or you can combine farming with being a butcher or cattle dealer. Most arable farms of 80–100 acres can be managed in evenings and weekends as you can subcontract a bit if necessary (in dairy farming, this size farm will keep you busy from dawn to dusk). A farm of 300–400 acres makes a comfortable family farm ('Don't even think of getting divorced'). Anything larger, you will need to employ staff to keep you going – dairy farming will need twice as many staff as most others. On a sheep farm, for example, you should assume you need about one person per 800 sheep. When it comes to crops, it depends what you grow – one acre of grass or peas will take the same time to harvest as two acres of corn. There is, finally, some government action to promote organic farming, so there are grants available for that.

Most farms change hands at auctions. These are advertised in the press and with estate agents: the more modest with the local agents and *Farmers Weekly*; large ones within commuting distance of London will be with West End estate agents and advertised in *Country Life*. These can end up being run by a manager on behalf of a landlord largely involved in other things. Farms that are waterlogged all winter will be sold in summer.

You can own the freehold of a farm or be a tenant farmer. With a tenancy, the landlord (often a large institution such as an insurance company or the CHURCH COMMISSIONERS FOR ENGLAND) owns the ground and the farm buildings. However, there are 'tenants rights', whereby, if you go, the new tenant pays you a sum (agreed between the valuers you have each appointed) towards improvements you have made. You own the farm machinery and buy seed, animals etc. Tenants have little interference from their landlords, except occasionally they press for more. Many landlords encourage tenant farmers to pass on the farm to a son (or, increasingly, a daughter, since the amount of physical work is relatively less these days). Heirs of the tenant who have drawn their principal source of income from working on the farm for five years are legally entitled to inherit the tenancy even against the landlord's wishes. Freehold farmers only have death duties as an impediment to passing on the farm – the higher the theoretical price of the land, the higher the duties. Once you own a farm and need to expand, you can 'share-farm'; you use land and buildings owned by someone else, you supply the seed, labour etc and the profit is divided between you both.

If you were not brought up on a farm, you will normally need a year's practical experience on a farm before being accepted for any agricultural course. You should then take a degree in agriculture or a course at a reputable agricultural college (better to stick to the straight practical course if you propose running your own farm rather than going for an agricultural management course).

Production of a number of farm products is controlled by EC quotas. This applies to eg milk, hops, sugar and potatoes. Quotas are valuable commodities and, if you don't need it yourself, there is a lively market in their sale or lease. There is not the same intervention with fruit and vegetables. Furthermore, you can cut costs by getting Joe Public to pick his own, if you are very accessible and can be highly professional – answerphone giving the current prices etc and perhaps combine it with selling other things such as bedding plants. For apple farms, you need a good cold store to get them to the market in proper condition when there is demand.

With animals, you can find a market if you go in for something different – goats, deer, or dairy sheep. And livings have been made farming garlic or leeches.

Farming is definitely big business, £60 will only buy you 100 new pullets or one very small new heifer calf. For £200–£700 you can buy a large white boar. Farm equipment and machinery is notoriously expensive (£20,000–£25,000 for a new tractor). But you can buy good second-hand equipment if you know what you're doing.

The growing trend is for farmers to set up co-operatives which store and sell their produce. You can also sell to specialist dealers or in the local market. If you are big enough, you can sell direct to a major user such as a supermarket chain. This means you have to contend with their obsessive size and quality control – most farmers with eg bullocks to sell find they are all different shapes and sizes.

There is plenty of bureaucracy and Joe Grundy-style resistance is not helpful. There are regulations governing the way you store your petrol; the logging of livestock in and out of the farm by ear numbers; the logging of crop sprays in and out; and the spraying records which must be kept (which fields they have been used on, the weather conditions and so on and so on). If you have the misfortune to get any notifiable disease on your farm, there will be more. For some, such as foot and mouth, you will get compensation although it will not stop you feeling as though you personally have leprosy. In case of accidents, eg Chernobyl, it can take the government an apparent age to decide whether or not you will get compensation. You can spend many hours alone on a tractor in this job; it is not for the gregarious. But you do need to be able to manage staff effectively and the local farmer is almost always an integral part of any rural community. You should not attempt this job if you are not very healthy – although you can get a contractor to do some of the work if you suddenly break a leg. It is still extremely hard work and it is vital that you love the work and the place you are farming. Farming is a complete way of life, since you live within the job. You must be prepared to work all the hours in the day for certain periods, depending on your product – lambing, sowing time or when the pease are ready for harvesting.

You should belong to and support the NATIONAL FARMERS' UNION. *Farmers Weekly* is useful reading. All farmers receive a host of farming freebies.

⁂ European Community Notes

British farmers are now looking seriously at France and also at Portugal and Spain, where the lower price of land is a real incentive to move. You may be able to pick up a farm in France for the price of your house in UK. All member states have agricultural attachés in their London embassies – start your enquiries there. The level of interest in France shown by northern farmers is such that the French embassy has a second agricultural attaché in Manchester. For France, the ANGLO-FRENCH PROPERTY GROUP is the leading agency handling French farms.

Farrier/Blacksmith

Qualifications/Training	Yes
Income bracket	Low–Medium
Licence	Farriers, yes
Town/Country	Country
Experience/Springboard	Essential
Travel	Local
Mid-career entry	Possible
Exit sale	Possible
Entry costs	£100–£30,000
Work at home	No

Mix and match	Possible.

You could think about: *Man with a van, Garage owner, Snail farmer, Gardener/garden designer, Saddler/leatherworker*

Enquiries
National Association of Farriers, Blacksmiths and Agricultural Engineering (NAFB & AE)

Farriery and blacksmithing are separate and highly skilled crafts. Farriers work with horses but need training in blacksmithing to enable them to make shoes properly. Blacksmiths work with iron and may never have contact with horses; although traditionally blacksmiths trained in farriery may shoe horses legally if authorised by the FARRIERS' REGISTRATION COUNCIL.

Farriers have to be capable of hard work and able to handle fractious animals and owners. You undergo an apprenticeship of four years with an approved training farrier and pass the examination before becoming registered. Find a training farrier through the FARRIERS' REGISTRATION COUNCIL or advertisements in *Forge*. Apprenticeships are interspersed with periods of residential training at the HEREFORDSHIRE TECHNICAL COLLEGE where you cover oestology (bones), shoe-making theory and veterinary science. You can also enter the trade if you have trained in the Army. Once qualified, a yearly registration fee is required to practise. The farrier should now be familiar with the work, and have built up contacts, confidence and business acumen. Few independent farriers can succeed without blacksmithing as a sideline. Be careful when finding a site that you do not encroach on other farriers. Farriers increasingly work from the back of a van (travel to hunts, shows, farms, riding stables) with cold-shoeing equipment (portable anvil £40, range of shoes, nails) or hot-shoeing (gas forge £300). Many make their own anvils and tools, otherwise a forge will cost £200, and anvils £70 each. A nucleus of loyal customers soon builds up, with publicity by recommendation. The work is immensely hard and the hours long but it is very satisfying.

Blacksmiths have a craft that is intellectually and aesthetically demanding. The whole field has recently expanded with contemporary design much in demand. You can train by taking a full-time degree or diploma course, usually included within art colleges' silversmithing/metals/sculpture syllabus; (Herefordshire Technical College run a one-year course in blacksmithing and metalwork). There are also apprenticeship/trainee schemes or you can take part-time classes. A full list can be obtained from the NATIONAL ASSOCIATION OF FARRIERS, BLACKSMITHS & AGRICULTURAL ENGINEERING (NAFB & AE) or SCOTTISH and WELSH DEVELOPMENT AGENCIES. On completing the training the smith can set up independently – many start with a homemade forge and anvil (approx £100), but more modern equipment would cost anything up to £30,000. Grants can be obtained from COSIRA. Publicity will be necessary – local papers, exhibit at art and craft shows, galleries, county shows, have your own showroom adjacent to the forge. Take portfolio and samples to architects and interior designers for commissions, whether traditional or contemporary. The BRITISH ARTIST BLACKSMITHS' ASSOCIATION (BABA), supply a quarterly magazine, *British Blacksmith* and hold annual conferences. Advertisements may be placed in *Forge*, a free bi-monthly trade magazine to members of NAFB & AE. Ornamental ironwork can be rewarding, with scope for creativity and physical work.

European Community Notes

The NAFB & AE organise youth exchange programmes both to Europe and the United States. The Association is considering establishing an EC enquiry point.

Fashion Designer

Qualifications/Training	Advisable
Income bracket	Low–High
Licence	No
Town/Country	Town
Experience/Springboard	Yes
Travel	Probably
Mid-career entry	Unlikely
Exit sale	No
Entry costs	£500
Work at home	Possible
Mix and match	Yes.

You could think about: *Illustrator, Fashion retailer, Magazine designer, Public relations consultant*

Enquiries
CFI International

The image of the sweat shop in the rag trade is not always so far from the truth. It is a very hard working, highly competitive and ruthless world where pressure to succeed, meet deadlines and supply on time can mount. Getting on with people is important, as are price, quality and punctual delivery. Independent designers have a choice of direction: freelance illustration for fashion magazines, freelance design work for others to make into clothes or hats, or designing and producing from their own workshop; all of these can be supplemented by part-time teaching.

Fashion courses at art school provide the basic technical skills and cover everything in the design room, from design and illustration through to pattern-cutting, garment construction and some business aspects. Specific courses are available for millinery. Good colleges have close connections with the fashion industry where you can make contacts at fashion shows. If you decide to set up your own workshop and design clothes which you produce yourself for sale, you should expect to spend at least a year working in a design or cutting room to gain experience. This is almost like an apprenticeship, ie low pay and hard work, especially before showing a collection. You'll learn about the panics and the problems.

For your workshop, you need enough space for large cutting-out tables, pressing table, dress stands, clothes rail and hanging space, an overlocking sewing machine (industrial or good domestic). You may be able to operate from home, but if you want to operate a retail outlet from the same premises you'll need a lot of space. You'll also need equipment like a yardstick, shears, scissors, set square, pins and needles. You'll need more specialist equipment for hat making, and leatherwork. For suppliers and trade information and second-hand goods for sale see the *Drapers Record* and *Fashion Weekly*. For choosing fabric you can see samples at the INTERNATIONAL INSTITUTE FOR COTTON and the INTERNATIONAL WOOL SECRETARIAT and choose swatches from a wholesaler. You can also get fabric specially designed or printed by a textile designer. It is cheaper to get cloth printed abroad. Rag trade shops generally group together in one area of a town. The rate of pay for a finished full figure drawing is £100 to £150. Many designers supplement their illustration work by part-time teaching.

Freelance designing is a difficult field to get into – big companies employ their own designer. Contacts are the most important thing. You have to hawk round your portfolio to the fashion magazines and design houses. Competition for freelance fashion illustration work is so fierce that it is crucial to have a rapport with the fashion editors. Decide which part of the market you are aiming at: high, middle or low, then make and price accordingly. You'll probably specialise, for example, in fashion, casual, evening gowns, bridal, rainwear, swimwear, leatherwear or whatever. Researching the market is important: there are fashion forecast companies which show business selling trends. It is important to get some advertising or editorial about your work.

With the considerable weight of imports flooding the UK market there may be some scope for a new sort of designer who acts as a link between foreign manufacturers and the British market. But, more than ever, this requires the designer to understand thoroughly the capability of the manufacturing resource where the clothes are to be produced. Workshops, factories, machines and operators are often less flexible than designers might hope.

Information and addresses from the *Clothing Industry Yearbook*, and the BRITISH CLOTHING INDUSTRY ASSOCIATION and CFI INTERNATIONAL.

European Community Notes

Europe – Italy especially – has long been recognised as receptive to British designers, for their style, training, ideas – even if the embrace is a little less whole-hearted than the 80s wonder years. Go somewhere they take fashion seriously!

Fashion Retailer

Qualifications/Training	Not necessary
Income bracket	Low–High
Licence	No
Town/Country	Town
Experience/ Springboard	Recommended
Travel	Some
Mid-career entry	Yes
Exit sale	Excellent
Entry costs	£8,000+
Work at home	No
Mix and match	Limited.

You could think about: *Fashion designer, Photographer, Magazine publisher, Artist*

Enquiries
Local fashion shops

There is a vast range of markets to choose from in fashion retailing depending on location, age and price range. Once you've chosen your market you have to move quickly to keep abreast of it. One successful outlet may lead you to opening up others (choose sites that will suit your established image). This brings a change in emphasis from acting as sole manager and spending a lot of time in the shop, to learning how to delegate responsibility and control increased stock and staff. Stock control and much other administration has been made a lot easier with the availability of computers.

You'll need some experience of working in a clothes shop. As well as being able to sell things, you have to know how to create an ambience for your shop, how to display goods and how to give your shop market appeal. It also helps if you have some idea of the sort of problems you may face from suppliers, unpleasant customers etc. As you expand you may find a management training course useful, or a course in running a small business. Fashion retailers need to have a good eye and an interest in clothes, they also have to enjoy serving people.

Before setting up, get a good accountant and a solicitor who can, among other things, give advice about leases and premises. For security and to enable reasonable insurance cover for your stock install a burglar alarm. You can't be insured against shoplifting which eats into profits, and so you may want to pay for a stock tagging system. It's important to build up a network of reliable suppliers. Initially, you'll find them at trade fairs or by visiting offices and showrooms (Soho is full of them). It takes time to find the right suppliers and to get used to the inevitable delays between expected and actual delivery days. Suppliers you can trust are also useful when you have to order clothes six months in advance for the next season – their stock should give ideas of style and colour ranges. If you're very enterprising you may branch out into manufacture yourself – this will increase your profit margins but needs a lot of organising.

The mark up on clothes is 100 per cent or more. Gross profit percentages are reduced by shoplifting, sales, promotions and mark downs to about 44 per cent. Aim for a complete stock turn around every eight–ten weeks. As long as you don't make too many buying mistakes, don't worry if you have to knock off about 20 per cent to get some things moving. All stock can be sold eventually by cutting

prices repeatedly and bringing out at subsequent sales. Through desperation, the Nineties have seen New Year sales that start 1 December and carry on until Easter. You should always have two sales per year in January and July, in which to clear old lines and make room for the new season's deliveries. Start with reductions of 25 per cent or 33 per cent depending on amount of stock left.

When you're opening up your new shop choose the site carefully; local competition is actually good in terms of drawing customers to the area as a whole as long as you use different suppliers, and you may in time have enough buying power to stop your suppliers from supplying other nearby shops. Managing a chain requires stringent stock control and the establishment of an image; you also need procedures for management, dealing with customer complaints etc. This may cramp your style a bit – a personal touch for one shop may not work for several when you don't have time to see to it yourself. Make sure that staff know what is expected of them, establish working relationships and keep tabs on what's going on. Introduce new blood, employ managers with training and experience different to yours. Once you've got several branches opening a central office is a help. You can buy from there and hold regular meetings as well as having a central address for invoices and post. Try to keep staff to a minimum to keep down overheads and create a busier, fast moving atmosphere.

Like all retailing, this is a full-time job made more so by the need to change stock every season in a very volatile market. Useful trade magazines include *Fashion Weekly* and *Women's Wear Resources*.

Festival Director

Qualifications/Training	Available
Income bracket	Low–High
Licence	No

Town/Country	Mostly town
Experience/Springboard	Essential
Travel	Yes
Mid-career entry	Good
Exit sale	No
Entry costs	£500
Work at home	No
Mix and match	Essential.

You could think about: *Events organiser, Artists' agent, Contemporary art gallery owner, Chamber group director, Opera director, Orchestral fixer*

Enquiries
Current festival directors

This work involves organising festivals, choosing venues and artists, raising sponsorship and subsidies from local and national sources. No particular academic qualification or arts administration course is needed, but a good general knowledge, enthusiasm, experience and love or arts and crafts is essential. Like planning a party, festival directors must be good at administration and delegation and be able to inspire a team. Being a good judge of people and getting on with sponsors, committees, artists and caterers is essential. The festival director must be able to empathise with the community and be able to produce a plan with which they can identify, but more imaginative than they themselves would choose. You must be able to balance your own ideas against the conflicting elements of audience appeal and the policy and finance of the city or town council.

Working as a gofer (often unpaid) at festivals can lead to contacts and a recommendation for paid administrative work; or get a job either in, or with, the arts – stage management, writing, editing, orchestral/operatic groups or with the local entertainment department. Form and run an unusual amateur dramatic/operatic venture or gallery so that you meet people and hopefully find sponsorship. Travelling and working abroad is valuable.

Get a cheap flat with a telephone or answering service and a typewriter or word processor. This job is normally part-time so you will need another to boost your income. A small festival will pay little, a large one maybe £50,000. You can compete for these jobs, or be invited. Once appointed, you should visit your festival town about once a week. There is no age, race or sex bias, but you must gain experience by travelling to performances and exhibitions at home and abroad, meeting sponsors and agents. A car is necessary. Hours are flexible but become demanding immediately before and during the event. A good way to meet lots of interesting and creative people, but not good for a conventional social life.

Film Director

Qualifications/Training	Available
Income bracket	Medium–High
Licence	No
Town/Country	Town
Experience/ Springboard	Not necessary
Travel	Lots
Mid-career entry	Good
Exit sale	No
Entry costs	£250
Work at home	No
Mix and match	Yes.

You could think about: *Journalist, Scriptwriter, Festival director, Opera director, Actor, Racehorse owner*

Enquiries
Directors' Guild of Great Britain, BECTU (Broadcasting, Entertainment, Cinematograph and Theatre Union).

A director might work in: features; TV drama; TV documentary and news; commercials; corporate films; pop videos; video promotions; or animation.

The factor common to all these specialisations is the employment of a camera but each specialisation demands skills not necessarily required by the others. Many individual directors cross over or do a combination of the different specialisations (for instance many distinguished feature directors have started their careers either in documentaries or in television or, more latterly, in commercials). Very few manage to keep a foot in all camps.

The director's function is to put the film on the screen. Directors are responsible for the visualisation of the film and are present at all stages in the production process, from the preparation of the script to the grading (the colour matching of the various shots) of the final show-print. Because they have a watching brief through all the technical areas of the production (all technicians are answerable to the director's interpretation), directors need a little technical knowledge across the board. They need not be expert – they employ the experts to do it for them. However, they must know enough to be able to describe the effect they wish to achieve.

In documentaries, a journalistic background is useful to be able to sift through unrelated information and create an ordered coherent argument. In video promotion, a sense of rhythm is obligatory. In film drama, be it for theatrical or TV release, a knowledge of actors' rehearsal techniques, though not essential, is helpful in finding a common language with the actors.

Because the skills used by directors are so varied, there is no set pattern by which would-be directors get their first film. The traditional route-in was via another film discipline. In features, your aspirants joined the camera or editing department (very seldom the art department and never the sound department) and worked their way up through the grades. This was a very lengthy process and only bore fruit by chance. In TV the promotion ladder is more secure. It is still possible to work up from the floor. The 1970s saw a proliferation of film schools and university film courses and many graduates of these institutions are working as directors in features and television. Even now, however, the best way to get started is to control a project (a script or a programme idea) which aspirant film-makers can use as a

lever to persuade producers or financial backers to give them the film to direct. The basic and absolute requirement for film directing is this ability to persuade others that you are to be trusted with a project that is probably costing vast sums to produce.

The most essential skills for successful directors are: charm and the ability to sell themselves; ability to manipulate and persuade others to their way of thinking; patience and dogged determination not to let the vagaries of the weather, the ever-decreasing budget and the intransigencies of actors, technicians and financiers obstruct their view of how the film should be made; unfailing optimism that someone will give them a film to direct and that they have something worthwhile to say on film.

How much you make will depend upon the area of specialisation and experience. Very few directors work for the BECTU minimum rates. Top feature directors can command fees (which are negotiated by agents) of up to 10 per cent of the film's budget and can secure 'points' in the profits of the film. At the other end of the scale, pop promotion directors working on shoestring budgets earn very little. In TV the rates are set by union agreements with the companies.

Many directors join the DIRECTORS' GUILD OF GREAT BRITAIN.

Film Extra

Qualifications/Training	No
Income bracket	Low
Licence	No
Town/Country	Both

Experience/Springboard	No
Travel	Yes
Mid-career entry	Yes
Exit sale	No
Entry costs	Nil
Work at home	No
Mix and match	Excellent.
You could think about: *Architect, Butcher, Taxidermist, Teacher, Sculptor, Pharmacist, Exhibition designer*	
Enquiries: Equity	

For those who aspire to a career on the silver screen, one route to stardom begins with working as a film extra. Even if the prospect of your name in lights doesn't prompt you to the grinding search for fame and fortune, those interested in other aspects of the cinematic art might wish to try their hand. Being on a film set can be an enlightening experience and an eye opener. Sometimes, it's even fun.

The quest begins, normally, with registration in EQUITY. (Many locations and studios are closed to you otherwise). Obtaining this presents something of a Catch 22: in order to qualify, one needs to show a work history of some length; logging such a history demands possessing the card. However, for the truly dedicated, this may be accomplished through a combination of perservance and luck. Begin by looking for productions where casting allows non-members to be used. If you know people in an advertising agency, this might be a good place to start. They will undoubtedly know other people working for film companies making adverts, serials or features. Or you can take the bull by the horns and begin to canvass the production houses themselves. Have photos and your vital statistics handy.

Once you manage to locate a job, be prepared for an early start; most days begin at the crack of dawn. There will usually be a production assistant to give you basic information and instructions, including the time, place and what you might reasonably be expected to wear. From then on, as Woody Allen says, 99 per cent is showing up.

Pay for work will usually be based upon a fixed day rate. If you are called upon to provide a car or some other skill apart from being there, then the amount goes up. Employment will generally be for a particular scene or set of scenes; the number of days will depend on how long the crew take to complete these scenes and the amount of 'exposure' which the director feels any single extra might have received. It is altogether possible to arrive on a location only to find that you do not perform at all. Don't worry; you will be paid regardless.

On the set, the numbers of skilled technicians (apart from the actors themselves) might come as a surprise. People deploy a daunting array of lighting and sound equipment with cables running everywhere. There are specialists to handle the wardrobe for the featured players, make-up artists and script people and someone looks after the continuity, making certain that characters and props are positioned correctly between takes. And the cameraman hardly touches the camera at all. That's the job of the 'grip'. All these people will utilise the opening hour (or hours) to organise the day's first 'set-up'.

The director or assistant director will then give the actors as well as the extras information as to what movements should be carried out. Once this has been done, everyone will probably go through one or more rehearsals of a particular scene. If all performances are acceptable (including yours), the next step will be for a 'take'. After a call for silence, the sound engineer will announce that his equipment is up to speed, the camera will begin to roll and the director will shout 'Action!' If all goes well, the scene will terminate with the equally famous 'Cut!' Unfortunately or fortunately (since you are paid by the hour) this simple procedure rarely works first time out.

When the fault is disclosed, be it an actor fluffing his lines, the sound man recording an inappropriate fire engine, the cameraman not being happy with the angle, or one of a thousand possible factors, everyone will return to their places for another try. And so the day goes.

Often, it will need hours to satisfactorily record minutes on film. For the extras, this means hours of waiting around while problems are corrected.

Having said this, the atmosphere on the set itself is often filled with a certain *esprit de corps*. The people are some of the most dedicated professionals in any walk of life and they undoubtedly enjoy their work. The pressures of time and budget which they carry are offset by a high degree of satisfaction with the end product and there are more than a few laughs to be had. You will also notice that, because of the pressures, little creature comforts are to be found: everyone on a shoot eats well.

If you do manage to find the first jobs which lead to an Equity Card, then you can move on to register with agencies or an individual agent to help in the further search for work: a star is born. On the other hand, should your goal be merely to pass the odd day in a unique environment and be paid well for the effort, then this is one of the best ways to do it.

Film Production Person

Qualifications/Training	Recommended
Income bracket	Medium–High
Licence	No
Town/Country	Town
Experience/ Springboard	Recommended
Travel	Lots
Mid-career entry	Yes
Exit sale	No
Entry costs	£500
Work at home	No

Mix and match	Limited.

You could think about: ***Film director, Typist, Market research interviewer, Artist***

Enquiries
BECTU (Broadcasting, Entertainment, Cinematograph and Theatre Union).

These are the people who are responsible for organisation and logistics and for getting films made on time and within budget. The production team is headed by a production manager who, under the auspices of the producer, prepares pre-production budgets and the shooting schedule. Production managers are usually helped by a production assistant, primarily a secretarial job that also involves dealing with any crisis that the production manager throws at them. Depending on the size of the shoot, there may also be a production designer who is in charge of the overall design of sets and costumes and a location manager who has to find suitable locations for filming, get permission to use them, ensure they have the right facilities etc. General fetching and carrying on the set and at the studio is done by runners.

Film, television and video are difficult to break into at the moment and you have to be able to work in all. There are no essential formal qualifications yet but NVQs are on their way. A qualification from a BECTU accredited school is useful for background experience, credibility and contacts. There are a number of courses which are mainly practical – they are listed in *Film and Television Training* from the BRITISH FILM INSTITUTE. A BECTU membership card is recommended, though not essential. The best way in is via a production company as receptionist/secretary/runner so that you can get an inside view of the industry and build up some contacts before moving on or starting to freelance. Get to as many shoots as possible so that you're seen and can be on site should any extra help be needed. Offer your services to anyone likely to use them. Ultimately it's a case of pushing; nag producers, they may hate you but at least they'll remember you and may pass you on to somebody else who can use you. Investigate the *Jobfit* scheme (*Cyfle* for Welsh speakers; *Scottish Film Training Trust* for Scots). These give on-the-job training and experience through temporary junior positions with various production companies.

Production people need to be methodical with good organisational skills and the ability to spot and solve problems. In the earlier stages you have to be prepared to do the running for other people (hence the term 'runner').

Once you go freelance, you'll need a telephone and an answering machine; better still register with a booking service which will run your diary while you're away. As you become better known and your circle of sources of work widens, it's probably worth getting an agent who can hustle and negotiate for you. BECTU sets minimum rates for production people. On the whole you can expect to earn more than they stipulate; commercials and promos command higher rates than feature films because the length of the booking is shorter.

Production people often work in informal teams, the producer appoints the production manager who then appoints assistants, etc. This means that you may do quite a lot of work with the same people but that you are free to work with others. Every shoot you go to will increase your network of useful contacts and gives you access to industry gossip. News travels fast so try not to make mistakes.

Having worked up the production team ladder, you should have useful experience for producing or directing. Read *Money into Light* for an account of producing a film.

Fish Curer and Smoker

Qualifications/Training	Recommended
Income bracket	Low–Medium
Licence	No
Town/Country	Country
Experience/Springboard	Essential
Travel	Local
Mid-career entry	Possible
Exit sale	Yes
Entry costs	£11,000
Work at home	Yes
Mix and match	Possible.

You could think about: *Oyster/Salmon/Trout farmer, Restaurateur, Wine bar owner, Caterer*

Enquiries
Aberdeen Fish Curers and Merchants Association, Agricultural Training Board

This job involves filleting, curing and smoking fish, giving it a unique flavour and a longer shelf life. This is becoming an overcrowded profession; you should be sure you can produce goods well above average quality in order to withstand the competition. You need a hardy physique as you will be standing for long hours in unheated premises in winter. You must be dextrous so you can fillet fish at speed with no waste. An excellent palate is essential, as the same critical qualities as those of a good cook are needed to test the taste of the cure (which is usually based on a mixture of salt and brown sugar). The best smoking methods are unchangingly traditional so you are relatively untouched by technical developments.

The AGRICULTURAL TRAINING BOARD runs short (two-week) courses in smoking and curing, or there are open learning modules run by the SEA FISH INDUSTRY AUTHORITY. In addition, you need at least two years working in a smokery with someone who is really skilled. Before setting up alone, do some market research. You must be prepared to spend the first year hawking fish around to find steady customers. It's useful to join the NATIONAL FEDERATION OF FISHMONGERS, which can give useful advice; find a good accountant.

You need a small building with a car park – near a main road for retail sales. The cost of buying or renting will depend on the area of the country. You must have planning permission and you will also receive the frequent attentions of the local environmental health officer (watch out for new food regulations). You need drains, hot and cold water and a separate septic tank (£5,000). A modern smoking kiln which draws smoke through a fan costs £3,000. Negotiate with the local saw mill for sawdust and oak or beech wood-chips for burning in the kiln. You can produce up to 130 sides of smoked salmon a week with this equipment. You will start with an income of £5,000 per annum rising to £10,000–£12,000. This job needs constant attention to detail and is normally a 50-hour week. It involves filleting all day; putting on the cure to soak all night; then smoking for anything from two to 24 hours; then slicing the flesh, as many chefs are nervous of this job.

Organisations such as the SCOTTISH SMOKED SALMON ASSOCIATION are useful for giving minimum specifications.

Food Manufacturer

Qualifications/Training	Available
Income bracket	Low–High
Licence	No
Town/Country	Either
Experience/Springboard	Useful
Travel	Some
Mid-career entry	Possible
Exit sale	Yes
Entry costs	£1,000+++
Work at home	Possible
Mix and match	Yes.

You could think about: *Snail farmer, Fish curer and smoker, Restaurateur, Psychotherapist, Shopkeeper*

Enquiries
Specialist food manufacturers

Current interest in healthy eating and real food, which has fewer preservatives and more taste than some mass-produced foods, means that you can make a living by producing and selling pies, mustards, pre-serves, cakes, biscuits, pizzas, filled rolls . . . as long as you're prepared to perse-vere. It can take a long time to turn a very small-scale cottage industry into a business with a reasonable turnover. For the less independently minded, one alternative would be to sell out to one of the larger food manufacturers and to exchange total autonomy for a seat on the board and what may be a lot of money; or to sell out completely and start doing something else. As long as you're relatively accessible to suppliers and for deliveries you can set up a food manufacturing business anywhere in the country.

To start up you need to have a product that you can make well, try it out on your friends to begin with, then you may be able to interest a local shop in testing how sellable it is. Find out, also, how long the shelf life of your product is – put some on one of your own shelves and see how long it lasts. All activities involving the pro-duction and distribution of food are be-coming more and more regulated. Before going into production check which bits of consumer protection legislation affect you. This will vary depending on what you're making but the two most likely things to consider will be the Labelling of Foods Act (which stipulates that your product must have a legible list of ingredients in des-cending order of weight or volume on every jar or packet) and the Weights and Measures Act (which subjects your weigh-ing and measuring equipment to periodic checks). Both of these fall under the juris-diction of the county council and some councils are more stringent than others. On the whole though, the approval of your own council is usually enough to satisfy the councils of any other county in which you sell your products so it pays to co-operate. You will also have to have your premises inspected by the environmental health office of your district council. They will continue to give regular checks which may become less frequent as you establish a reputation for being hygienic. Experi-ence in the food industry is useful: there are a lot of factors that make the manufacture and distribution of food very different from that of, say, shoes.

Set-up costs needn't be great. You can start production on a very small scale, baking a few cakes for a local baker every day or making a tray of sandwiches for an office. As you expand you can buy bigger and better equipment and premises; machinery for sticking on labels, measuring equipment. Most ingredients are readily available from wholesalers; if you're going to import from abroad check customs and import laws and make sure that you aren't going to end up with a load of rotting food because it was stuck on the quayside while you went through the necessary procedures. You will need a telephone and a van, a supply of stationery and labels and some packaging (some suppliers of jars are reluctant to supply the small quantities you may need in the early days). Base your charges on how much it costs to produce and how much you want to make per sale; people will pay more for specialist food but base your charges on the competition in the retail outlets you use – remember that the retailer will make a mark-up.

Because food doesn't last forever, your busiest times may be dictated by, for example, the lead-up to busy selling times or during certain seasons – these depend on what you're making (Christmas puddings or strawberry jam). As well as manufacturing you'll have to take orders and make sure that they're delivered, design promotional material and packaging and experiment with new lines. You also have to deliver to retailers, this can be handed over to a specialist distributor, who may help to extend your market field but the attention they pay to your range may be erratic – depending on what else they've got to distribute. Otherwise you can find your own retail outlets by driving around the country, using contacts and going to trade and food shows and exhibitions. This also means that you can, if you want, decide exactly which market you're aiming for (delicatessens, health food shops etc). If your product is good, retailers will approach you. Although you can have a very wide and varied range of retail clients you have to be very big before you can

supply supermarkets and once you're doing that you may have to drop your smaller specialist outlets who won't be able to compete with supermarket pricing. Another alternative is to market under someone else's label; small retailers often don't have the facilities to manufacture their own products.

Football Commentator

Qualifications/Training	Available
Income bracket	High
Licence	No
Town/Country	Town
Experience/Springboard	Essential
Travel	Essential
Mid-career entry	Yes
Exit sale	No
Entry costs	£100+
Work at home	No
Mix and match	Good.

You could think about: *Journalist, Public relations consultant, Sports retailer, Smallholder, Media trainer, Swimming teacher*

Enquiries
Television companies

Television sports commentators are self-employed and work under contract to TV stations and companies (radio commentators tend to be employed). Whoever you're under contract to has first call on your time but you're free to take on other jobs such as working on books, programmes and brochures; speaking at public and private functions and working on videos. The BBC won't let you take on any direct advertising but you can still work on material for football sponsors. Television football commentators have a high profile so spin-off work is likely, while you're working and after you've retired. Contracts last for about two–five years and are often renewed; the only risk is if the TV station you're under contract to loses *its* contract from the relevant sporting body to broadcast football matches. Clearly, in addition to ITV and the BBC, satellite and cable television channels are going to provide a lot of action.

There are no formal qualifications but you'll need experience of sports reporting. The way in is through journalism (information on journalism courses from the NATIONAL COUNCIL FOR THE TRAINING OF JOURNALISTS). You need a lot of determination; first push to be taken on by a local newspaper and, once you've some experience of football reporting, get on to local radio as a commentator. From there, if you're determined and good enough, you may get noticed and get on to TV. You need a good voice, to be quick with words, observant and quick to notice, identify and report what's happening. You must be passionate and knowledgeable about football, its history and that of the teams you're watching. Forget any flowery vocabulary you may have picked up from having to keep up a constant commentary on the radio; TV viewers are happy to have some minutes of silence from you; and they can see how beautiful the weather is and how vast the crowd. You have to add to what they can see, so specialist knowledge is essential as is the ability to concentrate on the game while still remaining in constant contact with the producer who directs the camera shots and decides which area of the field is being shown on the screen. Languages are useful when you're keeping up with what's going on abroad or commentating on a match with a foreign team.

The only equipment you need is a warm coat; a typewriter or word processor is useful while you're doing pre-match research. All technical equipment is provided by the TV company. Expenses include any books or magazines about football that you can lay your hands on. Keep up with what's going on at home from eg, *World Soccer*, *Match Weekly* and *Shoot*; read also overseas magazines like French *Onze*, and the sports pages of the national press. Contract fees roughly reflect the amount of work you're expected to put in; they range from about £35,000–£80,000 pa. Football commentating takes up an average of three–four days a week during the season. Fees for other work are negotiable; agents can help and are usually worth their 15–20 per cent commission.

You need a lot of contacts to do the job properly. That means getting to know football managers and players for after-match interviews; club secretaries who provide essential information about ticket allocation and crowd segregation as well as details of players' height, weight, age and biography; team physiotherapists for immediate information on any injuries during the game; commentators abroad who can tell you about visiting teams. Contacts will also get you work writing programme notes, club histories, articles for magazines and work on club videos.

Each match needs about two–three days of preparation. You'll probably only use a small proportion of the information you collect but before a match it's impossible to judge what you'll need on the day. By looking at the fixture list at the start of the season you'll have a pretty good idea of when you're going to be called on to commentate; expect to have about three weeks' warning of a definite booking. Get to know the teams playing, this may involve travelling to watch them in other matches. If one of the teams is foreign, get hold of videos and try to watch a training session as soon as they reach the country. Notice who wears which number and what each player looks like. Prepare notes on each of them, you won't necessarily have all this information in front of you but writing it down helps remember it. Prepare a card of essential information on each player. Find out too, all you can about the ground and make sure you know how to pronounce all the players' names.

The hours are irregular and there's a lot of travel including visits abroad and to tournaments like the World Cup. This gives you the chance to meet other commentators and build your network. It can be stressful and sore throats are an occupational hazard.

Foreign Correspondent

Qualifications/Training	Available
Income bracket	Low–High
Licence	No
Town/Country	Town
Experience/ Springboard	Recommended
Travel	Yes
Mid-career entry	Yes
Exit sale	No
Entry costs	£1,000
Work at home	Partly
Mix and match	Excellent.

You could think about: **Newsletter publisher, Radio reporter and presenter, Novelist, Farmer, Public relations consultant, Italian property finder, English language teacher**

Enquiries
Newspapers, BBC, Press agencies

There are three routes to becoming a foreign correspondent, a job which may sometimes be exciting (do you really want to get your legs blown off while covering the latest war?) but consists for the most part of reading foreign newspapers.

Route 1 is through the direct in-take of graduates to the BBC and REUTERS (or ASSOCIATED PRESS or other agencies) and is especially to be recommended. The on-the-job training is the best available and will open many other avenues on your way to the top. As a consequence it is also heavily over-subscribed and difficult to get in.

Route 2 begins on the Wigglesworth Evening News, from which you gradually elbow your way to one of the national newspapers, BBC, ITV, *Time Magazine* or any other employer who will undertake to send you abroad.

Route 3 is to take yourself off to a city or country of your choice – some like it hot, some like it cold – and set up as a stringer. A stringer is a freelance corres-pondent (whether the Wigglesworth Evening News' bowling correspondent or *The Times'* man in Outer Mongolia) who is usually paid per line published/minute on the air and if lucky may also receive a monthly retainer and expenses.

Route 3 is best practised after some ex-perience of Routes 1 or 2, but with luck, perseverance and good media connections it is possible to make a success of it with-out either. Why choose Route 3? In nine out of 10 cases, it's love that takes the unsuspecting Brit abroad without any vis-ible means of support.

Before leaving for your destination, trawl the foreign desks in London, visit magazine editors and so on, to establish connections and credentials. Having selected your city, you will almost certainly need to supplement stringer earnings by translation (don't be romantic: only undertake business translation, as you'll starve faster if you try the literary genre), teaching English to locals or with jobs for the English/American language pro-grammes of the local broadcasting media. Try charming your way to menial tasks for Reuters and other agencies: the local cor-respondent may be only too glad of someone prepared to relieve him of the late-night results for the Asian kayak championships, and once in with a finger you may be able to insinuate an elbow.

The going is probably slightly easier if you choose a big news centre (Brussels, Paris, Bonn, Tokyo, New York), where there are more opportunities but also more people competing for them, than in small news centres, where hungry local corres-pondents may chew up the newcomer for dinner. In Europe life is expensive, but you may be saved by the social security network. In some Far East centres (no personal experience) it is said that one can live quite nicely even on the pitiful rates which such as the Grauniad pays its stringers.

The rewards and style of life for the successful foreign correspondent are attractive, although the hours are long and unpredictable (which tends to upset co-habitants). You may meet The Great, sometimes face to face, more often with 500 other correspondents. You will eat and live well, and may influence the policy of nations. But don't underestimate the slog of getting established via bread-and-butter reporting (rape, mayhem, sports results).

Equipment: a portable computer is now essential. Forget typewriters. Get yourself, for example, a Tandy 200 with a communications program which will enable you to communicate with virtually all UK daily newspapers at the touch of a button – singly or collectively, as a kind of one-man news agency.

Franchisee

Qualifications/Training	No
Income bracket	Low–High
Licence	No
Town/Country	Town usually
Experience/Springboard	Useful
Travel	Varies
Mid-career entry	Good
Exit sale	Yes
Entry costs	£5,000–£5,000,000
Work at home	No

Mix and match　Depends on business. Not normally possible. You could think about: *Night care, Novelist, Smallholder*

Enquiries
British Franchise Association, Franchise Development Services

There are three ways to be involved in a business: employed; on your own; owning a franchise. More than 550 British companies are involved in franchising, and some 1850 franchisors within the rest of Europe. Frachise opportunities break down into: Job Franchises – vehicle tuning, glass engraving and other skill-orientated businesses, which can often be done at home; Sales & Distribution – for example, Snap-on Tools, Auto-Smart,

Retail – Body Shop, Benetton, Insurance brokers, etc; Management – fast food outlets, car-hire, etc; Investment – Holiday Inn, Hilton Hotels.

Provided you have the qualifications, owning a franchise can be fun and profitable. The main qualification is – capital: the more cash you have, the better the franchise you can choose. Operating within the safety of a group of other franchise owners does have a number of advantages – 'safety' being one of them. A franchise owner – the franchisee – purchases the rights to sell certain products or services from a franchisor. In exchange for paying a royalty to the franchisor, franchisees get initial training and advice with establishing and running their business and subsequent support and help as it develops. They also benefit from the reputation, marketing and experience of the franchisor but are restricted to running their business to the company format. Originally an American idea, the franchise industry is growing in Britain and now accounts for about £3 billion in annual sales and nearly 150,000 jobs. A handful of disreputable franchisors helped to give the concept a shaky reputation but this is improving, partly due to regulation of franchisors on the part of the BRITISH FRANCHISE ASSOCIATION, the FRANCHISE DEVELOPMENT SERVICES and also to greater media coverage of what's involved.

There are no formal qualifications but you may have to face some sort of vetting procedure from the franchisor to assure them that you suit their product. What they're looking for varies. Experience in a related field (eg, catering for pizza franchises) is useful but not necessary; in general franchisors are far more interested in proof of your ability to run a successful business and commercial experience is more useful. Franchisors know what they want to sell and how they want to sell it (they will usually train you in their ways and techniques) and you may find you don't have a lot of opportunity to experiment: innovative ideas are not usually greeted enthusiastically – what may work for your outlet wouldn't at others and any risks you take could reflect badly on the whole company if they didn't succeed.

Good franchisors, however, meet their franchisees regularly which gives you a chance to put forward any suggestions and some franchisees have found that, once they're established, the regular income they derive from the franchise allows them to set up their own separate businesses. You will have to be good at selling your product, capable of coping with customers and managing staff and prepared to work long hours.

A franchise will cost you anything from £5,000 upwards: say, Job franchise – £5,000–£25,000; Sales & Distribution – £15,000–£75,000; Retail – £35,000–£250,000; Management – £75,000–£450,000; Investment – £750,000–£5,000,000. For this you should get a ready-made business with necessary premises, equipment and initial materials plus advice about selection of staff etc. After that you will pay them an annual royalty of 4–10 per cent. Generally speaking, you'll be selling a product with an established image, reputation and market; this means that franchises are relatively safe ventures (statistics show a 4 per cent failure rate for the first two years as against 35 per cent for other new businesses). On the other hand, your autonomy is limited and thus your potential to cash in on successful experimentation. Profits are regulated because the company will probably provide the goods at their own price and set the selling price.

Franchisors help you with a lot of the customer finding and attracting that as a new business you'll need, through centralised advertising, marketing and market research. You can augment this with your own local campaign. You'll have to find a franchise that you can afford and are interested in. Do a lot of research before committing yourself, check out the company's financial standing and management structure. Talk to other franchisees to find out what support you have and how easy it is to succeed within the company's price and management structure. You can get help from the BRITISH FRANCHISE ASSOCIATION and FRANCHISE DEVELOPMENT SERVICES and read *Franchise International*, the *Franchise Magazine* and the *United Kingdom Franchise Directory*.

European Community Notes

Qualifications: UK qualifications recognised throughout EC and EC qualifications in UK.

Languages: To succeed, local language necessary.

Earnings: UK income generally lower than elsewhere in the EC.

Setting up: You will find it possible to succeed throughout Europe.

Advice/Training: Advice, information and training available for those wishing to work in Europe.

Exchanges: Formal job exchanges exist.

Financial help: Exists for study, training or travel in the EC, specific to this job.

Enquiry point for those wishing to work in the EC: FRANCHISE DEVELOPMENT SERVICES.

Funeral Director

Qualifications/Training	Recommended
Income bracket	Low–Medium
Licence	No
Town/Country	Town
Experience/Springboard	Useful
Travel	Local
Mid-career entry	Good idea
Exit sale	Yes
Entry costs	£50,000+
Work at home	No
Mix and match	Limited.

You could think about: *Embalmer, Garage owner, Jazz musician/singer*

Enquiries
National Association of Funeral Directors, British Institute of Embalmers

Although anybody can arrange a funeral, most people prefer to call on the professional help of a funeral director, also called undertakers, to take care of the corpse from death to burial or cremation and to make all the necessary arrangements. Exactly what this entails varies a lot – compare *What to do When Someone Dies* to the *American Way of Death*. Basic undertaking includes obtaining death certificates; providing a coffin and pallbearers; providing an embalming service and placing newspaper announcements if required; arranging the burial or cremation and transport of body and mourners to the funeral. Many funeral directors are small family businesses employing casual help at funerals. The recent emergence of body disposal units, which will remove a body from the place of death and dispose of it without ceremony, has posed a cheap alternative though it doesn't threaten traditional funeral directors at present.

In Britain there are no necessary qualifications or licences, which has led to the occasional cowboy undertaker setting up with no experience. But you are well recommended to obtain a diploma from the NATIONAL ASSOCIATION OF FUNERAL DIRECTORS and, if you're going to do your own embalming, join the BRITISH INSTITUTE OF EMBALMERS. Working for another undertaker is useful experience. Your clients, the bereaved, will need sympathetic and gentle handling, but you'll have to maintain a fairly detached outlook and not become emotionally involved with other people's death. On the whole age is a help. A mature appearance is somehow regarded as more appropriate, and undertaking attracts people who are retiring from other areas. You will need the organisational abilities necessary for arranging funerals without hitches and a non-squeamish attitude towards dead bodies.

There are no laws specifically covering the storage of corpses but planning permission is very difficult to obtain and you should check with your local council to make sure that you don't fall foul of local health regulations – you will almost certainly want to install refrigeration. Premises should have a reception area, a preparation room and possibly a small chapel for body viewing. Suitable cars cost about £15,000 each second-hand, and a second-hand hearse is about £22,000; you should also have a basic supply of coffins which can be furnished according to client demand. Allow at least £50,000 for set-up costs. You need at least one full-time member of staff for reception and telephone answering especially when you're at funerals, and a network of casual pallbearers, hearse drivers etc. You pay all the necessary fees on behalf of your clients, billing them for the whole funeral (between about £500 and £1,800), later.

Public opinion prevents you from going in for overt advertising so your premises have to be discreetly obvious. Clients will come to you because you are the local funeral director or because of personal recommendation (particularly from a doctor) or family tradition. It's better not to set up too close to other funeral directors. In addition to funerals, undertakers are sometimes called on to exhume bodies and some have body removing contracts with the police, eg to remove any dead body found in the local river; these do not include contracts for arranging funerals.

Clients usually contact you after a death although initial discussions may have taken place when it became imminent. There is about 10 hours work per funeral spread out over three to eight days. There are no legal controls over when bodies are buried, but conventionally all are disposed of within two years of death. Special arrangements have to be made with the MINISTRY OF AGRICULTURE for burial at sea. You will find yourself rather busier in the winter than the summer.

European Community Notes

Qualifications: UK qualifications recognised throughout EC.

Languages: To suggee, local language necessary.

Earnings: UK income generally lower than elsewhere in the EC.

Setting up: You will find it difficult to succeed in Denmark, Germany, Greece, Italy, Luxembourg, Netherlands, Portugal and Spain. You will find it easier in Belgium, Eire and France.

Advice/Training: Advice, information and training not available for those wishing to work in Europe.

Exchanges: Formal job exchanges do not exist.
Enquiry point for those wishing to work in the EC: EURO-SCHOOL OF FUNERAL DIRECTING.

Furniture Designer/Maker

Qualifications/Training	Recommended
Income bracket	Low–Medium
Licence	No
Town/Country	Either
Experience/ Springboard	Recommended
Travel	Local
Mid-career entry	Yes
Exit sale	No
Entry costs	£10,000+++
Work at home	Yes
Mix and match	Yes.

You could think about: *Wood carver, Tree surgeon, Sculptor, Interior designer*

Enquiries
Design Council, Craft Council

In spite of the ready availability of mass produced furniture, people and businesses are still prepared to pay for handmade furniture. It's possible to make a living from designing and making pieces of furniture to order but you'll need a lot of skill – it's time consuming; materials are expensive; and you're unlikely to make a fortune. However, you can set up a furniture business if either you've got the necessary dedication and good business sense, or you're an entrepreneur and can employ others to design and make the furniture. Craftsmen are notoriously short of business acumen and many of the best furniture makers prefer to work for other people. You won't need any formal qualifications but you do need to be taught how to make furniture. This includes design and construction

(you'll have to know how materials react to being treated in certain ways whether it's wood, stone, leather, glass, metal or plastics), drawing, technical drawing and model making. The traditional way of doing this used to be through a five-year apprenticeship; now you can do a course at an art school eg the JOHN MAKEPEACE SCHOOL FOR CRAFTSMEN IN WOOD, the LONDON COLLEGE OF FURNITURE, RYCOTEWOOD COLLEGE. Before setting up on your own get as much experience as possible; you'll have to know how long a job is likely to take and what to do if anything goes wrong. You'll also have to be good at dealing with people and coping with their demands. Good courses will include something on managing the business. (If you're in doubt about doing this yourself get someone else in – many furniture makers fail because they don't understand how to run a business.)

Setting up costs a lot. You'll probably have had to pay for your training (this can be £5,000). Then you need premises which, although they can be in cheaper rural areas, must be big enough to store large bits of wood and machinery. You'll also need a large car or van for transporting wood and furniture. Essential machinery and hand tools cost about £5,000 and can be added to as you expand; you could end needing about £50,000–£100,000 worth of equipment. Setting up with other furniture makers and sharing equipment cuts costs. Especially in the early days, you'll have to pay quite a lot for advertising (brochures, cards, advertisement in the local press). Customers are charged by job so make sure you're able to work quickly enough to earn something over the cost of materials and that you're adept enough not to have to do the same job several times over because something's gone wrong. You can regard yourself as doing quite well if you're making about £10–£12 per hour. The CRAFTS COUNCIL and the RURAL DEVELOPMENT COMMISSION can tell you about any grants or loans that are available. Banks aren't always very helpful; they like to see a clear-cut business plan and, unless you've got a well established range, the profits of furniture making are unpredictable.

Work comes from mail shots, good editorial in magazines or newspapers, exhibitions (starting at college) and building up a good reputation. Useful contacts are interior designers and architects, galleries and shops and anyone who can help you to track down the right bits of wood or leather. As well as making furniture for individuals or (in small batches) for shops, you may be able to get work making office furniture or shop fitting. For either of these it is essential that the job is finished in time – businesses are not indulgent to craftsmen and word will travel fast if you come up with the goods late. If you need extra help and can give some training you may find people prepared to pay you for allowing them to work for you. You can augment your income by teaching; or through design consultancy – if you get on to a DESIGN COUNCIL list of approved designers you can provide manufacturers with furniture designs for them to make up themselves (more cheaply). Days can be long, especially if you've got a deadline and something goes wrong; but the better the reputation you establish, the freer you are to pick and choose what you do and when you do it.

Futures Broker

Qualifications/Training	Yes
Income bracket	High
Licence	Yes
Town/Country	Town
Experience/Springboard	Essential
Travel	No
Mid-career entry	Yes
Exit sale	Possible
Entry costs	£20,000
Work at home	Possible

Mix and match   Yes.
You could think about: ***List broker, Accountant, Insurance broker, Greyhound trainer***

Enquiries
Securities and Futures Authority, Securities Institute

This job is changing fast. Futures brokers are intermediaries who are paid to execute, buy or sell orders for customers. Unless their customer defaults, they take no risk. Under the financial regulations they have a duty to exercise their discretion in a fair and honest manner.

You can be a floortrader (actually executing orders on the floor of the exchange); account executive (dealing with customers in a futures commission merchant's office); or a futures commission merchant – an individual, a partnership or a corporation. Your customers may be commercial and institutional hedgers, who take a temporary position in a futures market for the purpose of guarding against adverse movement in price and/or money rates; traders/investors, who take positions in the simple expectation of making a profit; arbitrageurs, who trade in order to profit from temporary price anomalies; fund managers, who see futures and options as an alternative investment.

There are five futures and options or 'derivative' exchanges in London: LIFFE (London International Financial Futures Exchange); LME (London Metal Exchange); IPE (International Petroleum Exchange); LONDON FOX (London Futures and Options Exchange); and OML (OM London Ltd). All are now regulated under a new regulatory framework and a good way of cutting through the complexities is to start your general enquiries at the JOINT EXCHANGE COMMITTEE.

A future is a contract which allows a commodity to be bought and sold in advance of delivery, at today's price. Between the day on which the future is issued and delivery this contract can be bought and sold many times in response to moves in the market. Financial futures and options are amongst the most modern and fastest growing categories in the world. Every commodity exchange has a futures department so that, not only can you buy and sell bauxite, say, or grain on current form (pork bellies does seem to be confined to the Chicago market) but you can buy ahead in anticipation. Futures are normally traded through brokers by instructing their trading representatives on the exchange floor when to act. Unlike commodity markets, the futures market is available to the public and much of the dealing is on behalf of private or institutional speculators, not the ultimate buyers and sellers of the commodity.

You must not only be qualified but individually registered by the SECURITIES AND FUTURES AUTHORITY (SFA) which means demonstrating that you are a fit and proper person to be registered. The SFA has introduced a futures and options representatives examination which is compulsory for most new entrants seeking SFA registration. Training is provided by a number of independent training organisations and the examination is delivered by the SECURITIES INSTITUTE on a regular basis. The Securities Institute is a new professional body for practitioners in the securities, derivatives and investment mangement sphere and is responsible for an expanding range of training and qualifications.

Experience of financial institutions and considerable knowledge of and expertise in the market are essential. This is best gained through a traineeship with another broker, getting experience of several of the areas of commodity broking and trading including working on an exchange floor for a while. Throughout this time you'll be working as part of a team so the ability to work well with others is essential. A background in economics or maths is useful; understanding of geology or agriculture can also help when you're dealing in a market based on natural or agricultural resources. Futures brokers must be intelligent, analytical and very interested; you have to keep in touch with any political or natural event which could affect the market. You'll also have to take a certain amount of flak; it's a high risk area where your advice may lose a client a lot of money.

It's not a cheap job to get into. As a broker you don't need to put up the £10,000–£144,000 needed for a seat on the exchange because you can trade through locals or another larger commodity firm. But you will need at least as much as this before the SFA will register you. This is to back up the traders you use (in case they lose vast sums in a crash for example) and so that you can afford a few short-term losses on the way to long-term gains. The relationship with traders is important as efficiency of trade execution will be one your main selling points. You'll need an office and administrative staff, equipped with telephones, typewriters and filing systems and, most important, with an information system from a specialist news agency (eg REUTERS) which will cost you about £10,000 a year. This is essential because you must have ready access to far more detailed and up to the minute information on current events and the market than the general press is likely to be able to provide; you also need it for pricing. You'll also need telex and direct links with other broking and trading firms and with your own representatives on the exchange floor. Other expenses include paying for outside consultancy and research and SFA fees. Money comes from the commissions you charge clients on deals; commissions charged to clients who generate large volumes of business is at a lower rate than commission charged to smaller private clients. Starting out as a small brokerage you're likely to attract more private clients than institutions. You can generate business through carefully placed advertisements but these cost a lot and you may prefer to use direct mail or the services of introducing brokers (also members of SFA who recommend your services to clients).

Each client must have an agreement with a 'clearing member' who will require 'margins' for each client in relation to the business expected. The clearing house guarantees all that client's trades. Each broker also has an arrangement with a clearing member who will guarantee his trades and be responsible for the broker's accounting, billing the clients etc. The clearer is paid a fee for each trade by both the client and the broker. The broker must lodge money with the clearer to cover potential mistakes (the amount depending on the volume of business envisaged). Each of the broker's employees must be a member of SFA (c. £500 pa) and relevant exchange if working on the floor (c. £500 pa). If a broker intends to trade of its own account it must lodge extra margin with the clearer.

This is an unpredictable, high stress job but there's the potential for great rewards if you're good (and lucky) enough. Hours are long to take in American trading hours; the working day can stretch from 9am to 10pm if you want or if the market's particularly busy. Read the national and financial press for background, look out for useful newsletters and develop contacts who can feed you the right information.

Current events play a very important role in the state of the market so books give only a general background to what it's like or how it's done. You could try the *GNI Guide to Traded Option, Trading in Oil Futures* (the same principles apply to all futures), commodity and financial yearbooks, *Controlling Interest Rate Risk* and the brochures produced by broking companies for their private clients. But the best starting point is the *British Derivatives Market*.

✶✶✶ European Community Notes

Qualifications: UK qualifications not recognised in EC, nor EC qualifications in UK.

Languages: To succeed, local language not now necessary but may become so.

Advice/Training: Advice, information and training not available for those wishing to work in Europe.

Exchanges: Formal job exchanges do not exist.

Enquiry point for those wishing to work in the EC: JOINT EXCHANGES COMMITTEE.

Recommended reading: The *British Derivatives Markets Handbook*, *Futures and Options World* and *Futures*.

London is the largest and most diverse trading centre in Europe but liberalisation of financial services in the Community means that cross-border services will probably increase. At present some member states restrict the carrying on of futures and options businesses and the rights of nationals to invest in futures. There are futures exchanges in Belgium, Eire, France, Germany, Netherlands and spain, the principal centres being France and Germany. While not absolutely necessary at the moment, the local language is likely to become more important as British brokers extend their operations in Europe.

The great advantage of London, which led to its pre-eminence, has been its uniquely liberal trading environment and this will inevitably be eroded with the development of a 'level playing field' within the community.

Gg

Garage Owner

Qualifications/Training	Recommended
Income bracket	Low–Medium
Licence	Yes, (MOT)
Town/Country	Town/Village
Experience/Springboard	Yes
Travel	No
Mid-career entry	Yes
Exit sale	Yes
Entry costs	£1,000+++
Work at home	No
Mix and match	Limited.

You could think about: *Man with a van, Motorcycle Racer, Courier service, Haulier*

Enquiries
Road Transport Industry Training Board

The motor trade is popularly believed to be full of dishonest people. This means that, no matter how law-abiding you are, once you own a garage you'll be regularly visited by official bodies, watching what you're doing and demanding to look at your books. Your customers will also be extra-vigilant and ready to assume the worst. If you think that a spot of second-hand car dealing is a good cover for any less legitimate activity – forget it.

Garages can do all or some of vehicle servicing: MOT tests; repairs, including crash repairs and panel beating; car and van hire; new and second-hand dealing; selling petrol. If you're going to sell vehicles with hire-purchase arrangements you'll need a standard credit broker's licence from the OFFICE OF FAIR TRADING; this costs about £300. For MOT tests you need a licence from the DEPARTMENT OF TRANSPORT. Unless you're taking over premises that are already used as a garage you will need planning permission. Otherwise to open up your own garage you don't need any formal qualifications but you'll need a lot of mechanical experience and contacts in the trade. You may have built these up through your own interest in car maintenance and practising on any old wrecks you can get your hands on. Any work in the trade is extremely useful; you'll have to know where to get spare parts as quickly and cheaply as possible so cultivate any contacts you make. The best experience is by working at another garage for a while. For this you probably will need to have some sort of City and Guilds, Btec (or Scotvec) qualification or a motor manufacturer's own certificate of competence (contact the ROAD TRANSPORT INDUSTRY TRAINING BOARD). Once cars have been repaired or serviced, you have to give them a road test so you'll have to be licensed to drive any of the vehicles you're repairing. To open your own garage you'll have to be a very good mechanic, quick at picking up new skills and techniques as there are new developments all the time and manufacturers change their models frequently. Although some garages specialise in one make of car, you have more flexibility if you are able to repair and maintain any make. You'll also have to be diplomatic in your handling of customers, many of whom have little idea of what's involved in repairing their car, find life difficult without it and think you may be cheating them anyway.

You could start off in a small way, mending people's cars in their own garages or streets. Ultimately, you need suitable premises with some sort of office, storage space for parts and equipment and as much off-street parking as possible, in an area where there's room for a few extra cars to be parked during the day. If you've room, you could have a couple of petrol pumps, a car wash, etc. You *could* start out with a box of tools and a telephone but you really need more than that to set up properly; electronic diagnostic equipment, exhaust gas analysers and vehicle hoists. Some of this is available second-hand. You also need insurance against theft of customer's cars belongings or damage and faulty repairs even though it's expensive and you may never need to use it. To begin with you might manage everything on your own or with a partner, but having somebody in the office as a receptionist and to help with the paperwork will stop you from spending half your time wiping oil off your hands on the way to the phone. Finding mechanics can be a case of trial and error. Although the qualifications mentioned above may have helped you to find a job, you'll soon find that they don't necessarily guarantee any great mechanical skill or initiative. The NATIONAL JOINT COUNCIL FOR THE MOTOR VEHICLE RETAIL AND REPAIR INDUSTRY sets minimum rates of pay for garage mechanics; expect to pay at least £150+ per week.

The charges you make are based on the spare parts needed and the number of man-hours taken (you set the rate for this, taking into account overheads, your own salary and the competition; you don't have to undercut as long as you can provide a consistently good service). You can get parts from manufacturers' own agents as you need them; for some old cars you may need to make or adapt your own spare parts and for a few foreign cars, less commonly used spare parts have to be ordered from abroad. The longer it takes to get a part the more impatient your customers will become so find a dealer you trust and who can come up with the goods quickly. Customers may want you to quote for a job in advance. This is risky unless you are absolutely sure you know what's involved; things can easily go wrong and you may end up spending far longer on the job than you anticipated. Once you've got a strong enough reputation you shouldn't need to quote in advance.

Work comes from your being known in the area. There is more work in towns but there is also room for garages in many rural areas. You may want to do some advertising to begin with. Mechanics have to be good at diagnosing cars' problems, if you get it wrong the first time it'll cost the customer more; if you get it very wrong it'll cost you – RETAIL MOTOR INDUSTRY FEDERATION policy is that you re-do or pay someone else to re-do any repairs that go wrong because of faulty parts or mechanics' mistakes. As well as repairs and MOT services, all cars are given regular services when they've reached certain mileages, these vary from manufacturer to manufacturer. Leasing companies are a steady source of work although they have fixed pricing. Doing your own car/van rental can be risky if you end up spending more on getting a car cleaned than you make from hiring it.

Working days are unpredictable, people bring their cars in at any time and may expect you to repair them on the spot – be wary of doing this, it may not be as simple a job as they or you think. Garage owners report that one of the greatest hazards is incessant telephone enquiries from customers asking when their car will be ready – the unpredictability of the work means you may have been working through a backlog or dealing with the results of a crash when they brought their car in for its service. It is easy to work 52 weeks a year so be forceful about taking holidays and time off. Rewards lie in the satisfaction of getting a battered heap back onto the road in full working order; frustrations, in finding that your hours of work have failed to do so.

Useful trade press, most of it free, includes *Garage and Transport*, *Car and Accessory Trader*, *Autotrade* and *Garage Equipment*.

Garden Centre Owner

Qualifications/	
Training	Strongly Recommended
Income bracket	Low–High
Licence	No
Town/Country	Either
Experience/Springboard	Essential
Travel	Local
Mid-career entry	Excellent
Exit sale	Good
Entry costs	£200,000++
Work at home	Yes
Mix and match	Yes.

You could think about: *Landscape designer, Smallholder, Village shopkeeper, Wine merchant*

Enquiries
Institute of Horticulture

Independent garden centres specialise in meeting the needs of gardeners right across the board – seeds, plants, shrubs, trees, fertilisers, insecticides, tools, machinery, greenhouses, garden furniture and horticultural know-how. They compete with huge garden centre companies with multiple outlets and tremendous purchasing strength – they can buy at least 20 per cent cheaper than you can and easily get away with pricing 20 per cent above you. They also compete with DIY shop, garages, department stores and supermarkets and of course nurserymen who have tacked a rudimentary garden shop onto their specialist business.

It's not an easy job to get into and it's expensive. There are too many garden centres, especially in the South-east; competition is beginning to thin them out. It's difficult to start up gradually in the way people did 20 years ago. You used to be able to start off by selling a limited range of your own plants and buy in only a few items, gradually broadening the range as the business grew. Now customers expect you to stock all their seasonal require-

ments, seven days a week, and probably won't come back again if you can't sell them what they want on their first visit. So if you are to be a one stop garden centre you'll need to carry a great deal of stock – £200,000–£250,000 worth on an annual turnover growing to perhaps £2–£3 million. As it's a very seasonal trade – you can expect about one third of your business to be done in just eight weeks (mid-April to mid-June) – your cash flow will need careful planning. Multiples and well-established businesses will get much of this stock on sale or return. To begin with, you won't, you'll have to buy. That means arranging substantial working capital to finance stock over and above finding the money to buy (or rent) the land and buildings.

Apart from the money, you'll need colossal physical stamina. Mid-career entrants beware – the physical demands on you will be a least five times greater than you are used to in your office job; you'll need to work seven days a week, with long hours; paperwork will get dealt with when your erstwhile office colleagues are watching TV and you'll find it almost impossible to take a holiday as it's a difficult job to delegate.

Why? Because your unique competitive advantage is your own horticultural know-how. Multiples and DIYs get away without it; you won't. Their staff can say 'Camelias? Never heard of them.' You can't. As an independent you must be able to answer technical gardening questions – you're the customers' resident expert on everything horticultural, everything you stock. Not only that, you are the stock control manager. Balancing your customers' spring, summer, autumn and winter needs against the the constant danger of overstocking is your key business skill. Employees are unlikely to match your combination of horticultural skill and business acumen.

To succeed on your own, you'll probably need three things: you'll probably need to have completed one of the formal training courses (one, two or three years; some colleges now run specialist horticultural plus garden centre management courses); you'll certainly need plenty of experience of working in garden centres before you go it alone; and – an absolute necessity – you'll need a real love of horticulture, a love sufficiently strong to survive your training, your work experience and the tedious paperwork (eg VAT, complying with the UK/EC regulations) with which your job is lumbered. With all three under your belt and still holding down a job in someone else's garden centre, you'll be poised to springboard to a garden centre of your own.

You can either acquire an existing business or start from scratch – not untypically in a failed nursery with rudimentary buildings and sufficient land. And you can choose a country, semi-rural or urban location – if you can find one. Some estate agents specialise in horticultural holdings and garden centres and it's worth keeping your eye on the property advertisements in the trade press. Whether you're acquiring or starting from scratch, favour the country or town, it's worth checking one or two points of general application before you let your gut feeling make the choice for you.

For instance, what's your proposed customer catchment area, what's the competition? In remote rural areas, customers are prepared to motor up to 100 miles on a round trip to get to their garden centre, passing perhaps half a dozen others on the way; this is unlikely to be the case in semi-rural and urban catchment areas where you'll need to 'count the chimneys' – is there room for a new business?

Then, land requirements vary greatly. If you intend to produce many of the plants, trees and shrubs you stock (some centres produce anything up to 95 per cent of their growing stock) then five acres and more are usually necessary; alternatively you may decide to buy in everything from nursery wholesalers and require no growing land. Whatever the case you'll need plenty of land for a car park.

Buildings including glass houses or space for covered plants are critical; they need to be adequate for your required business or you'll need to be sure there's land (with planning permission) available for expansion.

Think it all out from your customers' standpoint. Will your facilities be equally able to cope with your customers at the peak of the season in spring as they do in January? Almost all will come by car, take their purchases away by car and want guaranteed access for heavy loads and on-site parking. They may have driven for an hour or so to get to you. Do you need a tea room or loos?

Take all the advice you can get. Talk to local garden centres. Talk to the planning authorities. Consult the local branch of the NATIONAL FARMERS' UNION – it may be advising its members to diversify into your market now. Consider consulting ADAS. You'll have to pay but they have a wealth of horticultural experience.

Try reading: *The Garden Centre Manual* and *Profitable Garden Centre Management*. You must keep abreast of the trade press: *Nurserymen & Garden Centre* (*N&GC*) and the *Grower*

European Community Notes

The EC has far reaching consequences in the UK industry. A host of regulations are in the pipeline covering what you can do by the way of general practice and what you may sell. British garden centres doubt their value to the consumer and see no benefits whatsoever to themselves. While there is no EC finance for garden centres, EC financial incentives are offered to farmers to diversify into, among other things, garden centres; some British rural garden centres find themselves at a strong competitive disadvantage with farmers wielding EC diversification finance.

Garden Gnome Maker

Qualifications/Training	No
Income bracket	Low
Licence	No
Town/Country	Either
Experience/Springboard	No
Travel	Local
Mid-career entry	Yes
Exit sale	No
Entry costs	£500
Work at home	Yes
Mix and match	Essential.

You could think about: *Gardener/ garden designer, Toymaker, List broker, Chiropractor*

Enquiries
Local garden centres and craft shops

All you need for this is a suitably shaped mould, which will cost about £6+ from a craft shop, a bag of cement and sand (about a tenner from a builders' merchant), some suitable paints and a car. Then go into production, mix the cement, make the gnomes and paint them. You can probably make about 40 a day.

As well as the ability to mix cement to the right consistency, an imaginative attitude to the use of colour is useful. However, what is essential is the ability to sell. You need to operate in the right sort of area or be prepared to experiment in the hope that you may find a gnome that has widespread appeal.

Sell them through local garden craft shops, garden produce auctions or by advertising. Unless your gnomes are specialist ones you should probably sell them for less than the usual price. You may find that you have to be fairly persistent.

Gardener/Garden Designer

Qualifications/Training	Recommended
Income bracket	Medium
Licence	No
Town/Country	Either
Experience/Springboard	Useful
Travel	Local
Mid-career entry	Yes
Exit sale	No
Entry costs	£800+
Work at home	Yes
Mix and match	Yes.

You could think about: *Landscape designer, Property manager, Small-holder, Man with a van, Osteopath, Typist*

Enquiries
Institute of Horticulture

A living is to be made from helping other people to design, redesign or maintain their gardens. These can be small town gardens or rural estates, but on a smaller scale than projects tackled by landscape architects. The popularity of garden design is growing, helped by the media, the increase in house ownership and people simply getting fed up with the boring rectangle at the back of the house.

Many clients prefer a mixture of garden design and maintenance which makes for a job requiring flair but with regular work. You can drop the maintenance side as commissions for design come in, offering a service of layouts and planting plans either by post, or to a client in person.

This is a flexible business: you can operate in the town or the country, at home or abroad, and there is a great variety in scope and scale. You can sub-contract or include in your business clearing, paving, fencing, wall building, tree-felling and tree-surgery, turfing and so on. If you are designing only, acting as a mediator between your client and your sub-contractors, you need a room with a telephone and drawing board. You don't need to be involved with planning departments or architects unless you decide to include conservatories in your business. Once the garden is established you can mainain it yourself or leave it to your client.

Resources depend on the extent of the business. An answerphone will prevent you losing further business when you are on site. Order turf, paving stones, fertilisers and other bulky items for each job as and when you need them, and get them delivered direct; then you do not need storage space, except to house basics like wheelbarrow, secateurs, spades, forks and perhaps a few garden chemicals. You will need a car – estate car or van even better. Decide how much you are worth and charge per day or per hour; charging per job is always risky in case the job takes longer than you expect. Your rate can go up as you acquire more commissions and become more experienced. As a small business you won't be able to buy in bulk, but most garden centres/nurseries will give you discounts if you show your business card and spend over £100. If you sub-contract operations, try and ensure you have the money secured from your client before paying your sub-contractors; but don't risk spoiling good relations by withholding payment for too long.

Once you have completed your first commissions, the business will probably come to you via word of mouth. You can advertise in the local press and the *Yellow Pages*; *Thomson's Local Directory* is free. Obviously you need horticultural knowledge; apart from their innate usefulness in your pursuits, the letters after your name denoting qualifications, membership of professional bodies etc, create a good impression. Qualifications can be acquired on various courses: see the Department of Education and Science's booklet *Agriculture, Horticulture and Forestry (Choose your Course)*, or ask the INSTITUTE OF HORTICULTURE. Some private courses are advertised at the back of magazines such as the *National Trust Magazine* and the *Garden*; the ROYAL HORTICULTURAL SOCIETY runs courses and has many useful publications.

You will need to be able to get on with people and be fairly persuasive when the client wants something you know will not work; the ability to imagine what the garden will look like when it has grown to full size; an eye for colour and detail; some talent for drawing; knowledge of horticulture, and some key reference books. You may need to know about methods of construction; you should sub-contract heavy work such as paving if your back or constitution is not strong.

Other helpful publications are *Horticulture Week* and *Landscape Design* which is the journal of the LANDSCAPE INSTITUTE. For herbs, contact the HERB SOCIETY.

Glass Designer and Maker

Qualifications/Training	Recommended
Income bracket	Low
Licence	No
Town/Country	Either
Experience/Springboard	Useful
Travel	Some
Mid-career entry	Possible
Exit sale	No
Entry costs	£50,000
Work at home	Possible
Mix and match	Limited.
You could think about: *Silversmith/ jeweller, Interior designer, Potter, Beekeeper*	
Enquiries Craft Council	

Embarking on a glass-making business is a total commitment because of the equipment and premises needed. You need all the equipment (£10,000 plus) immediately you start. The kiln runs day and night, and you must produce enough work to run it continuously. You need premises large enough to house the kiln, electric furnaces and an annealing oven, with enough space to move around both comfortably and safely. The kiln must have a special ventilation duct (again expensive) to remove to the outside the lead oxide fumes created by melting glass. Setting up a studio will mean visits from fire prevention officers and if you set up a company with employees, a factory inspector. For electric furnaces (used for blowing, pressing and casting) you need three-phase electrics, which is also expensive. The size of the annealing oven depends on the size of the kiln. Other equipment will depend on what processes you use: electric or gas kilns for fusing, bending and enamelling; cutting, engraving and intaglio lathes for conventional decoration of glass; and if you are adding metal (such as silver) or wood to glass, you will also need the relevant special tools and silversmithing facilities.

The premises you choose must be big enough to house all these things plus craftsmen's benches. You need space to store a supply of cullet (broken glass) or batch (mixed glass whose fumes are more hazardous). If you are not on mains gas you will also need somewhere safe to store a supply of bottled gas. Because blowing glass is very hot work, you have to be able to create lots of draughts for the workers (but not on the actual glass or it will crack). A gallery area where you could display your finished work for sale is an advantage. Smaller items needed are blowing irons, wooden blocks for forming, colours, and clothes that do not catch in things.

Training for the studio glass-maker can be gained at art college, followed by an apprenticeship in a workshop. Some studios in Sweden, Finland and America also offer training. Czechoslovakia is a centre for glass; in the UK Stourbridge, Edinburgh, Sunderland and West Surrey are centres. Factory work is not useful to the studio designer/maker.

Tools and colours for glass-making come mainly from Germany. A lot of glass is sold to Germany, America, and – recently – to Japan. Trade Fairs (for example in Berne, Belgium, Germany and New York) operate but are very expensive if you are just starting up.

The only specific glass design magazine is *Neues Glas* (published in Germany), although general crafts magazines are sometimes useful.

You may find it helpful to contact the CRAFT COUNCIL.

Graphic Designer

Qualifications/Training	Recommended
Income bracket	Low–High
Licence	No
Town/Country	Town
Experience/Springboard	No
Travel	Local
Mid-career entry	Unlikely
Exit sale	No
Entry costs	£1,000
Work at home	Possible
Mix and match	Yes.

You could think about: *Book packager, Magazine publisher, Illustrator, Artist, Greyhound trainer, Wood carver, Mini-cab driver*

Enquiries
Design Council

Graphic designers are concerned with creating and projecting images for products, services and companies and with marketing, advertising and sales promotion. Much use of freelance graphic designers is made in design studios, publishing houses, advertising agencies, television companies and the film and video industries. Graphic designers usually specialise – eg in illustration, computer graphics, typography, poster design, book design, packaging, print-making, corporate image, photography and reprographics, animation, audio-visual.

Most graphic design work is in London and other big cities like Bristol, Birmingham and Manchester, because the big budget businesses are centre there. To begin with, graphic designers often back up their income with part-time teaching; a lot is available in London.

Start by looking at *Guide to Courses and Careers in Art, Craft and Design* and *Design Courses in Britain*. Graphic designers usually take a graphic design course and, during the last year of the course, choose which direction they want to work in: eg, towards design groups or advertising agencies or publishing. The DESIGN COUNCIL recommends graphic designers, through the Designers Selection Service, for consultancies and freelances; you have to fulfil certain criteria before they will recommend you. The Design Council also produces a number of useful publications. You can also advertise in *Creative Review, Design Week, Direction, Marketing Week* or *Marketing*. Join the CHARTERED SOCIETY OF DESIGNERS. If you specialise in illustration, the ASSOCIATION OF ILLUSTRATORS publishes a magazine and has a recommendation service.

You'll need a phone and some business cards as well as equipment such as drawing boards, pens and pencils. You can set yourself up as a graphic designer straight from college if you have managed to acquire the right contacts and have talent and persistence. To set up as a design consultant it probably takes about 10 years to get enough experience before you can form a group with confidence and have enough contacts, although some people leave the Royal College of Art and set up as consultants straight away. Develop a portfolio while you're at college and show it to contacts and potential clients.

The designer's role is to supply ideas. Clients may approach you thinking they know what they want. But it's up to you to interpret their ideas, help to think them through, find the solution and then commission illustrators, photographers, typesetters to produce the necessary work. You can present your design solution as a 'rough' which is then further discussed, amendments made, until the final design is arrived at. For example, a company might come to you wanting a new brochure, but you can tell them that what they really need is a whole re-think of their image – perhaps a new logo, letter-heading, reception area, and sign above the premises, which creates a new corporate identity for the public. This process applies whether you are dealing with corporate image, the selling power of consumer products, books or whatever. It is a world of deadlines and panics, and you have to be able to cope with that. It is very fast-moving and exciting and pretty ruthless. And if you're successful it pays extremely well.

European Community Notes

Qualifications: UK qualifications recognised throughout EC and EC qualifications in UK.

Languages: To succeed, local language not necessary.

Earnings: UK income generally higher than elsewhere in the EC.

Setting up: You will find it difficult to succeed in Belgium, Denmark, Greece, Luxembourg, Netherlands, Portugal and Spain. You will find it easier in Eire, France, Germany and Italy.

Advice/Training: Advice, information and training not available for those wishing to work in Europe.

Exchanges: Formal job exchanges do not exist.

Enquiry point for those wishing to work in the EC: DESIGN COUNCIL.

Graphologist

Qualifications/Training	Recommended
Income bracket	Low–Medium
Licence	No
Town/Country	Either
Experience/Springboard	Essential
Travel	Possible
Mid-career entry	Possible
Exit sale	No
Entry costs	£1,000
Work at home	Yes

Mix and match   Yes.
You could think about: *Careers consultant, Private investigator, Headhunter, Psychologist*

Enquiries
Graphology Centre

Graphologists can tell a lot about other people by looking at their handwriting. To a skilled eye, a specimen of writing can show how healthy the writer is, or how logical, reliable, punctual, self-controlled, systematic, garrulous, sensitive to beauty or emotionally stable. It can also indicate attitudes to a range of situations and even pregnancy at a very early stage. A new and undeveloped area, graphologists are already being used by many large employers to assess the personalities and suitability of job applicants or candidates for promotion.

To become a graphologist you should serve an apprenticeship with a qualified graphologist. If you think you may have the gift, read *The Secret Self: A Comprehensive Guide to Handwriting Analysis* to vindicate your instinct. To succeed you'll have to be good with people and have a very good eye and attention to detail. Extensive psychological knowledge is needed and the ability to convince clients of your ability is extremely important. Your credentials are those people whose writing you have diagnosed correctly.

The only set up costs are for advertising. Try the local press or newsagents for private clients, otherwise the trade and professional publications likely to be read by the management of large companies. Fees depend on the depth of analysis required: base these roughly on the amount of time and expertise involved; with experience and a reputation you could be getting up to about £35 an hour on some jobs, starting with about £5 for a very quick, basic assessment of suitability of an applicant for a job.

Private clients are people who want to know, for example, what sort of career they may be suited to or what particular skills (especially inter-personal ones) they have which could be developed. Employers are a very good source for volumes of work. They may want assessments of reliability for jobs involving the handling of money for example; on intelligence; ability to cope under stress; management or executive potential; mental and physical fitness etc. Employers like handwriting analysis because it's unobtrusive and doesn't overtly invade the candidate's privacy by asking specific questions. Handwriting can be judged as a whole as well as in separate components (width of margins, spaces between words) so any inconsistencies adopted by a writer who wants to create a certain impression can be ironed out. Forensic graphology is beginning to take off; you'll need to do some further training for this and anyone appearing in court as an expert witness needs a well established background, knowledge and experience.

You can work the hours you choose, as long as you get things done by deadline and are prepared to do some quick turnover work when an employer wants to weed out unsuitable job applicants as quickly as possible. Although Britain seems to be lagging behind many other countries in using graphologists as reliable sources of information about people, things are changing so persevere.

Further information from the GRAPHOLOGY CENTRE.

Greyhound Trainer

Qualifications/Training	No
Income bracket	Low
Licence	Yes
Town/Country	Country
Experience/ Springboard	Recommended
Travel	Yes
Mid-career entry	Possible

Exit sale	No
Entry costs	£5,000
Work at home	Yes
Mix and match	Yes.

You could think about: *Man with a van, Kennel/Cattery owner, Farmer, Book designer, Picture framer, Network marketing*

Enquiries
National Coursing Club, National Greyhound Racing Club

Greyhound trainers look after and train racing and coursing dogs for their owners. They have contracts with race tracks to supply dogs for races and are responsible for feeding the dogs and keeping them fit to run – dogs with bad track records can expect, at best, to be demoted to household pets. Greyhound racing is getting a lot of media coverage, due partly to increased middle-class interest in the sport, and this has broadened the market of dog owners that trainers can provide service for.

Trainers have to be licensed by the NATIONAL COURSING CLUB (for coursing) or to have a professional trainer's licence from the NATIONAL GREYHOUND RACING CLUB (NGRC) for racing. The most useful experience is as a kennel maid/lad for somebody else. You need to like dogs and to have friends who can put up with your smelling of dogs most of the time. Training the dogs requires experience, care and time. Between coursing and racing, one could say that while all greyhounds will chase a live hare not all will chase a dummy one. So the motivation to chase on the track needs to be carefully fostered from birth. You will need to know how to feed and exercise dogs so that they are in top form.

You'll need kennels to keep the dogs in and somewhere to exercise them; this means being somewhere fairly rural. You'll also need some way of getting the dogs from kennel to racetrack. You're paid a weekly fee by each owner (about £20 per week) and a retainer from racetrack owners who contract you to supply dogs for each race. Owning greyhounds is for fun rather than a serious way of making money, but

there are prizes for the owners of winning dogs and they like to see their animals run as often as possible. Track owners and bookies also like to see a lot of dogs running. The NGRC does not allow trainers to augment their incomes by using their knowledge of the dogs to gamble, nor to slow down dogs (by giving them water before a race for example) nor speed them up.

You'll need contacts among dog owners who don't want to train their dogs themselves, vets who will come out in an emergency and can advise about how to look after racing dogs and track owners who want supplies of dogs for their races. You need to be there most of the time because dogs need daily attention; holidays can be difficult if you don't have anyone to take over while you're away.

✪ European Community Notes
There are only three EC countries which have commercial greyhound racing: UK, Eire and Spain. No one in their right mind would set themselves up as a trainer in any of them without considerable experience of working with greyhounds.

Guardian ad Litem

Qualifications/Training	Essential
Income bracket	Low–Medium
Licence	No
Town/Country	Either
Experience/Springboard	Essential
Travel	Local
Mid-career entry	Vital
Exit sale	No
Entry costs	Nil
Work at home	Partly

Mix and match Yes.
You could think about: *Social worker, Journalist, Jazz musician/singer*

Enquiries
IRCHIN, Local panel managers

If you are a qualified social worker with considerable experience of social work in the child care field, you can apply to a local authority to join its panel of Guardians ad Litem (Curators ad Litem in Scotland) and Reporting Officers. If a court needs an independent report on a child (where there may be a conflict of interests between the child and the parents, say) a guardian may be appointed from the panel.

You must have undertaken the usual social work training – a course leading to the Certificate of Qualification in Social Work (CQSW) and at least two years' experience. Then five–ten years specialising in children is recommended (and a good range – fostering, psychiatric, residential etc). This means you are unlikely to be under 35. Once you have the confidence to go it alone, you can apply to local authorities before you resign from your conventional employment. Most local authorities should not appoint a social worker to their guardian panel if they have worked for that authority within the previous two–three years.)

In adoption cases, where the mother consents, you act as a Reporting Officer, discovering whether the natural mother truly understands the implications of her child being adopted. If she does not agree, and in all other cases, you act as Guardian ad Litem. In all cases you are formally the representative for the child's welfare in the case so you will need to get to know the child very well. You must be able to communicate with children quickly (a well-stocked box of toys helps) and be able to relate to parents and many other professionals. Your report will recommend what kind of order is in the child's best interests – which can be far from easy ('I want to go home but I want it to be nice again').

Cases can last up to six months (though this is undesirable). At the end of each case, you have to withdraw – both from the child and the people with whom you have worked closely while preparing your report. This can be a problem and is part of what can make the job isolated and lonely. You can discuss cases with other guardians and the child's solicitor who, in most cases, you are responsible for appointing (unless the court appointed the solicitor before the guardian). But you are not working with a team or within an established departmental policy – you are wholly dependent upon your own judgment.

The local authority social workers can be given a rough ride in court; but the Guardians ad Litem, although often subjected to tough cross examination, can be sure their views will be respected by the court itself. You need to have a sound understanding of the law relating to children, and to be able to defend your views in open court. Not for the weak-minded. You need both compassion and toughness.

An hourly fee for independent social work is fixed by the LAW SOCIETY but in some areas this is not paid to guardians in full. Some courts are more likely than others to use their panels but most guardians find work from two to three panels keeps them going; if you work for three or four you may get more variety – perhaps rural and urban communities and their different problems.

There is a newly-formed national support group, the National Association of Guardians ad Litem and Reporting Officers (NAGALRO). The CHILDREN'S LEGAL CENTRE will keep you in touch with what is happening in the field and publishes *Childright*. Also IRCHIN (Independent Representation for Children in Need) is a useful organisation for guardians and all social workers involved in independent representation, and publishes *Panel News*, a quarterly journal for GALs. You may find it useful to read *Adoption and Fostering* as well as general social work mags such as *Community Care* and *Social Work Today*.

The law relating to children was substantially altered with the implementation of the Children Act 1989, and the guardian's role is being extended and altered. Several publications from the DOH are essential reading.

⁎⁎⁎ European Community Notes

Qualifications: UK qualifications *not* recognised throughout EC but related EC qualifications are recognised in UK.

Languages: To succeed, local language necessary.

Advice/Training: Advice, information and training not available for those wishing to work in Europe.

Exchanges: Formal job exchanges do not exist.

Financial help: exists for study, training or travel in the EC, specific to this job.

Enquiry point for those wishing to work in the EC: IRCHIN.

Hairdresser

Qualifications/Training	Recommended
Income bracket	Medium
Licence	Not yet
Town/Country	Town
Experience/ Springboard	Recommended
Travel	Maybe local
Mid-career entry	Possible
Exit sale	Yes
Entry costs	£10,000+
Work at home	No
Mix and match	Possible.

You could think about: **Beauty consultant, Makeup artist, Interior designer, Newsletter publisher**

Enquiries
Local hairdressers and colleges

As a barber or hairdresser, you'll have to know how to wash, cut and style hair. Traditional barbers whose clients are men, may not go in for much perming or dyeing, but they do have to be able to shave their customers. Many hairdressers happily deal with both men and women clients.

You'll need some sort of training, through a course or better still an apprenticeship. Private hairdressing schools are not recommended and in any case are expensive (£5,000+ for an eight-month course). Within the trade, the LONDON COLLEGE OF FASHION is among the most highly thought of but there are good courses at a number of FE colleges which lead to City and Guilds certificates. The problem with college is that it is strong on theory but less useful from a practical point of view. You'll get a lot of stuff you may not want – like wig-making, make-up and beauty consultancy – and not enough practical – not least because of the problem of models: there do tend to be an awful lot of old ladies, which means loads of sets and perms and blue rinses but a distinct lack of modern styling and not enough *cutting*. On the whole, you need salon experience through, say, a three-year apprenticeship (much the best way of training), or traineeship with day release or night school courses. Top, established firms such as Vidal Sassoon have their own training programmes with a certificate – it's intense learning with lots of broad, day-to-day salon experience *and* of course, when you finish the training you are lined-up for work. It will take about five years to acquire the experience and standard of a top stylist and that's the stage at which you should open your own salon. Hairdressers obviously need to be dextrous, with an eye for what suits whom; less obviously but extremely important, you need to have good communication and understanding skills.

An excellent way in is to start out as an itinerant hairdresser visiting clients at home – increasingly popular especially if you are prepared to call during the evening or at weekends. If you're going to operate like that you need a car to carry you and your equipment (scissors, combs and materials) around in and a mobile phone is a plus, but with no overheads you can earn a fortune. Bear in mind though that since you'll be travelling back and forth you'll be lucky to get through even half the number of clients that you would in a salon where they come to you. But it is also a great way to build a rapport with customers and when you open your own place they will come with you.

Alternatively, you can work in a hotel or club and pay them commission on what you earn. Working on a ship is well paid as long as you don't mind long, hard hours. Otherwise, a 10-seater salon in the city centre costs about £30,000 to decorate and equip with heating, chairs, mirrors etc (about £12,000 in the provinces). Costs of buying or renting property are on top of this. You can raise the money through a bank loan. Most salons now are open plan. While a good location and a good-looking salon is extremely important you have to keep a sense of proportion. You are *only* cutting hair – there is *only* so much money you can make over the course of a year and if you spend a quarter of a million on bijou West End premises and hand-made Italian marble sinks you may find there aren't enough heads even at £50 a pop to make the sums work. Profile isn't everything – go for simple and nice to begin with. You'll need staff to help with the cutting, shampooing, drying, reservations etc. To find them, use your own network and the *Hairdresser's Journal International*. A relatively new scheme that's great for juniors has been set up by industry doyen Joshua Galpin, with government backing. They recruit and train apprentices. They'll come and check your salon out and, if you measure up, send you juniors (who you pay), give them a day's school a fortnight and constant assessment while they work. You want well qualified staff; they may work on commission or rent individual chairs from you. Most hairdressers want to open their own salons so you may find keeping staff difficult. Base your charges on overheads and local competition. Neighbouring hairdressers, unless they're aiming at very different markets, usually agree to charge similar rates. You can add to your hairdressing income by having sun beds (if you have the space), selling jewellery or introducing a manicurist or beautician to the salon on commission.

Clients come through word of mouth or because you're local. Your business is only as good as your staff are: you're selling their talents. When you first open, make sure you bring some clients with you – tell as many as possible, but keep quiet to your employers though. Expect *long* hours – especially if you're running a business as well. It's hard work, too, and very labour-intensive. You're dealing with people on a one-to-one basis, so you need to be patient and flexible. What do they want? Do they want to talk? If so, *how* do they want to talk? It can be stressful mentally, although perhaps surprisingly, it is not too bad physically, and it can be very rewarding. You will have to cope with difficult clients, and assorted disasters (clients hating what you've done or asking for miracles) but it does allow you to be creative and experimental.

Haulier

Qualifications/Training	Recommended
Income bracket	Low–High
Licence	Yes
Town/Country	Either
Experience/ Springboard	Not necessary
Travel	Yes
Mid-career entry	Possible
Exit sale	Yes
Entry costs	£40,000+
Work at home	Partly
Mix and match	Yes.

You could think about: *Garage owner, Snail farmer, Wine grower, Coal merchant, Antique dealer*

Enquiries
Freight Transport Association, Road Transport Industry Training Board

Hauliers arrange the transport of goods by road for their clients who are manufacturers and producers. This means providing lorries and drivers and delivering to anywhere in the UK, also in Europe if you get the necessary licence. It's a business which is fraught with regulations and you must know what you're doing; if you break any of the conditions laid down by the DEPARTMENT OF TRANSPORT you risk losing your licence and being forced to close immediately. For anyone who enjoys long distance lorry driving, it's a good way of making a living; you can operate on any scale from a one owner-driver business where you do all the driving yourself in your own vehicle, to owning a fleet of, say, 50 lorries and employing others to do most of the driving. You could mix and match this with something like specialist food manufacturer, making deliveries for other people while you don't need your lorry yourself. You need a standard (or standard international if you're going to work abroad) goods vehicle operator's licence from the DEPARTMENT OF TRANSPORT. This means you or a partner having a Certificate of Professional Competence for which you'll have to pass exams. There are residential, non-residential and correspondence courses to prepare you for these exams; the ROYAL SOCIETY OF ARTS can tell you about courses. In addition you have to show that you are a fit person to hold a licence; that your drivers will keep the rules governing working hours and records; that you will ensure your vehicles are not overloaded and that you have facilities and financial resources to keep them properly serviced. You will also have to have environmentally acceptable off-street parking for your vehicles while they aren't on the road. Before getting a licence you'll have had to advertise in your local paper, inviting any objections or comments on your business. Your licence permits you to operate the optimum number of vehicles that your facilities could support which means you can vary the size of your fleet within that limit. You're only charged for the vehicles you operate (currently £100 each), not for the maximum number for which you are licensed. Your operator's licence has to be renewed every five years.

If you're going to do any driving yourself, you'll need to have a Heavy Goods Vehicle (HGV) driver's licence, also from the DEPARTMENT OF TRANSPORT; once you've got one you'll be a very skilled lorry driver. In addition it's very helpful to be a qualified mechanic. To comply with the licence requirements you have to show that you have servicing facilities. You can contract with a local garage for this but it costs a lot because lorries need to be serviced every five or six weeks and may also need emergency repairs at anti-social hours. Hauliers need to be punctilious and patient about regulations and you'll need great organisational skills to make the business succeed and avoid having too many empty lorries on or off the road. As well as being good with lorries, you must be good with people to find suitable drivers and a ready supply of clients.

Each of your vehicles must of course be licensed and have its own ministry plate stipulating its maximum full weight. Vehicle licences are renewable every year at which point your vehicle is checked by the Department of Transport. If you buy a second-hand lorry in the middle of its licensing period, it needs an extra check when you take it over.

A new lorry tractor (the bit at the front) costs about £40,000, a trailer costs £12,000 (£20,000 if refrigerated). As an owner/driver you can just buy the tractor and work for people who have their own trailers. In addition you need off-street parking for the lorry and sufficient funds to keep it serviced. If you're out on the road yourself, you'll need a mobile phone to keep in touch with sources of work; you also need an office (this can be at home) and a phone with an answering machine.

You aren't allowed to use freelance drivers – though agency drivers can be employed on a temporary basis – so if you become an employer you must ensure that you've got enough work to make it worthwhile. Find staff by advertising in the local paper, there are usually plenty of drivers around but few stay at the same job for very long. You are held responsible for drivers and vehicles while they're on the road, even if you haven't seen either for days and aren't there when the lorry is being loaded. All lorries are fitted with tachographs which record their every move to ensure that drivers keep to legal working hours and speed limits. Tachograph records must be kept for at least 12 months. The tachographs are checked every two years and you're in trouble if one of yours is found to have exceeded the legal limit. The police keep a close eye on lorries to make sure that they're in good condition while they're on the road.

You need to find clients to give you regular work which matches your schedules; when you send a lorry from A to B you want it to return full. You'll have to cold call to start with and it can take a while to build up a clientele of people who know you. It helps to be able to provide a wide range of containers, eg for hazardous chemicals – though special training is required for dangerous goods – or for large industrial plant. You're responsible for carrying the right goods and weights in the right vehicles. You can find work from agencies. Some handle a lot of one-off trailers full, these are very useful for owner/drivers who can collect at short notice from, eg, the port. Others handle backloads for hauliers. Beware, these can lose you money; they usually don't pay much, believing that you'll take a pittance rather than to home empty, and you may end up losing a day waiting while the agent's client loads your lorry. If you're working overseas, your clients are responsible for any import/customs requirements but it's your time, not the clients', that is wasted at the borders/ports if they haven't complied with the regulations. 1992 should see the end of much of this nonsense within the European Community; also the opening of the Channel Tunnel in the mid-90s may reduce much of the physical aggro hauliers now suffer when the ferries are not working. Keep in touch by reading *Commercial Motor*, also *Freight* and *Motor Transport* and *Transport Week*. Further information from the FREIGHT TRANSPORT ASSOCIATION and the ROAD HAULAGE ASSOCIATION.

⁎⁎⁎ European Community Notes

Qualifications: UK qualifications recognised throughout EC and EC qualifications in UK.
Languages: To succeed, local language necessary.

Earnings: UK income generally same as elsewhere in the EC.
Setting up: You will find it difficult to succeed in Denmark, Germany, Greece, Italy, Luxembourg, Portugal and Spain. You will find it easier in Belgium, Eire, France and the Netherlands.
Advice/Training: Advice, information and training available for those wishing to work in Europe.
Exchanges: Formal job exchanges do not exist.
Enquiry point for those wishing to work in the EC: DTI.
Notes: You could find it difficult to succeed everywhere in the EC until the late 1990s. Fortunately for all concerned – and, conceivably, their customers – the dreaded 'cabotage' is on the way out as are the other restrictions on ferrying loads between or within other member states. Membership of the trade associations is advisable.

Headhunter

Qualifications/Training	No
Income bracket	Medium–High
Licence	Yes
Town/Country	Town
Experience/Springboard	Essential
Travel	Yes
Mid-career entry	Likely
Exit sale	Possible
Entry costs	£10,000+
Work at home	Unlikely
Mix and match	Possible.

You could think about: *Careers adviser, Marketing consultant, Accountant, Graphologist*

Enquiries
Institute of Employment Consultants, Institute of Management Consultants

Headhunters identify suitable people for their clients (employers), who are looking outside their own organisation for key staff

– top management and executive staff, also called recruiters or executive searchers. Headhunters often specialise, for example, in finding senior banking staff, or they can be genralists helping a wide range of clients fill a variety of top positions. It's a job set to develop as the demand for high calibre personnel increases; economics and competition make it more important than ever that businesses have the right person in the right role. Headhunters are well placed to supply this service because of their objectivity, their access to top personnel and ability to discuss opportunities without revealing the name of their client.

Some big recruitment companies offer management training which can be a useful springboard but isn't necessarily the best way into the business. Successful headhunters depend more on personal networks and flair than on professional testing methods to fit people to jobs. To succeed you should have personal credibility, well developed contacts, experience, and a good track record. The best way of gaining these is to work for another headhunter with experience within the industry in which you plan to hunt heads (absolutely essential if you're planning to specialise). Many successful head-hunting businesses are started by two or three people who pool their resources, experience and contacts. Some teams of headhunters stem from accountancy and management consultancy firms; people from both will normally have good business contacts and experience and are used to seeking new blood when helping to develop businesses. Clients must believe that you can find the right person. Candidates must believe that what you're telling them about a (possibly anonymous) client is worth listening to and, more important, following up. You need to be outgoing, confident and to know what you're talking about.

Although you should keep files on high calibre people you know are looking for a career move, headhunters are not dependent on job searchers seeking them out. Many of the people you're looking for won't have advertised the fact that they're looking for another job and some of them won't be unless the job is sold to them.

That means having a lot of information about a lot of people. You'll need up-to-date press reports on who's doing what; a library full of relevant *Who's Whos* and professional directories; a word processor/computer; files and a telephone. You'll also need at least one researcher/assistant who works with you (including going to client meetings) while you're tracking candidates down. Above all, you need excellent contacts who can point you in the right direction for likely candidates; who are likely to use your services themselves or to refer others to you. Networks like this are built up in a variety of ways; some date back to school or university; others are people you've met since, through your career or socially. Very often clients invite several headhunters to bid for a job. When this happens you put in a proposal outlining your approach to filling the specific vacancy.

Fees are usually paid in three instalments irrespective of delivery – first instalment on acceptance of the contract. Make sure your fee structure is clear; charges are usually based on the salary on offer. Headhunters make roughly the same as other employment consultants; they are paid more per assignment but have a more detailed, painstaking approach. After the initial client meeting, and the acceptance of your proposal, you usually have three months to complete the job. During this time you'll have follow-up meetings with the client. You may be expected to advise on suitable remuneration for the position you're filling and at the level at which headhunters are involved, this is usually high. You can advertise discreetly for candidates (in trade publications, the *Financial Times*, etc) but this is normally a last resort to be used only if your research and network of contacts fails. In some cases you may only track down one candidate, which doesn't matter so long as it's the right person. In others you may carry out the initial interviews and in-depth reporting in order to present clients with a shortlist of a few possibles after which you can either step down and leave it to the client to make the final decision, or continue to advise and attend interviews. There may be occasions when you can't fulfil a commission. This can't happen too often if you want to stay in business. Successful headhunters depend on their reputation and, while one high profile success can make you, credibility is rapidly lost if you don't deliver the goods.

Further information from the BRITISH INSTITUTE OF MANAGEMENT, INSTITUTE OF EMPLOYMENT CONSULTANTS and the INSTITUTE OF MANAGEMENT CONSULTANTS. The journal *Selection* is also worth reading.

European Community Notes

Qualifications: UK qualifications are *not* recognised throughout EC but some EC qualifications are accepted in UK.
Languages: To succeed, local language sometimes necessary.
Advice/Training: A modest amount of advice, information and training is available for those wishing to work in Europe.
Exchanges: Formal job exchanges do not exist.
Enquiry point for those wishing to work in the EC: INSTITUTE OF EMPLOYMENT CONSULTANTS.
Notes: It is very difficult to be precise about certain aspects, eg, earnings, prospects, as the industry is so different throughout Europe. Certainly, strict national legislation is in force regarding recruitment and employment.

Healer

Qualifications/Training	Not yet
Income bracket	Low
Licence	Not yet
Town/Country	Town
Experience/Springboard	No
Travel	Local
Mid-career entry	Yes
Exit sale	No
Entry costs	£2,000
Work at home	Possible
Mix and match	Yes.

You could think about: *List broker, Sculptor, Nursing home owner, Trout farmer, Potter*

Enquiries
Healers

Healers in terms of this job profile are defined as people used by 'God', 'the Creator', or 'the Power of Love' as an instrument through which patients are cured of their physical or emotional ills. This is achieved by the laying on of hands, or the healer's hands being held near the body of the patient.

Healers should be convinced that their ability to make people better is a gift, and that they themselves are just ordinary and imperfect human beings. It is also necessary that they believe and feel strongly that this reality is only part of a much longer spiritual life which began long before conception and will continue after death.

You should be interested in people and possess intuition, sensitivity and belief in some kind of higher spiritual power. It is not necessary, however, to belong to any organised religion, religious body or society.

Healers' career prospects depend wholly on their results; if they can heal they will always have plenty of patients. As soon as you have faith in your gift and believe you are fulfilling God's desire, you can set up on your own.

You need a quiet, warm, ground floor room, if possible near public transport and with parking facilities. It should contain two easy chairs and a stool. You will need a telephone and receptionist to make appointments if you are busy; you can organise your day to suit yourself. Donations are usually voluntary but you can expect some £15 an hour.

There is tremendous satisfaction and fulfilment in this job, but you must be careful to keep your work separate from family life if you are using a consulting room in your home. It's possible to do this job part time; you may need to travel to visit patients who cannot get to your consulting room.

The most useful sources of information are any books you can find in the public library on healing; and any literature, the more eclectic the better, which will broaden your awareness about man in relation to the unseen spiritual world. The COLLEGE OF PSYCHIC STUDIES has an excellent library.

Healthfood Shopkeeper

Qualifications/Training	No
Income bracket	Low–Medium
Licence	No
Town/Country	Town
Experience/Springboard	Useful
Travel	No
Mid-career entry	Good
Exit sale	Good
Entry costs	£7,000+
Work at home	No
Mix and match	Possible.

You could think about: *Restaurateur, Homeopath, Food manufacturer, Caterer, Fish curer and smoker, Potter*

Enquiries
National Association of Shopkeepers

If you go into this business you must decide what market you are catering for. Are you going to deal in pills and potions? Are your basic foodstuffs going to be priced below the local supermarket? How health/ecology conscious are your prospective customers? Will you stock books? Will you get involved in the community by supporting local groups or sticking notices in your window? In a nutshell are you for

lentils and beans or evening primrose oil? These two sides can be combined successfully but it is unwise to attempt this at the beginning. If you decide to go for the wholefood side think about wholesaling as well as retailing. Hospitals, other shops, cafés, restaurants, even burger bars could be wholesale customers, but you have to go out and find them or attract them through your retail business.

To start up you will need £7,000 for initial stock and retail premises (situation is important but not as much as for many shops as less passing trade is involved). Transport, owned or hired, is essential for collecting from your suppliers and delivering to your customers. You will need good management skills. Wholefood sales are labour intensive as bagging up sacks into small packages is necessary (you may need to employ a full-time helper to do this). You may like to sell home baked snacks/ bread and will need someone to cook these.

All food selling is a risky business as foodstuffs have a limited shelf life and can be subject to infestations. You will also have trouble persuading wholefood suppliers to supply the correct amount when you want it. This area of retailing is expanding fast thanks to better health education and a higher standard of living. Homeopathic cures are particularly on the increase – partly due to some disillusionment with traditional medicine and partly some American influence. Despite this growth you are highly unlikely to become a millionaire but should make a comfortable living. If you choose to get involved in community projects and have a feel for their needs, experience has shown that the rewards are personal rather than material.

All business involved with the production, distribution or retailing of food are becoming more and more regulated. It is essential to check the position with your local authority. Certainly, if you are planning to sell home-baked snacks, bread etc the preparation and cooking of such products, and the premises, are subject to inspection by environmental health officers under the Food Safety Act.

Hi-Fi Shop Owner

Qualifications/Training	No
Income bracket	Low–High
Licence	Yes for HP
Town/Country	Town
Experience/Springboard	Essential
Travel	No
Mid-career entry	Yes
Exit sale	Excellent
Entry costs	£12,000
Work at home	No
Mix and match	Possible.

You could think about: *Disco owner/ DJ, Music/Instrument retailer, Newsletter publisher*

Enquiries
Hi-Fi shop owners

There's a strong if finite market for good quality sound systems. Developments in hi-fi equipment have made people willing to splash out a great deal on quality CD and tape players, with amps and speakers to match. The ready availability of cheap equipment means that anyone entering the market will have to compete with high street shops and the cut prices they can offer with their large turnover. But if you're a good judge of hi-fi, you can build up a reputation for providing only the best at the more specialist end of the market. On the whole that will mean dealing in systems of £500–£750 upwards and components of £150–£200-plus.

Essential qualifications are a wide knowledge of what's available and what it sounds like, an excellent business sense and good selling skills. The best previous experience is working in someone else's hi-fi shop for at least a year, best in a fairly small one with a wide range of equipment. This will let you learn about the different components of hi-fi and give you some idea of the quality of various manufacturers' equipment so that you can start to develop your judgement of what's best. It will also put you in touch with suppliers' agents who may supply you in the future and with the hi-fi network which will help keep you abreast of developments. That's apart from giving you some idea of what to expect when you're selling hi-fi, how to deal with customers and what the pitfalls are. But working in an established shop will not show you what its like when you first start. You must be very interested in what you sell and it's unlikely that you'll enter this field unless you like music – much of the job involves listening to it. It's advisable to set up with a partner who can share the responsibility and who may concentrate on the accounts while you do the selling or vice versa.

Premises must be close to your customers, just off a main shopping street is ideal; probably not the cheapest you can find – it's worth getting the right shop to avoid expensive moves later (if you start off in the wrong place you may never be able to afford to move). Expensive hi-fi doesn't depend solely on passing trade (casual customers can waste a lot of time) but less specialist dealers may send customers to you and people don't travel far to buy hi-fi. Being near a business centre is useful for regular customers. You don't need masses of space for display or storage but must have an amenable demonstration room where people can listen to the equipment. To insure your premises you must have an alarm system. The telephone is essential, it's your link with prospective customers. To start with you don't need a lot of stock: about £10,000 worth will give you a fair range as long as your suppliers are reasonably fast. The amount of stock you hold will increase to several tens of thousands as you grow and widen your range of products. Providing a free delivery and installation service is good for customer relations so having a van is a plus. You can get a warehouse for holding stocks of best sellers when you're more established and turnover is higher. This saves you from moving to a larger shop but there are quite a lot of hidden costs in time and phone bills for communications. You'll soon have to employ help in the shop; find people with an interest in music and good product knowledge which will help you as well as the customers. Profit margins are approximately 30 per cent of turnover – good accounting is essential so that you know how much of this actually ends up in your pocket.

Buying an entire hi-fi system at once can cost a lot and many shops offer hire-purchase to customers. If you want to do this you need to have the protection of a credit company such as Lombard Tricity or North British Credit. You'll need a Consumer Credit Licence (costing about £40), available from the licensing branch of the OFFICE OF FAIR TRADING. If you decide to deal in second-hand equipment, or to operate a system of part exchange, make sure that you know how much it's worth to you.

Initial business comes from advertising; word of mouth and reputation will eventually take over; so your advertising budget should shrink quite quickly from an initial 5 per cent of turnover, the sort of figure you should expect in the early days. A spin-off from advertising is the good editorial you may get from publications you've advertised in. Get to know your competition; not only may they refer customers to you but suppliers will be reluctant to supply you if they think that doing so will upset existing local stockists.

Suppliers teach you to install equipment and also operate a one year parts and labour guarantee. For a specialist shop this isn't enough (customers won't like if it thousands of pounds worth of equipment packs up after 18 months because of a manufacturer's fault which wasn't obvious until then). You may want to extend the guarantee to two years for your customers. Some (not all) suppliers will do the same; when they don't, it'll be up to you to pay for repairs on any unsatisfactory equipment you sell. Using British suppliers (or the British subsidiaries of foreign manufacturers) speeds up delivery time and eases communication considerably.

You must keep up with developments: read the hi-fi press, *What Hi-Fi*, *Hi-Fi News* and *Hi-Fi Choice*, and get to know which reviewers or equipment are best. Don't be tempted to stock anything that isn't up to standard just because it completes a range; success depends on establishing a reputation for selling only the best. Customers will come back if you

provide a good service and if you're obviously well informed without being daunting. You have to listen to them and make sure you know what they want; don't contradict them if they want to buy something you wouldn't specifically recommend for them (another reason for being sure of everything you stock). They'll also come back to upgrade their equipment so make sure that you always have something rather better and more expensive for them to buy. As with any shop, hazards are shoplifting (against which there is no insurance) and unsellable stock. There's label snobbery in hi-fi too so only stock unknown names if you're sure that you can sell them.

High Street Photographer

Qualifications/Training	Recommended
Income bracket	Medium
Licence	No
Town/Country	Town
Experience/Springboard	Yes
Travel	Local
Mid-career entry	Possible
Exit sale	Yes
Entry costs	£10,000
Work at home	No
Mix and match	Possible.

You could think about: *Advertising photographer, Wedding shop owner, Contemporary art gallery owner*

Enquiries
British Institute of Professional Photography

If you want to work as a photographer in a small town, the most likely opening is in a high street practice. Many of the commissions may be repetitive (weddings and bar mitzvahs) and a large part of your business is likely to be in individual or family portraits. Another, less publicised, source of income is the less pleasant business of photographing people with injuries, to be used as evidence in court cases or insurance claims. You'll need to be able to be discreet when necessary (no one likes a pushy wedding photographer) and bring out the best in people (the gift of the gab can be helpful in getting subjects to relax). You'll also have to be able to charm children – and their doting parents. If you want to work for yourself, the best bet is to set up your own practice.

Training usually involves a spell at art school (vocational courses are recognised by the BRITISH INSTITUTE OF PROFESSIONAL PHOTOGRAPHY), and then an 'apprenticeship' working for a high street practice. To set up you may start in a small way, working from home and advertising your services in the local press, or you may raise the necessary capital to take over an existing practice, or lease premises to set up on your own.

You will need reliable equipment, and good processing facilities – some practices do their own processing, others send film to labs for developing and printing.

You may also find you are commissioned to do some commercial photography, for local industries, property companies or advertising agencies, for example. You will not be able to charge the same rate as commercial (advertising) photographers in the centre of London, but you should be able to negotiate fees which are more substantial than usual.

The *Photographer* is published by the BIPP, and is a useful way of keeping in touch with developments in the photographic field, and it carries a good range of advertisements for equipment.

✶✶✶ European Community Notes
Qualifications: UK qualifications recognised in EC except Belgium and Germany and EC qualifications in UK.
Languages: To succeed, local language necessary.
Earnings: UK income generally same as elsewhere in the EC.
Setting up: You will find it difficult to succeed in Belgium, France, Germany and Luxembourg. You will find it easier in Denmark, Eire, Greece, Italy, Netherlands, Portugal and Spain. This depends on individual talents, but Belgium, France, Germany and Luxembourg have a large indigenous threshold to break through. Languages are essential and intense market research to establish needs, trends and fashions.
Advice/Training: Advice, information and training not available for those wishing to work in Europe.
Exchanges: Formal job exchanges do not exist.

Hire Shop Owner

Qualifications/Training	No
Income bracket	Low–Medium
Licence	No
Town/Country	Town
Experience/Springboard	Useful
Travel	No
Mid-career entry	Yes
Exit sale	Yes
Entry costs	Highly variable
Work at home	No
Mix and match	Limited.

You could think about: ***Garage owner, Fashion retailer, Sub postmaster, Haulier***

Enquiries
Local hire shops

Hire shops own equipment and derive their income by charging people for borrowing it. There's a massive range of things that people would rather hire than buy: office equipment, cement mixers, sports equipment, televisions, even clothes. Some things can merely be collected from the shop by the customer – eg cutlery, others need to be delivered because they are too large for most customers to be able to transport – eg skips; and others need some additional service – eg public address systems to be wired up.

In general, hiring doesn't require any qualification but you may need some specialist knowledge of what you're hiring –

portable lavatories need to be plumbed into septic tanks, keyboards need to be tuned. Some experience in a field related to whatever you're hiring is useful; it'll give you an insight into some of the less obvious needs of your market and customers may want advice about which model to hire. You'll have to be meticulous to handle all the administrative paper work and to be good at coping with customers, a minority of whom will probably be very difficult or downright dishonest. It is probably best to have some experience of dealing with people before you start on your own if you are to avoid being taken to the cleaners.

Set-up costs vary a lot – obviously the value of what you're supplying affects this. Then there are premises and storage. If you're hiring carpet cleaners, your customers won't necessarily want to inspect a choice, you'll only need somewhere to store them and you can handle most bookings over the telephone. You may need to supply transport for the equipment if it's very large. Some hire businesses can be entirely run by one person; for others, eg marquees, you'll need help, often casual, to erect or install. As the business grows you'll probably want help with administration. Useful contacts, as well as people who may want to hire from you, include people who can lend you a hand from time to time and anybody who can repair and maintain equipment quickly.

Base charges on your overheads and the demand for your service. Hired goods tend to wear out more quickly than your own; they have a lot more use and aren't always treated well. Charge a deposit on anything breakable or, most important, stealable and check everything for damage as it's returned; some things, eg clothes, have to be cleaned between each hire. Make sure that you know where each item is – this will mean having customers' names and addresses; and for things like videos where you have a lot of customers and a lot of transactions it may be worth operating a membership system – issuing cards to customers and sending them regular bills.

Keep an eye on the trade press and add new equipment to your range as it becomes available and as you can afford it. For some things like cars or skis you may be able to sell off your stock from time to time when it is no longer hireable.

Publications for the hire market, *Hire News* and *Hireman*, tend to concentrate on the hire of plant and equipment.

Holiday Accommodation Owner

Qualifications/Training	No
Income bracket	Low–High
Licence	No
Town/Country	Either
Experience/ Springboard	Not necessary
Travel	Possible
Mid-career entry	Good
Exit sale	Excellent
Entry costs	Highly variable
Work at home	No
Mix and match	Yes.

You could think about: *Timeshare developer, Garden centre, Farmer, Import/export broker, Accountant, Riding school owner*

Enquiries
Tourist boards and other owners and agencies

This can involve managing a single cottage or a block of holiday flats: in rural Wales or round Victoria station. It is well suited as a family business. Unless you happen upon the premises before you start, it is highly capital intensive. The banks are generally cautious about the holiday business and you should expect to put up 50 per cent of the money yourself. Some grants from the relevant tourist board may be possible depending on their own cash flow and how keen they are to get tourists into the area.

You should think carefully about the size of the operation. A single cottage in your village may provide pocket money for you as well as headaches; a block of eg 20 flats will be more cost-effective. If you keep your income below the VAT threshold you need not become VAT registered. You will be able to price more competitively but your costs will be higher as you can't claim back the VAT you've charged.

Size is not the only consideration: the situation, whether to be beside the beach or near good salmon fishing; standard of accommodation, jacuzzis all round or just the basics; whether to stay open all year or just in the peak season; parking space for cars, boats or even caravans; whether to encourage singles/couples or families with children in which case you need somewhere for them to play, washing machines and relatively indestructible furnishings.

What you will charge will depend upon these conditions – and the prevailing weather expectations. The more you require payment in advance the fewer the risks of bad debts – though some areas of the country are worse than others for this. If you are well equipped, willing to help and reasonably priced, you can expect a number of recommendations and repeat bookings. This helps in reducing advertising costs. Where you advertise will depend upon your chosen market – the *Lady*, *The Times* or the post office window. There are a number of agencies and the tourist boards are very likely to help.

Whatever the size of your operation, your holidaymakers will need to be able to get hold of someone when they lose their key or the tap leaks, even if it is only a telephone number. You will also need to consider booking people in and out and cleaning on change-over day. If you have more than about a dozen units, you will probably need someone present most of the time although you may be able to inveigle eg a local shopkeeper to cover in emergencies.

The cost of setting up will depend on the cost of local property, the standard of your furnishings and the cost of local labour if necessary. You need good insurance.

You can regard owning holiday accommodation simply as an investment and pay others to manage the business on a day to day basis. Alternatively, you do everything yourself. If you do, you should be practical and resourceful in dealing with emergencies. As with all jobs associated with the tourist industry, you'll be a worker in a world of holidaymakers, and your clients will expect everything to be perfect throughout their stay in your holiday accommodation.

Homeopath

Qualifications/Training	Essential
Income bracket	Medium
Licence	Not yet
Town/Country	Town
Experience/ Springboard	Recommended
Travel	No
Mid-career entry	Yes
Exit sale	No
Entry costs	£5,000
Work at home	Yes
Mix and match	Yes.

You could think about: *Doctor, Journalist, Dispensing chemist, Illustrator, Music teacher*

Enquiries
Society of Homeopaths

Homeopaths heal illnesses ranging from colds to arthritis suffered by patients of any age or background, but using very different methods from conventional doctors. Homeopathy takes an holistic approach to disease, treating the whole patient rather than the symptoms. Not everyone will have the same response to an illness or to a cure; before any treatment is prescribed, the homeopath tries to find out as much as possible about the constitution of the patient as well as the history of the specific illness and its symptoms. In addition, the remedies used by homeopaths are quite different from those used in conventional medicine. Homeopathy stimulates the body's powers of healing itself by prescribing minute amounts of substances that in a healthy person would provoke the symptoms that are being treated. Currently, there is a shortage of homeopathic practitioners as the demand for alternative medicines increases in response to the growing number of illnesses and complaints with which conventional medicine has yet to devise ways of dealing.

There are two ways of qualifying as a homeopathic practitioner. As a registered doctor it is possible to become a homeopath by doing a course through the FACULTY OF HOMEOPATHY. Although this allows you to call on your conventional training as well as homeopathy, there are disadvantages; the approaches of both are so different that much conventional medical training has to be unlearned before you can practise homeopathy with complete conviction. (Homeopathic hospitals are staffed by members of the Faculty of Homeopathy, the only branch of alternative medicine recognised by the NHS.)

The alternative is to do a course at one of several colleges that are associated with the SOCIETY OF HOMEOPATHS. These last for four years, three of theory and one of clinical training. You don't need any special qualifications to get onto them and they're generally taught at weekends with a lot of home study (though there are also full-time courses). If you can't get an LEA grant it will cost you about £3,000 in tuition fees. When you pass the course you become a provisional member of the Society of Homepaths for two years during which you can practise while supervised and undertaking in-service training. After that, as long as you're at least 25, you're a fully registered member, although continued in-service training is expected. While there is no legal requirement for any licence to practise as a homeopath (though see below regarding dispensing) registration with the society is recommended. An EC licence *may* be required in the future. Many people come to homeopathy from other careers. It helps if you're mature enough to cope with some of the very great emotional stresses and strains of dealing with the sick. Patients die and leave friends and relations who need continuing support. Even those who aren't seriously ill can be distressed and distressing. You must be dedicated (and you will be if you've got through the course which is gruelling), be interested in health and healing and good with people.

Set-up costs aren't great as long as you've got somewhere to practise from. This can be in your own home but renting a room in a natural or alternative health centre is a good way of getting more widely known by patients and other practitioners. Also, doctors are increasingly inviting homeopaths to practise with them in GP clinics. Apart from that you need basic stationery and books. This could all cost as little as £200 but a computer with some special software will make life a lot easier and costs about £2,000. The software you need (obtainable from the HOMEOPATHIC BICYCLE CO) works out suggested prescriptions from what you tell it about particular cases and the *materia medica* that you are using – this can save hours of complicated calculations. Because of the amount of information you need to collect about each patient, first consultations usually last about an hour and a half; subsequently they'll be about half an hour. Most homeopaths are in private practice and charge patients per consultation; London homeopaths charge about £50 for the first consultation and £25 subsequently. Many operate a sliding scale, charging less for children, the elderly or those on low incomes. Annual earnings range from £10,000–£20,000 with £12,000–£15,000 being about the norm.

Once you've seen a patient, you have to work out and write the prescription which you either dispense yourself from stocks obtained from a pharmacy or send to a specialist homeopathic pharmacy. Because there aren't many of these around, most operate mail order systems. For the prescriptions you make up yourself you'll need a dispensing licence if you're going to charge but most practitioners avoid this by including the remedies in the basic consultation fee. Homeopathic remedies are inexpensive so this won't cost you much and saves time having to deal with a pharmacy for each prescription. Most patients will come to you (they have to pay extra for a home call) but some need home or hospital visits. Occasionally, you may need to get a patient into hospital as a precaution in case they need emergency surgery. Very rarely will you be called out on an emergency but you need to be on call all of the time unless you can make some arrangement with another homeopath; an answering machine is essential. As long as you can afford it and have a locum, you can have holidays whenever you like.

Although some patients will come to you as a last resort after all else has failed (currently many people with AIDS use homeopaths), there is an increasing number of people who are deciding not to use orthodox medicine and are turning to homeopathy for its own sake for themselves and their children.

For further reading, see the *Science of Homeopathy* and *Homeopathy, Medicine for the 21st Century*. The SOCIETY OF HOMEOPATHS, associate membership of which is open to all, publishes a register of practitioners, a journal and a newsletter.

✶✶ European Community Notes

Qualifications: UK qualifications are not recognised throughout EC but EC qualifications are accepted in UK because homeopaths practise under Common law – but for *registration* each person has to be examined.

Languages: To succeed, local language necessary.

Earnings: Vary in different countries.

Setting up: You will find it difficult to succeed in Belgium, France, Greece, Italy, Luxembourg, Portugal and Spain. You will find it easier in Denmark, Eire, Germany and the Netherlands (also Norway, Sweden and Finland).

Advice/Training: Advice, information and training not available for those wishing to work in Europe.

Exchanges: Formal job exchanges do not exist.

Enquiry point for those wishing to work in the EC: SOCIETY OF HOMEOPATHS.

Notes: There is a *very* wide variation of legislation in different countries.

Hotelier

Qualifications/Training	Recommended
Income bracket	Low–High
Licence	Yes for alcohol
Town/Country	Either
Experience/ Springboard	Recommended
Travel	Local
Mid-career entry	Ideal
Exit sale	Excellent
Entry costs	£150,000++
Work at home	Yes
Mix and match	Possible.

You could think about: *Restaurateur, Caterer, Holiday accommodation owner, Wine merchant, Farmer, Windsurfing school owner*

Enquiries
British Hospitality Association, Hotel and Catering Training Company, Hotel, Catering and Institutional Management Association

Anyone considering a career in the hotel business should think very carefully before going ahead; enjoying a stay in a hotel is very different from doing the entertaining yourself, seven days a week from 7.30 until late. Living over the shop, as is usually the case, may be tax-efficient but you never get away from the problems – no front door to shut the world away! This career is a way of life, its great joy is that a considerable degree of success can be achieved without a lot of training.

There are all sorts of formal courses in hotel management – at catering or FE college or degree courses at a poly or university. Check with the HOTEL AND CATERING TRAINING COMPANY (HCTC). But someone striking out on their own usually relies upon a short intensive course such as those offered by the HCTC, some of the FE colleges etc, and at private cookery schools such as CORDON BLEU or LEITHS; and the WINE AND SPIRIT EDUCATION TRUST runs excellent courses on the drinks side of the business. One way of getting the knowledge you'll need if you want to avoid costly mistakes is through working for a good hotel as a general assistant (badly paid and long hours) for at least a year. Find one similar to the sort of hotel that you want to set up. Staying in hotels (buying the product), is also essential research for anyone who hasn't been properly trained, and is something that you won't have much time for once you've set up yourself. If you want to serve wine and have a bar, you need a residential liquor licence, and for non-residential diners a restaurant licence. You can get these as long as you're considered suitable and as long as the building complies with certain regulations. It's more difficult to get a full on-licence that lets you serve booze without food. You need a fire certificate if six or more people are to be accommodated. Environmental health officers can walk in at any time to assure themselves that the premises – and staff – comply with regulations and if you're converting other property into an hotel you'll need to get planning permission. Certainly, the food side is heavily, and increasingly regulated. See Restaurateur entry for details, but essentially all 'eating houses' have to be registered with the local authority and all commercial preparation and cooking of food products, and the premises, are subject to inspection by EHOs – who can not merely shut you down but have you fined and even imprisoned if you don't come up to the mark!

Think clearly about the market you're aiming for before you set up as chopping and changing is bad for business. Affinity with your guests allows you to compete with large, impersonal but well-financed chains because of the friendlier atmosphere you can build up. There is a vast range of hotels from which to choose. One of the basic considerations is whether to cater principally for business visitors (in which case you'll most likely be in a town, serving bed, breakfast and, possibly, dinner from Monday to Thursday), or for people on holiday (when you'll most likely be in the country or at a tourist centre, and will have busier weekends than weeks). On the whole, business hotels need to emphasise efficient and professional service while people on weekend breaks are more impressed by your personality and the hotel's character. Rural hotels may be more pleasant to live in but tend to take longer to become established, require you to travel more to get your supplies and provide slower capital growth on your investment. Staff may also be difficult to find and are more likely to need accommodation/transport home when you do find them.

You can buy a going concern (agents or look in *Caterer and Hotelkeeper*, the *Morning Advertiser* or *Dalton's Weekly*). This may be good value if it is well done up but has been badly run. However, if you do this you may inherit an unwanted reputation or clientele that are hard to lose. Never underestimate the cost in time and money of a garden, therapeutic though it may be. Hotels aren't cheap, they start at about £150,000 and a modest-sized hotel in a good trading position can cost £500,000. (Buying a house and converting it won't cost much less.) However, people are prepared to pay for comfort and good food, and you can make a living although running costs cut what look like massive gross profits very quickly. Unless you've got a lot of working capital, you'll have to do most of the work yourself; consider a partner – 'two owners can do the work of six employees'. Staff create their own problems, however excellent they are and however well they get on with you personally. On the whole staff turnover is pretty high in this business.

For your first clients, contact local hotels and pubs for their turnaways and local businesses for their visitors. Advertising is expensive and can prove to be bad value if you haven't done enough research. The English and the Regional Tourist Boards have useful publications as does the BRITISH HOSPITALITY ASSOCIATION for its members. Get onto your local large town's accommodation register and, once you're good enough, try and get into guides like *Egon Ronay*, *Good Hotel*, *Good Food*, *Michelin*, *Ashley Courtenay*, AA, and RAC.

Running a hotel demands total commitment to the job which is, above all, about caring for people, both guests and staff. This might make it less suitable for people with young families but some manage, with notable success: it can even be one of the big attractions – a hotel where small persons are actively welcomed and properly accommodated rather than the customary freeze-out. The long and unsocial hours, with meals grabbed whenever they can be fitted in, require a strong constitution. The main advantage is that success lies mainly in your own ability as a host and your own sound financial judgment.

⁂ European Community Notes

Qualifications: A number of UK qualifications recognised throughout EC and EC qualifications in UK.

Languages: Whether local language is necessary or not to succeed will depend on the field and the country.

Advice/Training: Advice, information and training available for those wishing to work in Europe.

Exchanges: Formal job exchanges exist.

Enquiry point for those wishing to work in the EC: BRITISH HOSPITALITY ASSOCIATION.

Notes: It is hard to be specific when the range of possibilities is so vast. There are numerous stories of UK nationals succeeding in their pursuits; by how much tales of failure exceed them is not known.

House Converter

Qualifications/Training	Available
Income bracket	Low–High
Licence	No
Town/Country	Either
Experience/Springboard	Essential
Travel	Local
Mid-career entry	Yes
Exit sale	Possible
Entry costs	£50,000++
Work at home	Possible
Mix and match	Yes.

You could think about: ***Builder, Property developer, Surveyor, Property manager, Estate agent, Landlord***

Enquiries
Local estate agents

This entails buying up a single property, renovating or converting it and selling it again. It is not advisable to do this on your own home unless you and your family are able to cope with enormous disruptions in your domestic arrangements. Beware, it requires a rising house market; also it's a crowded market and in the South-east you'll need to find £100,000+ for the development and building before you start converting it.

You can make more money out of buying a house and converting it into a number of smaller units than simply renovating. You may lose friends if you acquire a reputation for buying up all the run-down cottages in the area, doing them up to a high standard and selling them as second homes.

Banks, by and large, understand lending money against bricks and mortar so are likely to be reasonably helpful; even so, they will only lend two-thirds of the sum and that on your own collateral. They need a well-presented package rather than a cigarette packet sketch. The amount which you will need to start off, and the profits you can make, will both depend upon local property prices and the state of the market. If house prices tremble while you're working on a house, you may be lucky to recoup your costs. Unless you are working in an area with exceptionally high property prices there is probably little profit to be had unless you can do the bulk of the work yourself, sub-contracting only the specialised work; on the other hand, it is quicker to subcontract all the work and co-ordinate it yourself. You need to know your contractors will work fast for you. To remain liquid you must be able to turn the property round quickly. If you're developing listed buildings or properties with preservation orders your plans may need to be passed by eg the VICTORIAN SOCIETY who will take time. Planning permission and building regulations can slow you down, depending on the local authority, and this needs to be considered when you are selecting properties. If you're operating as a business, you're subject to corporation tax or income tax; if it's a side line, to capital gains tax.

There are no formal qualifications except the eye for a property with potential; if you're in doubt about the structure, consult a surveyor before buying. If you are not a competent builder yourself, you should be able to communicate effectively with your contractors; local authority officials will always be part of your life and you should be able to live with them too. Your money needs to be tied up for as little time as possible and the vagaries of government economic policy, particularly the level of interest rates, need close monitoring if you are to come out with a profit. The work needs to be carefully scheduled, eg try not to change the roof of a house in January or put a seaside property on the market in November.

Hypnotherapist

Qualifications/Training	Yes
Income bracket	Low–Medium
Licence	No
Town/Country	Town
Experience/Springboard	No
Travel	No
Mid-career entry	Recommended
Exit sale	No
Entry costs	£1,000
Work at home	Possible
Mix and match	Excellent.

You could think about: *Counsellor, Music teacher, Market research interviewer, Graphic designer, Proofreader/copy editor*

Enquiries
Hypnotherapists

A hypnotherapist treats conditions, controlled by the subconscious, through the use of hypnosis. The best qualification for hypnotherapy is the experience of life, and it's therefore not a good choice for the very young person. It's not usually regarded as a full-time career on its own because it doesn't always guarantee enough money to live on. For these reasons, it is often practised by retired people and by those – usually women – who have some other form of income.

Hypnotherapy bears very little relation to the popular image of hypnosis as portrayed on the television. A hypnotherapist cannot – and would not want to – make a client do or say something against his or her will. The mind is a very powerful tool, and the hypnotherapist knows how to communicate with it at both conscious and subconscious levels.

The accepted formal qualification is a course in psychotherapy and hypnosis at one of the specialist colleges, like the UK TRAINING COLLEGE OF HYPNOTHERAPY AND COUNSELLING (this holds weekend and evening courses in central London, Bristol, Edinburgh and Dublin). Training takes three years and costs around £1,000 a year, but some of this can be recouped by going into practice once you've completed the first year. There are other hypnotherapy schools and training centres, many of which advertise in magazines, such as *Here's Health* and the *Journal of Alternative and Complementary Medicine*. Good books to read if you're interested in taking up hypnotherapy are *Hypnosis: Guide for Patients and Practitioners*; *Hypnosis*; and *Hypnosis: A Gateway to Better Health*.

It's useful to have experienced personal problems yourself and to have worked through them with the help of therapy. This will give you a good grasp of what it's all about and a healthy conviction that it can indeed work. The most important quality of all is an interest in people. You've got to be a good listener, to be highly sensitive and, above all, to care. There's no point in going into it for the money alone.

All you really need is a comfortable chair or couch, a telephone and, ideally, an answering machine which enables you to pull out the plug during a session so that the telephone doesn't disturb you. Some hypnotherapists use tapes, in which case you'll need a couple of inexpensive tape recorders perhaps costing £40 or so.

Hypnotherapy is not yet as popular a form of therapy, as, say, osteopathy, though it has the approval of many orthodox practitioners and is fast gaining ground. But it is not always easy to set yourself up in practice. Depending on where you live, you could start by charging around £15 an hour; £20 is about average. Once you're established, with good contacts and good publicity, you might be able to earn as much as £40 an hour, though this is not common.

Most hypnotherapists see five or six clients a day, and work only three days a week. It can be a draining process and some therapists feel that many more than that would be not only exhausting for the therapist but unfair on the clients. A few see up to 60 clients in a week, though that's far from usual. A lot of experienced hypnotherapists like to devote some of their time to teaching and to sharing some of their expertise with others.

The surest way of getting work is by recommendation. Advertising in local papers can work but word of mouth is the best way, particularly through any sympathetic local doctor. Application and perseverance are the key factors. You won't see many clients at Christmas or in the summer holidays but expect a sudden influx of clients if there's something about hypnotherapy on the television or in the press.

Ii

Illustrator

Qualifications/Training	Recommended
Income bracket	Medium
Licence	No
Town/Country	Town
Experience/Springboard	No
Travel	Some
Mid-career entry	Unlikely
Exit sale	No
Entry costs	£50
Work at home	Yes
Mix and match	Excellent.

You could think about: *Artist, Graphic designer, Artists' agent, Book packager, Greyhound trainer*

Enquiries
Association of Illustrators

Illustrating books, magazines and newspapers is one of the most attractive jobs available to artists who would like to make their name in their own right, but want to take on commissions to ensure an income. There has been an extraordinary boom in magazine and in-house journal publishing, and a strong demand for artwork for audio-visual presentations. This surge in demand coupled with easy availability of fax machines has provided stability in what has traditionally been seen as an insecure way of life.

The work can involve long hours and tight deadlines followed by periods of inactivity. Commissions come from book, magazine or newspaper editorial or art desks and range from imaginative book jacket illustrations to painstaking technical drawings of buildings or machinery to a caricature of the Prime Minister. Most illustrators specialise in a particular field and build up a 'stable' of clients. Successful illustrators can set their own fees – say, £200 for a decent drawing, and earnings of at least £500 per week when you're up and running.

A foundation course at art school, followed by a vocational course which includes options in printing, layout and design and illustration are the usual qualifications. If you want to go straight into freelance work, you will then have to put together a portfolio of work and start the long, weary business of selling yourself to the right people – the book, magazine and newspaper editors and designers who can give you work.

You will have to set up a studio, with a drawing board and storage space for materials. You may need some special equipment, such as a light box, a compressor for an airbrush, a Grant machine, and you may also need accounts with artists' suppliers, typesetting companies (if you are producing annotated artwork) and motorbike messengers.

To be successful, you need to be outgoing, able to sell yourself; your work must be fast, accurate and imaginative. You may have to work from a minimal brief – some book jacket illustrators have no more than a set of proofs to work from – or you may be given complicated instructions which must be followed to the last detail. If you want to specialise in cartoon illustrations you will have to be quick-witted – and since it's often topical you'll be expected to turn it round quickly. Contacts, as ever, are like old gold. It is an unavoidable fact that to really get on you'll have to come to London. Later you can wander wherever Red Star and a fax will take you but 99 times out of 100, if you want to make a viable splash you'll need to get known in London first.

The ASSOCIATION OF ILLUSTRATORS publishes a magazine and has a recommendation service. Illustrators may also be members of the GRAPHICAL, PAPER AND MEDIA UNION, the CHARTERED SOCIETY OF DESIGNERS or, on newspapers, the NATIONAL UNION OF JOURNALISTS.

Import/Export Broker

Qualifications/Training	No
Income bracket	Medium–High
Licence	No
Town/Country	Either
Experience/Springboard	Essential
Travel	Possible
Mid-career entry	Excellent
Exit sale	Yes
Entry costs	Bank credit
Work at home	Possible
Mix and match	Yes.

You could think about: *UK correspondent (overseas media), Foreign correspondent, Property developer, Shipbroker, Accountant, Holiday accommodation owner*

Enquiries
British Overseas Trade Board

You can import and export an enormous variety of products and services – legally – between two industrialised countries, between the East and West, and of course between the Third World and the industrialised North. Carpets, floodlighting, fruit and vegetables, oil industry supplies, books, print, machine tools . . . You can switch from product to product but the key to this job is to establish market know-how and a personal niche.

In this business, networks are all. If you have those, the only other musts are a telephone and access to a telex, fax or electronic mail. There are no essential qualifications and you do not need to be authorised by anybody to act as an import/export broker. You need to involve your own capital only until you start receiving income, apart from the cost of setting up an office. Banks finance thousands of transactions every week, using standard documentation and insurance, including government guarantees where appropriate – they usually want 23–30 per cent cover before opening a letter of credit. There is little personal risk so long as you stick to recognised well-established UK banks and ensure that your business is only conducted on terms of confirmed letters of credit for every transaction. A good relationship with a bank manager is important for speed and efficiency and because you'll need credit standing while you wait for payments to come through.

You can usefully team up with someone whose networks complement your own – and if you specialise in importing from or exporting to a particular country, a reliable and trustworthy local partner or agent and/or supplier is vital for distribution and quality control. You can work from a rustic cottage while renting a busy-sounding metropolitan address, complete with telephone number and telex, if that suits you. They will ring through telephone messages and telexes and forward your mail. You can start up with access to either demand or supply although starting with demand is easier.

Because of the need for networks, it is especially suited to people in mid-career – particularly those leaving an industry with good contacts in it. If you know that you want to set up as a broker in a particular industry, it often pays to take a job first to establish your networks.

You can do as much or as little work as you need; you will have to work odd hours if you are dealing with countries in very different time zones. The essence of the job is to introduce suppliers and purchasers at prices, quality and delivery dates acceptable to both. You can let them worry about customs, shipping, and red tape but it's worth your while making sure that they have all the right permits otherwise the goods won't get through the relevant customs, they'll lose the deal and you your commission. All you have to worry about is getting the price right. Remember that the market may be very competitive and that to gain a foothold you should be prepared to keep the margin for commission very low. Keep an open mind – people have succeeded in exporting flowers to Holland and snow ploughs to the Middle East but importers and exporters can lose a lot if they can't sell; in addition to shipping costs, VAT and customs duty are irredeemable and paid on nearly all imports.

Further information from the BRITISH OVERSEAS TRADE BOARD or through *Export*.

Impresario

Qualifications/Training	No
Income bracket	Low–High
Licence	No
Town/Country	Town
Experience/Springboard	Essential
Travel	Yes
Mid-career entry	Possible
Exit sale	Possible
Entry costs	£10,000++
Work at home	Yes
Mix and match	Yes.

You could think about: *Concert agent, Orchestral fixer, Music critic, Festival director*

Enquiries	
Impresarios	

Impresarios engage an orchestra, opera or dance company and take financial responsibility for their performance. The most important skill is an ability to work quickly and accurately with figures. Accountancy training is helpful but not essential. No academic or practical musical training is necessary. The local library can help you acquire the good general knowledge of music and musicians which is necessary. Ideal qualities are a phlegmatic temperament, patience, diplomacy and an organising ability. Physical and psychological stamina are required to withstand high levels of anxiety while waiting to see if your inspired idea for a concert series will attract the public or leave you financially drained. Confidence in your own judgement is vital.

Start by working as a gofer for an impresario and read the files. When you have acquired contacts and feel sufficiently confident to work alone, you need a room, telephone and typewriter. A computer, fax and more sophisticated office equipment will make life easier when you can afford it. You do not have to join a union. Useful books are the *British Music Year Book*, the *British Association of Concert Agents List of Artists*, *Grove's Dictionary of Music* and any record catalogues you can find.

Begin by approaching local authorities about promoting concerts jointly. Circularise artists about acting as their agent. For the first two years or so, earnings will be low, rising to over £90,000 when you are well established. Working hours will be irregular, up to 18 a day if you have to attend an evening performance. Allow some thinking time each day to create and develop your ideas. The job is lonely and you will be responsible for taking painful decisions and working in an area of high financial risk. There will be some travelling though a car is not essential. You meet interesting people and have the satisfaction of making things happen. The job is never boring.

In-Company Trainer

Qualifications/Training	Recommended
Income bracket	Medium–High
Licence	No
Town/Country	Town
Experience/Springboard	Essential
Travel	Yes
Mid-career entry	Essential
Exit sale	Possible
Entry costs	£20,000+
Work at home	Not recommended
Mix and match	Yes.

You could think about: *Marketing consultant, Computer consultant, Picture restorer, Gardener/garden designer, Journalist, Desktop publisher, Media trainer*

Enquiries
In-company trainers

There is growing demand to independent in-company trainers who will train other people's employees to do anything from answer the phone to manage a multi-national: many large companies with their own training departments augment their resources with outside help especially in specialist fields; many smaller companies don't want a permanent training staff themselves but find that they need to provide some sort of training from time to time. Independent trainers may also provide courses for the public in, for example, time management, sales techniques or marketing.

Client companies won't hand over their staff training to someone they know nothing about. You need credibility and contacts to set up on your own and, although some people get there earlier, you're unlikely to have collected enough of either until you're at least 40. In the meantime, there are two main routes you could follow. The first is through working in industry to management level and building up training experience in, say, personnel, sales or in the training department itself. The second is the academic route where, via a second degree (preferably an MBA) you are employed to teach but meanwhile develop contacts in industry and workable training programmes before springboarding. This second route is more prevalent in the US, where links between industry and higher education are stronger. Some trainers start after they have written a fantastically well received specialist book, using it as the flagship for a programme of training courses which they teach themselves, or front and delegate.

In-company trainers need to be at the forefront of training, able to identify new areas where there's a training need, and analytical enough to develop training programmes which succeed in filling those gaps. Communication skills and the patience to deal with trainees of a vast range of ability are also necessary. Essential equipment for setting up is an office and a manned telephone. You'll certainly need a car and should set up near a commercial or industrial centre. Training generates a lot of paper work (handouts for the training programmes etc) so a word processor and a photocopier are essential. In addition, although you can hire them, you're advised to have your own flip charts, projector and video equipment. You don't need your own training premises; they are expensive to maintain and anyway clients usually provide their own. If they don't or if you're running a course for the public you can hire college or university accommodation during the holidays or simply book into a hotel or conference centre. You can expect to spend £20,000–£30,000 pa on materials and administration.

Because training is intensive and hard work (you're talking to an audience all day), you shouldn't plan to do more than about three days a week actually training people. Set your fees accordingly. Start off by quoting your upper limit so that you can let yourself be bargained down. Some clients have fixed prices in which case you must decide whether the job's worth taking. If you're planning a course for the public you'll have to base your prices on competition and the number of people you expect to attend. You may develop a series of off the peg courses and this can work but many clients will want modifications to suit their own needs. It is most important for your business that you find out as much as you can about the organisational structure of the company whose employees you're training – you are, in effect, an intruder in a client's sub-culture when you're working there.

As an in-company trainer you may not need many different company clients as long as those you do have have large enough staffs. You won't need to advertise. You'll find that clients approach you through your network of contacts, and that people moving to another company will use you again there.

Clients will usually give you about two months' notice when they're going to need you; occasionally they may call on you in an emergency at only two–three weeks' notice. You almost always start with a preliminary meeting to discuss the nature of the course and its structure; it's there that you agree fees and settle payment schedules. After that meeting it's up to you to design and write handouts and other training material, inspect premises and hire the equipment you'll need if the client cannot provide it. The busy season is from September–April when companies are more likely to have new staff. Holiday times are quieter.

Independent Financial Adviser

Qualifications/Training	Recommended
Income bracket	Medium–High
Licence	Yes
Town/Country	Town
Experience/Springboard	Essential
Travel	Local
Mid-career entry	Yes
Exit sale	Possible
Entry costs	£12,000+
Work at home	Yes
Mix and match	Yes.

You could think about: *Stockbroker, Insurance broker, Futures broker, Disco owner/DJ, Timeshare developer, Novelist*

Enquiries	
FIMBRA	

These are the people who help private clients get the most from their money by advising them on the financial products and services offered by companies operating investment schemes, pension plans and life assurance policies. Independent financial advisers act as intermediaries between these companies and clients. You can if you want work as an agent for one of these companies but this restricts you to their products only.

In contrast, independent financial advisers may use any of the wide range of products on the market. You have great flexibility. Each transaction requires wide familiarity with the market and much of your time selecting what to advise. Clients usually prefer your impartiality and it's easy for you to extend your range of activities by offering (and charging for) a more general financial advisory service that doesn't always end with buying. Many people, including investors, home owners, the self-employed and small businesses, want help with financial decisions from someone other than their accountant and bank manager.

You must be authorised by a self-regulatory body before you set up on your own. For independent financial advisers this is virtually always FIMBRA (Financial Intermediaries, Managers and Brokers Regulatory Association) and means demonstrating that you are 'fit and proper' to conduct your proposed business. Exactly what this entails depends on the nature of the business you're going to carry out; roughly speaking you'll need at least three years' relevant experience to be registered as an individual able to deal directly with the public in an advisory capacity (1992 also sees the intoduction of the Financial Advisers' Competence Test and Financial Planning Certificate). As a company registered under the Financial Services Act, you must be solvent and trustworthy (no chance if you've got a criminal record). FIMBRA judges each case individually; it takes only four weeks on average to accept you into membership providing your application is straightforward and well presented and that there is no difficulty with collecting references.

You need to be creative and imaginative, with the experience and judgement to choose the best from a wide range and the ability to put your proposals into effect quickly. Seeing options is even more important than being a wizard figure juggler. This is very much a people industry, communication skills are important – clients must always understand what you're recommending and see you as someone whose judgement they can trust.

To set up you need to be easily accessible to clients, many of whom will want to see you outside normal office hours – at lunchtime and in the evening. As well as equipping yourself with a calculator, telephone, word processor/computer and filing cabinets make sure that you have a suitably professional image. Very rapidly, you may need to acquire an office and employ someone to answer the phone and deal with correspondence. Setting up as a partnership lets you share overheads.

Much of your income will come in commission from the companies whose products you are selling. Some companies offer massive commission, tempting, but long-term success depends on happy customers rather than a temporarily healthy bank balance. You are now obliged to disclose full details of the commission you will get on any of the transactions you recommend so your client can assess your objectivity. Partly in response to this and partly in a move to increase the overall professionalism of the business, some financial advisers now charge clients consultation fees or charge fees in addition to receiving commissions when business is placed, as it may not be appropriate to do business with a client at every client meeting.

A lot of clients come through personal recommendation. Start off with people you know; then try advertising, PR, and perhaps run seminars to tell people about what you do and how you could help them. Target a selected market (eg, self-employed, doctors, teachers) and become known as a specialist in that field, this may also help to increase the amount of media coverage and interest you generate. At your first meeting with new clients you must collect all relevant information about them and their finances. This helps you to see a wider range of options than the client may have realised existed. On the strength of this information you can make some general recommendations before selecting which products are best and transacting their purchase. It is important to keep in regular touch with clients (six months to a year) to ensure they are aware of any changes in financial legislation that may affect them (pension changes for example) and make sure that you keep up with their changing financial position. It can be a very time-consuming job, there's a lot of follow-up work from every meeting. Make sure that you book time off to avoid getting bogged down.

Read *Money Management* and *Marketing Week* to keep abreast of what's going on.

Indexer

Qualifications/Training	Recommended
Income bracket	Low
Licence	No
Town/Country	Either
Experience/Springboard	No
Travel	No
Mid-career entry	Good
Exit sale	Yes
Entry costs	£1,000+
Work at home	Yes
Mix and match	Yes.

You could think about:
Proofreader/copy-editor, Sub-editor, Word processor, Musician, Tourist guide

Enquiries: Society of Indexers

Indexers index. They don't catalogue. they don't compile contents lists itemising parts of a document such as chapters and tables. They do provide a key to a document in the enquirers' own terms – single words, technical terms, abbreviations, acronyms, phrases, or name, rank and number. All rather book-bound on the face of it but not necessarily so: indexers employ the term document generically to include not only a book/series of books or periodicals but audiotapes, videotapes, maps, pictures, computer discs – indeed any other print or non-print information-carrying artefact. So the job involves applying specific technical skills to any aspect of human knowledge, tackling an almost infinite diversity of concepts, terms, vocabulary and most subjects from the standpoint of an inquirer.

As an indexer you must be capable of confronting information that is entirely new to you. So you'll need to be able to recognise the chief concepts of a document, anticipate the ways users will look for information in it and choose the appropriate terms under which to index. In medical, scientific, legal and technical work you'll probably need at least a good first degree.

It's also claimed by the SOCIETY OF INDEXERS that good indexers require an innate talent for the task, that without it no amount of teaching will equip you. But you'll need technical training too. Believe it or not, there are closely defined British Standards for indexing which can be formally taught, learned and examined. The SOCIETY OF INDEXERS has an open learning programme which, after passing five formal exams, can give you the status of Accredited Indexer. That demonstrates theoretical competence. Professionally, you'll probably want to become a Registered Indexer which will require you to demonstrate practical competence by submitting an index you've compiled in the last couple of years that is published or about to be published.

Is it worth all the bother? As essentially a freelance occupation, you'll need to hustle for work, cultivate contacts with publishers' editors and organise your life to make concentrated work possible while surviving as a business. Don't expect to be paid much for your efforts and don't expect to be paid on time. The SOCIETY OF INDEXERS recommends a minimum fee for its members (currently £9.95 per hour for the simplest index, rising to £15.00 for the most taxing), but if you are not a fully-registered member you will probably be paid less than the recommended minimum rate. Publishers are willing to pay a higher rate to society members because they feel they will be guaranteed a certain standard of work. Simple indexes are often compiled in house or at a rate similar to that paid for proofreading. Some authors prefer to compile their own indexes, particularly when writing in a specialist area.

Your contribution is likely to be held in great esteem by the writer, desk editors and others concerned with the quality of the text; although the standard publishing contract dumps the cost of indexing firmly on authors, they value the indexer because they know that many of their peers (and almost all reviewers) start with the index. That's one advantage of the job for starters.

The entry costs are low, as all you need is a personal computer, word-processor or typewriter, telephone, desk and headed stationery. And it's a wonderfully flexible job. Each commission is firmly delineated in terms of the document you are indexing and you know when you are going to have to deliver. Otherwise your time is your own, although it is quite another thing to ensure a smooth flow of work. Indexers defy characterisation: it's an ideal job to mix and match so all sorts of people do it. The only characteristic common to successful indexers is a certain type of logical thinking combined with a good eye for detail. You can work anywhere you choose (providing its accessible for the dispatch and delivery of inevitably urgent proofs) and it's usual to work at home.

The SOCIETY OF INDEXERS publishes a list of indexers who undertake commissions and distributes it free to a large number of publishers; and publishers use it. To keep up technically, you'll want to read the Society's journal *The Indexer*. To find out what's involved in the job, try reading about the principles in G. Norman

Knight's *Indexing, the Art: a guide to the indexing of books and periodicals*, Margaret Anderson's *Book Indexing* and check out British Standards to see what's involved in practice, particularly computer indexing.

✳ European Community Notes

Specialist professional societies for indexers are known to be found only in English-speaking countries and Japan. We know of none within any European Community member state other than Eire, which has its own small but active branch of the British SOCIETY OF INDEXERS. This does not mean that they do not exist – they could easily be specialist divisions of professional bodies with a more general remit in the field of information librarian/scientist. Little is known about the position in the EC at the international level. *The Society of Indexers* is considering organising an international conference to attempt to elucidate the position.

Instrumental Soloist

Qualifications/Training	Essential
Income bracket	Low–High
Licence	No
Town/Country	Town
Experience/Springboard	No
Travel	Lots
Mid-career entry	Unlikely
Exit sale	No
Entry costs	£2,000+
Work at home	No
Mix and match	Probably essential.

You could think about: ***Orchestral musician, Music teacher, Conductor, Chamber group director, Counsellor, Photographer***

Enquiries	

Musicians' Union

This is someone who gives solo recitals and plays with orchestras. You need an aggressive agent, some talent, plenty of confidence and the will to succeed. Most important of all, you need a really good teacher – ask around amongst professional instrumentalists who play your particular instrument. Going to music college is not essential but it's more fun than private tuition. University will provide a wider view of life so long as you have regular lessons; a sport or a hobby will avoid an obsessional preoccupation with the instrument and provide the necessary balance. You must be independent and healthy. It's a lonely and tiring life with long hours or rehearsal, often in hotel bedrooms before a concert. Foreign languages are useful if you work internationally. Always look smart, organise yourself, answer letters and telephone calls promptly; it's all good PR. Learn to speak fluently to your audience, concert promoters and the media. The ideal soloist is an extrovert with charm, always amenable (temperamental tantrums are out of date) and more interested in music than self. The punters can spot someone on an ego trip.

You will need a really good instrument, telephone, somewhere quiet to practise (and avoid disturbing neighbours), cassette recorder for making demo tapes and taking timings for conductors, metronome and electronic tuner: concert pitch varies in different countries. Always have a good accountant and join the MUSICIANS' UNION. You need access to the *British Music Year Book* and *Grove's Dictionary of Music*.

It's important that your name gets known and stays known; so try and win a national or international competition. Solo engagements alone may not provide a living: you are always likely to need to supplement by orchestral work or teaching and adjudicating. Starting fee is £80 per concert but once you're successful, you can make £100,000++ pa.

Specialise in a certain style or period of music; make a name in that before expanding. Make sure your name is constantly in the press, on radio or TV. If you have £10,000 to spare you can hire an orchestra, conductor and hall for a concert in which you play concertos and invite agents and critics from the national press. You can make a recording the same way, as long as a good record company can be persuaded to accept and distribute it.

You are independent and free of organisational ties in this life but must be able to cope with loneliness and professional jealousy – a phenomenon of success. Constant travelling will interfere with your marriage and social life so your partner needs other interests. Maintaining your high standard of performance becomes difficult as you get older: you tire more easily. Arthritis can devastate your career.

European Community Notes

Highly international business. No problems working in other member states. Don't go on spec – get an engagement and your contract checked (the Musicians' Union will do this) before you set off.

Insurance Broker

Qualifications/Training	Essential
Income bracket	Low–High
Licence	Yes
Town/Country	Town
Experience/Springboard	Essential
Travel	Local
Mid-career entry	Good
Exit sale	Yes
Entry costs	£1,000
Work at home	Possible
Mix and match	Possible.

You could think about: *Estate agent, Conveyancer, List broker, Newsletter publisher*

Enquiries

British Insurance & Investment Brokers' Association (BIIBA)

Insurance brokers are independent registered intermediaries acting on behalf of their clients between insurance companies and underwriters. Their clients are people or businesses who want insurance cover; also advice on how to get the best and most appropriate cover. The amount of work, and the sum of money involved, varies a lot from insuring a second-hand car to providing the full range of cover required by a large manufacturing or retailing company. Your business will tend to depend on where you are and the size of your firm. Smaller firms tend to look after smaller policies leaving most large-scale business and industrial firms to larger brokers, most of which are in London.

Having discussed the client's needs the broker has to decide which insurance company or companies can provide the best deal. For example, to insure a house and contents you may want to use different companies to provide cover for the building, the contents, and individual valuable items in the house. You then liaise and negotiate with the company to provide cover and act on behalf of the client on any subsequent claims. Brokers who are members of Lloyd's of London deal directly with underwriters, otherwise, the insurance company does it for you.

As a broker you have to register with the INSURANCE BROKERS' REGISTRATION COUNCIL (IBRC). To qualify for that you need five years' experience or three years' experience and associateship of the CHARTERED INSURANCE INSTITUTE (this means passing exams – there are various ways to train for these, usually by day release, evening class or correspondence course). You'll also have to present accounts regularly to the IBRC and satisfy them of your solvency. If you're going to handle a majority of life assurance you also have to be regulated under the Financial Services Act by an appropriate regulatory body, eg FIMBRA.

Accountancy experience is a useful background. Brokers need to know a lot about insurance, to have sound financial sense and good communication skills so that they can negotiate effectively with companies and cope with clients. In many cases clients will be parting with a lot of money under your guidance so it's important that they should trust you.

To set up you need a telephone and a word processor. Answering machines don't inspire confidence or cope adequately with enquiries. You'll need some letterheads and a rubber stamp (so that insurance companies know your clients' policy application forms come from you and pay you commission). Reduce the risk of mistakes by organising an efficient logging system with records of daily incoming and outgoing post and money. You'll have to apply to underwriters to be their agent and they will probably want to have a reference from your bank. The more experience you have and the better known you are within the industry the easier this will be to arrange. Some underwriters will only grant agencies to brokers who sell a minimum annual premium on their behalf, this is usually quite low (about £5,000) but it has to be kept up. You're paid commission by the underwriter; this is usually 10 per cent of the premiums you generate for them.

A lot of clients come via word of mouth or advertising. One of the characteristics of a small brokerage is that they can get to know their clients better. Most of the work has to be done during office hours when insurance companies are open. This means a lot of time on the phone finding the best policies, reminding clients to fill in their forms, confirming premiums and policies etc. Make sure that you always quote the right premium to clients because you're responsible for any mistakes you make. Underwriters and companies will keep you informed of rate changes and will give a quotation for each premium.

This is a competitive business and although the bulk of your clients will stay with you for most of their cover some areas are unpredictable (eg car insurance) because people change their policies frequently.

The CHARTERED INSURANCE INSTITUTE publishes the *Insurance Journal* which gives news of what's going on in the industry.

European Community Notes
Qualifications: UK qualifications recognised throughout EC and EC qualifications in UK although each country has its own regulations concerning fitness to practise, capital, etc.

Languages: To succeed, local language necessary.
Earnings: Huge range of earnings by different individuals; impossible to generalise.
Setting up: You will find it difficult to succeed in Spain. You will find it easier in Denmark and Germany.
Advice/Training: Advice, information and training for those wishing to work in Europe available to members of the BIIBA.
Exchanges: Formal job exchanges exist through commercial contacts.
Enquiry point for those wishing to work in the EC: BIIBA.
Recommended reading: International Broker.

Get a thorough grounding in the business in Britain first; make sure you've learnt the language. Then start in a large UK brokers' office in the European country of your choice before becoming independent.

Interior Designer

Qualifications/Training	Recommended
Income bracket	Low–High
Licence	No
Town/Country	Mostly town
Experience/Springboard	No
Travel	Local
Mid-career entry	Yes
Exit sale	No
Entry costs	£5,000++
Work at home	Possible
Mix and match	Yes.

You could think about: *Antique furniture restorer, Upholsterer, Exhibition designer, Events organiser, House converter, Builder, Naturopath*

Enquiries	
Local interior designers	

Throughout the go-go Eighties, interior design was an expanding field. While the boom years have vanished people *do* still move home or, just as usefully, stay where they are and so feel the need to do the place up. Many people, having successfully 'designed' their own homes, are motivated to develop this into a career that calls for flair, professionalism and extremely hard work. It is not something that can be dabbled at if you want a thriving business. Formal training may not be necessary but you'll need a reliable team of builder / plumber / electrician / decorator/ carpet-layer/track-fitter (and that's just the start!).

You can train through specialist courses of one year to a few weeks, weekends or day/evening classes. A feel for cloth and precision cutting is helpful until you can afford outworkers. A sound business sense is needed (book keeping essential), a love of interiors and a willingness to constantly learn. Small commissions can be undertaken from home. If you're ambitious you'll soon find you want to buy or rent premises. The right location will bring passing trade. Publicity, if needed other than through recommendations, should be in local magazines and papers.

The initial cost of setting up at home is approximately £300, then you'll need probably several hundred pattern books, which cost £30–£60 each. The trade is very clannish; find a friendly trade rep, get taken seriously. Go to trade fairs, keep abreast of latest fashions through show-room open days, seminars, make contacts. Try designing fabric manufacturers' show-rooms and trade stands (good publicity and own stand very expensive). Keep trade fair catalogues for future reference. Many manufacturers require an initial order of £250.

It is most important that you take a 50 per cent deposit (or more) before ordering fabric, wallpaper, fittings. You will undoubtedly learn from your mistakes. A difficult customer can prolong payment on any pretext to reduce the final bill. It may be necessary to use a debt-collecting agency. Print your conditions clearly on the back of estimates. Outworkers will become necessary; the best tend to approach you, or train your own. Watch that they don't pass on trade secrets to competitors. Collect a stable of individual craftsmen:

ceramics (lamps, tiles), textiles (reflect a theme), artists (stencilling, wall murals). All will give you an individual style and prompt commissions.

It is possible to specialise, in fabrics (curtains, loose covers, cushions, lamp-shades etc). Stock a range of haberdashery (brings in customers). Beware of opposition and individuals questioning with no intention of giving commission and only cribbing ideas.

Only 50 per cent of estimates will result in commissions; there will be disappointments and frustrations, but it is enormously stimulating and rewarding.

Interpreter

Qualifications/Training	Essential
Income bracket	Medium–High
Licence	Recommended
Town/Country	Town
Experience/Springboard	Necessary
Travel	Yes
Mid-career entry	Yes
Exit sale	No
Entry costs	£500+
Work at home	No
Mix and match	Yes.

You could think about: *Tourist guide, Solicitor, Novelist, UK correspondent (overseas media), Import/export broker*

Enquiries
Institute of Linguists, Association Internationale des Interprètes des Conférences

At international conferences and meetings where the participants do not have a common language, interpreters translate simultaneously from one language into another so that everyone can follow what is going on. Although it's an international profession, it is also very small; the ASSOCIATION INTERNATIONALE DES INTERPRÈTES DES CONFÉRENCES (AIIC) has only about 2,000 members worldwide, about 100 of which are based in the UK. This is unlikely to change dramatically but demand will probably increase rather than decrease thanks to political developments in the EC, Russia, Eastern Europe and China, coupled with greater business links with the Middle and Far East. In the UK the centre for interpreters is London, although about 50 per cent of UK-based work is out of London; and there's far more regular work abroad in cities where international organisations have their HQs. If you want to make interpreting your main source of income you'll have to do a lot of travelling. With careful planning it's possible to mix and match your interpreting schedule with other work at home or overseas.

As a freelance interpreter you should be a member of AIIC and this means doing a course at an interpreting school (details from their Geneva headquarters indicate which are the best schools). There are nine main schools in Europe and the States (in the UK most go to the POLYTECHNIC OF CENTRAL LONDON SCHOOL OF LANGUAGES); courses are usually short (about six months) and intense. To be accepted on a course you should have a degree (not necessarily in languages) and proficiency in an appropriate language combination. English, French and Spanish are the most commonly used, with some Russian. A useful combination is what will get you work. That means having excellent French and English plus at least one other mainstream EC language (eg Spanish or German), Russian or Arabic plus a less common (often EC) language such as Danish or Greek. Interpreters divide languages into three groups: group A is the mother tongue into which they do most interpreting; group B is the language or languages other than mother tongue into which they may do some interpreting and group C is the languages from which they interpret. Most people have some work experience before they go to interpreting school in the late 20s. This usually, but not always, involves

languages or living abroad; teaching, couriering, working for a multi-national. Follow up this course with on-the-job training from a major organisation such as the EC or the UN which employs full-time interpreters as well as using freelance backup. To become a full member of AIIC you must be nominated by three existing members as a candidate and do 200 days of work that is vouched for by members with the same language combination as your own. As well as a facility with languages, interpreters need to be able to react quickly and spontaneously. You have to be able to communicate the speaker's ideas rather than giving a verbatim translation of what is being said and this, unlike translating where you tend to work alone and to have longer to check on the exact meaning of words, has to be done almost immediately. To do this requires wide general knowledge and understanding of people's motivations and it's for this reason that you're recommended not to come straight to interpreting from university or polytechnic; also to have lived for a while in at least the country of your major language. Interpreters don't necessarily do a lot of written translating.

Membership of AIIC is essential; it publishes a list of its members. You also need a phone and an answering machine. The complicated equipment needed to connect you in your interpreting booth with your listeners is provided by the conference organisers and the organisations you're working for. There are openings for interpreters in courts, the community and in business but these are often filled by language speakers within firms and organisations. The bulk of freelance interpreting work comes via the AIIC and will be for conferences and meetings or for organisations like the UN and the EC. That means that the main centres for interpreters are in Paris, Geneva, Strasbourg, Brussels and New York and you have to be able to travel to find work. Other sources of work are in smaller business or professional conferences in the UK (less often overseas as home grown interpreters are more often used for this) and, occasionally, for television; this is still a fairly unexploited area in the UK where TV viewers aren't always very interested in what foreigners have to say. The AIIC sets rates (officially these are minimum although few interpreters command fees that are far in excess of this minimum, unless they're working for TV) and daily expenses which are calculated to suit local prices. Travel costs are also charged.

When you're taken on for a job, you'll be paid for its duration regardless of how many hours' work you actually do; very often armies of stand-by interpreters will be called on to cover the possibility of several simultaneous multi-lingual meetings which do not necessarily occur. On these occasions there's a lot of hanging around which is a good way of meeting other interpreters; you'll also have plenty of chance to chat to whoever you're sharing your interpreting booth with, between bouts of interpreting; so the ability to get on with people is essential. Interpreters are taken on in teams to cover all the necessary language combinations. There are about four or five recruiting interpreters in London and they are the people to cultivate. To begin with it's difficult to get enough work but once you've had one good meeting where you did a terrific job this changes. It's a small world with a fast moving grapevine, which can be very useful, but also makes it difficult to live down a bad meeting.

Interpreting is very stressful. There's often a lot of long-haul travelling involved, sometimes at fairly short notice and, when you're on a job you have to concentrate very hard because what you're communicating to your listeners is usually important. The busy times are May/June and September/October when most of the conferences take place. January/February and July/August are a lot quieter but you should be able to make enough at other times to tide you over. Interpreters tend to take a long time to retire (irritatingly long for new blood) and, once you've got a good enough name, you can choose to do as many or as few jobs as you like. Contact also the INSTITUTE OF LINGUISTS for further information.

Inventor

Qualifications/Training	No
Income bracket	Low–High
Licence	No
Town/Country	Either
Experience/Springboard	Probably
Travel	Yes
Mid-career entry	Probably
Exit sale	Yes
Entry costs	Highly variable
Work at home	Possible

Mix and match   Probably essential. You could think about: *Computer consultant, Dentist, Furniture designer/maker, Garage owner, Fish curer, Proofreader/copy editor*

Enquiries
Institute of Patentees and Inventors

The British are superb at coming up with inventions, but notoriously bad at getting them onto the commercial market, a view upheld, interestingly enough, by the Japanese Ministry of International Trade. British inventions are hard to sell to UK manufacturers so very many British inventions are first developed and marketed overseas. Thus the path of the ordinary British inventor is difficult and can be long, expensive and dispiriting. But it is possible to make a lot of money out of inventing if you make sure that you take the right steps.

The first step is to protect your idea which involves the Patent Office. If you go direct to the PATENT OFFICE the initial application costs circa £20 giving you limited protection by just logging your idea. But this level of protection is far from adequate, and as a patent application is a complex legal and technical document, and useless if drawn up incompetently, most inventors do not apply directly but go through a patent agent (list obtainable from CHARTERED INSTITUTE OF PATENT AGENTS).

Once your patent application has been filed, you have 12 months to pursue it or let it lapse. The whole process up to obtaining a full patent is not cheap and although fees vary from patent agent to patent agent, getting a UK patent will cost you somewhere in the region of £1,000. If a European or other foreign patent is necessary the cost automatically rises. US, European and Japanese patents will cost you between £1,000–£1,500 on top of any existing UK patents. Even a full patent will not always protect you against the huge financial, legal and technical resources of a large company which may deliberately take advantage of your commercial or legal inexperience.

Marketing is the key to the successful exploitation of your invention. Traditionally inventors look to their patent agents but many are not qualified to help. There is nothing to stop you taking your brainchild to manufacturers and this can be very successful in spite of the many pitfalls. But remember, you are not the only budding inventor. Manufacturers often find it difficult to see the individual merits of different inventions, many of which purport to do the same thing, so your presentation is of the utmost importance. It is not much use inventing something highly technical if you do not have the technical know-how to put your dream into practice or to prove that it works and is cost effective, or even worth the expense of making a prototype. You also need thorough research into unit costs to make your idea more interesting to manufacturers.

There is rarely harm in getting publicity for your invention when it has been fully patented. If the idea is specialist you can try the specialist trade magazines. For more general publicity there is the national press, eg the Innovation Page of the *Sunday Times*, but it's not easy to get featured. There are also innovation, exhibitions, and competitions, like the Prince of Wales Award for innovation, the Toshiba invention awards – with appreciable prize money – and those run by major British companies like BP and the National Westminster Bank. Ask your patent agent or invention agency.

Once you have found a manufacturer to produce your idea your next problem is the licensing agreement. Like the original

patent it's a complex legal document under which you give the manufacturer the rights to produce your idea under licence while you retain the patent rights. Most licensing agreements involve an up-front payment and fixed royalties for the inventor. See that your agreements are not biased in favour of the manufacturer, who normally has much more legal muscle than you do. Contact the Licensing Executives Society and ask your patent agent or invention agency.

It's a good idea to work closely with an inventions agency or inventions sales company, using their commercial experience to help you with marketing, presentation and licensing. You are charged a fee at the beginning and they take a percentage of your royalties. Some research-based companies (eg BP) have venture departments which look out for new ideas. A useful address is the INSTITUTE OF PATENTEES AND INVENTORS; a useful book is *A Better Mousetrap*.

Investment Manager

Qualifications/Training	Recommended
Income bracket	Medium–High
Licence	Yes
Town/Country	Town
Experience/Springboard	Yes
Travel	No
Mid-career entry	Yes
Exit sale	Yes
Entry costs	£50,000+
Work at home	No
Mix and match	Possible.
You could think about: *Stockbroker, Solicitor, Accountant, Direct marketing consultant, Newsletter publisher*	
Enquiries IMRO, FIMBRA	

Investment managers advise on and manage sums of money (portfolios) on behalf of their clients who are private investors, pension funds, trusts and charity trusts. The aim is to make this money earn more by investing it; there is a variety of ways in which this can be done. Investment managers have to decide which is the most appropriate for the client's objectives. They operate as agents, with no direct access to or control over their client's funds. For a small firm this can be a difficult area to break into – your best bet is to woo the small investor (some of the larger managing firms only deal with investments of £100,000 or more). To succeed, you'll need credentials, experience and capital.

Investment management is regulated by a number of self-regulated bodies. All investment management companies now have to be registered with IMRO (Investment Managers Regulatory Organisation) or FIMBRA (Financial Intermediaries Managers and Brokers Regulatory Association). This means proving that you are 'fit and proper' before you set up. At the moment you'll need about five years' 'appropriate experience' (with another registered investment management company), a good past record and financial stability.

If you want to issue your own unit trust (and you probably will if you're managing for lots of small investors and don't want to go on putting money into other peoples') you should talk to the UNIT TRUST ASSOCIATION. You and your board will need to have a lot of financial experience and a paid-up share capital of at least £50,000.

Before you're allowed to give investment advice you have to pass the Stock Exchange Registered Representative's Exam. Any history of fraudulent practice reduces dramatically your likelihood of acceptance. You'll also have to convince them that your back office facilities comply with SE rules.

A qualification in accountancy or law or experience with a stockbroker or merchant bank is useful both for credibility and for what you'll learn. Small companies may give a wide range of experience because they aren't split into departments the way that large ones are. Large ones, however, may offer more structured training and a

large well-known company gives you more credibility. You'll need to know about financial and political trends, and enough about industry and technological developments to be able to give good investment advice. You must be good at getting on with existing and potential clients. This can be a precarious business where the more you know and the wider your range of interests the better. One of the advantages that a small non-specialist firm of investment managers has is that it can call on a variety of expert advisers including stockbrokers, merchant bankers, company and financial analysts and other investment managers. Use your contacts to keep in touch and co-opt anyone with kudos (economists, stockbrokers etc) onto your board if you can.

You'll need enough money to set up and run an office which is equipped and staffed to allow you to comply with SE regulations (eg all bargains must be reported to them within up to 15 minutes). You'll also need administrative and reception staff; clients don't like telephone-answering machines. The chances are that you'll be managing sums of money that are far greater than your own capital; although it's rare for clients to sue their investment managers, you should have professional indemnity insurance and fidelity bonding for your staff. Your income comes from acceptance fees from new clients; regular fees based on a percentage of the clients' portfolio capital; dealing charges on all transactions; and you may earn commission on some transactions. Some forms of investment (unit trusts for example) pay an additional commission (from the client's 'front load premium'); this will give you a quick income but at your client's expense.

Your first clients can come from friends and personal contacts. Small investors (with funds of as little as £7,000–£8,000 are likely to bring you more business by word of mouth; but any losses they incur will be proportionately more significant than for larger investors where you can easily make up for, say, a £2,000 loss. A balanced spread of interests, with units of several shares reduces the risk of clients losing all round but the units have to be large enough to make gains worth having.

Italian Property Finder

Qualifications/Training	No
Income bracket	Medium–High
Licence	No
Town/Country	Both
Experience/Springboard	No
Travel	Essential
Mid-career entry	Yes
Exit sale	Possible
Entry costs	£25,000+++
Work at home	Possible
Mix and match	Yes.

You could think about: *Property manager, Architect, Novelist, UK correspondent (overseas media), Timeshare developer, Travel agent, Art historian, Import/export broker*

Enquiries
National Association of Estate Agents, Department of Trade and Industry

Italian property finders look for and negotiate the purchase of property in Italy for clients who live elsewhere. They work on behalf of the buyer and charge a commission on purchases – this is standard practice in Italy where estate agents charge both sellers and purchasers commission on property sales. There is already a lot of demand for Italian country houses as holiday and retirement homes and this is likely to increase after 1992 when European communications and commerce becomes freer.

There are no formal qualifications but you have to know the language and the part of the country in which you're working extremely well. You should be familiar with Italian property law which is complex and subject to frequent changes; a course in legal Italian is useful. Experience in estate agency is not necessary but an interest in buildings and architecture is useful and enthusiasm for what you do, essential. You'll need perseverance and dedication combined with patience to sell Italian property successfully. The property market in rural Italy is less frenetic than in the UK and you'll have to be diplomatic in negotiating between Italian sellers and British buyers who will have very different expectations of how houses are bought and sold. If you like Italy and know it well this will be easier. Some sort of writing skill is useful when you're compiling particulars for clients who will want to know as much as possible about any house before they go out to Italy to view it.

You'll need two bases so it's advisable to set up with a partner; one of you can look after the UK end while the other is in Italy. Essential equipment is a phone, answering machine, stationery and a word processor so you can produce particulars on the properties you hope to sell. Your UK base must be somewhere close enough to a major airport to allow you to get to Italy quickly and easily. Yo need a car in Italy so you can get yourself and your clients around the countryside. You need cash for advertising and to finance frequent trips to Italy at short notice and a camera for photographing houses (a video camera is useful). Clients pay you commission on all sales – a sliding scale varying from about 2 per cent to 5 per cent. Many houses will have been empty for years and need a lot of work done before clients want to live in them. You may be asked to manage this, in which case charge commission (say, 5 per cent) on the work; alternatively, you can recommend local contractors as part of your service, and leave the client to manage the work.

You get clients by advertising in the UK press or in magazines and journals that are read by expats. Contacts in Italy are absolutely essential. You need to know both a *geometra* (an Italian surveyor/architect/conveyancer who can look over houses, advise on and organise any building work that needs to be done and check the history of each house to make sure that your client won't be lumbered with unpaid bills or taxes from the last owner) and a *notario* (public notary) who arranges the legal contracts for house sales. Building up a good working relationship with both of these will save you a lot of time, money and hassle.

Italian rural communities are close knit and more likely to help each other than someone from the UK or even an Italian city. It's important to use local people as much as possible, for example builders, architects and plumbers as they are likely to make sure they do a good job on any local property and cowboy firms are rare. If you are well known and liked in the community people will be pleased to let you sell their houses for them. You can pair up with a local estate agent, but make sure it's someone you can trust not to pass on their unsellable houses to you. *Geometri* often know of houses that are going on to the market. It is useful to have contacts in the local gas, electricity and telephone offices, who can speed up the transfer of accounts into your clients' names when they buy a house.

Although your annual schedule has to be flexible enough to allow several unplanned trips to Italy, there is a certain pattern. Most clients go to Italy over the Easter and August holidays so you have to be there to show them around. Once a sale is agreed, there are two stages of contract to be signed. The first part (the *compresso*) is a binding contract signed soon after the sale is agreed when 10–30 per cent of the price is paid; you can have power of attorney to sign the *compresso* on your clients' behalf and, although not a legal requirement, you're advised to do this in front of a *notai*. The second part of the contract is signed about two months later when you and your clients should be in Italy as it has to be signed in front of a *notaio*. A certified translation is required although a friendly *notaio* may allow you to provide your own. Some sales take longer than this but you should have several contracts to complete in October/November which is a good time to start looking for houses to put on your books for next year; aim to hold particulars on about fifty houses by the start of the buying season.

When you're in Italy working hours can be long and frustrating; Italian bureaucracy is notorious and there are public holidays when everything grinds to a halt. Some sellers suddenly changing their minds about the price or about selling their houses at all – something which can be incomprehensible to UK buyers. The DEPARTMENT OF TRADE AND INDUSTRY publishes useful information; membership of the NATIONAL ASSOCIATION OF ESTATE AGENTS is worth investigating.

Jj

Jazz Musician/ Singer

Qualifications/Training	Recommended
Income bracket	Mostly low
Licence	No
Town/Country	Town
Experience/Springboard	No
Travel	Lots
Mid-career entry	Possible
Exit sale	No
Entry costs	£1,000
Work at home	No
Mix and match	Yes.

You could think about: *Orchestral musician, Music teacher, Typesetter, Chemical engineering consultant, Solicitor, Mini-cab driver, Film extra*

Enquiries
Jazz Services, Musicians' Union

Music college is not essential if you want to sing or play in jazz style and the jazz repertoire in concerts, groups, clubs, on the radio and TV etc. But dedication and perseverance are required. Even with really good 'ears', you need instruction to focus on good instrumental or vocal technique and listening. This is the way to develop your own individual style. Listen to records, go to concerts, memorise songs, solos and chord sequences. You must have the rare ability to communicate musically, to forget yourself and give way spontaneously to other musicians when playing.

You will need a room for practising without disturbance and without wrecking your relationship with your neighbours. You also need a record player, telephone and answering machine or service. An amplifier is often provided or you can borrow or hire one, or buy one for £250.

Go to clubs in your local city (such as the Bass Clef or 606 in London), meet musicians and if you admire one, ask for a lesson. The democratic tradition in the jazz world is for even the most famous to be willing to chat. There you will meet fellow enthusiasts and can arrange to play together informally. There are now several vocational courses of a high standard as well as those at the ROYAL ACADEMY and GUILDHALL SCHOOL OF MUSIC AND DRAMA. For information on all these as well as possible venues in which you might work, get a copy of the Jazz Directory – *essential* reading, from JAZZ SERVICES which is the key enquiry and advice point.

Join the MUSICIANS' UNION. Although it tends not to intervene at gigs at the lowest levels, it does stipulate fees for major venues, recording, broadcasting and TV sessions. Financial reward for a jazz performer is minimal: £20 per gig, up to £60–£80 for an experienced group leader. An internationally known leader can get £600 per gig, which is exceptional; his musicians will receive much less. You therefore need another job, in a band or show, teaching or doing sessions.

You must be sociable, prepared to work long hours for little pay and be at the mercy of other musicians' private lives and moods. Successful groups may tour and you can travel if you also work in a show or rock band as a commercial musician.

Useful magazines are *Jazz Journal International*, *Jazz Express*, *Crescendo International* and, most useful, regional editions of *Jazz Newspapers*. Get any books on jazz theory and improvisation from a library with a jazz section.

Journalist

Qualifications/Training	Recommended
Income bracket	Low–High
Licence	No
Town/Country	Town
Experience/Springboard	Recommended
Travel	Yes
Mid-career entry	Possible
Exit sale	No
Entry costs	Nil
Work at home	Partly
Mix and match	Yes.

You could think about: **Foreign correspondent, UK correspondent (overseas media), Football commentator, Newsletter publisher, Radio reporter and presenter, Novelist, Proofreader/copy editor**

Enquiries
National Union of Journalists

' 'Ello dearie, would you undo your blouse buttons, just a few, for the snapper; it makes the picture, really.' Or 'If you don't come to the door and talk to the *Daily Sick* we'll tell your neighbours all about it' or 'Are you the dirty vicar or Griddlethorpe's blonde buxom live-in lover?' The popular contempt which regularly places journalists below politicians, social workers and (gruesome thought) even estate agents in opinion polls is well considered and, to an extent, justified.

But the public's attitude to the 'I was a vice thug's sex slave zombie' school of journalist is marinated in hypocrisy; the newspapers we most deplore are also the ones we most like to read. For example, a little less than half a million people buy the *Guardian*; a little more than four million people buy the *Sun*.

Sleaze sells. More importantly to anyone who is thinking about joining the Street of Shame, sleaze pays. Very early on in your journalist's career you will have to make hard decisions which turn on personal greed versus integrity; the hunger for a good story versus betraying, say, a promise to a contact who may have become something of a friend. That's part of the challenge of the job, part of its fascination. The test has to be is the story good enough or important enough to snap or curve your integrity. If it isn't, don't bother.

But you don't have to wallow in sleaze. Journalism can be better than that. For good journalism matters. A trip to pre-revolutionary Romania, where the only news story for the lapdog press was whom Ceaucescu was meeting that day at the airport, was the unanswerable argument in favour of a free press – and if that means the *Sun* too, so be it. A return visit to Romania after the Christmas revolution was to witness journalism at its thrilling best. Writers, photographers, cameramen, soundmen, reporters – we all witnessed history. Three lost their lives but it was hard not to be moved when you saw crowds of people run after lorries throwing out the first uncensored newspapers people had read in four decades. They ran like the hungry for bread. But it's not all like that; much of the time you're dealing with small stories or trying to find news at all. You must be able to write against deadlines and tailor your golden prose accordingly.

There are no rules, or none worth remembering. Membership of the NUJ, while not essential, is probably a prudent step while predators (like Murdoch and the late Maxwell) are on the loose. You can become a journalist in dozens of different ways; start up as a stringer in an exotic dictatorship; write soccer reports for a local freesheet; edit the school or college magazine. Even if you're aiming for the big time, a spell in the provinces is no disgrace; you'll find corrupt tyrants not just in banana republics but also in many a sleepy market town. They all need poking with a sharp stick and you've got to start somewhere.

Good books to read are Michael Frayn's *Towards the End of The Morning*, Robert Harris's *Gotcha – The Media In The Falklands War* and Harry Evans' *Good Times, Bad Times*. The Street of Shame column in *Private Eye* gives a fair impression of what a sweet and caring profession it is.

Many successful journalists have made it without taking a journalism course ('waste of time, giving knackered hacks an opportunity to bore you with stories of how they got their old scoops'); for ordinary mortals, in these hard times, they're probably a must. Shorthand is a gift; a necessity if you are going to be a full-time court reporter but many Fleet Street hacks go without. The late Patrick Donovan, an old *Observer* hand, once ended up an interview with the King of Greece with only a drawing of a large black cat in his notebook.

European Community Notes

There is a good deal of scope. Start with *Foreign Correspondent* and *UK Correspondent (overseas media)*.

Kk

Kennel/Cattery Owner

Qualifications/Training	Available
Income bracket	Low–Medium
Licence	Yes
Town/Country	Country
Experience/ Springboard	Recommended
Travel	No
Mid-career entry	Likely
Exit sale	Yes
Entry costs	£10,000+++
Work at home	Yes
Mix and match	Possible.

You could think about: *Greyhound trainer, Vet, Farmer, Tree surgeon, Taxidermist*

Enquiries
Kennel Agency, Feline Advisory Board, Canine Defence League, Animal Boarding Advisory Bureau

Kennels and catteries look after dogs and cats whose owners are temporarily unable to do so themselves, usually because they are on holiday. Some also offer a longer-term service for animals returning from overseas who must, by law, be kept in quarantine for six months. The job involves feeding, watering and exercising the animals, providing them with living quarters and arranging for any necessary veterinary attention. Another, though more unusual, way of being self-employed in this area is by offering your services as a freelance, temporary kennelmaid or as a canine beautician (groomer).

There are no necessary, formal qualifications for this but you'll need an unsentimental love of animals and genuinely care for the animals entrusted to you. Kennel work is extremely hard and attention to detail is essential. You can't be a clock watcher: this is a seven days a week, 24 hours a day job. A responsible person has to be on the premises at all times. You also have to remember that you're providing a service and to be prepared to put yourself out for others from time to time. A small animals course is held in AGRICULTURAL COLLEGES, eg, Sparsholt. Various residential kennelmaid courses are available (eg, from BELLMEAD KENNELS); the CANINE STUDIES INSTITUTE offers a correspondence course in kennel management and five-day courses in kennel and cattery management are organised by the Wood Green College of Animal Welfare. If you want a taste of what you're letting yourself in for you can do a working weekend as a kennelmaid. It helps if you enjoy being outdoors in all weathers, and can cope with mucking out kennels and the incessant noise and smell of dogs/cats. Contact also the FELINE ADVISORY BUREAU.

You'll need specially designed premises. You can buy an existing establishment or build your own. A licence is required for boarding kennels and/or catteries and is issued by the Environmental Health Officer of the local authority. Contact the RSPCA or get *Guidelines for the Inspection of Animal Boarding Establishments* for indications of the sort of building required. Location is important, not only for the sake of the animals but also because objections may be raised about noise, smell, hygiene, increase in traffic and general nuisance. In general you won't be able to set up business in town, but you will have to be accessible for your clients.

If you're proposing to take animals in quarantine, you'll need to apply to the MINISTRY OF AGRICULTURE and to nominate a veterinary superintendent who can be an owning partner or someone who lives nearby and is prepared to be on 24-hour standby. A licence is required for boarding, breeding and quarantine.

Set-up costs vary widely depending on the number of kennels, size of house and grounds etc. You need to spend £10,000 for the cost of an established property over and above the value of the property alone. You will need an animals' food preparation room with refrigeration, supplies of food from wholesalers, bedding etc. Again, depending on the size, you may want to employ help with the work. Charges depend a lot on what sort of service you're offering, how much attention you give to each animal and what clientele you are aiming for. You can, for example, specialise by boarding only small dogs, big breeds, dogs recovering from surgery or aged and infirm dogs, bitches in season or dogs all of one particular breed. £4.00 or more, per head, per day is the average price charged for the average dog. Your clients are liable for any vet bills incurred by their pets, so insist that the animals in your care are insured and sell policies to those who aren't.

Advertise in local (or as near to local as possible) shops and vets' surgeries for business. The *Yellow Pages* are very effective but costly. A lot should come via word of mouth as long as pets go home in good condition and happy (some grooming and attention helps). Pet owners who travel a lot are worth cultivating, as are vets for both their professional expertise and for their contact with animal owners. It's worth cosseting your regulars. Certainly the best advertisement is by word of mouth.

During a working day you'll have to feed the animals, clean them out and keep an eye on them. Dogs in particular need exercise, ideally a chance to run free for a while. There is also administration, taking bookings, dealing with arrivals and departures and, of course, bookkeeping, invoicing etc. Your busy times will be at weekends and holiday seasons so time off may be difficult unless you've either got reliable staff to take over in your absence, or are willing to close the business for a few days. Above all, you need to be physically fit; it's hard, continual slog – but an outdoor life is also both refreshing and rewarding.

Further reading: *Kennel and Cattery Management*, *Cat World*, *FAB Cattery Construction & Management Manual*, *Cats Magazine* and *Running Your Own Boarding Kennels*, also the *Dog Business*.

European Community Notes

It is difficult to be precise about the prospects and conditions for those wishing to work in the EC where the regulations and circumstances vary so widely from country to country. But one can identify a definite need in France and the Netherlands and possibly Germany.

Keyboard Hire

Qualifications/Training	Recommended
Income bracket	Low–High
Licence	No
Town/Country	Town
Experience/Springboard	Useful
Travel	Lots
Mid-career entry	Possible
Exit sale	Possible
Entry costs	£6,000
Work at home	Possible

Mix and match   Yes.
You could think about: *Man with a van, Musician, Music teacher, Hi-fi shop owner, Piano tuner, Music/instrument retailer*

Enquiries
Musicians' Union

This involves hiring out any form of keyboard instrument – piano, harpsichord, organ or synthesiser – transporting it to the performance or recording venue and tuning it to the pitch required. A good knowledge of the mechanics of keyboard instruments is useful but not essential; a really accurate sense of pitch and the ability to play are. You will also need to be physically strong, have a clean driving licence and own an electronic tuner. It's helpful to have good business sense and an accountant. You must also know the correct way to lift, without wrecking your back.

You can run your business from home in a large ground-floor room or garage. These should be dry but not centrally heated. It is possible to start with a small harpsichord, synthesiser or sampler; these will cost £2,000–£5,000 or you can buy them second-hand. You will also need a telephone, answering machine or service and a small light piano trolley. Hire a van to start with, but buy a second-hand one as soon as possible. There will be a lot of travelling so a basic knowledge of motor mechanics is useful should you break down in the middle of the night.

You will have to arrive before rehearsal and tune the instrument for the performer. Then you kill time all day, returning in the breaks, before the concert and in the interval to re-tune. Always talk to the performers: their recommendation could get you the next engagement. Porters at concert halls and theatres are generally reluctant to help and need tipping, so stamina is necessary for loading the van after an evening engagement and driving off early in the morning.

Allow at least £500 to get cards or brochures printed and distributed to music shops, recording studios, music societies, festivals, arts centres and dance halls. If using the post, investigate the first time small business delivery.

This is an energetic life. The bias tends to be towards men because of the physical requirements; a woman can organise, take bookings, and employ men to lift and transport. To succeed, you and your instrument must be reliable, punctual, in tune and of the best quality available. If you need to employ others, choose them with care and ensure they do not damage the instruments. Get good insurance cover. If you are accepted by a prestigious venue, musical show, orchestra or opera company you can make up to £50,000.

Union membership is not required but if you play and hire out yourself with your instrument you must join the MUSICIANS' UNION.

Ll

Landlord

Qualifications/Training	No
Income bracket	Low–High
Licence	No
Town/Country	Either
Experience/Springboard	No
Travel	Between properties
Mid-career entry	Yes
Exit sale	Excellent
Entry costs	£50,000++
Work at home	Yes
Mix and match	Yes.

You could think about:
Almost anything

Enquiries
Landlords

If you've got enough money to buy a flat or house outright you can let it to tenants and become a landlord. Alternatively, if you already own property (especially in an expensive and desirable area) you could let it and go and live somewhere cheaper and/ or more exciting. For anyone with several tens of thousands to spare, it's an excellent way of earning an income from an investment which should give you capital growth as well. Laws affecting the leasing of property have recently changed. In particular, rent fixing by rent assessment officers called in by tenants or housing benefit departments is changing for new tenants, which will remove the risk of an uncommercially low rent being set for your property. Being a landlord needn't be

a very time consuming job so is ideal for mixing and matching.

There are no essential formal qualifications but you must know what you're doing or you risk being caught out by unscrupulous (or over-scrupulous) tenants using a variety of legal loopholes. Arm yourself with a good solicitor to check all contracts and tenancy agreements. The more house maintenance you can do yourself the better – this saves the money you'd otherwise be paying to someone else and allows you to keep in touch with the property and its condition. Even better, if you have experience in construction buy unconverted or rundown property and convert it yourself into several letting units cheaply.

Setting up from scratch costs masses. On the whole, letting property on a small scale is only worth doing if you can buy somewhere outright; once you're personally involved in repaying a new mortgage it'll be difficult to raise enough rent to cover your expenses and make a decent profit. Apart from buying the property, you also need to furnish, decorate and equip it. Basically, the more you spend in the early stages, the more you stand to make from rent in the future, ie, you can charge more for a well decorated and equipped flat in an expensive area than for a grotty shack in a rundown area furnished only with a mattress and a broken chair. You'll also save on maintenance costs if you make sure the place is in good nick when you first let it. Other expenses include repairs and redecoration, solicitor's fees and the cost of advertising for new tenants. Telephone, electricity and gas bills are virtually always paid by tenants but, unless electricity and gas are supplied on a coin meter, the landlord may be responsible for tenants' unpaid bills including water charges. The Poll Tax is another hazard and, while it lingers on, your liability varies according to the type of letting. Get your solicitor to see that you, not the tenant, optimise your position. Always inform British Telecom, the gas, electricity, and water companies and local council of the names of new tenants and, when possible, give forwarding addresses of outgoing ones. Rents vary considerably across the country and also depend on what you're providing. Letting bedsits may maximise the income you can get from a property but you'll have to spend more time finding tenants and the property will suffer more wear and tear. It's normal to take a deposit from incoming tenants as some sort of surety against non-payment of rent or bills and against minor damage and breakages (allowing for reasonable wear and tear) – not always successful as tenants who leave without paying rent often owe money on bills and may have caused damage as well. Deposits are usually a month's rent, occasionally three months'.

Outgoing tenants may not give you much notice before they leave – contracts usually stipulate a month but that doesn't give you much time to find someone else, especially if you don't live in the area. You'll have to check the property over too, finding someone else to take on the lease as soon as possible usually means advertising in the local paper. Then it's up to you to show prospective tenants the property and decide who should have it. Be prepared for some prospective tenants to fail to show up at the time you've arranged.

It's pretty well up to you what restrictions you put into the contract (eg no pets, no noise after 11pm). It's normal for landlords to be responsible for external decoration and most prefer to maintain control over interior decoration (liaising with tenants) to avoid having to completely redecorate over someone else's dubious taste in interior design before you can re-let. Once you've found someone, check references from their bank or building society, employer and previous landlord. This may take a couple of weeks to clear but is important.

To minimise the risk of having a sitting tenant, draw up a shorthold lease (this is usually for a year or more); it also makes it easier to get rid of tenants who aren't paying the rent. If both you and the tenant are happy, shortlease contracts can be renewed. Long term non-payment of rent doesn't often arise but when it does, it's a great nuisance. You may have to get an eviction order from the local magistrate's court – this can mean that tenants are allowed some time to pay up or move out; they're given longer if they've got children (a situation which forces many landlords to refuse to let to families) and the period can sometimes be extended under other extenuating circumstances. In the meantime, you'll have no income from your property and the rent that you're owed could be paid by the tenant in small weekly instalments over several months. Moral: keep in touch with tenants on a fairly formal level. Although bad tenants are very bad, good tenants are more common and very good. They'll pay rent and bills regularly, let you know when anything needs to be done and leave the place as they found it allowing you to live in peace.

Landscape Designer

Qualifications/Training	Yes
Income bracket	Low–High
Licence	No
Town/Country	Either
Experience/Springboard	Essential
Travel	Yes
Mid-career entry	Unlikely
Exit sale	No
Entry costs	£2,000
Work at home	Possible

Mix and match Yes.
You could think about: *Gardener/ garden designer, Property manager, Timeshare developer, Architect, Surveyor*

Enquiries
Landscape Institute

There is a steady demand for landscape professionals, both at home and overseas, many of whom work as consultants receiving commissions from public authorities or private clients. The work is varied in type, scale and geographical range, as is the amount of time spent in office or on site. It ranges from wide questions of environmental impact and general ecology to urban and rural landscaping. Urban landscaping covers projects like housing, roadworks, parks, play areas and regeneration; rural landscaping covers agriculture, forests and tourist areas. Larger projects include industrial buildings, oil refineries, nuclear problems and so on.

You are the client's agent and your job includes the co-ordination of your designs' implementation. You nearly always work as part of a team involving planners, architects and contractors or various combinations of these. You have to be able to get on with people, and be prepared to tackle a certain amount of bureaucracy, for example when dealing with local councils. You need some talent for drawing, visual perception, imagination, an interest in the history of art and landscape design, architecture and building design, and in ecology and allied subjects such as horticulture and geology. You also need some knowledge of surveying, planning and contract law. All of these are covered in degree and diploma courses in landscape architecture. For information about courses apply to the LANDSCAPE INSTITUTE. To qualify for Associateship of the Landscape Institute (ALI) you must then work for two years for a landscape consultancy either in the public or private sector, after which you can take the professional exams. The terms 'landscape designer' and 'landscape architect' have been borrowed by many people who appear in the *Yellow Pages*,

but ALI is the only recognised professional qualification for landscape architects. Read *Landscape Design*.

The best thing about this career is the variety of choice: if you feel committed to developing countries you can work there; if you feel passionately about urban renewal you can do something about it; if your heart is in the countryside, you can live and work there; if you are against nuclear power, you can avoid designing power stations; or you can just work on small garden projects.

To set up as a consultant you have to be certain that you have secured the commissions and will be able to secure more. You will need to be employed for a while in order to gain experience. You can set up an office with a telephone and drawing board; the rest is reputation and persuading new clients to use your services rather than anybody else's. It is important to have a good working relationship with the contractors you choose and the planners and architects with whom you deal.

European Community Notes

Qualifications: UK qualifications recognised throughout EC.

Languages: To succeed, local language necessary.

Earnings: UK income generally same as elsewhere in the EC.

Advice/Training: Advice, information and training available for those wishing to work in Europe.

Exchanges: Formal job exchanges do not exist.

Financial help: exists for study, training or travel in the EC, specific to this job.

Enquiry point for those wishing to work in the EC: LANDSCAPE INSTITUTE.

Notes: It is difficult to go into individual detail about the EC member states as so many different factors apply. Conditions of practice and training vary considerably: they are being examined with a view to harmonisation by the European Foundation for Landscape Architecture. Certainly, UK landscape designers do practise successfully throughout Europe.

List Broker

Qualifications/Training	No
Income bracket	Low–High
Licence	No
Town/Country	Town
Experience/Springboard	No
Travel	Local
Mid-career entry	Good
Exit sale	Yes
Entry costs	£1,500+
Work at home	Possible
Mix and match	Yes.

You could think about: *Direct marketing consultant, Bookseller, Tourist attraction, Garden gnome maker, Newsletter publisher*

Enquiries
British List Brokers' Association, British Direct Marketing Association

Classified lists of names and addresses are a valuable commodity used in direct marketing and mailing campaigns. List brokers rent out lists (at about 20 per cent commission) on behalf of client companies. Customers who want to rent a list approach a list broker who will know which manager has the most appropriate list. To prevent the same list from being used more than once, the list owner will seed it with the names of friends (users should be advised of such seeding); pressure can then be applied on customers who infringe (litigation is costly and time consuming). The direct mail industry has doubled in the last five years; about £5 million is spent on it per annum and it looks set to grow. List broking is a fast moving business; in its early days it was a good way of making a fast buck and cowboy list brokers gave the industry a bad name. The BRITISH LIST BROKERS' ASSOCIATION has stepped in to regulate and tighten up on this.

There are no formal qualifications but you'll have to prove an ability to handle lists, and make good recommendations to potential list users. It's illegal to make money from other people's lists (*Yellow Pages*, professional directories etc) but difficult to make a prosecution case stick. List poaching is a hazard for established brokers. Successful list brokers need the self-discipline to work to their own deadlines. They also need to be good at selling and capable of inspiring confidence in their own judgement and ability in others.

Lists come from many sources. Specialising helps; the owner of one list may be interested in renting another in a related field. You'll get feedback from the lists you rent out which helps maintain their accuracy. Clients have lists based on magazine subscriptions, insurance policies, market research results etc. Ten company lists or a classified list of 200,000 can make your living. A good list lasts for about a year before it needs to be updated.

Set-up costs needn't be great. You can start up with £1,500 for a word processor and printer. Basic lists are presented on sticky labels but customers who want to send personalised letters need lists on magnetic tape – the machinery for this costs about £8,000–£10,000 or you can subcontract the conversion to a special bureau. Each list must be registered under the Data Protection Act – this costs £15–£20 for simple name and address lists but increases in price and complexity the more information you hold.

For a straightforward list expect to get about £15 per thousand names. For a good, response-generated list you can get up to £500 per 1,000 names. People to talk to are the BRITISH LIST BROKERS' ASSOCIATION, the BRITISH DIRECT MARKETING ASSOCIATION and the DIRECT MAIL SERVICES STANDARDS BOARD (a regulatory body). Also the MAILING PREFERENCE SERVICE who will remove any name from a mailing list on request.

European Community Notes
EC proposals on data protection could severely inhibit the list broker's activities although some of the early proposals, which could have proved very restrictive, have been toned down or dropped altogether. Try the DTI for updates.

Literary Agent

Qualifications/Training	No
Income bracket	Low–High
Licence	No
Town/Country	Town
Experience/ Springboard	Recommended
Travel	Yes
Mid-career entry	Probably essential
Exit sale	Yes
Entry costs	£3,500
Work at home	Possible
Mix and match	Limited.

You could think about: ***Bookseller, Book publisher, Novelist***

Enquiries
Association of Authors' Agents

Literary agents negotiate, sell, promote and protect the interests of authors. Most agencies are small businesses and are owned and run by one or two people who have been in the publishing industry for some time and have a lot of contacts. They operate by negotiating with publishers to get the best deal for their clients and making sure that agreements are kept – mistakes (conscious or unconscious) can be made easily. New technology, such as computers and fax machines, has streamlined a lot of the work involved.

Getting into the network is essential. Your success depends on getting people (especially publishers) to listen to you in the first place and they're far more likely to do so if they know who you are. Best ways of building your networks are through working for a publisher or a literary agent – a difficult area to get into. Many people start as secretaries (increasingly men as well as women), graduate trainees etc, and work their way up, moving from company to company. This takes a long time but will get you contacts. Get as broad a view as possible of the different areas. You'll need to know about copyright, rights and contracts (editing, production, marketing, sales etc are also useful).

Literary agents have to be sociable, self-starters and self-sufficient with an eye for detail. You won't have time to get lonely but neither (unless you've got a partner) will you have anyone with whom to discuss decisions. Life is a mixture of appointments and trying to fit in necessary follow-through with constant interruptions as things develop.

To start up, two telephone lines are essential (you'll lose business if people can't get hold of you) and an answering machine as well as the usual office files, desk, typewriter, etc. You may also want a computer, a photocopier, a fax and perhaps a telex or telex service. Regular expenses include letterheads, service agreements (strongly recommended) for your equipment, telephone bills and lunching publishers (a far more efficient way of finding out what they want and what's going on than telephone conversations).

You'll need some money to tide you over the first few months. Once you've got a client with a book to sell it's likely to take three months (for an established author) and up to a year (for a new one) before you see your first cheque for it. You retain commission (usually about 10 per cent) on whatever you manage to negotiate for your clients. This includes an advance against royalties (usually $1/3$–$1/2$ of the total expected); as well as royalties which are paid twice a year (once the advance has been earned) and any additional rights agreements such as translation, film, USS or serial rights. That means you'll need a turnover of £100,000 just to realise £10,000 for your own income and expenses. (The average author earns about £5,000 per annum.) You'll need an accountant and an understanding bank manager.

Clients will come through word of mouth, from other authors or even from publishers. You can hunt authors via reviews or the grapevine but you are not allowed to poach from other agents and must, when you approach a potential client, tell them to ignore you if they are already represented. You may find a few clients through your own slush pile of unsolicited and unintroduced manuscripts.

Handling the lists of foreign (especially American) publishers and agents for British editions is another source of revenue. There is growing use of contracts between agent and client which clarify the general agreement that agents should handle their clients' subsequent work. The material you handle depends on your experience (what you know how to sell) and interests; you can specialise if you want. There's little point trying to sell a book that you're not enthusiastic about but you may have to make exceptions for a regular, usually satisfactory author who turns out an aberration. Using the same publisher for an author's subsequent work will have a worthwhile knock-on effect – previous books by that author being re-released and the sales force will know something about what they're selling. You can continue to represent and reap profit from your clients' estates for up to 50 years after they have died, until the client's work is out of copyright.

You will need the *Writers' Handbook*, the *Writers' and Artists' Yearbook* and to contact the ASSOCIATION OF AUTHORS' AGENTS. Also read *Bluff Your Way in Publishing*, the *Bookseller*.

European Community Notes

Qualifications: For 'qualifications' read 'experience': UK experience recognised throughout EC and experience gained in EC is recognised in UK.

Languages: To succeed, local language necessary.

Earnings: Impossible to generalise about earnings in EC countries.

Setting up: You will find it difficult to succeed throughout Europe.

Advice/Training: Advice, information and training not available for those wishing to work in Europe.

Exchanges: Formal job exchanges do not exist.

Recommended reading: Trade magazines in each country.

Mm

Magazine Designer

Qualifications/Training	Recommended
Income bracket	Low–Medium
Licence	No
Town/Country	Town
Experience/ Springboard	Recommended
Travel	Local
Mid-career entry	No
Exit sale	No
Entry costs	£3,500
Work at home	Possible
Mix and match	Yes.

You could think about: *Book designer, Illustrator, Magazine publisher, Book packager, Wine merchant, Motorcycle racer*

Enquiries
Design Council (Young Designer Centre)

Although most magazine designers work on the staff of the magazine, there are openings for freelance designers – and the work can be well paid. On the staff of an ordinary magazine, an ordinary designer will earn, say, £15,000 a year. A freelance designer will earn upwards of £100 per day. A top designer will become an art editor or art director in a publishing company: a top freelance may become a design consultant (which is where fame, fortune and true independence lie), producing dummy layouts for publishers who are re-vamping existing magazines or developing new ones.

Most magazine designers start with a foundation course at art school, followed by a vocational course which will include options in magazine layout, printing and so on. There are a few specialist courses: the LONDON COLLEGE OF PRINTING and NAPIER POLYTECHNIC in Edinburgh are the two colleges best oriented towards the publishing trade. The first job is tradition-ally as a paste-up artist (on a small publica-tion, where finished copy and illustrations are mounted on a board ready for the printing process) or as a junior layout artist on larger publications, devising a layout to suit the copy and illustrations available. The advent of desk-top publish-ing, where all preparation is done on com-puter, has altered the nature of paste-up work: layout artists in many companies now need to be conversant with the new technology. If you intend to branch out and set up on your own, you may choose to work 'in-house' for different companies. If you want to work from home, designing house magazines for small companies or local interest magazines for estate agents, for example, you will need to equip a small studio (a room in a house is adequate). The equipment you need incudes a draw-ing board (if you like to work at one), a light box (for studying transparencies and checking colour, and black and white proofs), a Grant machine (a type of projec-tor which you use to blow-up transparen-cies, to trace on to the layout), plus stationery, storage space and work sur-faces. You will also have to learn how to cost a job, including an allowance for materials and typesetting where necessary. You may also find that you take on book design work to fill gaps between jobs, or you may combine the job with illustration work. On the other hand, if you are used to working to tight deadlines, you may diversify into the more lucrative field of newspaper layout (which involves working unsocial hours). You will have to build up a portfolio of work to show to prospective employers. Good contacts are vital, and it is useful to consult the *Writers' and Artists' Year Book* and the *Writers' Handbook* or *Willings Press Guide* to keep up to date with the names of editors of publications you intend to work for. You will also have to buy (or at least read) a wide range of magazines, including foreign ones, to keep up to date with style and design. Many designers are members of the CHARTERED SOCIETY OF DESIGNERS and subscribe to its magazine, *Design Review*. You can also advertise your services in *Publishing News*. *Creative Review* is the journal of the closely allied advertising world.

Most designers are members of either the NATIONAL UNION OF JOURNALISTS or the GRAPHICAL PAPER AND MEDIA UNION who run a call office where members can register themselves as available for freelance work.

✦✦✦ European Community Notes

Languages: To succeed, local language not necessary.
Earnings: UK income generally higher than elsewhere in the EC.
Setting up: You will find it difficult to succeed in Belgium, Denmark, Greece, Luxembourg, Netherlands, Portugal and Spain. You will find it easier in Eire, France, Germany and Italy.
Advice/Training: Advice, information and training not available for those wishing to work in Europe.
Exchanges: Formal job exchanges do not exist.
Enquiry point for those wishing to work in the EC: DESIGN COUNCIL, Young Designers Centre.

Magazine Publisher

Qualifications/Training	No
Income bracket	Low–High
Licence	No
Town/Country	Town
Experience/ Springboard	Recommended
Travel	Yes
Mid-career entry	Likely
Exit sale	Excellent
Entry costs	£5,000++
Work at home	Possible
Mix and match	Yes.

You could think about: **Book publisher, Book packager, Space sales agent, Direct marketing consultant, Nanny/ babysitting agent**

Enquiries
Periodical Publishers' Association

This is a vast area, covering a wide range of products from *Country Life* to soft porn; from free magazines deposited through your letter-box to highly specialist targeted products. Magazine publishing is fundamentally a commercial business; it's a high-risk activity with maybe a 40 per cent success rate. Big companies that can survive in spite of these high mortality rates dominate the industry. There is room for independent magazine publishers so long as they avoid competing head on with the giants of the industry and, instead, concentrate on producing a unique product, which means filling a gap in the market that you identify or create. Witness the extraordinary success of *Viz* – circulation one million-plus and still rising; *Viz* is something of an exception . . . Money is usually made primarily from advertising; circulation sales are secondary. Good circulation figures often boost advertising revenue. Once you have an established, successful product it might be bought out by one of the giant publishing houses. Alternatively the giants can wreck your profit or even force you to close down by launching a directly competitive product and achieving their circulation through promotional expenditure so enormous that you can't match it. If you sell (one free, local magazine was recently bought for £750,000 after three years) you can simply invest the money to set up a new magazine. The current trend in magazine publishing is towards narrower and narrower specialisation.

Although no formal qualifications are necessary to produce a magazine, any experience of the field, including working on an undergraduate magazine is useful. What you need is a target market (defined by age, socio-economic group, special interests, sex etc) and an idea to hit it with. You'll also have to decide how to distribute the magazine. You can do this in one of three ways. Firstly, from news-stands; for this you'll need wholesalers who will ensure that you get your target distribution through the retail trade (the wholesale trade and, to an extent, the retail trade is dominated by John Menzies and W.H. Smith, although there are thousands of outlets that may be better geared to your magazine). Secondly, you can operate a subscription list, which will save you the costs of retail distribution but will involve you in the time-consuming and equally expensive administration of the mailing list, although you can get the money up front. (Some magazines are distributed through a mixture of these ways.) Finally, you can hand it out or send it out free, deriving your income from advertisements alone.

Before you launch your magazine you have to get as good an idea as possible about how viable it may be. Major magazine distributors will help and may even try a regional test. By careful monitoring of the test, you might determine whether you have a success or not, but remember that the settle down circulation is usually only about 50–60 per cent of the initial sampling. Before you get this far you must have worked out production costs (paper, printing, quality etc) and revenue (from advertisers and/or cover price). Base your revenue calculations on the assumptions that you will penetrate only a small part of your target market; for news-stand sales you should expect to receive 45–50 per cent of the cover price per issue sold; the

trade regards sales of 85 per cent of an issue to be a 'technical' sell out. Of the 2,500 newstrade consumer magazines in Britain, only about 100 have circulations of more than 70,000. For subscription magazines, which are usually more specialised and with equally specialised advertisements, the market is more clearly defined and can be approached via list brokers. In any case, you have to get it right from day one. You'll soon find out if it's wrong; if you aren't reaching your target sales figures within four–five issues for news-stand distributed magazines (longer perhaps for subscriptions where there is a certain amount of buyer inertia), then you've probably failed. Advertisers will be monitoring the response that they get from your magazine and will stop using you if it isn't worthwhile. The success of free magazines is judged on advertising response.

Before you even start to think about revenue, your set-up costs will include financing all this research plus producing a mock up edition for distributors and advertisers. You probably should register as a company and you'll certainly need libel insurance and insurance against other disasters (floods, fires, etc). The absolute minimum of equipment is a telephone, typewriter and some printed stationery.

A bank manager who understands the needs of new enterprises (and preferably will know enough about magazine publishing to resist strangling the venture at birth if interest rates fluctuate wildly), is essential. If your own one doesn't, find one who does. Planning your cash flow is critical. If you are lucky, printers and paper merchants might give 60 days credit on bills (more if they know you). Advertisers are usually good at paying new companies quickly especially if they've had some direct contact with you and your magazine is small. Base cover price and rates card for advertisers on the research you've done and by referring to the competition.

Some people find having a partner with a different outlook useful for bouncing ideas off – not a friend though ('friendships never survive partnership'). Others find a partner only leads to clashes of ideas. Contacts are useful. You may want some freelance writers, editors and designers (try also the *Publishers' Freelance Directory*). You'll also probably want to employ help with ad sales, office administration etc. Young inexperienced staff are easy to find, enthusiastic and not blinkered by anybody else's training; they will need supervision though and employing some more experienced and expensive staff will give you more time to develop the business.

In the early days you have to establish confidence in your product. Get as much coverage in the media and in other magazines as possible. Make changes with caution and keep an eye on all competitors. Using established writers for regular features or columns helps to boost circulation as does satisfying any specific interest that you can identify in your market. As you expand you'll have to get used to spending an increasing amount of time managing staff, budgets etc.

Go to the PERIODICAL PUBLISHERS' ASSOCIATION for further information and read industry magazines like the *Publisher*.

Makeup Artist

Qualifications/Training	Recommended
Income bracket	Low–High
Licence	No
Town/Country	Town
Experience/Springboard Not necessary	
Travel	Yes
Mid-career entry	Possible
Exit sale	No
Entry costs	£500
Work at home	No
Mix and match	Possible.
You could think about: *Beauty consultant, Hairdresser, Yoga teacher*	
Enquiries Art colleges, model agencies, magazines	

It's every little girl's dream to earn her living by painting faces and that's exactly what a makeup artist does. It's a glamorous life involving a lot of variety – creating a fantasy makeup for a pop video one day and in a photographic studio making up models for the fashion shots in a magazine the next. But don't be misled by the glamour – it's also hard work, demanding a great deal of dedication and determination, particularly in the early days, and competition is stiff.

Most makeup artists are female, though there is no reason why men can't enter the field too. Most are self-employed and work on a freelance basis. A good eye for colour and interest in makeup are essential. You need to enjoy working with people and to be tactful, tolerant, discreet, outgoing and inventive. You also need to be able to work as part of a team.

Some cosmetic houses have trainee schemes for potential makeup artists but these tend to be short and invariably use only their own products. Art school is a good start, and beauty consultants, hairdressers and models often move on to become makeup artists. Television companies, such as the BBC and THAMES TELEVISION, run training courses but these are for employees only and there is fierce competition. The LONDON COLLEGE OF FASHION runs courses in London, and there are City and Guilds courses throughout the country. The many private schools can be expensive – a makeup course at COMPLECTIONS INTERNATIONAL, for example, will set you back over £4,000.

Alternatively, you can simply enlist the help of a few photogenic guinea pigs, find a good photographer and then tout your portfolio around as many outlets – magazines, photographic studios, advertising agencies, etc – as possible. If you've got the talent, someone will recognise it.

The initial costs and the money you can earn vary greatly, depending on ow you go about it and how successful you are. Earnings can be very high (£80,000 is not unheard of) but not everyone scores so high. You could even progress to opening your own beauty school, but you will really know you've made it when you're in constant demand for all the top magazines.

Most good artists have an agent who will do all their bookings for them and send their portfolio to prospective clients. Many of the model agencies also have makeup artists on their books.

Man with a Van

Qualifications/Training	No
Income bracket	Low–Medium
Licence	Driving Licence
Town/Country	Usually town
Experience/Springboard	No
Travel	Yes
Mid-career entry	Yes
Exit sale	No
Entry costs	£5,000
Work at home	No
Mix and match	Excellent. You could think about: ***Mini-cab driver, Disco owner, Painter/decorator, Events organiser, Hire shop owner, Musician***
Enquiries	Local removals companies, studios etc

A man with a van who knows his way about town can earn something in the region of £100 per day if he plays his cards right. Of course, there are overheads: tax, insurance, maintenance, parking tickets, a telephone paging account, not to mention the cost of the van itself, but if you enjoy driving, and want to be free to work when and as you please, this is the ideal job.

There are several different ways of setting up in the business – it depends on the type of people you are going to fetch and carry for. Many van drivers start off with mini-cab companies, breaking away to work on their own when they find that they are repeatedly working for three or four major clients: the clients may typically be in advertising, in film, publishing and TV, or be small manufacturing companies which have to distribute products. You can also build up a reputation independently,

if you know one or two people who need stuff moved at short notice. Another approach is to set yourself up as a small, local removals company; this tends to be less lucrative as you will need to be able to employ casual labour to help with hefty pieces of furniture.

One of the best ways to get yourself known is to have business cards printed to hand to anyone you do a small job for, send to office managers and leave pinned to noticeboards at offices, studios, warehouses and so on. If you are setting up as a small removals firm, a notice in the local paper is the best way to advertise yourself, plus an entry in the *Yellow Pages*.

You will have to keep careful accounts – some people will pay cash, but others will have to put your invoices through the system, which may cause cash flow problems. Some of the most successful van drivers specialise in moving props — easier as you gain experience: you will get to know the suppliers and the studios, and as you get to know them better, you build up a reputation among the people who hire you so that you become more popular. The problem comes when you are in such demand that you have to start turning work down. If you turn down a couple of jobs in succession, the hirer may not come to you again – so you have to find a balance between guaranteed, reliable delivery and an ability to take on any job at short notice.

Market Research Interviewer

Qualifications/Training	Yes
Income bracket	Low–Medium
Licence	No
Town/Country	Either
Experience/Springboard	No
Travel	Yes
Mid-career entry	Yes
Exit sale	No

Entry costs	Nil
Work at home	No
Mix and match	Excellent.

You could think about: *Actor, Musician, Novelist, House converter, Tourist guide, Antique dealer, Employment agent*

Enquiries
Market Research Society

Interviewing some 1,000 randomly selected people can, surprisingly, give an accurate idea of the characteristics, preferences, behaviour and opinions of a whole population. Market researchers use this data on behalf of clients with specific commercial or political interests – manufacturers, politicians, advertisers, broadcasters, etc.

Market research companies use a lot of freelance interviewers for specific projects, so you can work for a large company or several companies and get as much or as little work as you want. This makes it an excellent job to mix and match with another to keep the cash-flow positive between jobs or as you are building up (or for parents of young families). You can make your own interviewing schedules to suit your own constraints.

Interviews may be by telephone or 'in the field'. Research is either 'quantitative' or 'qualitative'. 'Sugging' is selling under the guise of doing market research – a reprehensible practice not undertaken by the respectable companies or interviewers.

Quantitative research is done on a nationwide sample of 1,000+. You interview Joe Public either on a random basis (every fourth person, every fifth house) within an electoral register, a region etc; or a sample carefully selected by region, age, sex, socio-economic group, working status. You'll have to cope with a lot of walking the streets, weather, finding nobody at home willing to talk to you. The clients may not have done much research themselves. (Wild goose chases such as researching opinions on the gas service where there is no gas are unusual but not unknown.) You may have to work at weekends and evenings especially if you're trying to reach people who are out during the day. You may be finding out what they think of a washing powder or what television they watch; sometimes a hall is hired for product testing and you invite people in off the streets; you may give people, say, a pair of tights and follow it up with a telephone call to find out how they've worn. Under MARKET RESEARCH SOCIETY rules, you must always show your identification on each occasion.

Once you've cut your teeth on quantitative research and shown some flair, you may be able to move on to depth interviewing. Here a smaller sample is interviewed in depth for two hours or so. This is more lucrative and commands a higher rate of pay.

Telephone interviewing is harder than interviewing people to their face, since you can't make eye contact, nod or give the other usual signs that you are listening attentively; and you have no visual aids such as show cards. You may have to complete a questionnaire on a computer screen (Computer Assisted Telephone Interviewing). There is scope here for linguists for international research so long as you don't mind working the hours necessary to ring different time zones.

There are no formal qualifications. You will usually receive some training on the job by the market research company; a couple of days is generally regarded as the minimum requirement. Otherwise, desirable qualities include persistence combined with tact; good health, good handwriting and a winning smile also count for a lot.

European Community Notes
Qualifications: UK qualifications recognised throughout EC and EC qualifications in UK.
Languages: To succeed, local language absolutely necessary.
Earnings: UK income generally same as elsewhere in the EC.
Setting up: You will find it possible to succeed throughout Europe; relatively easy in France, Germany and Spain.
Advice/Training: Advice, information and training not available for those wishing to work in Europe.

Exchanges: Formal job exchanges exist company to company.

Enquiry point for those wishing to work in the EC: ESOMAR and MARKET RESEARCH SOCIETY.

Recommended reading: European journal published by ESOMAR.

Notes: There are three things you should do: get a good grounding in a company in the UK before moving to Europe; get a command of your European language (top priority) which may also be possible from within a British office; start in a British-based firm in the country of your choice before springboarding.

Market Stall Holder

Qualifications/Training	No
Income bracket	Low–Medium
Licence	Yes
Town/Country	Town
Experience/Springboard	No
Travel	Local
Mid-career entry	Yes
Exit sale	No
Entry costs	£300++
Work at home	No
Mix and match	Yes.

You could think about: *Antique dealer, Caterer, Street entertainer*

Enquiries
Local markets or local authority

Market stalls have lower overheads than shops. They are an alternative small outlet for low value goods (collectables, costume jewellery, food, cheap clothes), but unsatisfactory for larger, more expensive things because they aren't secure. Although it is possible to use a market stall as a way into shop owning (more likely with antiques than with food) the vast difference in scale makes it a slow way in. Many towns have covered markets especially for antiques and crafts, some of these are privately owned; other markets are a collection of stalls on a street managed by the local council. It is illegal to sell from anywhere other than a licensed pitch in a market.

The only qualifications are having something to sell which suits the market and, in local authority markets, getting a licence from the local council. For a permanent licence, entitling you to a pitch on all market days (usually Monday–Saturday; sometimes only until Friday) you have to register with the council. There is usually a long waiting list (often two years or more) before you'll be offered a vacancy, subject to your commodity suiting the available pitch in the opinion of the council: eg no antiques in Smithfield. Licences can be passed on but only to a relation, some pitches stay in one family for generations.

Alternatively, get a casual licence; these are issued within a few days. With this you turn up early on market day, present yourself to the market inspector and are issued with any available pitch on either a first come or lottery system. There is no guarantee that you'll get a pitch when you want one but you can get a casual licence while on the waiting list for a permanent one; it's also useful for a one-off shot.

Costs of a pitch vary: up to £30 per week in a permanent market and about £10 per day for a casual licence holder. Additional set-up costs include about £5 registration fee to get a licence, your stock and something to sell it from that will protect both you and it from the rain (build your own stall or rent one), somewhere nearby (garage or shed) to store it in when the market is closed or a van. You'll also need something to carry the stock to market in.

The type of customer depends on the market. Food markets attract a high proportion of local shoppers while antiques and crafts have a less regular clientele of tourists, browsers, collectors and the trade. If you're selling your own craft work a market stall may lead to special commissions or interest from shops in stocking your goods. For some things reduced overheads may allow you to undercut shop prices and increase turnover.

It helps to have a partner or assistant; this will require your profits to support two but will allow you some time off. If you can't manage this, cultivate the friendship of neighbouring stall holders who will watch your stall while you have breaks during the day. You also need to find a stand-in to man the stall while you go on holiday. Market days are long, especially if you're selling food that has to be bought before you set up – this means starting work at about 5.00 am. Stalls have to be erected and displays set up before you open at about 9.00 or 10.00 and you'll have to pack up every night. Hours are even stranger for the specialist meat, fish and vegetable markets which serve the trade and are open all night. Those working outside will find bad weather may keep people away; but getting known at the market is important and your regular clientele will expect you to be there.

Marketing Consultant

Qualifications/Training	Recommended
Income bracket	High
Licence	No
Town/Country	Either
Experience/Springboard	A must
Travel	Lots
Mid-career entry	Essential
Exit sale	Possible
Entry costs	£5,000
Work at home	Yes
Mix and match	Possible.

You could think about: *Public relations consultant, Farmer, Timeshare developer*

Enquiries
Chartered Institute of Marketing

Marketing consultants sell one principal resource – their own skilled time. Businessmen buy this resource because they have confidence in the skill of the consultant to bring solutions to their particular businesses.

Marketing is an approach to business which holds that customers buy benefits or solutions to needs, rather than just products or services. It is concerned with the needs and attitudes of the customers and how to influence them in favour of given products, and with identifying market gaps to exploit competitors' weaknesses. Marketing is restless and dynamic; always trying to do things better, to improve market share and long-term profits. Market information gathered by a plethora of research methods underpins it.

Marketing is used in advertising to identify the best audiences and the most relevant benefits, in new product development, in sales promotion, in corporate design, in package design, and in multinational business – to explain how overseas markets are structured and work, and whether to enter them by means of joint ventures, by, say, starting from scratch or by acquisition. It is used in planning and executing mergers; in hiring and managing distributors; in building and running a sales force.

Marketing consultants must be able to persuade businessmen that they have some distinctive and sellable functional knowhow, or industry knowledge, or other personal attribute. It is – theoretically – possible to obtain such skills from outside industry (eg, as a business studies professor or industrial journalist) but in practice this is rare. The purchasers are businessmen used to demanding solid reasons to justify purchase decisions. The best reasons are the consultant's track record both as manager and consultant. Consultants must be seen to be able to deliver the goods.

The best way to start is to possess a CV which includes as many as possible of the following: good university degree, any subject; possibly an MBA – overrated unless from top institutions like Harvard, Columbia or Insead; basic marketing training in a highly regarded marketing and training company – eg, Unilever, IBM, Procter & Gamble; progressive career development, ideally to director level, in highly regarded companies; international experience; some language capabilities; marketing consultancy work with a leading consultancy such as McKinsey, Boston Consulting Group; demonstrable marketing record in a major industry sector such as retailing, liquor, banking, where many firms already value and understand your record; high visibility – eg, marketing writer, marketing media person, lecturer, public person; age at least 30. Paragons who boast all these CV attributes will already have sleek company cars and even sleeker salaries.

Starting out as a marketing consultant with a good CV is easy. You will already have a pool of potential buyers, ideally your first customers, waiting for you to begin. So start selling. You will need minimal capital since consultancy offers a generally positive cash flow, but budget to survive without income for the first six months. Keep down initial overheads, forgo the chauffeur, dispense with expensive trappings, at least until you are solidly established. The only essential start-up kit is top quality communications and top quality presentation, and much of this can be bought in.

The sort of people you sell to (their levels and their companies) will depend on what you are selling, what your skills are and whom you know. Do not try to sell acquisition studies to assistant brand managers, or sales promotion to the chairman. If the services you are selling fall within functional areas such as market research, PR, training, sales promotion, there will already be budgets you can feed on and specialists in the firm with a professional appreciation of your worth. But if you are selling solutions to ad hoc needs (such as acquisition searches, sales force reorganisations), no regular budget will exist. Unbudgeted projects are only approved at top level. Be persistent. The daily ratio of contacts to sales may be low but all contacts you make help prepare them for the time when they need you.

Firms engage consultants for a number of reasons: an overflow of work requiring your help temporarily; a young and untrained department needing to be galvanised by your new thinking; the specialist help which you can offer them. Firms often believe they already know the answer but want a second opinion, or face decisions laden with political and status risks to the managers who therefore need outsiders to identify solutions; take responsibility, and shoulder blame.

Marketing consultants come in all sizes: big-name consultancy companies and a host of smaller and one-man operators. Big companies charge the highest fees and often land the client when price is no object, or where the purchasers want to cover their backs by showing that they have used a top firm. But the key selection criterion is the confidence that the consultant can deliver and this confidence comes best from direct personal experience which leaves much scope for you to sell to people who know that you are good.

The amount of consultancy work is never just right for long. All projects are innovative (no problem, no consultancy project), and the work is demand-dedicated. Hence one more client may be one too many; but clients imagine they are your sole benefactors and if you prevaricate they will not come back. Uncomfortable as this can become, it does mean that life is seldom boring.

Demand for your services will vary between industry sectors, companies, management levels and problem areas. No two consultants will have identical experience. Projects handled by one marketing consultant in his first year of operation included: assessment of the 'brown ale' phenomenon in the UK beer market, for a French brewing group; review of the marketing plans for a new branded wine concept, to be launched in Belgium; sales force reorganisation and retaining, for a UK food manufacturer; development of incentive programmes for pharmaceutical reps, retailing to doctors in the UK; warehousing and distribution study for a cigarette company newly arrived in the UK market.

Whatever your stock in trade, it will be a wasting asset. The more you succeed in promoting and practising your skills, the more you will breed imitators. Imitators will compete by improving your product and undercutting your price. You must therefore invest in keeping your products modern and superior, and in placing them continuously before your audience. Never rest on your laurels. If successful, rewards are outstanding.

Read *Offensive Marketing*. Use the CHARTERED INSTITUTE OF MARKETING for its library and courses; and the Business Information Section of the British Library, located in the SCIENCE REFERENCE LIBRARY.

✯✯✯ European Community Notes

Qualifications: Some UK qualifications are affiliations recognised throughout EC and some EC qualifications in UK.

Languages: To succeed, local language necessary.

Advice/Training: Advice, information and training available for those wishing to work in Europe.

Media Trainer

Qualifications/Training	No
Income bracket	Medium
Licence	No
Town/Country	Town
Experience/Springboard	Essential
Travel	Possible
Mid-career entry	Essential
Exit sale	No
Entry costs	£3,000++
Work at home	No
Mix and match	Yes.

You could think about: *Journalist, Corporate video producer, PR consultant, Radio reporter/presenter, UK correspondent (Overseas Media), Film director, Actor, Football commentator, Conference organiser, In-company trainer*

Enquiries
Media Trainers

Media trainers help people to present a message on TV, radio or in the press. People who are likely to need media trainers include politicians, charity leaders, authors, senior businessmen and anyone else who may be called at short notice to comment on events or situations or to promote their work or organisation in the media. Media trainers provide practice and advice on how to communicate clearly and briefly; they also advise on personal presentation (which colours to avoid on television and how to control excessive hand gestures for example). Media training is not something you should expect to do full time, or as your first career. It's excellent for mixing and matching and to avoid going stale or losing touch with new developments, media trainers tend to continue to work in, for example, PR, newspaper or radio journalism to keep their own skills fresh while they train other people. There is likely to be increasing demand for media trainers as communications expand; deregulation is leading to the emergence of new TV and radio stations all with air time to fill, whilst promotional and training videos are produced by increasing numbers of businesses, companies and organisations. This means that many people with no media experience are likely to find themselves broadcasting at short notice and they'll want to be trained before this happens.

There are no formal qualifications but you need to have several years of experience of whichever media (TV, radio, video or the press) you intend to train in including having a good idea of the sort of approach interviewers are likely to take with your clients. This also gives you credibility amongst clients, who will, themselves, be experts in their own areas. Experience is also a good source of useful contacts. If you haven't worked in, for instance, TV it's a good idea to team up with someone who has and offer an allround media training package. Media trainers aren't there to tell their clients what to say but how to say it, so you'll have to be able to advise on how to present a wide range of, sometimes, contentious arguments in a way that audiences will understand. This means being openminded and diplomatic; you may disagree with the message you're helping to present. Media trainers should also enjoy meeting people and be patient and sympathetic to clients who may assume far too much knowledge from their audience or find the whole business of appearing on screen harrowing. Discretion is also important, the people you work with are often well known to the public and some of the material you deal with may be sensitive; it isn't a good idea to go running to the press with snippets of unpublicised information before your clients do.

You need to own a phone, an answering machine and some stationery. The rest you can hire when you need it. Media training is most usefully done by practical experience. You're working with busy, successful people who don't have time to waste and who will have to be prepared to condense what they have to say into as little as 10–15 seconds of air time. Allowing clients to see and hear themselves is sometimes brutal but an effective way of illustrating their weaknesses which works better than having you lecture on what to do and what to avoid. Video is especially useful for this, not least because anyone who has mastered the art of appearing in front of cameras is likely to find radio and the press considerably easier. This means hiring video studios, technicians and playback centres, also interviewers unless you're an experienced media interviewer yourself. You'll have to pay for this yourself before your clients pay you so make sure that you have a spare couple of thousand pounds to help cash flow. Clients usually book you for a day or half a day; charges work out at about £1,000–£1,300 per day. Work comes from advertising but, even more by word of mouth. Publicise your services to big businesses, politicians and PR companies. Once you've trained one senior employee you'll probably get others as well as running refresher courses for existing trainees. Jobs divide into two rough categories; those you train so that they are prepared for the media at some time in the future and more urgent jobs when, for example, a big story breaks and people need to be trained at short notice – when this happens you have to be especially sure of the discretion of everyone involved. It's a new and expanding area and there is a lot of co-operation: your contacts within journalism and PR are good sources of work as well as being on-call as potential trainers and interviewers themselves when your own expertise is not enough.

MEP

Qualifications/Training	No
Income bracket	High
Licence	No
Town/Country	Either
Experience/Springboard	Yes
Travel	Lots
Mid-career entry	Excellent
Exit sale	No
Entry costs	£1,000
Work at home	No
Mix and match	Excellent.

You could think about: *Solicitor, Public relations consultant, Landlord, Foreign correspondent*

Enquiries
Political parties

The work of an MEP is nothing if not varied. Covering anywhere between eight and ten parliamentary constituencies means the demands of local political parties, single-issue fanatics and genuine casework are larger than those of an MP. Conflicting priorities from all the above, the Whips (national and international) and the demands of working meetings in at least three countries give a whole new meaning to the word stress. Managing family life is difficult; although children under five can identify with the excuse 'I couldn't get home because the plane was delayed by fog,' which is easier to understand and accept than 'We had a three-line Whip at 10.00 p.m.'

Any job involving catching planes several times a week requires a strong grip on reality, steady nerves and good health. A life in hotel rooms requires an ability to sleep anywhere, and frequent airport delays and lack of time in any one place demand the ability to write speeches and articles in crowded public places on one's lap. Flexibility is the keynote.

MEPs have an office in Strasbourg, where they spend one week of every month; an office in Brussels, where they spend at least half of every remaining week, and, most importantly, an office in the constituency which will be run by trusted staff, and in which they may not set foot from one week to the next. Hi-tech communications equipment is a must.

It is necessary to cultivate the art of appearing to be in the constituency much more than one really is. This is because the main bulk of MEPs' parliamentary work not only takes place abroad, but seems remote and irrelevant to the ordinary people in the street, who require a 'local photo' event before they feel their MEP is working for them.

Members of the European Parliament first have to run the gamut of the same selection procedure as MPs (multiplied by eight or ten), and face the electorate once every five years. Clearly this requires a period of credibility building in the party of one's choice. For method, see **MP**. Added to this is an international outlook, possibly a foreign language or two (not mandatory), and an ability to turn European-level issues into something the local party and press can identify with.

Communications with party hierarchy and national MPs are spasmodic, mutually distrustful and sometimes downright acrimonious. Because the balance of power between the European and national Parliaments still favours the latter, a strong sense of identity is required (so as to survive observations such as 'Wouldn't you like to be a *real* MP?').

Once elected, culture shock is of mega-proportions. You are alone in foreign places where you forget the telephone dialling code. The staff never speak English when you want them to. Planes run late and you miss meetings about which the Whips get cross. You are exhausted, the rituals unfamiliar, and there is a new style of politics – consensus rather than confrontation – which means learning new rules from scratch. Political parties have different names – which ones to trust? You will start with no office and many demands requiring that you create a support infrastructure urgently. The hours are punishing. Parliamentary holidays are short (August only), allowing you to devote almost no time to your constituency, which makes constant and massive demands for your presence.

There are numerous possibilities for travel to exotic or other places scattered all over the world, for short periods of time crammed with meetings. This means family life is a disaster. It's best to be single, fit and childless.

Some MEPs are sponsored (mostly Labour, arranged before election). Many Conservatives have outside business interests. There is a voluntary register of interests, but nothing to stop, for instance, a landowner serving on the Agriculture Committee.

The development of specialisms is more important than at Westminster, if one wants to get any speaking time or have any measure of influence.

Elected representation is a risky job, but the redundancy pay increases over time (starting with three months' pay). A philosophical approach towards the future is therefore requisite.

The salary is meagre compared with local government, the civil service, law, consultancies or business – although the office expenses are sufficient to operate on a passing professional basis. Travel is paid for, and there is a daily allowance for days spent abroad, which is crucial for living in expense-account towns.

Useful reading: three daily newspapers, including the *Financial Times* – plus a glance at the tabloids; *The Economist*; lorry-loads of Eurodocuments and journals written in impenetrable prose; light novels for those hours in airports when you can't write or sleep. Any academic or economic book on Europe; the best single source on Europe is still the EUROPEAN COMMUNITY. A reasonable interest in foreign films and literature can help with relationships with non-British colleagues. Don't forget the vitamin tablets, ear-plugs and eyeshades!

Mini-cab Driver

Qualifications/Training	No
Income bracket	Low–Medium
Licence	Driving licence
Town/Country	Mostly town
Experience/Springboard	No
Travel	Local
Mid-career entry	Excellent
Exit sale	No
Entry costs	£3,500+
Work at home	No
Mix and match	Excellent.

You could think about: ***almost anything***

Enquiries
Local mini-cab companies

Mini-cab drivers use their own cars as taxis; legislation governing them is less stringent than for licensed cabs. They are self-employed and operate through companies who liaise between passengers and drivers. By and large cab drivers choose their own hours subject to the basic requirements of the company being fulfilled. This makes it a good job if you've got other commitments or want to mix and match with another job, or simply augment your income. There are more men than women mini-cab drivers not least because of the greater risks for women taking strangers in their cars. There is a market for all-women cab companies, to take women passengers only, which is not often tapped.

Anyone with a four-door car and a clean driving licence can become a cab driver. You pay rent to the controlling company which also provides (on payment of a fairly low rent) a radio phone which will keep you in touch with them while you're driving. Companies also arrange for advertising. By law mini-cab drivers may only carry passengers who have contacted the company (usually by phone) in advance – you cannot ply for hire on the streets without being a licensed cab driver. On the other hand there are no laws saying you must agree to carry passengers for certain distances and you can refuse to pick up any passengers you don't like the look of. The local police station will support you if any passenger refuses to compensate you for loss of income incurred by your having to clear up after they've been sick. Your insurance will probably stipulate the maximum number of passengers you can carry – usually four.

As well as a car and deposit for the radio phone, you will need hire and reward insurance which costs at least twice as much as standard motor insurance. The amount you earn depends on how many fares you can get which can depend on traffic conditions. Passengers are usually fairly local but, when they want to go for long distances, you may have an empty car on the way back. The cab company sets a rough fare scale (including a minimum charge for very short journeys, usually around £2.50 and extra charges for carrying baggage, animals etc). Mini-cabs don't have meters, fares and tips are paid in cash.

There are obvious risks. It helps if you're a good driver and also if you're careful about who you pick up (within reason). It's easy to get into; local mini-cab companies are often delighted to take on more drivers. Although there may be some routine work from regular customers (more likely during the day when local businesses or hospital out-patients may use you) most of this is unscheduled.

Trade press: *Cab Trade News*.

Motorcycle Messenger

Qualifications/Training	No
Income bracket	Low
Licence	Driving licence
Town/Country	Town
Experience/Springboard	No
Travel	Local
Mid-career entry	Yes
Exit sale	No

Entry costs	£1,000+
Work at home	No
Mix and match	Excellent.

You could think about: ***almost anything***

Enquiries
Local courier services

If you can ride well and have a good knowledge of a large city, the potential earnings may outweigh the thought of periods off work due to injury. But the danger element can be over emphasised. You're more at risk of collecting points for speeding and other traffic offences (traffic lights and one way streets are particular hazards) not to mention fines and fistfuls of parking tickets.

The upside is that not many other jobs provide you with the opportunity to cruise about on your mean machine all day long – often 8 am to 8 pm. Long motorway hauls can get a bit boring; shaft driven bikes have a big advantage over chain driven. You'll probably need to be your own mechanic to save cash.

While this is a good way to raise immediate cash the outgoings can knock you back a bit (petrol, repairs, maps etc) and the recession has not only decimated the customer base but led surviving businesses to economise on messengers. Many firms operate just inside the law and will rip you off rather than lose money eg they agree a legally impossible deadline with the client, you pay the speeding fine.

Very few despatch services provide much more than an agency for booking the services of their riders, so expect to take care of your own bike and other necessities (although a few agencies do provide bikes). Fees are on a piecework basis, with the agency taking a cut of the job. If you want to keep in business you will need a reliable bike and expect it to be worn out very rapidly – budget up to £1,000 or more. Find out what the agency provides in the way of insurance, an ordinary policy is likely to be invalidated by working as a messenger. Norwich Union will insure you with no age or experience considerations but a correspondingly high premium. A good agency will have plenty of work, so earnings depend entirely on how fast you are and how well you can find your way around but £7 an hour is easily possible. Many companies offer 'guaranteed' minimum earnings (in London commonly of £200 or £250 per week). Some specify minimum capacity bikes. Some charge a fee for the circuit and for the radio. There are also openings for bicycle messengers. Hours are basically the same as the businesses who use the service. *Despatch Rider* is a useful magazine.

Motorcycle Racer

Qualifications/Training	No
Income bracket	Low
Licence	Yes
Town/Country	Either
Experience/Springboard	No
Travel	Yes
Mid-career entry	Possible
Exit sale	No
Entry costs	£1,000+
Work at home	No
Mix and match	Yes.

You could think about: ***Motorcycle messenger, Pop group sound engineer, Garage owner, Sex therapist***

Enquiries
Auto Cycle Union, Amateur Motor Cycle Association.

Very few riders ever make it to a level where they can earn a living, but if you're good enough and lucky enough, you might land a 'works' contract from a major manufacturer or sponsor.

There are two organising bodies for motorcycle sport. The AUTO CYCLE UNION (ACU) covers all branches, while the AMATEUR MOTOR CYCLE ASSOCIATION (AMCA) caters only for off-road riding (such as moto-cross and trials).

You'll need to buy or borrow a suitable bike for the class of riding which interests you, then join a club affiliated to one of the organised bodies (they will supply lists).

You need to apply for a competition licence – the fee includes compulsory personal accident insurance. Expect to spend a year as a novice (you have to qualify at 10 events over at least three circuits) before obtaining a full licence. For details buy a copy of the *ACU Handbook*.

Trade magazines abound but the most useful are *Motor Cycle News, Road Racer* and *Dirt Bike Rider*.

MP

Qualifications/Training	No
Income bracket	Medium
Licence	No
Town/Country	Mostly town
Experience/Springboard	Yes
Travel	Yes
Mid-career entry	Excellent
Exit sale	No
Entry costs	£500+
Work at home	No
Mix and match	Excellent.

You could think about: *Barrister, Novelist, Public relations consultant, Journalist, Farmer, Teacher*

Enquiries
Political parties

The job of a Member of Parliament is several rolled into one. The demands of your electorate, your constituency party, the Whips' office and public life are all different. Conflict with family life is certain and the divorce rate is one of the highest. If you join a front bench, things only get worse. To be successful, you will need to be articulate, with a good line in 'flannel', the ability to think on your feet and excellent personal organisation. Life will be less gruelling too if you get on well with people, have plenty of self-assurance (critics call it conceit) and resilience to insult

and rotting fruit. Strong political convictions probably come next.

'Members of Parliament are selected not elected.' You can be bold, pay a deposit of £500 and stand as an independent but you're very unlikely to be elected. To stand any real chance you must be adopted by one of the major parties, whose selection practices vary. Find out more by contacting the head office of the party of your choice (CONSERVATIVE, LABOUR, LIBERAL DEMOCRATS . . .). Conservatives first attend the regular selection course and if you pass this stage, your name is placed on the list of candidates. When a vacancy occurs in a local constituency, you will be notified and you can apply if you wish. The local party committee will make a final shortlist after further interviews. Those on the final list are invited (sometimes with spouses) to a selection conference composed of around 200 paid-up constituency association members who take a secret ballot on the outcome.

In the Labour Party, every local branch of the Party and affiliated organisations (eg trades unions) can put forward a name to the constituency general management committee but the choice of candidate is made by a ballot of all the local Party members in conjunction with local trades unions (who make up 40 per cent of the vote). Canvassing is strictly prohibited once the process starts and this system now favours local talent.

How you finally get adopted as a candidate is largely a matter of chemistry, your face fitting in the locality and your political views matching any idiosyncrasies of the local party. There is an unofficial system whereby you cut your teeth in a no-hope constituency before getting the prize of a safe seat. But you can serve your 'apprenticeship' in other ways, working for the party HQ, local government, trades unions, voluntary work for the party etc. Your election campaign will be run by your election agent: you need someone who is efficient and who you can get along with under stress.

Once elected, many suffer from culture shock. You are exhausted, the rituals unfamiliar, you will start with no proper office and your support system may be a long way away. If you represent a constituency outside London, you have to decide how much of both your political and domestic operation to move to London. The hours are punishing. Parliamentary recesses are long, allowing you to devote some sustained time to your constituency and family (and get a holiday too if you can). You should either be single or be married to a saint. It's not a life recommended for single parents.

Some MPs are sponsored (mostly Labour, arranged before election) or use their position as an MP to gain eg consultancies outside Parliament. All interests should be declared in the parliamentary register of interests. Some MPs develop specialisms early, particularly if they are politically ambitious. Membership of select committees may then follow or maybe the front bench. If you don't mind not being re-elected, you can do nothing at all. Representing all but the safest constituency is a precarious business and political fortunes are made or lost very quickly. A second career is an asset, particularly if you can keep it going while you are an MP (difficult to find time); law is a popular one.

The salary is not excessive but you can claim additional costs – to stay in London if the constituency is distant; free rail warrants; and up to £28,986 pa for secretarial, research and office support. You can use your position to get some freelance work eg, writing and on television but you'll never get rich being an MP alone.

Useful reading is profuse; try the *House Magazine* and *Hansard*. Also, *Westminster Blues; Careers in Politics; Parliament and the Public; Westminster Man; A Tribal Anthropology of the Commons People; Honourable Member; Parliament in the 1980s; How Parliament Works.*

European Community Notes

See **MEP**

Music Copyist

Qualifications/Training	No
Income bracket	Low–Medium
Licence	No
Town/Country	Either
Experience/Springboard	No
Travel	Local
Mid-career entry	Yes
Exit sale	No
Entry costs	Nil
Work at home	Yes

Mix and match   Probably essential. You could think about: *Orchestral musician, Repetiteur/accompanist/ coach, Computer software author, Social worker*

Enquiries
Musicians' Union

This is someone who copies individual instrument parts from original scores so that the music can be performed by bands/ groups/orchestras. You need to be able to play and read music, have a good ear and knowledge of harmony. You should be able to write neatly and quickly, and known when to leave spaces so the player can turn the page without stopping in mid-phrase. The job requires patience, and an ability to work accurately and under pressure – possibly through the night, ready for an early morning recording session.

You can work from home with good light, a decent pen and a telephone. You can combine it with another job, which may be necessary as the pay is bad: £1.44 for single stave; £2.87 for double. Working flat out, and if you can stand the strain and loneliness, you can earn up to £1,000 a week for TV, but you're likely to end up having a nervous breakdown. If you own a motorbike you can earn more by charging for delivering your work. No computer is faster or more accurate than the human hand, but job prospects are poor. Join the MUSICIANS' UNION so that your name appears in the section on copyists in their directory. Send out cards advertising your services to music publishers, and recording, film and TV companies. Try to get in with TV, films, a successful conductor, composer or group who commission or are involved in new music.

Get the BBC pamphlet on copying from the music library at the BBC.

Music Critic

Qualifications/Training	No
Income bracket	Low–Medium
Licence	No
Town/Country	Mostly town
Experience/Springboard	No
Travel	Yes
Mid-career entry	Possible
Exit sale	No
Entry costs	£500+
Work at home	Partly
Mix and match	Excellent.

You could think about: *Scriptwriter, Journalist, Festival director, Novelist, Teacher*

Enquiries
Local papers or music critics

A real love of music is essential and if you can play an instrument (preferably the piano) it will help you to read a score. Take a degree course, not necessarily in music, which will provide training in writing creatively, organising, selecting and expressing your thoughts clearly. Playing regularly in an amateur orchestra or choir will remind you what it's like to perform, stimulate your enthusiasm for music and prevent your getting tired of it by always listening with a critical ear.

You must be aware of your subjectivity; your reaction is a very personal one. If a production or performance is bad, take the trouble to find out whether this was due to the conductor, the soloist, the orchestra or some external hazard. If you want to be devastatingly critical of some performer, composer or organisation, make sure they are in a position to withstand it – it is cruel and pointless to murder unknown beginners.

For the first few years it's wise to have other employment eg freelance journalism on another subject, a steady job in advertising, teaching or anything that leaves you enough energy to listen to concerts or records in the evening. All you need to start with is a room with a good record player and a telephone. Get to know as many journalists and musicians as possible. Write some sample programme notes or record reviews, submit them to an arts editor or record magazine. Seem confident in order to persuade them to try you out. There is now a wide range of magazines and newspapers which include music criticism: see them in your public library. Travelling to provincial productions in the UK is interesting and going abroad to festivals a bonus.

The job could be bad for your social life – though not if your social life consists of going to concerts and listening to music. If you enjoy doing background research and find pleasure in expressing yourself in writing, you should be able to endure enforced loneliness for the greater part of each day including weekends. If you use a computer terminal at home and type your article straight on to the page in the newsroom, this will increase your isolation, so visit your paper each week.

To start with, you can earn the odd £50 per article; probably up to £20,000 as a full-time critic.

You need access to *Grove's Dictionary of Music* and you should read *Classical Music* and the *Musical Times*.

Music/Instrument Retailer

Qualifications/Training	No
Income bracket	Low–Medium
Licence	No
Town/Country	Town
Experience/Springboard	Recommended
Travel	No
Mid-career entry	Excellent
Exit sale	Yes
Entry costs	£10,000+
Work at home	No
Mix and match	Limited.

You could think about: *Jazz musician, Music publisher, Musical intrument repairer, Music teacher*

Enquiries
Music Retailers' Association

This is someone who owns a shop which sells music and musical instruments. The only qualifications needed for this job are a knowledge of music and the ability to play an instrument. You must be resilient, be able to spot a good business prospect, have charm, tact and an eye for making attractive window displays. With these qualities the potential is limitless, but you need a good accountant.

You need a large amount of capital. If you have a partner, friend or relation with their own business who will act as your guarantor, this helps. Remember that accepting investment from outsiders takes away your independence, even though initially it might be useful financially. Borrow as much as possible from your bank, having sold your idea to the sympathetic manager. Find a suitable shop, possibly in a secondary trading position, making sure it is accessible and convenient for public transport and parking. The rent will depend on the area or region of the country. Allow at least £1,500 for buying second-hand display cabinets and counters or having them made by a friendly car-penter. Advertise in the local press, circularise musicians and music teachers; get addresses from the INCORPORATED SOCIETY OF MUSICIANS and the county music adviser. You will need good insurance cover for the instruments and music you are selling. Engage intelligent, reliable and cheerful staff – probably with a passion for playing, possibly on a part-time basis or job-share basis.

Working hours will probably be 10.00–5.30 but evenings will be spent pricing, checking deliveries, window displays, invoicing, doing accounts and chasing bad debts. When you can afford it, get a computer which suits your particular needs. You are vulnerable to changes such as schools reducing music lessons (because of strikes or cuts) thus reducing your sales.

If you survive the first two years you will be lucky to have made £8,000. After a while, you can combine the job with some teaching or playing part time. You will find music publishers are often out of date and out of touch; instrument makers on the whole are businesslike. You can join the MUSIC RETAILERS' ASSOCIATION. It's an enjoyable job if you like meeting interesting people, learning more about music and creating your own business.

Music Publisher

Qualifications/Training	No
Income bracket	Low – usually
Licence	No
Town/Country	Town
Experience/Springboard	No
Travel	Yes
Mid-career entry	Yes
Exit sale	Yes
Entry costs	£3,000
Work at home	Possible

Mix and match　　　　　　　Usually.
You could think about: *Musician, Music/Instrument retailer, music critic, Recording studio owner*

Enquiries
Music Publishers' Association

This is nothing to do with book publishing. It is a business venture in which the publisher searches for composers, procures their unpublished music, edits it and arranges for its printing and distribution to retailers under the publishing firm's own brand name. It is an area of endeavour paved with financial disasters. The few small independent publishers who succeed make little money and specialise in compositions of a well-defined historical period of music or for a particular instrument. You should be able to play an instrument, read music and like gambling. You also need enthusiasm, perseverance and a good accountant; a business management course is useful.

You can work from home preferably with £1,500 capital (a bank loan is not a good idea), telephone, typewriter, filing cabinet and storage space for stock awaiting distribution; a computer will help. Carry out careful market research to establish the most profitable area; it's best to go either for the top of the market or the bottom. Educational music (in book or sheet form) must be durable and therefore costs more to produce; books which always look good are also more expensive. At the other end of the market, the turnover of pop sheet music is quicker.

Maintain the goodwill of the composers and retailers; and, if you're publishing educational music, the teachers. Keep in touch with musicians or pupils to test the products and read musical magazines on your subject area; you will have to travel to keep in touch with the retailers who handle your list. With most music publishing it will be a year before you see a return on your money and your income will depend on how many works are published in a year. Find a good reliable printer and establish a good working relationship. You can sub-contract to sole selling agents but use only one to start with: they can deli-

berately suppress work to avoid competition. Membership of the IPG is useful for seminars on publishing information and advice; and join the MUSIC PUBLISHERS' ASSOCIATION when you are successful. You can do another job at the same time; if you are full-time, avoid becoming a workaholic by providing recreation periods during the day.

You must enjoy your work as you won't make any money unless you are very lucky in pop music. That said, these days there are many small independent pop music publishers who work with artists/songwriters and bands prior to them obtaining record deals. If the independents become associated with bands in the early days and develop them so that their songwriting later becomes successful, they will have made a major contribution both to the business and to their bank balances.

Music Teacher

Qualifications/Training	Recommended
Income bracket	Low–Medium
Licence	No
Town/Country	Either
Experience/Springboard	No
Travel	Local
Mid-career entry	Possible
Exit sale	No
Entry costs	£2,500
Work at home	Yes
Mix and match	Yes.

You could think about: *Musician, Orchestral fixer, Instrumental soloist, Classical singer, Counsellor, Hi-fi shop owner, Music therapist*

Enquiries
Incorporated Society of Musicians

This involves teaching people how to sing or play an instrument, or the history/theory of music, either privately or in a school or college.

If you want to have private pupils and teach an instrument from home it is useful first to get a practical teaching qualification: LRAM (ROYAL ACADEMY OF MUSIC) or the equivalent LRCM, LGSM or LTCM from one of the other colleges. Contact the INCORPORATED SOCIETY OF MUSICIANS (ISM) for the name of a really good private teacher. Going to music college or university will help to make contacts within the profession and get a wider musical education.

You need to enjoy communicating with people, especially children; be patient, understanding, enthusiastic and encouraging with your pupils. If you live in an area where parents can afford private lessons for their children, you can build up a practice quite quickly. Personal recommendation is the most effective way, but you can advertise in local shops and newspapers, the *Music Teacher* or *Classical Music*. The ISM fixes a minimum rate (£13.54–£14.32 per hour) for private teaching. Join ISM to benefit from standard contracts (essential for a secure income), legal advice, workshops and conferences and some social contact and stimulation as life can be isolated.

This is not the quickest way to the pot of gold at the end of the rainbow; but with a good reputation and pupils who go on to music college, do well in competitions and local festivals, you can earn as much as £15,000–£20,000 pa. Private lessons tend to be after school hours or in the evenings, which eats into your weekday social life. If you want to get some peripatetic teaching during school hours, write to your county or borough music adviser offering your services.

If you also want to teach music theory and harmony etc in schools or colleges of education, it is useful to get a Diploma of Education. This involves attending a suitable one-year course at poly, university or teacher training college, possibly one day a week over two years.

For private teaching you need a room, £1,500 to buy a second-hand or reconditioned piano, a telephone and neighbours who are tolerant of your pupils' musical efforts. You can work as a freelance performer so long as this does not interfere with your pupils, and they and their parents do not mind constantly changing lesson times. Allow another £1,000-plus for a car, particularly in the country and doing peripatetic work. You may be able to earn a bit more by teaching the organ, playing for the church or amateur choirs and musical societies; you have freedom to organise your life in this job. A free booklet, *Careers with Music*, is available from the ISM.

★ European Community Notes

Qualifications: Generally UK qualifications recognised throughout EC and EC qualifications in UK.

Languages: To succeed, local language necessary.

Earnings: UK income generally same as elsewhere in the EC.

Setting up: Is not easy anywhere. You will find it difficult to succeed in Denmark, Eire, France, Greece, Italy, Luxembourg, Portugal, Spain. You will find it easier in Belgium, Germany, Netherlands.

Advice/Training: Advice, information and training available for those wishing to work in Europe.

Exchanges: Formal job exchanges do not exist.

Financial help: exists for study, training or travel in the EC, specific to this job.

Enquiry point for those wishing to work in the EC: INCORPORATED SOCIETY OF MUSICIANS.

Music Therapist

Qualifications/Training	Essential
Income bracket	Low–Medium
Licence	No
Town/Country	Town
Experience/Springboard	Recommended
Travel	Local
Mid-career entry	Recommended
Exit sale	No

Entry costs	£2,500
Work at home	Possible
Mix and match	Yes.

You could think about: ***Music teacher, Musician, China restorer, Word processor***

Enquiries

British Society for Music Therapy, Association of Professional Music Therapists.

This is someone who uses a mixture of music and psychology to help people change both physically and psychologically. First you will need a diploma from a music college or a degree. Then apply for a one-year diploma at the GUILDHALL SCHOOL, ROEHAMPTON INSTITUTE or the NORDOFF ROBINS COURSE. All courses are in London. A PGCE is useful if you want to work in a school.

Primarily, you need the rare ability to listen and move others emotionally through your performance. You should be able to play an instrument well in all styles and have good keyboard skills, sight-reading and improvisation. You must be born with intuition and an awareness of others' feelings. You should enjoy working with other therapists, doctors or teachers in a team. Self esteem and hope are advantageous; good results do not come quickly. Do-gooders don't make good music therapists, but happy accepting people do.

Try to get experience working with a therapist in a local hospital or school before applying for a course. You should preferably be over 25 before starting training. It can be an isolated job so join the BRITISH SOCIETY FOR MUSIC THERAPY or the ASSOCIATION OF PROFESSIONAL MUSIC THERAPISTS, attend workshops and read their journals. You can work in hospitals, special schools or clinics; you can work with the deaf, mentally or physically handicapped, psychiatric, geriatric or the terminally ill, with recidivists and stressed workers of any kind.

You can work on your own from a large room at home with a telephone, tape recorder and, if you feel rich, a video. If you have to travel to visit your clients you will need a car, and £2,000 to purchase a good piano or synthesiser as well as various percussion and tonal instruments. You can negotiate your fees to match your clients' means.

Working in a private practice, you can mix work in a school or hospital, take private clients, and can teach music at the same time. There may be quite a bit of travelling.

Those in the music therapy field are sometimes looked upon as 'brown rice and sandals' do-gooders, not always understood or taken seriously by medics or teachers. It is a young and growing profession; practitioners see themselves as pioneers, needing to 'spread the gospel' so you should be able to speak confidently about your work.

European Community Notes

Qualifications: UK qualifications not recognised in EC, nor EC qualifications in UK.

Languages: To succeed, local language necessary.

Earnings: UK income generally lower than elsewhere in the EC.

Setting up: You will find it difficult to succeed in Belgium, Eire, France, Greece, Italy, Luxembourg, Portugal, Spain. You will find it easier in Denmark, Germany, Netherlands. The 'easy' ones have an established profession of music therapy.

Advice/Training: Advice, information and training not available for those wishing to work in Europe.

Exchanges: Formal job exchanges do not exist.

Enquiry point for those wishing to work in the EC: Amelia Oldfield, ASSOCIATION OF PROFESSIONAL MUSIC THERAPISTS

Recommended reading: Unlimited. Probably most helpful is the *International Newsletter of Music Therapy.*

Musical Instrument Maker

Qualifications/Training	Recommended
Income bracket	Low–Medium
Licence	No
Town/Country	Either
Experience/ Springboard	Recommended
Travel	No
Mid-career entry	Possible
Exit sale	Unlikely
Entry costs	£6,000+
Work at home	Yes
Mix and match	Possible.

You could think about: *Furniture designer/maker, Musical instrument repairer, Music/instrument retailer, Counsellor*

Enquiries
Other musical instrument makers

The degree of expertise needed for this means that most musical instrument makers specialise in one particular instrument and nearly all specialise to the degree of making only, eg string, brass, wood-wind. Some basic knowledge is needed of the principles of engineering and design draughtmanship, and a gift for working with wood or other natural materials is essential. It's obviously very useful to be able to play the instrument though you don't have to virtuoso – failing that you must have very close contact with someone who does and who can tell you what's good or bad about the instruments you make.

Courses at the LONDON COLLEGE OF FURNITURE, NEWARK or MERTON COLLEGES are a very good way of developing contacts and your own specialisations. If you want to go further afield, the best for strings is the NATIONAL SCHOOL OF VIOLIN MAKING in Mittenwald in West Germany or the Italian equivalent in Cremona. There are very few traditional apprenticeships still available; a good way of making contacts and gaining experience is to work for someone else (only bother with a well known maker) after you've done a course and gradually start to make your own instruments. Get to know as many musicians as you can. When you have sold one to a professional who likes it, then you can think about working part of the time for yourself. You must be able to empathise with your customers who tend to identify with their instruments to the point of neurosis. Makers need to be sympathetic, tactful, have physical stamina and an ability to trust their own judgement. Making an instrument involves the sensitivity of an artist which is why there are so few successful makers in the UK. The profession is overcrowded and the fall-out rate colossal.

To set up on your own you need either capital or a working partner to keep you for the first two years when there will be no income. Approach the NATIONAL FEDERATION OF SELF-EMPLOYED AND SMALL BUSINESSES for information and advice. Allow about £6,000 to purchase a workbench, band saw, circular saw, small drill and special wood etc. You can make your tools while in employment. Get accommodation of your own *before* you start; think about disturbance to the neighbours – musicians playing at all hours, the noise of electric tools etc. You can set up anywhere within reach of deliveries. Get a good accountant. After 10 years you can earn up to £25,000 pa. Charge by the hour plus materials; unlike furniture makers who quote for a job in advance and have to stick to what they've quoted, you can charge more if the job takes longer than usual. Contacts are best made within the profession.

Avoid becoming a workaholic by working a standard working day. Try to develop a sport or hobby to compensate for the enormous concentration which this exacting craft demands. But the job brings great personal satisfaction in the freedom to experiment with design and the pleasure of hearing your instruments played well.

Musical Instrument Repairer

Qualifications/Training	Recommended
Income bracket	Low–Medium
Licence	No
Town/Country	Town
Experience/ Springboard	Recommended
Travel	Local
Mid-career entry	Possible
Exit sale	Unlikely
Entry costs	£6,000+
Work at home	Yes
Mix and match	Possible.

You could think about: *Musical instrument maker, Music/instrument retailer, Piano tuner, Musician, Direct marketing consultant*

Enquiries
Other musical instrument repairers

This is someone who repairs and restores musical instruments. You must have a natural interest in mechanics and be good with your hands. You should be able to play the instruments you repair or to know someone who does and who is able to advise you on any additional modifications that would improve the instruments. Learn the basic principles of engineering and bookkeeping, either through the public library or at adult education classes. It is not necessary to go to a college such as MERTON or NEWARK (wind and brass) or the LONDON COLLEGE OF FURNITURE (which has specialist courses in a wide range of instruments) but colleges are a good source of contacts and work – musicians often ask colleges to recommend repairers. You can learn to make your own tools by going to an evening class. You should have a good ear for fine tuning and understand dynamics (playing loudly or softly). If you are accepted as an apprentice by an experienced instrument builder or repairer you will have to work under pressure. This helps you to get on with the job

quickly and efficiently; a professional musician may need an emergency repair just before a concert. You alone will be responsible for professional musicians' instruments, so must be able to do the repair quickly. It is important to socialise and listen to musicians' problems: sometimes it is the musician that needs a repair rather than the instrument.

When you feel confident and have made enough contacts you can work from home, if you can do so without interruption, or hire a small industrial unit. This must be central with good public transport and parking; because musicians travel in their work they are unwilling to do so to have their instruments repaired. This means that there are more opportunities in places like London than in small towns.

Most publicity comes by word of mouth. If you have a reputation for speed and accuracy, career prospects are good. Specialise in one particular instrument and corner the market. Advertise your service in the local press, the *Musician* and *Classical Music* magazines. Have business cards printed. Contact the local education office so that you can repair school instruments.

You will need £6,000 to buy new tools, which are more accurate than second-hand; a good drill, a lathe, pads for wood-wind and wood for stringed instruments. Better machinery is improving the quality and efficiency of the job. You can expect to start earning less than £5,000 pa; up to £15,000–£25,000 pa once you're established. Base your charges on time taken plus materials. You may have to modify these as some fairly straightforward repairs may take hours, while you can charge more for a quick job which requires a lot of expertise. You can also take into account the value of the instrument being repaired. A car is not essential, but may be useful for returning a large number of school instruments to an education authority some distance away. Make sure clients insure their instruments while they're with you; make sure you insure your hands as some of your tools are dangerous.

You can run a mail order business on the side, eg making reeds, reed boxes, tools, strings, music stands etc. To prevent interference with your repairing work, this and the packing must be done in the evenings. You can also sell instruments. To complete a job on time, plan a schedule; but you must be prepared for rush jobs late at night if players want their instruments next morning. Be prepared to work up to 12 hours a day. Work is sporadic. Build up a network of musicians and other repairers who may pass work to you when they're busy and take on some of yours when you are. Read any books on light engineering from your local library.

Musician

Qualifications/Training	Recommended
Income bracket	Low–High
Licence	No
Town/Country	Mostly town
Experience/Springboard	No
Travel	Yes
Mid-career entry	Unlikely
Exit sale	No
Entry costs	£1,000+
Work at home	No

Mix and match Probably essential. You could think about: *Music teacher, Music critic, Musicians' answering and booking service, Orchestral fixer, Food manufacturer, Counsellor, Wine merchant*

Enquiries
Musicians' Union

Work as a professional musician, whether in traditional, classical, pop or commercial music, is insecure, highly competitive, corrupt and has a very high stress rating. Only consider it as a career if you are so highly motivated that you cannot bear to do anything else. Working as a professional musician looks glamorous, seductive and romantic from a distance, but it is a tough business where resilience is essential. You need energy, excellent health, iron determination, and a belief in yourself. Life must be seen as a professional challenge with little hope of adequate reward. Being able to prove and express yourself must count for more than financial security.

All musicians require patience, tact and an ability to get on with people. It is a small world where everyone either knows or has heard of everyone else. The bush telegraph functions speedily and efficiently: your reputation will precede you. Contacts are essential and you need good friends.

The number of jobs is shrinking. This has forced musicians to seek commercial sponsorship. The MUSICIANS' UNION works at creating more opportunities for musicians to perform live. Some musicians feel the rates it sets for film and TV recordings have outpriced British musicians in the international market but the MU refutes this. Electronic synthesisers, like the Sampler, can reproduce any sound, providing new challenges – and threats – which musicians have to face.

Cuts have affected provincial opera companies, amateur choral and music societies all over the country. These used to employ professional artists for their concerts and now make do with music students whether performing as soloists, in chamber music or accompanying on the piano. Peripatetic teachers have been axed in many areas and the market for their services is shrinking.

It is absolutely essential to have a good accountant: disaster will strike without one. Professional musicians are constantly suspected of fiddling their books by tax inspectors. It is therefore important to keep copies of invoices, and receipts for all money earned. Being on tax schedule D you can claim relief for the room where you work, heating, lighting, telephone, costs of transport and printing, clothes, hairdressing, instruments, repairs and tools. Before starting out it is wise to have a financial plan which includes a partner who has capital or a steady income (casual orchestral rates are £46, or £55 for a Principal). Don't plan a family or take out a heavy mortgage until you are on a sound financial footing or you may find yourself sacrificing your art for money to pay the household bills.

Many professional musicians' jobs are bad for social life and marriage, especially when they involve long working hours and continual travelling. It helps to have a partner who believes in you and supports your ambition to succeed. Plan ahead. Many professional musicians' jobs, particularly in the pop scene, are for the young. By middle-age, if you have not already made a fortune so you can live off the income, you should be prepared to change jobs. You may have to do this earlier if you develop eg violinist's neck, clarinettist's thumb, although you may be helped by a musicians' clinic at St Bartholomew's Hospital.

Read *The Musician*.

✳ European Community Notes

Very itinerant profession. Don't go on spec; get engagements before you go and make sure your contracts are properly checked (the Musicians' Union will do this). No problems in the Community; Southern European orchestras are particularly receptive to UK musicians and audition openly. If you have difficulties, the Musicians' Union will help with local unions.

Musicians' Answering and Booking Service

Qualifications/Training	No
Income bracket	Low
Licence	No
Town/Country	Town
Experience/Springboard	No
Travel	No
Mid-career entry	Yes
Exit sale	Possible
Entry costs	£3,000+
Work at home	Possible
Mix and match	Possible.

You could think about: *Musician, Concert agent, Music/instrument retailer*

Enquiries
Musicians' Union

This is someone who arranges for phone calls to be answered for absent musicians and passing the information on to them. You need to be a performing musician, or have a partner who is, and know every fixer in town. You must be known and trusted by your clients and you must guarantee them total confidentiality – after all, you handle their private diaries. Your qualities should include calmness in a crisis – of which there will be many – diplomacy, patience and the ability to accept the judgement of a fixer or conductor whose opinion about who is a good musician may differ from yours – this is known as 'ghost fixing'. You will need some £3,000 to set up your service in a room, garage or shed with several telephone lines, a fax and a photocopier (second hand will do). You also need a computer and a good accountant. It is useful to buy the yellow pages for the whole country, have a telex book and the specialist directory for whatever line you specialise in. Your staff should be intelligent and willing to work till the early hours; international telephone calls may come at any hour of day or night, so you must be able to cope with interrupted sleep and have an understanding partner. Musicians are notoriously unreliable about checking regularly and after a night on the tiles may forget to collect urgent messages from their answerphone left by the service the previous evening. When fully developed, the new voice messaging computer will enable messages left with the service to be played back to the client. It is not possible to combine this with another job so for the first three years you must live on your savings or your partner's income. After that you can expect around £12,000 pa depending on your investment in equipment.

Your service can be blamed if a player does not perform well and players will blame you if they do not get enough work. The job is bad for your social life, but you will meet interesting people and can evolve ways of exploiting your equipment. You will not have to travel but it is vital that you join the MUSICIANS' UNION.

Nn

Nanny/Babysitting Agent

Qualifications/Training	No
Income bracket	Low–Medium
Licence	Yes
Town/Country	Town
Experience/ Springboard	Recommended
Travel	No
Mid-career entry	Yes
Exit sale	Yes
Entry costs	£1,000
Work at home	Yes
Mix and match	Yes.

You could think about: *Journalist, Childminder, Holiday accommodation owner*

Enquiries	
Employment Agency Licensing Office	

You don't have to be a City headhunter to make a living from finding staff for other people. There is an increasing demand, especially in the South-east, for nannies and mother's helps and many people would rather have a nanny agency send them one or two likely candidates than wade through masses of applications resulting from advertising. There is also a great demand for people who can supply good, reliable babysitters at short notice; once you, as a nanny agency, have placed a few nannies you'll have a pool of reliable, vetted nannies to choose from. One thing

to note: the recession of the early Nineties hugely increased this conversion rate. Full-time nannies were an early casualty – which, of course, increased the demand for babysitting services. Nanny and baby-sitting agents can easily work from home so this is an option for people wanting to spend time with their own young children or who want to mix and match. Nanny and babysitting agents are subject to the Employment Agencies Act, which stipulates that they must have a licence from the Department of Employment's EMPLOYMENT AGENCY LICENSING OFFICE. For this you'll have to give details of your past five years' employment history; you'll need two personal references; and you'll have to put notices in the local press and at your proposed place of business for 21 days in advance; you also have to have the terms and conditions of your business checked, these then have to be displayed in your office. Once you've done that you'll get a licence number to go on your stationery. Without one, nobody will accept or publish your adverts. After that, your premises will be inspected by, for example, planning and health authorities and you have to reapply for this licence every year.

There are no formal qualifications for nanny agents. Very useful previous experience is selecting and appointing nannies for your own children. You have to be able to spot good nannies and a lot of this is a case of using your instinct. There are nanny qualifications eg the NNEB (for details ask the NATIONAL NURSERY EXAMINATION BOARD) which requires full time attendance for two years at college. These give a good indication of proficiency but many excellent nannies with experience don't have them while some of those with impressive qualifications may prove to be useless when confronted by real children. Some clients will insist on formally qualified nannies only. Back up your instinct by checking nannies' references – do this by telephone: a glowing reference could have been written by one of the nanny's friends or an employer eager to get the nanny out of the home. You'll have to have good communication skills, to like people and to be good at summing them up – much of your success depends on being able to match nannies and clients.

To set up you need a telephone, a typewriter and some stationery (with your licence number). An answering machine is useful, especially if you're organising babysitting and people want to get hold of you in a hurry; a lot of people won't talk to machines so don't depend on it too much. Ultimately, you may want to install a second telephone line as a lot of this work is done by telephone. Advertising is probably your biggest expense. Use any suitable local press, free magazines etc and the *Lady*. Finding clients may well be less of a problem than finding suitable nannies and babysitters, bear that in mind when you're deciding where to put adverts.

As an agent you are paid a fee by the client for successfully introducing a nanny to them. You can decide to charge a set amount or to base the charge on how much the nanny is to be paid by the client (the drawback with this is that you'll have to do just as much work to find a nanny for £40 a week as you would to find one for £200). You won't get paid until the nanny has actually started the job – this may not always be immediately, so you can expect some cash flow problems. If you don't find a nanny you don't get paid; many agents charge clients a nominal registration fee (say £5–£10) to help cover time and expenses. For babysitting you may prefer to charge clients an annual fee rather than fiddly little amounts every time you get them a babysitter. You never charge the nanny or babysitter for finding work. As an agent you don't set the rates your clients should pay; you can, however, suggest guidelines and should be able to advise nannies on how much they can reasonably

expect to earn given their experience. You should also suggest babysitting rates; you'll find you need a lot of babysitters so it's worth making sure that they're happy.

On the whole, this job is fairly desk bound and you'll spend a lot of time interviewing and checking references but it's a good idea to visit clients to get a better idea of the sort of person they're looking for. The telephone rings a lot; clients and nannies often have problems they want to discuss with you; you may be asked to find a babysitter in the afternoon for that same evening. You'll also want to keep in touch with your babysitters so you know who you can call on at short notice. Ultimately you have to keep everyone happy. Make sure that employers are very clear about what they expect their nanny to do and if it seems more than normal check that they let the nanny know before the appointment's made. Is the appointment to be sole charge or not? Does the nanny know how much time off is allowed? Insist on letters of appointment – you're the one they'll turn to if anything goes wrong. Although you could be a part-time nanny agent by using an answerphone for several hours a day, it's difficult to take a whole day away; you're likely to have to deal with last minute emergencies, which is when a second (emergency only) telephone comes in. If you do go away you'll have to make sure that everybody knows and books their babysitters in advance. Ideally you should have someone else around just to keep the business going if you can't be on call yourself.

Naturopath

Qualifications/Training	Essential
Income bracket	Low–High
Licence	Recommended
Town/Country	Either
Experience/Springboard	Recommended
Travel	No
Mid-career entry	Possible

Exit sale	Possible
Entry costs	£4,000+
Work at home	Possible
Mix and match	Possible.

You could think about: ***Doctor, Osteopath, Acupuncturist, Potter***

Enquiries
General Council and Register of Naturopaths

Naturopaths deal with health and its maintenance. It is the oldest form of complementary medicines. Naturopathic medicine is a distinct system of healing – a philosophy, science, art and practice. Its philosophy is based upon three principles: the body possesses the power to heal itself through its internal vitality and intelligence; disease is a manifestation of the vital force so naturopaths seek to discover and remove the basic causes: chemical, imbalance of the body fluids due to dietary deficiency or dietary excess, retention of waste products due to inefficient functioning of the lungs, kidneys and bowels, or poor circulation of body fluids; mechanical, muscular tensions, strained ligaments, stiff joints, poor posture due to occupational factors, as well as spinal misalignments leading to an interference in the functioning of the nervous system and the musculoskeletal system generally; psychological, impaired function induced by stress and the third principle is that naturopathic medicine is a holistic approach to health, in other words, disease affects the whole person – body, mind and spirit, and not simply an isolated organ or system.

Naturopathic treatment employs six therapies:

– dietetics, including the prescription of a balanced, wholesome, natural diet, and specific, controlled diets when patients require a more rigid regime;
– fasting, as a treatment for obesity, high blood pressure, arthritis and rheumatism, various allergies and some psychiatric diseases;
– structural adjustments, by such methods as osteopathy, chiropractic, neuromuscular technique, postural re-education and remedial exercises, to balance and integrate the spine, muscles, ligaments and joints of the whole body;
– hydrotherapy, the use of water, both internally and externally in the form of baths, packs, compresses, sprays and douches;
– natural hygiene, including general bodycare, use of moderate physical exercise, cultivation of a positive approach to life and health, relaxation techniques, etc.; and
– education, explaint to patients why disease occurs and what patients can do to maintain the new, improved level of health given to them by naturopathic treatment.

The BRITISH COLLEGE OF NATUROPATHY AND OSTEOPATHY offers the only full-time course in naturopathy. The four-year course leads to qualifications as a Registered Naturopath and Registered Osteopath. Entrance requirements are three A-level passes in science-based subjects, although the college does offer places to mature applicants who may not have these requirements.

You can either establish a new practice, work in conjunction with an established practitioner or work at one of the health clinics. Here the work is more with chronic and more severe problems rather than those people who only require out-patient services as is found in a surgery-based practice. The GENERAL COUNCIL AND REGISTER OF NATUROPATHS is the professional body that governs the practice of qualified naturopaths; in conjunction with the British Naturopathic and Osteopathic Association they arrange lectures and postgraduate seminars.

Naturopathy is gaining wide approval as the acceptable face of complementary medicine. Many patients will come recommended by other practitioners and even registered medical practitioners are not averse to recommending the services of qualified naturopaths.

It is not difficult to find premises to establish a practice. The easiest way is to use one room in your own private house. The cost of establishing a practice is not great, the main essentials being a couch, a desk, chairs and a telephone. In time, filing cabinets and receptionists may be required.

The essential medical instruments will already have been bought during your period of training.

Most naturopaths work a five- or six-day week, but many are available on a seven-day-a-week basis to deal with those emergency situations that arise from illness not knowing which day of the week is which.

Initial earnings are low, in the order of £6,000–£10,000 but as one's experience and reputation grow so does one's earning potential.

The job satisfaction of being a naturopath is very high. Being able to see people transformed from only moderately healthy to vitally healthy is immense. The reward of a patient saying 'I feel so much better' makes all the study worthwhile.

Further information may be found from the General Council and Register of Naturopaths, The British College of Naturopathy and Osteopathy and The British Naturopathic and Osteopathic Association.

Qualifications: UK qualifications not recognised throughout EC but EC qualifications are in UK.
Languages: To succeed, local language necessary.
Earnings: UK income generally same as elsewhere in the EC.
Setting up: You will find it difficult to succeed in Belgium, Denmark, France, Italy, Luxembourg, Netherlands, Portugal, Spain. You will find it easier in Eire, Germany, Greece.
Advice/Training: Advice, information and training not available for those wishing to work in Europe.
Exchanges: Formal job exchanges do not exist.
Enquiry point for those wishing to work in the EC: GENERAL COUNCIL AND REGISTER OF NATUROPATHS
Notes: Conditions in EC may change from 1993 when legislation is expected to ease difficulties.

Network Marketing

Qualifications/Training	None
Income bracket	Low–High
Licence	No
Town/Country	Either
Experience/Springboard	No
Travel	Local
Mid-career entry	Excellent
Exit sale	No
Entry costs	£50–£500
Work at home	Partly
Mix and match	Excellent.

You could think about: *Dentist, MP, Hairdresser, Holiday accommodation owner, Wine bar owner*

Enquiries
Network marketing companies

If you have a wide network of friends and acquaintances, who you think you could sell to, try network marketing – also called multi-level marketing.

Network marketing works like a chain letter. Someone approaches you (and it will only be a matter of time before someone does approach you) with the opportunity of a lifetime. The deal will be that you sell a company's products (which may be water filters, car immobilisers, cleaning materials, make-up, perfume, books, videos – you name it), and sign up a couple more people, who sign up a couple more and so on. And all of you sell the company's products to people you know. You get your cut of the profits made by the people you've signed up *and* the people they've signed up and so on – so if you pick some real goers, you can (literally) retire to the Bahamas on the proceeds. If you pick some good people, are effective yourself and are prepared to put in some hard work you can make up to perhaps £40,000 pa. Most make less than that and lots find that they can't sell to their friends at all.

Unlike pyramid selling, where you have to buy lots of products which you may or may not be able to sell, with network marketing you buy as you sell. The idea is to get more people involved, although individually they are selling less product. You start by making an investment of £30 upwards, depending on the product; typically some £350. You need brochures, samples, demonstration equipment etc, enough to convince people to buy and to sell for you. A wide network is a must so it is ideally combined with an extensive coffee morning circuit or a job where you meet lots of people eg a dentist.

Be sure you are selling what is in demand in your particular network – no point in Aga cleaners in your high rise council block. The selling approach is deliberately low key ('I'm not trying to sell you this to you, just to share it with you'). Without a subtle approach, you may end up with no income and no friends either. What is successful is a mixture of perseverence, enthusiasm and an instinct as to when to shut up. There *are* a number of people who prefer the social contact of buying from someone they know who is knowledgeable about their product. This after all is in sharp contrast to most modern day purchasing.

Most companies have a somewhat evangelical approach – you are required to attend meetings to make sure you know your product and to be inspired by the success stories of others. The truly committed will be off to meetings in the US, where many of these companies have their home. You need to keep up with your paperwork and regularly visit your recruits to check up on them (as your sponsor will check up on you). And then, if you and your agents keep selling, the cheques just keep rolling in.

You may be able to get some general training from your company but most in-house courses teach specific company techniques. If you want to get a feel of what's really involved in the job (on both sides of the Atlantic) try reading Don Failla's *How to Build a Successful Multi-level Marketing Organisation*.

Newsletter Publisher

Qualifications/Training	No
Income bracket	Low–High
Licence	No
Town/Country	Either
Experience/Springboard	No
Travel	No
Mid-career entry	Likely
Exit sale	Good
Entry costs	£1,000+
Work at home	Yes
Mix and match	Yes.

You could think about: *Journalist, UK correspondent (overseas media), Book packager, Snail farmer, Contemporary art gallery owner, Estate agent, Para-legal*

Enquiries
Newsletter publishers

Roughly speaking, newsletters are periodical publications which seldom carry advertising and are neither large nor smart enough to call themselves magazines. Unlike Great Aunt Felicia's Christmas newsletter or Suckem & Sockem's giveaway to clients, newsletters as a means of earning a living, are normally based on one of two assumptions. The first is that there's always 1 per cent of the population barmy enough to buy anything (a standard direct marketing assumption). Enterprising newsletter publishers have made fortunes in the USA with newsletters for nutcases, like 'Stocking Your Cellar Against Nuclear War'. The second, more conventional assumption is that there are often small audiences who will pay well for highly-qualified information on subjects of insufficient general interest to sustain magazines. *Euromoney* and the *Financial Times*, for example, publish a wide range of newsletters for select sub-sections of the financial markets. Although some of them have subscription lists of only a few hundred, their prices are high so they still make good money. Big newsletter publishers are always searching for acquisitions so you can usually get out by selling a successful newsletter once it's got a track record.

It's not that difficult to start up. In general anything of narrow yet intense interest could work. As a rule of thumb, your subscribers will have to be prepared to pay about £300 pa in advance for what you're going to tell them. They could be all sorts of people: expats, for example, might subscribe to a UK educational newsletter if they are interested in schools for ex-pat brats or to a UK pensions newsletter if interested in good pensions for themselves; or, as one newsletter which went well for years, you could try a monthly sheet for non-English speaking businessmen on how to write correct English. Newsletters can be influential. Marshall McLuhan, of 'the medium is the message' fame, used this medium with some success to spread the message. All that's needed to start is a bright idea in an area where you have enough knowledge, experience and contacts to allow you to produce regular, up to date, specialist information. Capital requirements are low – as low as a typewriter, although a word processor and printer/copier are preferable, and you'd need access to a photocopier. The cash is up front – your subscribers are expected to pay at the beginning of the year – so your publication should be self-financing from day two (on day one you had to pay for your own stamps). You need to get enough subscriptions to make it worth your while. But, at £300 each, 200 subscribers will bring you in £60,000, from which you must then deduct costs, including production and postage.

Having dreamed up a bright idea, first identify your market, then catch it. Make a dummy edition (or, if you can afford it, make a complete first addition) and mail it, free, as widely as you can. This operation requires the names and addresses of potential subscribers. Advertising is normally too expensive and too diffuse a means of reaching your potential newsletter audience. You may have to create your own mailing list if your chosen market is not already served by ready-made lists (obtainable from list brokers at a cost, unless you can extract them free of charge by exercising charm). Beware. Once your mailing succeeds and you have banked your subscriptions, you must make sure you are able to come up with the year's worth of newsletters your subscribers paid for. Otherwise you'll risk being charged with embezzlement.

Night Carer

Qualifications/Training	Recommended
Income bracket	Mostly low–Medium
Licence	No
Town/Country	Both
Experience/Springboard	Yes
Travel	Possible
Mid-career entry	Yes
Exit sale	No
Entry costs	Nil
Work at home	No
Mix and match	Excellent.

You could think about: *Music teacher, Tutor, Scriptwriter, Gardener, Bartender, provided you don't need much sleep*

Enquiries
British Nursing Association

Not a job for the faint hearted, it's excellent for mixing and matching – provided you've got the stamina or don't need much sleep – because the day's your own. It's often physically demanding, especially if you are dealing with the immobile who may need lifting in/out of baths etc and it's obviously very responsible work caring for people who cannot look after themselves at night.

These can be of either sex and any age (teenagers to the senile) and require care for all sorts of reasons (broken legs, mental handicap, terminal disease). You'll need to be able to think on your feet and stay calm when dealing with the fragile, ill, dying, senile and incontinent. You need to be very patient and usually capable of holding your tongue with cantankerous patients (and impatient superiors) and not only kind and caring but strong enough not to get too emotionally involved. It can be very demanding work – trying to feed one patient while another two fight, a fourth fouls the sheets and the fifth walks out into the street stark naked (true story).

Caring requirements vary. Requirements for the institutional care of under 18s are stringent and you will have to be checked by police before you are taken on. Nursing homes often ask for some qualification and extensive experience – perhaps an NNEB (nursery nursing) and nursing experience or other care work. Old peoples' homes are more relaxed but you may need to talk your way into the first job. Family work is normally a matter of getting through an interview.

Once in, practical experience teaches you the basics in about a month. Jobs are advertised in local papers and there are specialist job agencies eg BRITISH NURSING ASSOCIATION (BNA). Surprisingly, travel is possible in this job – for example looking after a handicapped child on holiday with the family. Try the BNA.

Novelist

Qualifications/Training	No
Income bracket	Mostly low
Licence	No
Town/Country	Either
Experience/Springboard	No
Travel	No
Mid-career entry	Likely
Exit sale	Possible
Entry costs	£5+
Work at home	Yes
Mix and match	Probably essential.

You could think about: *Journalist, Scriptwriter, Radio reporter and presenter, Barrister, MP, Window cleaner, Shopkeeper*

Enquiries
Society of Authors, Local writers' clubs

If you are a well disciplined self-starter, with a real craving to write, you may succeed. Most novelists have always written – letters to the press, short stories in notebooks. It can become a time-consuming hobby and, if you are lucky, become a full-time job.

To start with, you will be lucky to get an advance of £1,000 for a book. You will normally get a royalty of approximately 10 per cent of hardback sales and 7.5 per cent of paperbacks. A handful hit the jackpot, but most reckon they are lucky if they are able to make a living from writing.

When you are unknown, it is extremely difficult to get published. First novels are a high publishing risk. Go to your local library and check which publishing houses are strong in your kind of novel. That way you'll be in with a chance. Ask their advice, don't just post your manuscript. Unsolicited manuscripts sent to publishers often get overlooked for several months before being returned to you with a cursory rejection.

The way to get publishers to take notice is to get a literary agent to submit your manuscript. But, Catch 22 – agents do not warm to first novels either, because they are difficult to sell to publishers and 10 per cent of your advance makes it hardly worth their while. So, it's not easy to get an agent – but difficult to get published without one. Get a published author to recommend an agent to you, or consult the *Writer's Handbook* which gives an excellent run-down on UK and US agents and publishers. An agent will want to see some work, but *not* neccessarily the entire manuscript – at least not to begin with: one chapter and a detailed synopsis might prove a better calling card.

Obviously the fastest way to fame and fortune is to win the Whitbread prize for a first novel but inevitably this eludes the majority. Most fit writing around another job for many years (and some never break the habit of writing at night). Take a course in journalism or a degree in a subject that will help you develop your writing style. Join your local Writers Club, where you can read out your work for criticism. Once you receive an offer from a publisher, you can join the SOCIETY OF AUTHORS (and receive the *Author*, guides for authors and advice on contracts) and the WRITERS GUILD (strong on writing for television). If you specialise you can also join the CRIME WRITERS ASSOCIATION, the ROMANTIC NOVELISTS ASSOCIATION etc as appropriate. The latter also takes probationary members and will provide professional criticism and a prize for a first novel which they will then submit and recommend for publication.

Outlay on equipment is minimal. All you need is some paper, pens or pencils and inspiration. Buy a secondhand typewriter when you can afford it and a word processor when you grow rich. A good dictionary, *Roget's Thesaurus* and the *Writer's Handbook* or the *Writers' and Artists' Yearbook* will be useful.

What starts off an idea for a novel is very individual. Some are prompted by a particular place; some a situation; some by commercial considerations, the inclusion of money/sex/power. Many authors find a book will take about a year, including a period of research and gestation; others take as much as 10 years; conversely, Barbara Cartland writes over 20 a year.

Writing is an isolated activity, in which you draw deeply on your own resources. Nevertheless your ability to cope with this must be combined with a strong understanding of and involvement with people. You need a fierce drive, great resilience, endless imagination and an unquenchable need to write.

Nurse

Qualifications/Training	Essential
Income bracket	Low–Medium
Licence	Yes
Town/Country	Either
Experience/Springboard	No
Travel	Local
Mid-career entry	Unlikely
Exit sale	No
Entry costs	Nil
Work at home	No
Mix and match	Yes.

You could think about: **Nursing home owner, Property manager, Gardener/ garden designer, Photographer**

Enquiries
Royal College of Nursing

Freelance nurses get their work through agencies usually by the day or week. They are available to nurse in every kind of situation for which they are qualified: in the NHS, in private hospitals or in the patient's own home.

You need to train at a school of nursing, usually in a teaching hospital. It takes three years to become a Registered General Nurse (RGN), usually followed by a year's experience as a staff nurse. You can then go on to take specialist training in orthopaedics, psychiatry, paediatrics (there is a shortage in this area), become a midwife or health visitor.

This is a tough and underpaid job so you need lots of dedication, good health and energy, a cheerful temperament, empathy, a liking for people, and a sense of humour. You will have to cope with difficult physical and emotional situations therefore you cannot be squeamish, faint at the sight of blood, or run away when someone has hysterics. If you have any problems dealing with authority, don't be a nurse, as the job structure is one of doing what you are told; responsibility can be considerable, but you must always answer to your superiors.

You can go freelance as soon as you are qualified; you don't need any special equipment. Having a car of your own makes travelling, usually at unusual and unsociable hours, much easier, especially when your job venue is always changing and no-one pays your fares. Don't expect to earn more than £10,000 per annum.

The advantage of this kind of job is the freedom you have to choose where and when you work; the disadvantages are that you are usually treated as an outsider by the permanent staff and have no holiday or sick pay. It's difficult to do another job at the same time as this work is very exhausting.

On the whole there are more women than men in this profession, and it's more difficult to get training as a really mature student for physical reasons – unless you are very fit. You can get more information from the ROYAL COLLEGE OF NURSING. Read the *Nursing Times* and *Nursing Standard*.

✯ **European Community Notes**

Qualifications: UK qualifications for RGN and midwife are recognised throughout EC (though other UK nursing qualifications are not necessarily accepted) and EC qualifications in UK. (British midwives may need an extra 18 months postqualification experience.)

Languages: To succeed, local language absolutely essential.

Earnings: UK income generally higher than elsewhere in the EC, excepting Greece (very low).

Setting up: You will find it possible to succeed throughout Europe but easier in Germany.

Advice/Training: Advice, information and training available for those wishing to work in Europe.

Exchanges: Formal job exchanges exist but arranged *ad hoc*.

Enquiry point for those wishing to work in the EC: ROYAL COLLEGE OF NURSING.

Recommended reading: Nursing: The European Dimension.

Notes: There is a great deal of interest in working in member states and the Royal College of Nursing runs an excellent advisory/information service from its overseas employment department – you must be a current member to access the service. You must have a good command of the local language to communicate with your patients. There are commercial nursing agencies recruiting in the UK for Europe which may teach you the necessary language in the UK before placing you. The one golden rule before going is: consult the Royal College of Nursing.

Nursing Home Owner

Qualifications/Training	Not essential
Income bracket	Medium
Licence	Yes
Town/Country	Either
Experience/Springboard	Preferable
Travel	No
Mid-career entry	Likely
Exit sale	Yes
Entry costs	£100,000+++
Work at home	Possible
Mix and match	Limited.

You could think about: *Nanny/ babysitting agent, Antique dealer*

Enquiries
Registered Nursing Homes Association, Royal College of Nursing

To run a nursing home for the elderly there are two essential ingredients: a good qualified nurse (RGN) in charge and sound management ability and acumen. If you personally fit neither bill you will have to acquire these services before you go any further.

Once the Cinderella of the medical world, with the increasing numbers of older people in the UK, geriatric nursing is now an expanding profession. When you start to run your own nursing home you must first register with and be inspected by the local health authority. The ROYAL COLLEGE OF NURSING has a really good reference library for members, and will provide legal advice, and information about relevant training courses. You must also be regularly inspected by fire and health and safety officers. You must make sure you have a good public liability insurance and an excellent accountant.

Costs vary through the country according to the price of property and overheads. Allow also for salaries and wages, buying beds, linen, disposable dressing pads, uribags, cradles, oxygen, suckers, dripstands etc, kitchen equipment and staff uniforms. There is also the cost of decorating, carpets and curtains. A nursing home with 30 patients should be modernised every seven years. Usually the patients like to bring some of their own furniture with them to make them feel at home and preserve their identities.

There are strict guidelines regarding the ratio of patients to each RGN; GPs or consultants usually visit their own patients. If patients are strong enough, outings to local sporting and cultural events or an occasional meal out is considered important to stimulate their interest.

While elderly patients are naturally happier with familiar faces, it is necessary sometimes to use agency nurses.

This is a satisfying job but potentially hard on your health. Don't attempt it if you are not prepared to work long hours. You must have the ability to settle new patients, as the first months can be traumatic – this can be difficult for everyone. You need personal qualities of tact, tolerance, patience and a genuine interest and affection for the elderly. You need to be able to adapt your nursing to the particular needs of each individual patient: they are too old to adapt to you. You also need to have plenty of energy and good feet. The prospects for those working with geriatric patients are excellent as the older population increases; there are now 10 million people in the UK over 65.

Since overheads are high, it is not cheap to live in a nursing home as a patient; many get some financial help from Income Support; the pension funds of larger banks and industrial organisations may also contribute to costs, and some charities will 'top up' if the individual's circumstances qualify them. Depending on the level of dependency, the DSS pays Income Support to qualifying patients in independent homes of between £270 and £280 a week (£305 and £315 in London); this can be well below the actual cost of care. So a potential proprietor will have to assess early on what balance – if any – of Income Support to fee-paying patients is realistic. There is also the question of ancillary services – anything from ambulances to chiropody and other 'extras' to nursing care and accommodation – and whether local authorities or nursing homes should have to pay for them. The RNHA has been lobbying on behalf of home owners to have Income Support levels raised and to clarify the ancillary position.

Useful books are *Geriatric Medicine and Gerontology, Laing's Review of Private Health Care,* you will also need to read the *Nursing Times.*

Oo

Office Cleaner

Qualifications/Training	No
Income bracket	Low
Licence	No
Town/Country	Town
Experience/Springboard	No
Travel	No
Mid-career entry	Yes
Exit sale	No
Entry costs	Nil
Work at home	No
Mix and match	Yes.

You could think about: *Opera singer, Teacher, Social worker, Novelist*

Enquiries
Advertisers in local papers.

If you reject office politics as a way of life then office cleaner could be the lifeline you're looking for. You work while they catch up with the paperwork at home; they work – ie write memos to each other, scheme, plot, huff and puff and, on a really good day, stab their best friend in the back – while you're miles away, living life, far from the action.

Good for the soul and excellent for mixing and matching. Many familiar faces on TV have used it as a lifeline while resting. You'll get between £3.00–£5.00 per hour, but rather more for weekends and early morning shifts. It's easy work to pick up through your local paper; very few checks on you are carried out. Skill is not of the essence, but personal trustworthi-

ness is: all offices, from the chief executive's/senior partner's downwards, will be open to your intimate inspection. To survive you'll need to be able to switch off, get into a routine and switch onto another wavelength – daydream, talk to yourself, ponder on life, love and everything. It's often lonely work.

Office cleaning takes place in small bitty shifts, one or two hours before the office opens and the two or three hours after every executive briefcase has been filled with the unexpired portion of the day's office memoranda and carried eagerly towards the exit. Then the office is all your own – until 9 o'clock approaches and it's time to put away the tools of the trade, lock up and return to another reality. Cinderella in reverse.

Office Services Bureau

Qualifications/Training	No
Income bracket	Low–High
Licence	No
Town/Country	Town
Experience/Springboard	Yes – for franchises
Travel	No
Mid-career entry	Yes
Exit sale	Yes
Entry costs	£2,000++
Work at home	Possible

Mix and match   Yes.
You could think about: *Book-keeper, Desk-top publisher, Network marketing, Dress agent*

Enquiries
Eurohouse; Local office services bureaux

For a large number of jobs in this book, it makes good sense for people to buy in office services from an office services bureau rather than set up an office and staff it themselves. The advantage to clients is that the office services bureaux can help to keep their overheads down while operating efficiently; most are now equipped with all the latest electronic gadgetry you would expect to find in a modern corporation and the staff to man it.

Services customarily offered include telephone answering, postal addresses (some people and businesses don't trust PO box numbers), photocopying, fax (incoming and outgoing), wordprocessing, book keeping, publicity (posters and flyers) laser printing, simple computer graphics and sales presentation packs etc. You don't have to supply all of them when starting from scratch, but your aim should be to supply the customer with a one stop service eg clients collecting mail may well want to photocopy some of its contents. Be prepared to make deals on any service you can provide.

To enter the business, it's best to start by talking to someone actually running a successful bureau. Make sure that you pick one miles from where you want to set up as nobody wants local competition. You'll find them helpful because they will probably be looking for ways to network/franchise their own business. Some will provide training if you are to become their franchisee. They themselves are usually looking to expand their outlets, particularly outside London and the main cities.

There are also various small business clubs and cash transfer arrangements that may help you get greater discounts and help your customer make instant use of office service bureaux in many parts of Europe.

You'll need less money than you may think because you can often get your start-up stock on sale or return and you should be able to rent rather than buy your equipment and the office. If you can start as a franchisee you may be able to get a back-up line of supply in your agreement. But one way or another, you'll need to be able to finance/rent/lease: office space, your photocopier, fax machine, telephones and telephone lines, computer/wordprocessor, laser printer, paper, stationery.

Exit prospects are excellent because all clients are logged in your books, their spending noted and the business's true form can be demonstrated in terms a potential purchaser's accountant can understand.

Opera Director

Qualifications/Training	No
Income bracket	Low–High
Licence	No
Town/Country	Mostly town
Experience/Springboard	Good idea
Travel	A must
Mid-career entry	Yes
Exit sale	No
Entry costs	£250
Work at home	No

Mix and match   Possible.
You could think about: *Film director, Festival director, Classical composer, Actor*

Enquiries
Opera directors

The opera director directs the singers on how to act, move and present themselves on stage. You co-operate with the conductor and designer to interpret the opera. The best way to enter this highly competitive field is to attend a university where there are ample opportunities for producing student operas (Oxford, Cambridge, Newcastle, Durham). An opera director should be a kind of renaissance person, with a wide knowledge of all the arts – music, painting, architecture, dance, literature and history. You also need the practical skills of basic human psychology and acting stage management. You should be able to read a vocal score and have a knowledge of French, German and Italian for international work.

You need to sell yourself and to communicate easily. Persuading a number of volatile personalities to realise your artistic ideas requires patience and sensitivity. Anxiety neurosis will help you to pre-empt things going wrong; you need a vivid imagination and to know about everyone else's job in the production team – lighting, designing and conducting an orchestra. You can learn by taking a job as an assistant stage manager and/or taking a course at eg the GUILDHALL SCHOOL or ROYAL SCOTTISH ACADEMY.

While at university, get introductions to as many influential people as possible. Write to directors or obtain good introductions to them. It's important to have done at least one production you can describe and if possible get them to come and watch. If you are lucky you may be taken on as an unpaid assistant for a production. Jobs become available at short notice, so you need a fixed address, telephone and answering machine or service. You must be free to travel. There are not many female or black directors but the numbers are increasing.

For a production, you will spend six–eight weeks on research in libraries and art galleries and listening to the opera on disc before meeting the designer and the conductor; the formulation of the designs can take 4–12 weeks, depending on the continuity of contact. Actual rehearsals will then last four–six weeks. It is possible to do an average of six productions per year with proper thought and preparation.

Earnings range from £20,000–£100,000 but can be as low as the minimum living wage. There is no time for another job if you are successful but throughout your career you risk long periods out of work which is depressing and a production may be jeopardised by bad notices from the critics. On the good side are the opportunities for self expression and, with a new opera, actually creating an interpretation of the composer's and librettist's ideas yourself.

Optician

Qualifications/Training	Essential
Income bracket	Medium
Licence	Yes
Town/Country	Town
Experience/Springboard	Useful
Travel	No
Mid-career entry	Unlikely
Exit sale	Yes
Entry costs	£25,000+
Work at home	Possible
Mix and match	Possible.

You could think about: *Shopkeeper, Silversmith/jeweller, Jazz musician*

Enquiries
General Optical Council, Association of British Dispensing Opticians, Association of Optometrists

Optician is the term used to describe an optometrist (opthalmic optician) or dispensing optician. An optometrist is trained to test sight and to supply spectacles or contact lenses, but a dispensing optician may not test sight or without a specialist qualification fit contact lenses. A dispensing optician may supply spectacles that have been supplied by an optometrist or doctor.

Optometrists examine and test sight, prescribe, fit and supply spectacles (and other optical appliances) and sometimes, if the practice is large enough to warrant a workshop, make up the lenses for prescription. The important part of this job is eye examination and care; some serious illnesses are first observed by optometrists who then refer the patient to a GP, also some symptom-free conditions (such as glaucoma) can lead to blindness if not treated in time. However, most optometrists have to subsidise their incomes by selling spectacles and other optical appliances. (Since the NHS stopped issuing spectacles this aspect of the job operates much like a shop although your patients may need some specific specialist advice.) There has also been deregulation of the selling of spectacles. This means that you will have competition from the new eye shops staffed by unqualified people. Eye tests are no longer free for most people on the NHS, so you recover most of your money from your patient.

Before practising you need to register with the GENERAL OPTICAL COUNCIL. This involves completing a three-year degree course in optometry, followed by a year's paid, pre-registration experience. You can also practise as a dispensing optician, fitting and supplying spectacles but not contact lenses, nor testing sight; for this you need a shorter training (details from the ASSOCIATION OF BRITISH DISPENSING OPTICIANS, ABDO). Opticians need a certain amount of manual dexterity, attention to detail and to be methodical. It also helps if you like people and enjoy being of service to them.

You can work from home but once you get going you'll probably need premises; in either case you'll need a consulting room as well as a showroom with space for display of spectacle frames. As an optometrist you'll also need the equipment for testing eyes which costs about £25,000 new although you can pick up bits and pieces secondhand. You can set up at home to begin with, perhaps keeping on a part time job with another practice until you've built up your own. Stocks of spectacle frames come from travelling reps and wholesalers. Lenses made up to the required prescription come from prescription houses; they charge you and you charge the patient. Usually these are made to order but eye shops keep stocks of some ready made-up prescriptions and supply them over the counter. You need an assistant to arrange appointments, look after the practice while you're testing eyes and help with administration.

People usually go to their nearest optician – at home or at work; bear this in mind when you're finding premises. They don't have to be referred by their GP, so make your presence obvious; advertising may not increase business but word of mouth probably will. Many opticians find working in a hospital for one or two days a week is a good way of increasing their experience and of keeping abreast with the profession. Read the *Optician, Optometry Today* and *Dispensing Optics* and contact the ABDO and the AOP.

European Community Notes

Qualifications: The acceptance of UK qualifications throughout EC and EC qualifications in UK is dependent on a newly implemented EC directive – it is not yet completely clear *which* qualifications are acceptable where.

Languages: To succeed, local language necessary.

Earnings: Earnings vary throughout Europe: UK income is probably lower than, say, Germany – but then so are costs. And in Portugal, say, the converse is true.

Advice/Training: Advice, information and training available for those wishing to work in Europe.

Exchanges: Formal job exchanges do not exist.

Enquiry point for those wishing to work in the EC: ASSOCIATION OF OPTOMETRISTS, ASSOCIATION OF BRITISH DISPENSING OPTICIANS

Euronotes: The provisions of the EC directive have yet to filter through entirely. It needs to be realised that in some EC countries, eg France and Greece, optometry can only be undertaken by a doctor. Only in Eire can the full range of an optometrist's services be easily operated. There is some form of restriction in all other EC countries. The position for a dispensing optician is easier.

Orchestral Fixer

Qualifications/Training	Useful
Income bracket	Low–Medium
Licence	No
Town/Country	Town
Experience/ Springboard	Recommended
Travel	Yes
Mid-career entry	Yes
Exit sale	No
Entry costs	£4,000
Work at home	Yes
Mix and match	Possible.

You could think about: *Festival director, Orchestral musician, Mini-cab driver*

Enquiries
Musicians' Union

This person procures engagements for an orchestra, arranges terms and engages players and conductors. No knowledge of music is necessary. You will be dealing with other people's money so it is essential to understand a balance sheet, bookkeeping and filing, and be able to type and use a word processor. You need to be organised, methodical, logical and a perfectionist; to be able to run an office, negotiate with tough artists' agents, demanding promoters, sponsors or public bodies; and ensure the booking of reliable and good musicians. Sympathy, warmth and diplomacy will enable you to see and understand the wider long-term implications of a complicated situation; you will require a steely determination when taking unpleasant or tough decisions.

Get to know as many people as possible in the profession – performers, agents, organisers and back-stage staff. To learn how to deal with musicians, it is best to work in orchestral management or arts administration. After a couple of years, when you feel really confident and have about £4,000 you can work from home. You will need a telephone with two lines, answering machine or service, typewriter or word processor, and about £1,500 worth of good stationery. Fax, telex and mailbox computer systems will make the job more efficient. Register as a contractor with the MUSICIANS' UNION.

On concert days, you may have to work at least 18 hours; try not to become a workaholic, and eat sensibly. Your social life will be virtually non-existent; travelling is constant. You must remain cool, smart, in control and patient even after days spent touring with unreliable artists, sorting out hotel arrangements and transport crises.

Grants to the arts are being cut and the future of music is becoming dependent on the whims of fickle sponsors. However, if you like achieving your own goals and you don't mind starting with a low income (5 per cent or 10 per cent fee per concert), after several years' success your income can rise to some £25,000.

Orchestral Musician

Qualifications/Training	Necessary
Income bracket	Low–Medium
Licence	No
Town/Country	Town
Experience/Springboard	No
Travel	Lots
Mid-career entry	No
Exit sale	No
Entry costs	£1,000+
Work at home	No
Mix and match	Probably essential.

You could think about: *Music teacher, Chamber group director, Instrumental soloist, Orchestral fixer, Antique dealer, Counsellor*

Enquiries
Musicians' Union

These people earn their living playing in orchestras; it is not a job for you unless you cannot bear to do anything else. The use of synthesisers means that this is a contracting area of work. Persevere if you are optimistic, outstandingly confident and talented and have good nerves. Only a small percentage of music students become successful performers: string players should find more work than those playing woodwind or brass. To receive really good tuition and make contacts, it's necessary to go to music college; either for three years or for a post-grad year if you are of a high enough standard. You should join the MUSICIANS' UNION.

The stress level is high; you must have enormous resources of stamina and energy to withstand endless travelling in all forms of transport, all over the UK and abroad.

You will be living and working in a group so need to be calm and good-humoured, sociable and able to put up with other people's eccentricities and problems. Getting on with other musicians is as important as playing well.

You need to gain experience of the orchestra/operatic repertoire by working for two–three years with a provincial orchestra, or better still abroad (jobs in Europe are advertised in international music magazines). You will find it difficult to manage without a steady part-time job, either teaching or something else which allows you time and energy to practise. It is important to have flexible hours as freelance work can come at short notice. You need a good accountant, telephone and answering machine; also an answering/diary service to deal with enquiries as to whether you are available to play. Permanent jobs are advertised in *Classical Music* magazine and the *Daily Telegraph*, usually on Saturdays.

Getting work probably means being in London. Telephone or write to orchestral managers, including opera and ballet, and the freelance fixers who manage the small chamber orchestras boasting and telling them of your experience. Let all your musical friends know that you need work and then you may be able to deputise for them in musical shows, dance bands or hotels. If you can play several instruments you will be more employable. Only the excellence of your playing or influential friends will help you get into the small but lucrative area of commercial TV and film recording sessions.

Earnings in this overcrowded scene are unpredictable. (Casual orchestral rates are £46, £55 for a Principal). If you like teaching, carry on as it will provide security. There is always the risk of injury of muscle overuse; the musicians' clinic at St Bartholomew's Hospital treats nearly 100 patients a year. It is likely to take at least five years to become established. There is a bias towards youth. If you become number three 'cello in an orchestra in your twenties, 10 years later you may have moved sideways but rarely upwards; there's not far to go!

You need a partner who realises that social events have to be cancelled at a moment's notice if a gig comes up and that you will be away travelling a good deal. A car is useful but other musicians will give you lifts. Read or have a hobby to keep you sane and relieve the anxiety about whether or not you are playing well, getting enough gigs or whether the fixers like you.

European Community Notes
Very itinerant profession. Don't go on spec; get fixed up and your contract checked before you go (the Musicians' Union will do this). No problems in the European Community. Southern European orchestras are particularly receptive to UK musicians and audition openly. If you have problems, the Musicians' Union will help you with local unions.

Osteopath

Qualifications/Training	Essential
Income bracket	Low–High
Licence	Professional register
Town/Country	Town
Experience/Springboard	Recommended
Travel	No
Mid-career entry	Possible

Exit sale	Possible
Entry costs	£2,000+
Work at home	Possible
Mix and match	Possible.

You could think about: *Doctor, Physiotherapist, Naturopath, Nursing home owner, Holiday accommodation owner*

Enquiries
General Council & Register of Osteopaths

This is someone who treats all mechanical problems of the body, bones and muscles, which can affect the nervous and circulatory systems as well as other organs. They use joint and soft tissue manipulation to restore normal function. You normally need three A-level passes, preferably in science subjects, to enter the BRITISH COLLEGE OF NATUROPATHY & OSTEOPATHY, the BRITISH SCHOOL OF OSTEOPATHY or the EUROPEAN SCHOOL OF OSTEOPATHY. It takes four years of intensive study to qualify as a registered osteopath; though, in spring 1992, the profession of osteopathy was not yet regulated by statute, as recommended to the Department of Health, statutory regulation seemed increasingly likely in the near future. If you are a qualified medical doctor, you need only 13 months at the LONDON COLLEGE OF OSTEOPATHY. You need to be really interested in people, have stamina and dedication. You should also be dextrous and physically fit as this is an energetic occupation.

It is sensible to gain experience by working as an assistant, either at one of the teaching institutions or with an established practitioner. This will allow you to make useful professional contacts as well as gain experience. The GENERAL COUNCIL & REGISTER OF OSTEOPATHS is the professional body to which registered osteopaths belong, with its own journal. It arranges lectures and conferences and gives careers advice on where a new practice may be set up.

When you start your own practice you will probably make no more than £5,000 in the first year. Later, in a fashionable area you could make upwards of £30,000 per annum. You first need to get known – circularise the local doctors and any other people who might send you referrals, such as the local orthopaedic surgeon. At present, you must work privately – only osteopaths who are already doctors or physiotherapists can treat patients on the NHS.

Your consulting room should be on the ground floor and near public transport as many of your patients will be old or disabled. You must apply to the local planning office for permission to use your room as a clinic. You need running hot and cold water in the room and a loo nearby. Allow £2,000, apart from premises, to cover equipment such as treatment plinth, chair, desk, filing cabinet, phone and answerphone as well as stethoscope etc. Conventional X-rays as well as CT scans and blood tests will help diagnose so access to these facilities is important. As soon as you can afford it, it is worth employing a practice manager to answer the door, the phone, and deal with payment. You also need good public liability and professional insurance, and also a good accountant.

You can work normal office hours but you need to have a flexible lunch hour to accomodate patients who cannot come during working hours. It is also worth having flexible working arrangements on Fridays, to avoid patients being ill or in pain over the weekend and then to be available to cope with emergencies.

This is a very rewarding profession with instant feedback – you actually see the results of your labours. But it is hard work and demanding both physically and mentally. You can't possibly do another job at the same time unless you work sessional hours in a clinic, with others such as psychotherapists and acupuncturists.

Apart from the GCRO, get information from the BRITISH HOLISTIC MEDICAL ASSOCIATION; and read *Clinical Biomechanics, Osteopathy*, the *British Osteopathic Journal* and the *Journal of Osteopathic Education*.

★ ★ ★
★   ★
★   ★
★ ★ ★
European Community Notes

Qualifications: UK qualifications not recognised in EC, nor EC qualifications in UK.

Languages: To succeed, local language necessary.

Advice/Training: Advice, information and training available for those wishing to work in Europe from GCRO.

Exchanges: Formal job exchanges exist.

Enquiry point for those wishing to work in the EC: GENERAL COUNCIL AND REGISTER OF OSTEOPATHS

Oyster Farmer

Qualifications/Training	Necessary
Income bracket	Low–High
Licence	Yes
Town/Country	Country
Experience/Springboard	Essential
Travel	Local
Mid-career entry	Likely
Exit sale	Excellent
Entry costs	£70,000
Work at home	Yes
Mix and match	Recommended.

You could think about: *Holiday accommodation owner, Sailing school owner, Tree surgeon, Smallholder*

Enquiries
Shellfish Association of Great Britain

Oyster farmers breed, grow and market oysters. You need to attend a specialist course in fish farming at INVERNESS COLLEGE, or at the AGRICULTURAL COLLEGE at Barony in Dumfries or Sparsholt in Hampshire. You must then have at least two or three years' experience working on different farms before starting on your own. You must have some mechanical skills, be able to swim and, if you run a hatchery, be neat, tidy and clean. You should enjoy a country open air life with irregular hours. Oyster farming is not necessarily a full time occupation and it is possible to do another job at the same time. But the process of establishing an oyster farm is a slow one.

You can set up by finding a mixed sea/fresh water site and negotiate Crown lease for foreshore rights – this will cost you anything up to £2,500 per annum. You can either buy oyster seed and keep and grow it over three years (this will cost about £14,000) or buy them half grown (£40,000) and sell after one year. You will need about £70,000 to start – apart from the oysters themselves, you need to spend £4,000 on the special bags which float on trestles; a pick-up truck and a shed.

You can sell locally or join a communal marketing association.

It's worth getting on the mailing list of the SEA FISH INDUSTRY AUTHORITY, to join the SHELLFISH ASSOCIATION OF GREAT BRITAIN and to take *Fish Farming International* and *Sea Food International* magazines.

★ ★ ★
★   ★
★   ★
★ ★ ★
European Community Notes

Qualifications: UK qualifications recognised throughout EC but EC qualifications not in UK.

Languages: To succeed, local language necessary.

Setting up: You will find it difficult to succeed in France, Germany, Greece. You will find it easier in Eire, Netherlands, Portugal, Spain.

Advice/Training: Advice, information and training available for those wishing to work in Europe.

Financial help: Exists for study, training or travel in the EC, specific to this job.

Pp

Painter/Decorator

Qualifications/Training	No
Income bracket	Low
Licence	No
Town/Country	Town
Experience/Springboard	Useful
Travel	Local
Mid-career entry	Yes
Exit sale	No
Entry costs	£1,000
Work at home	No
Mix and match	Yes.

You could think about: *Builder, House converter, Man with a van, Window cleaner, Actor, Musician*

Enquiries
Construction Industry Training Board, Local builders

Painting and decorating is regarded as a semi-skilled trade, and it is an area where there is plenty of scope to set up in a small way. You will need to have some idea of how to cost a job (calculate how much time and what materials you will need for a particular room) but you can get sufficient experience to do a convincing job just through doing your own decorating work on a DIY basis. However, if you do have the opportunity to do a basic course you will learn some of the tricks of the trade, and be able to do a more professional job.

Most decorators, however, do have some other skills (such as plastering or carpentry) so that they can offer extra ser-vices to those employing them. A rapidly expanding field of specialisation is in special paint finishes: scumbling, sponging, dragging, rag-rolling are the catchwords. These are skills you will have to be taught by an old hand, and practise so that you can produce an effective finish as quickly as possible. (Also read *Paint Magic*.) If you can also offer a convincing colour-scheming service, you will be able to work in more up-market areas – and charge higher prices.

As well as brushes, wallpapering equipment and other special tools, you will need a van – both to get you to the job and store the materials in while you are working on a job. Good overalls and plenty of dust sheets are also essential. You may work in partnership with someone, or employ assistants on a casual basis. Your income will depend on the area and the type of service you can offer.

Larger companies may join the NATIONAL FEDERATION OF PAINTING AND DECORATING CONTRACTORS (NFPDC), which is involved in administering the rules of the industry and sets safety and other standards.

✶ European Community Notes

There is always *scope* for skilled craftsmen – even if the recession has hammered the building trades more than other sectors; the Single Market could mean EC opportunities. Contact the DoE and the DTI, which are immensely Euro-conscious, and see *Builder* for more information on all construction industry trades and occupations.

Para-legal

Qualifications/Training	Recommended (essential for Legal Executive)
Income bracket	Medium–High
Licence	No
Town/Country	Town
Experience/ Springboard	Recommended
Travel	No
Mid-career entry	Possible
Exit sale	Unlikely
Entry costs	£20,000++
Work at home	Possible

Mix and match
Think about: *Conveyancer, Proofreader/copy editor, Greyhound trainer*

Enquiries
The Institute of Legal Executives

Para-legals are legal advisers. They are experts on, usually, one area of the law but can't represent clients in court. They are particularly useful to solicitors who from time to time need up to the minute detailed advice on a specific area of the law which their own firm can't provide. Other clients include institutions (such as banks) and people who want legal advice, on, for example, their rights as a soon-to-be-evicted tenant, without necessarily incurring the high costs of going to a solicitor. The areas in which para-legals are most likely to be needed include bankruptcy and insolvency, consumer rights, crime, family law, housing and welfare, tax law and wills. Demand should be increasing as the Lord Chancellor's overhaul of the legal system encourages the use of a wider range of qualifications in law offices, including professionally qualified legal executives. These reforms have coincided with the introduction of complex new welfare legislation and the closing (often due to lack of funds) of many of the benefit shops run by local authorities which used to give welfare advice; at the same time Citizens' Advice Bureaux often can't afford to offer the detailed help needed. In addition, many firms of solicitors who have their own departments of specialist para-legals (called legal executives) are finding that it is uneconomical to keep these on and have to go elsewhere for this detailed knowledge when they are working on a specific case. Para-legals cannot work in Scotland where the legal system is different and there are no equivalents of para-legals or legal executives.

There are no required qualifications for setting up as a para-legal but you need some relevant experience such as being a legal executive or working for a local authority welfare or housing deparment. The INSTITUTE OF LEGAL EXECUTIVES administers qualifying exams for Legal Executives which can be done through night classes and day-release combined with employment with a solicitor. This is a useful qualification for credibility, experience and contacts as well as giving you a good background to the law. Some of the larger solicitors' partnerships will help train you on the job while you work in one of their specialist departments. You must have deep knowledge and experience of your particular field. Apart from getting this through work experience, you can do courses run by Citizens' Advice Bureaux, colleges of further education or local authority action groups. Para-legals need to be good with people and have excellent communication skills combined with attention to detail to understand and interpret the law. You'll also have to be methodical and analytical to be able to see the repercussions of new legislation in general and of all the details of each case you advise. Some find first-hand experience of their speciality, for example, as a social security claimant themselves, a useful insight into the sort of help and advice they can most usefully offer. You're likely to be dealing with people who are worried, confused or angry and so patience is essential.

Setting up with others is recommended as a way of sharing costs and the workload. You may decide to offer a range of specialities for your local area or settle for being experts in one field serving a larger geographical area. Although individual clients may prefer coming to see you face to face, much of the business can be carried out over the phone, and once you've got a name, you can serve clients from all over England and Wales. This means that it doesn't matter which part of the country you set up in although it helps if you're in at least a small town.

To set up you'll need at least £20,000 to open an office equipped with phone, fax (essential when you're dealing with documents), photocopier, typewriters/word processors, stationery and filing systems. Running costs include paying for administrative and secretarial back-up. For many of your clients much of the attraction of your services will be that you're cheaper than a solicitor; para-legals charge by the hour; often operating a sliding scale and charging private clients less than corporate (banks, solicitors) ones.

Useful contacts are solicitors, accountants and banks who may need your advice themselves or refer other clients to you. Start by mailing all of these when you first open. Get to know local citizens' advisers and DSS employees who may refer people who need legal help to you, put up advertisements at Citizens' Advice Bueaux, DSS offices, community centres, libraries, etc. You'll work under pressure, solicitors need information fast and individual clients may be in dire straits so you need to be able to put in some long hours; much of the work is done during office hours and it's important that you're available throughout this time but it's also helpful if you can offer clients the option of meetings in the evening. As well as advising and doing any research needed for a specific job, you'll have to be well informed about all changes in the law and any recent court cases that are relevant to your area; this will mean a lot of reading of the national press as well as government department information and reports published by HMSO. You can get further information from the LAW SOCIETY and THE INSTITUTE OF LEGAL EXECUTIVES.

✦ European Community Notes

There are no actually recognised qualifications. However there are opportunities for employment overseas in a capacity similar to that of legal executive, often as legal assistants.

Patent Agent

Qualifications/Training	Required
Income bracket	Medium–High
Licence	No
Town/Country	Town
Experience/Springboard	Essential
Travel	Yes
Mid-career entry	Possible
Exit sale	Possible
Entry costs	£1,500+
Work at home	Possible
Mix and match	Yes.

You could think about: *Solicitor, Inventor, Computer Software author, Racehorse owner*

Enquiries
Chartered Institute of Patent Agents

Patent agents advise on, obtain and enforce patents for inventions throughout the industrialised world. The holder of the patent, usually an R&D-based company or a research-based academic or public institution, but still not infrequently a private inventor, has a legal right to prevent anyone else from exploiting the invention for a specified number of years – usually 20.

This is a highly technical area of law in which enormous commercial interests may be at stake: it's most emphatically not the sort of work that can be skimped or in which corners can be cut to get a cheaper or quicker result.

The job of the patent agent is first to research the area of the invention through the technical literature in order to ensure that the invention is sufficiently original to merit a patent at all and second to provide an exhaustive technical description of the invention to accompany the application for patent protection to the PATENT OFFICE. Some independent patent agents thus find it best to specialise in one area of technology.

In the UK it's a small profession – only about 1,250 in all. There's plenty of work for independent patent agents – from medium and small companies and private investors – even though the multi-national giants and major UK research-based companies may employ their own professional staff. As an independent professional yourself you can act before the EUROPEAN PATENTS OFFICE, which grants patents effective in 12 states in Europe, or through the offices of other agents overseas so that it is quite possible to handle the international aspects of the work effectively as an independent agent. And this is the area of rapid growth and potential, especially with 1992 and the opening of trade throughout Europe.

Patent agents need a combination of technical, legal and linguistic know-how. You must be registered by the CHARTERED INSTITUTE OF PATENT AGENTS. For this you'll need a broadly based science, technology or engineering degree followed by passing exams which require you to work for at least two years for a registered patent agent usually as a technical assistant. Registration with the European Patent Institute is also recommended and for this you'll need some knowledge of French or German and to pass more exams. Legal qualifications and experience are extremely useful as is a period in industrial research and development. The documents you are drafting will have to stand up in law courts so you need a deep knowledge of patent law, to have a logical, analytical mind and the ability to present specifications in clear, legally impeccable English. You should also be capable of understanding advanced ideas and keeping abreast of scientific developments. Finally, you may need to argue your case in and out of court so you'll need negotiating skills and an accurate and precise mind.

You can work from home. Set-up costs include a fax, a filing and a record keeping system. Patent agents generate a lot of paperwork, much of which has to be kept in case it's needed later to enforce a patent in court. You have to keep very careful records; the granting of a patent takes up to four-and-a-half years and involves presenting a series of documents at specific times; if you don't respond to the Patent Office within their deadlines the patent application may lapse, or cost more to be continued. Patent agents usually charge clients fixed fees for fulfilling each of these demands. In addition, clients pay an hourly rate for all the work you do; fees are similar to those charged by solicitors.

Clients for small patent agents are usually medium, or small and expanding, industrial companies. Work is generated through contacts and word of mouth; to begin with contact your local chamber of commerce who will have information on local companies. Other useful contacts are solicitors and some patent agents, especially those who have a solicitor's qualification, set up partnerships with solicitors: strictly only those who are qualified can enter into such partnerships but others are employed by firms of solicitors. When you're dealing with applications for patents outside Europe you'll need to contact patent agents overseas and work with them in their countries. A lot of the work is office bound, searching existing patent records before drafting technical specifications. In addition you'll have to visit clients, brief lawyers and appear in court as an expert witness in cases of suspected patent infringement. Patent agents are also needed to register trade marks and industrial designs such as the pattern on printed fabric. As long as you fulfil the schedule imposed by the Patent Office, you can set your own working hours making this a good career to combine with others. There is no need to operate from a particular part of the country although it's helpful to be near some of the developing industrial companies who are likely to use you.

European Community Notes

Qualifications: UK qualifications recognised throughout EC and EC qualifications in UK.

Languages: To succeed, local language not necessary.

Setting up: You will find it possible to succeed throughout the Community.

Advice/Training: Advice, information and

training available for those wishing to work in Europe.

Exchanges: Formal job exchanges do not exist.

Enquiry point for those wishing to work in the EC: CHARTERED INSTITUTE OF PATENT AGENTS

Notes: Patent agency tends to be an international career and links are good overseas. There is a European qualifying examination run by the European Patent Office in Munich.

Pharmacist

Qualifications/Training	Essential
Income bracket	Medium
Licence	Yes
Town/Country	Town
Experience/Springboard	Yes
Travel	None
Mid-career entry	Unlikely
Exit sale	Yes
Entry costs	£20,000
Work at home	No
Mix and match	Limited

You could think about: **Healthfood shopkeeper, Newsletter publisher, Sculptor**

Enquiries
Royal Pharmaceutical Society

Pharmacists dispense prescriptions, but it is unlikely you'll make a living from this so you need counter stock to augment the income from this. The National Health Service is your main customer, so you'll have to fulfil more requirements than other small, independent shops. You are contracted to specific opening hours (including late nights and Sunday opening) by the local Family Health Services Authority (FHSA). Small pharmacies cost the NHS more so it is trying to restrict their numbers; the FHSA now has to give per-

mission - before a new chemist will be granted an NHS contract and it's difficult to survive without one. By law a pharmacist must be on the premises whenever prescriptions are dispensed or certain other items sold. As well as making up and dispensing prescriptions pharmacists advise on the safe and effective use of medicines and act as readily accessible health advisors to the Great British Public.

Pharmacists have to register with the ROYAL PHARMACEUTICAL SOCIETY which means completing a degree course in pharmacy followed by a year's practical experience. Once registered, you can set up shop alone. Pharmacists have to be extremely meticulous – there is no room for error in making up prescriptions. They also need lots of patience and the ability at least to appear concerned; many of their customers are ill and require fairly specialist advice.

Set-up costs vary depending on size and location of premises etc. You will need somewhere to make up the prescriptions, and equipment for making them up (scales etc); storage for drugs (refrigeration for some) and retail goods; fixtures and fittings for the shop itself and a computer if you can afford it. In addition you need prescription drug stock – at least £10,000 and, depending on the size of your clientele and the sort of drugs they need, this could be up to £80–£100,000. You get stock from a drug wholesaler; some give credit to new chemists. There are initial cash flow problems; firstly because you will have to establish what drug stock you need (easier if you take over an existing business); secondly because the NHS takes about two months to pay for drugs, containers and dispensing fees. The NHS sets the rates for prescriptions and the prescription charges are deducted from what the NHS pays you. This means a lot of administration for pharmacists.

How much counter stock and what you stock is up to you. However, your customers will expect baby food, loo-paper, soap, contraceptives etc as well as non-prescription drugs; or you can specialise in eg homeopathic remedies, theatrical or hyper-allergenic toiletries.

Further information from the ROYAL

PHARMACEUTICAL SOCIETY which publishes the *Pharmaceutical Journal*. See also *Chemist & Druggist* and *Community Pharmacy*.

Photographer

Qualifications/Training	Recommended
Income bracket	Low–High
Licence	No
Town/Country	Either
Experience/Springboard	No
Travel	Probable
Mid-career entry	Possible
Exit sale	Yes
Entry costs	£5,000+
Work at home	Yes
Mix and match	Yes.

You could think about: ***Contemporary art gallery owner, Picture framer, Sculptor, Advertising photographer***

Enquiries
British Institute of Professional Photography, Association of Fashion, Advertising and Editorial Photographers, National Union of Journalists

Photography requires visual and technical talents. If you want to sell pictures as art, you will have to be prepared for long hours and a lot of foot slogging. There is much more money in specialising in editorial photography for magazines/ books or, better still, in advertising. Even most of Lord Snowdon's work is for glossy magazines in the first place.

Most photographers train at art school – foundation course followed by a vocational course at a college recognised by the BRITISH INSTITUTE OF PROFESSIONAL PHOTOGRAPHY. Press photographers are generally better off with courses in editorial photography at such colleges as NEWPORT or the LONDON COLLEGE OF PRINTING. The BIPP produce a publication called the *Photographer*, which is a useful source of small ads for equipment and jobs. The *British Journal of Photography*

is another publication in the field, but the design magazines, such as *Blueprint* and *Creative Review* are more fashion conscious.

If you have talent, and want to pursue a career as an art photographer, your most secure option is to look for sponsorship: some colleges and museums employ a 'photographer in residence'. Salary will be low, and you may be expected to lecture or run seminars, as well as organising exhibitions of your own work from time to time.

Another source of income may be from books, so cultivate relationships with people in publishing who could have helpful contacts. You can also place pictures with picture agencies, who sell rights on pictures for publication, but their needs are usually a bit commercial, and your style may not suit them.

You should also develop good relationships with small, private gallery owners, and persuade them to hold exhibitions (and sales) of your work – this helps to get your name known, as well as providing a small income.

Obviously, your main capital outlay will be on cameras and lenses: you will need at least a few thousand pounds worth of hardware, but the chances are you will start your collection while you are at college and build up from there. If you want to process your own film, you will also need dark room equipment, unless you have access to a dark room at an art college.

Your main overheads will be film, processing and framing pictures for exhibition. You may also need a studio, depending on the type of work you do. Income may be low for a long time, but if you do make the big time you can expect a very comfortable income.

European Community Notes
Qualifications: UK qualifications recognised in EC except Belgium and Germany and EC qualifications in UK. But no formal qualifications are needed in the EC as a freelance unless permanently relocating.
Languages: To succeed, local language necessary.

Earnings: UK income generally same as elsewhere in the EC.

Setting up: You will find it difficult to succeed in Belgium, France, Germany, Luxembourg. You will find it easier in Denmark, Eire, Greece, Italy, Netherlands, Portugal, Spain.

Notes: This depends on individual talents but Belgium, France, Germany and Luxembourg have a large indigenous threshold to break through. Languages are essential and intense market research to establish needs, trends and fashions.

Advice/Training: Advice, information and training not available for those wishing to work in Europe.

Exchanges: Formal job exchanges do not exist.

Photographic Assistant

Qualifications/Training	Recommended
Income bracket	Low
Licence	No
Town/Country	Town
Experience/Springboard	No
Travel	Maybe
Mid-career entry	Unlikely
Exit sale	No
Entry costs	Nil
Work at home	No
Mix and match	Yes.

You could think about: *High street photographer, Advertising photographer, Stage technician carpenter, Mini-cab driver*

Enquiries
Association of Fashion, Advertising and Editorial Photographers

As well as being a good career in itself, photographic assistants often go on to become top photographers. A thorough understanding of the mechanics of photography (how cameras work, and basic knowledge of lighting) is essential, and this is generally gained at a foundation course followed by a vocational (BTEC) course at art school. However, no art school can substitute for experience. The next step is the most difficult, finding a photographer who needs an assistant with no experience. As an assistant, your job will be to carry equipment, connect lights, check light readings, develop polaroids, label and arrange for processing of film, make the coffee and pour the wine. You may also have to organise invoicing, order background paper and film when necessary, get equipment serviced, arrange for the hire of extra lighting, keep the studio clean, and go out for last minute props (if there isn't a photographic stylist).

If you work full-time at one particular studio you *may* be paid as little as £100 per week, and you will be self-employed. Other photographers prefer to use freelance assistants and to use them on a daily basis for an agreed daily rate. If you are good at the job, and are based in London or another large city, you can make a fair living as a freelance assistant, working for several photographers, though the amount of work you get will be erratic and unpredictable.

One area of specialisation which can be fairly lucrative is in set building. Many photographers need a specialist assistant who can help to design and then build room sets (or outdoor scenes) in the studio – sometimes working from no more than a rough sketch, at other times following a brief to the last detail.

You do not usually need any equipment when you start, but most assistants build up a tool kit (electric screwdriver, hammer, scissors, handyman's knife, Blu-tack, superglue, pliers, a selection of adhesive tapes, pins and so on). Obviously, if you specialise in set building the tool kit must be extensive.

Photographic assistants should be aware of the activities of the BRITISH INSTITUTE OF PROFESSIONAL PHOTOGRAPHY, and their magazine, the *Photographer* may be a useful source of advertising for jobs. The ASSOCIATION OF FASHION, ADVERTISING AND EDITORIAL PHOTOGRAPHERS (AFAEP) holds careers talks for the benefit of people looking for their first work in advertising photography, monthly in London and four times a year in Manchester.

⁎⁎⁎ European Community Notes

Qualifications: No qualifications needed unless permanently relocating to work in EC on freelance basis.

Languages: To succeed, local language necessary.

Earnings: UK income generally same as elsewhere in the EC.

Setting up: You will find it difficult to succeed in Belgium, France, Germany and Luxembourg. You will find it easier in Denmark, Eire, Greece, Italy, Netherlands, Portugal, Spain.

Notes: This depends on individual talents but Belgium, France, Germany and Luxembourg have a large indigenous threshold to break through. Languages are essential and intense market research to establish needs, trends and fashions.

Advice/Training: Advice, information and training not available for those wishing to work in Europe.

Exchanges: Formal job exchanges do not exist.

Photojournalist

Qualifications/Training	Recommended
Income bracket	Low–Medium
Licence	Union card
Town/Country	Town
Experience/Springboard	Useful
Travel	Endless
Mid-career entry	Unlikely
Exit sale	Yes
Entry costs	£3,000+
Work at home	No

Mix and match   Possible.
You could think about: ***Advertising photographer, Cabaret performer, Motorcycle messenger***

Enquiries
National Union of Journalists

Every picture tells a story. That could be the motto of every photojournalist, whose job it is to take still photographs for magazines and newspapers. This can be done either on spec or, once you are known and if the event is a scheduled one – Tory Party Conference, for example – you may be commissioned to cover it.

It's a hectic, unpredictable life, dominated by men aged between 24 and 40. After that, most move into other sorts of photography that offer more stability if less excitement. It's difficult to get started because you probably won't be given any money up front until you get that all-important break. There's a high drop-out rate and only the most determined – and the luckiest – make it to the top.

New technology is set to change things, as the process of taking still photographs off video and TV footage is perfected. Thus the freelance stills photographer will increasingly compete with big news agencies who can afford the technology and get pictures out fast.

The first step is to take a BA or Diploma course both to gain a basic training and to sample the various directions in which you can go. However, more important than qualifications is your portfolio. If it shows a lot of potential, some agencies – such as REFLEX PICTURES LTD – will take you on and give you some training and a lot of encouragement, as well as selling your pictures for you. Some may even pay you a minimal retainer fee while you find your feet. The best training of all, of course, is working alongside someone who knows what they're doing so, if you can, become an apprentice to an established photojournalist. Some of the national dailies will let you follow a staff photographer around for a few days if you are on a recognized course. Another good way is to establish a rapport with some magazines and newspapers. Start at the bottom with the low-budget mags, charity papers, local rags and political tracts – and that can't afford to send their own staff photographer.

The most important personal qualities are initiative, determination, dedication, and an ability to elbow your way in and go for it. The downfall of a lot of would-be photojournalists is that they lack the ability to sell their work, which is an essential asset.

You can start with basic camera equipment costing around £500 and then add to it as you make money. You have to be prepared for a high wear and tear bill, especially if you cover stormy events like major demos, industrial disputes and wars. Insurance can be difficult and some insurance companies will quickly cancel your policy if you claim against it, so it's best not to claim for every minor mishap but to wait for the big ones.

If you work from home, an anwering machine and bleeper are a must. Other options include working for an agency or hiring your own agent, which is obviously the most expensive choice. The copyright laws have changed in favour of the photographer – the law now states that the copyright remains the property of the photographer – each magazine/newspaper is negotiating with individual photographers.

You might start by earning peanuts – as little as £25 a week. An average income after ten years is around £15,000, though some people obviously do a lot better. You can't count on a regular income, at least to start with, because you simply don't get paid unless you produce pictures that sell. Camera equipment and film are expensive, as are rail and air fares. You really need to have some degree of financial security – your own savings, another source of income or an understanding bank manager – before you set off on spec for eg Iraq. But there is money to be made if you hit the right spots: just one brilliant picture that no one else got, eg in the Gulf war, could have earned you £30,000. What's more, as you own the copyright you get paid every time one of your pictures is reproduced. So, over your career, if you're good you are building up a goldmine of a library either as a source of income or to sell outright to a picture library or agency – figures as high as half-a-million have been known to change hands for the work of an exceptional photographer.

You may find a NATIONAL UNION OF JOURNALISTS (NUJ) press card useful, although it is not essential and, if you plan to work abroad, an international press card. You will have to have a Metropolitan Police card, available from the METROPOLITAN POLICE PRESS BUREAU, if you intend to cover anything remotely connected with the law (including any major political event involving the security forces) in London and the equivalent from police forces outside London.

Useful books include *Making Waves, Freelance Photographer's Market Handbook, Photo Journalism* and *Pictures on a Page – Photo-journalism, Graphics and Picture Editing*.

A good place to buy books, see exhibitions, keep up to date, meet people and generally hang out is the PHOTOGRAPHER'S GALLERY in London.

Physiotherapist

Qualifications/Training	Essential
Income bracket	Low–High
Licence	Yes
Town/Country	Town
Experience/ Springboard	Recommended
Travel	No
Mid-career entry	Unlikely
Exit sale	No
Entry costs	£7,500+
Work at home	Possible
Mix and match	Possible.

You could think about: ***Counsellor, Sports retailer, Antique dealer, Acupuncturist, Window cleaner***

Enquiries
Chartered Society of Physiotherapy; Organisation of Chartered Physiotherapists in Private Practice

Chartered physiotherapists are skilled in massage, manipulation, movement and exercise techniques, as well as electrotherapy, heat, high frequency currents or ultrasonics to aid recovery from various ills. They also work in the preventative field as well as with post-operative rehabilitation, chest complaints, physical handicap, pregnant women, teaching, relaxation in psychiatric departments and treating sports and dance injuries, for individuals or teams.

To qualify as a state registered physiotherapist you'll need to do a three-year course at a teaching hospital, university or polytechnic. (The partially sighted can train at the NORTH LONDON SCHOOL OF PHYSIOTHERAPY FOR THE VISUALLY HANDICAPPED). You should join the CHARTERED SOCIETY OF PHYSIOTHERAPY which has useful lectures and seminars and keeps you in touch with latest developments. You'll need a healthy constitution and the ability to communicate with others; physios spend much of their life encouraging, persuading and explaining. Tolerance, empathy, patience, a sense of humour and initiative plus emotional stability are vital. The body can affect the mind and vice versa so it's necessary to take the holistic view of the patient. Career prospects are excellent, as the profession is expanding in many new directions, and the demand for physios in private practice is growing.

It's advisable to work and gain experience for at least five years in as many different fields as possible in the NHS. This is also a way of making contacts and building a good network of specialists in all fields to whom you can refer patients. You can practice from a ground-floor room in your house and you can start part time. You'll need £3,000–£15,000 to set up with a treatment bed, an ultrasound machine, a phone, answering machine, and filing cabinet. You also need hot and cold running water, to be near public transport and have car parking space. Average charges are about £20–£30 per treatment; in and around Harley Street nearer £40 or £45 for treatment at home. Private practitioners can earn up to about £50,000 a year.

Your day can be as long as you want it to be, but early morning and evenings are the best times for seeing patients, before or after their working day. When starting out, never refuse a patient referred at short notice by a local GP, as good relations with doctors are vital. This job is very satisfying as a high proportion of patients get better, and you're always gaining experience. But it is isolated unless you employ assistants. It's impossible to escape the clerical work even with a good secretary and it takes careful organisation to allow time to give or attend lectures and teach, both of which are rewarding.

Read *Physiotherapy*. The ORGANISATION OF CHARTERED PHYSIOTHERAPISTS IN PRIVATE PRACTICE produces an excellent handbook and runs courses to help you set up on your own.

European Community Notes

Qualifications: See *Notes*.

Languages: To succeed, local language necessary.

Earnings: UK income generally same as elsewhere in Europe.

Setting up: You will find it difficult to succeed in Belgium, France, Germany, Greece, Italy, Luxembourg, Netherlands, Portugal, Spain. You will find it easier in Denmark, Eire.

Advice/Training: Advice, information and training available for those wishing to work in Europe.

Exchanges: Formal job exchanges do not exist.

Enquiry point for those wishing to work in the EC: International Affairs Dept, CHARTERED SOCIETY OF PHYSIOTHERAPY

Notes: Conditions of work and salaries vary greatly throughout the EC. But the chief obstacle to success is the overproduction of fellow professionals. Since January 1991, EC law demands that professional qualifications are accepted as equivalent (not identical) by the competent authority for each member state. Few of the EC states have yet made the detailed provisions necessary to operate the system and it has got off to a slow start. In the meantime, there is a slow but steady flow of physios into the UK from the EC, largely due to our high number of vacancies and their high number of unemployed therapists.

Piano Tuner and Restorer

Qualifications/Training	Recommended
Income bracket	Medium–High
Licence	No
Town/Country	Mostly town
Experience/ Springboard	Recommended
Travel	Local
Mid-career entry	Yes
Exit sale	No
Entry costs	£1,000+
Work at home	Partly
Mix and match	Possible.

You could think about: *Musical instrument repairer, Keyboard hire, Wood carver, Jazz musician*

Enquiries
Piano Tuners' Association.

This is someone who restores, repairs and tunes keyboard instruments. A few with talent have picked up skills as they go. But you are advised to take a full-time course at eg LONDON COLLEGE OF FURNITURE. Evening classes are not so thorough. To detect absolutely accurate intonation and to be able to play the instrument, you need a really good ear. You should also learn bookkeeping, possess endless patience and a desire for meticulous accuracy. Work as an assistant to a tuner for at least two years. To go it alone you will need at least £2,000 to buy tools, a room or outhouse where you can do restoration work, telephone, answering machine or service and stationery.

Find your customers by passing the word around the local choir, and sending printed cards about your service to county musical advisers and local piano teachers (names from the INCORPORATED SOCIETY OF MUSICIANS). Join the PIANO TUNERS' ASSOCIATION and the GUILD OF MASTER CRAFTSMEN. Develop contacts at recording studios; pianos which are being recorded need to be absolutely in tune. It is possible to do without a car; you can ask your clients to employ a specialist piano remover if you need to take away an instrument for repair. It is dangerous both for you and the piano to try and do this yourself. You can find yourself working long hours – 12–18 a day if you have the energy – so it is unlikely that you can do another job at the same time. For most jobs you need speed to make money. To start with, you can charge £20 per tuning; the number you can do in a day depends on the age and condition of the piano, and how quickly you work. Modern electronic tuning devices make the work easier in noisy circumstances but are only as good as the ears that use them. Old pianos are likely to be affected by central heating; new pianos are seasoned to withstand these problems. Restoration work requires special care and training.

The advantages of this job are that it is one of the few in music that is expanding, and you can earn up to £25,000 pa if you establish your reputation with a concert hall. Hours are flexible but you may find yourself working at weekends and it's easy to become a workaholic. There is usually plenty of local work so it is unlikely you will have to travel far.

✦✦✦ European Community Notes
The prospects for this career in the EC are in many ways quite appealing – certainly financially: you'd get twice as much in France or Italy, for example, and tuning prices are considerably higher than the UK in a number of other EC countries. There is no obligation for a self-employed tuner to have any qualifications at all in the UK (unfortunately!) but there may be some local restrictions elsewhere. The PIANO

TUNERS' ASSOCIATION can provide details of local associations in other countries, which would prove useful contacts.

Picture Agent

Qualifications/Training	Useful
Income bracket	Low–High
Licence	No
Town/Country	Usually town
Experience/Springboard	Recommended
Travel	No
Mid-career entry	Yes
Exit sale	Yes
Entry costs	£2,500+
Work at home	Possible
Mix and match	Possible.

You could think about: *List broker, Newsletter publisher*

Enquiries
Existing picture libraries

A picture agency (or picture library) holds pictures (transparencies, negatives and prints) ready for use in newspapers, magazines, books, brochures and advertising material. The pictures may be bought direct from photographers, or they may come from magazines and books which have already been published. For example, a magazine like *Ideal Home* will commission photographers (at vast expense) to take shots of interiors, set up and photograph room sets, or do still life shots. Once the magazine has been published, the rights to reproduce the photographs will be handled by a picture agency. (In some cases, the agency will also syndicate the story that goes with the pictures.) The agency files and records all the original material, and sells rights to other publications or agencies for the re-use of the material.

Picture agents may have trained in librarianship or in art and design. It is important to keep meticulous records, and

be prepared for long delays in payment. The usual pattern is that a picture researcher contacts you asking for particular types of pictures (eg colour photographs of a specific plant, atmospheric pictures of happy, healthy families walking in the country, unusual pictures of construction workers climbing scaffolding – you name it!). You then go through your files (or make an appointment for the picture researcher to come in and look at what you've got), and then you send out the pictures (usually 'dupes' or duplicates). A picture researcher on a weekly magazine will probably make a selection within days and return pictures which are not wanted. But a picture researcher on a book may hold on to the pictures for several months while editorial and design decisions are made (and changed and re-thought). Payment is usually withheld until the picture has actually been published – which may be over a year in the case of a book (you may be able to demand a holding fee to help cover your expenses).

If you live fairly centrally, and depending on the subject area you specialise in, you can set up in your own home. Agencies specialising in a subject area such as plants, where researchers' needs are fairly precise (eg 'We want a picture of a buddleia with a butterfly on it' or 'a close up of a hydrangea petiolaris in flower') can usually manage very well working out of town. Indeed, some of these agencies are actually owned by photographers who specialise in plants and gardens, and their spouses or partners run the agency. However, if you specialise in news photographs, where pictures may have to be delivered to the picture researcher or picture editor on a magazine in a matter of hours (or even minutes) or an area like home interiors, where researchers have a feeling for what they are looking for, but don't know exactly what they want until they see it, you will have to set up your office in London.

The main requirements for the office are plenty of space to set up your library system, good light box facilities, and a computer to keep tabs on the whereabouts of all your pictures and to send and chase invoices. Most agencies have specialised stationery with multiple copy invoices to help both themselves and the picture researchers they deal with to keep records of payments, rights and so on.

Picture Framer

Qualifications/Training	Recommended
Income bracket	Low–Medium
Licence	No
Town/Country	Town
Experience/ Springboard	Recommended
Travel	No
Mid-career entry	Yes
Exit sale	Yes
Entry costs	£100–£5,000
Work at home	Yes
Mix and match	Yes.

You could think about: *Contemporary art gallery owner, Picture restorer, Antique furniture restorer, Art historian/critic, Healer, Sculptor*

Enquiries
Local picture framers

Picture framing seems to have been one of the growth industries of the Eighties; like many other Eighties' flyers it has taken a hammering, in the early Nineties but most high streets seem to have one framer. It's a good career to mix and match with something else – and often necessary unless business really takes off; even then the chains of high street framers are often able to undercut smaller framers. Framing combines especially well with picture and any other art dealing.

You can buy a franchise which will provide you with a shop, equipment and training. Otherwise you can start off by doing a course in commercial picture framing. Frame suppliers are a good initial contact: they sometimes send reps to advise and may offer training or have details of local courses. Or contact your local adult education centre. Course fees are £250 plus. WEST DEAN COLLEGE is recommended, with artistic, technical and business training. Working for someone else for a year or so is a good way of developing your own technique. You need to be good at doing fiddly jobs; this isn't something you can hurry (the machinery can be dangerous and frames are fragile) so you'll need to be patient; it's essential that you're artistic enough to be able to advise on good ways of framing pictures – clients often don't know what they want. As with anything that brings you into contact with a buying public, you'll have to be fairly long suffering and, at times, diplomatic.

You need a lot of space for picture framing. You can work from home if you've got a spare room or garage but, if you can afford it, a shop front will help to attract more business. Whichever you choose, aim to be as close to a town centre as possible, your customers will have to make two trips (one to deliver and one to collect) and the less they have to travel, the better; but make sure that there's enough parking nearby. Apart from a telephone, you don't need much equipment. You can start in a very small way with a mitre saw (£80) and a hand-held cutter (£5) but this will mean spending more time on each frame. It costs up to £5,000+ to equip yourself fully with: two large benches (one of which will get covered in glass splinters so don't use it for anything else); a mount cutter; a special saw or guillotine for cutting 45° angles in mouldings; a glass cutter and wooden measure; special pens; an under-pinner which holds the various bits of frame together; various rules and saws; a glazier's gun and points to fix it all in the frame. You're advised always to buy the best equipment available. You'll need supplies of glass and card for mountings; cord; wedges (to hold the corners of the frame together); rings, screws and clips, not to mention stretchers for oil paintings etc. Mouldings (the stuff that does the actual framing of the picture) have fashions – sometimes you'll sell a lot of metal ones, other times wood; keep a stock of about 50 different ones that your clients can choose from and make sure that you know a good fast supplier so that you can get hold of other ones at short notice if needed. Framing with perspex is very similar to framing with glass although it costs more, weighs less and is more difficult to cut; it's difficult to get large bits of perspex too. Another alternative is acrylic glass which is thinner than perspex. You'll need all-risks insurance cover for client's pictures while they're in your charge. Most framers calculate their charges on the dimensions or area of the frame, ie so much per square foot or inch. Charges have to cover glass, moulding, mount and other bits and pieces as well as your time. Most of the work you do will fall into the £60–£90 bracket; to customers it may seem a lot especially since high street shops have devised a way of framing quickly and cheaply. You can speed up your own production by working a sort of mini-production line, mounting several pictures at once, then framing them then cutting glass etc. This means that you have to collect work in advance, customers are usually happy to wait about two weeks for a frame and you can always do a special, quick job if someone wants theirs before that. You really need to be doing at least 40–50 frames a week to survive but you can augment your income by selling framed and unframed prints or posters either in your shop, if you've got one, or at fairs and markets.

Good sources of work and outlets for ready framed pictures are interior designers, antique shops which sell old prints, and gift shops. Much work comes by word of mouth. You can start off by going around antiques shows with a selection of framed prints for sale (see the *Antiques Trade Gazette*). Get yourself known at art suppliers who may be able to push some customers your way. If you can cope with bulk orders, art galleries generate great volumes of work but will probably want some sort of reduction; hotels and offices may also be interested in buying a set of inexpensive framed prints from you.

If you've got a shop you're tied to shop hours but, on the whole you're free to frame when you like. Christmas is a busy season. Occasionally you'll have to start a job from scratch again because frames are very easily broken during the last stages of their production.

Picture Researcher

Qualifications/Training	No
Income bracket	Low–Medium
Licence	No
Town/Country	Town
Experience/Springboard	Usually
Travel	Yes
Mid-career entry	Yes
Exit sale	No
Entry costs	£1,000
Work at home	Yes
Mix and match	Possible.

You could think about: *Magazine designer, Photographic assistant, Motorcycle messenger*

Enquiries
Society of Picture Researchers and Editors (SPREd)

Picture researchers are responsible for finding pictures and handling the rights to use pictures in a range of publications. They usually start by working on the staff of a newspaper, magazine or for a book publishing company before setting up alone. They may come straight from art school, they may have started as the office secretary, or they may drift into picture research from editing or design work. Part-time courses in picture research are available at the LONDON SCHOOL OF PUBLISHING and BOOK HOUSE TRAINING CENTRE. As a freelance picture researcher you tend to either work in-house on a newspaper or magazine, filling in while staff are off sick or while a new appointment is being made, or you work from home, researching pictures for a range of books.

The most common source of pictures is picture agencies, where you should have no problems in negotiating fees and rights, since these are set by the agency. However, good researchers will be ingenious and look for other sources – manufacturers (who often provide pictures free if they are given an editorial credit), historical archives (which may only charge a nominal fee for use of their material), private individuals who may be so excited that one of their pictures is likely to be published that they want to pay *you*, or may have such a limited knowledge of the system that they want to charge ten times the going rate.

One of the advantages of working freelance on several projects is that you can 'double up' when you visit agencies – researching pictures on a range of topics for different clients at the same time.

Picture researchers will charge by the hour or day, and expect to earn £150–£400 per week as a freelance. They must keep meticulous records, as the pictures they handle may each be worth up to £1,000. Working from home, a telephone and address book are the main pieces of equipment needed.

There is a professional association, SPREd (SOCIETY OF PICTURE RESEARCHERS AND EDITORS) which keeps a register of experienced, *bona fide* picture researchers who work on a freelance basis, so that editors and art directors can contact them. It has monthly meetings and produces a quarterly magazine to which non-members may subscribe. Other useful reading includes the *Picture Researchers Handbook*, the main source book, with picture agencies, museums etc both in the UK and abroad; *Picture Sources UK* is also valuable. When there are jobs on offer, Monday's *Guardian* and the *Bookseller* is where they may surface.

★★*★
★   ★
★★*★ **European Community Notes**
As far as setting-up in Europe is concerned, the general comments for all magazine and book publishing jobs apply. There are no standard qualifications; speaking the language – and knowing the market intimately – can only help; contacts are like old gold. Try SPREd for more details.

Picture Restorer

Qualifications/Training	Recommended
Income bracket	Low–Medium
Licence	No
Town/Country	Either
Experience/Springboard	No
Travel	Yes
Mid-career entry	Possible
Exit sale	No
Entry costs	£2,000
Work at home	Yes
Mix and match	Yes.

You could think about: *Antique furniture restorer, Picture framer, Contemporary art gallery owner, Artist*

Enquiries
Museums Association

Picture restorers mend damaged paintings and clean dirty ones. Paintings often change a lot after they've been cleaned – not only are the colours clearer and brighter but cleaning also shows up any modern additions that are not of the original painting. It is very intricate work, and sometimes controversial; there can be an outrage if the authenticity of works of art is seen as being under threat.

There are very few studentships or apprenticeships for picture restorers in this country at museums or art institutes. A few colleges offer training places: the COURTAULD INSTITUTE for oil painting restoration; GATESHEAD COLLEGE for prints and CAMBERWELL for prints and paper restoration. There are more training places in America.

You'll need a bit of capital to start with and may need to augment your income for a while. You are paid per job, not per hour, so you need to have a good idea of how long each job will take before you're ready to start quoting prices.

With training, there is quite a lot of freelance work available. Contacts and work of mouth are the normal ways to get work. Museums use freelance restorers (contact the MUSEUMS ASSOCIATION. They also keep lists of restorers and their particular specialism so that they can refer members of the public. Otherwise, finding work is just a matter of traipsing around likely clients like antique dealers. Once you've established a good reputation you'll get more and more work through referrals and clients coming back to you.

Pop Group Sound Engineer

Qualifications/Training	Not necessary
Income bracket	Low
Licence	Driving licence
Town/Country	Town
Experience/ Springboard	Recommended
Travel	Lots
Mid-career entry	Unlikely
Exit sale	No
Entry costs	£250
Work at home	No
Mix and match	Limited.

You could think about: *Landlord, Minicab driver, Bartender*

Enquiries
Recording studios

This is someone who transports, sets up and balances the sound equipment for a pop group. No formal qualifications are needed, but it is vital you understand how the equipment works so you can maintain and repair it, often quickly and under very difficult conditions. Youth, energy, strength, a good ear, and luck are all useful. You have to drive the van/car to gigs and on tours, so must have a clean driving licence.

Work in an equipment company, or as a gofer in a recording studio for a couple of years. You can meet groups there and do odd gigs with them. If they become successful, join them on tour. You will earn peanuts unless they are given a contract by a recording company, when your income can rise to £14,000 pa.

It's a good idea to have a house or flat and install a lodger when you are off on tour. You will need a telephone and answering machine or services; transport should be provided by the group. Working hours are likely to be 19 hours a day, seven days a week, so say goodbye to your private life.

A tour can last for up to three months and the group lives at close quarters, so you must be able to 'bend with the wind' and keep cool. The job can involve driving hundreds of miles to a gig, setting up heavy gear and doing a sound test before the concert; then loading up and possibly driving again. This is why the bias is towards fit young males.

Study the adverts in pop trade magazines, get the names of public address systems companies from yellow pages and apply for anything that sounds likely.

This job is a way of acquiring electronic and organisational skills. It's exciting and fun to travel around, but don't expect to enjoy it over the age of 30.

Potter

Qualifications/Training	Recommended
Income bracket	Low–Medium
Licence	No
Town/Country	Either
Experience/Springboard	Possible
Travel	Local
Mid-career entry	Possible
Exit sale	No
Entry costs	£3,000+
Work at home	Yes
Mix and match	Possible.

You could think about: *Photographer, Holiday accommodation owner, Book publisher, Tourist attraction*

Enquiries
Craftsmen Potters Association, Crafts Council

Decorative ceramics are now in demand in Britain (Scandinavia vigorously promoted it some 100 years ago) and the old image of beards and open-toed sandals has given way to a close co-operation between contemporary artist and craftsman. You can get advice on courses from the SOCIETY OF DESIGNER–CRAFTSMEN, the CRAFTS COUNCIL or ADAR. Or you can take recreational classes or do some odd-jobbing for a successful ceramicist if you have enough flair. You can work from home or share costs in a workshop or studio (advice on setting up a workshop from the CRAFTS COUNCIL).

Setting up costs (tools, material, publicity) are expensive – expect to pay £3,000–£10,000, plus the cost of premises or rent. Look out for second hand equipment in trade magazines (*Ceramic Review, Crafts, Tiles & Tiling*) and college noticeboards. Use college friends to design your publicity and take your own photographs: it all helps to reduce costs. Teaching can augment your income.

Contacts are invaluable. Exhibit your work locally – at Craft Fairs and Christmas Charity Fairs – where you pay a small amount for the stand and give a percentage of your takings to the charity. When you begin to succeed do what the big-time potters do: enter as many trade fairs as possible for publicity, trade and overseas buyers (World Ceramics Fair, Tilex, International Gift Show, Interior Design International). The DESIGN COUNCIL has lists of exhibitions/fairs and their costs; see also *Exhibition Bulletin*. Get yourself on the CRAFTS COUNCIL register – they also have one for the 'elite', those craftsmen who they consider are high-flyers. Forge links with as many interior designers as possible. Advertise in local newspapers and 'freebies'. Price your wares realistically. Most retailers want a mass-produced, yet specialised product. You have to be very good to seel a £400 plate to a discriminating customer. Make sure that you are capable of meeting all potential orders (as many as 500) before showing at a large fair – you risk 'sudden death' if you get a name for unreliability. The larger manufacturers use out-workers, but they want skills rather than designs. Specialist outlets (interior design, tiles) use designer craftsmen (on retainers) to supply ceramics to requirements – tiles reflecting a fabric design. There is a substantial shift towards selling to department stores taking limited editions or one-offs. Hawk your work around these outlets and use your imagination: would your product sell in designer giftware shops, garden centres? Supply samples and colour charts.

Potters must keep up with fashion (tiles, ornaments etc) and the times – for example, making dinner services which go in dishwashers.

Prep School Owner

Qualifications/Training	Necessary
Income bracket	Medium–High
Licence	Yes
Town/Country	Either
Experience/Springboard	Essential
Travel	No
Mid-career entry	Likely
Exit sale	Excellent
Entry costs	£175,000+
Work at home	No
Mix and match	Possible.

You could think about: ***Events organiser, Holiday accommodation owner, Sailing school owner, Music teacher***

Enquiries
Independent Schools Information Service

There is a growing demand for good, reliable independent schools. Currently some 600,000 (about 7 per cent) school children in the UK are being educated independently; this number increases by about 1 per cent per annum. Independent schools are often oversubscribed and in many ways there is room for more independent primary schools. There's more to opening a school than buying a blackboard and a couple of reading books before sitting back and waiting for enrolments. It's big business (the annual turnover of a large school can be £1 million or more) and needs a lot of financial backing and know-how if you're to succeed.

For help and advice while you're setting up and getting going, contact ISIS, the INDEPENDENT SCHOOLS INFORMATION SERVICE. Any school providing full time education for five or more children of school age must be registered with the Deparment of Education and Science. You can register provisionally as soon as you open; you'll then be visited by the local fire officer to check that the buildings are safe and comply with *Fire and Design of Schools*, and by HMI (Her Majesty's Inspectors of Schools) who want to ensure that you are equipped to provide a useful education, ie 'the opportunity to acquire a broad and balanced range of knowledge and skills . . . appropriate and effective teaching . . . develop the personal qualities of each pupil . . . (tuition) appropriate to age, ability and aptitude'. Although independent schools can employ teachers without formal qualifications, the DES will want to see some experienced and qualified staff. If it's a boarding school you'll need child care staff as well. Always check staff references before making appointments. You risk legal action if you employ staff deemed unsuitable to have access to children (usually because of a criminal record); *List 99* from the DES gives the names of banned teaching staff and the DES TEACHERS PAY AND GENERAL branch will help check anyone not on the list. It will take between several weeks and several terms to become fully registered; after that schools must keep daily attendance records of pupils and are subject to occasional HMI inspections. These are more in the nature of constructive visits and should be used by you as such. If you're failing to keep up to standard you'll be told how to improve or forced to close. There's a slightly different procedure in Scotland, details in *Notes of Guidance for Proprietors on the Registration of Independent Schools*.

Essential qualifications are teaching experience; good business sense/knowledge; contacts who may provide some of the financial backing or who'll help you recruit teaching and administrative staff; and, above all, enjoyment of working with chil-dren. You'll also need to present the right image; parents aren't going to hand their children into your care unless you're smart, obviously bright, businesslike and sympathetic; crisp rather than brusque. You're unlikely to have enough of any of this without several years' teaching experience and it's worth planning a combination of experience at a famous school (for credentials with parents) with working in a smaller school, closer to the size of the one you're likely to be opening (where you'll learn more about the overall school management). In addition, experience in business or finance is valuable; you'll need a very good idea of how businesses, as well as schools, are run and financed.

You can buy an existing school from about £175,000 from a school broker (eg SCHOOL TRANSFER CONSULTANTS). If you're starting from scratch you'll need planning permission and must ensure that you build in all the facilities required by the DES. You'll obviously need money for equipment and salaries. Start with a well-defined business plan. Appoint a board of governors. (Their role is to ensure the school is run in such a way as to be a success by suggesting policy on all aspects of running the school, including PR and fundraising). Contacts, the higher profile the better, are useful for this. When it's your school you appoint the governors yourself, something that many heads of established independent schools (most of whom are appointed by the governors) wish that they could do. Choose governors who share your aspirations for the school and what it should provide; the same goes for the staff you appoint.

Governors seldom put up money for the school; banks can be difficult. You can appoint a board of directors as a way of raising investment capital, they will be involved less in what goes on in the school than in how much money it's making. You'll have to draw up a full business proposal based on the initial plan and can offer shareholders incentives such as reduced fee for children they nominate. If you're operating as an educational trust you may qualify for charitable status, contact the CHARITY COMMISSION for further details. Once you're operating you'll probably find that parents are a good source of development finance if you want to expand.

Choose your location carefully. You can do your own market research by going around a chosen area and calling on people in their houses to find out how many are interested and likely to let you educate their children; the same people will also probably help to lobby for planning permission. This means selecting a rich area with insufficient independent prep schools, which doesn't always mean being the only independent school for miles. Once the school is opened, children will probably come from further afield. Premises must be big enough for the number of pupils, in a quiet area that's safe for children and easily accessible for parents but won't disrupt local residents too much with increased traffic at the beginning and end of the school day. The ISIS *Good Communications Guide* gives advice on how to publicise and market schools. Make sure that you can safely charge the fees you need to make the business profitable. Find out how much other schools charge; demand for places at independent schools is such that in many areas you'll be able to get into the top range, as long as your school's good. In top prep schools, in areas where you can charge top fees, day pupils now pay £1,500 a term.

For the first year calculate on operating at no more than 50 per cent of capacity, and probably making a loss. Once the school's opened, it should get up to capacity very quickly.

Schools have high profiles and are the subject of much dinner and cocktail party conversation; you'll need to keep an ear open for rumours about your school and make sure that the damaging ones aren't allowed to spread. Success depends on giving parents what they want; providing children with a good, useful education and offering something that parents feel is lacking at state schools. For many parents, at the moment, that means providing fairly traditional and disciplined education and getting your pupils through Common Entrance to the 'right' schools. Selling points include an emphasis on reading, writing, grammar, and arithmetic; a smart (but readily available) uniform and

encouragement of parental involvement. Keep up with what's going on in education by reading the *Times Educational Supplement* and there are organisations like the INCORPORATED ASSOCIATION OF PREPARATORY SCHOOLS and the INDEPENDENT SCHOOLS ASSOCIATION INCORPORATED which help their members through meetings with other independent school heads. Accreditation of your school via one of these associations gives automatic membership of ISIS.

Printer

Qualifications/Training	Recommended
Income bracket	Low–Medium
Licence	Union card recommended
Town/Country	Town
Experience/Springboard	Necessary
Travel	Local
Mid-career entry	Possible
Exit sale	Yes
Entry costs	£25,000+
Work at home	No
Mix and match	Yes.

You could think about: *Typesetter, Printmaker, Man with a van, Desk-top publisher, Book designer, Shopkeeper*

Enquiries
British Printing Industries Federation, Institute of Printing

Printing is in the top ten UK manufacturing industries. New technology has savagely depleted its workforce but there are still some 200,000 people working in approximately 6,000 firms. Having said that, forget about the giants of the industry. There is plenty of room for small, specialised suppliers; printers work for all businesses throughout the UK at some time or another. Financial printing is largely in London, books mainly in East Anglia and the West Country and cartons and packaging mainly in the Midlands and the North; notepaper, menus, brochures etc, everywhere.

Because of the enormous amount of work available, many printers set up on their own. The majority of small printers work with perhaps only one or two of the five main printing processes: lithography (most widely used), letterpress, flexography, gravure and screen printing. The connected finishing processes (collating, binding, guillotining, punching, stitching, folding) and the connected trades (retailing, stationery manufacture, distribution delivery) can either be handled directly by jobbing printers or sub-contracted.

Jobbing printers often employ no staff and act as their own sales team, quality controller, estimator, accountant and machine minder; not to mention being their own collator and supervisor of the print-run. It is very hard work, made more stressful by customers always wanting their print run in a hurry. You have to work late nights and over weekends, while somehow finding the time to seek your next orders.

You can compete on price, on quality, on delivery dates or on credit. If you can compete in all these and be reliable you will get repeat orders. Once you have successfully completed your first order you have the beginning of a portfolio to show potential new clients and something of a reputation to build on.

Work comes mostly through recommendation, but contacts can be made at business and social gatherings and trade fairs (eg IPEX, the major printing fair at Birmingham every four years) and packaging fairs. There are endless sources of printing orders: local freebie newspapers, magazine and book publishers, advertisers, products requiring packaging or labelling, posters, stationery, information bulletins.

New printing machinery is very expensive but there is a big second hand market (particularly in offset litho machines) because the technology is changing rapidly and the big firms often get rid of perfectly adequate models to keep competitive at their own level. As a jobbing printer you should find second hand machinery holds its value in a way that, for instance, computers do not. A good second hand offset litho machine with a single colour press might cost £15,000–£20,000; two, three and four colour presses will cost progressively more. Your work space has to allow for large machines and somewhere to collate the print-run; you can do some of the paperwork at home.

There are established courses for both beginners and professionals. Qualification is based on achievement of nationally-agreed standards laid down by the BRITISH PRINTING INDUSTRIES FEDERATION (the employers' organisation) in conjunction with the printing union: the GRAPHICAL, PAPER AND MEDIA UNION. The BPIF also acts as a training clearing house. Apprenticeship has been replaced by mutually signed training agreements so you can get an employer to train you before you set up on your own. The printing industry is still largely unionised, but there are many firms which are not closed shops. It can help to have a union card although you do not need one for many forms of printing.

The best college for the jobbing printer is the LONDON COLLEGE OF PRINTING. It offers courses in typography, graphic design, pre-printing and print finishing processes, graphic reproduction techniques, machine operation and maintenance, compositing, typesetting, quotations, packaging, plate-making, colour separation and print management. Contract printing is often considered more secure than jobbing but if you lose your contract you may find you have no work at all. Hedge your bets; do not get too high a proportion of your work from any one customer. Diversification, cash flow management, confidence and credibility are important. Never call in materials until you really need them.

Read the weeklies – *Litho Week* and *Printing World* for their recruitment ads, classified ads and the second-hand machinery on offer. Also read the *British Printer*. The INSTITUTE OF PRINTING is worth contacting for its courses and technical papers.

Print Maker

Qualifications/Training	Necessary
Income bracket	Low–Medium
Licence	No
Town/Country	Town
Experience/ Springboard	Recommended
Travel	No
Mid-career entry	Possible
Exit sale	No
Entry costs	£200+
Work at home	Yes
Mix and match	Possible.

You could think about: **Photographer, Contemporary art gallery owner, Graphic designer, Interior designer, Artist**

Enquiries
Print Makers' Council

Printmaking uses some of the same techniques as graphics but differs in that while graphics tend to be directly involved with the commercial world, printmaking is more of an art for its own sake. It can, however, be very lucrative.

After doing a course in printmaking which covers techniques such as etching, lithography, screen printing and relief painting, choose whether you want to specialise in fabric printing, collage design, art prints, posters, fine art or a combination. Useful experience is working as a technician and reproducing other peoples' work at a studio; this will give you an idea of what's going on in the field and may lead to contacts. It will help if you've got some idea of what people want to hang on their walls; this is obviously more important when you need to sell a lot of prints (eg posters) than if you're specialising in limited editions.

Screen printing is the cheapest form of printing to set up; all you need is the screen, inks and a table top. Etching is more complicated: you need a press, acids and an acid bath. For photographic reproduction you'll need to have access to a dark room. See *Artists Newsletter* for advertisements for equipment. Screen printing is at the commercial end of 'art for art's sake'; the market for prints is larger than for many other art forms because they tend to cost a lot less.

Once you've got a design for a print, you can sell several copies of it. Galleries charge 30–50 per cent mark up on anything they sell and sometimes need to be chased for payment. Many screenprinters augment their incomes with some part time teaching – this has the added advantage of getting you access to college facilities. There is a vast choice of small companies whom you can tap for work, perhaps via an interior designer, who may want prints for a client's boardroom or restaurant. Getting your work up in public places is a good advertisement, although large companies tend to be rather slow at paying. Exhibitions, especially national ones are a good source of commissions – the PRINT MAKERS' COUNCIL hold two or three a year.

Private Investigator

Qualifications/Training	Useful
Income bracket	Medium–High
Licence	No
Town/Country	Town
Experience/ Springboard	Recommended
Travel	Some
Mid-career entry	Likely
Exit sale	Possible
Entry costs	£5,000++
Work at home	Partly
Mix and match	Possible.

You could think about: **List broker, UK correspondent (overseas media), Conveyancer, Cabaret performer**

Enquiries
Association of British Investigators,
Institute of Professional Investigators

Private investigators do a lot of civil law

work, tracing people to serve writs and deliver affidavits – described by one as the faith healers of the legal world, as they get called in to handle cases that the police can't or won't deal with (matrimonial, industrial espionage and counter espionage, missing persons, etc). You may be asked to do work which is illegal (often under the Official Secrets Act); and to take on such work carries obvious risks and should be avoided.

There are no formal qualifications or legal requirements although NVQs are being developed. However, it may be useful to join one of the professional ssociations. These are the Association of British Investigators and, for experienced investigators, the NATIONAL ASSOCIATION OF PRIVATE INVESTIGATORS. Any sort of research experience (eg for a degree) is useful. Even more useful is a police (or army) background and this is the most usual route in. It gives you not only a training in the law and tracking down law breakers, but a network you can build up and call upon when you want specific information and advise. The INTERNATIONAL PROFESSIONAL SECURITY ASSOCIATION runs correspondence courses in general security but these are geared more towards those working for large investigating firms than for those setting up alone.

It is not an easy job to get with no relevant experience because most agencies are very small and have minimal staffing requirements. Most enter at mid-career, from the law, police and security work. Basic formal requirements for starters include a clean driving licence, good health and the capacity to work unsocial hours. Language skills, a working knowledge of photography or plan-drawing and some law would help.

To cultivate local police confidence and co-operation make sure you inform your local senior police officer before setting up – you'll then be checked over by the crime prevention officer (rumour has it that every private investigator merits a Special Branch file).

Necessary equipment is a car, a telephone, an answering machine, a typewriter and business cards. If you branch into industrial espionage you'll need some specialist, expensive equipment (anti-bugging devices, etc). Private clients may want to come to visit you so have somewhere suitable for this. Operate in an area with plenty of solicitors as, initially, they will provide most of your work, having people traced etc. You can approach them in person and with business cards. You may be required to write affidavits (for how to do this and other basics of the law see the *Penguin Guide to the Law*). If local solicitors do not provide enough work, advertise in the local press and the *Yellow Pages* for private clients. If may also be worth approaching the larger investigating agencies who sometimes subcontract some of their leg work when they are busy. Charging is by the hour, £10 is a competitive starting rate, up to about £25.

Contrary to the popular image, private investigators do not do a lot of dashing around the countryside in pursuit of criminals. Most of it is routine and can be done from home by telephoning your network and following up with some leg work at the end. This means you'll probably work office hours. You may occasionally have to meet a deadline (a missing witness required in court on a specific day) and sometimes you'll have nothing to show for the bill you present to your client. You can decide how hard you work but obviously your reputation will benefit from a few efficient successes.

Try reading a *Blueprint Guide to Private Investigation*; also *Pricing Your Work for Profit*, a study of the financial aspects of running an agency. *An Investigator's Library* is a select list of writings considered indispensable to working investigators.

European Community Notes

Europe is following British minds. As there are no statutory qualifications in the UK, Europeans are free to practice here but conversely there are no mutually recognised qualifications attainable here as yet, so British investigators wishing to practice in many European countries need to qualify locally.

Proofreader/Copy Editor

Qualifications/Training	Available
Income bracket	Low
Licence	No
Town/Country	Either if accessible
Experience/Springboard	Recommended
Travel	No
Mid-career entry	Yes
Exit sale	No
Entry costs	£10+
Work at home	Yes, usually
Mix and match	Excellent

with virtually anything. You could think about: *Musician, Continuity person, Alexander Technique teacher, Scriptwriter, Tourist guide, Nanny/ babysitting agency*

Enquiries
Society of Freelance Editors and Proofreaders, National Union of Journalists

Proofreaders read proofs of books, journals, reports and documents before they are printed to make sure that they don't have any obvious mistakes. Copy-editors read manuscripts of books before they are typeset, marking up how they should be set and checking that they make sense and are consistent in spelling and grammar usages. A lot of publishers, working to tight production schedules, prefer to have proofreading and copy-editing done by freelancers. While many people proofread and copy-edit full time, they are also an excellent lifeline and mix and match with almost anything else. Rates of pay and conditions of work vary vastly at the moment; a NEW SOCIETY OF FREELANCE EDITORS AND PROOFREADERS is, among other things, trying to establish an accreditation system and the NATIONAL UNION OF JOURNALISTS recommends minimum rates of pay for proofreaders and copy-editors.

There are no essential qualifications but you will need to know how to use the British Standard Printers' Marks. There are courses in proofreading and copy-editing at places like the BOOK HOUSE TRAINING CENTRE or through the Society of Freelance Editor and Proofreaders. Very useful reading is *Copy-Editing* and *Hart's Rules*. Working for a publisher is a good way of learning some of the skills and, even more important, of getting useful contacts – publishers like using ex-employees who know their house style and production systems for freelance work. You'll need strong eyes, good spelling and grammar, patience and attention to detail. You'll also need to concentrate hard: some books are so interesting that you stop noticing mistakes while others are so dull you'll hardly be able to read them. Copy-editors need to be diplomatic; while you have to allow a certain amount of authorial licence (for example, in quirky use of language or punctuation), facts must be correct and you're meant to be making the text as appealing to readers as possible which will sometimes mean suggesting alterations to sensitive authors. You'll need self-discipline to get on with the job without wasting time.

Set-up costs are minimal. A collection of red and blue pens, pencils, highlighters, Tipp-Ex, a ruler, a dictionary and the *Oxford Writers' Dictionary*. You'll also need a phone and some stationery; a typewriter or word processor would be useful, too. In addition you may need to buy the occasional specialist reference book when you're working on esoteric texts. You are unlikely to get rich as a proofreader/copy-editor. You're usually paid by the hour and many publishers set their own rates. The NUJ recommended minimum rates of pay are £10.50 an hour for proofreading and £11.50 for simple copy-editing but you'll be lucky to get this much as a beginner (the Society of Freelance Editors and Proofreaders found a range from £2.50– £12.00 but this includes other more lucrative freelance publishing work). On the whole you can expect to get about £6.50– £9.00 per hour. Don't forget to at least ask for annual increases; many publishers don't include freelance rates in their regular pay reviews.

You get work from advertising yourself to publishers and some large organisations with their own publishing departments. Write to editorial services managers with your CV and a list of the projects you've worked on so far, and follow up with phone calls; advertisements for freelance proofreaders and copy-editors appear in the *Bookseller* and Monday's *Guardian* from time to time. Although word of mouth recommendations tend not to operate amongst existing clients (publishers who like your work want to keep you to themselves), contacts in the trade are very useful as people prefer to use someone they know a little more about than they're likely to learn from a CV. A lot of the work is done at home. Sometimes you'll be expected to collect it or it will be sent by courier; this means that you need to be close to publishers in London, Oxford, Edinburgh, Glasgow, for instance. Scheduling is fairly flexible, although many of the jobs you'll be asked to do will need to be turned round quickly. Don't take on any work you don't have time to do properly (one botched job can lose you a client) and if you are going to have difficulty in meeting a deadline make sure that the client knows in advance so that they can make other arrangements. Isolation can be a problem unless you schedule work properly and make sure that you set time aside for meeting friends and colleagues. Workloads can vary; learn how to enjoy free time because you'll have plenty of chance to make up for any loss of income later on. Use quiet times to contact new potential clients.

Property Developer

Qualifications/Training	No
Income bracket	Low–High
Licence	No
Town/Country	Either
Experience/Springboard	Useful
Travel	Local
Mid-career entry	Likely
Exit sale	Yes
Entry costs	£50,000+++
Work at home	Possible
Mix and match	Yes.

You could think about: *Architect, Estate Agent, Surveyor, Builder, Tourist attraction, Landlord, MP*

Enquiries
Local estate agents, banks, etc

Property development companies come in all sizes – and are often not the most popular in town. At one end of the scale there are large public companies which buy up land and run-down commercial buildings to re-develop as shops and offices; at the other end of the scale are DIY enthusiasts, who buy (and sometimes live in) run-down property, do it up, sell it at a profit, and move on to the next project. Capital or large loans are required and the cost of money tied up in each project can be absolutely critical, especially in times of high interest rates and sluggish demand in the housing market.

There are no formal qualifications. Some developers just run a single project, and then let the finished units to bring in an income, others will sell and plough back their profits in a new development. Most developers have experience of some aspect of the business, either as estate agents or builders. An understanding of building construction, land law, planning and building regulations are essential; professional advice, from architects, solicitors and surveyors is usually taken.

To get started, approach local estate agents, study newspapers and ask around to find a suitable site to develop. To raise the finance you may be able to get a mortgage, but you will probably have to borrow from a bank, or go into partnership with an established businessman who has finance, or a property owner who is willing for you to do the work and share the profits. Bank managers may be cautious about lending such large sums of money, so when you approach them, make sure you have thought out every aspect of the project. On a larger scale, the *Directory of*

Property Developers, Investors and Financiers is a useful source of contacts.

The day-to-day work will depend on the role you play in the company: if you are developing individual homes or converting houses into flats, for example, you may find you are actually working on the site, or you may limit your activity to organising the subcontractors (bricklayers, roofers, plasterers, electricians, plumbers, carpenters, glaziers, painters and decorators and so on).

However you decide to proceed, you will need determination and entrepreneurial ability. The key is a high quality finished product so that you can sell as soon as you have completed it. Without that the possibility of over-borrowing and going bankrupt will always be hanging over you.

Property Manager

Qualifications/Training	No
Income bracket	Low–Medium
Licence	No
Town/Country	Either
Experience/ Springboard	Recommended
Travel	Local
Mid-career entry	Likely
Exit sale	No
Entry costs	£1,000+
Work at home	Yes
Mix and match	Possible.

You could think about: *Estate agent, Landlord, Builder, Holiday accommodation owner, Tourist guide, Naturopath*

Enquiries
Estate agents, solicitors, international companies

Property managers are responsible for looking after the houses and flats of absentee clients who may only spend a few weeks or months in their house but who may not want to rent it out. What you do depends to a large extent on what you are prepared to do; you should expect to provide at least a caretaker service, keeping an eye on empty houses, arranging for necessary work and the payment of regular bills and rates. In effect you act as the landlord without actually owning the property. In addition, while your clients are in residence, you may be called on to procure domestic staff, theatre tickets, chauffeurs, and catering services. Nearly all of the opportunities for this sort of work are in London and the South-east or in holiday resorts, as caretaker for holiday homes.

Essential qualifications are the ability to organise and a network of contacts which will grow as you develop. It helps to have experience of organising other people's lives: personal assistant, conference manager etc.

Many of your clients come from abroad – the ability to speak foreign languages is useful. You'll also have to be able to rise to the occasion, for instance, deal pleasantly with clients who ring at 5.00 in the morning because their pipes have burst.

Set-up costs are minimal; you'll need a phone and answering machine and a car is useful. Make sure you have a good solicitor and accountant. You're well advised to register as a limited company (thus reducing your personal liability) and to take out professional indemnity insurance and cover for any accidental damage caused by your contractors. Cash flow is less of a problem than for many other new businesses because your clients lodge money for your fees and expenses when they open an account with you (your solicitor will help to set this up).

You'll find clients are prepared to pay quite highly for good service in this area – not everyone wants to derive income from their property. Charge an annual rate for the basic caretaking service, based on the value of the property (£1,500 or so for London) and 15 per cent commission, on any job that you subcontract and on domestic staff salaries. You can also charge your contractors commission on the work you provide for them.

Getting into the network of overseas property owners is done through personal contacts and recommendation. Try large firms who are often the nominal owners of your clients' property – for tax purposes. Other essential networks are reliable domestic staff, gardeners, plumbers, etc whom you can call on at short notice. Build up trust by paying promptly, making sure that you're there to let them in and that they know what to expect. You'll find yourself tapping into more and more networks as you cope with various client requests.

During the day you'll do a lot of running around, letting plumbers into empty properties, recruiting casual staff etc, and you'll have to work at anti-social hours, meeting clients in the evening and coping with night-time emergencies. As a service industry you may find it difficult to reach the level of security to take on a full-time assistant so holidays can be difficult because you need to maintain a perpetual, comforting contact with your clients.

Psychoanalyst

Qualifications/Training	Essential
Income bracket	Low–High
Licence	No
Town/Country	Town
Experience/Springboard	No
Travel	No
Mid-career entry	Essential
Exit sale	No
Entry costs	£500
Work at home	Yes
Mix and match	Possible.

You could think about: *Gardener/ garden designer, Cabaret performer, Potter*

Enquiries
British Psycho-Analytical Society, Institute of Group Analysis, Society of Analytical Psychology

Psychoanalysts are trained to listen, observe and speak to their patients in such a way that they are able to analyse their patients' past, present and future life and problems. They meet and treat their patients once, twice or even five times a

week over a period – one or many years depending on the patient's problems and financial means.

You need a degree, as wide an experience of life as possible, and to be of a mature disposition. Then you can apply for the three–five year course at the BRITISH PSYCHO-ANALYTICAL SOCIETY; the SOCIETY FOR ANALYTICAL PSYCHOLOGY offers Jungian training and the INSTITUTE OF GROUP ANALYSIS is an organisation for training in groups. It is necessary to receive analysis for at least a year (preferably more) before you begin. You will not get a grant, though loans are available for students accepted for training; you will need at least £16,000 to cover the costs of the course and the analysis, which will continue. You need good concentration, an interest in people, an ability to listen and observe them carefully and a constitution which will allow you to work long hours without tiring. Full training involves seeing two patients five times a week under supervision. The number of patients you receive is dependent on contacts and the impression you make on those who teach you and those who learn with you, as it is they who will refer patients to you after you are qualified.

You need a consulting room, which can be in your own house, preferably near public transport, with two comfortable chairs, a couch, filing cabinet, phone and answerphone; a waiting-room, lavatory etc, are obviously necessary, too. Make sure that you are covered by insurance, for malpractice etc.

People may practise as part-time or full-time psychoanalysts – eg, they may hold other positions part-time in the Health Service. Many patients can only come before or after work so you may have to begin early and work late.

Go swimming or jogging to keep fit, as sitting in a chair is bad for your body if not your mind. Try and have a really interesting hobby, preferably physical, either an art/craft or gardening, to balance the intellectual and emotional stress of the job. A lively supportive family and circle of friends are very important and be careful you don't start analysing them from habit – they won't appreciate it!

This is an isolated job, you can't share your successes or failures or discuss your work with others as it's confidential. If you like people you will rarely be bored.

Most analysts belong to the BRITISH PSYCHO-ANALYTICAL SOCIETY; also of significance are the INSTITUTE OF GROUP ANALYSIS or the SOCIETY OF ANALYTICAL PSYCHOLOGY. All these will provide further useful information. Read anything you can find on Freud, Klein or Jung.

⁑ European Community Notes

Qualifications: UK qualifications recognised throughout EC and EC qualifications in UK.

Languages: To succeed, local language necessary.

Earnings: UK income generally lower than elsewhere in the EC.

Advice/Training: Advice, information and training not available for those wishing to work in Europe.

Exchanges: Formal job exchanges do not exist.

Enquiry point for those wishing to work in the EC: BRITISH PSYCHO-ANALYTICAL SOCIETY

Psychologist

Qualifications/Training	Essential
Income bracket	Medium–High
Licence	Recommended
Town/Country	Town
Experience/ Springboard	Recommended
Travel	Local
Mid-career entry	Yes
Exit sale	Possible
Entry costs	£1,000+
Work at home	Unlikely

Mix and match	Possible.

You could think about: *Musician, Football commentator, Landlord, Radio reporter/presenter*

Enquiries
British Psychological Society

Psychologists fall into several categories, but they are all people who through their knowledge and understanding of the human mind and human behaviour can solve psychological problems. Clinical psychologists if working with psychiatrists, and doctors in hospitals, assess and work therapeutically with individuals and groups who have personality and emotional problems. Educational psychologists concentrate on problems to do with learning such as dyslexia, physical and mental handicap and children's emotional difficulties in learning. Consultant, industrial or occupational psychologists use their expertise to solve problems in working situations, organisations and in industry and advertising.

You will need to do a degree in psychology and to become a member of the BRITISH PSYCHOLOGICAL SOCIETY (BPS) and register as a Chartered Psychologist. A consultant occupational psychologist may find it useful to have a qualification in management. Read the *Psychologist*.

Clinical psychologists need perception, to be observant, reflective and have the capacity to sit and listen for long periods. A wide life experience, an appreciation of pain and an endless curiosity about people are essential. There are good prospects in private practice.

An educational psychologist (see job profile on child/educational psychologist) must share the same personal qualities but must also enjoy children and be able to relate easily to those who are mentally or physically handicapped; a sense of humour is useful. With educational cuts, this area is not very encouraging as a career, and to work freelance you must have a good professional reputation based on solutions to problems that have been shown to be effective in the private sector.

Industrial or consultant psychologists have excellent prospects if they have the ability to deal with complex data, to stand back and view their position in a complicated or difficult organisational situation, and can take a high level of anxiety in a very competitive field. You are employed on contract to solve a problem, or show where it lies, and if you can do this scientifically in the shortest possible time, your reputation will increase accordingly.

It's best to do regular work in your chosen area for at least three years, with good supervision to gain contact and experience. You can often devote part of your time to your private work while still doing sessions for the NHS or education authority, or an industrial job. You can start by charging £15–£30 an hour for clinical or educational work. For consultative work the rate is £200 per day rising to £500 or even £1,000 if you are very successful. You can work from your home and only need a phone, answerphone, typewriter and filing cabinet.

Your working days are as long as you make them while you are on contract, usually for a designated number of weeks. In educational work your day can be long, as you tend to see problem children after school or have meetings when parents, teachers and administrators are available. This also applies to clinical work when you tend to see clients outside office hours.

Being a clinical or educational psychologist is stimulating if you like working with people; if you are analytically minded, consultancy or industrial work is interesting and challenging. Clinical and educational psychologists have the disadvantage of long hours which interfere with family life and consultative work which can involve a lot of travelling and a high level of anxiety. It is possible with good organisation to do another job at the same time. Video, fax and word processor make this job much easier.

✴ European Community Notes

Qualifications: UK qualifications recognised throughout EC and EC qualifications in UK (as per EC Directive 89/48).
Languages: To succeed local language necessary.
Advice/Training: Advice, information and training for those wishing to work in Europe is produced by individual countries.
Exchanges: Formal job exchanges do not exist.
Notes: The problem of assessing prospects and conditions for UK psychologists working in Europe is that there is so little evidence or experience of UK citizens setting up in private practice in the EC and the primary reason must be the language barrier. To be effective as a psychologist in another country one would have to be completely fluent in the language of the local people, including slang, dialect and so on. The problems presented by trying to handle a person's difficulties in a foreign language can be readily imagined.

Psychotherapist

Qualifications/Training	Essential
Income bracket	Low–High
Licence	No
Town/Country	Town
Experience/Springboard	Useful
Travel	No
Mid-career entry	Essential
Exit sale	No
Entry costs	£15,000
Work at home	Yes
Mix and match	Possible.

You could think about: *Furniture designer, Proofreader/copy editor, Holiday accommodation owner*

Enquiries
British Association of Psychotherapists, Tavistock Institute of Human Relations

A psychotherapist is someone who is trained to sit and listen confidentially to the personal or relationship problems presented by the patient. The patient is seen at an agreed regular time, usually at least once a wek for 50 minutes. Through this professional relationship, psychotherapists are able to facilitate psychological growth and understanding in the patient through their warmth, patience and expert observation both of the conscious and unconscious.

You need a degree (the most useful is pyschology), to be over 30 years old and to have received psychotherapy for at least one year. The latter is not to be underestimated: intensive personal psychotherapy three times a week for at least a year before starting, in order to understand oneself, is a vitally important part of the training. After that you can apply for a three-year part-time course at a reputable organisation (there are many disreputable ones) such as the BRITISH ASSOCIATION OF PSYCHOTHERAPISTS or the TAVISTOCK INSTITUTE OF HUMAN RELATIONS. There are many others, which follow different theoretical beliefs and practices; and some starting in the provinces which are still in their early days. You will get no grant so, with the ongoing psychotherapy throughout your training, you should expect to spend about £15,000. The most usual route is via a background in psychology, social work or medicine but this is not essential – a varied life experience is helpful. You need a good constitution; an interest in people; patience; warmth; good listening, concentrating, and observing skills; and a sense of humour. A full rich personal life is vital to keep you balanced and to preserve a sense of proportion.

If you are shown to be good and will have patients while you are training, other psychotherapists will refer patients to you – so it's important to start building contacts while you are learning. Make sure you have good insurance cover.

It's possible to start a private practice as soon as you qualify. Depending on your contacts and rate of successful and satisfied patients you can expect to make about £3,000 pa to begin with working part-time, but this can rise to £40,000.

You can use a room in your house or flat as long as it's fairly quiet and those you live with are well disciplined. It must contain two comfortable chairs, a couch and a filing cabinet. Patients can pay at the end of each session or on invoice. You also need a phone and an answerphone; a loo with washbasin nearby is useful. If you can be near public transport this makes you available to more patients.

As a lot of patients can only attend before or after working hours you must be prepared to start work early and finish late. However it's sensible to have a long lunch with another activity – sport or jogging – as sitting in a chair all day is very unhealthy. Many psychotherapists prefer a three-day weekend to keep really fit. It's possible to work part-time, combining it with teaching or doing research or a completely different job.

This is a relentlessly isolated and tiring occupation; you can't cancel a patient when you don't feel like seeing them. The plus is that you can work from home and it's always fascinating, rewarding work. It's very important that it doesn't interrupt your family and social life.

Useful sources of information are the various associations such as the BRITISH ASSOCIATION OF PSYCHOTHERAPISTS. Windy Dryden's book *Individual Therapy in Britain* or Anthony Storr's *Art of Psychotherapy* can be found in public libraries.

European Community Notes

Qualifications: Negotiations are underway for UK qualifications to be recognised throughout EC and EC qualifications in UK.

Languages: To succeed, local language necessary.

Advice/Training: Advice, information and training not available for those wishing to work in Europe.

Exchanges: Formal job exchanges do not exist.

Notes: It is not easy to provide much detail on the prospects for UK citizens throughout the EC. Very few members of the British Association of Psychotherapists have ventured to practise in other member states – and those that have have been nationals of that country, returning after training in the UK. Communication is everything, so one's grasp of the other language and culture must be total.

Public Relations Consultant

Qualifications/Training	Recommended
Income bracket	Medium–High
Licence	No
Town/Country	Town
Experience/Springboard	Essential
Travel	Yes
Mid-career entry	Likely
Exit sale	Possible
Entry costs	£7,500
Work at home	Possible
Mix and match	Yes.

You could think about: *Direct marketing agent, Events organiser, Media trainer, MP, Advertising agent, Exhibition designer, Desktop publisher*

Enquiries
Institute of Public Relations

Public relations is the practice of helping to build and sustain a good relationship between a company, an organisation or a brand (the client) and its public. In this case public means virtually everyone and anyone who directly or indirectly is used by the client to achieve an objective – usually profit. Public relations works alongside, but should not be confused with advertising and sales promotion. PR can be directed at the factory floor, at politicians, at the financial community, at businesses or directly at the consumer. It might involve lunch with a government minister; a press conference; a sponsored event; a company newsletter; a radio or television interview. All of these and more are simply a means to an end, and the end is the communication of the right message to the right audience. Small consultancies with good client lists are very attractive to large PR and advertising agencies – make a success of this and you could sell out for a massive amount in a few years' time.

There are numerous courses available for would-be PR executives and the INSTITUTE OF PUBLIC RELATIONS will help you to locate them; it can also arrange careers counselling sessions, in your local area. These give a basic background. However, there's no substitute for learning at first hand and your initial step should be to join a large consultancy as a trainee. This is not always an easy task as most don't have a formal training programme. A traditional route is to join as a secretary and move on from there. For those with no secretarial experience the way in is through persistence and using and developing contacts. Some PR consultants come from marketing, journalism or the media. The essential qualities for anyone entering public relations are common sense, enthusiasm, good writing skills and the ability to get on with others. The hours can be long and the industry is highly competitive, but the work is very varied and can be creative.

When you feel you have sufficient knowledge and have decided on your area of operation, you can set up on your own. Different areas of PR (financial, corporate and consumer) operate at different paces and in different markets so, for small consultancies particularly, specialisation is important. You can do some direct advertising or sales promotion as part of a PR campaign; some consultants specialise in getting sponsorship for sporting or cultural events, others in one area of consumer marketing, fashion, travel or health for example.

Set up costs include an office with a word processor and printer, fax, telex and a photocopier. You will need a good secretary/PA. Cash flow has two elements; your fees which are based on the amount of time you expect the job to take and calculated as a monthly charge payable in advance. Then there are out of pocket or operation expenses incurred by you on the client's behalf; these are usually charged a month in arrears with commission; alternatively you can try to get them in advance and avoid having to charge clients commission.

Good contacts with journalists, photographers, printers and graphic designers are essential. Get hold of a good media contact directory such as *PIMS Media Directory*. This lists the names of media contacts according to category – the same company also handles mailing and distribution of press releases if you need it. Above all you need clients. Public relations is a part of marketing so get yourself known to potential clients through adverts or, better still, good editorial in the trade publications such as *Campaign* and *Marketing Week*. Other clients come through the network and through word of mouth. (Get into the trade press for your particular specialisation, that way you'll catch new businesses as they set up and established ones as they need new PR).

Clients provide you with a brief which may or may not include their budget. From this you draw up a proposal for a recommended PR programme, including how much it's going to cost. At this stage you may be in competition with other agencies. Each job needs a slightly different structured campaign. This may involve large scale media relations (press releases and launches) or very small scale wooing of opinion formers, eg members of a pressure group. It may also involve boosting your client's media profile by encouraging them to set up a spokesperson who can be contacted to give a trade reaction to relevant new legislation. On the whole campaigns can be planned well in advance and emergency PR is rare although clients may want extra work done quickly from time to time. *PR Week* is suggested reading, also *Offensive Marketing*.

European Community Notes

Qualifications: UK qualifications recognised throughout EC and EC qualifications in UK.

Languages: To succeed, local language necessary.

Earnings: UK income generally lower than elsewhere in the EC.

Setting up: You will find it difficult to succeed throughout Europe.

Advice/Training: Advice, information and training available for those wishing to work in Europe.

Exchanges: Formal job exchanges do not exist.

Enquiry point for those wishing to work in the EC: INSTITUTE OF PUBLIC RELATIONS

Publican

Qualifications/Training	Recommended
Income bracket	Low–High
Licence	Essential
Town/Country	Either
Experience/ Springboard	Recommended
Travel	Local
Mid-career entry	Likely
Exit sale	Excellent
Entry costs	£25,000++
Work at home	Yes
Mix and match	Possible.

You could think about: *Caterer, Restaurateur, Wine bar owner, Wine merchant, Hotel keeper, Caravan park owner, Holiday accommodation owner, Musician*

Enquiries
Licensed Victuallers' Association

To run a pub, you will need a strong liver, sound business sense and physical stamina. It has the advantage of being a career you can move into later in life but it is a full time job and more, not a halfway house to a rosy retirement, so be sure it's what you want before you take the plunge. There are two self-employed options: to buy your own pub (leasehold or freehold); or be a tenant, where you own the licence but the brewery owns the pub. It is a highly regulated area of work. You have to be licensed personally by the local magistrate every year as being fit and respectable; and to comply with all sorts of government regulations such as control of opening hours, age of your customers, hygiene etc.

You will need to know something about the business. Many breweries run short training courses for their tenants; there are useful short and part-time courses on the licensed trade run by FE colleges. The BRITISH INSTITUTE OF INNKEEPING, will also give advice. It is then generally best to get some practical experience before investing, either behind a bar or as a relief manager learning the ropes at someone else's expense.

Tenancies are advertised in the *Morning Advertiser*, as are Public House Brokers who specialise in matching pubs with potential publicans. They will vet your qualifications, check that you have got the money and that you comply with any brewery requirements for that pub (most are predisposed husband and wife teams unless, for example, they are keen to get a gay pub in the area). Once over that hurdle, the broker will introduce you to the pub and the brewery. Getting this far probably means you are on a small shortlist. The brewery will want some surety before finalising the contract. If you are after a freehold, you can also use Licensed Property Agents, both national and local (see the property pages of the *Morning Advertiser*). If you want to run a 'real ale' pub, look in CAMRA's monthly publication *What's Brewing*.

A tenancy costs relatively little capital. You buy the fixtures and fittings (even if they're not to your taste or clapped out which is likely) and current stock (in a well run pub, about 10 days trade) from the outgoing tenant. The price is normally fixed by a broker. For a middling sized pub with a take of £150,000 you might expect to pay £19,000 (brewery deposit, £5,000; fixtures and fittings, £12,000; stock, £2,000). An annual rent to the brewery will be £15,000 and upwards (peppercorn rents are a thing of the past), depending on annual beer sales, called barrelage. Look for a pub selling at least four barrels a week; below that level you will find it difficult to make a living. Tenants, traditionally, were tied by the brewery to buying much of their stock from it exclusively – at least the beer – with a major effect on profits. The Monopolies and Mergers Commission's report recommended substantially lessening the breweries' hold on pubs. The DTI's watered-down Beer Orders insisted on a far less radical break between brewers and outlets. On the plus side tenants are now allowed to sell at least one guest beer. The brewery will expect a cut on takings from the fruit machine (but not bed and breakfast, if you've the energy to organise that) and increasingly they want to dictate the style of operation. You will be expected to live in the pub.

More leaseholds are available now. Without the freehold, you are still tied to the brewery to some extent – and the lease agreements can vary enormously. Some will try and insist you buy their beer – one lease even included a clause allowing the brewery to de-licence and develop the site if the whim took it! Most allow the leaseholder independence – take legal advice, read the lease carefully yourself and negotiate.

Freeholds or Free Houses are easier to find since the breweries stopped buying and wrecking every pub in sight and started selling pubs they didn't want. They may not now own more than 2,000 pubs so they are being forced to sell some which may bring pub prices down. You don't have to convince the brewery that you are a suitable pubican but you still need to convince the magistrates who award your licence. You will need to buy the building as well as the stock. The building will probably cost at least £250,000 in the South, less in the North depending on the size and turnover; the sky is the limit in Central London – though Beer Orders and recession, not to mention the state of the property market, will have substantially altered rates downwards. If a brewery is selling a pub cheap, it probably means it's falling down or in the middle of nowhere – good if you like a quiet life but no good for business. Certainly, don't buy, whether lease or freehold, without getting hold of the last five years' accounts. In fact, don't buy anything without your accountant having a very good look at the figures. Don't skimp on the structural survey and, if a lot needs doing, think carefully before planning to shut a pub for alterations; it has been fatal. You may be able to borrow the money from the bank or sometimes from the brewery – perhaps in exchange for selling its beer. Brewery loans at low interest rates may be available without a charge on your property. Other than that, the pub is yours and there's no-one else you can blame if it doesn't work out.

Most pubs need something other than booze these days – games, music, fruit machines, cigarette machines, videos and almost always food. Be advised: food is an increasingly regulated area. Commercial preparation and cooking of food, and the premises, are subject to inspection by enviromental health officers under the Food Safety Act. 'Eating houses' have to be registered with the local authority and staff handling food now have to be trained. You'll need licences from the PRS and the PPL to play music and a licence for gaming machines above a certain prize limit – currently £7. 'Games of skill', you're all right. You will have to think hard about added attractions or events to drag in customers on a wet Wednesday evening in these straitened times – anything from general knowledge contests to wet T-shirt competitions. There's a market for providing office services in some areas, if you stay open all day (one rural pub in the West country incorporates the local office of a building society); or you can try pub theatre. You will need to think strategically about how to place your pub in your local market, eg whether to offer your locals chip butties or Sole Veronique, darts or discos.

A word of warning: if you are married you must have a very strong marriage to survive the rigours of a publican's life and both partners must be prepared to be totally involved in running the business. Running a pub is a way of life – seven days a week, 364½ days a year (most shut on Christmas night).

And now you may find yourself under pressure to extend your opening hours beyond the traditional. Holidays are difficult – a relief manager will mean total stocktaking before and after. 'There is no such thing as an honest stand-in; if they don't help themselves to the cash, they regard themselves as totally honest.' Conviviality is an asset but it doesn't pay to get too matey with your customers. At the end of the day, what counts is a sound business sense (good management of cash, stock and staff – and no 'slates'), stamina, patience to listen to the 'pub bore' and the ability to stay sober until closing time.

Join the LICENSED VICTUALLERS' ASSOCIATION and read their publication *Licensee*. Read also *Caterer & Hotel Keeper*, *Free House* and *Publican*.

Puppeteer

Qualifications/Training	Available
Income bracket	Low
Licence	No
Town/Country	Either
Experience/Springboard	Not essential
Travel	Constant
Mid-career entry	Yes
Exit sale	No
Entry costs	£2,000+
Work at home	No
Mix and match	Yes.

You could think about: *Street entertainer, Cabaret performer, Actor, Stockbroker, Radio reporter and presenter*

Enquiries
Puppet Centre

Puppeteering covers a vast range of styles and methods; from formalised, traditional story telling where each life sized figure is manipulated by several operators using rods and strings; to shows where one person is responsible for the actions of several puppets. Whichever branch you choose, it isn't easy to make a living on puppetry alone. Although there are possibilities in alternative or community theatre funding for these is spasmodic (many local authorities have been forced to cut their arts funding, and the few permanent puppet theatres there are don't provide a lot of work for many puppeteers). If you're prepared to persevere, perhaps combining puppetry with another part-time occupation, there is work in cabarets or at children's theatres, schools and (at weekends) parties and fetes.

There aren't many courses in puppetry but a one-year post-graduate course in puppetry skills is available at Central School of Speech and Drama. Formal qualifications aside, what you do need is the imagination to create stories or satire (eg Spitting Image) and a combination of acting ability and dexterity to present them with puppets. The PUPPET CENTRE can advise on any puppetry or puppet-making courses you may be interested in, they also provide information on resources and funding. You can work for one of the permanent theatres such as NORWICH PUPPET THEATRE, LITTLE ANGEL or POLKA THEATRE or PLAYBOARD – which does a lot of TV work – for initial experience, but most theatres are very small (about two to five performers), financially insecure and difficult to get into. The best way of starting out is to get a show together and go for it. You'll need to be co-ordinated, versatile, adaptable and capable of living with an erratic source of income. If you're looking for cabaret work you'll probably have to travel on the circuit. Anyone working with children, especially children who are being entertained, should like them a lot. It helps if you can respond to their interruptions other than by telling them to shut up and sit down but you may have to discourage the noisier ones so that they don't spoil the show for the others. If you are going to specialise in children's entertainment it is useful to have experience of working at a playscheme, for instance. Involving children in the show with singing or holding props is often successful and some puppeteers offer a full party package with games and other entertainment.

The best puppeteers are those who have a real knowledge of how children (and sometimes adults) respond to puppets. They must understand what themes and stories work best using puppets (go and see other shows and talk to the puppeteers and read some books on the subject); have a wide range of craft skills; be able to play one or more musical instruments; and above all have good dramatic skills. Puppetry is a difficult and demanding art but the rewards are good for those who set their standards high and are committed to producing good quality theatre for children.

You don't need a lot of money to start up. You can make your own puppets, props and theatre which needn't cost much. Add more expensive equipment, a cassette player for background music for example, as you expand. A car is vital and a telephone answering machine will ensure that you don't lose too much business by not being at home. You may want to have cards printed to hand out at engagements, drop through letter boxes or put in local shops.

A lot of work comes via word of mouth especially for children's party entertainment. To get started you'll need to be seen; some local communities arrange showcases for performers, these often take place in parks or community centres during the holidays; build up a network of other puppeteers and offer to stand in for them when they can't keep an engagement (useful too if you can't make one of your own because you're ill – once you've got an engagement it's essential that you keep it one way or the other). Contact local schools for end of term puppet shows; the organisers of local fetes; managers of cabaret theatres and clubs. Once you're established you may be able to get some stand in or regular work on television shows like Spitting Image. An entry in the *Yellow Pages* costs about £130 or try your local *Thomson's Directory*. Other directories worth investigating are the *Directory of Puppeteers*, the *British Alternative Theatre Directory*, the *Special Needs Drama Directory* and the *British Performing Arts Yearbook*. Charges are up to you. Some regular cabaret spots have fixed fees for performers and these vary. Otherwise base your charges on what you need to make; take local competition into consideration and any extras that you provide. In London an hour's slot at a children's party costs about £35–£45, hourly rates may be less than that if you're providing a full party's worth of entertainment. You may also want to charge travel expenses on top of that.

As with any entertainment, the audience can be the greatest hazard; you'll learn from experience how to gauge the amount of audience participation that works best and how to adapt the show to various contingencies without losing control all together. Co-ordination is essential and you may occasionally drop something or forget your lines while you're concentrating on something else. Whatever area of puppetry you choose the chances are that you'll have some quiet patches which you can use for making and repairing puppets, looking for new sources of work and working on ideas for new shows. According to one, all puppeteers are prima donnas and, although you may not make a fortune, you'll certainly have plenty of chance to be in the limelight as a puppeteer.

Read *Animations* magazine.

European Community Notes

Qualifications: UK qualifications are *not* recognised throughout EC but EC qualifications are in UK.
Languages: To succeed, local language not necessary.

Earnings: UK income generally lower than elsewhere in the EC.
Setting up: You will find it difficult to succeed throughout Europe, but it is slightly easier to make headway in Denmark, Eire, France.
Advice/Training: Advice, information and training available for those wishing to work in Europe.
Exchanges: Formal job exchanges do not exist.
Financial help: exists for study, training or travel in the EC, specific to this job.
Enquiry point for those wishing to work in the EC: THE PUPPET CENTRE

Rr

Racehorse Owner

Qualifications/Training	No
Income bracket	Nil–High
Licence	No
Town/Country	Country
Experience/Springboard	No
Travel	Yes
Mid-career entry	Likely
Exit sale	Possible
Entry costs	£10,000+
Work at home	No
Mix and match	Yes.

You could think about: ***Almost anything***

Enquiries
Racehorse Owners' Association, Jockey Club, Federation of Bloodstock Agents

Racehorse owners buy horses, pay for them to be trained, stabled and ridden by others, then pocket most of the prize money that their horses win in races. It's not so much a way of earning a living as a way of disposing of some of the money you've made at other things. Horses cost a lot to buy and keep and only about 20 per cent of those that pass through the sales ever win a race. There is the potential for massive gains, however, if your stallion is a successful enough winner for you to put him out to stud, charging hefty fees from breeders. The capital value of stud horses has been known to reach £15 million, or more.

Essential qualifications are money and either lots of knowledge of horses and trainers or access to it. Horses are first sold when they are yearlings. There are annual sales of yearlings in September and October at Doncaster and Newmarket. Although you may be lucky and a sound enough judge to pick up a winner for less than £10,000, the average price of a yearling with winning potential is around £100,000 with some horses fetching seven or eight times that amount. On top of this you have to pay for stabling and training at around £150 per week. A successful year's winnings is around £30,000 although you stand to make a lot less or more (£300,000 for a Derby winner) than this. The better your horse's track record, the better its stud value. You can reduce your financial outlay (and potential gains or losses) by joining a racehorse-owning syndicate or partnership. This is known as owning a leg and allows people to buy shares in one or more horses. Trainers or syndicate managers set them up and will be able to help you if you want to find out more. If you want to set up your own syndicate, contact the JOCKEY CLUB.

Horses bred to be flat racers are either sprinters, milers, middle-distance or stayers; sprinters are best at short distances, they need shorter time in training and are often ready to race the spring after you bought them. Stayers need more stamina; all horses have to be two years old before they should be raced and stayers may require that bit longer to get up to strength. Yearlings are valued on the strength of their pedigrees and unless you're an expert on bloodstock, it's worth seeking advice from a bloodstock agent; they usually charge 5 per cent commission.

Contact the FEDERATION OF BLOODSTOCK AGENTS (GB) LTD for help with this. Horses with form (ie, those that have raced and have a track record of wins or failures) are valued according to this form. Horses for jumping come a lot cheaper but the prize money is correspondingly lower, although they are likely to have a far longer working life than flat horses. Equally, they are unlikely to end their careers 'entire' – ie, they'll be gelded for racing – which means no stud value.

Finding a good trainer who is close enough to allow you to visit your horse regularly is equally important; bloodstock agents can help here as well. The most fashionable trainers are at Newmarket and Lambourn but there are plenty of others especially in the South-east and near racing courses. If your horse is immensely distinguished it will race in the Classics (the Derby etc) or other important 'Group One' races. There are principal meetings at Newmarket, Cheltenham, York, Goodwood, Ascot – and other glamorous courses – but even on a wet winter Wednesday there can be four or five meetings, from Towcester to Taunton. It's usually the trainer who decides whether or not your horse should race and, if so, which jockey should ride it. Jockeys race in your colours. There is little point in owning a racehorse if you don't like going to races or don't have time to travel around the UK and Europe watching your horses race. And even less if you can't afford the occasional lean year while you wait to race a winner.

Read *Racing Post*, and almost any novel by Dick Francis.

✦✦✦
✦   ✦
✦✦✦ **European Community Notes**
Qualifications: UK qualifications recognised throughout EC and EC qualifications in UK.
Languages: To succeed, local language not necessary, but very helpful.
Earnings: UK income generally higher than elsewhere in the EC.
Setting up: You will find it difficult to succeed in Eire, France. You will find it easier in Belgium, Denmark, Germany, Italy.
Advice/Training: Advice, information and training not available for those wishing to work in Europe.
Exchanges: Formal job exchanges do not exist.
Enquiry point for those wishing to work in the EC: RACEHORSE OWNERS' ASSOCIATION
Notes: VAT rates vary greatly, eg UK 17.5 per cent, France 5.5 per cent, Eire 2.1 per cent.

Radio Reporter/ Presenter

Qualifications/Training	Available
Income bracket	Low–Medium
Licence	No
Town/Country	Town
Experience/Springboard	Essential
Travel	Yes
Mid-career entry	Yes
Exit sale	No
Entry costs	£2,000+
Work at home	No
Mix and match	Yes.

You could think about: *Journalist, UK correspondent (overseas media), Snail farmer, Antique dealer, Book publisher, Conference organiser, Public relations consultant, Media trainer*

Enquiries
BBC, Local radio stations

As a radio reporter you create the package that is broadcast; that means collecting a lot of material (interviews, readings, music, linking script) on tape and editing it down to the length needed. A presenter sits in the studio while the material is being broadcast and provides linking scripts between each report. Presenters tend to be well established radio people; it takes a long time to build up a good enough reputation to be asked to present radio shows as a freelance.

Very few people make a living from freelance radio reporting and presenting alone. It's badly paid and there aren't many sources of work. However, if you're reasonably flexible, it can tie in quite well with other careers, for example there are radio reporters who are also magazine journalists, writers, conference organisers or public relations consultants. Although some very successful radio reporters manage to cope with having young families, it's a lot easier if you're free to travel at short notice, visit people at any hour of the day or put in long hours editing your material.

There are no essential formal qualifications. Most of what you need to know – how to edit tape, where to put your microphone when you're interviewing, how to use various machines – can be picked up easily; see the *Technique of Radio Production*. The BBC runs courses for reporters to help them develop their skills free if you're working for them. A journalism degree or course is useful. In particular the post graduate degree in journalism at CARDIFF UNIVERSITY, which includes a placement in your chosen specialisation – an excellent way of picking up some experience and contacts. Otherwise, hang around your local radio station and pester. You may be allowed to make tea and answer the telephone for a pittance but you'll be able to learn a lot from being there. Local stations may broadcast one of your reports if you don't ask them for anything in return; or you may be able to work on one of their access programmes. Once you've got some experience you've got some hope of getting a short term research contract on national radio; these are few and far between but are an excellent way of getting contacts and a track record. You can use any other qualification you've got as a way of building a reputation for a specific type of programme eg, a zoology degree for wildlife programmes. To succeed as a radio reporter you must be creative and have a humble attitude. You don't have to have any particular accent although there seem to be fashions when certain regional accents are prevalent on the radio. You have to get on with people and be good at getting people to talk; to be curious enough to want to investigate whatever you're reporting on fully; flexible enough to be able to put in long hours at other people's convenience; confident and able to put up with inevitable cricism. It takes a long time to gain a reputation.

You need a car, to carry recording equipment, and a telephone. You don't need to buy any equipment – you can borrow a tape recorder from the radio station, this has to be an extremely good machine or your reports won't broadcast well, (they cost about £1,000 new). You can edit at the studio using their editing machine to cut and splice the tape (a second-hand machine costs about £100). The radio stations you're working for decide what you'll get paid; virtually nothing if you're working for local radio, not much more for others. You're paid per minute on the air regardless of the hours of background research and work that you put into that minute. BBC network radio rates start at around £40 for up to six minutes of straightforward interview; £120 for up to seven minutes of report. You can regard yourself as doing pretty well if you manage to make about £11,000 pa from freelance radio work. However if a programme repeats any of your material, you may get about 75 per cent of the original fee – depending on your initial contract. There are spin offs from radio work; you may be able to get some voice over work for adverts or company training videos (you'll need contracts for these); to run or teach courses for people who want to be trained in how to speak on radio. You'll have to persevere to get work. Theoretically, you can operate from anywhere. Much of the work for freelance radio reporters comes from Radio Four (Woman's Hour, You and Yours, Today) based in London. You're bound to have to do some travelling to find interesting material and interviewees. Make sure you're clear about the sort of material the producer wants; length, might they want some music or dramatised readings rather than a straightforward interview? What sort of audience are they aiming at? In the early days you'll have to come up with all the ideas for reports; later you'll find yourself approached as someone suitable for a particular report. Get to know producers, hang around radio stations as much as possible so that you're on the spot when a job comes up. Keep an eye open for new material – pressure groups and self help groups are useful – often having press releases which are good sources of stories. Build up as wide a contact file as possible so that you can easily get hold of the sort of people you want for a particular programme.

Expect to spend as much time travelling to an interview as the interview itself. People are more relaxed on their own territory and you may get some appropriate background noises. You'll also have to do background research, write linking scripts and edit interviews. There are hazards – people who were garrulous on the telephone may dry up completely when you put a microphone in front of them; learn how to encourage people to speak. Working for the BBC you'll have access to legal experts and advisers; on local radio you're less well protected (read *Essential Law for Journalists* and seek legal advice if you're in doubt). Interviewing can be harrowing, eg if you're talking to people who have suffered a lot. Have someone you can unload on (the producer of the programme is the most obvious) and make sure that you don't leave your interviewee in a state of distress; worth getting some counselling skills.

Making a radio report is very much a solo effort but you are at others' convenience – producers and interviewees. The time you have for each assignment varies – sometimes you may be commissioned to do an item weeks in advance; at other times you'll be expected to turn the piece around within a day. Generally, the faster you can work without compromising accuracy or standards the more cost effective it is. Whatever happens, you can never miss a deadline!

Record Company Owner

Qualifications/Training	No
Income bracket	Low–High
Licence	No
Town/Country	Town
Experience/ Springboard	Recommended
Travel	Local
Mid-career entry	Possible
Exit sale	Good
Entry costs	£15,000++
Work at home	Possible
Mix and match	Essential to start. You could think about: *Mini-cab driver, Bartender, Market research interviewer*
Enquiries	Record shops, recording studios, musicians

This is an overcrowded, tough but not unglamorous job. You need real knowledge and love of music; it involves owning and taking financial responsibility for a record label. You decide the content of the record, organise the engagement of artists, recording studios, engineers and backing musicians and arrange distribution of the product. You need good business sense; an ability to manipulate and co-ordinate people and their skills to create a special kind of record; enthusiasm, diplomacy, an accurate prediction of what people will buy and enjoy, and lots of luck. You must be highly motivated to succeed, have faith in your own judgement, be sociable and have endless energy. Don't leave your current employment until you have found another where you can learn the mechanics of selling records. Get a job in a leading record shop, read every kind of catalogue you can find, go to lots of concerts and read about composers in the public library. Learn about public relations, printing, pressing records, distribution. Start saving until you have about £15,000; you will need another job for the first few years, eg driving a mini-cab at night, and a friendly accountant or someone to handle your books.

Find a small room with a typewriter, telephone and answerphone, then start setting up a record. You will need a few thousand pounds to book a studio and artists, engineer and producer. The cost of a run of 2,000 compact discs, including design, printing and manufacture, will set you back another £5,000–£6,000. Cassettes will be extra.

The work is obsessive and you can find yourself working 18 hours every day – very bad for your social and family life. It's exciting, full of variety and you meet interesting people, but if you're inclined to worry, don't do it: the risks are high and you will make no profit for the first three years. If you're successful, the sky's the limit financially.

Recording Studio Owner

Qualifications/Training	Recommended
Income bracket	Low–Medium
Licence	No
Town/Country	Town
Experience/Springboard	Essential
Travel	Some
Mid-career entry	Possible
Exit sale	Yes
Entry costs	Highly variable
Work at home	Possible
Mix and match	Essential to start.

You could think about: *Record company owner, Disco owner/DJ, Mini-cab driver, Bartender, Painter/ decorator*

Enquiries
Association of Professional Recording Services

This is someone who owns their own recording studio; who not only makes the equipment work but also has the musical expertise to help the musicians create a good artistic product. To be a good recording engineer it is useful but not essential to have a qualification such as BMus from SURREY UNIVERSITY or take a Recording Techniques course at any of a number of polytechnics or private training schools. You do need a real knowledge of electronics (how the equipment works so you can use it properly and maintain it) and sound general knowledge about all types of music.

You need business management skills, a discriminating ear, tact, a calm personality to deal with stressed musicians and stamina for the very long hours. It's best to be a gofer in a studio for two years so that you learn to work under pressure, gain experience and make contacts. To set up on your own, you will need a lot of luck and ideally £500,000 or more to buy a studio or mobile van containing your equipment; you can make one yourself in any sound-proofed premises but you will need planning permission. You must also have proper coverage of fire insurance and public liability cover, and meet the requirements of Health & Safety (Noise at Work) legislation. You can work from home if others can stand the noise and nuisance of people tramping in and out at all times of the day and night. The golden rule is to spend as much as you can on really good equipment; you will need savings or another job for the first few years as there will be little income.

Make contact with publishers and advertising companies, national and local. Advertise in the pop and classical press. Record local choirs and orchestras, make demo tapes for aspiring pop groups or young classical musicians.

This job is not glamorous. The hours are appalling: you may have to record/edit for up to 24 hours. You shouldn't expect to earn more than £10,000 to £30,000 pa. The advantages are endless variety in the work and the sense of enjoyment of helping in an artistic enterprise. It is both possible and necessary to have some other form of employment, eg teaching your skills or using them in other ways. Black or female recording engineers are relatively few increasing. Classical music is often but recorded on location – which means the use of a mobile – while pop recording is mostly within the studio. The only organisation you may need to join is the ASSOCIATION OF PROFESSIONAL RECORDING SERVICES (APRS). You will need to upgrate your equipment periodically. Consult *Studio Sound, Home & Studio Recording* or *ProSound News*. Also read *Sound Recording Practice* (APRS).

✶✶✶ European Community Notes

Qualifications: UK qualifications 'recognised' throughout EC and EC qualifications in UK, but they are not regarded as necessary.

Languages: To succeed, local language necessary.

Setting up: You will find it easier to succeed in Denmark, Eire, Germany, Italy, Netherlands. It will not be *easy* anywhere, but easiest in these countries – not least because UK citizens would be able to work in English to a large extent.

Advice/Training: Advice, information and training not available for those wishing to work in Europe.

Exchanges: Formal job exchanges do not exist.

Reflexologist

Qualifications/Training	Necessary
Income bracket	Medium–High
Licence	No
Town/Country	Town
Experience/Springboard	No
Travel	Local, perhaps

Mid-career entry	Yes
Exit sale	No
Entry costs	£1,000
Work at home	Possible
Mix and match	Limited.

You could think about: *Musical instrument repairer, Novelist, Greyhound trainer*

Enquiries	

Dallamore College of Advanced Reflexology

Reflexology works on the principle that if certain specific points on the feet or hands are pressed in a certain way, this pressure creates a reflex action in another part of the body, stimulating that part to improve its functioning. Thus reflexology facilitates the body to use its own resources to heal itself.

No formal academic qualifications are needed to enter the DALLAMORE COLLEGE OF ADVANCED REFLEXOLOGY. To be really well-qualified, students must attend weekend courses over a period of three to five years, depending on the individual's ability. This covers human physiology and anatomy, and how to recognise what diseases must be referred to conventional medical practitioners. Reflexologists cannot diagnose or prescribe drugs. After the course, students become members of the Dullamore College, the highest qualifications being Fellow and Teacher. You can, do the course at any age – in your seventies if you will.

You need to be interested in people and be naturally dextrous. Career prospects are limitless and the demand far exceeds the number of qualified people. Reflexologists often have patients with chronic degenerative diseases which conventional medicine cannot improve further.

Most students begin their own private practice within a year of starting training but are always supervised by their teachers. By the time they are qualified they will have enough patients but will continue to consult with other reflexologists on difficult cases. Make sure you are insured first. It's best to have a consulting room on the ground floor, near public transport, either at home or in a clinic shared with other complementary medics. Depending on the part of the country you live in, the fee for a $^1/_2$ hour session can be £4–£5. For an experienced reflexologist in London, the average is £20 an hour and £45 for a 'call out' visit to a patient.

The only equipment you need is a comfortable reclining chair for the patient, a stool for the practitioner (second hand cost about £50), telephone, answerphone, filing cabinet, running hot and cold water and a loo. A receptionist is essential if you are working a long day. It's normal to treat patients before or after work and in the lunch hour so surgery times are flexible. The advantages are seeing people improve and learning new techniques.

Useful reading includes *Reflexology*, *Advanced Reflexology* and *Here's Health* magazine.

European Community Notes

Qualifications: UK qualifications recognised throughout EC and EC qualifications in UK.

Languages: To succeed, local language necessary.

Earnings: UK income generally same as elsewhere in the EC.

Setting up: You will find it difficult to succeed in France, Germany. You will find it easier in Belgium, Denmark, Eire, Greece, Italy, Luxembourg, Netherlands, Portugal, Spain.

Advice/Training: Advice, information and training available for those wishing to work in Europe.

Exchanges: Formal job exchanges do not exist.

Enquiry point for those wishing to work in the EC: DALLAMORE COLLEGE OF ADVANCED REFLEXOLOGY.

Repetiteur/ Accompanist/Coach

Qualifications/Training	Essential
Income bracket	Medium
Licence	No
Town/Country	Town
Experience/Springboard	No
Travel	Yes
Mid-career entry	Highly unlikely
Exit sale	No
Entry costs	£2,000+
Work at home	No
Mix and match	Yes.

You could think about: **Music teacher, Music copyist, Conductor, Mini-cab driver**

Enquiries
Musicians' Union, Incorporated Society of Musicians

An accompanist accompanies other musicians by playing the piano; teaching singers their music by coaching them, or in an opera company, they are known as repetiteurs or coaches. It is important to go to music college or university, preferably both, as high musical and technical standards, and good contact with your peers and in the profession, are essential. You should have excellent sight-reading, transposition and a basic knowledge of voice production and instrument playing, and be able to play all kinds of keyboard instruments in the correct style, from early music to modern jazz and pop.

You must possess an excellent ear, be sensitive and tactful with other artistes, and when accompanying them be prepared to adapt your own musical ideas in favour of theirs. An outstanding accompanist should be able to arrange music, speak foreign languages and empathise with the soloist's thoughts and feelings.

Before starting you should consider joining the MUSICIANS' UNION or the INCORPORATED SOCIETY OF MUSICIANS. The ISM has a good standard contract, and can provide legal back-up. Standing in for friends playing the musical shows, accompanying choirs or ballet classes, deputising in an orchestra, coaching or accompanying young singers for competitions, auditions and recitals are all ways to gain work. It is possible to audition for the BBC accompanists' list, or to apply for work as a repetiteur in an opera company.

Your income will be very low to start with and you will need either to play the organ on Sundays, teach, copy/arrange music, or develop another skill, as this is a highly competitive career. Luck and availability have a lot to do with success so a telephone and answering machine/service are vital. The need to travel constantly, both in the UK and abroad, may deter those with families. To start with, you only need a piano tuned to concert pitch, and a room in which you can practise all day without the neighbours objecting. Later on you will need a car. Stamina is needed to practise every day and, when you can afford your own synthesiser or harpsichord, to move that about.

To be taken on to the books of a concert agency is useful for getting work, but to be known by orchestral fixers and other musicians is just as good. Read the *Unashamed Accompanist*. A free booklet *Careers with Music* is available from the ISM.

The music profession is under pressure from government cuts, reduced sponsorship and film work going abroad. The introduction of the 'Sampler' synthesiser (which reproduces the sound of all instruments) provides new challenges – and threats – which musicians have to face.

⁂ European Community Notes

Qualifications: Generally, UK qualifications recognised throughout EC and EC qualifications in UK.
Languages: To succeed local language not necessary.
Earnings: UK income generally same as elsewhere in the EC.
Setting up: Is not 'easy' anywhere. You will find it difficult to succeed in Denmark, Eire, France, Greece, Italy, Luxembourg, Portugal, Spain. You will find it easier in Belgium, Germany, Netherlands.

Advice/Training: Advice, information and training available for those wishing to work in Europe.
Exchanges: Formal job exchanges do not exist.
Financial help: exists for study, training or travel in the EC, specific to this job.
Enquiry point for those wishing to work in the EC: INCORPORATED SOCIETY OF MUSICIANS

Restaurateur

Qualifications/Training	Recommended
Income bracket	Low–High
Licence	Alcohol – yes
Town/Country	Usually town
Experience/ Springboard	Recommended
Travel	Local
Mid-career entry	Likely
Exit sale	Excellent
Entry costs	£20,000+++
Work at home	No
Mix and match	Possible.

You could think about: *Caterer, Wine bar owner, Publican, Hotelier, Wine merchant, Wine grower, Franchisee*

Enquiries
Hotel and Catering Training Company, British Hospitality Association, Restaurateurs Association

Sandwich bar or three-star Michelin, hamburger joint or Chinese restaurant, there are as many different styles of catering operation as there are people running them. Fifty new ones open every month in London alone. Lots go bust, and quickly. Success depends on a mixture of good food, atmosphere, planning and successful cash flow. Decide on a style that suits you; do you want just to make a living or do you search for self-expression, to indulge in fantasy, to create a lifestyle? Why should customers visit you? Once you move beyond sandwich bars and fast food joints, clients are also looking for entertainment, novelty, ambiance or simply want to impress their guests. Arguably, catering is part of show biz ('20 per cent food, 40 per cent atmosphere and 40 per cent bullshit'). If your customers are only with you because they're hungry, you have to be well placed for passing trade eg, town centre, next to an office block or factory. On the other hand clients will travel for something new and individual.

Get experience, if possible, by working in a show similar to what you have in mind. Cooks can hone up their skills on part-time and short courses by FE colleges, as well as countless private cookery schools. Many colleges, polys and universities offer hotel and catering management courses, and the HOTEL AND CATERING TRAINING COMPANY runs short courses for people wanting to open their own restaurant. The time to attend a course is before you start off, not after, as in the case of many publicans opening restaurants, because you can easily get a bad name if you are using your customers to learn on. At the upper end of the scale, many years of training and experience are needed as well as large capital; lower down the scale, motivation counts for a lot and many restaurants are successfully run by very young people, particularly outside London.

As well as a cook, you need someone for the front with sound business sense and the tact and patience to deal with the general public. Swot up on hygiene. The local environmental health officer will take a keen interest in your activities. Hardworking, overstretched EHOs may appear opinionated and even capricious, but you need their help with the complex hygiene regulations so it's best to have a good working relationship with them. They cannot stop you opening up but they can close you down – and you could face unlimited penalties and up to two years in prison! Consult them early in any plans for alterations to kitchens and bars (the new Food Safety Act requires 'eating houses' to be registered with the local authority and futher regulations require all food handlers to be trained). You will also have the attentions of the fire officer and consumer protection officer from time to time and, if licensed, magistrates and police. Nowadays there is little obstruction to granting restaurant licences which permit the sale of alcohol only with food. The BRITISH HOSPITALITY ASSOCIATION and RESTAURATEURS ASSOCIATION give expert advice to their members on catering laws, contracts, licensing, hygiene, fire precautions, planning, insurance etc. Be prepared for contradictory advice; what pleases one lot won't necessarily satisfy them all.

Set-up costs include premises, either rented or owned. Look for low overheads – prestigious surroundings are for the big boys. Don't overlook the Uniform Business Rate in your calculations – it can be very burdensome. It's easy to start catering in a pub; if you buy an existing operation, you avoid planning problems for change of use (but find out why it was for sale). You'll also need equipment for the kitchen, furniture for the front and an opening stock of cooking supplies, wine, drinks etc. It helps if you've got contacts in the trade who'll give credits for this. Otherwise raise a bank loan and a mortgage for the premises (you'll need some collateral for that – your own house for example). It's worth paying for service and maintenance contracts for your equipment so that you are guaranteed quick service should anything go wrong. Unless your operation is very small, you'll need to employ some help in the kitchen and with waiting and cleaning. Profit margins need to be quite high; a common formula is: materials × 3 + VAT, giving 66 per cent gross on selling. But percentages don't always work satisfactorily and many operators work on a cash mark-up. Thus, decide on the cash profit needed, and the formula becomes: materials + cash amount + VAT. This has the effect of making cheap dishes relatively more expensive and expensive dishes, less so, which can be a good marketing ploy. You can apply this formula to wines too; this will encourage your customers to sample the finest wines on your list.

Before deciding on your menu you need to consider a check list that includes: your equipment; the capability of the cook; seasonal availability of the food at reasonable prices; type of clientele; price strategy;

amount of preparation required. Making your own restaurant succeed is hard work and involves long hours, much more than meets the eye – one ex-Savoy restaurant manager returned to the Savoy after trying to go it alone for a while. You're dependent on having a reliable staff and it may take time to establish one – they won't necessarily be as committed to your operation as you are. Husband and wife teams often work well, but remember, fatigue is endemic and you could find domestic fracas on the menu.

European Community Notes

Qualifications: A number of UK qualifications recognised throughout EC and EC qualifications in UK.
Languages: Whether local language is necessary or not to succeed will depend on the field and the country.
Advice/Training: Advice, information and training available for those wishing to work in Europe.
Exchanges: Formal job exchanges exist.
Enquiry point for those wishing to work in the EC: BRITISH HOSPITALITY ASSOCIATION
Notes: It is hard to be specific when the range of possibilities is so vast. There are numerous stories of UK nationals succeeding in their pursuits; by how much tales of failure exceed them is not known. Find out as much as you can from anyone who has tried.

Riding School Owner

Qualifications/Training	Essential
Income bracket	Low–Medium
Licence	Essential
Town/Country	Mostly country
Experience/Springboard	Yes
Travel	Little
Mid-career entry	Yes

Exit sale	Good
Entry costs	£100,000
Work at home	Yes
Mix and match	Possible.

You could think about: *Farmer, Smallholder, Caravan park owner, Holiday accommodation owner*

Enquiries
Association of British Riding Schools, British Horse Society

So you are mad about horses and fancy running a riding school. Before committing yourself, you need to be sure that you also like people, really want to teach, you're a glutton for long hours and don't expect to make much money. The price of land being what it is, the proposition is only likely to be a starter if you already own land (or have the capital to acquire it) and have at least a small amount of stabling at your disposal.

To begin, you need to take a reputable course in horse management and in instruction. It's useful to be qualified. There is an increasing number of different courses – degrees in equine studies, Btec courses at a local college or, probably most practical, the exams run by the BRITISH HORSE SOCIETY and the ASSOCIATION OF BRITISH RIDING SCHOOLS (ABRS). To run a riding school, you should aim to pass at least the BHS Assistant Instructor's Award, preferably the Intermediate Instructor's Certificate and the ABRS Groom's Diploma – especially necessary if you are going to deal with liveries. You should work in a good school (or yard) where you can get loads of practical experience at the same time. Once you are a qualified instructor, you can start a school in the UK – or work in Europe where the qualifications are recognised and there is considerable demand.

You might start with a small amount of stabling and work as a freelance instructor, maybe with the odd horse in livery as a sideline. You can build up in a number of different ways. You can teach local children; run courses for local schools; provide riding for the disabled, local psychiatric patients, or children in care;

keep horses in livery or breed; link up with a local FE college running horse management courses; do Pony Club work; take clients hunting; run residential courses; or start a tack shop. Most riding schools will do a mixture, depending on where or who they are. If you are an international show jumper, people will pay sizeable entry fees for your show jumping competitions. If you are in a resort area, you must reckon on hard work all the holiday season and go for what you can get the rest of the year. How you run your school will depend partly on your market (small children need small ponies) but also on how much money you can put into your school and expect to take out.

Unlike the rest of agriculture, where capital (machinery, tractors etc) has replaced most of the work formerly undertaken by farm labourers, horses are very labour-intensive. If you are more interested in profit than the welfare of your horses, you can work on a ratio of one stable hand to 20 horses by keeping your horses boxed up the year round, bedded on rubber or plastic and minimal grooming. This way you can do with a minimal amount of land (say 12–15 acres). Other measures such as selling off underused ponies over the winter and making sure you have large numbers of riders on each of your rides will ensure you make some money. However, if you care for the welfare of your horses, you want to have them out in the paddocks, not stressed, properly groomed, fed and bedded, and for small groups tuition you should budget on one stable hand to 10 horses. You won't make much money but there are many who wouldn't exchange their lifestyle (land rover, horses, hunting, shows) for any other.

You need to do a realistic tally of your costs – insurance, rates, fencing, hay and bedding, feed, shoeing and labour. A good stable hand will cost you something in the order of £100–£150 a week living-in. You may want an indoor school so you can keep teaching when it rains. You need a licence from your local authority, third party insurance and a copy of the Riding Establishment Acts 1964 and 1970. Much useful information is available from the ABRS, which has a starter pack and after six months you can apply for approved membership.

Without doubt, it's a seven-day-a-week job. As well as a total devotion to horses, you do need to be able to get on well with people and to be able to delegate. You (or your stable hands) will also need the organisational skills required to sort out the work programme of your horses over a range of riders. It pays to stay under the VAT threshold if you want to avoid being desk-bound and see your horses and riders. Useful reading includes a British Horse Society book, *Where to Ride*; and the magazine *Horse and Hounds*.

European Community Notes

The UK qualifications in horse management and riding instruction are not only recognised in the EC but highly regarded and there is considerable demand. You will need to speak the local language unless you can find a large enough ex-pat community to teach. All countries will have their own local regulations on animal establishments.

Ss

Saddler/ Leatherworker

Qualifications/Training	Essential
Income bracket	Low–Medium
Licence	No
Town/Country	Either
Experience/ Springboard	Recommended
Travel	Local
Mid-career entry	Possible
Exit sale	Unlikely
Entry costs	£2,000+
Work at home	Yes
Mix and match	Yes.

You could think about: *Shoe designer/ maker, Fashion designer, Farrier/ blacksmith, Taxidermist*

Enquiries
Saddlers Company, British Leather Federation

A lot of saddles on the market are cheap imports. As a British saddle maker, your commissions will come from people who want to have a saddle made to fit a particular horse; you'll also have some repairs and alterations. This is a small market and many saddle makers have to combine saddlery with making other leather goods or selling riding equipment; others go in for livery, providing stabling for and at times looking after other people's horses. You can set up a workshop in the country or in town. The number of horses used for competition and leisure is increasing all over the country. You can learn to make saddles by being apprenticed to a master saddler. The SOCIETY OF MASTER SADDLERS may be able to help you find a suitable master but such openings are increasingly few and far between. Alternatively you can attend courses at CORDWAINERS COLLEGE in London or the WALSALL LEATHER TRAINING CENTRE – both have good contacts with industry and will help with planning your further career. The BRITISH LEATHER FEDERATION runs courses in selling, judging leather quality etc. You need technical and design expertise for leatherworking together with business acumen for your own business. Most of the work is done by hand so you'll need strong fingers.

For saddlery, you need a small shop with enough space for a heavy grade sewing machine, a bench, a 'horse' or two to hold the finished saddles and somewhere to store leather. You may also want attached shop premises if you're going to sell other riding equipment. Excluding rent/mortgage for premises this will cost about £2,000. For general leatherwork you'll need to spend a bit more on a sewing machine (£800 second hand, £1,000–£1,500 new); a skiving machine for trimming the edges (£700–£800 second hand, £1,200 new); and a press (£1,000–£2,000). These can be rented or bought through *Fashion Extras* or *Shoe and Leather News*. Saddles sell for about £180–£500 each, averaging around £300.

Before you start on repair work to saddles and bridles, it is necessary to have your skills assessed by the trade. The SOCIETY OF MASTER SADDLERS administers a national skill assessment and qualification: you can have your skill tested at basic, intermediate and advanced level. (Similar qualifications will be recognised as NVQs). The safety of a rider depends on the quality of his tack – it would be dangerous to attempt repairs without ensuring your work is up to nationally recognised standards.

Small leather goods such as purses, wallets, luggage, handbags and belts can be sold to small shops and boutiques. Exclusive stores may be interested in commissioning you to provide them with their own line of belts or filofaxes. You can seek more clients by taking samples of your work around potentially interested shops. There is also a big market for leather clothing.

The main trade exhibition is the International Leathergoods Exhibition in Birmingham in February. Also of note is the British Equestrian Association International Trade Fair.

European Community Notes

EC saddlers compete with the best British saddlery. Any opportunities to work in the Community are advantageous. Try the SADDLERS' COMPANY as an enquiry point.

Sailing School Owner

Qualifications/Training	Yes
Income bracket	Low-Medium
Licence	RYA
Town/Country	Either
Experience/Springboard	No
Travel	No
Mid-career entry	Likely
Exit sale	Yes

Entry costs	£8,000+
Work at home	No
Mix and match	Yes.

You could think about: *Holiday accommodation owner, Windsurfing school owner, Swimming teacher, Sports retailer, Shopkeeper, Smallholder, Potter*

Enquiries
Royal Yachting Association

This is something that you can start on a small scale, with just one boat, and build up until you have several boats.

You'll have to pass the ROYAL YACHTING ASSOCIATION's (RYA) yacht master and instructor exams before you can teach. The RYA has a list of training establishments which it recognises to run RYA courses. Most people who go in for running a sailing school have been interested in sailing for a long time; but you need to be good at teaching as well as being good at sailing.

Your most expensive initial outlay is for the boat; you'll also need life jackets and distress flares, charts and navigating equipment. The RYA can supply information on the safety equipment required by the Department of Transport. You'll need some sort of office, with a telephone, from which to operate and take bookings. You'll need easy access to the open sea.

You can run weekend, weekly or fortnightly courses, and can combine teaching with cruises. If your school is in a holiday resort, you may increase your trade when the tourists arrive. Safety is very important at sea and your boats have to be checked regularly for seaworthiness, and quite a lot of time will be spent in the winter on maintenance and repairs.

You can advertise in *Yachting, Yachts and Yachting* or *Practical Boat Owner*.

European Community Notes

Qualifications: UK qualifications recognised throughout EC, but not necessarily by formal agreement. RYA-recognised schools normally require RYA qualified staff.

Languages: To succeed, local language necessary.

Earnings: UK income generally lower than or same as elsewhere in the EC.

Advice/Training: Advice, information and training not available for those wishing to work in Europe.

Exchanges: Formal job exchanges do not exist.

Notes: Most countries, including the UK, require their own national qualifications and regulations to be followed to ensure that standards are maintained.

Sales Agent

Qualifications/Training	No
Income bracket	Low-High
Licence	No
Town/Country	Either
Experience/Springboard	Essential
Travel	Essential
Mid-career entry	Yes
Exit sale	Possible
Entry costs	£3,000
Work at home	Partly
Mix and match	Possible.

You could think about: *Direct marketing agent, List broker, Photographer, Motorcycle racer*

Enquiries
Sales agents

Sales agents, reps or representatives, sell their clients' products to retail outlets, by visiting them and taking orders. The client arranges delivery, payment and, almost always, debt collection. Sales agents work for commission on behalf of the manufacturers and producers of almost anything; for example, books, toys, cigarettes, whisky, chocolate, cleaning stuff and sex aids. Sometimes freelance sales agents handle all the sales for smaller clients; otherwise they may be used to promote a

particular product or range or to reach remote places that don't fall within the client's usual sales area. Sometimes they can join 'drive teams' and work for a set time promoting one (usually new) product with demonstrations and leaflets. Drive teams are usually paid a set fee based on the services that they are providing and the amount of time it takes them.

There aren't any formal qualifications but you'll need selling experience; firstly so that you have some idea of what's involved in selling whatever it is you're selling, and secondly, so that you have some proof of selling ability for potential clients. The best experience is in the sales team of a company in the field that you're going into or for another agency (one that is expanding or taking on extra help over a busy time). You'll usually be trained by either of these. Selling encyclopaedias, brushes, etc is another way of finding out what it's like travelling and selling, even though, of course, in these cases you're selling directly to the customer rather than to a shop. Successful sales agents have to inspire their clients' and customers' confidence and trust. You have to put up with long hours in a car and with the possibility of being phoned at unreasonable times by demanding clients who are used to employing a sales force who will do exactly what it's told; although you need to give satisfactory service to your clients, you don't have to agree to all their requests.

To set up you need a car and if you can't arrange to have somebody there to answer your phone a telephone answering machine (preferably one that will play back your messages to you when you phone in during the day). You don't need to buy any stock, clients supply samples and specifications. You're paid commission on net invoice so you lose out if customers return goods to your client. Be prepared for about six months with very little income; some companies have very slow accounts departments and it's worth having a contract with them laying down how often you are to be paid (monthly, quarterly, etc) otherwise you may have to wait for years with no easy legal recourse. In any case, many orders are taken several months before the product is available which adds to the time you have to wait for payment. Another useful contract clause is one about termination. This avoids the possibility of your losing clients over night because they've decided to set up their own sales force or have been bought by somebody else. Your clients will tell you what they want you to sell; this may sometimes mean taking on products that you or your customers don't like and you have to decide whether or not that's worthwhile.

You can find clients through contacts and your experience in the trade. More come through word of mouth and you'll develop a network of regular customers in the same way. You look for more all the time. Some products are suitable for outlets other than the ones you usually use and any additional sales that you make earn more money. You can also find clients through adverts, trade shows and local magazines. Read *Campaign*. Before visiting a potential client, make sure that you know a lot about them (this is good interview technique) and you also need to know that they're reliable, liquid etc before you want to represent them. Although sales agents usually have several clients, they tend to stick to one area of products so that they can represent most of their clients at each customer they visit. It's better and fairer, however, not to take on two products that are in direct competition. If you expand, you may want to take on other agents, you can recruit these through contacts in the trade, from reps you know who want a change or by taking on and training novices. You can join in partnership with others, each taking a territory and ensuring national distribution.

It can be a 24-hour job. Most days you're on the road, visiting all the customers in one area; they all need to be regularly visited and occasional lunches, drinks etc can be useful. You may well be the customer's most direct contact with the manufacturer and so will have at least to act as go-between with some of their problems if you can't sort them out yourself. On top of this there is the necessary paperwork and follow up, making sure that orders reach your clients and that appropriate action is taken.

Salmon Farmer

Qualifications/Training	Necessary
Income bracket	Low-Medium
Licence	No
Town/Country	Country
Experience/Springboard	Essential
Travel	Local
Mid-career entry	Good
Exit sale	Yes
Entry costs	£200,000
Work at home	Yes
Mix and match	Yes.

You could think about: *Fish curer and smoker, Sailing school owner, Holiday accommodation owner, Novelist*

Enquiries
Scottish Salmon Growers Association, Shetland Salmon Farmers Association

This is someone who breeds, grows and sells salmon. It may be useful but not essential to attend a specialist one or two year course in fish farming at INVERNESS COLLEGE or the AGRICULTURAL COLLEGE at Sparsholt in Hampshire. Most learn the job on site and at least two or three years' experience working on different farms is important.

You must learn the business thoroughly, and particularly how to sell, before going alone. When you do, you will succeed if you either stay small or become very very large. You will need a really good accountant. There is no need to join a union but the SCOTTISH SALMON GROWERS ASSOCIATION is very useful and undertakes the marketing for the industry.

You will have to be brave to start at the moment, with the quantity of Norwegian salmon around. You will start by making somewhere between nothing and £5,000; but a successful one-man business can make £15,000–£20,000 a year. You need a total of £150,000 working capital – for the site, a shed with a phone in it, £50,000–£60,000 for a few floating cages to hold the fish, a motor boat and pick-up truck and the smolts (young salmon). The Crown lease rights for use of the sea bed; the cost is very variable but you might expect to pay £2,500 plus. There are few good sites left, so you may have to buy an existing farm. You need access to both fresh and salt water but not the fluctuating salinity of an estuary. As well as leasing the foreshore you need discharge consent from the National Rivers Authority.

You need to be practical and able to swim. It is a good life if you dislike fixed hours but it is difficult to get away. There should always be someone around to feed the fish every day and guard them against thieves, ice, ravenous seals and cormorants. As well as feeding the fish, you must remove any that are dead and establish the cause of death; look for damage or pests; take out the smaller fish and put into a separate pen; and maintain the automatic feeders. You also have to kill those ready for market, gut and pack in ice and send off to market or customers. This can be made easier by communal marketing with other farmers for chiller transport. Some salmon farmers have contracts with multinational companies who buy and process all their fish.

You will need to travel to see customers, attend the annual fish farm conference and keep up to date with equipment. There are always new machines to count and grade fish. Useful organisations are SCOTTISH SALMON GROWERS ASSOCIATION and the SHETLAND SALMON FARMERS ASSOCIATION. Useful magazines include *Sea Food International*, *Fish Farming International*, *Scottish Fish Farmer* and *Fish Farmer*.

★☆★☆★
★☆★☆★ **European Community Notes**
Qualifications: UK qualifications not recognised in EC, nor EC qualifications in UK.
Languages: To succeed, local language not necessary.
Earnings: UK income generally lower than elsewhere in the EC.
Advice/Training: Advice, information and training not available for those wishing to work in Europe.
Exchanges: Formal job exchanges do not exist.

Financial help: Exists for study, training or travel in the EC, specific to this job. Not much salmon farming in Europe except in France and Scandinavia.

Scriptwriter

Qualifications/Training	No
Income bracket	Low–High
Licence	No
Town/Country	Either
Experience/Springboard	Advisable
Travel	Sometimes
Mid-career entry	Yes
Exit sale	No
Entry costs	£10+
Work at home	Yes

Mix and match   Essential to start.
You could think about: **Actor, Novelist, Film director, Market research interviewer, Bartender, Mini-cab driver, Proofreader/copy editor**

Enquiries
Writers' Guild of Great Britain

Not an easy thing to get into, but if you make it, there are three main areas: complete one-off plays written for TV and radio; long-running series for which you may write one or more episodes; and serialisations of novels and stories. There is some overlap between these but TV companies tend to have different departments for different areas and are more likely to accept a script that will fit neatly into one of these. There's a lot of re-writing and working of scripts for TV but this has been made far easier with the advent of word processors.

The TV industry has been going through a particularly difficult time. The downturn really came in 1991 and while things are starting to improve, life is not at all easy for established TV writers, let alone beginners. For the beginner, radio is a good area to gain experience – there are more opportunities in radio than anywhere else for scripts, and many distinguished playwrights and TV writers began their careers in radio. Having said that, the competition is fierce. The BBC recieves at least 10,000 unsolicited television scripts a year. Some 9,000 are totally unsuitable being badly presented, unoriginal or just totally illiterate. That, you can do something about.

Knowledge of how TV works is extremely useful. You need to be able to set scenes and suggest shots and it helps to know about shooting both on location and in front of a live audience as well as having a vague understanding of the techniques involved. Although you don't have many of the physical restrictions of writing for the stage, you will have to contend with a fairly unadventurous market. Learning how to write for TV is a bit like learning a new language. Reading a TV script helps to see what is involved but they are not often published – however, see *Adventures in the Screen Trade*. Once you've got a foot in the door, you can get valuable experience of the discipline of TV writing by working on the scriptwriting team of a long running soap-opera – this is not easy to get into though, producers don't want to take risks and tend to use only writers they know something about.

Any work you can do at a TV company, from scene-shifting to acting, is useful. It will put you in contact with the script editors and producers who decide what is going to be produced. On the whole, people are pretty cautious about what goes on to TV and the bigger the name, and therefore influence, the more useful the contact. If you can't get the producer's or script editor's ear, try a well known actor who may like one of the roles in your script enough to push for its being produced. Whatever you do, find an agent (try *Contacts* if you don't know any) who can advise and cope with the complexities of TV writers' contracts; these include international rights, syndication rights, repeat fees (100 per cent of original fee), royalties and rights to write subsequent episodes of series. Agents can also tell you about which TV companies are worth trying. Once you've had a script produced you can join the WRITERS' GUILD OF GREAT BRITAIN. Radio is one of the greatest users of new writers' work and, although the cross over from radio to TV scriptwriting is difficult, it can be done. Radio is a good starting point for anyone who wants to derive an income from writing (eg Alan Ayckbourn). Set up costs are virtually nil, but it will take a long time to derive income from TV scriptwriting and you'll need another source of income in the meantime. Original scripts can take from six months to 10 years from conception to broadcast – average probably two years. You are paid 50 per cent on commission (whether for your own idea or for something you have been commissioned to do) and the rest on acceptance (about two–three months later by the time you have reworked the script to the necessary style and length and the company have decided that they definitely want it).

Present your ideas attractively and succinctly. Producers don't have much time for reading but a straightforward precis will be rather dry. Illustrate with quotations, background information, even pictures if it helps to capture the flavour of your idea. If you want to serialise a novel, you are well advised to buy the rights to it, subsequent scriptwriting is then a case of adapting the existing text. Presentation of your ideas is also important when you have been approached to write an episode for a series. Some scriptwriters find it helpful to work with a partner with whom they can thrash out ideas and who can help to produce an acceptable and polished script. No play exists until it has been produced. A lot of other people are involved in interpreting the script and you may find that the final broadcast doesn't appear as you expect.

Many without talent attempt to become scriptwriters. Don't. It's one of the most hopeless jobs in which to conceal your self-delusion. If in doubt about the real depth of your creative talent try this test: if you entertained your family at the dinner table as a child, if people laugh at your lavatory grafitti or if your poetry brings tears to the eyes of your loved ones then there is an outside chance of success; when an audience fails to laugh at your comedy, fails to cry at your tragedy or fails to be tremendously entertained by your drama then you won't do. Only those with a burning desire to see their work on the screen and a genuine belief that what they have to say is worth saying should write for the screen. Good luck!

Read *The Way to Write Radio Drama*, *Writing for Television*, *Writers' and Artists' Yearbook* and *Writers' Handbook*. Think about writing courses, such as those run by the ARVON FOUNDATION, which are possibly the best in the country and give you the chance to meet top professionals who will offer a good deal of guidance. Talent *may* out!

Sculptor

Qualifications/Training	Helpful
Income bracket	Low-High
Licence	No
Town/Country	Either
Experience/Springboard	Useful
Travel	No
Mid-career entry	Possible
Exit sale	No
Entry costs	£1,000+
Work at home	Possible
Mix and match	Good.

You could think about: *Photographer, Caterer, Man with a van, Antique dealer, Contemporary art gallery owner*

Enquiries
Art colleges, Sculptors

The aim of the sculptor is pure art. Any money you make will either be from commissions (eg busts for private clients; perhaps large pieces for businesses, or maybe trophies) or by finding a buyer for non-commissioned work. You can choose to sculpt from almost anything including fibreglass, terracotta, plaster, wood, stone and metal, even junk.

You'll have to be artistic and creative but also to know how to handle your medium, how it reacts to different treatments and

what you can do with it. Although self-teaching is quite common, most sculptors take a degree or diploma course at art college; see the *Student Book*. This is useful not only in order to learn the techniques but to have access to the prohibitively expensive materials/foundries etc without which you will not be able to experiment. Working at a casting foundry for a while after your course is useful experience and you may pick up good contacts; otherwise work as an assistant to an established sculptor.

Sculptors need to derive a great deal of satisfaction from sculpting and not to mind periods of poverty. The enterprise allowance scheme is a must; mixing and matching is important and temporary work of any kind useful until you've got enough work to show for sale.

When you're setting up your studio, you need a space big enough to house the size of sculpture you are going for, also electricity and maybe heating. You could operate in an old barn or shed. If you're using fibreglass, you'll need to have special ventilation because the fumes are dangerous. You will have to spend money to get going. You'll also have to pay for materials long before you get paid for the finished work; it's worth becoming acquainted with cheap processes like welding or woodcarving. Making a living comes more quickly and cash flow problems are less if you specialise in small pieces, which need less financial outlay on materials, can be churned out more quickly and, on the whole, have a larger market. It will cost £500–£1,000 for a life size head in bronze at a foundry; it will also take you a minimum of 10 hours to model a portrait head out of clay or wax before you take it to the foundry. That means you have to charge at least £600 for each head in bronze.

The more you can spend on publicity, the better. It's worth paying hundreds of pounds for some decent photographs of your work if you can't use a photographer friend from college. Most galleries like to have slides of your work so you need to get lots of duplicates of the same slide. Publicity is important. A good art college makes sure the right people in the art world are invited to your degree show.

You may be able to pick up some orders there. Look out for competitions in the local and national press. The more contacts you have, the better, especially art gallery contacts, but you might find that your work has to sit around for some time before it finds a buyer. Just keep sending out slides to galleries, architects and agents. Enter all competitions and open exhibitions. Make your presence known to your regional arts association. Exhibit in theatre foyers and restaurants and wine bars. Prepare and distribute a full CV – people will only commission you if they know about you so tell them.

The biggest money comes from modern art collectors but don't be choosey – all well known sculptors had humble beginnings. There is also an expanding market in garden sculpture, which has its more technical problems – it must be waterproof and vandal proof. Also 'sculptural' furniture, chess sets and candle sticks are in vogue.

To keep up with what's going on in the art world, read *Artists News Letter* and *Arts Review*; visit contemporary sculpture exhibitions.

Sex Therapist

Qualifications/Training	Necessary
Income bracket	Low-High
Licence	No
Town/Country	Town
Experience/Springboard	No
Travel	No
Mid-career entry	Recommended
Exit sale	No
Entry costs	£400
Work at home	Yes
Mix and match	Yes.

You could think about: *Doctor, Journalist, Furniture designer/maker*

Enquiries
Medical schools

No job in the world is right for everyone – this one is less right than most. Sex therapists counsel people to help them overcome sexual problems or disfunctions that can result from physical, mental or emotional causes or from pure ignorance. To be taken seriously – especially by the medical profession and the NHS – you have to take one of the three or four recognised courses in Britain, eg the medical schools at Edinburgh or London University (normally part-time). If you don't already have a medical or counselling background it may take some work to persuade them of your bona fides. You need a broad knowledge of anatomy and of everything that might affect sexuality from hormone production to behavioural psychology. Sex therapists need to be able to deal with other people's problems, this means having self confidence and sanity. Deeply held religious or moral principles of acceptable sexual practice don't help.

You'll need to have suitable premises, on your own or as part of a group practice with other medical specialists. Some of your clients may prefer home visits. You can charge from about £10 per hour to about £100 (if you're on Harley Street). Most people who try to live exclusively from ST fail – not least because of people's reluctance to admit to sexual shortcomings and inadequacies.

Most work comes through contacts and networks. Visit local doctors and try to get referrals from them. This can be difficult because doctors tend to be happier advising marriage guidance rather than assistance with specifically sexual problems; this means that there is a great need for your services if you can manage to tap it. Advertising isn't very successful, it goes against the medical tradition and so people tend to be suspicious of those who do.

Like VAT men or prison officers, you don't always want to tell people at parties what you do. Your own relationships can suffer – even the most cool partner will tend to overreact to your casual comments about your sex life and you may get very involved with your subject and your clients (it's difficult not to take work home with you). Your clients may resent having to come to you and won't always thank you for the help that you've given them. However it can be very fulfilling because the results are often quick; you can see someone for four hours and clear up a problem they've had for 15 years – 'so that's what a clitoris is'. Once you know what you're talking about most problems are easy to solve.

Shepherd/ Shepherdess

Qualifications/Training	Useful
Income bracket	Low
Licence	No
Town/Country	Country
Experience/Springboard	Essential
Travel	Between jobs
Mid-career entry	Possible
Exit sale	No
Entry costs	£2,000
Work at home	No
Mix and match	Yes.

You could think about: *Tree surgeon, Man with a van, Proofreader/copy editor, Holiday accommodation owner . . .*

Enquiries
National Sheep Association, National Farmers' Union

This is someone involved in lambing, foster mothering, clipping and dipping sheep, gathering them off the hills and taking them to sales. Farmers are using fewer full time shepherds so if you are prepared to travel around, there is plenty of work.

Work on a farm in the school holidays to make sure you like the work. Formal qualifications are not necessary but you can take a course, including some animal husbandry, at an agricultural college. You must work on a farm for at least one year assisting an experienced shepherd. Look for jobs in the farming press or ring up your local agricultural college who may have block release work contracts. It may be useful to learn to ride a motorbike as on many farms these are replacing the shepherd and his dog for gathering and checking. It is not necessary to join a union but the local branch of the Young Farmers is good for contacts and a social life.

You will start by only earning £30 a week, rising to £160–£200 for a really experienced shepherd, though accommodation is usually provided. If it isn't you will need a cheap base to work from, with a phone. Invest in a secondhand van (£1,000), warm waterproof clothing (£200) and a good sheep dog (£600). A crook is not vital and other shepherds will make and give them to you. It is usually a 40-hour week except during lambing when it can be 18 hours a day. The lambing season can last from December till May if you are prepared to move jobs frequently. It is hard work but with lots of variety. It is possible to combine it with forestry work in the autumn after weaning the lambs.

You must have considerable physical stamina and not mind working in cold, wet and windy conditions. You must be able to cope with long hours alone taking responsibility and using your own initiative especially during the lambing season. On the other hand, you will have to work in a team when clipping, dipping etc. An understanding of animals and lots of patience are essential as sheep are inclined to suicide.

Young experienced men are preferred to women on the whole – although many farmers find girls are better for lambing as they have small hands and are more understanding.

Useful information can be gained from the NATIONAL FARMERS' UNION, the NATIONAL SHEEP ASSOCIATION, the AGRICULTURAL TRAINING BOARD, the MINISTRY OF AGRICULTURE, the YOUNG FARMERS' CLUBS and the agricultural colleges. Read *Farmers Weekly*, the *Scottish Farmer* and the magazines of all the different sheep breeders' societies.

Shipbroker

Qualifications/Training	Recommended
Income bracket	Medium–High
Licence	No
Town/Country	Town
Experience/Springboard	Essential
Travel	Possible
Mid-career entry	Yes
Exit sale	Possible
Entry costs	£10,000
Work at home	Partly possible
Mix and match	Possible.

You could think about: *Import/export broker, Futures broker, Jazz musician, Landlord*

Enquiries
Baltic Exchange, Institute of Chartered Shipbrokers

Shipbrokers work in an international freight market to bring together cargo interests such as commodity dealers with shipowners. They also buy and sell ships on behalf of principals, handle the management of ships and the administration of ships' affairs throughout the voyage and in ports. The broker's job is to match available cargoes which need to be transported anywhere in the world from exporters, importers, oil companies, grain traders and mining companies with available and suitable vessels at the best possible price. So, a food manufacturing company with 60,000 tonnes of grain to be moved from Canada to Japan would use a broker to find a ship or ships which were suitably positioned and able to carry the cargo safely and securely at the minimum price available in the market. Contact will be made with brokers representing shipowners and negotiations between the two sides would result in a fixture – a contract between the manufacturing company and shipowner for the carriage of the goods either in terms of a single voyage or perhaps hiring a ship for a fixed period of time. The rates involved reach tens of thousands of dollars a day and the broker earns a commission of around 1.25 per cent. Other brokers concentrate on buying and selling ships on behalf of clients. International shipbroking is located fairly tightly around the BALTIC EXCHANGE in the City of London and there are domestic shipping exchanges in some major European ports as well as New York and the Far East. London is important because it provides a good time zone for dealing with both North America and the Far East; it has a major maritime insurance market as well as established maritime law (English law is the dominant system in the maritime world), arbitration, ship classification, banking and finance.

Shipbroking relies heavily on fast and effective communications – the telephone and fax most of all, although electronic data interchange and the information services available through networked computers are important for background market information. The BALTIC EXCHANGE (which got its name from early trade with the Baltic Seaboard a couple of hundred years ago) has an international trading floor which allows brokers to meet each day to gather market information, to discover what cargoes will be available and what suitable ships are around. Baltic Exchange members handle most of the world's bulk cargo chartering, including tanker fixtures, and the market is regulated through its own code. Those involved in ship management or handling the administration after the fixture has been made can be involved in foreign travel.

It would be impossible to set up as an independent shipbroker straight from school or university. You need experience and a lot of contacts in the freight market and to be trusted and respected before anyone is likely to use you. Entry could be through a larger firm where you can receive training on the job and work under supervision. To become a member of the BALTIC EXCHANGE you have to pass their examination. The more formal INSTITUTE OF CHARTERED SHIPBROKERS is the professional body which provides a graded series of professional qualifications starting from the basics of the industry. Stepping stones to higher levels of membership are available for those making a career in broking.

Details of vacancies can be found in specialist shipping journals such as *Lloyd's List* and by direct contact with the companies. You will need the ability to take responsibility and mix well with other people as well as expressing yourself logically and clearly both in writing and in speech. General commercial experience, coupled with specific knowledge of ships, import and export arrangements, commercial and political geography, and ship management are all experience you will need to gain. Negotiating flair is key as well as making and maintaining your contacts. Shipbrokers have to be tough and resourceful negotiators to get the best deals for their clients from the shipowner or the charterer who have their own interests (for example, keeping their ships fully occupied at all times) to consider. You will need a lot of tenacity to conclude some deals. These qualities are often more important than higher level educational qualifications.

You'll need a telephone, a fax and a telex (this is a competitive business and it's important for you to contact people quickly). You may want some secretarial help but most business is done immediately over the phone so you don't need a massive staff. You will have to work long hours yourself. Because of global time differences this is not a 9–5 job. You may be on 24-hour call to cope with any problems your clients, subcontractors or colleagues meet on the other side of the world – and at senior levels you may have to travel at very short notice. When the contract has been achieved arrangements need to be made for loading and unloading the cargo, customs clearance and perhaps the management and crewing of the ship.

European Community Notes

A totally international market, the European Community's arrangements are not central to individual brokers. Shipping is already highly competitive internationally. The INSTITUTE OF CHARTERED SHIPBROKERS' professional qualifications are recognised throughout the European Community.

Shoe Designer/ Maker

Qualifications/Training	Necessary
Income bracket	Low-High
Licence	No
Town/Country	Either
Experience/Springboard	No
Travel	Yes
Mid-career entry	Unlikely
Exit sale	No
Entry costs	£500
Work at home	Possible
Mix and match	Yes.

You could think about: *Fashion designer, Fashion retailer, Saddler/ leatherworker, Cabaret performer, Advertising photographer*

Enquiries
British Footwear Manufacturers Federation, CFI International

Unlike the conventional industry where people are used to producing component supplies, the fashion shoe maker carries out most of the processes from design to production. It is normal, however, to subcontract last-making to specialist firms to your specification.

The independent shoe designer/maker has emerged in this country as a reaction against an old fashioned, long established shoe industry which has neither the inclination nor the investment to produce new lines. People are tired of limited choices in their shoes and fashion shoe design is booming. UK designers are eagerly sought after abroad – notably in Italy – but the opportunities for the designer in this country are fairly small. There is some resistance to new ideas and a certain resentment of young designers.

You can't design shoes if you don't know how to make them. There are specialist courses in the technical expertise, the design ability and business skills necessary to go it alone – eg CORDWAINERS COLLEGE in London and SOUTHFIELDS

COLLEGE in Leicester. CFI INTERNATIONAL has details of courses and some are listed in *Design Courses in Britain*. A more general fashion course will not enable you actually to make shoes. The industry has almost lost its apprenticeship scheme; what there is tends to concentrate on component-making rather than the whole shoe.

A fashion shoe maker can operate in a fairly small space – you can make a pair of shoes over a last on your knees. All you need is a place to store a small amount of leather and your equipment. You need a hammer, knives, pincers, an industrial sewing machine and a roughing wheel. You can farm out some operations like last-making to specialist firms who implement your design to your specifications. If you get a big order you could consider sub-contracting to a manufacturer. Italy is a good place to go because factories there are much smaller than their British counterparts and much more adapted to wide variation in design on their advanced machines (eg, laser pattern grading, and computer control). They might produce 500 pairs of shoes a week retailing at between £80 to £150 a pair.

You have to secure commissions by hawking round your portfolio and range of sample shoes to likely outlets eg, small exclusive designer shops who may commission more. You can get a collection of shoes ready while still at college. Contacts are very important and designers will help each other. Word of mouth, fashion shows etc will get you more orders. You have to be very sure of your ambition and product and not be afraid to go out and sell.

Handmade shoes are bought for their fine workmanship, variation in design and colour, beautiful leather, handstitching, embroidery and innovation. They are therefore more expensive than other shoes and are sold at the exclusive end of the market. For the designer the aim is the product, not to save pennies. You can go in for zany products but these retail for a lot because of the work involved. You have to make sure that you charge enough for your work, currently about £85 to £100 a pair for men's fashion shoes and perhaps £120 for ladies' shoes – prices that compare pretty well with the quality end of the ready-made market. A one-off special might cost £250. You may have cash flow problems when you've had to pay for eg shipping shoes and then have to wait weeks until delivery for the pay off. Distance creates its own problems when selling. The first year is particularly difficult until orders pick up.

Pitfalls of the business can be learned as you go along. Producing too much variation on a design theme, for instance, is expensive. One good motto is 'if it's not there they won't ask for it'. Another problem is taking too many orders and being unable to fulfil them, or taking too few and not having enough work. After a while you get the balance right.

For supplies and service, *Shoe and Leather News* and the *Shoe Trade Directory* are useful. Also contact the BRITISH FOOTWEAR MANUFACTURERS FEDERATION. The BRITISH KNITTING AND CLOTHING EXPORT COUNCIL produces a useful yearbook and also organises exhibitions for fashion, including shoes. CFI INTERNATIONAL also provides a yearbook and footwear journal.

European Community Notes

As noted above, like all areas of the fashion trade UK designers are sought after abroad, particularly in Italy, where fashion is taken seriously. Go where a prophet is not without honour – nor profit.

Shopkeeper

Qualifications/Training	Available
Income bracket	Low-High
Licence	No
Town/Country	Mostly town
Experience/ Springboard	Recommended

Travel	Local
Mid-career entry	Likely
Exit sale	Excellent
Entry costs	Highly variable
Work at home	No
Mix and match	Possible.

You could think about: ***Franchisee, Sub postmaster, Wine merchant, Wine bar owner, Novelist***

Enquiries
College for the Distributive Trades,
National Association of Shopkeepers

If you are thinking of opening a shop some considerations will depend on what you are going to sell (whether you need refrigeration, how much storage etc). However, some things apply to nearly all shop owners. You'll almost certainly have to work long hours; being open six days a week with extra time needed for accounts, buying and ordering of stock, stocktaking, maintaining and cleaning of premises etc. Even with a partner or employee to help, holidays and time off may be difficult especially to begin with. Some shop owners are subject to legislation affecting, for example, who they can sell to, storage provision, opening hours, health and safety provisions. You must be aware of these before setting up rather than risk the expense and inconvenience of being caught breaking the law. New technology (especially in computerised equipment) can make stocktaking, accounting and ordering easier. Legal Sunday opening (already widespread in Scotland) is sporadically under discussion for England and Wales. This would have obvious repercussions for shop owners.

No qualifications are necessary unless you are offering a specialist service such as dispensing prescriptions for which you will need special training and/or registration in a profession. It is extremely useful to have had some relevant experience so that you have some idea of what working in a shop can be like and are aware of some of the potential pitfalls. Knowledge of running your own business is useful, try local colleges and institutes or the COLLEGE FOR THE DISTRIBUTIVE TRADES who run a course on 'Your Own Shop'. The NATIONAL ASSOCIATION OF SHOPKEEPERS helps its members with advice and resources. You'll have to be organised and patient enough to cope with customers.

The amount of money you need varies. Budget for suitable premises, storage and display, cash registers, heating and lighting, transport if necessary (eg to get your fish from market), enough stock to open with, security for valuables, advertising and insurance. Choose premises carefully and consider: do you need to provide parking or will most of your customers be local? How much storage space do you need? Do you need changing rooms? Are you too close to the competition or, alternatively, too isolated? Two bookshops on the same road may be too many while three or four expensive dress shops may actually do better than one on its own because it's worthwhile for customers to travel. Do you need passing trade? As well as doing as much initial market research as possible, you should follow up by keeping abreast of developments in your particular section of the market (there are fashions in virtually everything from meat to spectacle frames) and also by getting to know your own customers so that you can gather some idea of the sort of things that they want. You'll also find it helpful to cultivate suppliers. Your success will depend upon your suppliers, what you are selling, the profit margins that you can charge, overheads including staff and your own ability to experiment successfully.

You should recognise that this pursuit is becoming more and more regulated – you should contact your local authority for full details. And if you are involved in production or retailing of food the fun really starts. For example, on all produce you need to display the country of origin – do you really know where those oranges are from? If your selling home-made snacks, bread or what-have-you then the preparation and cooking of such products, and the premises, should be subject to inspection by environmental health officers under the provisions of the Food Safety Act.

Silversmith/Jeweller

Qualifications/Training	Recommended
Income bracket	Low-Medium
Licence	No
Town/Country	Both
Experience/Springboard	No
Travel	Yes
Mid-career entry	Possible
Exit sale	No
Entry costs	£2,500
Work at home	Yes
Mix and match	Yes.

You could think about: *Fashion clothes/hat designer, Dealer in small antiques and collectibles, Man with a van, Contemporary art gallery owner*

Enquiries
Goldsmiths' Company

This is a small, highly competitive craft industry, with outlets concentrated (apart from the tourist routes) in a few centres such as London, Birmingham, Glasgow, Basle, Paris and Tokyo. Vocational degrees, diplomas or certificates are no guarantee of success. Most who are independent are designers or designer/craftsmen although some independent craftworkers act as outworkers for established companies. Specialisation is usual. Fashion and jewellery are more rapidly lucrative. In gold and silversmithing, working in precious metals or stones, objets d'art or trophies, it's slower to get established but rewards are greater, especially at the top. Contacts are invaluable – trade fairs and competitions the way to get your name known and get to the top. You need persistence to get commissions or work as well as making what people will buy.

The most usual way to start is to take a degree or diploma course and then start on your own – the better courses give some basic grounding in running a business; the Goldsmiths' Company sponsors a useful course for all newly qualified students. Less usually, you can, at 16, take a pre-apprenticeship course at an art college, followed by a four-year apprenticeship. A very small number of successful designers are self-taught, or have taken short or part-time courses (eg, courses leading to the GEMMOLOGICAL ASSOCIATION exams). But to succeed untrained you must be both good and lucky.

To start up on your own you'll have to equip yourself with tools, publicity, materials and premises. You need more tools for silversmithing than for jewellery. The cost of materials will depend on what you will make – feathers and plastics are obviously cheaper than gold (prices quoted in the newspaper). Some grants are available (CRAFT COUNCIL, local councils etc). Use all your contacts to reduce your costs – any college mates who can do art work for your publicity? You can try sharing costs through joint workshops or co-operatives – which give moral as well as financial support. There is a drift away from the towns where rents are so high. A small inexpensive fax machine can keep you in touch. Look out for second hand equipment in the *Retail Jeweller* (the trade bible). Some shops such as Hyper Hyper in Kensington rent out units and manage publicity – but at a price. Others use markets one or two days a week. In the early stages it usually pays to combine your own work with other sources of income; teaching or selling others' work along with your own (out-working for an established company is possible but you will need a specialist skill such as pearl stringing). Your time is largely under your own control, so it's possible to mix and match.

Your biggest early problem is to get known. Use all your contacts, get known and *sell*. If you are going to make a real name for yourself, you should exhibit at the trade fairs (eg London, Basle, Tokyo); start with local craft fairs and work up to the UK craft/trade fairs then upgrade to Europe and elsewhere overseas – and enter the competitions (eg, Platinum Award sponsored by Ayrton Metals and De Beers in alternate years; annual competitions run by the GOLDSMITHS' COMPANY). Competitions are advertised in the trade mags: *Retail Jeweller, Goldsmiths' Gazette,* and *Design.* Winning is worth a lot. Exhibit where you can – libraries, boutiques, galleries. Send photos to magazines and slides to designer groups promoting new designers. Wear your own jewellery to parties; write, phone visit, hawk your samples/portfolio around. Be organised; keep a record of people you have met, and which shops you have visited. Take commissions and don't be too proud to do repairs which might result in further work. Also desirable is multiple production to spread costs.

Knowing your market and what it will pay is important – the English, for example, prefer 'safe' jewellery when they are spending a lot of money – the Americans often prefer something more showy. In fashion jewellery, the more different the better. You should, incidentally, check out copyright laws – it's important for the protection of designs and products. There is always a small market for objets d'art which can pay for its exclusive taste. There is some published market research. One study identified silver items which sell and the price range; it established that way-out design doesn't sell and the most popular item singled out was a silver mounted nightcap decanter. Need we say more?

⁑ European Community Notes

Qualifications: UK qualifications recognised throughout EC and EC qualifications in UK.

Languages: To succeed, local language necessary.

Earnings: UK income generally lower than elsewhere in the EC.

Setting up: You will find it difficult to succeed in Belgium, Denmark, France, Germany, Greece, Luxembourg, Portugal, Spain. You will find it easier in Eire, Italy, Netherlands.

Advice/Training: Some advice, information and training available for those wishing to work in Europe. Some agencies such as EURODESK offer limited advice and training opportunities – mainly for Scotland, but will advise rest of UK.

Exchanges: Formal job exchanges do not exist.

Financial help exists for study, training or travel in the EC, specific to this job.

Enquiry point for those wishing to work in the EC: Goldsmiths' Company

Recommended reading: DTI reports, foreign journals, eg *l'Orefo, Argento, G.Z. European Jeweller*.

Smallholder (horticultural)

Qualifications/Training	Recommended
Income bracket	Medium
Licence	No
Town/Country	Country
Experience/ Springboard	Recommended
Travel	No
Mid-career entry	Possible
Exit sale	Excellent
Entry costs	£10,000+++
Work at home	Yes
Mix and match	Excellent.

You could think about: ***Beekeeper, Gardener/garden designer, Caterer, Tree surgeon***

Enquiries
Institute of Horticulture

For many town dwellers, the prospect of making a living from a smallholding with all the attractions of life in the open air and close contact with nature has a strong appeal. The reality though is invariably far removed from the idyllic vision. To make a living out of a few acres calls for specialisation and ensuring a market for the comparatively few lines grown.

Whatever crops you choose to grow you must set your sights on producing high quality which usually means an appreciable level of investment. You will need an eye for detail and, above all, a willingness to work long hours, seven days a week. One correspondent knew of several couples running smallholdings who had not been able to leave the place, apart from the odd day, for more than five years. But a lot of people have built up successful horticultural businesses from scratch; some of them with comparatively little experience of plant-growing, save in their own gardens. In many cases they have used redundancy money or a legacy to finance the start-up. It is also quite possible for younger people (and others!) to start their own business by running a smallholding as an ancillary occupation to their full-time job. But this requires tremendous dedication and prodigious energy. Many have trodden this path, comparatively few last the course.

There is certainly no sure-fire prescription for those who wish to establish a horticultural business, but there are some guidelines worth noting. Commercial horticulture embraces a wide range of crop production and marketing. Ignore top fruit (apples, pears, plums, cherries) if you're considering starting up on your own – unless money is no object. Soft fruit (strawberries, raspberries, blackcurrants, gooseberries) presents limited scope except possibly a pick-your-own holding if located in a part of the country where the competition is minimal (difficult to find). And it's a high-risk operation. While new varieties provide a longer picking season than used to be the case, two or three wet weekends at the crucial time can still ruin your budget. Field vegetables (cabbage, cauliflowers, carrots, onions, beans, peas, etc) are best left to the big arable farmers. The exception – and an increasingly important one – is the 20–30 acre organic holding but you will need capital of at least £40,000–£50,000 to tide you over the early non-productive years. Protected crops (tomatoes, cucumbers, lettuce, mushrooms, cut flower crops, pot or bedding plants) represent one of the best areas for a newcomer to start; either by buying second-hand glasshouses or new plastic tunnels. Renting is possible in some areas; otherwise be prepared for an investment of around £20,000 an acre for plastic tunnels erected and equipped on site. Nursery stock includes raising of trees, shrubs, herbaceous plants, alpines. Many new nurseries have started up on a small scale by people specialising in a few lines, eg ground cover plants, ornamental grasses, alpines, and it's probably the best bet for anyone intending to run a holding as a part-time operation to begin with. Some produce plants solely for the trade, ie the larger wholesale and retail nurseries and/or the landscape industry and garden centres. Others deal with the public direct; a natural progression is the ploughing back of profits into bought-in stock and developing into a garden centre. Dried flowers have so far been the start-up success story of the Nineties, but do obtain guidance from the BRITISH DRIED FLOWERS ASSOCIATION. Herbs are also well worth considering; contact the BRITISH HERB TRADE ASSOCIATION for more information.

In spite of the success stories of those who have flourished without any formal training, it *is* advisable to spend a year or two at a horticultural college (contact the INSTITUTE OF HORTICULTURE for a list of courses) followed up with working experience at a well-run horticultural business, ideally in the field in which you propose to establish yourself. Membership of a professional institute or local growers group is also helpful. From the *Grower* you can learn more about the industry, get the latest market prices and find out second-hand prices for equipment, machinery and so on.

✳✳ European Community Notes

As with FARMERS, British producers are looking seriously at, for example, France and at Portugal and Spain where the lower price of land and property is a considerable incentive to move. Equally, the state of the UK property market of the early 1990s has done a lot to flatten – or worse – the differential, and the ease with which you could unload your house in exchange for another property with acres of land. Add to that, the smallholding tradition is already far more firmly entrenched in the South than the UK. Start enquiries with the agricultural attachés of the EC members' embassies and, as ever, anybody who has ever done it.

Snail Farmer

Qualifications/Training	Useful
Income bracket	Medium
Licence	No
Town/Country	Country
Experience/ Springboard	Recommended
Travel	No
Mid-career entry	Yes
Exit sale	Excellent
Entry costs	£10,000++
Work at home	Yes
Mix and match	Possible.

You could think about: *Restaurateur, Fish smoker and curer, Sculptor, Holiday accommodation owner, Tourist attraction*

Enquiries
Snail Centre, British Snail Farmers' Association

Heliculturists breed and prepare edible snails for sale to restaurants and hotels, either frozen or vacuum-packed. It is a potentially expanding market; while protein-rich snails are becoming an increasingly popular food in Britain, France consumes countless millions of snails every year and produces less than 2 per cent of what it eats; snail eggs are also something of a delicacy in parts of France, a sort of caviar. At the same time, a combination of factors have prevented eastern Europe from supplying the snails it used to provide.

It's been claimed by snail farming enthusiasts that snails may yield up to £6,000 per acre. There are no UK qualifications for snail farmers. The WELSH OFFICE, AGRICULTURAL DEPARTMENT produces an introductory information folder on snail farming. French connections are useful for contact with the suppliers of your first breeding snails, though these are now available in the UK. Other useful organisations are the SNAIL CENTRE (for advice and stock; subscription £100 pa) and the BRITISH SNAIL FARMERS ASSOCIATION, a supplier and franchise contractor, membership of which costs £1,800 for which you get advice and support in your venture including a guarantee to sell all the stock you produce. The SNAIL CENTRE also runs three-day training courses. You need contacts in the food and wine world so experience as a chef, wine merchant or in another branch of specialist farming or food production is useful. Snail farming is becoming increasingly recognised as a normal form of agriculture in the UK but you'll have to be patient to build up the business into a profitable concern.

Most snails in the UK are now grown indoors so soil, surroundings and predators such as moles and field mice are no longer the factor they were. You will still need planning permission though. You'll need premises – a building of approximately 500 sq ft, heated and insulated. You will also need, at least eventually, a mechanical system processing unit, at a cost of £20,000. Bulk snail selling is best done through the French or British snail market co-operative (BRITSNAIL); snails will reach about £4,000–£4,500 a tonne (approximately 65,000 snails). Fully prepared snails ie, in the traditional French manner (bourguignonne) should fetch between £2.80–£3.50 a dozen, sold direct to local outlets such as restaurants and specialist food shops. When established you should be looking at a net income of around £20,000 pa on a turnover of £90,000..

Snails are quiet, relatively inactive animals; very peaceful – some people get quite a taste for them.

Social Worker

Qualifications/Training	Essential
Income bracket	Low-Medium
Licence	No
Town/Country	Either
Experience/Springboard	Essential
Travel	Local
Mid-career entry	Usual

Exit sale	No
Entry costs	Nil
Work at home	No
Mix and match	Yes.

You could think about: ***Counsellor, Guardian ad Litem, Nursing home owner, TV and film music composer, Potter***

Enquiries
British Association of Social Workers (BASW), Central Council for Education and Training in Social Work

While the vast majority of social workers are employed by local authorities and the voluntary organisations, a small proportion are freelance. To become a freelance inevitably means springboarding as you'll need a good range of reliable contacts and proven skills that can only be gained by first being in conventional employment. People will need to know and trust you personally to give you freelance work.

You'll need to be properly trained and qualified – take a course leading to the Certificate of Qualification in Social Work (CQSW) (information from the CENTRAL COUNCIL FOR EDUCATION AND TRAINING IN SOCIAL WORK). Then you need a good deal of social work experience – and probably specialist experience too – before you can think of going solo.

Some social workers go freelance in order to continue their social work part time while changing direction to eg counselling. But there is a full time living to be made as an independent – so long as you are working in an area of the country where people will pay for your services and particularly if you have specialised in eg psychiatric, geriatric or family work. Most freelancers are specialists in children and work part of their time as guardians ad litem. Others get work from eg local solicitors and doctors. It may involve regular visiting of the elderly, writing reports on conditions in which children are being kept, some family therapy, maybe some teaching, social work and consultancy work for local authorities. The latter will depend upon your credibility with the social workers in your local authority – by and large they don't smile upon their independent colleagues.

Working without the support of a team can be isolated and lonely. Join BASW. You need the qualities routinely required of social workers, including compassion and toughness. Read *Community Care* and *Social Work Today*; read (and make sure the editor knows about you) *Search*, the BASW directory of independent experts.

European Community Notes

Qualifications: UK qualifications not recognised in EC, although some EC qualifications recognised in UK.
Languages: To succeed, local language necessary.
Earnings: UK income generally lower than elsewhere in the EC.
Setting up: You will find it difficult to succeed throughout Europe except Eire.
Advice/Training: Advice, information and training not available for those wishing to work in Europe.
Exchanges: Formal job exchanges do not exist.
Enquiry point for those wishing to work in the EC: BRITISH ASSOCIATION OF SOCIAL WORKERS which will put you in touch with local professional associations.
Recommended reading: In Europe: Social Work Education and 1992
In Europe: Links and Exchanges

Solicitor

Qualifications/Training	Essential
Income bracket	Medium-High
Licence	Yes
Town/Country	Local
Experience/Springboard	Essential
Travel	Yes
Mid-career entry	Possible
Exit sale	Excellent
Entry costs	£20,000+

Work at home	Yes

Mix and match	Possible.

You could think about: *Property developer, Landlord, Patent agent, Estate agent, MP, Sailing school owner, Jazz musician*

Enquiries

Law Society, Law Society of Scotland

Solicitors give their clients appropriate legal advice on anything from buying a house to what to do if they are arrested on a murder charge; increasing specialisation means it is unlikely the same solicitor will be called upon to do both. Most solicitors (nearly three-quarters of the 70,000) are in private practice; 24,000 are partners and 4,000 are sole practitioners. The trend is away from setting up entirely alone and towards either staying in established partnerships, or a small group of partners from an established partnership setting up together. This is partly for financial reasons (it costs a lot to set up a solicitor's office) and for practical reasons, for example, allowing the responsibility and administration to be shared, pooling of expertise and ensuring the partnership is never left unattended. There is an increasing trend towards larger firms with a greater degree of specialisation. Practices are broadly on three levels of profitability; some take rich pickings from the financial services revolution, largely London-based with corporate clients; most are the steady local solicitors; the least profitable are the legal aid practices in large cities. Increasingly, solicitors are opening up links with Europe to take advantage of the single market in 1992. This will increase opportunities for solicitors, especially those with language skills.

All new legislation has some effect on the legal profession. Recent examples include the loss of the conveyancing monopoly and the increased use of other professions for tax advice. Another possible change comes from plans to allow solicitors to act as advocates in the higher courts, in addition to the lower courts in which they can act at present; this may spread solicitors' work further. The need for solicitors to specialise is growing as the demand for legal advice spreads.

It is usual to be a graduate to become a solicitor and then to take professional exams (fewer if the degree is in law) before becoming an articled clerk for two years. As an articled clerk you will get a taste of most of the departments in the partnership (see ROSET for details of available clerkships). Articled clerks do some routine jobs but in most cases the work is varied and interesting and you only have to stick it for two years. In some cases articled clerks are very well paid and have considerable responsibility. After that you will need to work for an existing practice for at least three years before the LAW SOCIETY allows you to run your own office. (This and other regulations are explained in the Law Society pamphlet, *Professional Conduct of Solicitors*.) Over half of newly qualified solicitors are women. It is possible (if you don't mind being an articled clerk) to come to the profession later in life. Training is slightly different in Scotland, where law graduates or non-law graduates who have a three year training contract with an employer, do a year's full time course leading to a diploma in legal practice followed by two years' post diploma training with a firm before qualifying. Details from the LAW SOCIETY OF SCOTLAND. In Scotland intending sole principles may set up any time after they have become fully qualified.

It takes between five and ten years to become a full partner in an existing firm, often following a stint as a salaried partner (it can take longer, the older and larger the firm). You may have to accept established customs and conditions – scales of profit-sharing, office management – but you avoid some of the headaches of a new practice. It can be a good thing to change jobs until you find the firm in which you want to stay and become a partner. It is best to do this straight after qualifying or after two or three years. But don't change too often.

If you are setting up a new partnership, raising the necessary capital (although important) is less of a problem than building up your clientele. Some have set up practices where the partners are all ethnic minorities or women, obviously with a particular clientele in mind. The number of clients you can take with you when you set up will depend on the prestige of the firm you are leaving and, more importantly, there are likely to be restrictive covenants. It is wise to consider how long the clients will be with you – you may set up as a divorce specialist with 50 clients, whose cases may all have settled within a year, by which time you must have made your reputation. Location is also important. Clients, in general, don't like travelling to see their solicitors; nor do they like them to change address too often so find somewhere with room to expand. You may have covenanted not to set up a new partnership within a certain radius of the one you are leaving, which can force you into an area where your particular specialisation is less likely to flourish. If you want to move right out of the area, the Law Society provides lists of members, with date of qualification, and location of practice. You can therefore identify a town where many solicitors are near retiring.

Apart from premises, office equipment and an extensive library, you will need an absolute minimum of one member of staff who is prepared to act as secretary, receptionist, telephonist etc. Such people are difficult to find and before you have established a reputation, you may have difficulty finding articled clerks and assistants. Banks are quite helpful to professionals setting up on their own.

Office procedure is important for solicitors – it is not a job for people who can't stand filling in forms. There is a lot of paperwork so it helps if you're methodical. However the days when solicitors acknowledge acknowledgements seem to be over. Much of your time is spent talking and writing to people. You need to be able to maintain a detached judgment but to inspire the trust of your clients by being patient, sympathetic and capable of understanding what their needs are.

There is a variety of videos about the profession (try your careers office). The Law Society publishes pamphlets on becoming a solicitor. *The Legal 500* is an excellent digest of the major law firms in England, Wales and Scotland with a description of each and the work they do.

⁎⁎⁎ European Community Notes

Qualifications: UK qualifications recognised throughout EC and EC qualifications in UK.

Languages: To succeed, local language necessary.

Setting up: You will find it possible to succeed throughout Europe.

Advice/Training: Advice, information and training available for those wishing to work in Europe.

Exchanges: Formal job exchanges exist.

Financial help: Exists for study, training or travel in the EC, specific to this job.

Enquiry point for those wishing to work in the EC: The LAW SOCIETY, LAW SOCIETY OF SCOTLAND

Notes: It must be stressed that the whole position of the legal profession throughout the EC is very complex and diverse. As the Law Society says, the organisation and scope of practice of the legal professions differ widely throughout the member states, and superficial impressions can be extremely misleading. But, the wide scope of activities of UK solicitors and their relative flexibility means that they are by far the largest exporters of legal services in the Community and, with caveats as above, prospects continue to look rosy.

Space Sales Agent

Qualifications/Training	No
Income bracket	Low–High
Licence	No
Town/Country	Either
Experience/Springboard	Essential
Travel	Some
Mid-career entry	Yes
Exit sale	Possible
Entry costs	£500
Work at home	Yes

Mix and match   Yes.
You could think about: *Direct marketing consultant, Advertising agent, Magazine publisher, Motorcycle racer*

Enquiries
Space sales agents, Magazine and newspaper publishers

Media space sales people are responsible for getting advertisements into books, magazines and newspapers. They do this by contacting potential advertisers (or their advertising agencies) and encouraging them to book advertising space in the publication. Their client is the publisher. Publishers may also want advice on charges, target advertising revenue and so on. Space salesmen sell to people who already have advertising budgets, many of them running to literally millions of pounds, so the emphasis is on advertising in the client's product rather than on having to sell the idea of advertising itself. It's a fast moving, competitive business, you work under pressure to meet deadlines and have to keep up momentum and enthusiasm for what can be a fairly thankless job, by being constantly on the move, phoning, writing and visiting.

There are no formal qualifications but you'll need some experience. National newspapers are always recruiting space salesmen; there is a fast turnover because people soon get bored with a product and want to try selling on another publication. Many newspapers and magazines train their sales staff and, as long as you've got a reasonable telephone manner and are suitably persuasive, you shouldn't have any trouble getting in. Appropriate experience on an undergraduate magazine or any magazine/book production experience is also useful.

You can operate from anywhere with a telephone so set-up costs are minimal. You may find, especially as you expand, that you want to be closer to your clients and to media buyers. If your client is productive enough, you'll only need one. You can get this client through contacts or by approaching one and suggesting that you sell space for them. You'll have to have a reasonable idea about the sort of advertiser your client will attract. You have a rate card, describing the publication (competitors' rates are easily established from BRAD – British Rates and Data), its value to advertisers, cost per thousand readers and so on. The price on the rate card is often calculated to allow you to cut some of the margins for advertisers. You'll usually get between 15 and 30 per cent commission on your client's yield from advertising. Advertisers pay the publisher; you are paid by the publisher after you've sold the space. Sometimes you may be given an advance for outgoings; these include arranging the printing of a rate card. For magazines, newspapers and journals you want to book as many series as possible – ie, a space regularly filled by the same advertiser. Rates vary according to size and positions of the advertisement and whether it's colour or black and white.

You'll spend a lot of time on the phone, but you may need to entertain major media buyers from time to time. There's a certain amount of cajoling involved but when you are dealing with advertising agencies you'll find that many are delighted to buy space on behalf of their clients. If you decide to expand the operation and take on your own staff you can pay them a small flat rate and a percentage of the commission that you're getting. It's a competitive business in which clients often move their accounts. You can't rest on your laurels for long.

Sports Retailer

Qualifications/Training	No
Income bracket	Low-High
Licence	No
Town/Country	Town
Experience/Springboard	Essential
Travel	No
Mid-career entry	Likely
Exit sale	Excellent

Entry costs	Highly variable
Work at home	No
Mix and match	Possible.

You could think about: ***Sailing school owner, Windsurfing school owner, Football commentator, Physiotherapist, Holiday accommodation owner***

Enquiries
Sports associations and local sports shops

General sports shops tend not to be able to offer the expert advice that is needed by people buying specialist equipment, eg riding or watersports. This means that there is little point in opening a specialist sports shop without having a lot of experience and enthusiasm for the sports involved. If you combine two sports, pick eg windsurfing and ski-ing whose seasons complement one another.

Shop experience is essential so you'll know how the business is run. It's particularly useful if you've worked for another specialist sports shop and so have a better idea of what you're getting into. As well as the usual attributes of a shopkeeper, you'll have to have the patience and stamina to spend a lot of time with each customer (allow about an hour to sell a set of ski-ing kit for example). They need individual attention so you should have at least one partner or employee with the necessary expertise to man the shop.

You'll need to rent or buy a shop with suitable storage space. Location is important, customers will travel up to about 35 miles but most will be local; don't open up too close to competition unless you think you can take over or survive on half its clientele. Most sports gear is bulky so you should try and have parking facilities.

Initially you have to get dealership of the brands you want to sell – this means convincing the manufacturers or their British distributors that you are a credible outlet for their goods and are not too close to a rival stockist. For some reason, although people only use sports equipment seasonally, many people buy bits and pieces (for tennis etc) throughout the year.

Aim to turn round your stock about four or five times a year.

Ski buying is different – about 90 per cent of the year's stock is delivered in September and October having been ordered the previous spring via trade fairs and visits to dealers. The equipment that you stock will be made to order by companies in France, Switzerland, Austria etc. This means that your requirements will have to be carefully predicted (not made easier by dependence on the weather and changing fashions in ski-wear and equipment). You may be able to make a few negotiations during the season but not many. You can pay for ski stock under various instalment schemes from the supplier. You'll build up a regular clientele, who will return to you every year to add or replace equipment and you can stock bits and pieces of more general equipment to keep people coming in regularly.

You can hire out ski equipment. Unless you're near one of the Scottish centres, most of your equipment will be used abroad (people don't like using new kit on dry slopes) so you won't have a demand for ski hire. But you may be able to hire out basic ski-ing outfits several times a season, which pays for them very quickly. Windsurf hire is totally dependent on access to water and good weather. You'll have to keep abreast of what's going on in the sport via the press – *Watersports Trade News, Ski Survey, Equestrian Trade News* etc. Contact the relevant body – eg SKI CLUB OF GREAT BRITAIN or the ASSOCIATION OF PROFESSIONAL BOARDSAILING CENTRES.

Stage Designer

Qualifications/Training	Necessary
Income bracket	Low-Medium
Licence	No
Town/Country	Town
Experience/ Springboard	Recommended

Travel	Local
Mid-career entry	Possible
Exit sale	No
Entry costs	£50
Work at home	Partly
Mix and match	Yes.

You could think about: *Illustrator, Artist, Stage technician carpenter, Book packager, Yoga teacher*

Enquiries
Theatrical agents, Equity

Stage designers design and build sets appropriate both for the production and the stage. They usually work from scale models, making sure that the lighting works and that a special scenic effect isn't going to block the audience's view. Commercial theatre is the most lucrative, but there are also openings in repertory, fringe and youth theatre, ballet and opera. Stage design is also used in film and TV, creating special effects, models of monsters and fantasy worlds, costumes and interiors. There are other openings in industrial theatre, eg for large promotional conventions which have to be produced, stage managed and publicised in much the same way as a piece of theatre. Most opportunities are in London but there is scope anywhere with a theatre – Edinburgh, Glasgow, Birmingham, Stratford etc.

As a designer, you don't have to be a member of EQUITY but it's advisable; they lay down minimum rates of pay but if you are sought after you get better rates. A course in theatre production and design is the starting point for anyone who wants to work in the theatre. As well as set design and construction you'll need to have a background knowledge of theatre, scene painting, props, lighting, management, publicity, special effects, costume cutting and making, construction and model making, technical drawing etc. Most freelance designers have been assistant stage hands at theatres before setting up on their own. Other good sources of experience and contacts are annual festivals, Glyndebourne etc, where freelance stage builders and painters are needed for the season. You'll need contacts (your college may have some

initial contacts with commercial, youth, repertory or fringe theatre); and it helps if you can offer some impressive experience (helping with designs for a West End show etc). Once you have established a reputation people will come to you, so you have to make a splash with your first designs. Read the *Stage*.

To find your first job you have to show people your portfolio and go to theatrical agents; you'll have to pay them commission for any work they get you, but they have contacts and will push for somebody they think is worth promoting. It is a competitive world and is often pressured. The theatre has tight deadlines to meet.

Stage Technician Carpenter

Qualifications/Training	Available
Income bracket	Low-Medium
Licence	No
Town/Country	Town
Experience/Springboard	Essential
Travel	Maybe
Mid-career entry	Possible
Exit sale	No
Entry costs	£250
Work at home	No
Mix and match	Possible.

You could think about: *Stage designer, Furniture designer/maker, Mini-cab driver, Photographer, Wood carver*

Enquiries
FE and drama colleges or local theatres

This is someone who builds, repairs, sets up and takes down stage scenery, in the theatre, or for TV or films.

Experience in the building trade is useful if you are lucky enough to get a rare apprenticeship. You can take a carpentry course at a further education college or a theatre technicians' course at a drama college. You need to be physically strong, and have practical skills, intelligence and quick reactions for striking or setting up a set at speed. You must be able to get on well with other people; not only to work in a team but, if you work as a master carpenter eventually, to organise and direct others. Punctuality is vital. It's essential to join the BECTU if you do TV and film work but not necessary in the theatre. To set up, you can get part-time work as a flyman (who pulls scenery up and down with a panto or musical where there are many scene changes). If reliable you can find a job as a full-time assistant carpenter. You will start by getting £90 a week plus overtime as a flyman (£40–£50 part-time) rising to £200+ a week as a master carpenter. Film and TV companies will pay £100 a day.

Setting up you will need to outlay a minimum of £80–£100 on tools. However, a proper tool kit is £600. You need a base with a phone, and someone or an answerphone to answer it.

There is a shortage of carpenters. Once it is known that you are good at your job, everyone wants you. You can work in the theatre; freelance with commercial TV and film companies, where there is a lot of money; or you can work for large set-building companies. It is possible to set up your own set-building business if you have good contacts and a good accountant.

The advantages of the job are the lack of routine and the interesting people you mix with. These make up for the lack of social life outside the theatre. In film and TV the work is irregular – it's possible to work 24 hours a day. This can also happen when you are changing complicated sets in opera, particularly if you are working on tour. You must be prepared to travel to find work unless you have plenty of contacts in a large city but it's possible to do other jobs between assignments. There are few women in this job because of the heavy lifting. New fly technology and developments such as rechargeable drills improve the job all the time. Useful magazines are the *Stage*, *TV Today* (for jobs), *Spotlight*.

Stockbroker

Qualifications/Training	Essential
Income bracket	Medium-High
Licence	Yes
Town/Country	Town
Experience/Springboard	Essential
Travel	Possible
Mid-career entry	Possible
Exit sale	Possible
Entry costs	£100,000++
Work at home	No
Mix and match	Possible.

You could think about: *Farmer, MP, Cabaret performer*

Enquiries
Stock Exchange, Securities Institute

Stockbrokers give advice to private clients, companies and institutions on investments. They also buy and sell these investments on behalf of clients. Private clients may be: discretionary – where the stockbroker has the power to buy/sell investments without reference each time to the client; or execution only – where the stockbroker merely does what he is asked to do. There are many different types of investment, but those considered for a private client's portfolio might include government stocks, debentures, loan stocks, shares in listed companies and 'derivatives' from them such as options and warrants, and unit trusts. There is no guarantee that the value of securities will go up and successful stockbroking depends on knowing the market well enough to be able to predict with some accuracy which investments are likely to realise the maximum profits, and to decide on a suitable strategy within each client's own investment needs – whether primarily income, capital growth or a combination of the two.

Almost all trading in shares in public companies and government stocks is carried out by registered dealers or representatives through the STOCK EXCHANGE, to which stockbroking firms must belong. London is one of the major world markets and dominates trading in the European time zone.

Since Big Bang, many City partnerships have been bought by financial institutions, some of them gigantic American, French, Japanese and Swiss banks. The trend has been for these to shed private investors. This means there are good opportunities for independent stockbrokers, especially outside London, who live amongst their clients and get to know them. Big Bang has also meant that all stockbrokers can deal directly by computer (the Stock Exchange Automated Quotation System – SEAQ). Recent Government policy aimed at wider share ownership, combined with Big Bang, has led to greater public awareness of the SE and to larger numbers of small investors using the services of stockbrokers – often through their own clearing bank.

First, join a member firm as a trainee (there are no formal requirements; trainees can be graduates, school leavers or from a related field). Your firm will provide training to help you pass the formal SE exams. After that you need £1,000 to pay to the SE and you're a member. A new professional body, the SECURITIES INSTITUTE, for practitioners in the securities, derivatives and investment management sphere, has taken over from the Stock Exchange the responsibility for the existing securities industry examinations and diploma and provides a range of qualifications and training.

Before a new firm can trade it has to be registered under the Financial Services Act (as a member of a self regulatory organisation or an exempted or 'Europerson'). A new firm must also become a corporate member of the SE which means conforming to its rule book on, eg, activities of directors and minimum liquidity margins, which are a significant percentage of your annual trading budget – a lot of money. Entry to the SE costs £10,000–£50,000, with a subscription of £1,000 pa thereafter. On top of this come the costs of running an office, settlement, secretarial and administrative back-up. Stockbrokers are paid commission on their transactions. Commission rates are no longer set by the Stock Exchange and are usually around 1.5 per cent of the value of the shares bought or sold, with a minimum charge rather like a cover charge in restaurants to protect the stockbroker against the cost of executing very many tiny transactions.

You'll need a good understanding of how investment works in general and to keep up with what's going on in various sectors. There are over 7,000 different securities traded on the Stock Exchange so most stockbrokers specialise in one sector (retail, heavy industry etc), keeping an eye on any changes or developments likely to affect long or short term investment prospects. Firms tend to have partners with complementary specialisations. A network of City and financial analyst contacts is useful for keeping up with what's going on. You will certainly need to read the *Financial Times* and *Investors Chronicle*.

By the time you're a partner/director in a new or existing firm, clients will come via personal and professional referrals. Small investors are likely to enthuse about their stockbrokers (as long as you're good) and provincial stockbrokers can provide a more personal service. You are likely to concentrate on the UK market when trading securities; diversify overseas through unit trusts if you want to develop a private client's portfolio into, say, Japan, rather than attempt to be expert in overseas securities yourself. There are opportunities for working an 18 or 20-hour day by dealing on foreign markets, but most stockbrokers manage not to. It's a stressful life especially in a bear market.

✦ European Community notes

As things currently stand you need to deal through a local broker in order to trade on continental exchanges. However, many European shares are traded in London, especially Blue Chips. Liberalisation of financial services in the Community means that cross-border services will probably increase and restrictions on foreign nationals trading disappear – so brush up your languages. The downside is that as foreign markets emulate London's uniquely liberal trading environment, its pre-eminence as the largest and most diverse trading centre in Europe will become eroded. All the more reason to investigate Europe.

Street Entertainer

Qualifications/Training	Useful
Income bracket	Low
Licence	Usually
Town/Country	Town
Experience/Springboard	No
Travel	Local
Mid-career entry	Possible
Exit sale	No
Entry costs	Nil
Work at home	No
Mix and match	Essential.

You could think about: *Cabaret performer, Puppeteer, Actor, Musician, Accountant*

Enquiries
Street entertainers

You can earn money, if not a particularly secure living, from entertaining passers-by in the street. Sometimes called buskers, street entertainers are quick to distinguish themselves from the image of tired old men shuffling through a few tap dance steps. The hours are flexible, so it's a good way of making extra money, especially for musicians, children's entertainers, actors or cabaret performers who may have stretches of free time during the day or evening while they aren't fulfilling conventional appointments. You aren't necessarily going to be picked up by a talent scout but you will be able to develop your skills while keeping the wolf from the door. Some prefer to limit outside performances to the summer; others find it a good way of helping to finance overseas travel. The street entertaining network is worldwide.

There are no formal qualifications. However, laws govern where and when you may perform on the street and (although arrests are rare) these are often rigorously enforced by the police and local traders who will send you off no matter how big the, as yet unpaying, crowd you may have attracted. It's advisable to work only in legally defined patches (and that means no straying even by a few yards) and for that you'll often need to get a licence. For this you have to pass an audition and your performance has to be unoffensive, socially and politically sound in the view of the licensers. In London the main centre for street performers is at Covent Garden (licences are controlled by the COVENT GARDEN MARKET MANAGEMENT); out of London performers are often allowed in market towns or at festivals and carnivals like EDINBURGH and GLASTONBURY. For some of these you'll have to book in advance so check with the organisers. Street entertainers are encouraged in many countries, especially in tourist centres, like Paris, Amsterdam and Copenhagen. Some street entertainers happen to be members of EQUITY but this is useful only when you're mixing and matching this with other professional performing.

Success is largely a matter of trial and error. Unlike conventional theatre where the audience shells out for a ticket in advance, street audiences only pay after they've seen the show – if they weren't amused or impressed they won't pay. You must be able to make people stop, stay, watch and pay. Everyone has their own ways of doing this; planting generous stooges who will ostentatiously give you fivers, borrowing money from a member of the audience, getting the audience involved, playing music, leaving open violin cases in the path of passers by, bullying the crowd to get them to pay and ridiculing anyone who doesn't. You can pick up some basic skills at a part- or full-time performance course and then develop your own show and extra skills such as magic tricks. No matter how well you may perform in front of the mirror or your admiring parents, there's no substitute for an audience. Good starting experience is in children's entertainment or for cabaret audiences; neither is likely to sit in polite silence if you haven't grabbed their attention. Street entertainers need to be outgoing, self-confident, sensitive to audience response and quick thinking enough to be able to capitalise on audience reaction and involvement. You have to please the audience which may mean being subtly patronising. Apart from props, there are no set up costs for street entertainers, but in general anyone who makes a living from entertaining or performing is likely to have to pay more for things like insurance (household insurance can carry as much as 50 per cent loading) and pension plans. For a half-hour show at somewhere like Covent Garden, you can expect to make anything from about £3 upwards (occasionally very good performers may collect £100) and for that you'll have had to do a lot of hanging around waiting for your pitch.

The network is extremely active. Read *Cascade*, the juggling monthly which has details of what's going on including the addresses of jugglers all over the world who will put up any visiting colleagues. You may be able to pick up some ideas from other performers especially if you're prepared to hand over any of your own which you can't use yourself (eg, time-sensitive jokes about current events). The downbeat of this is plagiarism; don't discuss the material you're developing for future use unless you want to see it being used by someone else.

European Community Notes

Some European tourist centres such as Paris, Amsterdam and Copenhagen seem almost to encourage street entertainers: no footage of the Metro exists without a flash of a whited-up mime artist or beret-toting saxophonist. Whatever the strict legal position, which varies with location, it takes some doing to match the officious hostility encountered on the London underground, for instance. Besides, the continental street life is so much greater, and the weather – in the south, at least – so much more clement – beaches, too – that your audience and opportunities are greatly increased, if nothing else then, to subsidise travelling. As ever, the best source of information is others who have tried it.

Stylist

Qualifications/Training	Useful
Income bracket	Low-High
Licence	No
Town/Country	Town
Experience/Springboard	Essential
Travel	Yes
Mid-career entry	Possible
Exit sale	No
Entry costs	£300+
Work at home	Partly
Mix and match	Yes.

You could think about: *Magazine designer, Graphic designer, Illustrator, Wine merchant*

Enquiries
Association of Fashion, Advertising and Editorial Photography

For all but true photo-journalism, every photograph has to be styled (or arranged) to some extent. Often the photographers themselves will do the work, but with more elaborate pictures, a stylist is involved, collecting necessary props, and arranging them, or helping to arrange them, to create the desired effect.

On major home interest and fashion magazines, for example, a stylist will be employed to check that all the necessary accessories (flowers, clothes etc) are borrowed from manufacturers or agencies, hired or bought when necessary, and brought to the studio or location where the photography will take place, so that the photographer's valuable time is not wasted. They are usually employed by the magazine but there are openings for good freelance stylists – to help with rush jobs, take over when in-house stylists are not well, or fill in if there is a gap between one stylist leaving a magazine and a new member of staff being found.

When it comes to photography for advertising, the advertising agents will dictate a style, and it will be up to the stylist, usually in conjunction with the photographer, to select appropriate props. Some are hired, others have to be bought. So for an advertising shot for, say, wine, involving a glamorous lady lying back on a chaise longue in a stately home, the stylist may have to find and hire a location, hire any furniture that is needed, book a model, hire or buy a suitable outfit, choose the right style of glass for the drink, and hire a make-up artist. And be ready to change everything at the drop of a hat if the model turns up with a boil on her nose, the chosen glass is dropped half way through the session, or the owner of the location refuses to let the photographer run his electric cables across the hallway.

Most stylists start by working on magazines as full time employees, as layout artists, editorial assistants or sub editors, depending on the structure of the magazine. They may also come from the advertising side, moving on from copywriting or designing. Some design qualifications are useful, but not essential. It is helpful to get to know plenty of photographers, photographic editors of magazines, and art directors of advertising agencies. Being in the right place at the right time is all-important.

Stylists are usually paid on a daily rate: from about £60 for editorial work to £300 for top notch advertising work. The only essential equipment is an answerphone and a huge contacts (address) book. It is also useful to have your own business cards. Which you can pin up on noticeboards in photographers' studios close to the phone, to keep your name in front of as many of the right people as possible. You can usually work from home, or use the studio where the photo session is to be.

A cheerful disposition, wit, and an ability to manipulate people who are too big for their boots are essential qualifications.

⁂ **European Community Notes**
Qualifications: UK qualifications recognised in EC except Belgium and Germany; in UK, no required qualifications, unless permanently relocating.
Languages: To succeed, local language necessary.

Earnings: UK income generally same as elsewhere in the EC.
Setting up: You will find it difficult to succeed in Belgium, France, Germany, Luxembourg. You will find it easier in Denmark, Eire, Greece, Italy, Netherlands, Portugal, Spain. This depends on individual talents but Belgium, France, Germany and Luxembourg have a large indigenous threshold to break through. Languages are essential and intense market research to establish needs, trends and fashions.
Advice/Training: Advice, information and training not available for those wishing to work in Europe.
Exchanges: Formal job exchanges do not exist.

Sub editor

Qualifications/Training	Recommended
Income bracket	Low-Medium
Licence	No
Town/Country	Town
Experience/Springboard	Yes
Travel	No
Mid-career entry	Possible
Exit sale	No
Entry costs	Nil
Work at home	No
Mix and match	Excellent.

You could think about: *Novelist, Proofreader/copy editor, almost anything*

Enquiries
National Union of Journalists

The sub-editor is the link between the written article and the printed page for newspapers and magazines, including part-works (cf copy editors for books). You are the process through which the masters of the written word – the fevered reporter with a story that burns, the pungent star columnist with telling bon mots, the dazzlingly witty award-winning feature writer

– reach the outside world. No wonder it's so bloody tricky sometimes.

Generally, you're working in a team, under a chief sub-editor or production editor feeding you tasks to discharge at great speed and send back to him or her, often via a 'revise sub' making encouraging remarks like 'the title is *Carrington*, the family name is *Carington*' or 'Call that a headline?'. The level of input varies, but in essence, as a common or garden 'downtable' sub, when the copy comes to you you'll have to take care of some, most or all of the following areas.

Facts (to a point): some titles notoriously have a 'fact thing', where nothing appears in print that hasn't been laboriously checked – so, knowing how to look things up helps. Most of the time you'll take *some* of the writer's efforts at face value. But you'll need to add what they left out, eg things they think they have explained but haven't because they are too overburdened with specialist knowledge or too close to the subject to accommodate those who unfortunately aren't.

Spelling, grammar, punctuation: the concept is straightforward, the practice not always (see Style). Cutting stories to fit the allotted space, and the 'furniture' – headlines and any cross-heads, picture captions, introductions or 'standfirsts', 'readthroughs' or quotes pulled out of the copy and so on. Other tasks, though less likely to devolve to casuals or new bugs, include some input on the layout and design front and, on some systems, dealing with typesetting instructions and even electronic page make-up, undeniably the coming thing.

Then there is Style – not necessarily as interesting as it sounds, this is sometimes reduced to 'Is worldwide one word, two words or hyphenated?' As arbiter, some insist on the *Oxford Dictionary for Writers and Editors* – and *Oxford Dictionary* to match – but this is rather retarded on *real* usage, as appropriate for live publications. Far richer is the *Economist Style Guide* – like the magazine, informative, entertaining and at times ineffably smug – and, like the magazine, know your way round it and (if nothing else) you'll certainly give a convincing appearance of knowing your

way around. Good dictionaries include Chambers and Collins.

But ultimately, house style is the guide to house practice. Does the publication make a point of avoiding capitals on eg trade secretary, general election; full points after initials; titles and honorifics at every repetition – famously the affectation of mediocre columnists ('Mr' Mick Jagger), but widely preferred in stories? Obviously, too, on a specialist journal, say, you would make more use of jargon, acronyms and so on because of the readers' familiarity with the subject. You just have to find out and then follow whatever they do wherever you are.

Finally, inevitably, you have to deal with the writing – and that's where the problems can really start. Just as no man is a hero to his valet . . . wait till you see your favourite columnist in the raw. But if they're worth their salt they'll recognise 'your contribution' – certainly anyone who's suffered at the hands of bad subs will. The old advice for subs was to take out the first line, last line, most of the adjectives, all of the jokes – but that may have been a joke (though it sometimes bears thinking about . . .). But there are writers so precious that they can't conceive how a single iota of their copy can possibly be modified. Some writers complain about you removing all their colour. 'You've taken out all my nunceal values' complained one columnist, who regularly writes of 'new stars in the fundament', 'going off at a tandem', and – a particular favourite – things that 'really get up my goat'. If it's wrong, or bad, or stupid, change it – that's what you're paid for; but be ready to justify the change.

As far as getting started goes, there are sub-editing courses – eg LONDON COLLEGE OF PRINTING, and so on. But qualifications won't get you work like experience will. Trade mags are the traditional way in, or perhaps provincial newspapers. As far as job ads go there is the *Guardian* on Mondays and the *UK Press Gazette* for newspapers. Once you're up and running though, this is one of those deeply networky roles where people are forever asking other people: 'Do you know any decent subs?' – let the answer be

Yes and the name yours. You can write to the chief sub-editor of a publication or particular desk on it (phone the switchboard to establish the name first) then follow up with a phone call; if they're hiring they are at least *interested*.

If you want to work around, especially on newspapers, it's probably essential that you are properly steeped in technology. There are courses which will help if you can't learn as you work: a few years ago it was easier, when the technology was new and the publication was more likely to give you a grounding in how to use it. Now more often than not you'll be expected to know it already. The more systems you're familiar with the better: word-processing software, mainly for PCs, for many mags – though Apple Macs are widely used – and in-house systems for newspapers eg SII, Atex. Also, as noted, full electronic page make-up is increasingly common, with mags asking for Quark Xpress experience or similar.

Diligence, accuracy, speed, unsurprisingly, are highly regarded, but 'cleverness' gets you noticed as a casual/freelance, especially good headlines with plenty of word play, punning, etc, and hired again. While as a sub you will never attain the heights that other freelance journalistic roles do, good subs are always valued (partly because there are so many dopey ones) and – when there is any – you should always reasonably well paid work.

NATIONAL UNION OF JOURNALISTS minimum rates for newspapers and the richer or glossier mags are around the £100 a day mark (ie, eight-hour shift including an hour break) – up to £20 less for more modest mags, provincial papers – plus £10–£15 per hour beyond that; not too deadly if there's a lot on and when the chief sub declares shifts-and-a-half all round. And you could work from breakfast-time through till the middle of the night, seven days a week on different publications with different schedules – though it is not recommended you do that too often.

As a freelance, obviously work is precarious. You want to get a reputation as being available at short notice and ready to oblige – especially more antisocial hours such as working Sundays or covering on a Bank Holiday when regular staff are off – but do try and give yourself some time off, holidays etc otherwise you go bananas. Part-time contracts can be had – say Saturday afternoons throughout the soccer season or press day on a weekly magazine, to mix in with your other work, such as writing at home (journalism gets you out of the house). A mixture of different types of publications and offices is definitely recommended to stop things becoming too stale.

Sub Postmaster

Qualifications/Training	Yes
Income bracket	Low–Medium
Licence	Yes
Town/Country	Town/Village
Experience/Springboard	No
Travel	No
Mid-career entry	Excellent
Exit sale	Yes
Entry costs	£1,000++
Work at home	No
Mix and match	Yes.

You could think about: *Shopkeeper, Publican, Kennel/cattery owner, Garden centre, Calligrapher*

Enquiries
District postmaster

Sub-post offices are a popular escape from the rat race because they offer a secure way of running your own business; sub postmasters are paid by the post office, which they can combine with another business (village shop, chemist, newsagent, pub etc) from the same premises. The post office brings in trade for this.

You can apply to the Head Postmaster of the district to start a sub-post office, but as (in the Post Office's view) there are too many already this is unlikely to prove successful. Alternatively you find one up for sale in *Dalton's Weekly* (price ranges from about £75,000–£300,000). In either case you apply to the district Head Postmaster and are called for an interview. The two main planks of the interview are reliability and cash/collateral, so that you are unlikely to be caught with your fingers in the till.

If accepted, you get four weeks free tuition with someone from Head Office sitting beside you. Post Office Counters ask for 15 per cent of the previous year's takings in advance. Income is based on units which in turn are based on varying percentages on all transactions including pensions, stamps, Giro, National Savings, etc. There is a range of about 140 different items for an average sub-post office to select from. Income ranges from about £1,100 to about £60,000. If you're working alone you should be able to cope with enough PO work to earn you about £12,500 pa.

It is recommended that a first-timer buys a post office without mails (ie no vans, postmen's pay, deliveries etc) which includes most sub-post offices in towns and cities. Also that you obtain a good lease rather than a freehold.

Head Office carries out an audit about twice a year, although this tends to be irregular. The business can be built up by applying for more transactions such as Motor Vehicle Tax, normally carried out by GPOs, so increasing your units and so your income.

Losses in a sub-post office come out of the sub postmaster's pocket, so accuracy is of prime importance. The principal requirements for the job, other than re-liability and cash are a basic knowledge of mathematics and the ability to be polite and friendly to infuriating customers who don't know what they want and become abusive because you haven't got it.

Surveyor

Qualifications/Training	Essential
Income bracket	Medium-High
Licence	For financial advice
Town/Country	Both (+ sea)
Experience/ Springboard	Recommended
Travel	Yes
Mid-career entry	Possible
Exit sale	Possible
Entry costs	£7,500++
Work at home	Possible
Mix and match	Possible.

You could think about: *Estate agent, Property developer, House converter, Landlord, Builder*

Enquiries
Royal Institution of Chartered Surveyors

Wherever there is land, property or construction, you will find chartered surveyors at work. They are instrumental in developing and maintaining the very visible environments which effect all of our lives: shopping, leisure complexes, airports, industrial buildings, industrial estates, office blocks, docklands, housing, historic buildings, woodlands, oil rigs, theme parks, mineral deposits, agriculture, navigation channels, golf courses, pipelines, process plants, antiques . . . The ROYAL INSTITUTION OF CHARTERED SURVEYORS (RICS) issues rules and codes of practice and news of any relevant new technology or legislation.

Before establishing a practice as a chartered surveyor you will need to be either an associate or a fellow of the RICS. For this you need an accredited surveying degree and two–three years' probationary experience culminating in a professional exam. Alternatively if you have a non-related degree you can do an MSC lasting one–three years to qualify. You may also need a licence (eg if you're going to give mortgage advice). Surveyors need to be meticulous and painstaking; able to alternate between working from an office and scrambling around on roofs. You have to work under pressure and are often involved with other professions (solicitors, etc) which can entail conflicts of schedule.

Get as much experience as possible (public authorities can provide good varied work, if you can stand it). Once you feel ready to set up on your own, you'll need to decide whether to be a sole practitioner or whether to set up or join a partnership or a company. Consult an accountant and solicitor before entering into partnership. You can buy into an existing partnership, usually one where you have done your probation or associateship. Set-up costs (or the costs of buying into an existing partnership) can be advanced from banks, merchant banks, and insurance companies.

The RICS Professional Conduct Department has a very useful package for members who wish to set up their own business. The main expense is insurance, as well as public liability, you should insure against loss of fees and have personal insurance. The RICS outlines rules which stipulate that you have professional indemnity which costs around £50.00 per week. The RICS will also help with recommended scales of charges for quantity and certain building surveying services. The RICS pack also provides wording for letters to new clients as it is vitally important for you to survive. Once successfully established the RICS helps you recruit professional staff as your workload increases.

✸✶✱ European Community Notes

Qualifications: There is no equivalent qualification to the chartered surveyor in Europe. Not all UK qualifications recognised in EC, nor EC qualifications in UK. It varies by activity and country; there is no complete match between what British surveyors do and what is done by professionals in each European country.

Languages: To succeed, local language necessary.

Earnings: UK income comparable to elsewhere in the EC.

Setting up: You will find it possible to succeed in Belgium, Denmark, Eire, France, Germany, Italy, Luxembourg, Netherlands, Portugal. You will find it difficult in Greece and Spain.

Advice/Training: Advice, information and training available for those wishing to work in Europe from RICS which will put you in touch with local professional bodies for detailed regulations.

Exchanges: Formal job exchanges do not exist.

Enquiry point for those wishing to work in the EC: ROYAL INSTITUTION OF CHARTERED SURVEYORS (European Section, International Affairs)

Recommended reading: General Practice Guide to the Single European Market

Because of the very different professional practices in each country you are particularly ill-advised simply to head off to the country of your choice and try to open up a new practice. Before you set off, learn the local language and get a job in British firms already operating locally. Learn the local ropes, then begin to look around for your own opportunity.

Swimming Teacher

Qualifications/Training	Essential
Income bracket	Low–Medium
Licence	No
Town/Country	Town
Experience/Springboard	Useful
Travel	Local
Mid-career entry	Good
Exit sale	No
Entry costs	Nil–£50
Work at home	No

Mix and match Excellent. You could think about: *Teacher, Yoga teacher, Puppeteer, Musician, Football commentator, Driving instructor, Stylist, Book-keeper*

Enquiries
Amateur Swimming Association, Royal Life Saving Society

It's not enough to like swimming and enjoy working with people in this job, you've got to have a real interest and ability in teaching too. The bulk of your clients will be children, so you need to be able to get along with them – and their parents. But more adults are taking swimming lessons as they find themselves conspicuous in the Mediterranean (or beyond) if they don't swim, in the way they weren't on Blackpool Sands. So it's an advantage to be able to manage tactfully macho-men with a self-image dented by admitting to a fear of water. Some will need to be got afloat, others to improve their strokes.

You shouldn't consider teaching swimming without a recognised first-aid qualification and lifesaving training (eg Bronze Medallion of the ROYAL LIFE SAVING SOCIETY). Although some private clients may take you without, you should also have the appropriate AMATEUR SWIMMING ASSOCIATION (ASA) qualifications – the Preliminary Swimming Teacher's Certificate (allows you to assist a qualified teacher), a Teacher's Certificate (qualifies you to teach on your own) and maybe even an Advanced Teacher's Certificate. These courses allow you to get people afloat and to perfect their strokes, start diving and learn some water skills and safety. The are specialist courses (and a variety of ASA specialist certificates) which qualify you to teach eg disabled children, antenatal swimming, synchronised swimming, diving, or to coach professional swimmers. Typically, a Teacher's Certificate course can take one week residential, a day a week for six weeks or four hours a week for 12 weeks, the ASA will tell you where courses are run locally. Once you are qualified, you can keep up-to-date with the help of the ASA, which runs swimming seminars, has an excellent teaching book and publishes *Swimming Times*. Other useful books are *Swimming Teaching and Coaching to Level 1* and *Teaching Your Child To Swim*; *ASA Teaching and Coaching Certificates* spells out the details of each ASA qualification.

Although many schools and swimming pools have swimming teachers on their staff, many also use freelancers; approach them direct. Once you have your own clients, you can pay your local swimming pool to allow you to teach in their pool; this can give you more flexibility about your clients and hours. Your clients will range from three-year-olds to adults, although 90 per cent are likely to be children. The majority will be able to float and swim to some extent but want to improve their technique and breathing; few are up to butterfly standard in the average pool. Adults have often developed bad habits which need correcting; non-swimming adults take a long time to get going.

It is a job which can easily be combined with one or more others, as you can choose your own hours, within reason – no point in expecting children to flood in during school hours if you're not working for a school. Best time for *them* is after school (4 pm–7 pm) and at weekends. If you are paid by the school/pool, you will get around £7 per hour for teaching individually, £8 per hour for group teaching, slightly more for teaching in schools; if you are paid by your clients, you can charge what you think they will pay – up to £12 per hour.

Very few people are unable to learn to swim and, for the right person, there is a real buzz to be got from turning the timid mite who is terrified of the water into a confident swimmer somersaulting for fun. The kids who have not had much of a chance are more rewarding than the spoilt brats – and aspiring parents are major wreckers of the job satisfaction. You need to be energetic and it is a physically demanding job – eight hours a day, five days a week will more than take it out of you, even if you're fit. Chlorinated water will ruin your skin and scalp and you'll need the voice of a sergeant major to be heard in most swimming pools.

European Community Notes

The ASA qualifications are recognised all over European Community and by swimming associations in all EC countries. It is obviously helpful (and arguably safer) to be able to speak the same language as your clients; so either go where you speak the language or where there are English-speakers in residence or on holiday.

Tt

Tailor

Qualifications/Training	Available
Income bracket	Low–Medium
Licence	No
Town/Country	Town
Experience/ Springboard	Recommended
Travel	No
Mid-career entry	Possible
Exit sale	Possible
Entry costs	£2,000
Work at home	Not recommended
Mix and match	Possible.

You could think about: *Fashion retailer, Wedding shop owner, Costume designer, Import/export broker, Graphologist*

Enquiries
Tailors

In spite of the ready availability of off-the-peg suits from chain stores there is a demand for independent tailors who will make suits to their clients' measurements and carry out repairs on their own and other suits. Although from time to time you may be asked to fit and make suits for women, most of your clients will be men who want suits of traditional design with a few modifications according to current fashions (size of lapel, cut of trousers etc). Most tailors' clients tend not to be interested in innovative suit design although you could make a name for yourself in that area and attract those who are.

The traditional way in involves years of hard and badly paid apprenticeship. It takes three years to learn the basics of the trade. After that you need another two years at least specialising in cutting, trouser-making, jacket-making, or fitting. If you don't want to do it this way, you'll have to be very good at fitting and making suits, have some contacts who will use you and have some experience of working in a tailor's shop so that you can give your customers the sort of service they expect. Each tailor has a slightly different style and uses slightly different methods so, the more you see, the more variety you will have from which to develop your own style. As well as being good at sewing, you'll have to keep full records of customers' details.

To set up you need a sewing machine, needles, scissors, tape measure etc and also a work room. Ideally, premises should be fairly central to attract passing trade and also near offices so that customers can visit you easily for fittings. This means that it costs a lot to rent or buy a suitable shop and some tailors visit their customers at home or the office for fittings.

You can charge a deposit when you take an order but the bulk of what you're paid comes once the suit has been finished to the customer's satisfaction. Customers select the fabric from samples that you have from the suppliers. Fabric comes from the mills in Scotland, Yorkshire etc. You may have to shop around until you find one that will supply the comparatively small quantities that independent tailors need. Initially clients come from contacts; people you have fitted at previous employers; clients spread the word and the suits themselves are a walking advertisement. New clients are attracted by competitive prices, and good cuts and fits. Once you're off the ground, you'll have to employ assistance or subcontract some of the work.

It is important not to rest on your laurels once you start being successful. You have to keep in with your clients and not neglect your old customers. A lot of success depends on your ability to get on with your clients. You also have to be very exacting with those who work for you and be prepared to work long hours yourself.

Tattooist

Qualifications/Training	No
Income bracket	Low-Medium
Licence	Yes
Town/Country	Town
Experience/Springboard	No
Travel	No
Mid-career entry	Possible
Exit sale	No
Entry costs	£5,000
Work at home	Possible
Mix and match	Possible.

You could think about: *Makeup artist, Private investigator, Antique dealer, Taxidermist*

Enquiries
European Tattoo Artists Association

Unless you have a lot of contacts in the trade or have been born into it, there is little point in attempting to set up a new tattooing business in most places. There are more men than women but this matters less than who you are and where you come from. Recent Aids and hepatitis scares have made some people wary of tattoos – although the risks are reduced by the

health and safety regulations. But then, in some circles now, a tattoo is a must.

No formal qualifications or training courses are available. Tattooists learn through practice on family and friends until they feel confident enough to start charging. By law, you must be registered by your local Health Authority who will inspect the premises and check up on you from time to time to make sure that your practice is hygienic. Tattooists have to be able to make their own designs and to reproduce them on human skin, so there is no room for error. Some also do ear-piercing or removal of old tattoos, and there is some cosmetic work on scars etc. A few work on animals for identification purposes but a completely different set of equipment is needed for this. You need a very steady hand. The hours you work are up to you and depend on the amount of business you get.

As well as premises you will need needles, sterilising equipment, colours etc. Most of this is handed on from other tattooists, but to buy it new would probably cost about £5,000. Tattooists mix their own colours from natural lead and zinc-free pigments. This is a very secret operation because there are certain tricks to mixing colours that will keep under the skin. What you charge varies, probably from about £1.50 for a name to £30 for a large tattoo. A good tattooist can expect to do a large tattoo eg, arm-sized, in about two hours as long as the client can bear it.

Much work comes from regular customers who know and trust you. Contacts are all important because the existing tattooing business has a strong hold over suppliers etc and without their co-operation you probably won't be able to open. The EUROPEAN TATTOO ARTISTS FEDERATION is a self-regulating body. Tattooists see an unusual view of life. They have to cope with a great many of their clients passing out and should know how to cope with that. It also helps to be fairly tough (black belt in karate perhaps) because you will have to deal with some fairly strange people and may not want to have to comply with their requests.

Certainly, tattooing will never make you rich. For most of those who practise it, it is a part-time occupation, but the cost of equipping a studio far outstrips any compatible pursuit. Most practitioners have a main occupation like engraving or sign-writing and tattoo by appointment. One noted practitioner ('Painless Jeff') always recommends sign-writing – initially at least – to aspiring tattooists: the techniques are similar, it's far cheaper to start up and any damage is more easily remedied.

Read any graphic art mags, *Memoirs of a Tattooist* and *Pierced Hearts and True Love*.

European Community Notes

Qualifications: UK qualifications recognised throughout EC but EC qualifications not accepted in UK.

Languages: To succeed, local language necessary

Earnings: UK income generally lower than elsewhere in the EC.

Setting up: You will find it difficult to succeed in France, Greece, Italy, Luxembourg, Portugal, Spain.

You will find it possible in Belgium, Denmark, Eire, Germany, Netherlands.

Advice/Training: Advice, information and training not available for those wishing to work in Europe.

Exchanges: Formal job exchanges do not exist.

Enquiry point for those wishing to work in the EC: M. Bernard, 18 rue de l'Abbé Groult, 75015 Paris, France, tel. 45 32 06 44.

Notes: On the whole, most European countries do not at present have the regulations governing tattooing that the UK does – always enquire locally about special restrictions. Tattooists in Europe are accused of any number of nefarious activities to supplement their incomes – though in major sea ports they are said to make ends meet from tattooing alone. But tattooing is most popular in the UK – and in religious/Latin countries it is really abhorred!

Taxi Driver

Qualifications/Training	Yes
Income bracket	Low-High
Licence	Yes
Town/Country	Either
Experience/Springboard	No
Travel	Yes
Mid-career entry	Yes
Exit sale	No
Entry costs	£500++
Work at home	No
Mix and match	Possible.

You could think about: *Garage owner, Street entertainer, Bookie, Painter/decorator*

Enquiries
Licensed Taxi Drivers Association

As a licensed cab driver you can ply for hire in the streets and taxi ranks which mini-cab drivers can't. You can also take passengers who contact the taxi company. The vehicles cabbies drive tend to be of a standard design, to carry up to five passengers and baggage. In major cities they are often built to a special design with diesel engines, still often referred to as black cabs although the colour can vary.

To get a licence you will have to pass various tests which vary depending on the local authority that governs them. These are especially stringent in London where after registering at the PUBLIC CARRIAGE OFFICE you will go through medical and police vetting before going on to 'The Knowledge' which is details of all routes and street names within six miles of Charing Cross. You learn this by driving around on a motor bike teaching yourself the routes from specially provided maps; alternatively some garages run schools. This culminates in a driving test in a taxi; it usually takes about a year and a half to pass.

Once through all of that you can work. Taxi drivers are self-employed and operate through companies (rather like co-operatives). You can hire a cab from the company for either a weekly rent or a cut of your takings but to make proper money you really need your own cab – they cost up to £16,000 new, though they can be bought secondhand, and will need to be well-maintained. The local authority which awards licences controls maximum fares and taxis have meters which indicate how much to charge on each journey. Tips are always in cash.

Licensed cab drivers are subject to certain rules (depending on where they are). For instance, once you've stopped to pick up a passenger you must carry them anywhere within a six mile radius; but you don't have to stop for anyone. There is no legal limit on the number of hours you can work. The busy times are usually in mornings and evenings. You can expect to cover about 30,000 miles each year – more if you work at night, which avoids the stress of driving in traffic jams all day.

Further information from the LICENSED TAXI DRIVERS ASSOCIATION which also publishes *Taxi*.

Taxidermist

Qualifications/Training	Available
Income bracket	Low
Licence	Yes (to sell British birds)
Town/Country	Either
Experience/ Springboard	Recommended
Travel	Local
Mid-career entry	Yes
Exit sale	No
Entry costs	£100+
Work at home	Yes
Mix and match	Yes.

You could think about: *Artist, Book packager, Embalmer, Accountant*

Enquiries
Guild of Taxidermists

Taxidermists preserve dead animals. Popular taste and legislation aimed at protecting endangered species has lessened the demand for mounting pets or big game trophies. Most of the work you'll do will be on fish, legal game birds, deer and road casulties. There's no need to work regular hours so you could mix and match taxidermy with another job. The way to learn is to find a commercial taxidermist who is willing to teach you; the GUILD OF TAXIDERMISTS may be able to help, and its journal is worth reading. The Guild have meetings with lectures in specialist areas such as bird mounting, modelling rocks and mounts, and there's a range of books from the general *Taxidermy* to specialist works like *Symmetric System of Big Game Head Mounting*. If you want job experience, try approaching a local taxidermist and your local museum, You'll need a good knowledge of natural history to be dextrous and artistic enough to finish up with something that looks very like a living animal.

Basic equipment costs about £50–£100. You need knives, scalpels and forceps, scissors and supplies of syringes, pins, wire, thread, needles, tape and glue. In addition you need supplies of preserving chemicals, modelling materials (tow and wood pulp) and putty. Once you've got a commission you have to select imitation eyes and an animal form on which you sew the preserved skin. Base your charges on materials plus time. If you're hiring out mounted animals, charge a percentage of their value; remember they may need to be cleaned when you get them back and make sure clients know they're responsible for damages. Repairs are difficult because of having to match, for example, legs or beaks, and it is hard to 'relax' mounted specimens. Mounted animals must be kept in a dry cool place and be treated carefully. Replacement, especially of endangered species, can be very difficult.

Taxidermy isn't a glamorous career, many lay people find it funny and do not understand the skill required. There is a small market for preserving pets but this is a very difficult area and perhaps worth avoiding as the customer will expect the finished piece to show a character that they alone could see when it was alive. Most work comes by word of mouth, but *Yellow*

Pages is a good place to advertise. Never handle an endangered or protected species unless you're sure and can prove that it died of natural causes. Under the Wildlife and Countryside Act you risk heavy fines even if it's someone else's illegal acquisition you're in possession of; big auction houses have been known to suffer heavy penalties for handling – unwittingly – illegally obtained specimens. Full records must be kept of all specimens in your possession showing that they were obtained legally. British birds and protected mammals cannot be sold without a licence from the DEPARTMENT OF THE ENVIRONMENT.

European Community Notes

Qualifications: UK qualifications recognised throughout EC and EC qualifications in UK.
Languages: To succeed, local language necessary.
Setting up: You will find it difficult to succeed throughout Europe, though Eire is easier. You will need to check local laws.
Advice/Training: Advice, information and training not available for those wishing to work in Europe.
Exchanges: Formal job exchanges do not exist.

Teacher

Qualifications/Training	Essential
Income bracket	Low
Licence	Yes (state schools)
Town/Country	Either
Experience/ Springboard	Not necessary
Travel	Local
Mid-career entry	Yes
Exit sale	No
Entry costs	Nil
Work at home	No

Mix and match	Excellent.

You could think about: ***Classical singer, Tutor, Novelist, Potter, List broker, Desk-top publisher***

Enquiries
Teaching as a Career (Department of Education & Science)

If you like children, are flexible and a good communicator and want to run your own life, you can be a supply teacher – a qualified teacher who covers for absent teachers in state schools, rather like a locum does for a GP. (In the independent sector, it is up to the school what qualifications are demanded.)

It's largely a graduate profession but there are now four routes into it. The traditional routes are by taking a four-year degree which gives qualified teacher status (usually a BEd but increasingly a BA/BSc Ed); or taking a degree (usually three years) followed by a PGCE (post-graduate certificate in education). Some believe the BEd route is better because you get more teaching experience; others that a standard degree + PGCE keeps your options open for longer and gives a wider experience. Two rather different routes have now been opened which allow you to earn as you learn. If you are over 26 and have spent at least a couple of years in higher education, the Licensed Teacher scheme enables you to learn by working under licence for one–three years, paid by the local education authority; it's a way of attracting mid-career entry. If you want a professional training but feel you have had enough of college learning, you can become an Articled Teacher for two years; 80 per cent of the training is on the job, the rest in college although the college is involved in the school training too. You get paid £5,500–£6,500 (plus £1,000 in London).

Whichever route you take, you qualify to teach in either a primary or a secondary school. As a primary teacher, you are expected to teach everything from science to music, regardless of your own skills or enthusiasms (you can also do some secondary teaching). As a secondary teacher, you will cover two subjects only but must be able to cope with adolescents.

You can be a supply teacher straight after qualifying and you'll sort out your ideas on the job fast; some reckon you'll learn more about education in a year as a supply teacher than two or more years in one school. The choice of work for the supply teacher increases with teacher shortages. You can do the odd day/week or settle in for a term or school year. You register with your local education authority(ies). They will check your qualifications; some will interview you; *each* will check for any criminal record (which is with you for life if you are working with children) and this can take up to two months before you can be added to their list. Then you will be contacted when work arises, either by the education offices or directly by the Heads. You can always turn down a particular job without giving your reasons but you won't be the teacher asked first if you do it too often. If you don't want regular work, you can phone the offices when you are available.

Each school has a different ethos so you need to be adaptable and should leave most of your preconceptions at home. In a primary school, starting the day with something fun can help – the children may resent your being there and play you up, so you need to be able to assert yourself. For the odd day/week, it is best to plan the day so it doesn't matter too much what they've already covered – don't go in determined that today is the day for them to learn fractions. As a secondary teacher, you are more likely to be given a room for the day and different groups of children will pass through every forty minutes or so. In many subjects they will be busy on their set syllabus; what you cover and how well you are briefed is likely to depend on how close they are to public exams.

Unless you visit the school often, you will not know the school's discipline code and may find a surprising variety in the standards of behaviour. The Head and staff are normally supportive and you will usually be included in the traditional Friday pub sessions.

You will gain confidence very quickly and be able to observe different teaching methods. You can become a supply teacher at any stage, so can easily mix it with another job – provided you don't expect to make any money from it. Read the *Times Educational Supplement*.

✶✶✶ European Community Notes

Qualifications: UK qualifications not at present recognised in EC; EC qualifications accepted in UK from 1993. EC governments are dragging their feet and the position is not likely to change until a government is taken to court – then it may change fast.

Languages: To succeed, local language necessary unless teaching English.

Setting up: You will find it difficult to succeed, particularly in France and Germany.

Advice/Training: Advice, information and training not available for those wishing to work in Europe.

Exchanges: A few formal job exchanges exist for those employed in schools. If you can work as an English language assistant as part of a design course, it will give good experience.

Enquiry point for those wishing to work in the EC: DES

Telesales Person

Qualifications/Training	No
Income bracket	Low-Medium
Licence	No
Town/Country	Both
Experience/ Springboard	Not necessary
Travel	No
Mid-career entry	Excellent
Exit sale	No
Entry costs	Nil
Work at home	Yes
Mix and match	Good.

You could think about: *Desk-top publisher, Interior designer, Magazine publisher, English language teacher*

Enquiries
Telesales companies advertising in local and national newspapers

As you slam down the phone on yet another telesales person wanting to know why you haven't replaced nasty Victorian windows with nice new aluminium ones you may be inclined to think that you, the potential customer, are telesales' sole target. Wrong: much of telesales effort is business to business, selling office equipment, space (in magazines and newspapers), office accommodation, recruitment, financial, travel and a host of business services. While there's certainly room for the salesperson who'll charm the pants off the average housewife, a businesslike approach to business is essential.

It's a person-to-person job so, apart from the need to be able to brandish perhaps a GCSE or two (maths and English are usually enough to demonstrate your fit and active mind), your voice is your principal asset. You can't do much about your sex – it's said that men do as well as women on the whole – but, fat businessmen being fat businessmen, the female voice is highly valued for its persuasive qualites. Regional accents can be an advantage for the sake of a fresh approach, but some accents are more persuasive than others: Scottish and Irish are persuasive; unclear or muffled voices a turn-off. Mature voices are preferred.

Apart from your voice you'll need quite identifiable personal qualities: a competitive nature (the whole thing is a bit of a game – Who Sells Wins), ambition and confidence; you'll need to be alert and a good communicator (friendly and charming but efficient); and the most taxing of all, you need to be able to keep a positive frame of mind to ride out the countless rejections.

Statistically, you get most rejections when cold calling, and it's cold calling where you'll inevitably start. After you've won your spurs phoning secretaries whose general reaction is to hang up on you, you may be trusted to move up to dealing with account customers and, later still, negotiating deals with company directors. At this stage you may be invited to become an established rep, abandoning the telephone + jersey + jeans for an executive briefcase + calling card + collar and tie. Telesales persons by tradition tend not to stay long in one job. It's easy to get stale, bored or disheartened and the grass always looks greener in this week's job ads.

Training is almost always provided by the company hiring you – it's in their interest that you succeed and tell the correct story.

✶✶✶ European Community Notes
This job recognises no national boundaries; languages are the main constraint. Mobility within the Community depends on the line of business – whether you are selling for a multinational corporation or a local business.

Textile Designer

Qualifications/Training	Recommended
Income bracket	Low–High
Licence	No
Town/Country	Either
Experience/ Springboard	Not necessary
Travel	Yes
Mid-career entry	Possible
Exit sale	No
Entry costs	£100+
Work at home	Yes
Mix and match	Yes.

You could think about: *Interior designer, Fashion designer, Market stall holder, Print maker*

Enquiries
Design Council

For the individual designer, selling to the British market is extremely difficult and many designs go overseas to more receptive markets. Selling is then largely through overseas trade fairs and buyers. Formal training is usual, but on the smaller scale (printing) occasional classes or similar can be adequate. There are opportunities to specialise in many fields (scarves, buttons, printed ribbons). Contacts are invaluable. A large amount of hard sell and publicity will be required involving long hours. A flamboyant nature is an asset.

Numerous degree and diploma courses are available (details from ADAR). These cover some commercial aspects of the textile trade and often offer opportunities to be placed short-term with experienced designers, colour consultants etc. Colleges exhibit students' work in their own shows and abroad (enter as many as possible). This provides good experience in presentation (which is 50 per cent of the ingredients of success), recognition and contacts.

Set-up costs are minimal (paint, brushes, boards, paper). Producing material from your own designs can be low (batik) or high cost (screen printing). Colleges will rent out use of equipment and you can operate from home. The alternative is to set up a small concern and print your own and others' designs. Take a market stall for one or two days a week, in eg Covent Garden.

Use all contacts, wear your own designs made up, and go out and sell. Trade fairs and shows are vital (see *Exhibition Bulletin* in reference libraries; DESIGN COUNCIL for lists and costs); but they are expensive, especially abroad (£500–£1,000). Get an agent (they go to all the shows) who will take your portfolio to the fairs for you, for 30–40 per cent commission. Personal contact is better. Sell designs to suitable retailers (Next; Designers' Guild). If you have an interest in interior design, approach individuals and outlets to supply designs, to order or original. This is an under-exploited area but it can be extremely satisfying and lucrative.

Textile design has a large fashion turnover, so make the most of opportunities and success can be achieved. Follow current trends through fashion and interior design magazines eg, *Craft*, *Designer's Journal*. Seasonal colour forecasts, part of a style and design package, are available from the INTERNATIONAL INSTITUTE FOR COTTON, and the INTERNATIONAL WOOL SECRETARIAT.

Thatcher

Qualifications/Training	Essential
Income bracket	Low-Medium
Licence	No
Town/Country	Mostly country
Experience/Springboard	No
Travel	Yes
Mid-career entry	Good
Exit sale	No
Entry costs	£5,000+
Work at home	No
Mix and match	Possible.

You could think about: *Builder, House converter, Import/export broker, Man with a van, Gardener/garden designer, MP*

Enquiries
Thatching Advisory Service, Rural Development Commission

This is a traditional craft that is attracting refugees from the rat race. Thatchers spend most of their time rethatching houses or barns either from scratch or by building on an existing foundation of thatch. Thatched roofs are fashionable and are sometimes put on new houses or to replace tiles; thatching is also used for garden sheds etc. Most work comes from private house owners but there are opportunities for thatch building in film and TV sets, for exhibitions and occasionally on showpiece factories. A thatch should last anything from about 15 years to more than 50. Although repairs are sometimes needed, you should only expect to spend about three weeks a year repairing. So you'll need to travel and work away from home. Traditionally a men-only job, there are now some women around, but they are regarded as exceptional.

You can learn how to thatch by serving a five-year trade apprenticeship with an established thatcher, this includes some courses on day and block release at local FE colleges. Alternatively the THATCHING ADVISORY SERVICE (TAS) runs a franchise system where for a fee of £15,000 (get a bank loan) you will be given a six-month training (and paid £900 a month while you do it) before becoming a franchise holder with them. This scheme is over subscribed and only about 2 per cent of applicants can be accepted. The TAS offer continuing guidance through their magazine *Thatch* (their managing director has written the authoritative book on the subject, also called *Thatch*; also recommended is the *Thatcher's Craft*). Either of these ways of learning gives you the qualification to thatch and will have taught you enough to be able to work for yourself.

Obviously thatchers have to enjoy being outside, have good balance and a degree of physical strength. You can decide how long you work and when. Some thatchers choose not to work during the winter, while others are prepared to work whenever they can. You'll probably get more work in the summer and can use longer daylight hours. Rain needn't stop you from thatching, but may make the job less agreeable; winds can be a hindrance.

You will have collected the necessary tools and equipment during training – hammers, legget, ladders, needles, mallet, knives and shearing hooks. In addition you'll need insurance to cover damage to your clients' houses and contents for which you are liable while thatching (£1 million plus of cover). You'll need to buy the reed for your first commission in advance. It will cost about £3,000 (bank loan) and is usually brought from the South of France, Hungary or Poland by lorry. Importing direct from the supplier cuts out the reed dealer, saving about £700 a load, and giving you a sideline to thatching. The average charge for a cottage (about eight weeks' work) is between £8,000 and £10,000. Rather than work alone you may prefer to employ assistants which means you'll get jobs done more quickly but your profits will be smaller, so it depends on how much local work there is. The TAS recommend a minimum monthly turnover of £4,000 during the first year (about £1,450 of that goes on salaries and profit). They also suggest that you should wait until your third or fourth year before gauging profitability.

Thatched roofs are usually a luxury, so clients may be demanding and will want some say about what you do. You can opt to specialise in certain designs, eg for the ridge (often decorated and a job you may be called upon to do on its own), and you will have to give expert advice on which sort of reed to use and the basic structure of the roof. Reputation counts for a lot so keep your customers satisfied.

Further information from RDC and TAS.

⁂ European Community Notes

Qualifications: At present UK qualifications recognised throughout EC and EC qualifications in UK.
Languages: To succeed, local language not necessary, but a distinct advantage.
Earnings: UK income generally same as elsewhere in EC.
Setting up: You will find it difficult to succeed in Belgium, Greece, Italy, Luxembourg, Portugal, Spain.

You will find it possible if not easy, in Denmark, Eire, France, Germany, Netherlands.
Advice/Training: Advice, information and training not available for those wishing to work in Europe.
Exchanges: Formal job exchanges do not exist.
Enquiry point for those wishing to work in the EC: THATCHING ADVISORY SERVICE

Theatrical Agent

Qualifications/Training	No
Income bracket	Low–Medium
Licence	Yes
Town/Country	Town
Experience/Springboard	Yes
Travel	Some
Mid-career entry	Possible

Exit sale	Possible
Entry costs	£2,000+
Work at home	Possible
Mix and match	Limited.

You could think about: *Scriptwriter, Calligrapher, Potter*

Enquiries
Spotlight, Theatrical agents, Casting directors

Theatrical agents help actors to find work and make sure that they are fairly treated (given reasonable contracts, pay etc) when they are working. Particularly for young actors who don't always know the ropes and who are vulnerable to unscrupulous directors and producers, agents are very important to their clients; helping them to cope with problems and crises in their private lives as well as sorting out their professional affairs. Agents can also represent well-known and established clients, actively promoting actors both 'on stage' and off – arranging for them to write books, open village fetes etc, and becoming more involved in all aspects of their client's life that could have a bearing on their career.

There are no formal qualifications but you'll need to have had some experience of working in a theatrical agency so that you have some idea of what's involved and, more importantly, have a grounding in actors' contracts and how they work. You have to balance being businesslike, efficient and tough, with being prepared to listen sympathetically to your clients at times when they are having difficulty in coping with the problems of long rests or difficult working conditions. Acting experience gives you useful insights into actors' problems. It's a good idea to set up with a partner – having someone to consult often helps you to make decisions. You may find that one of you is better suited to concentrating on the business/legal side of the agency while the other spends more time with clients and work hunting. The more you know about plays and drama the better for when you're looking for suitable parts for which your clients can audition.

Set up equipment includes typewriter, stationery, an efficient filing system and perhaps a computer. Later it may be worth investing in a fax machine; this is a very visual business and casting directors like to see what you're sending them. You'll spend so much time on the phone that you need at least a second line for incoming calls and somebody to answer it as well as to help with administrative and secretarial back up. Once you get busy a secretary is essential to cope with the paperwork and invoicing and a book-keeper for the accounts. You're paid commission on the fees that your clients get. Every agent has his own scale of commission. For example, some may charge 12.5 per cent across the board; others may charge, say, 10 per cent for theatre, 12.5 per cent for TV and films and 15 per cent for commercials.

Actors normally have exclusive arrangements with agents, but might by arrangement have a separate voice-over agent. You aren't expected to try and poach another agent's clients, although big agents often do successfully grab up-and-coming actors. You can, however, take on anybody who approaches you because they want a different agent and you'll probably be able to take quite a few of your clients from wherever you were before you opened on your own. (Remember this when you start to employ assistants in your own agency.) Otherwise, contact SPOTLIGHT, and send them details and they can give you advice about setting up an agency. SPOTLIGHT helps actors to find agents and will tell them about you if you seem to be right for the actor. After that, new clients come via word of mouth and reputation.

When you're choosing clients you have to select those you can get work for; this will usually mean having one or two examples of each of a wide range of age and appearance. It is highly unlikely that you would take on an actor without having seen him or her working ie, in the theatre or on TV. There is a lot of work for very young actors, but also a lot of them around and when your clients are resting (ie, not earning any money from acting), you are not earning commission. Some agents have different partners to handle different areas (theatre, TV etc), others split the work load by sharing out clients. Most agents would represent more men than women, which is a reflection of the casting opportunities. You need a network of contacts who will listen to you when you're trying to promote your clients. That means getting to know producers and more importantly casting directors; you won't necessarily meet them very often but you'll spend a lot of time talking to them on the phone when you're finding out what they're casting so that you can promote your clients. You may not have a lot of time to yourself during the week. You spend days on the phone, meeting clients and casting directors; then you have to visit the theatre or studios perhaps once or twice a week, watching how your clients are doing and looking out for parts that may suit them. Some agents choose to spend their weekends touring around the country watching other companies or their own clients on tour.

⁎⁎⁎ European Community Notes

The future holds much more potential for European co-productions – or so it is fondly hoped. So contacts should be actively pursued in Paris, Rome, Madrid and so on.

Timeshare Developer

Qualifications/Training	No
Income bracket	Low-High
Licence	No
Town/Country	Either
Experience/Springboard	No
Travel	Between sites
Mid-career entry	Likely

Exit sale	Yes
Entry costs	£100,000++
Work at home	No
Mix and match	Yes.

You could think about: *Holiday accommodation owner, Landlord, Builder, Direct marketing agent, List broker, Estate agent, Import/export broker*

Enquiries
Timeshare Council

You can sell and manage units of holiday accommodation on a timeshare basis – either refurbishing property you already own or, if you are brave, building it specifically for the purpose. But if you can't sell quickly once you've started investing the money, you will follow many others and go bust. This is a business with high capital risks but is also one of the fastest growing areas of tourism.

You need at least 10 units of accommodation which must be furnished to luxury standard and on a good site. There is no point trying to run this alongside the letting of standard holiday accommodation, except in the short term, since the standard of the amenities must be excellent and cannot be justified by ordinary holiday rents. And amenities not provided locally – shops, swimming, videos, good play facilities etc – will have to be provided on site.

Before you start, you are wise to commission a feasibility study from a reputable timeshare consultant. Once you have started renovation and have sample accommodation to show, you can apply to an international timeshare organisation, such as RESORT CONDOMINIUMS INTERNATIONAL (RCI) for affiliation. This allows those who buy your units to exchange their holiday for another within the organisation (in the case of RCI, this gives the possibility of exchanging for a holiday in any one of 2,000-plus resorts, from China to the United States). So you can make buying your timeshare attractive to British buyers, even to people who live fairly locally, but have the place full of Yanks and Swedes.

A professional selling operation is essential and it is worth employing specialists. You will probably need several people selling in peak season to get it right, as well as any on-site management. You are, after all, persuading people to make a capital investment. Your buyers will usually be over 40, largely with kids off their hands. They will need to be satisfied as to the security of their investment and the proper running of the operation – so you need to have thought all that out before you start. A sound legal framework is essential, so you should find a solicitor who is familiar with timeshare. A trust company will also have to be formed to protect buyers. You may want to join the new TIMESHARE COUNCIL.

Banks are extremely cautious because they cannot repossess the accommodation once time has been sold on it; 50 per cent is the maximum you should expect to be able to borrow. You may find others who are more adventurous but beware of interest rates. If you do not sell a basic minimum quickly, to service the initial loan, the whole operation will abort. You need a cool business head.

To be successful, you should also have a good selling technique, sound management skills, and the ability to design the accommodation with flair or to select others who will. It's worth very careful research before starting.

An EC directive and UK timeshare legislation are in drafting stages, both of which will affect the manner in which timeshare accommodation can be sold – both will legislate for a 'cooling-off' period for example.

✷✷✷ European Community Notes

Those with overseas operations must ensure they comply with local legislation, which has tightened up appreciably in certain areas over the past couple of years, and you will need to comply with the forthcoming EC directive once in force.

Toastmaster

Qualifications/Training	Available
Income bracket	Low-High
Licence	No
Town/Country	Mostly town
Experience/Springboard	No
Travel	Yes
Mid-career entry	Recommended
Exit sale	No
Entry costs	£500++
Work at home	No
Mix and match	Excellent.

You could think about: *Radio reporter/ presenter, Taxi driver, Media trainer, Puppeteer, Market research interviewer*

Enquiries
Guild of Professional Toastmasters

Toastmasters introduce speakers, propose toasts and preside over public and private events such as dinners, weddings and other ceremonies. It's not necessarily a job that you would go into straight from school or college. A lot of the work is done over lunch or in the evening and it's up to you how many jobs you do so toastmastering is an excellent mix and match with other careers and an option for mid-career changers.

You don't need a qualification but THE IVOR SPENCER SCHOOL FOR PROFESSIONAL TOASTMASTERS runs courses which, although they are expensive (£3,000), teach you some of the basics of toastmastering including work experience assisting toastmasters at events. It also helps you to find some work after you've completed the course. You'll need to know the proper way of introducing speakers and toasts as well as how to conduct formal events; you can find out about these in *Debrett's Correct Form*. Essential attributes are a loud voice; a good memory for names and faces; tact; the ability to sit through speeches and to remain sober while nobody else is. You'll need a phone and answering machine, white tie with red, toastmaster's jacket and a gavel. Also a car so that you can get home easily after events without having to dash off to catch the last train before you've proposed any toasts. The amounts you earn as a toastmaster vary depending on how established you are and how important the event is. As well as being paid you'll also usually be fed with the guests.

Work comes from anyone who is putting on a formal event or presentation. Contact local party organisers, domestic help agencies and PR companies. Companies and organisations are also likely to use toastmasters at annual dinners and ceremonies and other useful contacts include established toastmasters who may pass on work that they don't have time for themselves. Although most major public events take place in large cities there are opportunities for toastmasters in more rural areas for instance at weddings. In most cases you'll be booked up several weeks in advance so your schedule is easy to predict and control. Most work will be in the evenings and over lunchtime. There's some travel involved both locally and to events further afield especially as you get well known. You'll have the opportunity to meet famous people and to eat well but not to drink much. You can get special toastmasters' glasses which are made out of very thick glass and hold far less wine than they seem to, this is so that you can down several toasts without getting tipsy. In addition to attending the events you'll have to do some preparation on who is speaking and to whom so that you can make the right introductions. Toastmasters can also be asked to make speeches themselves. There is a GUILD OF PROFESSIONAL TOASTMASTERS which advises potential toastmasters.

☆ European Community Notes

Qualifications: UK qualifications recognised throughout EC.
Languages: To succeed, local language not necessary.
Earnings: UK income generally same as elsewhere in the EC.
Setting up: You will find it possible to succeed throughout Europe.

Advice/Training: Advice, information and training available for those wishing to work in Europe.
Exchanges: Formal job exchanges exist.
Financial help: exists for study, training or travel in the EC, specific to this job.
Enquiry point for those wishing to work in the EC: Ivor Spencer, GUILD OF PROFESSIONAL TOASTMASTERS.
Notes: Ivor Spencer, the doyen of professional toastmasters, sees scope for a great deal of business in Europe where the trained British style is apparently very highly regarded.

Tourist Attraction

Qualifications/Training	No
Income bracket	Low–High
Licence	No
Town/Country	Either
Experience/Springboard	No
Travel	No
Mid-career entry	Likely
Exit sale	Excellent
Entry costs	Highly variable
Work at home	Yes
Mix and match	Yes.

You could think about: *Farmer, Wine grower, Zoo keeper, Contemporary art gallery owner, Silversmith/ jeweller, Landscape designer, Accountant*

Enquiries
Local Tourist Board, Historic Houses Association

This assumes you have something that the Great British Public (GBP) will pay to come and see. You may have inherited or bought a house, garden or area which is of historical or natural significance (eg, Windsor Castle, Land's End); or you may have developed a model railway or built up a unique collection of Georgian thimbles.

You must clearly identify the sort of visitors you want to attract. Do you want families, coach parties, Volvo estate drivers or the Aldeburgh Festival set? Some owners ban coaches; others are into the mass market. Location is important: there is probably no point in having the best doll collection in the world on the north-east coast of Scotland – though fishing nets do well. Your price will be linked to location and what you're offering – more in London than outside; more for something good that will take at least an hour to see as opposed to something mediocre that a bored child will skip through in 10 minutes. One crude rule of thumb is to charge £2.00 for each hour the average visitor takes to go round. Tourist boards are usually a great help – both with advice and promotional literature (you pay but they distribute it). There is a caveat: tourist boards are interested in promoting a particular area. To generate visits, they are obviously keen on new attractions but, as one respondent put it, it is 'not unknown for them to create a misplaced sense of optimism' and when that optimism proves unjustified it is the new entrant that pays for it. Join any local association of tourist attractions. If you are selling entry to an historic house and/or garden, join the HISTORIC HOUSES ASSOCIATION. It provides seminars and information on topics such as broadcasting rights; also advice on the appropriate price and the best arrangements to make. Make sure you get on all local lists (and national, if you're big enough) of houses/gardens/museums open to the public.

You can increase the 'spend-per-head' by having a cafeteria or a shop stocked with postcards and a range of branded goods – teatowels, coasters, etc – all good on the gifts market. Then, in addition to their admission fee, visitors will hopefully buy postcards and gifts as well as tea and cakes. If you are into this on a large scale, you will need to employ people to help so this will drastically increase your costs.

Before you open, you will need to ensure that the place is well presented, clean and tidy (particularly the loos) and properly decorated. Think also about security and GBP's sticky fingers (Sissinghurst lost all but the stump of a rare plant that was planted close to a path because GBP took cuttings). You must be tolerant of GBP and its rubbish – although by and large if your presentation is smart and tidy, GBP will also leave it tidy. You need no special licence to open to the public but you are foolish not to have public liability insurance. Keep your opening hours simple so as not to confuse the public – if you can, stay open seven days a week.

You have to do this well to succeed. GBP is becoming much more sophisticated and will judge you against what is seen on television and at Euro Disney. If you are not worth visiting, or are overpriced, you will be rumbled very quickly; even if you still attract the odd passer-by, you will not get the coach parties and others directed to you by the local tourist board, so will never make your fortune. If you are successful, you should not expect to get rich though you may get a reasonable return on your capital. It can combine well with another job. In the end success depends not just on a good product and value for money but on your *enthusiam*: you have to genuinely enjoy welcoming the GBP, not just their money.

Tourist Guide

Qualifications/Training	Necessary
Income bracket	Medium
Licence	In some cases
Town/Country	Either
Experience/Springboard	No
Travel	Yes
Mid-career entry	Yes
Exit sale	No
Entry costs	£1,000
Work at home	No
Mix and match	Yes.

You could think about: *Mini-cab driver, Interpreter, Costume designer, Tourist attraction, Smallholder*

Enquiries
Local tourist boards

With tourism in the UK becoming a leading industry, tourist guides play an important part in entertaining visitors from home and abroad, by sharing their knowledge about places, people and life in the most imaginative and informative way possible. Tourist guides en masse are a disturbing force with each endeavouring to out-face the other, but no two tourist guides are alike when it comes to leading a group of visitors through our national heritage, and it is the individual's love of his or her own subject that makes one guide different from another. Tourist guiding is open to all creeds and races, but beware, there is an unhealthy majority of the retired headmistress type. Young blood of both sexes is desperately needed to swell the ranks, and graduates are coming into the industry in their twenties. Training is through one of the Blue Badge courses operated by tourist boards in conjunction with local authorities and tourism related businesses. Courses vary in length and entry qualifications. THE LONDON TOURIST BOARD trains guides over six months, involving a considerable amount of on-site training, and successful candidates are then registered and qualify to work in and near London. Other regions run shorter courses. Courses include local history lectures and core knowledge covering law, religion, geography, etc. Languages are of immense help in winning a place on a course which might be over-subscribed. Less well-known languages such as Chinese, Japanese or Arabic will assist and in time, bring financial reward. Tourist guides come from all walks of life: road-sweepers, bus drivers, housewives, air stewards, nurses and publicans to name a few. All have to be good listeners. Academics, whilst knowing their subject, do not necessarily have the expertise to put it across in the world outside the classroom. You must keep up to date with developments such as excavations or the opening of new attractions. Other Blue Badges and endorsements should be sought out and thereby increase your chances of employment.

Most tourist guides run an office from home. Along with a telephone, you'll need a reliable answering machine, and given time, even a fax or telex; suitable letter headings for your stationery, and business cards to match; beware of how you advertise yourself in travel trade publications until you can justify the expense and have sufficient expertise as a guide. Having drafted suggested itineraries, mail shot tour operators, travel agencies, tourist boards, . . . informing them of your services which could complement theirs in your neck of the woods. Tourist guides often put packages together by co-ordinating travel, a meal stop and places of interest through a knowledge of the area. Given time, most business comes direct through personal recommendation. Tourist guides are well known for passing business amongst themselves, but as you develop your own standards, you soon learn who to pass work on to and who not. Income in the first year or so will not be that forthcoming. It takes time to establish your own niche, especially in the major tourist destination centres where so many guiding organisations ply for a living. It takes just one hi-jacking of a North American aircraft to put you out of business. If you've got another job, hang on to it until you can afford to concentrate on tour guiding. It's a good thing to mix and match with others, especially in the depths of winter when supplies of tourists dry up.

There's no such thing as an average day; no two tourists are the same, and no question is ever stupid even though the enquirer thinks so. When you get to the point of having to explain the purpose of a flying buttress in driving rain, just remember how far some of your visitors have flown to listen to you.

The season is usually for six months or so. Few work all year round, but with earnings for some in excess of £15,000 per year, you can forget your summer holidays, and spend Christmas in the Bahamas (at the cost of not having a day off for weeks or even months on end).

Avoid ruts! Doing the same old tour day in day out becomes stale, so keep extending your areas of interest. For example, driver-guiding is a specialist form of touring small groups in the tourist guide's own car, often setting up complete itineraries to include accommodation. Some guides lecture on cruise ships, others join forces with tourist boards and work on promotions overseas. Some painstakingly develop tours for the handicapped. As long as you can combine tact, diplomacy and have the ability to bring history alive through public speaking, along with the odd story or two, you're well on the way to becoming a tourist guide.

Useful organisations for courses: contact local tourist information centres, local authorities/regions tourist boards and regional colleges. Read *Please Follow Me* and contact the GUILD OF GUIDE LECTURERS.

Toymaker

Qualifications/Training	Available
Income bracket	Low-Medium
Licence	No
Town/Country	Either
Experience/Springboard	No
Travel	No
Mid-career entry	Yes
Exit sale	No
Entry costs	£500+
Work at home	Yes
Mix and match	Yes.

You could think about: *Wood carver, Builder, Antique dealer, Farmer*

Enquiries
British Toymakers' Guild, Guild of Master Craftsmen, British Toy and Hobby Association

A lot of modern toys are necessarily mass-produced in factories. But there is a market for traditional handmade toys – rocking horses, porcelain dolls, soft toys, dolls houses etc and collectors' pieces (for adults rather than children), such as toy soldiers and mechanical toys. You can sell directly to the customer or to a retailer. If you don't want to or can't make the toys yourself, with or without assistance, you can sell new designs for toys to other manufacturers; make sure that any agreement you enter into with the manufacturer will let you benefit if your idea really takes off. You don't need any special qualifications. There are various courses in toymaking (evening classes in puppet-making for example). But, if formally trained at all, toymakers are more likely to have done a course in woodwork, pottery etc. Toys must satisfy stringent safety rules before they can be sold for children. The BRITISH STANDARDS INSTITUTION will send you a list of these rules. Toymakers have to be consistently good craftsmen; innovative in their ideas for new toys and market places; business-like and reliable, clients aren't impressed by unexplained late delivery or ignored customer enquiries. Initially you'll need a lot of confidence and determination to make your ideas succeed.

As well as the tools and equipment you need to make the toys, set up costs include a workshop. Small toys can be made in a spare room at home, otherwise a garage, shed or barn if you don't want to buy a workshop straight away. You can change premises as you grow. As long as you're relatively accessible, so that materials can get in to and toys out from your workshop, you don't have to be particularly close to big towns. Banks aren't always helpful but are more likely to listen if you present them with coherent and realistic business plans and proposals. You'll need some capital to keep you going until your business takes off. Charges are based on costs of equipment and time. Keep an eye on competition but make sure that you're earning enough to make the business worthwhile.

Your first few orders will probably come from friends and then, if your work is good, your reputation will spread by word of mouth. Sell to a prestigious name like Harrods, it helps with further orders. Publicity is important. Advertising is expensive so try and get some write-ups (which are free) in the local and national press. Try and get onto children's TV (not easy) if your products are particularly appealing and you're comparatively charismatic. Also, try toy and gift exhibitions. Develop your contacts all the time.

For publicity purposes, it looks good to be a member of the BRITISH TOYMAKERS' GUILD or the GUILD OF MASTER CRAFTSMEN; they also give advice to their members. The BRITISH TOY AND HOBBY MANUFACTURERS ASSOCIATION has useful information especially on toy safety matters although it caters for mass producers rather more than craftsmen.

You can find useful facts about toy marketing and trade associations in the *British Toy Industry HandBook* (£8.50 incl p & p).

Travel Agent

Qualifications/Training	Recommended
Income bracket	Medium
Licence	Recommended
Town/Country	Town
Experience/Springboard	Essential
Travel	No
Mid-career entry	Good
Exit sale	Yes
Entry costs	£40,000
Work at home	No
Mix and match	Limited.

You could think about: **List broker, Sports retailer, Novelist**

Enquiries
Association of British Travel Agents,
ABTA National Training Board

Travel agents reserve, issue and sell tickets for air, rail, sea and coach travel. They also sell package holidays offered by tour operators, give advice and help with passports, visas, foreign currency and insurance, arrange reservations for hotels and car hire and compile tailor-made packages.

To open your own travel agency approved by the ASSOCIATION OF BRITISH TRAVEL AGENTS (ABTA), you must lodge a bond of £7,500 (this goes towards the rescue of any stranded customers if a member goes bankrupt). ABTA also requires you to have capital of at least £10,000 and to have two people working full time, one with two years' ABTA experience. If you want to issue, rather than merely reserve, air tickets you have to be a member of the INTERNATIONAL AIR TRANSPORT ASSOCIATION having lodged a bond equal to 50 per cent of a month's air turnover (based on the reservations you have made) and to have a year's air ticket selling experience. Although no additional qualifications are formally necessary, there are ABTA-approved courses which you are well-advised to investigate. See also *Travel Trade Gazette*, *Travel News* and *Airline World* for help with getting the necessary travel agent experience.

Travel agents have to be methodical and meticulous (a mistake on an air ticket is serious), long-suffering enough to cope with long hours on the telephone and patient enough to do all of this in spite of constant interruptions from customers. You'll need some sort of office; theoretically, the only equipment you need is a desk and a telephone but it's useful to have a computer link with airlines (Travicom) and/or tour operators (Prestel) which give quicker access to details of availability. Altogether, allow about £40,000 to open. You will be paid on commission ranging from 7–15 per cent, by the companies whose tickets you sell (including British Rail and National Express coaches). Turnover will seem vast – half-a-million per month isn't unusual for air sales alone. But commission is paid on profits only so don't get too excited.

People use their local travel agent, so set up in an area which will provide enough business and check out local competition. Nearby offices will buy tickets for business travel, residential areas may want more package holidays (but not always the same ones). In either case, your customers will have some idea of where they want to go and when; the bulk of your job is finding out how to get them there, which may mean offering them compromises. Make your presence obvious, and advertise the services you offer, the companies you are agent for, and any special offers (cut-price late bookings etc) that are available. Tour operators and travel lines do a lot of their own advertising on TV and in the press.

Holidays are sold all year round but there are seasonal variations in clientele; some stick to school holidays, some off season; sun lovers and skiers. Cultivating contacts in the trade is useful for speeding up enquiries and getting hold of unobtainable tickets; a spot of ostentatious use of contacts is impressive for customers.

✳ **European Community Notes**

Travel qualifications and practices vary greatly across Europe. All that can be said for certain is that conditions in the EC vary from country to country and it is very different from the travel industry in the UK. ABTA has been engaged in a project to determine standards in the industry across the EC.

Tree Surgeon

Qualifications/Training	Recommended
Income bracket	Low-Medium
Licence	No
Town/Country	Town and country
Experience/Springboard	No
Travel	Yes
Mid-career entry	Possible
Exit sale	Yes
Entry costs	£2,000+
Work at home	No
Mix and match	Yes.

You could think about: *Gardener/ garden designer, Man with a van, Farmer, Thatcher, Smallholder, Accountant, Osteopath*

Enquiries
Forestry Training Council

Tree surgery (arboriculture) is mainly concerned with the health of trees. Tree surgery focuses on individual or groups of trees as opposed to forestry which is more of an agricultural approach. The work, for private and public customers, is on trees which are in need of attention. That can mean routine maintenance – pruning for aesthetic or utilitarian reasons. It also means dealing with trees which are diseased or wind damaged, or which have grown too large – basically, and especially in town, *trees under stress*. There is a need

for people trained in the science and technology of trees, from their planting to their felling

The FORESTRY TRAINING COUNCIL provides courses for the private sector – employees, self-employed contractors and specialist advisers – in a wide range of skills and technical management. This is a relatively new industry and training programmes are still being developed. ASKHAM BRYAN HORTICULTURAL COLLEGE is recommended and MERRIST WOOD AGRICULTURAL COLLEGE offers a one-year course. And you can do short courses in safety, including chain saw handling and tree climbing.

Professional tree surgeons, apart from their specialist knowledge of tree identification, tree disease and solving problems, are also concerned with felling. The problems of felling say a chestnut tree over 100ft tall are considerable. You'll need to be good at climbing trees, have a good head for heights and love trees in the way that vets love animals – ie recognise when they need to be destroyed.

To set up you need ropes, harnesses, a chain saw, a ladder and a hard hat. It can be a very noisy occupation so you may want ear protectors too. A vehicle that can cope with rough terrain is useful. You could cause a lot of damage if you miscalculated and allowed a tree to fall in the wrong direction, so substantial risk insurance and professional liability cover is essential, not just for the physical damage to you or helpers or property but also for eg, making the wrong diagnosis of a complaint. You should also top up your legal knowledge regarding handling of trees in a conservation area or preserved under the Town and Country Planning Act. Like most professions, the charges are based on the amount of time taken on the assignment; bear in mind also you may have to deal with a considerable amount of timber and brushwood, which can also be time-consuming. You need to operate in an area where people have big gardens. This is a dangerous job. You can't do it single-handed – it's too dangerous – so you will need to have a ground crew as well. The rate of serious personal injury is probably higher among tree surgeons and fellers than any other group of horticultural workers but if you know what you are doing there's no need for alarm. And if the risks are high so are the rewards – tree-felling like steeplejacking and other high risk solitary occupations has a great appeal and satisfaction for a certain type of person. There is also the fulfilment from knowing that ultimately you are working for the future, for more and better trees. A good thing.

Trout Farmer

Qualifications/Training	Necessary
Income bracket	Low-Medium
Licence	Yes
Town/Country	Country
Experience/Springboard	Essential
Travel	Local
Mid-career entry	Good
Exit sale	Excellent
Entry costs	£50,000
Work at home	Yes
Mix and match	Yes.

You could think about: *Holiday accommodation owner, Restaurateur, Fish curer and smoker, Wind surfing school owner*

Enquiries
British Trout Association

Trout farmers breed, grow and market trout. Start by taking a specialist fish farming course at the AGRICULTURAL COLLEGE in Dumfries or Sparsholt in Hampshire. Then get some experience working on several farms over two or three years to build up good contacts and learn the business thoroughly. Join the BRITISH TROUT ASSOCIATION. You will make somewhere between nothing and £10,000 in the first few years, rising to £24,000 per annum. Trout farming has a quicker turnover than salmon farming and the small fish or eggs are cheaper. You need around £50,000, depending on the cost of your site. You also need to negotiate with the

local water authority and/or the NATIONAL RIVERS AUTHORITY to remove and replace water from the river. This will involve you with a lot of bureaucracy.

You will have less babysitting to do than your salmon counterparts, as there are fewer marauding animals or birds and you are more protected from the extremes of the weather and force of the elements. It is essential that you can take part in communal marketing with other fish farmers in your area which will cut costs. Get a good accountant.

As well as feeding your fish, you must also remove any that are dead and diagnose the cause; look for damage or pests; take out the smaller fish into separate cages to allow growth and prevent them getting attacked by the others; kill, gut and pack in ice for transport those that are ready for market.

You must be practical and able to swim. If you run a hatchery, you should be clean and tidy. Only go in for this is you enjoy the open air and irregular hours. Attend the annual fish farm conference and visit customers and watch new developments in equipment. Read *Fish Farming* magazine.

European Community Notes
There is little trout farming in the Community other than in France – although the Scandinavians are starting to be involved too.

Tutor

Qualifications/Training	Recommended
Income bracket	Medium
Licence	No
Town/Country	Mostly town
Experience/Springboard	Essential
Travel	Local
Mid-career entry	Yes
Exit sale	No
Entry costs	Minimal

Work at home   Yes

Mix and match   Excellent.
You could think about: *Teacher,
Barrister, Mini-cab driver, Cabaret
performer, Racehorse owner, Desk-
top publisher*

Enquiries
Incorporated Association of Tutors

Many people use private tutors – largely
children supplementing their school work
but also adults needing some specialist
knowledge. If there are enough of them
round you, and you are qualified to teach
what they want to learn, you're in luck.
But you'll need to enjoy teaching one-to-
one and to arrange your own life so that
you are available to teach when your pupils
are not at school.

You are recommended to be a qualified
teacher. If you are working with children,
you should also have real working experience in a school; you cannot help children
under-pin their school work without it and
it will get you used to dealing with
parents.

Some tutors specialise in particular
subjects such as languages; others cover a
general curriculum for younger children
(state or independent primary schools).
You can also run short courses in half-
terms and holidays, do educational assessments (for which you do need lots of experience) or teach English as a Second
Language for foreign employees in this
country. Whatever area you choose to concentrate on, you need to check first that
there is a market.

Most tutors start with one or two children; success with a few children breeds
success as word of mouth is the best way of
ensuring a steady flow of pupils at your
door. With the right contracts and reputation, you could even be recruited as
private tutor to children of Middle Eastern
potentates in school holidays. If you are a
member of the INCORPORATED ASSOCIA-
TION OF TUTORS, your name will appear
on its list which is available to the general
public. The association also provides some
useful information and holds the DES List
99 (which lists those no longer permitted
to hold a teaching post).

If you're tutoring children at home,
make sure you have a room and furniture
appropriate to the child's size. It won't
help children to learn if you sit round a 24-
seat dining table or place them in grand-
father's favourite chair, although either
might impress parents. Make it clear
whether you or your pupil are responsible
for providing materials and avoid future
acrimony by making it crystal clear that
you charge for cancelled lessons unless
given appropriate notice. You can charge
whatever the market will bear, around
£15–£20; more if you visit pupils in their
own homes as you will lose time travelling
between jobs. Working around school
hours, you could fit in about 25 pupils a
week and be busy about 40 weeks a year
(long holidays are part of the attraction).
Some adults may be able to come during
the day but there is likely to be a good deal
of evening work.

Teaching one-to-one can be a strain, not
only on the pupil (some can't take it) but
also on the tutor. You'll need to prepare
proper lesson plans for each session so as
to make the best use of time – the relationship between your time and their cash
makes people conscious of progress. The
plus of this is you will find parents generally ensure kids do their homework.

You will find children's exams focus
parents' minds. So there is scope for tutoring children for one term to two terms
towards the end of their primary education
(state or independent) if they need to sit an
exam for a secondary school and those
needing extra help before GCSE or A-
level. Some children with learning problems (or aspiring parents) have longer-
term tuition to cope with the curriculum.
There is great satisfaction from helping
children meet their own maximum
potential.

Parents can be their children's largest
handicap. You need to be sufficiently
mature (and professional) to tell parents
when their aspirations are unrealistic
('Adrian will never get into Eton') or,
perhaps most difficult, that their children
would do better if parents modified their
own behaviour – switch off the TV or
make English the language of conversation at home. Education, like pet food, is

seldom purchased by the final consumer so you need to balance your professional judgment against parental caprice.

European Community Notes

Qualifications: UK qualifications not at present recognised in EC; EC qualifications accepted in UK (from 1993). EC governments dragging their feet.

Languages: To succeed, local language necessary unless teaching English.

Enquiry point for those wishing to work in the EC: DES

TV and Film Music Composer

Qualifications/Training	Recommended
Income bracket	Low–High
Licence	No
Town/Country	Either
Experience/Springboard	No
Travel	Possible
Mid-career entry	Possible
Exit sale	Possible
Entry costs	£5,000
Work at home	Yes
Mix and match	Essential.

You could think about: *Impresario, Festival director, Conductor, Repetiteur/accompanist/coach*

Enquiries
Association of Professional Composers

This involves writing music, all kinds of styles. Going to music college is not essential but useful for making contacts and learning to play keyboards. It is vital to be able to write easily in folk, jazz, pop and classical styles; look at other composers' scores (in public libraries) and try to copy them. Time is money in the commercial music world. You must be flexible and able to work fast and to change and accommodate producers, directors and performers during rehearsals. To succeed, you need talent, persistence and a lot of luck. It is not necessary to join a union, but do join the PERFORMING RIGHTS SOCIETY and the MECHANICAL COPYRIGHT PROTECTION SOCIETY.

Do another job which leaves you time and energy to write or arrange; persuade musicians and friends to perform your work. You can form your own group, give concerts and hope that TV, radio or commercial fixers will come and hear your work. Send out scores and tapes to TV, Radio 2 and theatrical producers. One success may encourage you to set up on your own.

You will need a telephone and answering machine or service; and over £3,000 to purchase a synthesiser; multi-track tape recorder or sequencer (a computer which records direct from a keyboard) for demonstration cassettes; small upright piano and special calculator which transfers the metronome speed to the timing of the film track. When successful you will need a publisher and an agent to get you work and negotiate fees.

To start with you are paid either by the bar or the number of minutes in the music, at very variable rates. If you hit the jackpot and write a television theme, you can probably live off the proceeds. Top income is £150,000 plus, with recording royalties and performing rights. Improvements in electronics are making recording easier and more accurate; but to avoid getting stale do not concentrate solely on TV work. Accept less lucrative but more challenging commissions from impoverished classical musicians to keep your creative process going. The ASSOCIATION OF PROFESSIONAL COMPOSERS publishes a book *The Composers Guide to Music Publishing*

You can usually work from home; the job keeps you on your toes, pays well and you meet interesting people who are good at their jobs.

A useful book is Cecil Forsyth's *Orchestration*; study scores by Tchaikovsky and Ravel.

Typesetter

Qualifications/Training	Recommended
Income bracket	Low–Medium
Licence	No
Town/Country	Town
Experience/Springboard	Useful
Travel	Local
Mid-career entry	Yes
Exit sale	Possible
Entry costs	£5,000+
Work at home	Yes
Mix and match	Yes.

You could think about: *Word processor, Computer software author, Shopkeeper, Book packager, Proofreader/copyeditor, Desk-top publisher*

Enquiries
Typesetters, Graphical Paper and Media Union

This has nothing to do with the old printer's craft of setting type. It is still part of the printing process but is much closer to word processing, indeed it follows on from that. New technology has changed printing probably more than any other 'traditional' industry.

You must be able to type accurately and quickly and you must understand the process of taking a manuscript, converting the author's words into machine-readable form, visualising the finished book and inserting the necessary codes to control the photosetter. Membership of the GRAPHICAL PAPER AND MEDIA UNION used to be essential; that is no longer the case, but you are unlikely to be able to work for any of the established publishing houses which has union agreement without GPMU membership. That could limit your market. You need an eye for detail and an ability to remember all the codes (and sometimes these can be fairly complex) if you are not to waste time (and money) by having whole paragraphs in the wrong typeface. You need to understand all the old terms – fount, measure, type-

face, etc if you are to produce a 'book' which conforms to the book designer's specification; also in order to suggest changes to that specification which can drastically affect efficiency or cost of production of the finished job.

The only equipment you need to begin with is a desk, a computer and a supply of disks. You will be subcontracting the photosetting and (if required) preparation of artwork to other specialists. But you are responsible for the final product so it is essential that you understand all the processes and can prepare an accurate quotation that is likely to be accepted by the publisher. Luck will play a great part in your eventual success but you will almost certainly need to know somebody in publishing to get your first job. No-one is likely to give you work unless you can prove that you are capable of producing the goods. Initially your earnings will be nil, and you are unlikely to get paid for any job until it is completed, so cash flow will be a real problem – the bigger the job the greater your cash problems.

The work involves liaising with the publisher (and possibly the author) to understand their requirements, keying-in the manuscript, transferring data to the photosetter of your choice and supervising the output. You will find the most satisfactory arrangement is to deal with one or two photosetting specialists who understand you and your requirements and who, at the same time, offer you the best financial terms. Mistakes can be expensive and, as sub-contracting forms such a large part of the work you need to be confident that those who are working for you (and who represent a large part of the overall costs in your calculations) do not eat up your profit. Before the whole job goes to the photosetter get a large enough sample set to bring to light any problems before they become catastrophes. You need to be able to understand the needs of the writer, the publisher, the designer and the machine operator. Before beginning work spend time with the publisher so that you are absolutely clear about what is required. Do a good job at the right price and you will be able to hope for more work from the publisher but don't expect any favours.

There are too many people around offering the same services as you for you to be able to rely on loyalty for the future. On the other hand you must be prepared to pester publishers to allow you to quote for more jobs – emphasise any areas in your favour – preliminary mailings of questionnaires to collect data, fast efficient updating for second and subsequent editions, sub-editing ability etc. Remember that the data on your disk is not your data and the publisher may well require you to supply copies of any disks on completion of a job.

Typist

Qualifications/Training	Recommended
Income bracket	Low-Medium
Licence	No
Town/Country	Town mostly
Experience/Springboard	Yes
Travel	Local
Mid-career entry	Yes
Exit sale	No
Entry costs	£5++
Work at home	Yes
Mix and match	Yes.

You could think about: *Word processor, Typesetter, List broker, Proofreader/copy editor, Bookkeeper, Novelist, Sculptor*

Enquiries
Secretarial agencies

It is easy to learn to type if you have time to practise. But to be convincing when looking for work it is useful to have certificates to show you have reached good speeds and are competent. You can pick up the skills at evening classes, private secretarial schools, further education colleges (some are tailored for graduates) or from a book. Some offer courses leading to their own certificates; others to qualifications such as RSA (ROYAL SOCIETY OF ARTS). Like learning to ride a bike, touch-typing may seem impossible at first, but once you've mastered it you'll never forget it. Straight typing is being replaced in more and more offices by word processing – a closely related job.

Typists can specialise – shorthand and typing, audio typing (where the material has been dictated on to a special tape recorder) or copy typing (where the material is handwritten or a revision of something that has been typed or printed before). If you don't want to work for a company, you can find work typing at home (eg students' theses, book manuscripts) or do temp work, getting jobs through an agency.

Either way, you can usually work the hours or days that suit you. It is a useful job to fall back on if, for example, you are trying to get into another career but the work is not coming in as regularly as you would like.

If you want to do more than be a typist you can go on to use a word processor or become a secretary or personal assistant. Working as a temp is a good way of getting a taste of different types of business – you can pick up information on office management and see exactly what people do in a range of different offices – before making a final decision on your career. You can also temp while you travel around if you choose.

If you get fed up with working for an agency, who take a cut of the money paid out by your temporary employer, you can try volunteering yourself as a freelance typist with companies who know you; they can call on you when their own staff are on holiday or off sick. If you are working from home, advertise your services with local business, university, colleges etc.

As a typist you may be paid by the hour (£5–£10) or by the page if you work at home (so you need good speeds to make a living). You will need a supply of stationery and your own electric typewriter if you are working at home, and should also consider developing skills in computing (or at least word processing), as much of this work can now be done at home and transmitted to the appropriate destination via the telephone.

Uu

UK Correspondent (Overseas Media)

Qualifications/Training	Available
Income bracket	Low-Medium
Licence	No
Town/Country	Town
Experience/Springboard	Essential
Travel	Yes
Mid-career entry	Yes
Exit sale	No
Entry costs	£2,500
Work at home	Partly
Mix and match	Good.

You could think about: *English language school owner, Journalist, Interpreter, Insurance broker, Tutor*

Enquiries
International news agencies, Overseas media

You can make money as a freelance journalist working for overseas newspapers, magazines, radio and TV companies. The amount of work you can get depends largely on who and what you know but it's an excellent thing to mix and match with virtually anything else and you may be able to make it pay for some overseas travel.

There are no formal qualifications but you must be fluent in the language you're working in and familiar with the culture of the country you're reporting to. It helps also if you're an expert in an area that people are likely to be interested in reading about: art, theatre, food, economics, pop-music . . . and you need to have a supply of good ideas for material as well as being in touch with current events in the UK and the country you're writing for. You need good writing skills, imagination and the ability to work quickly. You also need contacts who can help with research; journalists and others, both in your field of speciality and in other areas which may be of interest to your overseas audience or readership. Unless you're working for a very large publication or broadcasting company which uses a wide range of special correspondents in the UK, you should be prepared to cover stories on virtually anything including current events and special features tailored to your overseas audience/readership.

Set-up equipment is minimal: you need a phone and a typewriter or word processor. Depending on the work you're doing and the sophistication of your client, you may also need a tape recorder, a fax and/or a modem. The amount you're paid varies a lot but is usually calculated on the final number of words or air-time minutes you produce. You definitely need to be pushy to get into this job. Write to, telephone and visit international news agencies. Get the names of people to contact at overseas publications and broadcasting companies. This is best done while you're in the country you want to write for. Talk to anyone you know who's already involved in the area: journalists, researchers, producers, editors. Then send out your CV and visit as many people as you can see. It's easier if you're a national of the country you're hoping to report to, if not, you should have spent some time there and have family or friends living there. If you aren't a national, you'll improve your chances by having good credentials; these can be either in doing similar work in the UK or by having a lot of experience or expertise in a sexy area. Once you've found someone who's interested in what you've got to offer, you can work out between you how much work you do for them. Some correspondents have a regular slot, reporting on current events in the UK or on subjects of general interest when events aren't exciting. Others do occasional work or do series on, for example, British painters, from time to time. You can work for as many people as you like as long as you're careful about copyright ownership when you use the same material for more than one.

What you write about is largely up to you as long as you know your audience. Virtually everywhere is interested in hearing about the Royal Family so following them around can be lucrative. In many ways it's up to you how much time you spend on being a correspondent. You may have to do some intensive research for a story, alternatively you could use your own experience in the UK or abroad and turn it into publishable or broadcastable material at the drop of a hat.

Upholsterer

Qualifications/Training	Recommended
Income bracket	Low
Licence	No
Town/Country	Town
Experience/ Springboard	Recommended
Travel	Local
Mid-career entry	Possible
Exit sale	Possible
Entry costs	£1,500+
Work at home	Possible
Mix and match	Possible.

You could think about: *Furniture designer/maker, Man with a van, Antique dealer, Interior designer*

Enquiries
Local upholsterers, Guild of Master Craftsmen

In spite of an increase in throw-away furniture, there is a demand for upholsterers, especially to refurbish antiques. The work you do is meant to last up to 50 years and requires extensive knowledge of fabrics, stuffing, wood and the best ways of using them; an appreciation of antiques and their value is essential. Women may encounter a certain amount of sexism from more old fashioned practitioners of the trade; ('a woman just can't do some of this work') but clients are usually broader minded. You need skill to set up a new business and the more experience you have the better.

You can learn the trade by taking a course leading to a City and Guilds certificate. This will give you the rudiments but not the vast range of experience and practice that is regarded as essential. Traditionally upholsterers serve a five-year apprenticeship including time at a technical college before they are let loose on commercial work. During this time you will earn very little and if you're a woman, may find you are expected to be more interested in curtains and soft furnishings than in stuffing, caning etc. Some people drift into upholstery mid-career, without this training or experience. There are obvious exceptions but, by and large, they have neither the skill nor the speed to make a living – usually doing this as a sideline to something else. Experience and practice are essential; you will have to have attained a certain degree of speediness before it is worthwhile operating as an upholsterer. You can charge around £25 for the seat of a dining chair, £600 for refurbishing a three-seater sofa, so if you can't work fast enough, you won't make money.

You need large premises, to work in and to store both the materials (stuffing, springs, buttons, braid, hair etc) and the pieces you are working on. You also need tools, hammers, needles, shears, etc. A very basic kit costs a minimum of £20, but you will want to build on that (heavy-duty sewing machine, web stretcher), and to replace tools with better quality (shears range from £7–£150 for a pair). Covering fabrics are usually bought to client specification. A van is useful so that you can collect from and deliver to your clients. Insurance is essential, especially if you are going to work on valuable antiques.

Upholsterers have to be painstaking, dextrous and able to work to deadlines. Clients believe they are paying a great deal (although you may disagree) for their upholstery service so it is important to get everything right as business comes from word of mouth.

There are no definitive texts on upholstery. However, *Upholstery* and *Practical Upholstering and the Cutting of Loose Covers* give a good introduction and you will find the GUILD OF MASTER CRAFTSMEN helpful.

Vv

Venue Manager

Qualifications/Training	No
Income bracket	Low-Medium
Licence	No
Town/Country	Town
Experience/ Springboard	Recommended
Travel	No
Mid-career entry	No
Exit sale	Yes
Entry costs	£5,000++
Work at home	No
Mix and match	Very limited.

You could think about: *Disco owner/ DJ, Racehorse owner, Landlord*

Enquiries
Local venues, booking agents

Venue managers are in business to provide the 'theatre' in which bands and groups perform to their audiences. It is a young person's job and the secret of success is to get in at an early age. Often the most successful people are graduates and ex-students who managed to cut their teeth arranging concerts and events while still at university or polytechnic. Many social secretaries leave without their degrees because they've spent all their time arranging gigs (eg Harvey Goldsmith). At college there is a ready-made structure for arranging events with an eager audience but without the economic pressure of the real world.

The first step is to join the Ents society at your college. Get to know everyone and work your way to becoming the Ents secretary. Normally these are sabbatical posts that you can take up during the end of your course.

Take an interest in the music industry and what's being written up in the music newspapers; follow local bands. The newspapers give you some idea of who's up-and-coming across the country from which you can identify possible candidates for college bookings. Contacts you make at this early stage can prove invaluable to you later when you start up on your own.

Having got some experience at college and made initial contact with some of the people established in the industry, your next move must be to London if you aren't already there. Nearly all the major booking agents are London-based, as is the music industry itself, so there's really no alternative. Start by working for a booking agent. They are the lynch pin between bands and promoters, choosing and arranging venues throughout the country and therefore ideal people to work for in order to find your feet. But beware, the music business is not for slackers. It's a ruthless business and the only way you can justify yourself is by earning your booking agent money. The experience should be good – you'll learn all about contracts and the organisation of the business – but the salary is likely to be bad, perhaps £7,500 or £8,000 if you're lucky.

From here, you can springboard into venue management. It is important to have some idea of the sort of place you would like to run and the types of band or music you want to put on. The next step is to find a suitable venue and a financial backer. If all this is forthcoming, you can concentrate on the job in hand which, apart from a lot of hard graft, largely boils down to PR. The best approach is to try and build a reputation for an individual or specialist type of music that will distinguish your venue from others. The work is very tiring and demands your complete attention; a six-day week is normal; working 14 days on the trot, 12 or 13 hours each day, is not uncommon. You'll need good man-management skills, as there'll be a high staff turnover. You'll have to be willing to get your hands dirty since much of the work will involve you in shifting heavy equipment.

Financial rewards may not be high – probably no more than £14,000. However, you could have the satisfaction of turning an empty space into a successful venue and the kudos that goes with it.

Vet

Qualifications/Training	Essential
Income bracket	Medium-High
Licence	Yes
Town/Country	Either
Experience/Springboard	Yes
Travel	Local
Mid-career entry	Unlikely
Exit sale	Excellent
Entry costs	£15,000+
Work at home	Possible
Mix and match	Yes.

You could think about: *Farmer, Novelist, Property developer*

Enquiries
Royal College of Veterinary Surgeons

A large number of vets work in private practice; some are in towns dealing with small animals; there are also openings in rural practices (farm animals, horses etc). Variety can be achieved if you have a small zoo in your area.

Before being allowed to practise vets must, by law, become members of the ROYAL COLLEGE OF VETERINARY SUR-

GEONS (RCVS). To do this you face very fierce competition for a five- or six-year degree course (400 places for 1,600 applicants – you will need very good grades in science A-levels).

There is a trend for newly qualified vets to set up in partnership as soon as possible after gaining experience as an assistant or locum. This is partly due to the poor pay and conditions normally offered to assistants. If you are setting up your own practice, it is important to have had experience of as many different practices as possible so you see the work vets do at first hand and also the business aspects. (The BRITISH VETERINARY ASSOCIATION has started to run courses on the business aspects of running a practice.) Students can always visit practices but, once you are qualified, the best way of doing this is by working as a locum for a while.

Vets sometimes share the responsibility of their practice with one or more partners – this involves a very great commitment ('more difficult to get out of than marriage'). A male/female combination allows you to pander to any client preference. On the whole, sexism is no longer rife although farmers may expect to see a man doing things like calving or trimming cows' feet. You are dependent on good nurses and lay staff to help run the practice and establish good client relations. You can buy yourself into an existing practice but you will usually need to be known first because of the amount of financial and professional dependence between partners. These opportunities arise from contacts or by working as an assistant in the practice for a year or so (look for jobs 'with prospects' in the *Veterinary Record*). To set up a new practice you need planning permission. This can take three to six months and involves providing eg sound-proofing, an efficient waste disposal system and agreeing to run an appointments system. Then you can apply for a mortgage – 100 per cent available from some such as the Royal Trust Company of Canada. People tend to use their nearest vet so choose your site carefully and know your competition (animal hospitals etc). You will need about £8,000–£10,000 worth of equipment (although secondhand can be bought from hospitals etc) and about £4,000–£5,000 stock of drugs. A good relationship with your bank is essential for loans and because you will probably not make any profit for several years.

Theoretically you can charge what you like but the NHS has made people unaware of the real cost of treatment. You can expect to make up to £20,000–£30,000 as a partner. You will put about 25 per cent of what you charge back into the practice. Specialism is restricted by the fact that the RCVS insists that all practices treat any sick animal that is brought in. So you cannot advertise yourself as being a specialist for any particular type of animal or problem (unless you have been recognised as a specialist by the RCVS), although other vets will get to know and refer particular problems to you if you have a specialist knowledge or experience. You have to provide 24-hour emergency cover every day of the year.

You need to be able to cope with people who may be anxious or distressed about their animal and it helps to have some business sense. It is important to keep abreast of medical and veterinary developments through journals, books, continuing education courses and contact with local hospitals, dentists etc. You should have a strong liking for animals, lots of stamina to cope with the physically and mentally demanding work and sometimes long hours. You should not be squeamish.

⁎⁎⁎ European Community Notes

Qualifications: UK qualifications recognised throughout EC and EC qualifications in UK.

Languages: To succeed, local language necessary.

Earnings: UK income generally same as elsewhere in the EC.

Setting up: You will find it difficult to succeed in Italy. You will find it easier in Eire, Luxembourg.

Advice/Training: Advice, information and training available for those wishing to work in Europe.

Exchanges: Formal job exchanges do not exist.

Financial help: Exists for study, training or travel in the EC, specific to this job.

Enquiry point for those wishing to work in the EC: ROYAL COLLEGE OF VETERINARY SURGEONS

Recommended reading: Veterinary Record

Village Shopkeeper

Qualifications/Training	Available
Income bracket	Low–Medium
Licence	No (but alcohol licence)
Town/Country	Village
Experience/ Springboard	Recommended
Travel	No
Mid-career entry	Good
Exit sale	Excellent
Entry costs	£20,000++
Work at home	No
Mix and match	Limited.
You could think about: *Sub postmaster, Holiday accommodation owner, Scriptwriter*	
Enquiries	
National Association of Shopkeepers	

Supermarkets pose a severe threat to traditional small shops. Survival depends on adapting; rather than being a main stop for your customers, you'll depend on having a large clientele who buy a few essentials.

If you're opening a shop in residential premises, you apply for planning permission to change the use of the property. Objectors will most likely be the next door neighbours and the nearest competition. Alternatively you purchase an existing shop for a given sum plus the valuer's assessment of the value of the stock at takeover.

You can do a course at the COLLEGE FOR THE DISTRIBUTIVE TRADES or, as most people do, use their common sense and buy a book on VAT. Keep what your predecessors stock until you find it wrong. The stock value from scratch is approx

£15,000 to £20,000. Join the NATIONAL ASSOCIATION OF SHOPKEEPERS.

Get yourself onto a wholesaler's books and/or get a card from the best local cash and carry. Once a week, check what is left of each item and re-order or dash down to the cash and carry. Some items, such as milk, bread and fresh vegetables, need daily deliveries from the local milkman, baker etc.

If you're going to sell newspapers, you'll find that all areas are currently covered by franchise; unless you buy the newspaper round with your shop, you may find it impossible to get any newspapers or magazines from the wholesalers. However, if there is no competition from an existing newsagent, depending on the wholesaler's attitude *and* subject to a survey by the wholesaler, an application for the supply of newspapers and periodicals *may* succeed.

If you wish to stock alcohol you must apply to the magistrates and appear before them for a licence. If it is granted, you have to put your name over the door and keep your alcohol in a secure way. Find out the law about selling alcohol to youngsters before you appear before the magistrate. A friendly police sergeant appears in your shop about once a year to see if all is well with the sale of alcohol. It is unclear what this achieves but it happens. Aspects of shopkeeping are becoming more and more regulated, especially if you're handling food. For example, you'll need to display the country of origin for food (do you know where those oranges really come from?) and if you are preparing any food for sale you enter a whole new realm of regulation. Check with your local authority about *everything*.

To run a successful village/corner shop you need to know your customers, be willing to vary your stock according to their wants, ensure your staff are polite and courteous and be prepared to stay open for long hours to fit in with customer demand – this will mean that you'll probably be at your busiest when other people are on holiday, coming home from work etc.

Ww

Wedding Shop Owner

Qualifications/Training	None
Income bracket	Low–Medium
Licence	No
Town/Country	Town
Experience/ Springboard	Recommended
Travel	None
Mid-career entry	Yes
Exit sale	Yes
Entry costs	£500+
Work at home	No
Mix and match	Yes.

You could think about: *Fashion designer, Fashion retailer, Photographer, Caterer*

Enquiries
Local bridal retailers

There are nearly 350,000 weddings a year; a lot of these are traditional church weddings for which the bride and her attendant bridesmaids want to wear special dresses and accessories. For these they will pay anything from about £80–£1,500+. That means that there is a demand for shops which make, sell and alter wedding dresses, artificial floral headdresses and bouquets and sell wedding accessories.

You could start off in a very small way, making dresses for friends and contacts to your own or their designs; from this you may be able to build up a good enough reputation to make a living. On the whole though, if you want to make a commercial success from outfitting brides and bridesmaids, you'll have to have a shop and to do more than make dresses. For this it's very useful to have experience of bridal retail, which is quite different from selling other clothes. Customers want a lot of attention, they'll probably expect this to be a once in a lifetime occasion; remember this when you're putting up with yet another panic stricken phone call about whether or not the flowers will match the bridesmaids' dresses. You need to advise on what to wear with what; to know how to alter dresses; and it helps if you can think ahead and predict when an apparently calm bride is going to start worrying. Expect to have to put in some long hours from time to time, making sure that everything's ready in time. This is one job where you can't miss a deadline. You'll need, at the very least, a sewing machine, some scissors, tape measure and other sewing kit. Once you've got a shop you'll have to spend something on making it suitably pretty – buy some chairs and little tables and have flowers around, this puts people into the right mood. As well, you need enough space to store dresses before customers pick them up. Premises needn't be on the High Street, people are willing to travel some distance to the right wedding dress shop.

There's a vast range of ready-made wedding dresses available; for these you'll have to know your market. Hold a supply of samples of each style and order the right size as customers want them; for most you'll have to make some alterations. You should always have a supply of bridal accessories. Base your charges on what you're providing and on the time you expect to take making everything ready; you may need to employ some extra help during busy times so don't under-value this. Customers pay half of their bill when they place an order and the rest when you deliver. Other sources of income include altering wedding dresses under contract with larger shops and de-partment stores; making headdresses and bouquets (if you limit this to artificial flowers you'll avoid having to work franti-cally on the morning of the wedding with live ones and will be able to sell them to other retail outlets); your sample dresses can also generate income if you hire them out – it's normal to charge about half the retail price for this but hire customers will probably expect just as much attention as buying ones. You can also make money by making special wedding dresses to order.

You won't have many regular cus-tomers; most come through word of mouth; getting some good editorial in a local paper helps in the early days. Other-wise use leaflets, ads in the local press (you may get lost in the national press or in specialist magazines). Customers approach you about six months before the wedding and may want to make evening appoint-ments to see you and often use you as an agony aunt as the day approaches and they are finding their bridesmaids unobliging about dress fittings. The busiest season is from April to September so you can forget summer holidays; the only truly quiet time is over Christmas. During the quiet times you can build up your stock and keep an eye on slow moving wedding fashions by reading *Brides*.

Town/Country	Either
Experience/Springboard	No
Travel	Local
Mid-career entry	Possible
Exit sale	No
Entry costs	£300+
Work at home	No
Mix and match	Yes.

You could think about: *Painter/ decorator, Thatcher, Man with a van, Novelist, Physiotherapist*

Enquiries
Window cleaners

Window cleaners are very rare birds in many places – all you have to do is choose the right area. You need a ladder, a bucket, cloths and some sort of transport, also preferably a telephone number and busi-ness cards. Start off with a bit of practice at home; make sure that your balance is good and heights don't make you dizzy.

To begin with you'll have to establish a clientele – once you've established a repu-tation people will start to search you out rather than vice versa. Put cards through lots of letter boxes and wait to find out which areas give the best response. Even in London people don't want to have their windows cleaned more than once a month or six weeks so build up enough customers to keep you going. Charge from about £3 for a flat to about £12–£15 for a large house; more to clean inside as well as out. Most of it is outside work so there may be times when you won't be able to do as much as usual.

Phone your customers to make an appointment beforehand; if they're going to be out you'll have to make special arrangements. It also shows that you're reliable – worth doing because window cleaning is a well known cover for house-breaking.

You can also go for contract work on offices, shops and industrial establish-ments. This is another game normally re-quiring a group of you to tender and have access to equipment like cradles which you may not wish to acquire or rent. Or you can stay small – say working a couple of

Window Cleaner

Qualifications/Training	No
Income bracket	Low
Licence	No

days a week as a window cleaner and mix and match. Window cleaning is one of the easiest ways of mixing and matching because you can always choose when and where you work.

Windsurfing School Owner

Qualifications/Training	Necessary
Income bracket	Low-Medium
Licence	No
Town/Country	Country
Experience/Springboard	Useful
Travel	No
Mid-career entry	Good
Exit sale	Good
Entry costs	£5,000+
Work at home	No
Mix and match	Yes.

You could think about: *Sports retailer, Sailing school owner, Swimming teacher, Motorcycle racer, Magazine publisher*

Enquiries
Royal Yachting Association

The popularity of this relatively new sport has led to a demand for windsurf instruction. This is usually done by windsurfing schools – on small lakes, gravel pits or sheltered coastal sites; usually only the most advanced part of the ROYAL YACHTING ASSOCIATION (RYA) Scheme is taught on the sea. Running a school is a risky business due largely to the seasonal nature of demand (many fail) with little chance of a long-term future unless you run it alongside another business (a specialist sports shop, for example) which allows cross-fertilisation between your two businesses (pupils will buy equipment and customers will take courses).

The RYA's windsurfing training scheme allows you to award RYA certificates to successful pupils. If you want to use this scheme (which also gives credibility to your school) you will have to become an RYA Level 2 Instructor. This costs about £200 and the course lasts five days. You'll also need a first aid certificate and windsurfing experience. It's helpful to have had some previous instructing experience – not all good windsurfers make good teachers. As well as enjoying water sports (especially windsurfing) you'll need to have some organisational and business skills to run the school or the wherewithal to delegate.

Rent a lake to teach on. These are not easy to come by and usually cost at least £2,000 and sometimes up to £10,000 pa in rent with rates and any bills on top of that. On the whole motor and sail water sports can't operate on the same lake unless you time-share. You may be paying for the lake all year round even though the windsurfing season only lasts from about April to September. Find a lake that is accessible, (pupils won't want to travel too far) with adequate parking. Get the owner's agreement before you open the windsurfing school. If you're teaching on the sea you will need the permission of the local authority.

Basic equipment includes boards and sails, wet suits, buoyancy aids, marker buoys and a first aid kit. Also a rescue boat with outboard motor (£500–£1,000). In addition to boat and motor it costs about £2,000–£3,000 to equip a windsurfing school. You'll probably want to have at least a storage shed on the lake, and may need planning permission for it. This can grow and double up as a club house for regular lake users. You will need third party and liability insurance, also cover for the equipment. Build up a network of qualified freelance instructors. You'll need to have someone there all the time to stop people from using your lake without paying for it and to generally keep an eye on it. You may also need office staff to take bookings, deal with correspondence etc. You can enlist enthusiastic school-leavers to help issue pupils with boards and getting them waterbound. Occasionally, ready-made facilities will come up for tender – see the windsurfing press.

Advertise in local sports shops and newspapers. You may also get groups from local schools, clubs and businesses. Courses can be of any length from an hour to two weeks; groups are ideally of about three–six pupils. (The RYA will tell you which aspects of the sport you should cover at each level.) Get your pupils to pay in advance and make sure that they sign a responsibility disclaimer. Cancelled lessons, eg due to the weather, lose money because you have to fit them in at another time without charging. Business will also come from ex-pupils who hire boards, and use the lake for practice (charge about £5 per hour for hire and the same for access to the lake, with own board, per day) and taking additional courses. Many schools have clubs attached allowing use of the lake for an annual fee, Clubs also work as a way of keeping in touch with lake users over the winter so that they'll remember to come back again for the new season.

Useful publications include *Boards* and *Windsurf* magazines.

★★★★
★   ★ **European Community Notes**
★★★★

Qualifications: UK qualifications are recognised in many EC countries, EC qualifications may be in UK.

Languages: To succeed, local language necessary.

Earnings: UK income generally same as elsewhere in the EC – again, seasonal in nature.

Setting up: You will find it difficult to succeed in France, Germany, Greece, Italy, Luxembourg, Portugal, Spain.

You will find it easier in Belgium, Denmark, Eire, Netherlands.

Advice/Training: Advice, information and training not available for those wishing to work in Europe.

Exchanges: Formal job exchanges exist.

Enquiry point for those wishing to work in the EC: Mr. J. Jameson (Vice-Chairman ISSA), RYA Scotland, Caledonia House, South Oyle, Edinburgh EH12 9DQ, Tel: 031 317 7388.

Recommended reading: RYA publications

Notes: Check with appropriate national authority concerning licence/instructional qualifications.

Wine Bar Owner

Qualifications/Training	Recommended
Income bracket	Medium
Licence	Yes
Town/Country	Town
Experience/Springboard	Essential
Travel	Local
Mid-career entry	Good
Exit sale	Excellent
Entry costs	£25,000+
Work at home	No
Mix and match	Possible.

You could think about: *Wine merchant, Wine grower, Restaurateur, Antique dealer, Contemporary art gallery owner, Tourist attraction*

Enquiries
Wine and Spirit Education Trust, British Hospitality Association, Wine bar owners

Although wine bars are opening all the time, a great many of them go bust very quickly so it's worth doing some research before deciding where to open. Thanks to breathalysers and health consciousness, food is becoming increasingly important in wine bars. A good cook is essential as is some idea of local tastes. It's a full-time job, certainly to begin with, and it helps if you have a partner to share eg bookkeeping, front of house, planning menus and buying supplies; that way you may be able to take a few hours off without having to close.

No formal qualifications are necessary, but some experience working in a wine bar (at least a few months) is essential and is a good way of establishing contacts in the trade. You should know something about wine or have a dealer you trust. A catering or business training is useful. To survive, you'll have to be sociable and diplomatic and to balance friendliness with the ability to run a successful and profitable business.

Before opening, you'll need to have a licence obtained by applying to the magistrates' court. Brewers may put up opposition to this on behalf of local pubs especially if you're applying to sell draught beers or spirits. But on the whole, a wine-only licence is quite straightforward unless you have any sort of criminal record in which case your chances are slim. Unless you're taking over an existing wine bar premises you'll need permission for change of use from the local planning department. They will make stringent checks on fire, safety and health as well as considering objections from local residents. The food side is also heavily, and increasingly, regulated. All 'eating houses' have to be registered with the local authority and all commercial preparation and cooking of food, and the premises, are subject to inspection by environmental health officers under the Food Safety Act. Involve EHOs early with plans for kitchens, bar etc; they cannot stop you opening but they can shut you overnight – and you could face unlimited fines and imprisonment, to boot! Choose premises that are not too small (seating at least 40–50) in a mainly residential area ideally with some local business too for lunchtime trade. You can buy freehold or a special catering lease – say 15 years with three/five-yearly rent review (always up). Premises – in the past, at least – come with a premium: sellable 'goodwill' goes with a big turnover, so if you're doing well not only is your income buoyant but your exit sale goes up. So if you are buying premises from a business that's up and running get a *good* look at the books – at least three years' worth – and get your accountant to check them out thoroughly.

The costs of setting up, apart from premises, vary. It will cost about £20,000 to equip from scratch, with ovens, storage fridges, loos etc, and you will need about £2,000–£3,000 worth of stock (trade contacts are useful for credit for this). Apply for a mortgage or bank loan but expect to have to put up about 50 per cent of the opening costs yourself. On top of any staff costs, you also need to budget for heating,

lighting, accountant and solicitor, a good laundry service, and maintenance back up prepared to answer any emergency calls. You can charge approximately three times cost price, plus VAT. The obvious hazard is the ease with which you can become an alcoholic; you also have to deal with occasional drunks and under-age drinkers, listen to bores, act as confessor and put up with patronising customers. If you come from a non-catering background and are used to being treated with some deference, you may be surprised by the churlish attitude of some customers; wine-bar owners in Britain report on a national disdain for the catering profession. That's another reason for getting plenty of experience before going it on your own – finding out about *having to deal with people*. It's easy to fall foul of the finer details of health and safety regulations so it's important to be familiar with them all. The WINE AND SPIRITS EDUCATION TRUST COURSES vary from the most elementary to the most sophisticated. *Decanter* is the bible of the trade. For someone who enjoys socialising and doesn't mind working very hard it's rewarding. As with restaurateurs, husband and wife teams often do well – one can do food, say, the other the wine and front-of-house side – but fatigue is endemic and it can be 'a real marriage wrecker'.

Wine Grower

Qualifications/Training	Recommended
Income bracket	Low-Medium
Licence	Yes
Town/Country	Country
Experience/Springboard	Useful
Travel	No
Mid-career entry	Good
Exit sale	Excellent
Entry costs	£90,000+
Work at home	Yes

Mix and match   Essential to start.
You could think about: *Wine bar owner,
Tourist attraction, Holiday
accommodation owner, Gardener/
garden designer*

Enquiries
English Vineyards Association

A vineyard – what a marvellous idea! The
imagination conjures up a picture of sunny
days spent lovingly tending the vines,
which have plentiful bunches of juicy,
disease-free grapes, swelling magnificently
just ready for picking. Reality is of course
entirely different.

To start, you will need access to plenty
of money and a willingness to put up with
a negative cash flow (ie, no income) for the
first five years and the subsequent risk that
the enterprise fails and you lose the lot.
You will need a well-sheltered site in the
south of England, south-facing, with free-
draining soil, not in a frost pocket nor too
high. If tourism is a consideration, it needs
to be well placed for that too. The smallest
commercially viable vineyard is about 10
acres. Once you have the site, it will cost
about £40,000 to establish the vineyard,
plus at least £25,000 for a tractor and
related machinery and equipment. You
should expect to harvest 5,000 bottles
from 10 acres in your third year (for sale in
your fourth), building up to 30,000
bottles after five–six years – so you will
need a second income to live on at least in
the short term. You ought to know how
you are going to sell your wine at the
outset. There are a remarkable number of
vineyards with bonded stores full of
unsold wine and it is difficult to establish
an unknown brand – especially through
the wine trade which is, not unnaturally,
able to be choosy as to whose wines it will
stock. English wine is a premium product
but many people still confuse it with the
totally different British Wine.

It makes sense to open a tourist-related
enterprise too. You can then promote your
wine direct to the public and sell at full
retail prices. You need to be near where
tourists go or be able to offer something
pretty special if you are to persuade them
off the beaten track. To do it properly you
will need further capital to build a car park,
wine bar or tasting room, interpretation
facilities – and loos, of course. Selling a
premium product needs to be done properly; it's hard work convincing someone to
spend £5.00-plus on a bottle of wine when
you're selling it out of a tin shed.

To succeed you will need to be able to
grow what is a high value and very
demanding crop – diseases and disorders
need to be recognised and acted on swiftly
or they can write off your whole crop. A
formal horticultural or agricultural qualification is desirable. If you are going to
make your own wine, then a science and
mathematics background is useful as wine-
making is much more science-based than it
used to be. Many growers send their
grapes away to another vineyard or a contract winemaker who comes back a few
months later with their (usually well-
made) wine in bottles – and a bill. You will
need to be able to cope with interference
from the Trading Standards Officer (they
check how full your bottles are), the Wine
Standards Board (who administer all the
EC regulations on wine), and of course
Customs and Excise (who license you to
make wine and collect the duty). This
means careful record keeping. But you are
allowed four bottles a day, duty free, if you
can drink that much.

If you send a large SAE to the ENGLISH
VINEYARDS ASSOCIATION they will send
you a list of vineyards open to the public
and membership details. They also produce a useful quarterly magazine, the
Grape Press. Read also the *New English
Vineyard*, *Vinegrowing in Britain*, *The
Vineyards of England* or *A Tradition of
English Wine*. Visit as many vineyards as
you can – most growers are gregarious and
friendly, if a little odd.

You will be watching for diseases during
the summer and picking grapes in October
so you should have an enthusiasm for winter holidays. It is a very pleasant way of
life, if not wildly profitable. But it is possible to succeed, with a good dose of realism injected into initial plans. It's too easy
to get carried away and nothing would be
worse than to find 10 years later that it
doesn't work after all and the best years of
your life have gone.

⋆⋆⋆⋆
⋆   ⋆
⋆   ⋆ **European Community Notes**
⋆⋆⋆⋆
Prospects for independent wine growers in the EC are alluring, especially France, Germany, Portugal and Spain (Greece, Italy and Luxembourg could prove difficult), with the promise of higher income than in the UK – though of course it is necessary to buy your own vineyard and/or winery.

Wine Merchant

Qualifications/Training	Recommended
Income bracket	Low-High
Licence	Yes, if you sell single bottles
Town/Country	Either
Experience/Springboard	No
Travel	Yes
Mid-career entry	Good
Exit sale	Yes
Entry costs	£5,000++
Work at home	Yes
Mix and match	Essential to start.

You could think about: **Wine bar owner, Restaurateur, Direct marketing consultant, List broker, Events organiser**

Enquiries
Wine and Spirit Education Trust, Wine merchants

Don't become an independent wine merchant if you have to make money to start with; there are too many people at it, margins are too low, and big customers are surprisingly loyal to existing suppliers. But, if you are looking for a means of earning while following your wine tasting hobby or giving some commercial purpose to your wine tasting holidays then maybe you are on to something. There are many merchants operating successfully who started by bringing a few cases back from holiday and selling to friends. But bear in mind that the wine trade generally tends to suffer from chronic cash flow problems and fierce competition, although the rivalry is friendly.

You will need to take the courses run by the WINE AND SPIRIT EDUCATION TRUST (they are short and part-time). If, like many aspiring merchants, you are an enthusiastic amateur (member of a wine tasting club and reader of eg *Wine Magazine* or *Decanter*), you can probably skip the first certificate course. But you will need to take the higher certificate and diploma courses to know enough about wines (regions, labels, tasting etc) in order to be able to speak reasonably knowledgeably to your customers. (A very few progress to Master of Wine and it is not really necessary.) It is possible, though not advisable, to take the courses at home. Expect to take about three years to get the diploma. Languages are useful, especially if you want to use small suppliers who may not speak English.

The traditional structure of the trade is: producer – shipper – wholesaler – retailer – consumer. Though still discernible, this is crumbling as wholesalers sell direct to the public and shippers direct to retailers. And, of course, supermarkets and wine warehouses ship many of their products direct from producers to the final consumer. This has the effect of shattering margins on wines coming through the old set-up, making some of them quite uncompetitive. But the big chains require large volumes of totally consistent wine so they have to buy from the large producers, co-operatives and negociants or shippers.

Most wine regions still have plenty of independent growers whose production is nowhere near the size to interest the big buyers, so here is an opportunity for the small specialist. (Small providers often have less modern equipment so quality could be less consistent though.) As wine consumption increases, so will the sophistication of the consumer and a market exists for those looking for wines with individuality in the middle and upper price range. Here the independent can give personal attention and advice unlikely to be found in a supermarket.

Buying from producers is not difficult and can be great fun. Shipment is generally easy; 25 cases can be viable, using group-age through freight-forwarders, but rates reduce dramatically as quantity rises. However, the more prestigious proprietors will already have UK customers or agents they will expect you to use and, though there are plenty of others, you cannot always be certain that the wines they send will be the same as tasted in the cellar. If you are exporting, you should be able to reclaim the VAT but will have to pay excise duty when you import it to this country.

If you buy from producers you will get the best prices but have to carry stock which requires capital. If you buy from shippers they will have a minimum order of five or six cases, perhaps with a discount structure for larger quantities, so you need only modest stocks. If you buy from wholesalers they will sell you a single case (at a higher price, of course) but your stocks are minimal. The same rules apply as in any business – a quick turnover can be done at a low margin; a slow turnover needs a margin to cover the capital involved.

Restaurants are often interested in lesser-known wines but they may take extended credit, can be quite demanding about delivery and may want contributions towards printing the wine list; cash from the general public is best. Mail order is a ripe market for some specialist wines; national advertising is needed and delivery costs can be very high (less significant with more expensive wines). No licence is required to sell by the case but don't get caught selling single bottles. Or you can buy an off-licence as a base so you can display and sell single bottles. If you want to sell specialist wines, there is no need to get involved in cut-price spirits and beers but choose your site carefully. Here you would need magistrates' approval of yourself and your activities but there should be no problem with an existing off-licence. To get permission to convert a property to an off-licence is much more difficult, requiring planning consent and probably attracting objection from other off-licence holders and the local residents.

✦ European Community Notes

Qualifications: UK qualifications recognised throughout EC and EC qualifications in UK.

Languages: To succeed, local language necessary.

Earnings: UK income generally same as elsewhere in the EC.

Advice/Training: Advice, information and training not available for those wishing to work in Europe.

Exchanges: Formal job exchanges do not exist.

Financial help: exists for study, training or travel in the EC, specific to this job.

Enquiry point for those wishing to work in the EC: WINE AND SPIRIT EDUCATION TRUST.

Wood Carver

Qualifications/Training	Recommended
Income bracket	Low–Medium
Licence	No
Town/Country	Either
Experience/Springboard	No
Travel	No
Mid-career entry	Possible
Exit sale	No
Entry costs	£2,500
Work at home	Yes
Mix and match	Yes.

You could think about: *Furniture designer/maker, Psychoanalyst, Sculptor, Carpenter*

Enquiries
Guild of Master Craftsmen

Much of this work involves commissions for clients who want pieces custom built to their own specifications. In addition to an expert knowledge of wood and how to treat it, you will therefore need tact, patience and determination. Within reason you can set your own deadlines but these must be met so if things go wrong, you may have to do some quick thinking.

You will need to rent or buy somewhere to work (possibly a converted garage), £700–£1,000 worth of equipment and tools (these can be bought secondhand), publicity material and a ready source of wood. Some form of transport is useful for larger jobs away from your workshop. Setting up on your own as a craftsman is difficult but you can survive by producing small items for local craft shops/markets and the tourist trade.

To learn the trade you can become an apprentice for several years before qualifying. This will provide regular employment but restrict your artistic freedom; and apprenticeship tends to be available only to those of school-leaving age. Or you can take a degree course in three-dimensional design (find one specialising in wood; or apply to ADAR). The CITY & GUILDS OF LONDON ART SCHOOL and the JOHN MAKEPEACE SCHOOL are the only places in the UK offering courses specifically for craftsmen wood carvers; but even with this qualification you will need perseverance.

Contacts are all-important. Most work will come via interior designers and those who desire those extra touches, eg special carving, panelling, plinths etc, for their dream homes, so you should cultivate an artistic aura. Try approaching the specialists direct (see *Yellow Pages*), get some cards printed – design them yourself. The most likely route is to pool resources with others, invest in a workshop or join an established group of fellow craftsmen.

A newly qualified wood carver can expect to earn about £50 per day by calculating the cost of each piece produced plus a charge for time and materials, not forgetting any special effects or finishes but you are almost bound to have slack periods. Having become established, commissions are likely to come through word of mouth so get as much exposure for your work as possible. Arrange joint exhibitions with other craftworkers. The local press may be interested in writing a short article, with photographs, about an especially decorative or outrageous item (but check with the owner first), particularly if it's for a local celebrity. Some shops, galleries or restaurants may be willing to exhibit samples of work, or display your cards.

If you are working with others, this can be a sociable, relaxed job but you are likely to have to devote a lot of your time to repetitive jobs, eg friezes, panelling. Your clients may not share your taste, but if you find that some of your ideas are commercial, you may have to spend more time on them than being creative.

Useful books about wood carving include *Practical Woodworking*, the *Craftsman's Handbook*. Join the GUILD OF MASTER CRAFTSMEN.

Word Processor

Qualifications/Training	Useful
Income bracket	Low-Medium
Licence	No
Town/Country	Mostly town
Experience/ Springboard	Recommended
Travel	Local maybe
Mid-career entry	Yes
Exit sale	No
Entry costs	£4,000
Work at home	Yes
Mix and match	Yes.

You could think about: ***Typist, Typesetter, Shopkeeper, Proofreader/ copy editor, Jazz musician***

Enquiries
Word processing agencies

Almost all offices are now equipped with micro computers and use word processors and their secretarial staff are expected to have word processing skills. To make a career as your own boss in word processing you have to be able to offer something not otherwise available, or in short supply, to clients who already have offices equipped with micros. If you can offer specific skills like languages, mathematical or engineering knowledge for example, you may be able to carve out a specialist niche for yourself.

You don't need any formal skills to become a word processor. What you do need is intelligence, good spelling, common-sense, a capacity for working accurately for hours at a time, often on a boring job. Computers are marvellous machines (if you are afraid of them don't become a word processor) but they don't correct your mistakes. The fewer mistakes you make at the initial keying stage, the more time you have to take on more work. Word processing is a competitive business (just look at the *Yellow Pages*) and the rates you charge are generally restricted by the competition. But do a good job once, and however small it is put something into it that your competition doesn't offer (often sensible comments before you start) and your client will undoubtedly come back to you next time.

You need at least one computer (preferably two identical ones in case one goes wrong), a reliable and high quality printer, computer stationery (disks, labels, paper), a telephone and electricity. You will need to advertise your service (not in newspapers or other short life publications) but this will not bring you an immediate response. Your first source of work will probably be through a carefully selected mailing of possible clients in your region. In general it isn't worth looking for work outside a radius of more than 30 or 40 miles.

You are very unlikely to make a fortune (unless you can afford to branch out into related fields, such as translation, recruitment, publishing) but you should expect to make a living after a couple of years – if you don't, try something else.

A good computer will cost approx £1,000 (including cables and word processing programs), a printer £2,000; allow at least £100 for floppy disks and £100 for stationery. If you are starting with a bank loan or HP be warned that you will probably only be offered a three-year agreement, although if you have enough clout you may get this extended to five. You will find that all machines you buy will outlive the technology they represent so it is important to get advice before committing yourself to ensure that data will be transferable to future generations of equipment.

You must be prepared to work seven days a week. Anybody who wants you to do a job for them wants it very quickly – that is why they come to you. It is worth trying to get some sort of arrangement with another word processing office, or having a network of outside contacts (ideally with their own machines and certainly able to produce compatible disks) so that you never need to turn a job away because it is too large. You must be interested in every job that you do – typing a list of names and addresses is very boring but you have got to find something in it that interests you. If you don't you will make silly mistakes and lose that client.

All word processing work has three parts. 1) Keying in data. Typing skills are essential for this. 2) Correcting data. Here you need an ability to read quickly and accurately and a thorough knowledge of your word processing program. 3) Printing. This is a mechanical process but it is surprising how much time you can save by knowing how to ensure that machines are set up correctly for each job. By and large clients will bring their work to you (often they want to see what your equipment is like) but you may well need to deliver proofs and final copy.

You should always insist that your client reads and corrects a proof: resist as far as you can any pressure to take a job through to final output without your client seeing it. Always expect copy to be a mess (and quote on that basis) and never believe anyone who says they won't need to make changes to the manuscript. Your clients will vary enormously, from academics writing books on abstract technical subjects to the local builder who wants you to type a quotation for building a public urinal. Each has its own challenge and each must be equally important to you. Before you take on any work satisfy yourself that you have considered all the possible problems before you give a quotation and make sure you allow for subsequent 'extras'. You must have a schedule of rates for all types of work (keying, correcting, printing) even if you depart from these rates for any reason. It is all too easy to give a figure for a job and then forget how you worked it out! You will need *Yellow Pages*, any local trade directory or Chamber of Commerce directory to find potential clients.

Yoga Teacher

Qualifications/Training	Yes
Income bracket	Low
Licence	No
Town/Country	Either
Experience/Springboard	No
Travel	Local
Mid-career entry	Yes
Exit sale	No
Entry costs	£480
Work at home	Possible
Mix and match	Yes.

You could think about: *Healthfood shopkeeper, Beekeeper, Healer, Furniture designer/maker*

Enquiries
Iyengar Yoga Institute, Yoga teachers

The very essence of yoga is that it is for most people strictly non-competitive, so the concept of 'making it to the top' is not an appropriate one. Having said that, only very few yoga teachers do more than scrape a living. Most teach part-time rather than as a full-time pursuit.

Most yoga teaching in this country is by the method practised by the IYENGAR YOGA INSTITUTE. To qualify as a teacher you need to have done a minimum of two years' 'Iyengar' yoga (most people do more). This means regular attendance at classes run by a qualified Iyengar teacher, after which you have to attend a teacher training course (one class a week for a minimum of two years). This is followed by an assessment of your own practice and understanding of the postures to be taught under your relevant syllabus, and of your teaching abilities. On passing you are awarded a teaching certificate, of which there are four further grades.

The most important qualities required to succeed as a yoga teacher are a thorough knowledge of the postures and breathing techniques, with the ability to practise and demonstrate as well as to teach them. You need to be mature and sensitive and acutely observant. Dedication to the subject and to the pupils is also necessary.

Expenses to set up depend on where you intend to teach. Many local education authorities employ yoga teachers. If you use a suitable room in your own house, costs will be minimal; you may be able to teach in other people's houses, in which case you'll find it useful to have a car; some companies organise yoga classes for their employees at their offices; or you can hire premises, such as a church hall, which is obviously more expensive. Start by spending just a few pounds on a mat for yourself and some belts. You can also buy various items of equipment such as wooden and foam blocks, blankets, back stretchers, ropes and bolsters.

How much you earn will depend on the number of pupils you teach and how much time you are prepared to spend. Most people do not feel able to teach for longer than three hours a day because they find it too demanding and physically exhausting, though some manage to teach for perhaps four or five hours. Few teachers earn enough to be able to support themselves. You can start by taking two classes a day, say, which would earn you a maximum of £25. Even if you did this for five days a week, it's obvious that we're not talking big money. An established teacher hiring a hall and teaching yoga weekends can charge students £40 for the weekend. A few internationally known teachers earn more and spend considerable amounts of money on travel. By being very organised about advertising you can do better too; though for most people word of mouth is the best way of getting work.

Yoga is not an easy option and demands a great deal of personal practice. It's also important to keep up to date with new developments and ways of thinking. One magazine which will help is *Yoga and Health*. Three good books to read are *Light on Yoga* and *Light on Pranayama*, and *Yoga a Gem for Women*.

⁎⁎⁎ European Community Notes

Qualifications: UK qualifications recognised throughout EC and EC qualifications in UK.

Languages: To succeed, local language necessary.

Earnings: UK income generally lower than elsewhere in the EC.

Setting up: You will find it easier to succeed in Eire, France, Germany, Italy, Netherlands, Spain.

Advice/Training: Advice, information and training available for those wishing to work in Europe.

Exchanges: Formal job exchanges do not exist.

Enquiry point for those wishing to work in the EC: IYENGAR YOGA INSTITUTE

Zz

Zoo Keeper

Qualifications/Training	Recommended
Income bracket	Medium
Licence	Yes
Town/Country	Either
Experience/Springboard	Essential
Travel	Yes
Mid-career entry	Likely
Exit sale	Possible
Entry costs	£1 million+
Work at home	No
Mix and match	Possible.

You could think about: *Tourist attraction, Vet, Restaurateur, Novelist*

Enquiries
Federation of Zoos, Association of British Wild Animal Keepers

Britain has lots of zoos – over 250 – so you should be quite certain this is what you want to do before you think of starting up another. If you want to make money, do something else. All but a few commercially owned large zoos are owned by charitable foundations. If you have a strong commitment to animals and their preservation, and can stand people as well as animals, then it's worth considering. By law you must have a licence.

Zoos see themselves as being in the conservation business. They are keen to scotch the myth that zoos are full of animals snatched from the wild. A tiny proportion of zoo animals in this country have ever caught sight of the wild (mostly the geriatrics) and many are bred in captivity with a policy of then returning them to the wild. Although there are some 250 licensed zoos in Britain only about 50 are what would be generally recognised as zoos ie, with some of the larger mammals and birds traditionally associated with zoos.

You can start with a small number of animals if you choose to be very specialised and have, say, just a few great apes or, more likely, just monkeys – or small mammals, birds and so on. Once you are established and have started a breeding programme, you probably won't have to buy animals because there is strong co-operation between zoos in the UK and abroad. But to start up, you should expect to spend sums in the order of £400 for a marmoset to £25,000–£30,000 for an Asian elephant. And this is only the beginning. To start up a zoo is wildly expensive – millions to start a reasonably sized one. The animals must be satisfactorily housed, cared for and fed – so you will need to obtain planning consent and staff and be able to foot substantial food bills. In addition, your visitors will need facilities – somewhere to park, loos, food, a shop or play area – all of which have to be built and then staffed. You must have a good head for business and be able to manage staff.

As well as the financial considerations you must have worked in a zoo, to get to know the business, and have a good theoretical and practical knowledge of animals. Most take a City and Guilds Diploma (you can take it by correspondence) or some other animal husbandry course. You must also have a sound concept of the wider issues of conservation. Approach the FED-ERATION OF ZOOS and the ASSOCIATION OF BRITISH WILD ANIMAL KEEPERS.

Understandably, this area is much governed by regulations. To open at all you must be licensed. This involves being inspected by the local authority together with two specialised inspectors (a zoo curator and a zoo vet), appointed by the DEPARTMENT OF THE ENVIRONMENT. You are also controlled by the animal health regulations administered by the MINISTRY OF AGRICULTURE. Britain is a signatory to the Convention on International Trade in Endangered Species and this is administered in this country by the DEPARTMENT OF THE ENVIRONMENT. Imported animals are covered by the usual constraints – blood tests on zebras, specialist dockside quarantine for antelopes, six months rabies quarantine on cats, primates and most other species.

Your visitors will be seasonal – you'll get more winter visitors in an urban zoo. But Easter and the school summer holidays and weekends are the favourite zoo visiting times. You will need good insurance cover, including a large public liability insurance. However, most of your claims are likely to be for people falling over, rather than being savaged by a tiger – a well-run zoo has a safety record comparable with a farm. One zoo owner believed the biggest danger on his zoo was visitors parking their cars.

European Community Notes

Qualifications: UK qualifications not generally recognised in EC (except The Netherlands), EC qualifications occasionally in UK.

Languages: To succeed, local language necessary.

Earnings: UK income generally same as elsewhere in the EC.

Setting up: You will find it difficult to succeed in Greece, Italy.

You will find it easier in Eire, Germany, Netherlands, Spain.

Advice/Training: Advice, information and training not available for those wishing to work in Europe.

Exchanges: Formal job exchanges do not exist.

Recommended reading: International Zoo Yearbook, International Zoo News, Ratel.

Notes: Very few UK nationals work in zoos abroad.

Independent
Job Search Index

Job	Qualifications/ training	Licence	Experience/ springboard	Mid-career entry	Entry costs	Income bracket	Town/ country	Travel	Exit sale	Work at home	Mix and match
Accountant	Yes	Yes, to audit	Necessary	Possible	£20,000	Medium–High	Town	Yes	Yes	Possible	Possible
Actor	Recommended	Union card essential	No	Unlikely	£100	Low–Medium	Town	Yes	No	No	Often essential
Actuary	Essential	Yes	Essential	Possible	£2,000+	High	Town	Yes	Possible	Yes	Possible
Acupuncturist	Yes	Recommended	Yes	Possible	£100+	Low–Medium	Town	No	No	Yes	Yes
Advertising Agent	Useful	No	Essential	Unlikely	£7,000	Medium–High	Town	Possible	Yes	Unlikely	Yes
Advertising Photographer	Recommended	No	Recommended	Possible	£6,000	Medium–High	Town	Yes	Yes	Yes	Yes
Alexander Technique Teacher	Yes	No	Recommended	Yes	£500	Low–Medium	Town	Local	No	Yes	Possible
Antique Dealer (Large antiques)	Not formal	No	Recommended	Excellent	£50,000+	Low–High	Town/ Village	Essential	Yes	Possible	Yes
Antique Dealer (Small antiques and collectibles)	Not formal	No	Recommended	Excellent	£5,000+	Low–High	Town/ Village	Yes	Possible	Possible	Yes
Antique Furniture Restorer	Recommended	No	Essential	Yes	£5,000	Low–Medium	Either	Possible	No	Possible	Yes
Architect	Essential	Yes	Yes	Possible	£2,000+	Medium–High	Either	Yes	Yes	Possible	Possible
Art Historian/Critic	Recommended	No	Essential	Yes	Nil	Low–Medium	Either	Yes	No	Yes	Yes
Artist	Recommended	No	No	Yes	£50	Low	Either	Possible	No	Yes	Yes

Job	Qualifications/training	Licence	Experience/springboard	Mid-career entry	Entry costs	Income bracket	Town/country	Travel	Exit sale	Work at home	Mix and match
Artists' Agent	No	No	Helpful	Yes	£5,000	Low–Medium	Town	Local	Possible	Not recommended	Yes
Assistant Film Director	No	Union card	Yes	No	£500	Low–Medium	Town	Yes	No	No	Limited
Barrister/Advocate	Essential	Yes	No	Unlikely	£1,000+	Medium–High	Town	Yes	No	No	Possible
Bartender	No	No	No	Yes	Nil	Low	Either	No	No	No	Yes
Beauty Consultant	Recommended	No	Recommended	Possible	£2,000	Low–Medium	Town	Local	No	Possible	Possible
Bed and Breakfast	None	No	No	Excellent	£200–£750	Low–Medium	Either	No	Minimal	Yes	Excellent
Beekeeper	Available	No	Useful	Yes	£5,000	Low	Country	Local	Yes	Yes	Yes
Book Designer	Recommended	No	Recommended	Doubtful	£1,000–£5,000	Medium	Town preferably	Local	No	Yes	Yes
Bookie	Available	Yes	Essential	Yes	£1,000 (on-course)	Highly variable	Town or on-course	Yes (on-course)	Possible	No	Possible
Book-keeper	Available	No	Recommended	Yes	£2,000	Low–Medium	Either	Some	No	Yes	Excellent
Book Packager	Available	No	Essential	Likely	£5,000–£10,000++	Medium	Either	Possible	Yes	Possible	Yes
Book Publisher	Available	No	Essential	Possible	£20,000	Low–High	Town	Yes	Yes	Yes	Possible
Bookseller	Available	No	Recommended	Yes	£20,000	Medium	Town	None	Yes	Yes	Possible
Brewer	Available	Yes	Essential	Likely	£60,000+++	Low–High	Either	No	Excellent	Yes	Possible

Job	Qualifications/ training	Licence	Experience/ springboard	Mid-career entry	Entry costs	Income bracket	Town/ country	Travel	Exit sale	Work at home	Mix and match
Builder	Yes	No	Recommended	Unlikely	£1,500++	Medium	Either	Local	Possible	No	Possible
Butcher	Available	No	Essential	Possible	£20,000	Medium	Town/ Village	Local	Yes	No	Limited
Cabaret Performer	Recommended	No	No	Possible	£2,000	Low–High	Town	Yes	No	No	Probably essential
Calligrapher	Necessary	No	Good idea	Possible	£200	Low	Town preferably	No	No	Yes	Yes
Camera Crew	Recommended	Union card necessary	No	Unlikely	£500+	Low–Medium	Town	Lots	No	No	Limited
Caravan Park Owner	No	No	No	Good	£125,000	Medium	Country	No	Yes	Yes	Excellent
Careers Adviser	Recommended	No	Usual	Yes	£2,000	Medium–High	Town	Local	Possible	Possible	Yes
Carpenter	Recommended	No	Recommended	Possible	£2,000	Low	Either	Local	No	No	Possible
Caterer	Useful	No	Useful	Yes	£2,500+	Low–Medium	Town or nearby	Local	Possible	Yes	Yes
Chamber Group Musician Manager	Essential	No	Vital	Yes	£6,000	Low	Town	Lots	No	No	Yes
Chemical Engineering Consultant	Essential	No	Essential	Yes	£12,000+	Medium–High	Town	Yes	Possible	Possible	Yes
Child/Educational Psychologist	Essential	Recommended	Essential	Possible	£1,500	Medium–High	Town	Local	Possible	Yes	Possible

Job	Qualifications/ training	Licence	Experience/ springboard	Mid-career entry	Entry costs	Income bracket	Town/ country	Travel	Exit sale	Work at home	Mix and match
Childminder	No	Yes	Yes	Yes	Nil	Low	Town/ Village	None	No	Yes	Limited
China Restorer	Recommended	No	Recommended	Possible	£1,000	Low	Town preferably	Local	No	Yes	Good
Chiropodist/ Podiatrist	Vital	No	Recommended	Yes	£5,000	Medium–High	Town	Local, possibly	No	Possible	Possible
Chiropractor	Essential	No	Yes	Unlikely	£9,000	Medium–High	Town	No	No	Possible	Limited
Classical Composer	Recommended	No	Recommended	Possible	£1,000	Low	Either	Possible	Yes	Yes	Essential
Classical Singer	Recommended	No	No	Unlikely	£500+	Low	Mostly town	Yes	No	No	Essential
Cleaning Contractor	No	No	No	Yes	£3,000+	Medium	Town	Local	Possible	Not recommended	Possible
Coal Merchant	Recommended	Yes, if new	Recommended	Possible	£5,000	Low–Medium	Either	Local	Yes	Possible	Possible
Company Doctor	No	No	Essential	Essential	Nil	Medium–High	Town	Yes	No	No	Yes
Computer Consultant	Available	No	Vital	Usual	£8,000+	Medium–High	Town	Local	No	Yes	Yes
Computer Hardware Engineer	Necessary	No	Recommended	Yes	£5,000+	Medium	Town	Local	No	Possible	Possible
Computer Software Author	Usual	No	Recommended	Possible	£2,000+	Medium	Town or nearby	Local	No	Possible	Possible

Job	Qualifications/training	Licence	Experience/springboard	Mid-career entry	Entry costs	Income bracket	Town/country	Travel	Exit sale	Work at home	Mix and match
Concert Agent	Recommended	Yes	Essential	Possible	£5,000	Low–Medium	Mostly town	Yes	Possible	Yes	Possible
Conductor	Recommended	No	Yes	Possible	£2,000–£5,000	Low–High	Town	Endless	No	No	Yes
Conference Organiser	No	No	Essential	Yes	£5,000++	Medium–High	Town	Yes	Possible	Yes	Yes
Contemporary Art Gallery Owner	No	No	Recommended	Yes	£20,000+	Medium	Town	No	Yes	No	Yes
Continuity Person	No	No	Yes	Yes	£100	Medium	Town	Yes	No	No	Limited
Conveyancer	Essential	Yes	Essential	Yes	£5,000	Medium	Town	Local	Possible	Possible	Yes
Corporate Video Producer	Recommended	No	Recommended	Possible	£2,000	Low–High	Town	Essential	Possible	No	Yes
Costume Designer	Yes	No	Recommended	Difficult	£100	Low–Medium	Town	Yes	No	No	Limited
Counsellor	Essential	No	No	Essential	£600+	Medium	Town/Country	No	No	Yes	Excellent
Courier Service	No	No	Recommended	Excellent	£10,000	Medium–High	Town	No	Yes	No	Limited
Dancer	Necessary	No	No	No	£200	Low	Town	Lots	No	Limited	Yes
Dance Teacher	Essential	No	Recommended	Possible	£200	Low	Town	Local	No	No	Yes
Dental Practice Broker	Recommended	No	Useful	Yes	£5,000	Medium	Town preferably	Yes	Possible	Possible	Yes

Job	Qualifications/ training	Licence	Experience/ springboard	Mid-career entry	Entry costs	Income bracket	Town/ country	Travel	Exit sale	Work at home	Mix and match
Dental Technician	Recommended	Not Yet	Essential	Unlikely	£65,000	Medium	Town	Local	Yes	Unlikely	Limited
Dentist	Essential	Yes	No	Highly unlikely	Highly variable	Medium–High	Town	None	Yes	Possible	Yes
Desk-top Publisher	Recommended	No	Essential	Yes	£10,000+	Low–High	Either	No	Yes	Yes	Yes
Dietary Therapist	Essential	Yes	No	Good	£1,000	Low–Medium	Town	Local	No	Yes	Yes
Direct Marketing Consultant	Useful	No	Essential	Yes	£1,000+	Medium–High	Town	Yes	Possible	Possible	Yes
Disco Owner/DJ	No	No	No	Highly unlikely	£5,000	Medium–High	Town	Lots	Possible	No	Yes
Doctor (GP in the NHS)	Essential	Yes	Recommended	Limited	Highly variable	High	Town/ Village	Local	Possible	Possible	Yes
Doctor (Private GP)	Essential	Yes	Recommended	Highly unlikely	Highly variable	High	Town	Local	Yes	Possible	Yes
Dress Agent	No	No	Useful	Ideal	£2,000	Medium	Town	No	Yes	No	Yes
Driver (Hire Cars)	No	Yes	Yes	Yes	Nil	Low	Both	Yes	No	No	Excellent
Driving Instructor	Essential	Yes	Recommended	Good	£12,000	Medium	Town	Local	Possible	No	Yes
Editorial Photographer	Recommended	No	Recommended	Possible	£5,000+	Medium–High	Town	Yes	Yes	Possible	Yes
Embalmer	Essential	No	Recommended	Yes	£500	Low–Medium	Either	Local	No	No	Yes
Employment Agent	Possible	Yes	Recommended	Yes	£2,000+	Medium	Town	No	Yes	Possible	Yes

Job	Qualifications/ training	Licence	Experience/ springboard	Mid-career entry	Entry costs	Income bracket	Town/ country	Travel	Exit sale	Work at home	Mix and match
English Language School Owner	Recommended	Recommended	Recommended	Yes	£8,000	Medium	Town	No	Yes	No	Yes
English Language Teacher	Recommended	No	No	Yes	Nil	Low–Medium	Town	Yes	No	Excellent	Yes
Estate Agent	No	No	Essential	Yes	£10,000+	Low–High	Town	Local	Yes	No	Yes
Events Organiser	No	No	Recommended	Likely	£3,000	Medium–High	Town	Yes	Possible	Partly	Possible
Exhibition Designer	Yes	No	No	Unlikely	£2,000	Medium	Town	Yes	No	No	Yes
Farmer	Recommended	No	Useful	Yes	£100,000 +++	Low–High	Country	Local	Yes	Essential	Excellent
Farrier/Blacksmith	Yes	Farriers	Essential	Possible	£100–£30,000	Low–Medium	Country	Local	Possible	No	Possible
Fashion Designer	Advisable	No	Yes	Unlikely	£500	Low–High	Town	Probably	No	Possible	Yes
Fashion Retailer	Not necessary	No	Recommended	Yes	£8,000+	Low–High	Town	Some	Excellent	No	Limited
Festival Director	Available	No	Essential	Good	£500	Low–High	Mostly town	Yes	No	No	Essential
Film Director	Available	Union card	Not necessary	Good	£250	Medium–High	Town	Lots	No	No	Yes
Film Extra	No	No	No	Yes	Nil	Low	Both	Yes	No	Limited	No
Film Production Person	Recommended	Union card	Recommended	Yes	£500	Medium–High	Town	Lots	No	No	Limited
Fish Curer and Smoker	Recommended	No	Essential	Possible	£11,000	Low–Medium	Country	Local	Yes	Yes	Possible

Job	Qualifications/ training	Licence	Experience/ springboard	Mid-career entry	Entry costs	Income bracket	Town/ country	Travel	Exit sale	Work at home	Mix and match
Food Manufacturer	Available	No	Useful	Possible	£1,000++	Low–High	Either	Some	Yes	Possible	Yes
Football Commentator	Available	No	Essential	Yes	£100+	High	Town	Essential	No	No	Good
Foreign Correspondent	Available	No	Recommended	Yes	£1,000	Low–High	Town	Yes	No	Partly	Excellent
Franchisee	No	No	Useful	Good	£5,000– £5,000,000	Low–High	Either	Varies	Yes	No	Not normally possible
Funeral Director	Recommended	No	Useful	Good idea	£50,000+	Low–Medium	Town	Local	Yes	No	Limited
Furniture Designer	Recommended	No	Recommended	Yes	£10,000+++	Low–Medium	Either	Local	No	Yes	Yes
Futures Broker	Yes	Yes	Essential	Yes	£20,000	High	Town	No	Possible	Possible	Yes
Garage Owner	Recommended	Yes (MOT)	Yes	Yes	£1,000+++	Low–Medium	Town/ Village	No	Yes	No	Limited
Garden Centre	Strongly Recommended	No	Essential	Excellent	£200,000+	Low–High	Either	Local	Good	Yes	Yes
Garden Gnome Maker	No	No	No	Yes	£500	Low	Either	Local	No	Yes	Essential
Gardener/Garden Designer	Recommended	No	Useful	Yes	£800+	Medium	Either	Local	No	Yes	Yes
Glass Designer/ Maker	Recommended	No	Useful	Possible	£50,000	Low	Either	Some	No	Possible	Limited

Job	Qualifications/ training	Licence	Experience/ springboard	Mid-career entry	Entry costs	Income bracket	Town/ country	Travel	Exit sale	Work at home	Mix and match
Graphic Designer	Recommended	No	No	Unlikely	£1,000	Low–High	Town	Local	No	Possible	Yes
Graphologist	Recommended	No	Essential	Possible	£1,000	Low–Medium	Either	Possible	No	Yes	Yes
Greyhound Trainer	No	Yes	Recommended	Possible	£5,000	Low	Country	Yes	No	Yes	Yes
Guardian ad Litem	Essential	No	Essential	Vital	Nil	Low–Medium	Either	Local	No	Partly	Yes
Hairdresser	Recommended	Not yet	Recommended	Possible	£10,000+	Medium	Town	Maybe local	Yes	No	Possible
Hauler	Recommended	Yes	Not necessary	Possible	£40,000+	Low–High	Either	Yes	Yes	Partly	Yes
Headhunter	Yes	No	Essential	Likely	£10,000+	Medium–High	Town	Yes	Possible	Unlikely	Possible
Healer	No	No	No	Yes	£2,000	Low	Town	Local	No	Possible	Yes
Healthfood Shopkeeper	No	No	Useful	Good	£7,000+	Low–Medium	Town	No	Good	No	Possible
Hi-Fi Shop Owner	No	Yes for HP	Essential	Yes	£12,000	Low–High	Town	No	Excellent	No	Possible
High Street Photographer	Recommended	No	Yes	Possible	£10,000	Medium	Town	Local	Yes	No	Possible
Hire Shop Owner	No	No	Useful	Yes	Highly variable	Low–Medium	Town	No	Yes	No	Limited
Holiday Accommodation Owner	No	No	Not necessary	Good	Highly variable	Low–High	Either	Possible	Excellent	No	Yes
Homeopath	Essential	Yes from 1992	Recommended	Yes	£5,000	Medium	Town	No	No	Yes	Yes

Job	Qualifications/ training	Licence	Experience/ springboard	Mid-career entry	Entry costs	Income bracket	Town/ country	Travel	Exit sale	Work at home	Mix and match
Hotelier	Recommended	Yes for alcohol	Recommended	Ideal	£150,000++	Low–High	Either	Local	Excellent	Yes	Possible
House Converter	Available	No	Essential	Yes	£50,000++	Low–High	Either	Local	Possible	Possible	Yes
Hypnotherapist	Yes	No	No	Recommended	£1,000	Low–Medium	Town	No	No	Possible	Excellent
Illustrator	Recommended	No	No	Unlikely	£50	Medium	Town	Some	No	Yes	Excellent
Import/Export Broker	No	No	Essential	Excellent	Bank credit	Medium–High	Either	Possible	Yes	Possible	Yes
Impresario	No	No	Essential	Possible	£10,000++	Low–High	Town	Yes	Possible	Yes	Yes
In-Company Trainer	Recommended	No	Essential	Essential	£20,000+	Medium–High	Town	Yes	Possible	Not recommended	Yes
Independent Financial Adviser	Recommended	Yes	Essential	Yes	£12,000+	Medium–High	Town	Local	Possible	Yes	Yes
Indexer	Recommended	No	No	Good	£1,000+	Low	Either	No	No	Yes	Yes
Instrumental Soloist	Essential	No	No	Unlikely	£2,000+	Low–High	Town	Lots	No	No	Probably essential
Insurance Broker	Essential	Yes	Essential	Good	£1,000	Low–High	Town	Local	Yes	Possible	Possible
Interior Designer	Recommended	No	No	Yes	£5,000++	Low–High	Mostly town	Local	No	Possible	Yes
Interpreter	Essential	Recommended	Necessary	Yes	£500+	Medium–High	Town	Yes	No	No	Yes

Job	Qualifications/ training	Licence	Experience/ springboard	Mid-career entry	Entry costs	Income bracket	Town/ country	Travel	Exit sale	Work at home	Mix and match
Inventor	No	No	Probably	Probably	Highly variable	Low–High	Either	Yes	Yes	Possible	Probably essential
Investment Manager	Recommended	Yes	Yes	Yes	£50,000+	Medium–High	Town	No	Yes	No	Possible
Italian Property Finder	No	No	No	Yes	£25,000+++	Medium–High	Both	Essential	Possible	Possible	Yes
Jazz Musician/ Singer	Recommended	No	No	Possible	£1,000	Mostly low	Town	Lots	No	No	Yes
Journalist	Recommended	No	Recommended	Possible	Nil	Low–High	Town	Yes	No	Partly	Yes
Kennel/Cattery Owner	Available	Yes	Recommended	Likely	£10,000+++	Low–Medium	Country	No	Yes	Yes	Possible
Keyboard Hire	Recommended	No	Useful	Possible	£6,000+	Low–High	Town	Lots	Possible	Possible	Yes
Landlord	No	No	No	Yes	£50,000++	Low–High	Either	Between properties	Excellent	Yes	Yes
Landscape Designer	Yes	No	Essential	Unlikely	£2,000	Low–High	Either	Yes	No	Possible	Yes
List Broker	No	No	No	Good	£1,500	Low–High	Town	Local	Yes	Possible	Yes
Literary Agent	No	No	Recommended	Probably essential	£3,500	Low–High	Town	Yes	Yes	Possible	Limited
Magazine Designer	Recommended	No	Recommended	No	£3,500	Low–Medium	Town	Local	No	Possible	Yes

Job	Qualifications/ training	Licence	Experience/ springboard	Mid-career entry	Entry costs	Income bracket	Town/ country	Travel	Exit sale	Work at home	Mix and match
Magazine Publisher	No	No	Recommended	Likely	£5,000++	Low–High	Town	Yes	Excellent	Possible	Yes
Makeup Artist	Recommended	No	Not necessary	Possible	£500	Low–High	Town	Yes	No	No	Possible
Man with a Van	No	Driving licence	No	Yes	£5,000	Low–Medium	Usually town	Yes	No	No	Excellent
Market Research Interviewer	Yes	No	No	Yes	Nil	Low–Medium	Either	Yes	No	No	Excellent
Market Stall Holder	No	Yes	No	Yes	£300++	Low–Medium	Town	Local	No	No	Yes
Marketing Consultant	Recommended	No	A must	Essential	£5,000	High	Either	Lots	Possible	Yes	Possible
Media Trainer	Not essential	No	Essential	Essential	£3,000++	Medium	Town	Possible	No	No	Yes
MEP	No	No	Yes	Excellent	£1,000	High	Either	Lots	No	No	Excellent
Mini-Cab Driver	No	Driving licence	No	Excellent	£3,500+	Low–Medium	Mostly town	Local	No	No	Excellent
Motorcycle Messenger	No	Driving licence	No	Yes	£1,000+	Low	Town	Local	No	No	Excellent
Motorcycle Racer	No	Yes	No	Possible	£1,000+	Low	Either	Yes	No	No	Yes
MP	No	No	Yes	Excellent	£500+	Medium	Mostly town	Yes	No	No	Excellent
Music Copyist	No	No	No	Yes	Nil	Low–Medium	Either	Local	No	Yes	Probably essential

Job	Qualifications/ training	Licence	Experience/ springboard	Mid-career entry	Entry costs	Income bracket	Town/ country	Travel	Exit sale	Work at home	Mix and match
Music Critic	No	No	No	Possible	£500+	Low–Medium	Mostly town	Yes	No	Partly	Excellent
Music/Instrument Retailer	No	No	Recommended	Excellent	£10,000+	Low–Medium	Town	No	Yes	No	Limited
Music Publisher	No	No	No	Yes	£3,000	Low – usually	Town	Yes	Yes	Possible	Usually
Music Teacher	Recommended	No	No	Possible	£2,500	Low–Medium	Either	Local	No	Yes	Yes
Music Therapist	Essential	No	Recommended	Recommended	£2,500	Low–Medium	Town	Local	No	Possible	Yes
Musical Instrument Maker	Recommended	No	Recommended	Possible	£6,000+	Low–Medium	Either	No	Unlikely	Yes	Possible
Musical Instrument Repairer	Recommended	No	Recommended	Possible	£6,000+	Low–Medium	Town	Local	Unlikely	Yes	Possible
Musician	Recommended	No	No	Unlikely	£1,000+	Low–High	Mostly	Yes	No	No	Probably essential
Musicians' Answering and Booking Service	No	No	No	Yes	£3,000	Low	Town	No	Possible	Possible	Possible
Nanny/Babysitting Agent	No	Yes	Recommended	Yes	£1,000	Low–Medium	Town	No	Yes	Yes	Yes
Naturopath	Essential	Recommended	Recommended	Possible	£4,000+	Low–High	Either	No	Possible	Possible	Possible
Network Marketing	None	No	No	Excellent	£50–£500	Low–High	Either	Local	No	Partly	Excellent

Job	Qualifications/training	Licence	Experience/springboard	Mid-career entry	Entry costs	Income bracket	Town/country	Travel	Exit sale	Work at home	Mix and match
Night Carer	Recommended	No	Yes	Yes	Nil	Low–Medium	Both	Possible	No	No	Excellent
Newsletter Publisher	No	No	No	Likely	£1,000+	Low–High	Either	No	Good	Yes	Yes
Novelist	No	No	No	Likely	£5+	Mostly low	Either	No	Possible	Yes	Probably essential
Nurse	Essential	Yes	No	Unlikely	Nil	Low–Medium	Either	Local	No	No	Yes
Nursing Home Owner	Not essential	Yes	Preferable	Likely	£100,000 +++	Medium	Either	No	Yes	Possible	Limited
Office Cleaner	No	No	No	Yes	Nil	Low	Town	No	No	No	Yes
Office Services Bureau	No	No	Maybe	Yes	£2,000+	Low–High	Town	No	Yes	Possible	Yes
Opera Director	No	No	Good idea	Yes	£250+	Low–High	Mostly town	A must	No	No	Possible
Optician	Essential	Yes	Useful	Unlikely	£25,000+	Medium	Town	No	Yes	Possible	Possible
Orchestral Fixer	Useful	No	Recommended	Yes	£4,000	Low–Medium	Town	Yes	No	Yes	Possible
Orchestral Musician	Necessary	No	No	No	£1,000+	Low–Medium	Town	Lots	No	No	Probably essential
Osteopath	Essential	Professional register	Recommended	Possible	£2,000+	Low–High	Town	No	Possible	Possible	Possible
Oyster Farmer	Necessary	No	Essential	Likely	£70,000	Low–High	Country	Local	Excellent	Yes	Recommended

Job	Qualifications/training	Licence	Experience/springboard	Mid-career entry	Entry costs	Income bracket	Town/country	Travel	Exit sale	Work at home	Mix and match
Painter/Decorator	No	No	Useful	Yes	£1,000	Low	Town	Local	No	No	Yes
Para-legal	Recommended (Essential for Legal Executive)	No	Recommended	Possible	£20,000++	Medium–High	Town	No	Unlikely	Possible	Yes
Patent Agent	Required	No	Essential	Possible	£1,500+	Medium–High	Town	Yes	Possible	Possible	Yes
Pharmacist	Essential	Yes	Yes	Unlikely	£20,000	Medium	Town	No	Yes	No	Limited
Photographer	Recommended	No	No	Possible	£5,000+	Low–High	Either	Probable	Yes	Yes	Yes
Photographic Assistant	Recommended	No	No	Unlikely	Nil	Low	Town	Maybe	No	No	Yes
Photojournalist	Recommended	Union card	Useful	Unlikely	£3,000+	Low–Medium	Town	Endless	Yes	No	Possible
Physiotherapist	Essential	Yes	Recommended	Unlikely	£7,500+	Low–High	Town	No	No	Possible	Possible
Piano Tuner/Restorer	Recommended	No	Recommended	Yes	£2,000+	Medium–High	Mostly town	Local	No	Partly	Possible
Picture Agent	Useful	No	Recommended	Yes	£2,500+	Low–High	Usually town	No	Yes	Possible	Possible
Picture Framer	Recommended	No	Recommended	Yes	£100–£5,000	Low–Medium	Town	No	Yes	Yes	Yes
Picture Researcher	No	No	Usually	Yes	£1,000	Low–Medium	Town	Yes	No	Yes	Possible
Picture Restorer	Recommended	No	No	Possible	£2,000	Low–Medium	Either	Yes	No	Yes	Yes
Pop Group Sound Engineer	Not necessary	Driving licence	Recommended	Unlikely	£250	Low	Town	Lots	No	No	Limited

Job	Qualifications/ training	Licence	Experience/ springboard	Mid-career entry	Entry costs	Income bracket	Town/ country	Travel	Exit sale	Work at home	Mix and match
Potter	Recommended	No	Possible	Possible	£3,000++	Low–Medium	Either	Local	No	Yes	Possible
Prep School Owner	Necessary	Yes	Essential	Likely	£175,000+	Medium–High	Either	No	Excellent	No	Possible
Print Maker	Necessary	No	Recommended	Possible	£200+	Low–Medium	Town	No	No	Yes	Possible
Printer	Recommended	Union card recommended	Necessary	Possible	£25,000+	Low–Medium	Town	Local	Yes	No	Yes
Private Investigator	Useful	No	Recommended	Likely	£5,000++	Medium–High	Town	Some	Possible	Partly	Possible
Proofreader/ Copy editor	Available	No	Recommended	Yes	£10+	Low	Either if accessible	No	No	Yes, usually	Excellent
Property Developer	No	No	Useful	Likely	£50,000+++	Low–High	Either	Local	Yes	Possible	Yes
Property Manager	No	No	Recommended	Likely	£1,000+	Low–Medium	Either	Local	No	Yes	Possible
Psychoanalyst	Essential	No	No	Essential	£500	Low–High	Town	No	No	Yes	Possible
Psychologist	Essential	Recommended	Recommended	Yes	£1,000+	Medium–High	Town	Local	Possible	Unlikely	Possible
Psychotherapist	Essential	No	Useful	Essential	£15,000	Low–High	Town	No	No	Yes	Possible
Publican	Recommended	Essential	Recommended	Likely	£25,000+++	Low–High	Either	Local	Excellent	Yes	Possible
Public Relations Consultant	Recommended	No	Essential	Likely	£7,500	Medium–High	Town	Yes	Possible	Possible	Yes
Puppeteer	Available	No	Not essential	Yes	£2,000+	Low	Either	Constant	No	No	Yes
Race Horse Owner	No	No	No	Likely	£10,000+	Nil–High	Country	Yes	Possible	No	Yes

Job	Qualifications/ training	Licence	Experience/ springboard	Mid-career entry	Entry costs	Income bracket	Town/ country	Travel	Exit sale	Work at home	Mix and match
Radio Reporter/ Presenter	Available	No	Essential	Yes	£2,000+	Low–Medium	Town	Yes	No	No	Yes
Record Company Owner	No	No	Essential	Possible	£15,000++	Low–High	Town	Local	Good	Possible	Essential to start
Recording Studio Owner	Recommended	No	Recommended	Possible	Highly variable	Low–Medium	Town	Some	Yes	Possible	Essential to start
Reflexologist	Necessary	No	No	Yes	£1,000	Medium	Town	Local, perhaps	No	Possible	Limited
Repetiteur/ Accompanist/ Coach	Essential	No	No	Highly unlikely	£2,000+	Medium	Town	Yes	No	No	Yes
Restaurateur	Recommended	Alcohol – yes	Recommended	Likely	£20,000 +++	Low–High	Usually town	Local	Excellent	No	Possible
Riding School Owner	Recommended	Essential	Yes	Yes	£100,000	Low–Medium	Mostly country	Little	Good	Yes	Possible
Saddler/ Leatherworker	Essential	No	Recommended	Possible	£2,000+	Low–Medium	Either	Local	Unlikely	Yes	Yes
Sailing School Owner	Yes	RYA	No	Likely	£8,000+	Low–Medium	Either	No	Yes	No	Yes
Sales Agent	No	No	Essential	Yes	£3,000	Low–High	Either	Essential	Possible	Partly	Possible
Salmon Farmer	Necessary	No	Essential	Good	£200,000	Low–Medium	Country	Local	Yes	Yes	Yes
Scriptwriter	No	No	Advisable	Yes	£10+	Low–High	Either	Some- times	No	Yes	Essential, to start

Job	Qualifications/training	Licence	Experience/springboard	Mid-career entry	Entry costs	Income bracket	Town/country	Travel	Exit sale	Work at home	Mix and match
Sculptor	Helpful	No	Useful	Possible	£1,000++	Low–High	Either	No	No	Possible	Good
Sex Therapist	Necessary	No	No	Recommended	£400	Low–High	Town	No	No	Yes	Yes
Shepherd/Shepherdess	Useful	No	Essential	Possible	£2,000	Low	Country	Between jobs	No	No	Yes
Shipbroker	Recommended	No	Essential	Yes	£10,000	Medium–High	Town	Possible	Possible	Partly	Possible
Shoe Designer/Maker	Necessary	No	No	Unlikely	£500	Low–High	Either	Yes	No	Possible	Yes
Shopkeeper	Available	No	Recommended	Likely	Highly variable	Low–High	Mostly town	Local	Excellent	No	Possible
Silversmith/Jeweller	Recommended	No	No	Possible	£2,500	Low–Medium	Either	Yes	No	Yes	Yes
Smallholder	Recommended	No	Recommended	Possible	£10,000+++	Medium	Country	No	Excellent	Yes	Excellent
Snail Farmer	Recommended	No	Useful	Yes	£10,000++	Medium	Country	No	Excellent	Yes	Possible
Social Worker	Essential	No	Essential	Useful	Nil	Low–Medium	Either	Local	No	No	Yes
Solicitor	Essential	Yes	Essential	Possible	£20,000+	Medium–High	Town	Yes	Excellent	Yes	Possible
Space Sales Agent	No	No	Essential	Yes	£500	Low–High	Either	Some	Possible	Yes	Yes
Sports Retailer	No	No	Essential	Likely	Highly variable	Low–High	Town	No	Excellent	No	Possible
Stage Designer	Necessary	No	Recommended	Possible	£50	Low–Medium	Town	Local	No	Partly	Yes

Job	Qualifications/training	Licence	Experience/springboard	Mid-career entry	Entry costs	Income bracket	Town/country	Travel	Exit sale	Work at home	Mix and match
Stage Technician Carpenter	Available	No	Essential	Possible	£250	Low-Medium	Town	Maybe	No	No	Possible
Stockbroker	Essential	Yes	Essential	Possible	£100,000+	Medium-High	Town	Possible	Possible	No	Possible
Street Entertainer	Useful	Usually	No	Possible	Nil	Low	Town	Local	No	No	Essential
Stylist	Useful	No	Essential	Possible	£300+	Low-High	Town	Yes	No	Partly	Yes
Sub-editor	Recommended	No	Yes	Possible	Nil	Low-Medium	Town	No	No	No	Excellent
Sub Postmaster	Yes	Yes	No	Excellent	£1,000++	Low-Medium	Town/Village	No	Yes	No	Yes
Surveyor	Essential	For financial advice	Recommended	Possible	£7,500++	Medium-High	Both (and sea)	Yes	Possible	Possible	Possible
Swimming Teacher	Essential	No	Useful	Good	£50+	Low-Medium	Town	Local	No	No	Excellent
Tailor	Available	No	Recommended	Possible	£2,000	Low-Medium	Town	No	Possible	Not recommended	Possible
Tattooist	No	Yes	No	Possible	£5,000	Low-Medium	Town	No	No	Possible	Possible
Taxi Driver	Yes	Yes	No	Yes	£500++	Low-High	Either	Yes	No	No	Possible
Taxidermist	Available	Yes	Recommended	Yes	£100+	Low	Either	Local	No	Yes	Yes
Teacher	Essential	Yes	Not necessary	Yes	Nil	Low	Either	Local	No	No	Excellent
Textile Designer	Recommended	No	Not necessary	Possible	£100+	Low-High	Either	Yes	No	Yes	Yes
Telesales Person	No	No	Not necessary	Excellent	Nil	Low-Medium	Either	No	No	Yes	Good

Job	Qualifications/training	Licence	Experience/springboard	Mid-career entry	Entry costs	Income bracket	Town/country	Travel	Exit sale	Work at home	Mix and match
Thatcher	Essential	No	No	Good	£5,000+	Low–Medium	Mostly country	Yes	No	No	Possible
Theatrical Agent	No	Yes	Yes	Possible	£2,000+	Low–Medium	Town	Some	Possible	Possible	Limited
Timeshare Developer	No	No	No	Likely	£100,000++	Low–High	Either	Between sites	Yes	No	Yes
Toastmaster	Available	No	No	Recommended	£500++	Low–High	Mostly town	Yes	No	No	Excellent
Tourist Attraction	No	No	No	Likely	Highly variable	Low–High	Either	No	Excellent	Yes	Yes
Tourist Guide	Necessary	In some cases	No	Yes	£1,000	Medium	Either	Yes	No	No	Yes
Toymaker	Available	No	No	Yes	£500+	Low–Medium	Either	No	No	Yes	Yes
Travel Agent	Recommended	Recommended	Essential	Good	£40,000	Medium	Town	No	Yes	No	Limited
Tree Surgeon	Recommended	No	No	Possible	£2,000+	Low–Medium	Either	Yes	Yes	No	Yes
Trout Farmer	Necessary	No	Essential	Good	£50,000	Low–Medium	Country	Local	Excellent	Yes	Yes
Tutor	Recommended	No	Essential	Yes	Minimal	Medium	Mostly town	Local	No	Yes	Excellent
TV and Film Music Composer	Recommended	No	No	Possible	£5,000	Low–High	Either	Possible	Possible	Yes	Essential
Typesetter	Recommended	No	Useful	Yes	£5,000+	Low–Medium	Town	Local	Possible	Yes	Yes
Typist	Recommended	No	Yes	Yes	£5+++	Low–Medium	Town mostly	Local	No	Yes	Yes
UK Correspondent (Overseas Media)	Available	No	Essential	Yes	£2,500	Low–Medium	Town	Yes	No	Partly	Good

Job	Qualifications/ training	Licence	Experience/ springboard	Mid-career entry	Entry costs	Income bracket	Town/ country	Travel	Exit sale	Work at home	Mix and match
Upholsterer	Recommended	No	Recommended	Possible	£1,500+	Low	Town	Local	Possible	Possible	Possible
Venue Manger	No	No	Recommended	No	£5,000++	Low–Medium	Town	No	Yes	No	Very limited
Vet	Essential	Yes	Yes	Unlikely	£15,000+	Medium–High	Either	Local	Excellent	Possible	Yes
Village Shopkeeper	Available	No (but alcohol licence)	Recommended	Good	£20,000++	Low–Medium	Village	No	Excellent	No	Limited
Wedding Shop Owner	None	No	Recommended	Yes	£500+	Low–Medium	Town	None	Yes	No	Yes
Window Cleaner	No	No	No	Possible	£300+	Low	Either	Local	No	No	Yes
Windsurfing School Owner	Necessary	No	Useful	Good	£5,000+	Low–Medium	Country	No	Good	No	Yes
Wine Bar Owner	Recommended	Yes	Essential	Good	£25,000+	Medium	Town	Local	Excellent	No	Possible
Wine Grower	Recommended	Yes	Useful	Good	£90,000+	Low–Medium	Country	No	Excellent	Yes	Essential to start
Wine Merchant	Recommended	Yes, if you sell single bottles	No	Good	£5,000++	Low–High	Either	Yes	Yes	Yes	Essential to start
Wood Carver	Recommended	No	No	Possible	£2,500	Low–Medium	Either	No	No	Yes	Yes
Word Processor	Useful	No	Recommended	Yes	£4,000	Low–Medium	Mostly town	Local, maybe	No	Yes	Yes
Yoga Teacher	Yes	No	No	Yes	£480	Low	Either	Local	No	Possible	Yes
Zoo Keeper	Recommended	Yes	Essential	Likely	£1 million+	Medium	Either	Yes	Possible	No	Possible

Part 2

How To Go About It
A–Z

This A–Z spotlights many of the
matters you'll need to know about
en route to becoming your own boss
– from choosing an independent
career, through getting job
experience (probably working for
others), then springboarding to
independence and making sure you
stay independent.

How To Go About It A–Z

Accessibility
Accounting and Book-keeping
Advertising
Advice – General
Ageism
Application Forms
Application Game
Aptitude Tests
Bankruptcy
Banks
Biodata
Blockers
Borrowing
Budget
Bumf
Bureaucratic Benefits
Business Courses
Business Plans
Capital Needs/Entry Cost
Career Choice
Career Development Loans
Careers Advice
Careers Guidance (Private)
Careers Information
Charm
Choosing Your Clients and Suppliers
Communication Skills
Company Information
Compartmentalising Your Life
Conferences
Constraints
Consultancy
Co-ops
CV
Decision-making Strategies
Disability
Displacement Activity
Divorce
Driving Licence
Employing Others
Entrepreneurial Skills

Equal Opportunities
Equipment
Europe and You
Europe Open for Business
Exhaustion
Exhibitions and Trade Fairs
Exit Sale
Experience
Family Commitment
Family Tradition
Finance
Finance Checklist
Financial Control
Franchising
Freelancing
Getting Things Done
Growth Planning
Handling Information
Health
Home-based Work
Insurance
Interpersonal Skills
Interview
Job Hunting
Job Sharing
Keeping in Business
Lifelines
Lifestyle Choices
Limited Companies
Location – Office and Home
Luck
Management Skills
Manual Skills
Market Research
Marketing
Mid-career Moves
Mix and Match
Moonlighting
Mortgages
Motivation
Names – Business

Accessibility

Whatever type of work you go for, people have got to be able to get in touch with you.

Phones are the most direct method of contact, and here you have several options. If you can't be by your office phone all the time you could get an answerphone (a phone which records messages). There is a range of systems you can use to be contacted if you're always on the move, eg a bleep, paging system, cell phone, car phone. Find out more about all these in *Yellow Pages* (communications equipment and telephone answering services) or from British Telecom. A radio phone extension to your household or office line may be useful – eg if you run a small plant nursery, and spend a lot of time in the potting shed, or if you let holiday cottages, and spend time away from your office while you are cleaning them. Message taking services can also be a smart answer.

A fax allows you to send and receive documents by phone. This speeds up transactions a great deal and is particularly useful for negotiations where a number of drafts are needed. What's more, they're a lot cheaper than they were a year or two ago.

A smart address is another useful asset: you probably won't be able to afford an office in Central London, but you can get your mail sent to one. Check the entries in the *Yellow Pages* under Accommodation agencies – business. Many agencies offer more than just an address and mail service: they provide office space and have telex and fax machines, photocopiers, secretarial services and so on.

If you want something cheaper, and anonymous, a PO Box number may be best: ask the post office.

Accounting and Book keeping

Boring, boring – but without it, you sink.

Rule one: get a good accountant. To find one, you're best off asking people you know who already have one. Initially you may be better off with a small firm/self-employed accountant who lives in your world. Only if you are thinking of raising venture/development capital do you need one of the big six accounting firms to get you past bankers for whom 'meaningful cash flow' is only 'meaningful' if authenticated by one of the great firms!

Rule two: get a system. Your accountants will help so you need to talk to them before you start. You must keep careful records to check your business is profitable. Make sure you know a bit about basic book-keeping.

Rule three: make sure you have a system for invoicing clients/customers punctually and you follow it up until you see the cash.

Note all expenses when they occur: simply keep receipts and put them in a box. It's easy to forget things and lose track. Keep a notebook with a list of unreceipted expenses (fares, drinks with contacts) and get in the habit of checking it daily. Pay by credit card where possible: this gives you up to six weeks free credit, and provides a monthly record of payments made with names and dates. Pay credit card bills when they are due: there are cheaper sources of finance if you want to borrow.

Try asking for part-payment for a job in advance: to cover paint and wallpaper if you are a decorator, or an advance on royalty if you are an author. Demand interim payments if the job is a long one. The quicker you send out your invoices, the sooner they'll get paid. Conversely the slower you pay your bills the more money you will have in your own bank.

Big companies often have gigantic accounts departments which deliberately sit on your invoices, especially at times of high interest rates. This is now so prevalent as to constitute a national scandal. Even if they do not deliberately hold onto your money, they may well take a long time to pay and have their own systems which don't lend themselves to eg partial payment in advance. Get clear at the outset what their system is and make it work for you.

All invoices must show: your name and address and preferably phone number; your VAT number if you have one; the date; who the customer or client is; what the invoice is for (goods, services – some customers demand detailed information); any order number of yours or the customer's. Make sure your system includes all this automatically, and also chases up unpaid invoices every month. If customers and clients are not forthcoming with the cash, consider employing a debt collecting agency – addresses from the NATIONAL ASSOCIATION OF TRADE PROTECTION SOCIETIES. Never part with your file copy of an invoice.

You will find *Working for Yourself* useful; also some business courses.

Advertising

Get your name known to the people who need you.

The most basic form of advertising is a business card or leaflet: leave them in likely places, slip them through the front door of private households, hand them out at exhibitions – whatever is relevant to your job.

Other forms of advertising depend on your job: entries in the Yellow Pages and Thomson's Directory are useful and local papers are effective for advertising your services if you are a small company in the building industry, for example. In certain professions (eg medical and legal) there are restrictions on advertising, so check with the appropriate professional body.

Placing an advertisement costs anything from 30p per week for a notice in the local newsagent to £30,000 for a colour spread in a national magazine. Outlets to consider are trade press listings, local business directories, poster sites (including hoardings, buses and tubes, taxis, any public places), mass leaflet drops (some services are provided by the post office), mail shots (based on mailing lists purchased from agencies), exhibitions (from art school graduation shows to major international exhibitions in your field). On top of the cost of placing the ad, there is the cost of producing it – negligible for a notice in the small ads in a paper, phenomenal for a snazzy ad with snappy copy put together by a top advertising agency.

Before placing an ad think about: your target market (if you know what publications they are likely to read, what sort of tastes they have and what sort of budget they have for your goods or services, this will not only help you tailor your output to suit them, it will point the direction for advertising outlets as well); your unique selling proposition – what is special or unique about your product or services and why people/companies might prefer to do business with you.

Any ad has got to answer the questions: who are you, what are you offering, when, where, why and how can people purchase your goods or services or find out more?

If you can offer any special discounts or freebies, this may help to attract people to you – the important thing is to give people the idea that you provide value for money and are unique in your field.

Consider the more direct face to face approaches first.

Short business courses normally cover some advertising. Special courses are also run by CAM, The Communication, Advertising and Marketing Education Foundation. Or you can read *Spending Advertising Money*, *The Fundamentals of Advertising*.

Advice – General

Never take advice uncritically. Listen to it, then decide what you will do. It's your life; live it your way. Don't boggle your mind by reading too much before you get started: the most important thing is knowing who to go to when you've got a particular problem. You'll find that most books and courses say much the same thing – sift through them and just buy a couple of books which are relevant to your particular needs. Consult your local (Thomson) directory for help in your area.

Keep up with new developments by reading the financial pages and weekly supplements in the national press. Most of all, don't forget to ask – friends, family, colleagues – for advice. They may not know the answer, but they might know someone who does.

Ageism

'Graduates required, under 25'; 'Likely age of successful candidate: 24–27'.

When you see ads like this, you realise that in some occupations there is bias against the over-30s never mind the over-50s.

Mature graduates often have to fight harder to get jobs: a survey of poly graduates showed that although older graduates got better degrees, they were less likely to be employed than younger graduates. This may be changing as the demographic time-bomb ticks away – there's a shortage of under-25s.

Many jobs in this book are well suited to the victims of ageism. There is really no substitute for experience and a well-developed network of contacts.

Application Forms

For most people, filling in application forms is a pain in the proverbials. Tough. Most bureaucracies use them to find out more about you, your qualifications and your experience. They vary in shape, size and complexity and to complete them fully and to do yourself justice can take many hours of work. Once you have sorted out the relevant information, each one becomes easier to complete. But beware of completing them mechanically. Each form is a peculiar medium of communication with a handful of identifiable bureaucrats, just as an examination paper is a method of communicating with one or two known examiners. Use the application form as an opportunity to sell yourself – your skills, abilities, achievements, interests, motivation and attitude to work. (Remember that your covering letter is a part of your application; a good covering letter can lift you above the crowd. Also remember that you can only communicate with the employer if you fill in the form LEGIBLY.)

There are many courses, leaflets and even videos available on this dreary skill. Ask your careers adviser.

Application Game

For many independent careers there's no alternative: you'll have to springboard from employment to independent. Which means first getting a job. The thing about applying for jobs is to concentrate on selling yourself to your prospective employer. It's just like any other form of selling: not every consumer wants to buy a green tie with pink spots, not every employer wants someone just like you. But you cannot begin the game until you have been noticed, which means getting shortlisted. Concentrate on getting shortlisted.

Get your formula established – decide on your strong points.

Present them: by putting them in the appropriate box on the application form, or including them in your CV.

Decide what the selector wants: trained selectors will have a clear idea of the skills, knowledge and attitudes they are looking for – they may even have a checklist of them, against which evidence of your skills, as shown on the application form, are assessed.

Answer the questions: few employers are going to be interested in someone who skirts a question, or has unexplained gaps in their employment record. And when it comes to questions about general interests, for example, employers are not really bothered about how large your stamp collection is or how many different sports you watch on television – they look at what your interests say about you and your ability. If propping up the bar and going to the cinema are your main pastimes, then this may indicate that you are sociable and enjoy passive cultural activities. But if you can say that you run a social club, arranging a varied annual programme and have doubled the membership in the last six months, the prospective employer can conclude that you are someone who can organise, plan ahead and achieve results. Whatever you say will be interpreted subjectively by the interviewer so that a contrary conclusion, that your energies are dissipated and certainly not directed to your work is equally possible. That's a risk you have to run but you might as well write what you think is true about you because if you get the job you'll have to live with what you have written – that is until you become your own boss.

Put across your experience: even if the work you have done so far does not seem relevant to the new job, some aspects may be useful – for example if you have had to work under pressure or deal directly with the public, then you have developed skills which can be transferred and developed in the new job.

Also have a look at *CV Game*. Try to get offered this job, even if you are pretty sure that you do not want it. It's all good experience and you can always turn it down.

Aptitude Tests

You probably know (or think you know) where your natural abilities lie, but your view will have been influenced by many factors: general interests, parents' and teachers' advice, motivation, abilities of your peer groups at school and college.

Aptitude tests are used mainly to test prospective employees of major organisations, as part of their selection procedure. At the simplest level they involve tests of manual dexterity and clerical data handling. At the graduate recruitment level they include:

Verbal reasoning: This is to test your ability to distinguish levels of information, make reasoned answers and evaluate a situation in a logical way. Analogies are often used (puppy is to dog as kitten is to ---); or statements are made and you are asked to make appropriate deductions based on the information given.

Numerical reasoning: Some tests simply ask you to select the next number in a series – 3, 9, 27, . . . to show you have the ability to manipulate numerical information, or you may be given sheets of data and asked to interpret and present information drawn from them.

Diagrammatic reasoning and spatial visualisation: This involves the ability to judge shapes and sizes and to visualise the relationship of objects to each other.

Remember when taking aptitude tests

that they are demanding – you're not supposed to finish, as they are testing your speed and accuracy at the same time. You can practise tests to help improve your score and assess your aptitudes; some tests are available through all university and polytechnic and some college careers services. Eysenck's books *Know your own IQ* and *Check your own IQ* have some examples that you can practise. Before taking a test, throw away your calculator for a week and think figures; aptitude testers seem to think there are merits in being able to do long multiplication in your head.

Psychological/motivational testing: This gets to the basics of what sort of work you're most suited for and will enjoy. You may want to have yourself tested to make sure you are making the right career decisions, or you may find that you want to employ someone, and would like to check their abilities. You can get this done by professional agencies – check the Yellow Pages under Careers advice. Watch out for high charges. College careers centres can sometimes provide the service free.

You can't always rely on the results; remember they are produced by computers (or people who think like computers). In one (apocryphal) case, someone was told her aptitudes pointed to a career in the church; the computer had neither asked her sex nor whether she believed in God.

Bankruptcy

There's a lot of it about.

If you can't pay a particular bill at the time it is due, the people you owe money to can go to court and petition for bankruptcy. If you still don't pay up, a licensed insolvency practitioner will move in to sort out your assets and pay your debts.

Some creditors have a greater claim than others, for example, the taxman and secured creditors.

The main lesson to be learned from the bankruptcy of others is that it is usually a muddled approach to financial management or half-hearted marketing, rather than a failure in the underlying business, which gets you into deep water. The most common causes of business collapse are: over-rapid expansion (too much anticipated on the basis of the first contract); income being over-estimated and costs under-estimated; and lack of financial control. Keep your plans and books orderly, and you can pull out before it is too late. If it happens to you, don't be put off trying again – you'd be surprised at who has gone bankrupt en route to wild success.

Banks

Much as you hate them, it's difficult to do without them. They have no shame. Not content with throwing billions of pounds into irrecoverable Third World debt during the 70s, they lent millions to Maxwell et al in the 80s, and compounded their folly by financing property development as if there was no tomorrow (which there wouldn't be for most managements with this sort of record).

Shamelessly, small businesses will be expected to pay for their delusions of grandeur. It'll be harder for you to get working capital, the costs will be greater and the conditions will be more onerous (they'll want your house as collateral as a start). Their power to pull the rug from under your feet will be enshrined in every subclause of every interminable loan document. While they smother more small businesses, their top management floats effortlessly to the top of the Honours list.

You, of course, won't be dealing with the great lenders, you'll be dealing with a local bank manager, possibly masquerading as a Small Business Adviser. These are different **in kind**. They'll be short on the readies, long on advice about your business. Many won't bother to get a feel of what you are up to by visiting you – they probably don't want to know. All too often they'll retreat into accounts, forecasts, references to higher authority and the whole bureaucratic smokescreen employed by risk-averse managers whose main concern is to avoid mistakes being pinned on them.

There are exceptions, we know some. But always remember, you may have built up a good relationship with one bank manager but his capricious successor could close you down overnight if he decides to call in your loan. Consult your accountant and make sure of your position.

What this means to you is:

(1) Watch them like a hawk
(2) Read the small print
(3) Give as little by way of personal guarantees as you can.

Having said that you'll probably still have to live with them. Some are human – ours is.

Biodata

Trends come and go in recruitment and selection, and this approach to application forms appears to be increasing. It is a computerised method of preselection, based on the information provided on the application form. Factual information such as exam results is marked, together with manner of approach to study, outlook on life, sociability and so on. Questions are usually presented on a form, on which you tick the relevant box, so that results can be fed into a computer and analysed. It's worth bearing in mind that there is little point in 'cheating' on these forms – they are not always looking for the straight 'A' grades and sensible 'time-planned' approach to exam studies.

Blockers

Blockers which stop you getting on may be real or apparent:

Real: too little money
too little time
no premises
no support from others
no constructive ideas
no creative inspiration
no confidence
no ability to organise
no success with selling
no negotiating skills

Apparent: The belief that these real blockers can't be overcome

Work out ways of getting around blockers: eg borrow money, learn to manage your time, ask for help – people might not know you feel a lack of support, identify your strengths and if necessary employ someone else to do the things you can't do, or take a relevant training course.

Borrowing

Borrowing equipment is cheaper than hiring; for example, you may be able to borrow cameras or studio space from a photographer friend; or borrow help from your spouse or family in producing an advertisement for a trade magazine; or borrow time from friends who are happy to help you get started – they might service your van, or give you advice on people to approach with ideas for new products.

Borrowing money is often vital for business; most small businesses start with bank finance. On the whole, banks and institutions prefer lending large rather than small amounts of money because it takes them the same amount of time to manage a loan/investment of £5,000 as it does to manage £500,000. The margin they charge over bank base rate often reflects this, which penalises the small borrower.

Banks are primarily responsible to their shareholders, not to you their customer. Even if they may seem ridiculously worried about granting loans to what you know is your excellent business, persevere. They are in business to lend *you* money. If you're approaching a bank manager, go armed with a watertight case for needing a loan in which you are confident – and in which you can appear convincingly confident. Know how you are going to repay it. Ask for more than you think you'll need (but not more than you can afford) – you don't want to waste time working out another case for more money, and the bank manager may offer a smaller loan than you ask for. Remember that bank managers are often perverse: they only like to lend you money when you do not need it, and the way to cope with that is to get your cash flow worked out and walk into the bank when you look most flush with cash and fix up the borrowing arrangement from a position of strength.

Budget

Your budget is the amount of money which has to be spent to achieve your targets (your expenditure), balanced against the amount you expect to make on sales and services (your income). Professionals will project an annual budget, breaking it down into monthly figures. You may just think in terms of 'I must earn another couple of grand before Christmas, so I can buy a new computer' but if you haven't a budget plan with monthly figures as targets and guides you won't know how well things are going. One way of reducing the risk of overspending is to allow for 12 months' expenditure and only 10 months of income in your calculations.

The monthly budget should list estimates of income and outgoings, both fixed – rent, rates, loan repayments, insurance etc – and variable – costs of materials, day-to-day expenses. Armed with these lists you can juggle the bills to ensure the best cashflow; try to withhold payment on certain bills until your invoices have been paid. Remember that one cause of disaster in small businesses is not lack of profit, but lack of liquidity (or cashflow). If there isn't the cash to cover immediate, short term outgoings, you may be forced out of business even though your business idea is sound.

By drawing up a budget which works, you can convince the banks that you can look after their money and are creditworthy. And if the figures aren't reaching the planned targets, you can take appropriate action – pick up small jobs to fill the gaps, or sell off something to see you through the hard times until the big jobs pay off.

Your bank may offer courses or leaflets and advice on setting up a business – they don't want your enterprise to go down the tubes any more than you do. And for high powered advice the major accountancy firms provide information in the form of private consultancy, leaflets, books and courses.

Bumf

Business bumf proliferates; business studies departments, central and local government, accountants, newsletter and paperback publishers are all guilty. There's far too much of it about in the Enterprise Era. Don't let yourself be swamped by it – bin most of it.

Bureaucratic Benefits

If you do intend to springboard, take advantage of your position in a bureaucracy to reap the benefits provided most readily to bureaucrats by the financial services industry. For instance, you should:

- arrange a good line of credit/borrowing facility with your bank while you still have a regular monthly salary
- get adequate health insurance: health is a key to success as your own boss and ill-health the cause of many failures
- get a personal pension plan (avoid employers' pension schemes like the plague): personal pension plans can sometimes be used as collateral or to buy premises for your new business if you make sure before you begin that such uses are written into the rubric of the plan

You could:

- get credit cards: gold cards in particular offer sufficient unsecured credit to get many small businesses off the ground (at a cost!)
- get a mortgage for as large a house as you can afford in an area which will be fashionable by the time you need to sell it
- get a second mortgage on your house so that you can buy a second property, eg a cottage in the country: you can use this as collateral when financing your new enterprise without hazarding your prime residence.

Business Courses

Local business training/teaching is now the name of the game although a few renowned courses such as the excellent CRANFIELD Enterprise Development Programme may yet survive the government's new emphasis. There is a huge range of courses on offer.

Start by looking locally, checking that at least some of your course is being taught by presenters running their own business. Your easiest way of finding what's on offer is to look at the Open Learning Directory at your nearest JOBCENTRE. It lists some two thousand options and the staff should be able to help you find what you need; check it out for yourself before enrolling.

Nationally, apart from the business courses run by polytechnics, universities and business schools you could consider two open learning routes: the OPEN UNIVERSITY and the OPEN COLLEGE. The OU now has its own business school and has long taught business subjects such as accounting. Its emphasis is professional and academic and you can pick up an MBA part-time. In contrast, the Open College concentrates on practical subjects and works towards NVQs. And your own professional body may run tailor-made courses; specialist courses are offered not only by leading firms of accountants and management consultants but by small training firms such as BREAKTHROUGH.

Business Plans

These are a must.

They are an (apparently) boring method of sorting out your ideas, enthusiasms and personal feel for the market in a way that both makes them mesh together sufficiently to make some sort of operational sense and also enables you to explain them to bank managers. You'll need one in any of the jobs in this book, from actor to zoo keeper, but the structure, content and depth of analysis required obviously varies from job to job. Try writing one and you'll probably become intrigued. Keep it and review it regularly – half yearly at least. Most small businesses overestimate their income and underestimate their costs. Make sure you are realistic.

Here's a checklist to help you get going with a pretty thorough business plan:

- your idea expressed as a business idea and why people should buy it;
- the market;
- competition;
- objectives, qualitative and financial
  - money in and out
  - start up costs
  - funding
  - pricing;
- operational strategy – how it will all work in outline;
- communication strategy, selling and media;
- action timetable.

A book that takes you through all this, and helps you think out your own plan is *Breakthrough*.

Capital Needs/ Entry Cost

These vary enormously from job to job. Each of our job profiles gives a very rough indication of the entry cost, excluding your own personal costs of qualifying, training and living. For some jobs your need to get your hands on prestige premises, expensive equipment, valuable stocks or have access to large sums of money to demonstrate 'capital sufficiency'.

Do not despair – loads of other jobs just need a battered van, a telephone in your home or use of somebody's garage as a workshop. You can get a rough idea of what you can do with the amount of capital/borrowing that you would feel comfortable in investing in your job – from £1.00 to £1,000,000 – from the *Independent Job Search Index*.

Career Choice

When choosing a career, there are thousands upon thousands of different jobs you could consider, but only five points to investigate:

- **You** – your skills, aptitudes, interests and values
- **The occupational area** – find out about types of work within the field
- **The job** – what will you actually be doing all day?
- **Who you will be working for** – (employers if you are spending some time in conventional employment; clients in other cases) who they are, what they want and whether you want to work for them
- **The job market** – if you can understand how it operates, you're half way to a job.

Career Development Loans

This government-backed scheme enables you to borrow between £300–£5,000 to cover up to 80% of the cost of the fees, books and materials of your job-related training course. This can be professional, managerial, scientific or technical and last between one week and one year.

Repayment terms are generous. While training you need not repay any of the loan and the government pays the interest; at the end of your training you begin to repay the loan and interest, usually over a period of three to five years. The scheme is run by three banks – Barclay's Bank, Clydesdale Bank and the Co-operative Bank – and you can talk to any of them about it but it is probably best to start by telephoning free for an information pack on *0800 585505*.

Careers Advice

The main source of formal careers advice is through the careers advisory service at your school, college, polytechnic or university. You may still be able to use their services once you've left, too. There are private advisers if you can afford to pay.

The problem with careers advisers is that they are such a mixed bunch you are taking pot luck when you consult them. But their experience of how different students' careers have progressed and knowledge of the job market should put them in a good position to point you in the right direction.

Most careers advisers are employed and always have been. So, on the whole, they are more useful to those wanting to work in bureaucracies than to the entrepreneur.

To make the best of your time, do a bit of research and preparation before going for a careers interview. It's not the adviser's responsibility to set you on the road to a career. It's yours.

Before the careers interview identify clearly what you want from the session. If you have no idea what you want to do you can't expect to come away with a career planned in detail. Don't expect the careers adviser to do all the work. Read up about various different jobs and occupations and start to analyse your skills and interests. Find out how the careers information room is organised, so that you can use it to your best advantage. Try some of the careers choice computer-assisted questionnaires available at your careers centre (Gradscope, Cascaid). They can generate some job ideas and set you thinking about where your talents lie.

During the interview remember that it is a two-way process. If advisers are going to be helpful, you must build up a rapport with them. If you don't feel this is possible, you may be able to work with another adviser at the centre, so check out the interview booking procedures and find out as much as you can about the personnel.

Careers interviews usually start with the adviser finding out about your ideas. These are far more important than anything they can suggest – after all, they only met you five minutes ago.

After the interview follow up the ideas. Go back, even if you didn't feel the interview was particularly helpful. There's no point in just writing off any advice you were given: tell them, so they can look at further ways of helping you. And if the adviser has suggested some careers which you hadn't thought of you need time to chew the ideas over – you can't decide your whole future on the basis of only one interview.

Careers advice after college You may be able to go for a careers advisory interview at your old college as an ex-student (particularly if you are a recent graduate). There is a Mutual Aid System, whereby ex-students can get interviews at colleges closer to home, but since careers advisers' first loyalties are to current students, you will be unlikely to get an interview through this system at busy times. There is usually no restriction on using the careers centre's library, so check opening hours, and use the information service. Local authorities may run education advice centres, but they tend to focus on courses rather than careers.

Careers Guidance (Private)

Private careers guidance companies are even more of a mixed bag than careers services at institutions, and they charge hefty fees. Before consulting one, find out what they offer, what they specialise in, how much they charge and what guarantees they offer. Typical charges for 3–4 hours, including interest inventories, tests and discussion, are £200–£300. Some centres are much more expensive – charging up to £3,000; check very carefully what is included and what services are offered. The Yellow Pages list advice centres in your area.

Careers Information

Beware. Most careers information is written and published by bureaucrats with the aim of selling you the proposition that you too should become a bureaucrat; it's usually disseminated uncritically by careers officers. Careers directories and encyclopaedias derive much of their content from the same sources. If you happen to want to make your way up a bureaucratic ladder to (say) Air Chief Marshal, Chairman of

Shell, or Permanent Secretary at the Ministry of Agriculture this is fine. It's also OK if you have less ambitious bureaucratic aspirations, eg to lead a modestly prestigious and not unrewarded life in a secure job with the prospect of an adequate occupational pension when you retire. Some graduates want just that; many do not. For those who want to become their own boss, conventional careers information may seem worse than useless. If you are one of them, the simple message for you is find out for yourself. Nobody can do it for you. Read this book; if the jobs you are interested in are covered by other directories read them too (*Careers Encyclopaedia*; *Occupations 92*; other guides published by COIC). Talk to people in the jobs you have shortlisted. Try working at any level in the area that interests you, even for a few weeks in the vacation. Meanwhile don't ostracise your careers service – USE IT to help you further your own career. Its sources of information are much wider than the published documents that you will see in the careers library.

Charm

Charm will get you a lot of jobs, and out of a lot of tricky situations. It is also a great asset in dealing with staff and getting the best out of people. You needn't go as far as going to Charm School, but there are always new books on executive manners and charm. Try browsing in a business bookshop.

Choosing Your Clients and Suppliers

Concentrating effort is the name of the game. Straightforward clients who know what they want, tell you what that is and then pay for it quickly are easy to deal with. But the unproductive parts of your business can take up a lot of time. The main culprits are clients who pull out at the last minute after hours of discussions and suppliers who fail to come up with what they promised. These rules shoud help cut down on time wasting:

1 Work only for people/companies who will pay you.
2 If in doubt, take a substantial deposit.
3 If they object to this, you're right to have asked.
4 Don't part with any money until you're sure you know what you're getting.
5 Don't put all your eggs in one basket. Make sure you've got enough clients and suppliers to ensure that even if one or two get into financial trouble, *you* won't. Many businesses go bust because they were started on the back of one contract and others don't follow – beware.

Communication Skills

Communication is a two-way process. Getting your message across is vital in any job: skills may be oral or written, informational or persuasive. You must also be able to extrapolate the right information from communications addressed to you.

Oral skills As well as the gift of the gab, these involve other interpersonal relationships and body language, which may affect how information is perceived and received by the audience. You may need to develop skills in the following areas:

asserting yourself
public speaking
lecturing
teaching
debating
presenting
persuading
chatting/small talk
conversing
telephone manner
interviewing

On the receiving end, you may need to be good at:

listening
reflecting
responding
questioning
clarifying
summarising

Written skills You may not need to be able to write exquisite prose, but you may need to be able to present relevant information in written documents.

Can you write:

letters
memos
quotes
reports
essays
project proposals
business plans
CVs
publicity material (selling copy)
press releases?

On the receiving end can you:

analyse
synthesise
collect
collate
classify
evaluate
summarise?

If you haven't got all the skills you think you need, you can take INDUSTRIAL SOCIETY courses, read books, or employ someone to do the work for you.

Visual/spatial skills Another field of communication skills you may need to develop is visual communication: if you are a trained designer, your course will have included work on illustration and presentation, which are often essential in putting your message across. Recognising the importance of the visual message is vital in successful advertising and publicity. You may need professional help from a graphic designer to produce your publicity material.

Company Information

If you're a graduate looking for a first job in a company (or any bureaucracy) from which you intend to springboard into your own enterprise when you have sufficient contacts and experience then you'll need to find out as much about prospective employers as possible. Sources include: the free directories, such as ROGET, DOG or GET, which provide thumbnail sketches of major graduate recruiters, the type of organisation, what jobs they have available for graduates and the geographical areas they cover; ROGET also provides very useful job descriptions from which you can identify the main tasks in the various work areas; more detailed information is usually given by each company in its own graduate recruitment brochures, available from careers services or by direct application to the company concerned; some companies/organisations produce videos, organise presentations to final year students, or run work experience programmes and may organise open days where you can go along and see what they have to offer.

Once you are in business you need to know about other companies in the field – possible competitors, suppliers or purchasers of your goods and services – what size they are, whether they could put business your way, how healthy their turnover is. This type of information is available in trade directories (Mintel, Extel, Market information) in trade and reference libraries (eg CITY BUSINESS LIBRARY).

Trade magazines keep you abreast of personnel changes, new developments and trade gossip. You can also find out a good deal from the information companies supply at COMPANIES REGISTRATION OFFICE.

Compartmentalising Your Life

If you want to lead an entirely separate job life and personal life, then bureaucratic jobs are for you. If you are your own boss, there are various degrees of possible compartmentalisation. An actor in the third year of a walk-on part in a television soap opera may be able to separate work and play; a resident owner of a country-house hotel cannot. Those with young families may not want their life compartmentalised – but beware of working with small children under your feet without adequate childcare arrangements. Either your work or your children are likely to suffer, probably both.

If you let your work get in the way of your family life you may find that stress and tension build up and you have nothing but problems, instead of the support you need. Compartmentalise your time and your space, and you might find working for yourself a lot easier.

If you are based at home, you have the advantage that you don't have to travel to a place of work but at the same time you require self discipline. This works in two ways. If you're a workaholic, you will have to draw the line and STOP when it's time to – or you'll go stale. On the other hand, you may be the type of person who gets diverted and would rather spring-clean the cellar than sit down to send out invoices (in which case, don't work at home).

Conferences

The main aim of most conferences is to make money for the conference organiser. Your aim in attending should be to stimulate your own ideas about your industry, profession or field of study. You can use them to make and develop contacts, to meet recruiters if you are looking for traditional employment and potential clients if you're self-employed. They can be expensive to attend throughout; part-time attendance may be all you need to make contacts (there are often special rates for full-time students). If you can't attend, write for conference details and copies of the proceedings. Conference attendance lists provide a useful source of information on companies and personnel.

Constraints

You may have real constraints to contend with – you may be handicapped, have a young family to look after or be responsible for the well-being of an ancient granny. Be realistic when choosing your job.

If you're in a wheelchair, for example,

you would probably find it hard to manage as a GP but you could well be a successful solicitor.

Consultancy

When you've worked successfully for some years, the knowledge you acquire becomes useful to others. So you can take off on your own into consultancy work. This can be combined with other jobs – if you're an architect, for example, you may find yourself working as a consultant to a large firm or government organisation, while at the same time you do some teaching work, or take on some private refurbishment projects. Fees to consultants are usually massive compared to fees for more mundane work. In many fields, there is a trend towards reducing the number of permanent jobs and increasing the use of consultants for specific tasks.

Co ops

A co-operative is a formal agreement between a group of people working together. It may involve a group of workers getting together to buy the company they work for, or a group of people with similar or interdependent skills getting together to market those skills. As a co-op, you may be able to get a grant or loan from a local authority, or specialist agency (eg agencies which specialise in providing advice and training for ethnic groups).

CV

A CV (curriculum vitae) is your way of presenting yourself to prospective employers or clients. It is essential that you put across basic information such as: name, address, telephone number, age, experience and educational details, and maybe add information on personal interests, special skills, and the names of people who can provide references for you (academic, as employers, or personal). When presenting yourself to potential clients, forget most educational details and personal interests; concentrate on your experience and list clients who are willing to give recommendations or references.

The way in which you present the information is all part of the CV game. If in doubt, get help.

Presentation: is all-important; you'll need a perfect typescript and a clear layout. If you can't guarantee to produce this yourself go to a word processing/office services bureau and pay for it to be done properly; it's worth the money. Consult *Yellow Pages* and ring round for prices. Never send photocopies of CVs; employers want to feel that you have chosen the advertised job because you are particularly suited to it – not that you are applying for everything.

Tailoring the CV: It is important to tailor each CV to suit the job you are applying for: emphasise experience in a related field, even if it was only a holiday job. For example, if you had a temporary job working as a typist for a travel agent, it is worth mentioning if you are applying for a job as a courier but not necessarily if you are applying for a job as a cookery writer. You may need very many versions of your CV, to send with different job applications. This is where a word processor pays handsome dividends; once your CV is on disc you tailor it much more easily and produce a new top copy in seconds.

Creating a CV: If you are a full-time student, your work experience may be minimal, but look out for vacation jobs to embellish your CV, however lowly or poorly paid. If you can't find paid work, consider voluntary work, so that you can demonstrate some work experience on your CV.

Chronological or reverse chronological order? Usually, for the first two or three jobs after graduation it is best to arrange your CV in chronological order. As you gain more experience, start your CV with the most recent jobs you have done. The more experience you have, the less relevant early jobs and education are to

a prospective employer; so you can lose some of the detail, eg by the time you are 30 you no longer need to list exam grades (unless you are particularly proud of them).

Covering letter: Remember that while the CV will be accompanied by a covering letter it should **always** speak for itself. Keep the covering letter to a single page. It should explain where you saw the advertisement and why you feel you are particularly interested/suited to the job. Also look at the *Application Game*.

Decision-making Strategies

Decide quickly (but not hastily). Change your decisions slowly.

Making the right decisions is an essential part of being your own boss. You cannot pass the buck like the vast majority of bureaucrats. The first point is that the decisions must be made – not put off for a couple of days. Problems which need a decision rarely go away, and you'll only have to make the decision in a week's time.

So how do you make the decision? Here are some well-established strategies.

Strategy 1: Arbitrary: toss a coin.

Strategy 2: Toss a coin and analyse your reaction. This helps you to identify your feelings about an arbitrary decision. Once your feelings are clearly exposed you can start to analyse the information available, which should be the basis of your decision making.

Strategy 3: The rational approach. Start to identify the facts, and project the consequences of different courses of action.

- List all the facts, as you know them;
- list all the difficulties and problems associated with each fact;
- list all your options, however bizarre;
- weigh up the likelihood of achieving each option and give it a percentage score;
- list what you have to give up if you pursue a particular action (the opportunity cost) and analyse how much it matters to you;

- look for any compromises that might be possible;
- identify a priority/preference scale and place the options in order;
- choose between the more certain and riskier options.

Review the situation: if it's a major decision, sleep on it and take a fresh look at your options in the morning. If you haven't time for that, just go through the options again, make sure you've considered all the possibilities, consult colleagues to see if they can see any alternatives you have not considered and look again at the likelihood of success for each course of action. If all else fails, go back to strategy 1.

Then make your decision *and act on it*.

Disability

Remember that physical disabilities need not prevent you working as your own boss. And new technology now makes it easier to work with only the aid of a computer terminal and a telephone line.

Consult your careers advisers. Read *Employment for Disabled People* which includes a chapter on running your own business, outlines information available, and gives some inspiring examples of disabled entrepreneurs.

Displacement Activity

Classic examples of displacement activity are sharpening pencils or worrying about tax, instead of getting on with the business. Don't worry, almost everyone does it. The key is to know when you are doing it so that you can make sure you begin to get on with the job as soon as it's over.

Divorce

There is plenty of it around, but research indicates that the self-employed are no more likely to suffer marital breakdown

than anyone else. If your business is jointly owned, divorce could have dire consequences and pole-axe the entire enterprise. So draw up a written agreement at the start, and seek legal advice if things start to go wrong. Know who owns what within the business.

Driving Licence

Get one and keep it. The younger you are when you take your test, the more naturally it will come to you and the fewer lessons you will need. The experts reckon on one lesson for every year of your life. So take your test as soon as you can.

Employing Others

Employing others immediately involves you in office politics, office socialising and office administration. Whether they are casual labour, part-timers, full-timers or freelancers, once you start employing others your headaches begin. You're not just responsible for making a success of your life, you're responsible for the livelihood of others as well. Likewise, the success of your business is no longer entirely dependent on you.

Delegating effectively can be very difficult, particularly in a new business which has always been your baby. You have to accept that employees are unlikely to work as hard for your business as you will. One business owner reckoned it took three employees to do the work of one owner.

Once you've realised you need someone, make sure that you get them personally involved as the more personally fulfilled they become the better job they'll do. Decide precisely what it is that you want them to do and make sure they know; then make sure both you and they are clear on the terms and conditions of employment. They'll need a job description (even if it's just 'general dogsbody').

Get professional advice on:

- Contracts of employment
- National Insurance contributions

- PAYE, income tax
- Statutory sick pay
- Unfair dismissal
- Redundancy
- Sex/race discrimination

Business courses can help a lot.

Find out more from the leaflets published by the Department of Employment, at your local office and read the *One Minute Manager*.

Entrepreneurial Skills

If you want to be your own boss, entrepreneurial skills always help. Initiative, confidence, energy, persuasiveness, tact, salesmanship, reliability, ability to work under pressure, efficiency – the list is a challenging one, but these are the qualities you need to be a successful entrepreneur.

Don't be put off if you don't feel particularly entrepreneurial yet: few do when they start. Most of this can be developed in you, once you have identified what you want, by tapping into local courses through your local Jobcentre.

Equal Opportunities

If you are a member of a disadvantaged group (such as a racial minority, women) working for yourself may be a way of doing the sort of job you want. Don't forget you still have to contend with the attitudes of the public you deal with, even if you can avoid prejudice in your workplace. But don't see your ethnic background as an insuperable disadvantage – it gives you access to some markets that are closed to others. Marginality is often the drive to get you going: how do you think M & S started? A number of agencies can help eg PAUL BOGEL FOUNDATION, WOMEN RETURNERS ASSOCIATION.

If you are employing staff, all jobs advertised must be open to all racial groups. Only the smallest of employers are exempt from equal opportunities legislation.

Equipment

In some fields of work, good equipment is vital. When you're setting up, you may be able to borrow, you may have to hire (keep a close eye on the amount you are spending on hire fees) or buy secondhand. There soon comes a point when you are better off borrowing the capital to buy equipment new. Always build an allowance for replacement of equipment into your budget. You'll never make money if your word processor is always broken or you're always mending the car. The same applies of course to one's telephone service but regrettably that's not in your control.

Europe and You

The European Community matters. Forget what Europe looks like now; concentrate on what Europe is going to be like by the time you have trained/qualified and gained sufficient experience to become your own boss.

In principle, any professional – accountant, actuary, barrister, chiropodist . . . veterinary surgeon – can automatically be entitled to become a member of an equivalent profession in any other member state *without* having to requalify. In practice, the detail varies from profession to profession, depending on the state of negotiation between the governments and professional bodies of the member states – dentists have few problems; for teachers working in Europe is more difficult. But things are changing fast. For more detailed information on the position, get hold of *Europe: Open For Professions*.

Meanwhile do what you can to pick up European languages. The best place to do this is at school; if you've missed that, try when you are a student; and if you've missed that, you'll have to try to study in your spare time when you are not at work. Many schools, universities and polytechnics run exchanges with Europe, which is an excellent way of familiarising yourself with other countries. (For information on

EC universities and colleges, see *Student Handbook*.) There are loads of European initiatives which it is worth making the most of when you can – the Lingua programme, run by *Eurydice*, aims to improve language learning; *Erasmus* enables students to spend part of their degree course in a university/poly in another EC state; *Comett* helps students get work experience in the EC; *Petra* allows young people to get vocational training in the EC when they leave school; there are other exchange programmes run by the *Central Bureau* and *Youth Exchange Centre*. However you do it, it is essential both to be able to speak the language fluently and be familiar with the culture of the country in which you propose to work.

Europe Open For Business

In many of the jobs in this book, your future as your own boss cannot be isolated from the single European market. You should worry less about what Europe looks like now, and concentrate on what it is going to be like in a few years time. The best way of getting to grips with what Europe means now is to get hold of a copy of *Business Europe*.

But things are changing fast. In principle, any professional will automatically be entitled to become a member of an equivalent profession in any other member state without having to requalify (see *Europe: Open for the Professions*). In addition, a vast variety of business and creative endeavour will be able to make the move to Europe. By the end of 1992 the national trade barriers which have prevented you from conducting your business freely in any member state will have come down: Europe will be open to your business and the UK will be open to theirs. Realists say it will be a further five years until the process is completed. They may be right but don't let that deflect you.

Working from a base in the UK, you should be free to sell your services, farm your own land or make those products in any member state, ie Belgium, Denmark, Eire, France, Germany, Greece, Holland, Luxembourg, Portugal, Spain and of course the UK. By the time you need to know about the small print things will be clearer. The position for many of the jobs (so far as we have been able to unearth it) is given in the *European Community Notes* in the *Independent Jobs A–Z*.

Before you start, pick up European languages and make sure your job experience is gained with people keen to exploit the single market. You need to be familiar with the culture, and preferably have some experience of the countries you wish to work in *before* setting up on your own. Our general advice is to springboard from local employment – that is, to work in someone else's office, farm, school, business, studio or surgery in the country where you wanto work, before striking out on your own. Either do that by getting a job with a local firm, or an international or UK organisation with a branch in the area in which you're interested. You can look for a job through an employment office which collaborates with the Sedoc network (an EC-wide network exchanging job information); ask the *Employment Service*. You have the right to spend up to three months in another member state looking for a job. Have a look at *Working Abroad* from the Employment Service.

However you do it, make sure you are well prepared before launching into Europe. Some entrepreneurs have persuaded a number of British dentists moving to Europe that the problems were almost insuperable and have taken huge sums for their services. In fact, for dentists, the transition to Europe is fairly simple, so make sure your information is authoritative. Professional bodies and trade associations often have lots of useful information (though some have surprisingly little; but always ask). The DTI produces a number of booklets including *Action Checklist For Business*, covering the free movement of goods and capital between member states; *Single Market: The Facts*; and a newspaper, *Single Market News*. If you want detailed information, telephone the DTI's Hotline (081–200–1992).

Exhaustion

When you're working for yourself, it is easy not to notice how long and hard you're working. The result can be that you exhaust yourself, which is counter-productive. If you're working on your own, you need to force yourself to take proper breaks. It is a matter which only you can determine in the light of your job and your own stamina. Research shows that most small businessmen work more than 50 hours a week.

Exhibitions and Trade Fairs

Vital sources of information and contacts if you are your own boss. Try to get to any that are relevant – in the UK or overseas – even if only for a few hours. They are advertised in trade publications. Entry fees are not usually prohibitive although fees to exhibitors often are.

You will not only see what the competition is up to, you will be able to meet suppliers, pick up trade and find out more about the structure and future trends of the trade.

The catalogues from these exhibitions are full of useful information, so get hold of any that are relevant even if you don't get to the exhibition.

Exit Sale

Once established, you can often sell all or part of the business (that is, the expectation of the future income), usually as a capital sum. This is obviously so in the case of businesses that are not entirely dependent on your own unique contribution as a craftsman or expert, eg an established magazine; less so where the income derives from intangible rights eg performing rights, copyright, film rights; and less obvious still when you're simply selling good will eg many professional practices. There are quite a lot of jobs where you can be

your own boss and still, like a bureaucrat, find your income ceases when you stop working. Working out the permutations of earned income, pensions and capital in financial terms is a highly technical matter on which it is almost certainly necessary to take proper advice. It is worth thinking about exit sales before you start; if you decide that you want to work towards an exit sale consult your accountant and solicitor before taking the plunge.

Experience

In some jobs there is no real substitute for experience: you can go on doing courses and reading books, but until you actually get on with it out in the field you won't really get to know the business. Getting a job in the traditional job market is one of the best ways of gaining experience – and it's a useful springboard to setting up on your own. You can find out a lot about how specific organisations work by getting employment – temporary, part-time or a full-career post. But beware of getting sucked into permanent employment.

Family Commitment

Family commitment to your job is often vital. This is quite unlike many bureaucratic jobs, where the bureaucrat's family knows little or nothing about the job that pays the bills. All they see is the company car and the company dinner-dance, the company pay-slip, the company pension, and, increasingly, the company's redundancy cheque. On the whole it's all they need to see.

Not so if you are your own boss. The levels of family commitment will depend on the job but in general if you cannot rely on the commitment of your immediate family join a bureaucracy. Family help can also play a vital part: look at the success of the Asian families in the newstrade, takeaway and corner shops.

Family Tradition

Some families have a tradition of self-employment and it's easier to cope with the risks and uneven income if you've been brought up with it. Other families don't. If yours hasn't don't worry – why not be the first?

If your family has a traditional line of business, you will be in with a flying start. You will have instant contacts and experience derived from older generations and you can reduce a lot of the initial risks. It may seem like a cop-out to join the family profession or the family firm, but you could also regard it as a challenge: look at the way it works and improve upon it.

Finance

Loans, grants, bursaries, sponsorship, family capital, redundancy payments – all these have been used to start up businesses. It's important to do your sums before you start. Work out how much finance you will need, then decide which is the most appropriate source. If you are thinking of setting up a small, soft toy making business, for example, your local bank manager should be able to lend you the few hundred pounds you need to get started. On the other hand, if you want to go into property development you may need to approach the big city financiers. Anything is possible; they are in business to lend *you* money, not do you a favour. You no longer need simply to distinguish between being rich and poor; it is a matter of who is creditworthy and who is not. Make sure you are. Most accountants should be able to suggest who to approach where.

Beware. Sales are the only real source of finance. The rest comes from borrowing/using other people's money to provide working capital. This is useful to get your business off the ground. But it can be counterproductive; many people find it easier to spend their time seeking further 'injections' of money than selling their products or services. That route only leads to failure.

Finance Checklist

Always talk to your accountant; many people should also ask their bank manager. Here are some of the places you could look at if you need to use other people's money.

Banks The major source of borrowing. You don't necessarily have to be a customer of the bank you approach. All banks produce literature on obtaining finance. Even if you don't need any capital to start with, it is worth talking to your bank manager to arrange a loan and/or overdraft facilities in case you have cash flow problems; they'd rather know about possible problems before you start. Make sure you are talking to a manager who has authority to make the arrangements you want, otherwise you may be fobbed off because he does not want to lose face by telling you he's too junior.

Local Authority Grants There are some schemes administered by local authorities which may be useful.

Enterprise Allowances If you are unemployed you may qualify for an enterprise allowance until your business starts to bring in a regular income. The precise amount and the period of your allowance are decided locally. Ask your local *Jobcentre*.

Under-30s There are several schemes which are specifically designed to help young people setting up businesses. The PRINCE'S YOUTH BUSINESS TRUST will provide loans of up to £3,000 and bursaries for young unemployed people who want to start up their own businesses, or loans, training grants and ongoing support for new or expanding businesses. LIVEWIRE give awards for promising business ideas.

Small Firms Loan Guarantee Scheme This is a government-backed loan scheme, with the loan being arranged through a bank. The government provides a guarantee for 70 per cent of the total loan agreed. It may be for property purchase, extending premises, purchasing business assets, setting up costs and/or working capital. The maximum you can borrow under such schemes is £75,000, over 2–5 years, at a cost of 1–2 per cent over the base rate.

Government Finance There are cash

grants and special loan schemes for companies in development areas.

EC Money Loans may be available for up to 50 per cent of capital costs at reduced rates from the European Investment Bank. Your accountant or bank should be able to tell you whether you are eligible.

Financial Institutions Many large institutions and companies have money to invest in start-ups and venture capital. Consult the list published each year (available in libraries) called Development and Venture Capital, reproduced in the *Investor's Chronicle* and also in *Working for Yourself*. Look up *Crawford's City Directory*, the best source book. The Bank of England also produces a useful guide – *Money for Business*.

Other sources you may consider:

There are local co-operatives offering a variety of loans, advice, support and shared back-up facilities (childcare, photocopying) – eg BOOTSTRAPS – currently in Hackney but planning to expand.

If you're creating jobs in a mining area or in a British Steel Opportunity Area you may be eligible for a bank loan from BRITISH COAL ENTERPRISE or BSC INDUSTRY.

Private Loans If you are borrowing money from friends and relatives, draw up a proper agreement, listing the terms of repayment and rate of interest so that there is no misunderstanding. Consult a solicitor. Business courses guide you round many of the pitfalls.

A book to put you into the right frame of mind is *Think and Grow Rich*.

Financial Control

A prior condition of success is financial control. Take instructions from banks and accountants (all of which may sound deadly boring) and follow it. Do not attempt to devise your own original approach; install a well-tried, foolproof financial control system. Many failures are not business failures but are simply attributable to lack of financial control, particularly control of cash flow.

Franchising

This is where the owners of business (franchisors) allow others (franchisees) to sell their products or services under their own nationally promoted name. The franchisor sets standards; the franchisee sets up with reduced risks.

For more information read *Working for Yourself*. Also the BRITISH FRANCHISE ASSOCIATION produces background information sheets, a checklist of questions to ask a franchisor (also available in the Department of Industry's Small Firms Advice Service booklet no. 3), and many other services. Or see *Franchisee* in the *Independent Jobs A–Z*.

Freelancing

There is increasing scope for freelance work, from the area in which it originated (mercenaries) to the area in which the term is most commonly applied (journalism).

Most freelancers train in employment first. Many start to take on extra, part-time jobs (moonlighting) before using the contacts they have developed to set up on their own. Many go freelance because the idea of working for themselves appeals; to earn more for the same work; or to give them control over their working hours.

For some jobs you may find *The Freelance Alternative: Working for Yourself* is useful reading.

Getting Things Done

You won't get anywhere if you procrastinate. If you're the sort of person who tends to leave things until it's too late, working for yourself might not be the right thing for you. However, you can change if motivated. Write down what has to be done and when. Then check it every morning before you start work. Make sure you're doing things that are worthwhile, not just trivia. Do the really important tasks first.

Growth Planning

Creating a new business needs different skills from those needed in the day-to-day running of an established business. People who are good at setting up may find it difficult to keep things going, so find a structure that works easily and keep the business interesting for you. Many businesses fail because they have expanded too rapidly. So plan your growth realistically.

Handling Information

Computers have revolutionised this. For most jobs at least a word processor is a must. Try to get at least a rudimentary grasp of word processing, by taking a course or doing a vacation job in a company where word processors are used.

If you're hell-bent on living without high tech you could get a filofax, a card index or a filing cabinet. Be methodical.

Health

In spite of the long hours and extra stresses of self-employment and running small businesses, research indicates you are likely to be healthier than your counterparts in employment. Remember reliability is essential to your good name; you can't have frequent days off sick. Many self-employed people take out health insurance to protect their income (usually more expensive for women than for men).

Smoking, alcohol, over-eating and anxiety are the main causes of ill health so deal with them positively NOW. You can try worry beads.

Home based Work

Home is often a good place to start. It saves you both the cost of premises and the time spent on travel to and from work. It can also be a good place to continue once you're up and running, especially in London and the south where the rents can be prohibitive.

But beware; your work needs its own space. It needs space for you and your clients, contacts and suppliers (childproof if you have a family). It needs secure accommodation for your equipment (eg word processors, telephone, fax or drawing board, work benches, library). Entertaining can be done in local wine bars, hotels, etc. Provided this space is available, it has many advantages but the down side can be a feeling of isolation and the lack of any clear differentiation between the time you work and the time you play. So it is often difficult to know when to stop working. There is a network that supports home-based workers worth investigating – OWNBASE.

Insurance

Make sure you are properly insured. Depending on your job, you will almost certainly need to insure your premises and equipment. You may also need public liability insurance, professional indemnity, partner or key man insurance, insurance to cover accidental injury, vehicle insurance, fidelity insurance (or bonding), to insure your income and so on. Some professional institutes and trade associations run special schemes. Whatever your job you have to pay national insurance for yourself and any employees. And find out about life insurance and pension schemes *before* you get old and grey.

Interpersonal Skills

Interpersonal skills are important when you're your own boss. You'll have no big company image to hide behind. You'll need good relations with customers, clients and suppliers – you can't just leave it to the sales department. Try reading *The Psychology of Interpersonal Behaviour*.

Interview

An interview is simply a conversation with a purpose, eg:

- your job interview with recruiters
- a job interview you conduct with a prospective employee
- a financial interview with a bank or accountant
- an interview about the possibilities of going into business with an agency or grant-giving body.

You the Interviewee

Preparation: When you go for an interview of any kind, make sure you've got a clear idea of what you want to get out of it. Bring with you anything you think the interviewer may be interested in (eg qualification certificates for a job interview; bank statements and accounts for a financial interview).

Think about any likely questions so you are one step ahead.

Prepare a list of the questions that you genuinely want to ask, to satisfy yourself about the job/loan scheme/product involved.

Presentation: Whatever your attitude to outward appearances, there is plenty of evidence to show that first impressions count. Clean, appropriate clothes and a minimum of nervous habits are all positive assets. Make eye contact (but don't stare). While you don't want to look like a stuffed dummy, interviewers will be put off by wild gesticulations, fidgeting and nose-picking.

Tactics: There are professional tutors in interview techniques. Their services are usually aimed at executives and spokespeople who are in a position to be called on at short notice for radio and TV interviews, and their media techniques have some general application to the interviewing you may do, or be subjected to, as your own boss.

Here are some of the tactics they teach:

- **The message:** On the way to the interview, list on a postcard the points you want to put across.

- **The no-go areas:** On the other side of the card, list the points you don't want to come across: consider ways of avoiding (not evading) issues. Don't let the interviewer see the card.

- **Delaying and diversionary tactics:** If you're stumped by a question, think on your feet. In the meantime, cause a diversion by taking a sip of water, having a coughing fit, or saying 'Now that's a very interesting question, but before I answer could I just add one or two points about the last matter we were discussing . . .' Also you don't have to answer the question as given – eg 'The real question is . . .' A further diversionary tactic is to pick up on one of the words in the question and deflect with your prepared answer which will now include the 'picked' word.

- **Be honest:** If the interviewer persists, and you don't know the answer to the question, tell them you weren't prepared for that one but will go away and check your facts. People are impressed by honesty. If you are presented with information which contradicts your story, politely thank the interviewer for pointing this out and explain you would like to look into the matter further before commenting.

- **After the interview:** If you are the interviewee, wait a week, then ring up to see what the outcome of the interview was. Don't be too pushy – if you haven't heard anything it may be because the interviewer is still making a decision and doesn't want to be harassed. On the other hand, they may have forgotten about you, in which case the odd phone call can produce results. If you are the interviewer, follow up with a letter. For a job interview this may be a straight letter of rejection or a letter offering the post; or, if a different type of interview, send a letter summarising the main points made and decisions reached.

When you're your own boss, you need to be able to ask the right questions: listen, establish rapport, respond appropriately. Whether the interview is in the form of a meeting, for example with a prospective supplier, or interviewing an assistant you must decide what information you are looking for and work out a strategy for getting it.

Prepare for the interview by finding out all you can about the other party. Read the letter of application; ring referees; or it may involve looking into the background of a company to find out how big an operation it is, what other clients it has and so on. Use your contacts.

For job interviews, decide what qualities you are looking for and organise the interview so that the interviewee can demonstrate them. If you want someone who can perform under pressure, you may want to take a formal approach. If you are looking for an easy-going, accurate typist, hold an informal interview, and give them a typing test.

Job Hunting

If you want to find a first job in employment, as a springboard to being your own boss, here are the main sources of information about vacancies:

AGCAS: Vacancy lists are available at all graduate careers advisory services. The forward list, available from October to March, gives vacancies starting the following summer; and the current list hs immediately available jobs. Start to pick up the forward list during your last year at college and use the current lists nearer the time you graduate and whilst still job hunting.

College careers office: Your careers office may also have its own list of vacancies, either with local firms, or with firms with a special link with your college.

Trade publications: These are widely used for jobs in specialised areas. Some publications are more useful than others. It's worth consulting trade magazines regularly at your local library both to keep you informed of job vacancies and to widen your knowledge of the industry.

National and local papers: Most newspapers advertise particular types of jobs on particular days: find out which days your area comes up in which paper, and make sure you get to see it.

Professional bodies and trade associations: Many professional bodies and trade associations produce lists of vacancies.

Vacancy directories: Your careers office will have directories such as ROGET, DOG, GET and so on, which list major organisations and may be worth consulting. Also perhaps *Graduate Post* and *Executive Post* which list jobs and training opportunities.

Milk round programme: Your careers service will organise open days and interviews towards the end of the academic year.

Recruitment fairs: These are increasing not only during summer but are now held in some places at other times. Check with careers offices for details.

Jobcentres: Don't forget your local Jobcentres.

Speculative applications: There's nothing to stop you writing to organisations to offer your services or talking your way into an appointment with the boss. If you don't have any links with firms in your field, consult business directories, professional year books or *The Financial Times Top 1,000 Firms* or the *Personnel Managers Yearbook*. If firms are successful they're likely to have more vacancies. Write to the personnel manager of larger companies, the managing director of small ones. Many companies need extra help at busy times of the year, or when staff are on holiday, so you may at least find you get a short-term job which will tide you over and give you an insight into how firms work.

Networking: Once you've got contacts in the field, networking is the most helpful source of jobs. Ask everyone you know if there is anything going, write to companies you have worked for in the past and keep your ear to the ground.

Job Sharing

Formal job sharing is where two or more part-timers share one full-time job. For example, some education authorities will employ two teachers to share one job. This gives the job sharers a regular income, plus time to go out and do their own thing – perhaps a part-time course, voluntary work, look after their families or start out to become their own boss.

If you want to be your own boss but don't want to take the plunge all at once, why not suggest such a scheme to your employer, particularly if you have a possible job sharer lined up.

Keeping in Business

People who provide workshops and consultancy for new businesses often assert that new businesses often seem to run out of money and energy 22 months after they first set up. Whatever the precise timing, very many people are exhausted and overwhelmed by the business they've created within a couple of years and may need help to survive what is akin to nervous exhaustion. Lots of people underestimate the time it takes to set up – allow at least three years and make sure that you'll have enough to live on over this time.

Getting the right amount of money into a business is not as simple as it sounds. If you have too much you may not be able to afford to service the loan/capital; if you have too little you may strangle the business at birth. With a modest loan/capital base you need a good overdraft facility which will allow you to borrow more money as your business expands and you can afford to pay more interest. If you start small and build up from a sound base it's difficult for the business to get out of financial control. If you start off with loads of other people's money and no business base you're likely to find all you succeed at selling is shares in your business right up to the point at which it collapses.

Start small and let the business grow slowly. Keep overheads as low as possible; no smart offices until you're sure you can afford them. This needs commitment and patience but gives you time to learn more about how to run your business. You can get things to happen with very little outlay by subcontracting (say) manufacturing, sales, etc.

Lifelines

These are jobs that you have to do while you're trying to do what you want to do – or decide what that might be. There are plenty of them in this book – not by any means onerous or uninteresting or useless. Many are worthwhile pursuits in their own right, such as Sub-editor or EFL Teacher. But they are also well-suited to slipping in and out of or mix-and-matching, by taking advantage of a skill or qualification like a driving licence or the ability to speak your own language – viz. EFL teacher.

Lifestyle Choices

Conventional career planning often forgets about life styles. To a large extent, in choosing your job you choose your lifestyle. Do you want to grow strong local roots? Join the jet set? Develop an exquisite judgment of the wines of the Côte d'Or? Work 18 hours a day? Drive a battered Land Rover or a snappy new Porsche?

As your own boss nobody will dictate to you. The thickness of your office carpet, which lavatory you use, or what car you drive will be your decision, not some senior bureaucrat's. Nevertheless, within the job you have chosen, constraints of behaviour, dress and business manners will remain, so make sure they suit you.

Limited Companies

It may be to your advantage to turn yourself into a limited company. If your business is a private limited company, it means that the shareholders are not responsible for the company debts in the case of bankruptcy (unless the company has been trading fraudulently). Read

Working for Yourself. Your accountant will tell you if you should do this – then get your solicitor to set it up. Don't try it yourself unless this is your patch. There are disadvantages to being limited (eg higher accounting charges) and in many crucial ways it does not even limit your risk. Many people, however, find it easier to handle their suppliers and clients as a limited company than as a sole trader. COMPANIES HOUSE has a centre in London and one in Cardiff.

Location – Office and Home

When you are your own boss, you can choose where you work. You can work at home, thus avoiding time spent travelling to work. Modern telecommunications, faxes, word processors make it possible for lots of people to work at home who would not have been able to a few years ago – even if it means entertaining clients in a nearby wine bar. On the other hand you may need to be able to visit customers and clients easily, so an office close to theirs cuts down travelling time during working hours. Consider also your business address; a solicitor may be more plausible at a High Street address than 'Primrose Cottage', for example.

If you are setting up a venture where you are dependent on the public at large coming to you, location is very important. For example, a clothes shop or picture gallery would have to be very special to attract people to come out of their way. Groups of similar retail outlets often stimulate demand, eg in Bond Street; watch out for developments in your area. Groups of photographers will want equipment suppliers and photo lab facilities nearby; useful if that's what you are offering.

Many people use their homes to fund new ventures – either selling up and moving to a cheaper area, or selling their home and using the profits to buy a property which will provide both income and housing (eg hotel or old people's home). You

may need to increase your mortgage when starting up.

As long as you don't make a nuisance of yourself or have a lot of visitors, it is usually all right to work from home as far as local authorities are concerned. However, if you ask them they are likely to say No. So . . .

Luck

Have you got it? If not, you can offset the deficiency by joining a bureaucracy, but do not start out on your own.

If you aren't sure, look at it another way. Luck can be something you yourself create – by seeing opportunities and being open to receive it.

Management Skills

Courses
Some management skills can be taught, but fewer than are sometimes claimed in the more glossy management education prospectuses. Before signing on a course check that the syllabus matches your job requirements. Local enterprise centres may have details of local courses.

Text books
Skim-read general management textbooks (see your local or college library), then identify the area of knowledge you need to develop.

Management training
Most graduate level jobs offered by major organisations for new graduates in the milkround/recruitment fairs are part of that company's management training scheme. One option is to get a job with a major organisation and learn about management through their training schemes; then move on to be your own boss.

Manual Skills

You may have been shunted into an academic education, when in fact your manual skills are your greatest asset. Don't be afraid to let go and move on if you feel that your interests are different to your educational qualifications. You can do evening classes to polish up your skills – and everyone knows that plumbers get paid more than teachers these days.

Market Research

Before taking the plunge look carefully at the market to ensure there is an adequate demand for the goods or services you plan to produce.

- You can start in a simple way by asking friends and contacts what they think of your ideas.
- You can look at others in the field to see how they are trading.
- You can ask groups of potential customers if they would be interested (eg ask local shoppers if they would visit your proposed coffee shop).
- You can call in a professional market research company to advise you.
- You can run your own 'pilot' launch to help you develop your product or service before getting too committed to something that needs changing.
- Some major reference libraries stock copies of published market research reports eg tourist authorities data.

The *Small Business Guide* is a good guide to sources of market and other information. For a more expansive view of trends in the world have a look at *Megatrends* and the *Third Wave*.

Marketing

Finding, getting and keeping more customers so you can live – ie the essence of business. Selling is one of the primary tools of marketing.

Books to read: *Marketing*, *Marketing for Small Firms* and *Breakthrough*.

Mid career Moves

Research into the problems facing people moving from large organisations into their own businesses at mid-career established that most of their problems were psychological rather than practical and administrative. They were made brutally aware of the true cost of much of their job support services – offices, tea-ladies, photocopiers and telephones – all of which they had taken for granted in their sheltered, organisational environment. As a result, they experienced greater anxiety and need for reassurance. Their real problem was isolation – from colleagues, mutual support, organisational beanfeasts and people with whom to share professional worries.

As this is the most common single complaint of people starting up on their own it's worth thinking about before you jump at mid-career and worth considering before you become your own boss. Get into the small business world. Look at professional associations, clubs and workshops for the self-employed, eg the BREAKTHROUGH CENTRE.

Mix and Match

It's important to remember you can mix and match jobs – as your own boss you can do two or more jobs in parallel and may be well advised to do so. Barristers are often MPs; MPs may write bestsellers; most writers do almost anything else while waiting for royalties and some playwrights are barristers. Don't be frightened of apparently bizarre career mixes. One of the country's best known opera directors is also a medical researcher who trained as a doctor; one successful restauranteur and wine merchant (mix and match again) is a professional musician. You can do two (or more) related jobs such as publisher and book editor; or two that are totally unrelated, such as counsellor and musician. Make sure your combined jobs make sense in terms of: time (you can't run any kind of shop with a job involving erratic schedules such as photojournalist); money (find a steady earner while you get known as a composer); and stress (psychotherapist and potter or futures broker and artist).

Moonlighting

This is taking on work 'by the light of the moon' in addition to a full-time job. It can give you the chance to hold on to one main job whilst experimenting in a new area of work to gain experience or to 'test the water'.

BE WARNED Some companies' terms of employment prohibit you from taking on extra work without permission and the Inland Revenue has 'Moonlighting squads' whose aim is to check up that moonlighters pay tax. You also run the risk of getting so exhausted that you don't do yourself justice anywhere.

Mortgages

A domestic mortgage can be a useful source of long-term borrowing for your job. Most building societies only give mortgages to self-employed people on the basis of three years' trading figures, so get fixed up before starting out.

You can take out a second mortgage on your home, especially if it has increased in value, to fund a business. It's essential to go into this with your eyes open; consult your accountant, bank manager, building society, financial consultants, and mortgage brokers to get the best deal. Remember – as they say in the building society ads, your home may be at risk. . .

Motivation

Motivation is one of the keys to success. You've got to motivate yourself first, then motivate others. For some, it's simply a question of sitting at their office desk with a picture of their children in front of them, to remind them that they need a good income to provide for their family. For others, it's a question of getting this contract finished quickly so they can spend the summer in Bordeaux. Everyone has their own reasons. Identify your reasons for wanting to do something, and you'll find it easier to be enthusiastic and confident.

Names – Business

Your business name is what hits people first and first impressions count. You can trade under your own name but in some fields a catchy, memorable tag is an asset.

Once you've decided on a name, you can make it official in a variety of ways.

- The Department of Trade and Industry have a free pamphlet, 'business names – guidance notes'.
- If you buy an off-the-shelf company you can apply to change the name for £10 through the REGISTRAR OF COMPANIES.
- You can trade under a name that is different from the official company name, but you must disclose the names of the owners and the registered office address.
- You can register your trading name with the Trade Marks Registry at the Patents Office, as well as your trade mark or logo (the emblem you use at the top of your stationery and on your products). This is usually more complicated than it sounds and you probably need a patent agent to get anywhere.

National Vocational Qualifications (NVQs)

NVQs are a new attempt to rationalise the British vocational qualifications offered through bodies such as BTEC, City and Guilds and the RSA. New standards are being set for each job skill at four levels ranging from basic skills to management, professional and technical. You can find out more from your *Jobcentre* or Careers Office.

National Insurance

When you're self-employed, you have to arrange this yourself. Ask your accountant.

Negotiating Skills

Before you can negotiate, you've got to get round a table. Whatever type of negotiations you want to enter into, there are some basic points to remember.

- Talk to the right person ie the person who has the power to make decisions or if the company uses an agent, the right agent.
- Find a point of mutual interest or benefit and emphasise it.
- Be flexible in your approach.
- Listen to what the other person has to say – negotiations are two-sided by their very nature.
- Start by asking for the maximum (or offering the minimum) to give yourself room to manoeuvre.
- Identify the other person's point of view, and use it to your advantage.

The aim is not to crucify the other guy; the aim is for you both to feel you have won.

Useful reading: *Managing Negotiations*; *The Skills of Negotiating*.

Networks

Your contacts are your lifeline when you are setting up on your own. You need a well established network of clients and suppliers, and to keep a record of it. The same applies when you're job-hunting. Many jobs are never advertised – you get them by knowing somebody who knows somebody who heard about it on the grapevine: the kind of people who are always being asked 'Do you know someone who . . .?'. Make sure they can answer, 'You'.

Journalists pinched the idea of a complete contacts book from the Army and the Church: Filofax originally produced their diaries - cum - address - books - cum - information - sources - cum - notebooks for these groups. Now they have been taken up by everyone. Whenever you meet someone or read about someone who you feel might be helpful, **write it down**. Include friends, friends of friends, organisations listed in directories, work colleagues, contacts you have made in traditional employment and so on. Write down as much information as you can spare the room for. Where appropriate, make a note of when and how you came across the name; having a mutual friend can often be the basis for much faster development of a new business relationship.

Numerical Skills

Numerical skills are the ability to calculate, manipulate and interpret numbers, together with an understanding of basic statistical approaches. Such skills are often equated with maths – but don't think you're not numerate just because you did miserably at maths at school.

Life will be easier if you are:

- quick at arithmetic or adept with the calculator
- accurate
- figure-minded.

Part-time Work

Part-time work is growing. This is mainly due to the increased numbers of working women, but there is speculation that the time is coming when the majority of people working in Britain will be part-timers, many with more than one job.

Working part-time can give you *time*:

- time to develop another job where you are your own boss;
- time to complete studies on a part-time basis, or to take extra courses to further your career;
- time to pursue leisure or family activities or simply do nothing at all.

Partnership

There are few restrictions on setting up a partnership. An important point is that all members are equally liable for the partnership's debts (even if clandestinely entered into by one partner) and for each and every partner's tax liability from the income of that partnership. Liability for hefty tax bills can arise from your partners' muddle as well as from their dishonesty.

Before entering into a partnership make sure you know your partners well, their strengths as well as their weaknesses, and find someone who complements your own. Have a written partnership agreement stating what will happen when (rather than if) the partnership ends.

Further reading: *Professional partnerships – Facing the future*; *Working for yourself – The Daily Telegraph guide to Self-Employment.*

Pensions

Personal pensions are the most tax-effective method of savings and also a useful form of collateral for financing your job. Avoid other employers' company pension schemes (other than your own!) like the plague – ask any Imperial Tobacco employee.

Unless you are a pensions expert, get advice.

Personal Financial Circumstances

Your personal financial circumstances help to determine what you can do – eg if you haven't got any money, start small; if you've got a dependent family, don't take risks that'll make them suffer. Having a lot of money may actually be a hindrance if you're worried about losing it all. Your personal financial gearing, the ratio of your borrowing to income within limits accepted by the bank, may be the absolute constraint on your investment decisions.

Personal Qualities

Before taking the plunge try some self-analysis. Jot down at least six descriptive adjectives in answering the following questions:

– What type of person do you think you are?
– How would your best friend describe you?
– How would your family describe you?
– How would your colleagues describe you?
– What would your worst enemy say about you?

When you've decided on a shortlist of jobs, write down the attributes you believe those jobs need. Do they match?

You may find life more pleasant if you get on with the people around you, but the qualities you look for in a friend aren't necessarily those needed to get on, especially in a bureaucracy, where the absolute rule is that from the day you are taken on, at least one person will be trying to stab you in the back.

Personality Tests

These can be a useful way of identifying your qualities (ask your careers service). Large firms tend to use them as part of their selection procedure so an acceptable profile in a personality test may not be a prerequisite for success as your own boss.

For example a recent survey of sacked or redundant managers found them to be intelligent, imaginative, conscientious, calm and independent thinkers. However, they were also found to be less manipulative, too trusting and didn't plot and scheme enough. Being good at your job and interested in excellence is not enough in bureaucracies; you need to be good at the power game as well. If you don't want to play other people's power games, why not set your own rules and go it alone.

Premises

Whatever you do, you have to have somewhere to do it.

There are various alternatives: work at home; lease or buy business premises; share premises through local authority schemes, co-ops etc.

Before deciding remember:

- Working at home may be the cheapest and easiest option, but if your neighbours complain you'll have to move or close;
- Your lease, deeds or local authority restrictions may prevent trading from home;
- If you are renting business premises, check planning restrictions with your local planning officer, get the fire department to look it over before taking it on, and make sure you know how long you are committed for;
- Never sign a lease without consulting a solicitor;
- Read *How to choose business premises*.

Presentations

These range from a simple meeting, where you present your ideas to a prospective client or new business plans to your bank, to a full-blown advertising agency presentation. A professional approach is essential; scrappy ideas, badly presented do not win contracts – and winning contracts is what presentations are about.

Pricing

If you're selling goods or services, you'll need a pricing policy. Charge too little and you won't be able to meet your costs; too much and customers will go elsewhere. Find out what competitors offer and how much they charge.

The correct price is what the market will stand. Simple 'cost plus' pricing is a bit of a blunt instrument, although it can be useful to start off and it does give you a base price. You won't always have to be the cheapest.

Publicity

It can be good or bad; paid for or free. On the whole, you'll have to pay for it if you want to control it.

Many professions have strict rules on publicity and some allow none at all. Anyone else has a wide choice:

- Advertisements (newspapers, local radio, shop windows, hoardings)
- Press releases
- Taking a stand at an exhibition
- Giving talks/demonstrations
- Writing and broadcasting
- Sponsorship
- Competitions
- Direct mail and leaflet drops
- A clearly identifiable logo
- Free trials; free samples; free bags and badges; free information packs.

Once you are established, the main publicity is the product or service itself.

Qualifications

Degrees in themselves do not normally license you to practise a profession. There are legal requirements for many professions (eg solicitors). Appropriate qualifications (in anything from piano tuning to midwifery) increase public confidence while membership of professional associations will get you into the network.

However, in other cases, people who are their own boss can worry less about qualifications than those looking for employment. You may just need to be able to do the job properly and let your track record speak for itself.

Recruitment Fairs

Go to recruitment fairs if you're looking for a suitable employer to give you the appropriate experience before becoming your own boss. Graduate recruitment fairs are held in various locations about the country. Keep in touch with your careers centre for details. There are specialist recruitment fairs, to attract experienced staff in shortage areas – national and trade press give details.

CVs and shin pads are essential equipment.

Refugees

The BRITISH REFUGEE COUNCIL has an enterprise training unit, which offers advice, support and training courses on self-employment. Refugees can also obtain general careers advice from the Council.

Science and Technology Students

Those reading for science and technology degrees who want to become their own boss have special problems if they want to remain within their discipline. Most science and technology jobs are bureaucratic jobs because only large bureaucracies can afford the equipment and the R & D budgets. Even university research is being heavily concentrated. Pressure from politicians, the media, careers advisers and your own teachers to become a science/technology bureaucrat is insidious. But consider your own interests first. Remember it's your life not theirs. Ask yourself if your interest in your subject and its practical applications is sufficient to outweigh your ambition to be our own boss, and make sure you know what is going on in your own science park.

Self-employment

If you are self-employed, you are not alone: the proportion of the working population working for themselves has vastly increased in the past 10 years. The NATIONAL FEDERATION OF THE SELF EMPLOYED was set up to promote and protect the interests of the self-employed. Their leaflet 'Be you own boss' is useful, as is *Working for Yourself*, and there are many courses.

If you want self-employed status however (for tax and National Insurance purposes), you may find it more difficult than you think. It varies by occupation and industry, partly depending on which job is the victim of the month at the DSS or Inland Revenue. Our advice is simple – consult your accountant before you start.

The underlying principle is that you must be working at your own risk. Some of the things that might keep them all off your back include:

- spreading your income over several sources, anyway at least two or three;
- avoiding committing yourself to working at a specific time and a specified place for long: irregularity helps;
- invoicing for your income; don't be paid automatically on a specified date;
- using your own tools and equipment – eg word-processor, bulldozer, acupuncturist's needles, musical instrument, chain saw – not your client's;
- if you sign a contract with a client, making sure it's a contract to supply services, not a contract of service;
- if you are in the building trade, getting the correct form from the Inland Revenue;
- considering registering for VAT.

If you think that your clients will need proof of your status before giving you work/paying you, get a Certificate of Self-Employment from the Inland Revenue. Always *consult your accountant*.

Self-presentation

Remember that, for most people, there are two forms of presentation – you in person and you on paper. You must get the right image across.

- **Personal presentation:** If you don't feel up to scratch, take courses in public speaking, presentations, interviewing, negotiating and selling, preferably when you are a student or trainee, and can take advantage of cheap rates or company training schemes.

- **Written presentation:** This covers CVs, application forms, business cards and letterheads, leaflets, brochures, price lists, reports. Take note of how the competition presents itself and make yours better or different.

The more professional the presentation, the more convincing you will appear to prospective purchasers of goods and services. Courses are available, and there are plenty of books on the subject – consult your local library.

Selling

Selling is the main way you present your product or service to people you feel will want it. To be a whizz at selling:

- Believe in it yourself (most salesmen don't).
- See who will benefit (most products don't have benefits).
- Present it to people who need it (not just to everyone regardless).
- Help them buy (don't ram it down their throats).

Two good books on selling are *How to Win Customers* and the *One Minute Sales Person*.

Initially the main problem may be that nobody knows you from Adam and you lack credibility. To overcome this

- Start with people you know.
- Drop names, piggy-back (do subcontracted work for) established traders.
- Tap into the people who influence sales.
- Use commission agents already known in your market.

Before you set up, you should know clients' names – at least ten for service businesses, 100 customers for shops – who will actually buy, rather than make promises.

Sex

Research has shown that sex discrimination is alive and well, but often at a hidden level.

Working for yourself may be a good route round residual prejudice. However, women still have to tackle additional constraints arising out of, eg childcare responsibility. A shortage of competent managers is gradually shifting this prejudice; and successful, well-publicised female entrepreneurs are doing the same for the self-employed.

Shiftwork

Don't forget that you can mix and match with a full-time job where the work is clearly divided into shifts, eg Bartender.

Social Skills

Social skills are your ability to handle cutlery, glasses, formal invitations and other people. They form part of self-presentation: affability, good conversation, charm and knowing when to wear a tie can be your passport to success; picking your nose when you visit your bank manager is unlikely to help.

Sole Trading

Not what fishmongers do, it's the term given to a one-person business. There is little to stop anyone setting up as a sole trader. You must:

- Inform the tax inspector (or get your accountant to do so)
- Look into the need to register a business name
- Be aware that if the business fails you will be liable for all the debts of the business

THE NATIONAL FEDERATION OF SELF-EMPLOYED AND SMALL BUSINESSES aims to promote the interests of the sole trader and has good literature.

Springboarding

Beware! For many jobs in this book you will need to 'springboard'. That is, you will need first to succumb to employment (very often within a bureaucracy) as a necessary/advisable step to working for yourself. This is self-evident in the case of most professions, eg accountancy, architecture and the law, where it is an integral part of the process of qualifying and obtaining a licence to practise. In many other jobs it is essential in order to acquire sufficient expertise, business know-how and job contacts before setting up on your own, eg consultancy. So, if your strategy is to become your own boss the first thing paradoxically may be to get a job. Tough. But at least you will be able to start up with your job networks in place.

Stress

Some people perform well under pressure, but research shows that people under stress do not perform well.

Stress is not necessarily caused by overwork, but by setting unrealistic targets and attempting the impossible. There are also external stress factors, including: bereavement, divorce, moving house, having children.

To avoid suffering under stress:

- Have realistic plans and goals;
- Talk over problems – a fresh view often helps;
- If you're totally stuck, do something else.

Taking the Plunge

There are two ways of doing this:

- Diving board: all-or-nothing approach – often used by the most successful

entrepreneurs (essential in retailing, for example).
- The steps: easing yourself in through moonlighting or part-time working, until you've built up the contacts and workload you need for the deep end.

Tax

Tax evasion is illegal; tax planning isn't. Indeed, it is a substantial industry in its own right. If you are working for yourself, your tax bill may well be lower, since you will be able to offset certain costs against your tax eg your car, stationery, materials, reference books and so on. If you work from home, you may be able to count a certain proportion of your heating and lighting bill as business expenses. Get an accountant to sort it all out. Make sure the Inland Revenue is aware of your tax status. Keep a careful note of all business expenses, plus receipts where possible. It's very boring but saves you lots of money. If you have turned yourself into a company, you will be liable for corporation tax; if you are registered for VAT, for that too. Make sure you anticipate large tax bills and have a good accountant.

Thinking Skills

You can develop your thinking skills, particularly if you have worked mindlessly as a bureaucrat for some time. Here are some approaches:

- Develop your lateral thinking by reading *The Five-day Course in Thinking*.
- Develop problem-solving techniques with systematic problem analysis (select, define, record, examine, develop, implement and monitor progress). If you don't like that approach, use the questions What? How? Why? When?
- Brainstorming (think tanks). Get a group of people together to focus on a situation or problem: everyone must present their ideas with a minimum of criticism, so that you can draw together

areas of similarity, common associations and so on. It is essential to record all the ideas.

Time Management

Two valid approaches:

'Never leave till tomorrow that which you can do today.' (Benjamin Franklin)

'I like work; it fascinates me. I can sit and look at it for hours. I love to keep it by me.' (Jerome K. Jerome)

Many people have some of the qualities needed for success as their own boss (self-motivation, risk-taking), but it is clever use of time that is often the essential ingredient for success.

Essential for success
- Identify your goals, both immediate and long term
- Decide when you work best: up with the lark or burning the midnight oil
- Analyse what you actually do with your time
- List what you have to do, with any deadlines
- Anticipate how much time a particular project ought to take
- Use a diary or a planner
- Review your achievements
- Delegate where it's cost-effective and saves you time
- Tie up loose ends as you go along
- Plan breaks and time off

But don't
- Spend too much time analysing, planning, and over-accounting
- Stick by your plans doggedly if the situation changes
- Be too perfectionist

Watch out for time wasters
- The telephone: is this chat necessary for business? Plan your calls and know what points you want to cover.
- Paperwork: read priority post first; learn how to write business letters, develop standard phrases and formats.
- Meetings: don't attend too many, or the wrong sort of meetings.
- Decisions: learn how to make the right ones.

- Plans: inform others and stick to them.
- Systems: develop systems to deal with common tasks (eg invoicing). Develop good filing systems and stick to them.
- Tidiness: saves time looking for things (so does filing).
- Unfinished business: finish it.
- Time management is particularly important when working at home with a family. Physical boundaries (a room set aside) will help you manage your time better.

Training and Enterprise Councils (TECs)

TECs are companies run by local business and community leaders which now assess local training and enterprise needs and ensure that they are met by local individuals and services. Through others, they help people wanting to set up on their own and ensure that skills programmes they provide normally lead to NQVs.

You should be able to find your TEC in the local telephone book, or try the JOBCENTRE or your bank. As TECs try to work through other organisations you will be referred onwards to the appropriate local organisation.

Unemployment

If you're working for yourself you must be prepared to keep the wolf from the door when work is not coming in. You may be able to rely on your savings but you may have to look at other forms of work to keep you going. Typical casual jobs taken up by 'resting' actors include promotional work at exhibitions, secretarial work, gardening, cleaning, bar work, market research interviewers. You must be prepared to 'mix and match' so that, if your main aims are in a highly competitive or seasonal field, you can fall back on other work, eg drive a mini-cab or hearse, babysit.

Vacations

While you are a student, you can use the long vacs to give you useful experience and help you identify your priorities, what you want to do and what skills you enjoy developing. You can do this by vacation jobs (which provide useful contacts and make your CV look better) or take vacation courses; these are often well run and cheap.

VAT

If your annual turnover (ie your charges for goods or services) is more than the VAT minimum (about £37,000 at the time of writing, though the figure usually changes with the Budget) you must register for Value Added Tax with the CUSTOMS AND EXCISE and you can register even if it is not that high. Consult your accountant. VAT is an involved tax. You have to pay 17½ per cent of the value of your outputs, but can offset against that any VAT which you have been charged by your suppliers. VAT is deadly boring, but it has advantages. First, when you are starting up you are likely to be spending money faster than you are earning it, so the VAT man pays you, not you the VAT man. Second, it forces you to keep proper accounts. (The VAT man can launch a dawn raid and inspect your books at any time.)

Other reasons for registering are:
- It makes you look bigger than you are.
- Your business is zero-rated.
- You're selling mainly to people who can claim back VAT.

Being VAT registered isn't as complicated as a lot of people think – you'll need an extra column in your accounts book and you have to fill in four more forms a year and that's it!

Talk to your local VAT inspector – contrary to popular belief they're usually delightful people!

Wills

Make one and take advice. If you've got a business and you die intestate you can easily leave your partners and family with nothing.

Women Returners

Women who want to get back to the job they did before bringing up their families have traditionally found the going hard. RETURN, the Women Returners Training Consultancy, can point you towards employers who might value you; they also run courses to help you get the act together. If you want to become your own boss, you may be well advised first to find employment in order to brush up your know-how and revitalise your network of contacts before springboarding. If you can't face that, take a pretty beady look at your income projections and make sure that they do not underestimate the time it will take to regain your old network.

Work Familiarisation Events

Many organisations offer introduction days and work familiarisation events. Treat them as free seminars and use them to help decide if you want to join their bureaucracies.

You

Here are five questions to ask yourself:

Q1 What do you want out of life:
  A to get by or
  B to get ahead?

Q2 Do you always want to work:
  A for somebody else or
  B for yourself?

Q3 What sort of person are you?
  A Do you value stability or
  B can you cope with and enjoy uncertainty?

Q4 When working do you:
  A enjoy routine and being part of a machine or
  B prefer to see the job through from beginning to end?

Q5 Which do you prefer:
  A taking orders from somebody else or
  B being in charge?

If the answers are mainly **A**s, you will probably be happier in a bureaucracy.

If the answers are mainly **B**s, you should probably be aiming for a top job in a bureaucracy or being your own boss.

Running your own business is one of the best places to find out about and develop yourself. Some books that help with this are *Think and Grow Rich*, *Pathfinder* and *Breakthrough*. But beware; some people who have spent a long time in employment can't cope with the prospect of unpredictable income, so make sure you're not one of them.

Part 3

Reference

Abbreviations

The job world is peppered with abbreviations and acronyms. Here are some which you may come across.

ABTA	Association of British Travel Agents
ACU	Auto Cycle Union
AFAEP	Association of Fashion, Advertising and Editorial Photographers
AFBD	Association of Futures Brokers and Dealers
AGCAS	Association Graduate Careers Advisory Services
AMCA	Amateur Motor Cycle Association
APRS	Association of Professional Recording Studios
ASM	Assistant Stage Manager
BABA	British Artist Blacksmiths' Association
BBC	British Broadcasting Corporation
BECTU	Broadcasting, Entertainment, Cinematograph and Theatre Union
BIBA	British Insurance Brokers' Association
BIE	British Institute of Embalmers
BIPP	British Institute of Professional Photography
BMA	British Medical Association
BTEC	Business and Technician Education Council
C & G	City and Guilds
CAM	Communications, Advertising and Marketing
CAMRA	Campaign for Real Ale
CHE	College of Higher Education
CII	Chartered Insurance Institute
COIC	Careers and Occupational Information Centre
CoSIRA	Council for Small Industries in Rural Areas
CV	Curriculum Vitae
DE	Department of Employment
DFE	Department for Education
DIY	Do It Yourself
DJ	Disc Jockey
DoE	Department of the Environment
DOG	Directory of Graduate Appointments
DSS	Department of Social Security
DTI	Department of Trade and Industry
EC	European Community
ET	Employment Training
FDR	First Destination Return
FE	Further Education
FHSA	Family Health Services Authority
FIMBRA	Financial Intermediaries Managers and Brokers Regulatory Association
GCE	General Certificate of Education
GCSE	General Certificate of Secondary Education
GBP	Great British Public
GO	Graduate Opportunities
GP	General Practitioner
GPMU	Graphical, Paper and Media Union
HE	Higher Education
HGV	Heavy Goods Vehicle
HMSO	Her Majesty's Stationery Office
IBM	International Business Machines
IEE	Institution of Electrical Engineers
IMRO	Investment Managers' Regulatory Organisation
IPM	Institute of Personnel Management
ISE	International Stock Exchange
ISM	International Society of Musicians
ITB/TB	Industrial Training Board/Training Board
ITDG	Intermediate Technology Development Group
ITV	Independent Television
LAUTRO	Life Assurance and Unit Trust Regulatory Organisation
LEA	Local Education Authority
LGSM	Licentiate of the Guildhall School of Music
LRAM	Licentiate of the Royal Academy of Music
LRCM	Licentiate of the Royal College of Music

LTCM	Licentiate of Trinity College of Music	PER	Professional and Executive Registry
MEP	Member of the European Parliament	PGCE	Post Graduate Certificate of Education
MOT	Ministry of Transport	PR	Public Relations
MP	Member of Parliament	RAD	Royal Academy of Dancing
MSc	Master of Science		
NATTA	Network for Alternative Technology and Technology Assessment	RCVS	Royal College of Veterinary Surgeons
		RGN	Registered General Nurse
NFPDC	National Federation of Painting and Decorating Contractors	RHS	Royal Horticultural Society
		RICS	Royal Institution of Chartered Surveyors
NFSE	National Federation of Self-Employed and Small Businesses	RSA	Royal Society of Arts
		ROGET	Register of Graduate Employment and Training
NFU	National Farmers' Union		
NHS	National Health Service	RYA	Royal Yachting Association
NICIEC	National Inspection Council for Electrical Installation Contracting	SAE	Stamped Addressed Envelope
		SDP	Social Democratic Party
		SFEP	Society of Freelance Editors and Proofreaders
NME	New Musical Express		
NMFB & AEA	National Master Farriers, Blacksmiths & Agricultural Engineering Association	SIAD	Society of Industrial Artists and Designers
		SIB	Security and Investments Board
NRA	National Record of Achievement	SRO	Self Regulatory Organisation
NUJ	National Union of Journalists	TEC	Training and Enterprise Council
NVQ	National Vocational Qualifications	TSA	The Securities Association
OND	Ordinary National Diploma	TSB	Trustee Savings Bank
		UCCA	University Central Council for Admissions
PC	Personal Computer		
PCAS	Polytechnic Central Admissions System	VAT	Value Added Tax
		YES	Youth Enterprise Scheme

Acknowledgements

We are very grateful for the help we have received in producing this book from a wide range of institutions, and the very many individuals who have helped in the preparation of the job profiles –

ANTONIO, Vas (Hairdresser)
ARMITAGE, Aileen (Novelist)
ASHBY, Barry of Ashby PR (Public Relations Consultant and others)
BARKER, Noel (Classical Singer)
BARNES, Hilary (Foreign Correspondent; Newsletter Publisher)
BEARN, E.M. (Dentist)
BEGG, Sally (Potter)
BESCH, Anthony (Opera Director)
BICKERSTETH, Jane (Print Maker)
BLOODWORTH, Colin (Timeshare Developer; Holiday Accommodation Owner; Import/Export Broker)
BODGENER, Beste (Picture Restorer)
BOLTON, Rohan (Europe)
BONCZYK, Philip (Caterer)
BOOK HOUSE TRAINING CENTRE (Book Packager; Book Publisher)
BOWDAGE, Ruth (Picture Framer)
BIGGS, Vivien (Guardian ad Litem; Social Worker)
BRIGGS, Stephen (Furniture Designer/Maker)
BROOKES, Anna (Fashion Designer)
BROWN, Ashley (Book Packager)
CAIRNS, David (Music Critic)
CAMPBELL, Alan (Greyhound Trainer; Space Sales Agent; Advertising Agent)
CARR, Antonia (Hypnotherapist)
CATTO, A.G. (Chiropodist)
CHADWICK, Anna-Mei (Contemporary Art Gallery Owner)
CHADWICK, Brian (Publican; Restaurateur; Wine Merchant)
CHILD CONSULTANTS (Child/Educational Psychologist)
CLODE, Alex (Futures Broker, Stockbroker)
CONNOR, Julie of Job Shop (Employment Agent)
COOKE, Richard of Head South (Hairdresser)
COPPOCK, Ted (Builder)
CORBETT, Nigel of Summer Lodge (Hotel Keeper)
CRIGHTON, Veronica (Media Trainer)
CROUCH, Colin (Thatcher)

CUMING, Hugh (Kennel/Cattery Owner)
CUMMINGS, Joe (Illustrator)
CURTIS, P.J. (Chiropractor)
DALAMORE, Robert (Reflexologist)
DAVIS, Gretal (Actor; Market Research Interviewer)
DAWSON, Adam (Various)
DAY, D.F. (Smallholder)
DEAN, Lee (Stage Designer)
DEWHURST, Barbara (Antique Dealer)
DICKENS, Richard (Contemporary Art Gallery Owner; Picture Framer)
DILL, ROSANNE [Property Manager]
DOGGART, W.L. (Embalmer)
DONOVAN, Paul (Film Director; Scriptwriter)
DUNWOODY, Dr John (GP in the NHS)
EDWARDES, Phil (Healer)
EVANS, Deborah (Various)
EYNON, Mark (Festival Director)
FERGUSON, Andrew of Breakthrough Centre (How To Go About It)
FORD, Kevin (Caterer)
GARLICK, Bill (Desk-top Publisher)
GIBBS, Michael (Bookseller)
GIBSON, Janet (Riding School Owner)
GILBERT, John (Printer)
GODDARD, Anthony (Wine Grower)
GODDAR, Jennifer of the Law Society (Solicitor)
GOFF, Anthony (Literary Agent)
GRAINGER, Ashley (Direct Marketing Agent)
GREENSHIELDS, Anne (Caterer)
GREGORY, Jane (Literary Agent)
GUBBAY, Raymond (Impresario)
HANKIN, Christine (Music/Instrument Retailer)
HARCUS, James of Gordon Dadd (Solicitor)
HAYES, Geogg (Book Designer)
HONEYMAN, Louise (Orchestral Fixer)
HOPKINS, Brian (Dental Technician)
HUGGINS HAULAGE (Haulier)
JOHNSON, Brian (List Broker; Garden Gnome Maker)

JONES, Robin L. (Chemical Engineering Consultant)
JOYCE, Christine (Swimming Teacher)
KAWALL, Kieron (Dancer)
KAY, Andrew (Various)
KIDD-HEWITT, Jan (Insurance Broker)
KILPATRICK, Di of Tuscany Inside Out (Italian Property Finder)
KING, Chris (Film Director)
KING, John (Courier Service)
KINMONTH, Fergus (Tree Surgeon)
KNOWLES, J. (Zoo Keeper)
KOREN, Anna (Graphologist)
LANGFORD, Philip (Pop Group Sound Engineer)
LASCELLES, Roger (Antique Dealer; Antique Furniture Restorer)
LEA, Liz (Gardener/Garden Designer)
LEE, Lilly (Calligrapher)
LEFEVER, Dr Robert (Doctor – Private GP)
LIDDELL, Edward (Publican)
LINDLEY, John of Activ Sports (Sports Retailer; Windsurfing School Owner)
LIVINGSTONE-LEARMONTH (Various)
LONERGAN, B. (Osteopath)
LOWDELL, Paul (Musical Instrument Repairer)
LOWRY, Stephen (Actuary)
LUKAS, Andrew (Bed and Breakfast)
MACARTHUR, Norma (Dentist)
McCAUSLAND, Tina (Acupuncturist)
McCULLOCH, Andrew (Scriptwriter)
MANSELL, Ros (Silversmith/Jeweller)
MARINE, R.P. (Sailing School Owner)
MARLOWE, Linda (Actor)
MATTHEWS, David (Classical Composer)
McGRATH, Tony (Editorial Photographer)
MEINHARD, Gillian (English Language Teacher)
MELLUISH, Sarah of Cameo Events Organisation (Events Organiser)
MILMAN, David (Musicians' Answering and Booking Service)
MILLS, Simon (Tourist Guide)
MILLS, Steve (Street Entertainer)
MOON, Noel (Kennel/Cattery Owner)
MOORE, John (Shoe Designer/Maker)
MORRIS, Sandra (Architect)
NEAL, Vickie (Acupuncturist; Physiotherapist)
NEWMAN, Edward (Saddler/Leatherworker)
OLIVER, John (Bookseller; Sales Agent)
ORME, David (Magazine Publisher)
OULTRAM, Kenn (Kennels/Cattery Owner)
OWENS, Tuppy (Sex Therapist)
PARKER, Jim (TV and Film Music Composer)
PARKIN, Lynd (Direct Marketing Consultant)
PEPPER, Mark (Editorial Photographer; Photojournalist)
PERRY, Ted (Record Company Owner)
PHELAN, Brian (Private Investigator)

PHIPPEN, David (Garden Centre)
PICKETT, Maggie (Music Therapist)
PIERCEY, Jacqui (Teacher)
POLLACK, Anita (MEP)
PRICE, Fiona of Fiona Price and Partners Ltd (Independent Financial Adviser)
RANGER, Helen (Concert Agent)
RANGER, John (Piano Tuner)
REISS-McCULLOCH, Amanda (Theatrical Agent; Dress Agent)
RENNIE, Mike (Music Copyist)
REYNOLDS, J.G. (House Converter; Property Developer)
RICHARDSON, Ilana (Artist)
RICHARDSON, N.W. (Shipbroker)
RIGBY, Penny (Magazine Publisher)
ROBERTSON PRESS (Printer)
ROBINSON, Sarah (Nanny/Babysitting Agent)
RUSSELL, Peter of the Driving Instructors Association (Driving Instructor)
SANDYS-RENTON, David (Publican; Brewer)
SANDYS-RENTON, Harriet (Inventor)
SANDYS-RENTON, Tim (Sculptor)
SHEERMAN, Barry (MP)
SMITH, Ainsley (Optician)
SMITH, Catherine (Various)
SMURTHWAITE, A. (Chiropodist)
SOLON, Jackie (Various)
STEELE-PERKINS, Crispian (Instrumental Soloist)
STEVENSON BROTHERS (Toymaker)
STILL, M. (Tree Surgeon)
STORCH, Christopher (Hi-Fi Shop Owner)
STRICKLAND, John (Cleaning Contractor)
STROMAN, Scott (Jazz Musician/Singer)
SWEENEY, John, writes for the *Observer* (Journalist)
THOMAS, Kathy (Sub Postmaster; Village Shopkeeper)
THOMAS, Pete (Musician)
THOROGOOD, John (Estate Agent)
TOMLINSON, James (Typesetter; Word Processor)
TOOKEY, Fleur (Glass Designer/Maker)
TREFTZ, Mark (Tutor)
VINCENT, Sidney (Publican, Restaurateur)
WALLIS, Elizabeth (Indexer)
WARHURST, Fiona (Film)
WESTRAY, Katharine (Costume Designer)
WHEELER, F. (Coal Merchant)
WHITE, Malcolm (Graphic Designer)
WHITING, John (Antique Dealer)
WHITING, Stephanie (Dance Teacher)
WILLIAMSON, Malcolm (Alexander Technique Teacher)
WILTSHIRE TRACKLEMENTS (Food Manufacturer)
WOODMAN, Peter (Landlord)
WOODMAN, Trevor (Carpenter)
YOUNG, John (Funeral Director)

and many others who prefer to remain anonymous.

Addresses

Aberdeen Fish Curers and Merchants Association
South Esplanade West,
Aberdeen AB9 2FS
tel 0224 897744

Actors Centre
4 Chenies Street,
London WC1E 7EP
tel 071 631 3599

ACTT see BECTU

Acupuncture Association
34 Alderney Street,
London SW1V 4EU
tel 071 834 1012

ADAR (Art and Design Admissions Registry)
Penn House,
9 Broad Street,
Hereford HR4 9AP
tel 0432 266653

ADAS
Look up Ministry of Agriculture in the local telephone directory or ring ADAS Information tel 0242 226077

AGCAS (Association of Graduate Careers Advisory Services)
University of Manchester Careers Service,
Crawford House,
Precinct Centre,
Oxford Road,
Manchester M13 9QS
tel 061 275 2828

Agricultural Colleges
Hampshire –
Sparsholt College Hampshire,
Winchester SO21 2NF
tel 096 272 441
Dumfries and Galloway –
Barony Agricultural College,
Parkgate,
Dumfries DG1 3NE
tel 038 786 251

Agricultural Training Board
Summit House,
Glebe Way,
West Wickham,
Kent BR4 0RF
tel 081 777 9003

Allied Brewery Traders' Association
85 Tettenhall Road,
Wolverhampton WV3 9NF
tel 0902 22303

Amateur Motor Cycle Association (AMCA)
Darlaston Road,
Walsall WS2 9XL
tel 0922 39517

Amateur Swimming Association
Harold Fern House,
Derby Square,
Loughborough LE11 0AL
tel 0509 230431

Anglo-European College of Chiropractic
13–15 Parkwood Road,
Bournemouth,
Dorset BH5 2DF
tel 0202 431021

Anglo-French Property Group
150 Northgate,
Darlington DL1 1QU
tel 0325 381304

Animal Boarding Advisory Bureau
c/o Blue Grass Animal Hotel,
Little Leigh,
Northwich,
Cheshire CW8 4RJ
tel 0606 891303

Approved Driving Instructors National Joint Council
121 Marshalwick Lane,
St Albans,
Herts AL1 4UX
tel 0727 58068

Architects Registration Council of the UK
73 Hallam Street,
London W1N 6EE
tel 071 580 5861

Arels-Felco Ltd (Association of Recognised English Language Schools and Federation of English Language Course Organisers)
2 Pontypool Place,
Valentine Place,
London SE1 8QF
tel 071 242 3136

Arts Council
14 Great Peter Street,
London SW1P 3NQ
tel 071 333 0100

Askham Bryan Horticultural College
York YO2 3PR
tel 0904 702121

Arvon Foundation
Lumb Park,
Hebden Bridge,
West Yorkshire HX7 6DF
tel 0422 843714
and
Totleigh Barton,
Sheepwash,
Beaworthy,
Devon EX21 5NS
tel 040 923338

Associated Press
12 Norwich Street,
London EC4A 1EJ
tel 071 353 1515

Association Internationale des Interprètes de Conferences (AIIC)
14 rue de l'Ancien Port,
CH 1201,
Geneva,
Switzerland

Association of Authors' Agents
79 St Martin's Lane,
London WC2N 4AA
tel 071 836 4271

Association of British Dispensing Opticians
6 Hurlingham Business Park,
Sulivan Road,
London SW6 3DU
tel 071 736 0088

Association of British Investigators
10 Bonner Hill Road,
Kingston upon Thames,
Surrey KT1 3EP
tel 081 546 3368

Association of British Riding Schools
Old Brewery Yard,
Penzance,
Cornwall TR18 2SL
tel 0736 69440

Association of British Travel Agents (ABTA)
55–57 Newman Street,
London W1P 4AH
tel 071 637 2444

ABTA National Training Board,
Waterloo House,
11–17 Chertsey Road,
Woking,
Surrey GU21 5AL
tel 0483 727321

Association of British Wild Animal Keepers
12 Tackley Road,
Eastville,
Bristol BS5 6UQ
(SAE with all enquiries)

Association of Certified Accountants
29 Lincoln's Inn Fields,
London WC2A 3EE
tel 071 242 6855

Association of Consulting Actuaries
Rolls House,
7 Rolls Buildings,
Fetter Lane,
London EC4A 1NH

Association of Educational Psychologists
The Secretary,
3 Sunderland Road,
Durham DH1 2LH
tel 091 384 95112

Association of Fashion, Advertising and Editorial Photographers (AFAEP)
9–10 Domingo Street,
London EC1Y 0TA
tel 071 608 1441

Association of Illustrators
1 Colville Place,
London W1P 1HW
tel 071 636 4100

Association of Optometrists
233 Blackfriars Road,
London SE1 8NW
tel 071 261 9661

Association of Pension Trustees
James Hay Pension Trustees Ltd,
Albany House,
3–5 New Street,
Salisbury,
Wiltshire SP1 2PH
tel 0722 338333

Association of Professional Composers
34 Hanway Street,
London W1P 9DE
tel 071 436 0919

Association of Professional Music Therapists
c/o The Administrator,
38 Pierce Lane,
Fulbourn,
Cambs CB1 5DL
tel 0223 880377

Association of Professional Recording Services
2 Windsor Square,
Silver Street,
Reading,
Berks RG1 2TH
tel 0734 756218

Autocycle Union (ACU)
Miller House,
Corporation Street,
Rugby,
Warwick CV21 2DN
tel 0788 540519

Baltic Exchange
1 Lime Street,
c/o Lloyds 4th Floor,
London EC3M 7HA
tel 071 623 5501
(until end July 1992)

BBC
Broadcasting House,
Portland Place,
London W1A 1AA
tel 071 580 4468

BBC Publications
80 Wood Lane,
London W12
tel 081 576 2000

BECTU
(Broadcasting, Entertainment, Cinematograph and Theatre Union)
111 Wardour Street,
London W1V 4AY
tel 071 437 8506

Bee Farmers Association
Sec: K.A.J. Ellis, DFC,
22 York Gardens,
Clifton,
Bristol BS8 4LN
tel 0272 738506

Bellmead Kennels
Priest Hill,
Old Windsor,
Berks
tel 0784 432929

BIIBA
14 Bevis Marks,
London EC3A 7NT
tel 071 623 9043

Book House Training Centre
45 East Hill,
Wandsworth,
London SW18 2QZ
tel 081 874 2718/4608

Booksellers Association
Minster House,
272 Vauxhall Bridge Road,
London SW1V 1BA
tel 071 834 5477

Breakthrough Centre
7 Poplar Mews,
Uxbridge Road,
Shepherds Bush,
London W12 7JS
tel 081 749 8525

Brewers Society, The
42 Portman Square,
London W1H 0BB
tel 071 486 4831

**British Antique Furniture Restorers'
Association**
37 Upper Addison Gardens,
Holland Park,
London W14 8AJ
tel 071 603 5643

British Artist Blacksmiths' Association
c/o Alan Evans,
Hon Sec,
2 Police House,
Cheltenham Road,
Bisley,
Glos

British Association of Concert Agents
28 Wadham Road,
Putney,
London SW15 2LR
tel 081 874 5742

British Association for Counselling
1 Regent Place,
Rugby,
Warwickshire CV21 2PJ
tel 0788 578328

British Association of Psychotherapists
37 Mapesbury Road,
London NW2 4HJ
tel 081 452 9823

**British Association of Social Workers
(BASW)**
16 Kent Street,
Birmingham B5 6RD
tel 021 622 3911

British Chiropractic Association
Premier House,
10 Greycoat Place,
London SW1P 1SB
tel 071 222 8866

**British Clothing Industries'
Association**
7 Swallow Place,
London W1R 7AA
tel 071 408 0020

British Coal Enterprise Ltd
Hobart House,
40 Grosvenor Place,
London SW1X 7AE
tel 071 235 2020

British College of Acupuncture
8 Hunter Street,
London WC1N 1BN
tel 071 833 8164

**British College of Naturopathy and
Osteopathy**
Frazer House,
6 Netherhall Gardens,
London NW3 5RR
tel 071 435 7830

**British College of Ophthalmic
Opticians**
10 Knaresborough Place,
London SW5 0TG
tel 071 373 7765

British Computer Society
13 Mansfield Street,
London W1M 0BP
tel 071 637 0471

British Council
10 Spring Gardens,
London SW1A 2BN
tel 071 930 8466

British Dental Association
64 Wimpole Street,
London W1M 8AL
tel 071 935 0875

British Direct Marketing Association
see Direct Marketing Association

British Dried Flowers Association
4 St Mary's Hill,
Stamford,
Lincolnshire PE9 2DP
tel 0780 51513

British Film Institute
21 Stephen Street,
London W1P 1PL
tel 071 255 1444

**British Footwear Manufacturers'
Federation**
Royalty House,
72 Dean Street,
London W1V 5HB
tel 071 437 5573

British Franchise Association
Thames View,
Newtown Road,
Henley on Thames,
Oxon RG9 1HG
tel 0491 578050

British Herb Trade Association
Agriculture House,
25–31 Knightsbridge,
London SW1X 7NJ
tel 071 235 5077

**British Holidays and Home Parks
Association**
Chichester House,
31 Park Road,
Gloucester GL1 1LH
tel 0452 526911

British Holistic Medical Association
179 Gloucester Place,
London NW1 6DX
tel 071 262 5299

British Horse Society
British Equestrian Centre,
Stoneleigh,
Warwickshire CV8 2LR
tel 0203 696697

British Hospitality Association
40 Duke Street,
London W1M 6HR
tel 071 499 6641

British Institute of Embalmers
21c Station Road,
Knowle,
Solihull,
West Midlands B93 0HL
tel 0564 778991

British Institute of Innkeeping
51/53 High Street,
Camberley,
Surrey GU15 3RG
tel 0276 686664

British Institute of Management
Management House,
Cottingham Road,
Corby,
Northamptonshire
tel 0536 204222

**British Institute of Professional
Photography**
Fox Talbot House
Amwell End,
Ware,
Herts SG12 9HN
tel 0920 464011

**British Insurance & Investment
Brokers' Association**
14 Bevis Marks,
London EC3A 7NT
tel 071 623 9043

**British Knitting and Clothing Export
Council**
7 Swallow Place,
London W1R 7AA
tel 071 493 6622

British Leather Federation
Leather Trade House,
Kings Park Road,
Moulton Park,
Northampton NN3 1JD
tel 0604 494131

**British Library, Business Information
Service**
Reference and Information Service,
25 Southampton Buildings,
London WC2A 1AW
tel 071 323 7454

**British Library, Official Publications
Library**
Official Publications and Social Sciences
Service,
Great Russell Street,
London WC1B 3DG
tel 071 323 7536

British List Brokers' Association
see Direct Marketing Association

British Medical Association (BMA)
BMA House,
Tavistock Square,
London WC1H 9JP
tel 071 387 4499

British Nursing Association
443 Oxford Street,
London W1R 2NA
tel 071 629 9030
(see telephone directory for local
branches)

British Overseas Trade Board
1 Victoria Street,
London SW1 0ET
tel 071 215 5000

British Printing Industries Federation
11 Bedford Row,
London WC1R 4DX
tel 071 242 6904

British Psycho-Analytical Society
63 New Cavendish Street,
London W1M 7RD
tel 071 580 4952

British Psychological Society
St Andrews House,
48 Princess Road East,
Leicester LE1 7DR
tel 0533 549568

British Refugee Council
Bondway House,
3 Bondway,
London SW8 1SJ
tel 071 582 6922

British School at Rome
Regents College,
Inner Circle,
Regent's Park,
London NW1 4NS
tel 071 487 7403

British School of Osteopathy
1 Suffolk Street,
London SW1Y 4HG
tel 071 930 9254

British Snail Farmers' Association
Mr Jacques Aubree,
Barrow Farm,
Rode Hill,
Rode,
Somerset
tel 0373 830 300

British Society for Music Therapy
c/o Mrs Denise Christophers,
69 Avondale Avenue,
East Barnet,
Herts EN4 8NB
tel 081 368 8879

British Standards Institution
2 Park Street,
London W1A 2BS
tel 071 629 9000

British Toy and Hobby Association Ltd
80 Camberwell Road,
London SE5 0EG
tel 071 701 7271

British Toymakers' Guild
c/o Mr R. Brookes,
124 Walcot,
Bath,
Avon BA1 5BG
tel 0225 442440

British Trout Association
Fishfarmers Trade Association,
104 Parkway,
London NW1 7AN
tel 071 911 0313

British Veterinary Association
7 Mansfield Street,
London W1A 0AT
tel 071 636 6541

Broadcasting and Entertainment Trades Alliance (BETA)
see BECTU

BSC Industry
Canterbury House,
2–6 Sydenham Road,
Croydon CR9 2LJ
tel 081 686 2311

Building Employers Confederation
82 New Cavendish Street,
London W1
tel 071 580 5588

Business in the Community
227a City Road,
London EC1V 1LX
tel 071 253 3716

Camberwell (School of Art)
Peckham Road,
London SE5 8UF
tel 071 703 0987

Cambridge Venture Management
Unit 136,
Cambridge Science Park,
Milton Road,
Cambridge CB4 4GD
tel 0223 423618

CAMRA (The Campaign for Real Ale)
34 Alma Road,
St Albans,
Herts AL1 3BW
tel 0727 867201

Canine Defence League
1 Pratt Mews,
London NW1
tel 071 388 0137

Canine Studies Institute
London Road,
Liby Hill,
Bracknell,
Berkshire RG12 6QN

Cardiff University
University College,
Cardiff,
PO Box 68,
Cardiff CF1 3XA
tel 0222 874000

Central Bureau (for Education Visits
and Exchanges)
Seymour Mews House,
Seymour Mews,
London W1H 9PE
tel 071 486 5101

**Central Council for Education and
Training in Social Work**
Derbyshire House,
St Chad's Street,
London WC1H 8AD
tel 071 278 2455

CFI International
Suite 105/6 Butlers Wharf Business
Centre,
45 Curlew Street,
London SE1 2ND
tel 071 403 9926

Charity Commission
St Alban's House,
57–60 Haymarket,
London SW1Y 4QX
tel 071 210 3000

**Chartered Association of Certified
Accountants**
29 Lincoln's Inn Fields,
London WC2A 3EE
tel 071 242 6855

**Chartered Institute of Management
Accountants**
63 Portland Place,
London W1N 4AB
tel 071 637 2311

Chartered Institute of Marketing
Moor Hall,
Cookham,
Maidenhead,
Berks SL6 9QH
tel 06285 24922

Chartered Institute of Patent Agents
Staple Inn Buildings,
335 High Holborn,
London WC1V 7PZ
tel 071 405 9450

**Chartered Institute of Public Finance
& Accountancy**
3 Robert Street,
London WC2N 6BH
tel 071 930 3456

Chartered Insurance Institute
20 Aldermanbury,
London EC2V 7HY
tel 071 606 3835

Chartered Society of Designers
29 Bedford Square,
London WC1B 3EG
tel 071 631 1510

Chartered Society of Physiotherapy
14 Bedford Row,
London WC1R 4ED
tel 071 242 1941

Children's Legal Centre
20 Compton Terrace,
London N1 2UN
tel 071 359 6251

Church Commissioners for England
1 Millbank,
London SW1P 3JZ
tel 071 222 7010

City and Guilds of London Art School
124 Kennington Park Road,
London SE11 4DJ
tel 071 735 2306

City Business Library
106 Fenchurch Street,
London EC3
tel 071 638 8215

City University
Northampton Square,
London EC1V 0HB
tel 071 253 4399

Coal Merchants' Federation
Victoria House,
Southampton Row,
London WC1B 4DH
tel 071 405 8218

College for the Distributive Trades
(London College of Printing and
Distibutive Trades)
30 Leicester Square,
London WC2H 7LE
tel 071 839 1547

COIC
Room W1108,
Moorfoot,
Sheffield S1 4PQ

College of Psychic Studies
16 Queensberry Place,
London SW7 2EB
tel 071 589 3292

College of Radiographers
14 Upper Wimpole Street,
London W1M 8BN
tel 071 935 5726

College of Speech Therapists
Harold Pastor House,
6 Lechmere Road,
London NW2 5BU
tel 081 459 8521

College of Traditional Chinese Acupuncture
Tao House,
Queensway,
Royal Leamington Spa,
Warwick CV31 3LZ
tel 0926 422121

Comedy Store, The
28a Leicester Square,
London WC2 7LE
tel 0426 914433

Comett
c/o Department of Education and Science
Room 6/7A (E M A Moss),
Elizabeth House,
York Road,
London SE1 7PH

Communications, Advertising and Marketing Foundation (CAM)
Abford House,
15 Wilton Road,
London SW1V 1NJ
tel 071 828 7506

Companies Registration Office
Companies House,
55 City Road,
London EC1Y 1BB
tel 071 253 9393
and Companies House,
Crown Way,
Maindy,
Cardiff CF4 3UZ
tel 0222 380801

Complection International (London School of Makeup)
47 Lamb's Conduit Street,
London WC1N 3LE
tel 071 242 0778

Composers' Guild
34 Hanway Street,
London W1P 9DE
tel 071 436 0007

Conservative Party
32 Smith Square,
London SW1P 3HH
tel 071 222 9000

Construction Industry Training Board (CITB)
Careers Advisory Service,
Bircham Newton,
King's Lynn,
Norfolk PE31 6RH
tel 0553 776677

Cordon Bleu Cookery School (London) Ltd
114 Marylebone Lane,
London W1M 5FX
tel 071 935 3503

Cordwainers' College
182 Mare Street,
London E8 3RE
tel 081 985 0273

CORGI (Confederation for the Registration of Gas Installers)
See local telephone directory

CoSIRA (Rural Development Council)
141 Castle Street,
Salisbury SP1 3TP
tel 0722 336255

Council for Dance Education and Training
5 Tavistock Place,
London WC1H 9SS
tel 071 388 5770

Council for Licensed Conveyancers
3 Caingorm House,
203 Marsh Wall,
London E14 9YT
tel 071 537 2953

Council of Legal Education
The Inns of Court School of Law,
4 Gray's Inn Place,
London WC1R 5DX
tel 071 405 4635

Council of Legal Education (Northern Ireland)
Institute of Professional Studies,
Queen's University,
Belfast BT7 1NN

Council for Professions Supplementary to Medicine
Park House,
184 Kennington Park Road,
London SE11 4BU
tel 071 582 0866

Courtauld Institute (of Art)
Somerset House,
The Strand,
London WC2R 0RN
tel 071 872 0220

Covent Garden Market Management
41 Central Avenue,
The Market,
Covent Garden,
London WC2E
tel 071 836 9136

Crafts Council
44a Pentonville Road,
London N1 9BY
tel 071 278 7700

Craftsmen Potters Association
21 Carnaby Street,
London W1V 1PH
tel 071 437 6781

Cranfield
Cranfield Institute of Technology,
Cranfield,
Bedford MK43 0AL
tel 0234 750111

Crimewriters' Association
PO Box 172,
Tring,
Herts HP23 5LP

Crowcraft
Orchard Farm,
Escrick Road,
Wheldrake,
York YO4 6BQ
tel 0904 89727

Customs and Excise, Department of
New Kings Beam House,
22 Upper Ground,
London SE1 9PJ
tel 071 620 1313

Cyfle
Gronant,
Penrallt Isaf,
Caernarfon,
Gwynedd L55 1NW
tel 0286 671000

Dallamore College of Advanced Reflexology
50 Sydney Dye Court,
Sporle,
King's Lynn,
Norfolk PE32 2EE
tel 0760 725437

Dance UK
80 Ulster Gardens,
London N13 5DW
tel 081 803 0535

Dankworth Summer School
The Stables,
Wavendon,
Milton Keynes,
Bucks MK17 8LT
tel 0908 582522

Department of Education and Science
see DES

**Department of Employment
Employment Agency Licensing Offices**
(1) London and South-East
2–16 Church Rd,
Stanmore,
Middlesex HA7 4AW
tel 081 954 7677

(2) Midlands, South-West and Wales
Cumberland House,
200 Broad Street,
Birmingham B15 1PQ
tel 021 631 3300

(3) North and Scotland
City House,
Leeds LS1 4JH
tel 0532 438232

**Department of Employment's Loan
Guarantee Unit**
SFPB2, Level 1,
St Mary's House,
CO Moorfoot
Sheffield S1 4PQ
tel 0742 597373

Department of the Environment
2 Marsham Street,
London SW1P 3EB
tel 071 276 3000

**Department of the Environment
(Endangered Species Branch)**
Tollgate House,
Houlton Street,
Bristol BS2 9DJ
tel 0272 218694

Department of Trade and Industry
1–19 Victoria Street,
London SW1
tel 071 215 5000

**Department of Trade & Industry
Internal European Policy Division**
Room 405,
1–19 Victoria Street,
London SW1H 0ET
tel 071 215 5610
    071 215 4648
Hotline 081 200 1992

**DES (Department of Education and
Science)**
Sanctuary Buildings,
Great Smith Street,
London SW1P 3BT
tel 071 925 5000

Department of Transport
2 Marsham Street,
London SW1P 3EB
tel 071 276 3000

**Department of Transport (Marine
Directorate)**
Sunley House,
90–93 High Holborn,
London WC1V 6LP
tel 071 405 6911

Design Council
28 Haymarket,
London SW1Y 4SU
tel 071 839 8000

Despatch Association
17 Lavington Street,
London SE1 0NZ
tel 071 620 0755

Dietary Therapy Society
210 Tufnell Park Road,
London N7 0PZ

Direct Marketing Association
Grosvenor Gardens House,
35 Grosvenor Gardens,
London SW1W 0BS
tel 071 630 7322

Direct Mail Producers Association
see Direct Marketing Association

Direct Mail Services Standards Board
26 Eccleston Street,
London SW1W 9PY
tel 071 824 8651

Directors' Guild of Great Britain
Suffolk House,
Whitfield Place,
London W1
tel 071 383 3858

Disabled Living Foundation
380 Harrow Road,
London W9 2HV
tel 071 289 6111

DoE
Department of the Environment
2 Marsham Street,
London SW1P 3EB
tel 071 276 3000

Driving Instructors Association
Safety House,
Beddington Farm Road,
Croydon CR0 4XZ
tel 081 665 5151

Driving Standards Agency
2nd Floor,
Stanley House,
Talbot Street,
Nottingham NG1 5GH
tel 0602 474222

Edinburgh Fringe Festival
180 High Street,
Edinburgh EH1 1QS
tel 031 226 5257/9

Employment Agency Licensing Office
2 Church Road,
Stanmore,
Middlesex
tel 081 954 7677

Employment Consultants Institute
6 Guildford Road,
Woking,
Surrey GU22 7PX
tel 0483 766442

Employment Service,
Department of Employment
St Vincent House,
30 Orange Street,
London WC2H 7HT
tel 071 839 5600

Employment Service
Overseas Placing Unit (OPS 5)
c/o Moorfoot,
Sheffield S1 4PQ

English Tourist Board
Thames Tower,
Blacks Road,
London W6
tel 081 846 9000

English Vineyards Association
38 West Park,
London SE9 4RH
tel 081 857 0452

Equity (British Actors Equity
Association)
8 Harley Street,
London W1N 2AB
tel 071 636 6367

Erasmus
The University
Canterbury
Kent CT2 7PD

and at
rue d'Arlon, 15
B-1040 Brussels
Belgium

ESOMAS
European Society for Opinion and
Market Research
Amsterdam
tel 010 3120 664 2141

Eurodesk
Scottish Community Education Council,
90 Haymarket Terrace,
Edinburgh EH12 5LQ

Eurohouse
11 Lime Hill Road,
Tunbridge Wells,
Kent TN1 1LJ
tel 0892 518490

European Council of Thanatopractic
Associations
Anubis House,
21c Station Road,
Knowle,
Solihull,
West Midlands B93 0HL
tel 0564 778991

European Patent Office
Erhardstrasse 27-D-8000,
Munich 2,
Germany
tel 010 49489 201 7080

European School of Osteopathy
104 Tonbridge Road,
Maidstone,
Kent ME16 8SL

Euro-School of Funeral Directing
75 Station Road,
Great Billing,
Northampton NN3 4DS
tel 0604 405085

European Tattoo Artists' Association
108 High Street,
Deal,
Kent CT14 6EE
tel 0304 636006

Eurydice
(European Unit of the Eurydice
Network)
rue Archimède 17
Bte 17B
B-1040 Brussels
Belgium

Faculty of Actuaries
23(a) St Andrew Square,
Edinburgh EH2 1AQ
tel 031 557 1575

Faculty of Advocates
Advocates Library,
Parliament House,
11 Parliament Square,
Edinburgh EH1 1RF
tel 031 226 5071

Faculty of Homeopathy
Royal London Homeopathic Hospital,
Great Ormond Street,
London WC1N 3HR
tel 071 837 3091

Farriers' Registration Council
PO Box 49,
East of England Show Ground,
Peterborough PE2 0XE
tel 0733 234451

Federation of Bloodstock Agents (GB) Ltd
The Old Brewery,
Hampton Street,
Tetbury,
Gloucestershire GL8 8PG
tel 0666 503595

Federation of International Competitions
104 rue de Carouge,
CH-1205 Genève,
Geneva,
Switzerland
tel 010 41 22 213620

Federation of Master Builders
14 Great James Street,
London WC1N 3DP
tel 071 242 7583

Federation of Recruitment and Employment Services
36–38 Mortimer Street,
London W1N 7RB
tel 071 323 4300

Federation of Zoos
Zoological Gardens,
Regent's Park,
London NW1 4RY
tel 071 586 0230

Feline Advisory Bureau
235 Upper Richmond Road,
London SW15 6SN
tel 081 789 9553

Fellowship of Engineering Institutions
2 Little Smith Street,
London SW1P 3DH
tel 071 222 2688

FIMBRA (Financial Intermediaries and Brokers' Regulatory Association)
Hertsmere House,
Hertsmere Road,
London E14 4AB
tel 071 538 8860

Forestry Training Council
Forestry Commission,
231 Corstorphine Road,
Edinburgh EH12 7AT
tel 031 334 8083

Franchise Development Services
Castle House,
Castle Meadow,
Norwich NR2 1PJ
tel 0603 620301

Freight Transport Association
Hermes House,
St John's Road,
Tunbridge Wells,
Kent TN4 9UZ
tel 0892 526171

Gateshead College
Durham Road,
Gateshead NE9 5BN
tel 091 477 0524

Gemmological Association (of Great Britain)
27 Greville Street,
London EC1N 8SU
tel 071 404 3334

General Council and Register of Naturopaths
Frazer House,
6 Netherhall Gardens,
London NW3 5RR
tel 071 435 8728

General Council and Register of Osteopaths
56 London Street,
Reading,
Berkshire RG1 4SQ
tel 0734 576585

General Council of the Bar
3 Bedford Row,
London WC1R 4DB
tel 071 242 0082

General Dental Council
37 Wimpole Street,
London W1M 8DQ
tel 071 486 2171

General Medical Council
44 Hallam Street,
London W1N 6AE
tel 071 580 7642

**General Nursing Council for England
and Wales**
23 Portland Place
London W1N 3AS
tel 071 637 7181

General Optical Council
41 Harley Street,
London W1N 1DJ
tel 071 580 3898

Glastonbury (Festival)
Enquiries to Michael Eavis,
Worthy Farm,
Pilton,
Shepton Mallet,
Somerset BA4 4BY
tel 074989 254

**Goldsmiths' Company (Worshipful
Company of Goldsmiths)**
Goldsmiths Hall,
Foster Lane,
London EC2V 6BN
tel 071 606 7010

Graphical, Paper and Media Union
Keys House,
63–67 Bronham Road,
Bedford MK40 2AG
tel 0234 351521

Graphology Centre, The
tel 071 262 0198 (telephone enquiries
only)

Guild of Guide Lecturers
2 Bridge Street,
London SW1A 2JR
tel 071 839 7438

Guild of Master Craftsmen
166 High Street,
Lewes,
East Sussex BN7 1XU
tel 0273 478449

Guild of Professional Toastmasters
12 Little Bornes,
Alleyn Park,
Dulwich,
London SE21 8SE
tel 081 670 5585

Guild of Taxidermists
Membership Secretary,
Art Gallery and Museum,
Kelvingrove,
Glasgow G3 8AG
tel 041 357 3929

**Guildhall School (of Music and
Drama)**
Barbican,
Silk Street,
London EC2Y 8DT
tel 071 628 2571

Hambros
Hambros Bank Ltd,
41 Tower Hill,
London EC2
tel 071 480 5000

Herb Society, The
tel 0712 284417

Hereford Technical College
Folly Lane,
Hereford HR1 1LS
tel 0432 352235

Hippodrome
Cranbourn Street,
London WC2H 7AJ
tel 071 437 4311

Historic Houses Association
2 Chester Street,
London SW1X 7BB
tel 071 259 5688

HMSO Bookshop
tel 071 873 0011 (enquiries)
tel 071 873 9090 (orders)

Homeopathic Bicycle Co
Flat 2,
18 The Avenue,
Brondesbury Park,
London NW6 7YD
tel 081 459 8530

Hotel and Catering Training Company
International House,
High Street,
London W5 5DB
tel 081 579 2400

Hotel Catering and Institutional Management Association
191 Trinity Road,
London SW17 7HN
tel 081 672 4251

IMRO (Investment Managers' Regulatory Organisation)
Broadwalk House,
5 Appold Street,
London EC2A 2LL
tel 071 628 6022

Incorporated Association of Preparatory Schools (IAPS)
138 Kensington Church Street,
London W8
tel 071 727 2316

Incorporated Association of Tutors
27 Radburn Court,
Dunstable,
Bedfordshire LU6 1HW
tel 0582 605920

Incorporated Society of Musicians
10 Stratford Place,
London W1N 9AE
tel 071 629 4413

Incorporated Society of Valuers and Auctioneers
3 Cadogan Gate,
London SW1X 0AS
tel 071 235 2282

Independent Film, Video and Photography Association
79 Wardour Street,
London W1V 3PH
tel 071 439 0660

Independent Schools Association Incorporated (ISAI)
Former Boys British School,
East Street,
Saffron Walden,
Essex CB10 1LS
tel 0799 23619

Independent Schools Information Service (ISIS)
56 Buckingham Gate,
London SW1E 6AG
tel 071 630 5013

Industrial Society
48 Bryanston Square,
London W1H 7LN
tel 071 262 2401

Institute of Actuaries
Education Service
Napier House,
4 Worcester Street,
Oxford OX1 2AW
tel 0865 794144

Institute of Chartered Accountants in England and Wales
PO Box 433,
Chartered Accountants' Hall,
Moorgate Place,
London EC2P 2BJ
tel 071 628 7060

Institute of Chartered Accountants in Scotland
27 Queen Street,
Edinburgh EH2 1LA
tel 031 225 5673

Institute of Chartered Shipbrokers
24 St Mary Axe,
London EC3A 8DE
tel 071 283 1361

Institute of Employment Consultants
6 Guildford Road,
Woking,
Surrey GU22 7PX
tel 0483 766442

Institute of Group Analysis
1 Daleham Gardens,
London NW3 5BY
tel 071 431 2693

Institute of Horticulture
PO Box 313,
80 Vincent Square,
London SW1P 2PE
tel 071 976 5951

Institute of Inventors
19 Fosse Way,
London W13
tel 081 998 3540

Institute of Legal Executives
Kempston Manor,
Kempston,
Bedford MK42 7AB
tel 0234 841000

Institute of Linguists
24a Highbury Grove,
London N5 2EA
tel 071 359 7445

Institute of Management Consultants
32 Hatton Garden,
London EC1N 8DU
tel 071 242 2140

Institute of Patentees and Inventors
Suite 505a Triumph House,
189 Regent Street,
London W1R 7WF
tel 071 242 7812

Institute of Plumbing
64 Station Lane,
Hornchurch,
Essex RM12 6NB
tel 04024 72791

Institute of Printing
8 Lonsdale Gardens,
Tunbridge Wells,
Kent TN1 1NU
tel 0892 38118

Institute of Professional Investigators
31a Wellington Street,
St Johns,
Blackburn,
Lancashire BB1 8AF
tel 0254 680072

Institute of Psychoanalysis
63 New Cavendish Street,
London W1
tel 071 580 4952

Institute of Public Relations
Old Trading House,
15 Northburgh Street,
London EC1V 0PR
tel 071 253 5151

Institution of Chemical Engineers
Davis Building,
165–171 Railway Terrace,
Rugby,
Warwickshire CV21 3HQ
tel 0788 578214

Institution of Electrical Engineers
Savoy Place,
London WC2
tel 071 240 1871

Insurance Brokers' Registration Council (IBRC)
15 St Helens Place,
London EC3A 6DS
tel 071 588 4387

International Air Transport Association (IATA)
15 Kingsway,
London WC2B 6UN
tel 071 497 1048

International Commodities Clearing House Ltd (ICCH)
Roman Wall House,
1 Crutched Friars,
London EC3N 2AN
tel 071 488 3200

International House
106 Picadilly,
London W1V 9FL
tel 071 491 2598

International Professional Security Association
292a Torquay Road,
Paignton,
Devon TQ3 2EZ
tel 0803 554849

International Register of Oriental Medicine
Greenhedges House,
Greenhedges Avenue,
East Grinstead,
Sussex RH19 1DZ
tel 0342 313106

International Wool Secretariat
6 Carlton Gardens,
London SW1Y 5AE
tel 071 930 7300

Inverness College (of Higher and Further Education)
3 Longman Road,
Inverness IV1 1SA
tel 0463 236681

Investors in Industry (plc)
91 Waterloo Road,
London SE1
tel 071 928 3131

IPE (International Petroleum Exchange)
International House,
1 St Katherine's Way,
London E1 9UN
tel 071 481 0643

IPG (Independent Publishers Guild)
25 Cambridge Road,
Hampton,
Middx TW12 2JL
tel 081 979 0250

IRCHIN (Independent Representation of Children in Need)
23A Hawthorn Drive,
Heswall,
Wirral,
Merseyside L61 6UP
tel 051 342 7852

Ivor Spencer School of Professional Toastmasters
12 Little Bornes,
Alleyn Park,
Dulwich,
London SE21
tel 081 670 5585

Iyengar Yoga Institute
223a Randolph Avenue,
London W9 1NL
tel 071 624 3080

Jazz Services
5 Dryden Street,
London WC2E 9NW
tel 071 829 8353

Jobcentres
See Employment Service in local telephone directory

Jobfit
5 Dean Street,
London W1V 5RN
tel 071 734 5141

Jockey Club, The
42 Portman Square,
London W1H 0EN
tel 071 486 4921

John Makepeace School for Craftsmen in Wood
Parnham House,
Beaminster,
Dorset DT8 3NA
tel 0308 862204

Joint Exchange Committee
28–29 Threadneedle Street,
London EC2R 8BA
tel 071 283 1345

Labour Party
150 Walworth Road,
London SE17 1LJ
tel 071 701 1234

Landscape Institute
6/7 Barnard Mews,
London SW11 1QU
tel 071 738 9166

LAUTRO (Life Assurance and Unit Trust Regulatory Organisation) Ltd
Centre Point,
103 New Oxford Street,
London WC1A 1DD
tel 071 379 0444

Law Society
113 Chancery Lane,
London WC2A 1PL
tel 071 242 1222

Law Society Careers Office
227–228 Strand,
London WC2R 1BA
tel 071 242 1222

Law Society of Scotland
26 Drumsheugh Gardens,
Edinburgh EH3 7YR
tel 031 226 7411

Leith's (School of Food and Wine)
21 St Alban's Grove,
London W8 5BP
tel 071 229 0177

Liberal Democrats
4 Cowley Street,
London SW1P 3NB
tel 071 222 7999

Licensed Taxi Drivers' Association
9–11 Woodfield Road,
London W9 2BA
tel 071 286 1046

Licenced Victuallers' Association
Boardman House,
2 Downing Street,
Farnham,
Surrey GU9 7NX
tel 0252 714448

LIFFE (London International Financial Futures Exchange)
Royal Exchange,
Cornhill,
London EC3V 3PJ
tel 071 623 0444

The Little Angel
Marionette Theatre
14 Dagmar Passage,
London N1 2DN
tel 071 226 1787

LME (London Metal Exchange)
Plantation House,
Fenchurch Street,
London EC3M 3AP
tel 071 626 3311

Livewire
60 Grainger Street,
Newcastle upon Tyne NE1 5JG
tel 091 261 5584

London and Provincial Antique Dealers' Association
Suite 214,
535 King's Road,
London SW10 0SZ
tel 071 823 3511

London College of Fashion
20 John Prince's Street,
London W1M 0BJ
tel 071 629 9401

London College of Furniture
City of London Poly
41 Commercial Road,
London E1
tel 071 247 1953

London College of Osteopathy
8 Boston Place,
London NW1 6QH
tel 071 262 5250

London College of Printing
Elephant and Castle,
London SE1 6SB
tel 071 735 9100

London Enterprise Agency
4 Snowhill,
London EC1A 2DH
tel 071 236 3000

London FOX
1 Commodity Quay,
St Katharine's Dock,
London E1 9AX
tel 071 481 2080

London Retail Meat Traders' Association
27 Central Markets,
London EC1
tel 071 248 0732

London School of Publishing
47 Red Lion Street,
London WC1R 4PF
tel 071 405 9801

London Tourist Board
26 Grosvenor Gardens,
London SW1W 0DH
tel 071 730 3450

London Traded Options Market
Royal Exchange,
Cornhill,
London EC3V 3PJ
tel 071 623 0444

Mailing Preference Service
1 Leeward House,
Square Rigger Row,
Plantation Wharf Street,
London SW11 3TX
tel 071 738 1625

Management Consultants Association Ltd
11 West Halkin Street,
London SW1X 8JL
tel 071 235 3897

Market Research Society
15 Northburgh Street,
London EC1V 0AH
tel 071 490 4911

Marriage Guidance Council
see RELATE

Mecca (Leisure) Ltd
76 Southwark Street,
London SE1 0PP
tel 071 928 2323

Mechanical Copyright Protection Society
41 Streatham High Road,
London SW16 1ER
tel 081 769 4400

Merrist Wood Agricultural College
Worplesdon,
Guildford,
Surrey GU3 3PE
tel 0483 232424

Merton College
Morden Park,
London Road,
Morden,
Surrey SM4 5QX
tel 081 640 3001

Metropolitan Police Bureau
New Scotland Yard,
Nroadway,
London SW1H 0BG
tel 071 230 1212

MI Group
Centrepoint,
New Oxford Street,
London WC1A 1DD
tel 071 379 5995

Ministry of Agriculture (Fisheries and Food)
Whitehall Place,
London SW1A 2HH
tel 071 270 8080

Ministry of Agriculture (Veterinary Division)
Government Buildings,
Toby Jug Site,
Hook Rise South,
Tolworth,
Surbiton,
Surrey KT6 7NF
tel 081 330 4411

Ministry of Transport (MOT)
Department of Transport,
2 Marsham Street,
London SW1P 3EB
tel 071 276 3000

Motor Cycle Association
Staley House,
Eaton Road,
Coventry CV1 2FH
tel 0203 227427

Museums Association
34 Bloomsbury Way,
London WC1A 2SF
tel 071 404 4767

Music Publishers' Association
103 Kingsway,
London WC2B 6QX
tel 071 831 7591

Music Retailers' Association
PO Box 249,
London W4 5EX
tel 081 994 7592

Musicians' Union
60/62 Clapham Road,
London SW9 0JJ
tel 071 582 5566

NACRO (National Association for the Care and Resettlement of Offenders)
169 Clapham Road,
London SW9 0PU
tel 071 582 6500

Napier Polytechnic
Craiglockhart Campus,
219 Colinton Road,
Edinburgh EH14 1DJ
tel 031 444 2266

National Association of Bookmakers
Tolworth Tower,
Ewell Road,
Surbiton,
Surrey KT6 7EL
tel 081 390 8222

National Association of Estate Agents
21 Jury Street,
Warwick CV34 4EH
tel 0926 496800

National Association of Farriers, Blacksmiths & Agricultural Engineering (NAFB & AE)
Avenue R,
7th Street,
National Agricultural Centre,
Stoneleigh,
Warwickshire CV8 2LG
tel 0203 696595

National Association of Funeral Directors
618 Warwick Road,
Solihull,
West Midlands B91 1AA
tel 021 711 1343

National Association of Shopkeepers
Lynch House,
91 Mansfield Road,
Nottingham NG1 3FN
tel 0602 475046

National Association of Trade Protection Societies
c/o 14 Parkside Groby
Leicester LE6 0EB
tel 0533 876672

National Childminding Association
8 Mason's Hill
Bromley,
Kent BR2 9EY
tel 081 464 6164

National Children's Bureau
8 Wakeley Street,
London EC1V 7QE
tel 071 278 9441

National Council for Drama Training
5 Tavistock Place,
London WC1H 9SN
tel 071 387 3650

National Council for the Training of Journalists
Carlton House,
Hemnall Street,
Epping CM16 4NL
tel 0378 72395

National Council for Vocational Qualifications
222 Euston Road,
London NW1 2BZ
tel 071 387 9898

National Coursing Club
16 Clocktower Mews,
Newmarket,
Suffolk CB8 8LL
tel 0638 667381

National Farmers' Union
Agriculture House,
Knightsbridge,
London SW1X 7NJ
tel 071 235 5077

National Federation of Fishmongers
Pisces,
London Road,
Feering,
Colchester,
Essex CO5 9ED
tel 0376 571391

National Federation of Music Societies
Francis House,
Francis Street,
London SW1
tel 071 828 7320

National Federation of Painting and Decorating Contractors (NFPDC)
82 New Cavendish Street,
London W1
tel 071 580 5588

National Federation of Self-Employed and Small Businesses Ltd
32 St Anne's Road West,
Lytham St Annes,
Lancs FY8 1NY
tel 0253 720911

National Federation of Spiritual Healers
Old Manor Farm Studio,
Church Street,
Sunbury-on-Thames
tel 0932 783164

National Graphical Association (NGA)
see Graphical, Paper and Media Union

National Greyhound Racing Club
Shipton House,
24 Oval Road,
London NW1 7DA
tel 071 267 9256

National Inspection Council for Electrical Installation Contracting
Vintage House,
36 Albert Embankment,
London SE1 7TL
tel 071 582 7746

National Joint Council for the Craft of Dental Technicians
64 Wimpole Street,
London W1M 8AL
tel 071 935 0875

National Joint Council for the Motor Vehicle and Repair Industry
201 Great Portland Street,
London W1
tel 071 580 9122

National Nursery Examination Board
Chequer Street,
St Albans,
Herts AL1 3XZ
tel 0727 867333

National Schools of Violin Making
Instituto Internazionale per l'Artigianato,
Liutario e del Legno 'Antonio Stradivari',
Palazzo dell'Arte,
Piazza Marconi 5,
26100,
Cremona,
Italy
tel 010 39 372 457297

**Staatliche Berufsfach und Fachschule
für Giegenbau,**
Parten Kirchener Str. 24,
8102 Mittenwald,
Germany

National Sheep Association
The Sheep Centre,
Malvern,
Worcester WR13 6PH
tel 0684 892661

National Union of Journalists (NUJ)
Acorn House,
314 Gray's Inn Road,
London WC1X 8DP
tel 071 278 7916

Newark College
Friary Road,
Newark,
Notts NG24 1PG
tel 0636 705921

**Nordoff-Robins (Music Therapy
Centre Ltd)**
3 Leighton Place,
London NW5
tel 071 267 6296

**Northern Ireland Council for Nurses
and Midwives**
216 Belmont Road,
Belfast BT1 2AT

**North London School of
Physiotherapy for the Visually
Handicapped**
10 Highgate Hill,
London N19 5ND
tel 071 272 1659

Norwich Puppet Theatre
St James,
Whitefriars,
Norwich,
Norfolk NR3 1TN
tel 0603 615564

Office of Fair Trading
Field House,
Breams Buildings,
London EC4A 1PR
tel 071 242 2858

**Office of Population Censuses and
Surveys**
St Catherine's House,
10 Kingsway,
London WC2B 6LH
tel 071 242 0262

OM (London Ltd)
Milestone House,
107 Cannon Street,
London EC4N 5AD
tel 071 281 0678

Open College
Freepost TK1006,
Brentford,
Middlesex TW8 8BR

Open University
Walton Hall,
Milton Keynes MK7 6AA
tel 0908 274066

**Organisation of Chartered
Physiotherapists in Private Practice**
c/o Chartered Society of Physiotherapy,
14 Bedford Row,
London WC1R 4ED
tel 071 242 1941

OWNBASE Association
57 Glebe Road,
Egham,
Surrey TW20 8BU

Oxford Polytechnic
Gipsy Lane,
Headington,
Oxford OX3 0BP
tel 0865 741111

Patent Office
State House,
66–71 High Holborn,
London WC1R 4TP
tel 071 831 2525

Paul Bogle Foundation
189 Kentish Town Road,
London NW5 2JU
tel 071 267 0980

Pensions Management Institute
124 Middlesex Street,
London E1 7HY
tel 071 247 1452

Performing Rights Society Ltd
29 Berners Street,
London W1P 4AA
tel 071 580 5544

Periodical Publishers' Association
Imperial House,
15–19 Kingsway,
London WC2B 6UN
tel 071 379 6268

Petra (Appui Technique Petra)
Ifaplan
Square Ambiorix 32
B-1040 Brussels
Belgium

Photographers' Gallery
5 Great Newport Street,
London WC2H 7HY
tel 071 831 1772

Piano Tuners' Association
10 Reculver Road,
Herne Bay,
Kent CT6 6LD
02273 68808

Playboard
Playboard Puppets,
94 Ockendon Road,
London N1 3NW
tel 071 226 5911

Polka Theatre, The
240 The Broadway,
London SW19 1SB
tel 081 542 4258

Polytechnic of Central London School of Languages
309 Regent Street,
London W1R 8AL
tel 071 911 5000

Prince's Trust
8 Bedford Row,
London WC1R 4BA
tel 071 430 0524

Printmakers' Council
31 Clerkenwell Close,
London EC1R 0AT
tel 071 250 1927

Public Carriage Office
15 Penton Street,
London N1 9PU
tel 071 278 1744

Puppet Centre
Battersea Arts Centre,
Lavender Hill,
London SW11 5TN
tel 071 228 5335

Racehorse Owners' Association
42 Portman Square,
London W1H 9FF
tel 071 486 6977

Reflex Pictures Ltd
83 Clerkenwell Road,
London EC1R 5AR
tel 071 405 8545

Registered Nursing Home Association
Calthorpe House,
Hagley Road,
Edgbaston,
Birmingham B16 8QY
tel 021 454 2511

Registrar of Companies
Companies Registration Office,
Crown Way,
Maindy,
Cardiff CF3 3UZ
tel 0222 388588

RELATE (National Marriage Guidance)
Little Church Street,
Rugby,
Warwickshire CV21 3AP
tel 0788 73241

Resort Condominiums International (RCI)
Parnell House,
19 Wilton Road,
London SW1V 1LW
tel 071 821 5588

Restaurateurs Association (of Great Britain)
190 Queensgate,
London SW7 5EH
tel 071 581 2444

Retail Motor Industry Federation
201 Great Portland Street,
London W1N 5HA
tel 071 580 9122

**RETURN
The Women Returners Training Consultancy**
33 Lausanne Road,
London N8 0HW
tel 081 986 5105

Reuters (Ltd)
85 Fleet Street,
London EC4P 4AJ
tel 071 250 1122

Riverside Studios
Crisp Road,
Hammersmith,
London W6 9RL
tel 081 741 2251

Road Haulage Association, Ltd
104 New King's Road,
London SW6
tel 071 736 1183

Road Transport Industry Training Board
Capitol House,
Empire Way,
Wembley,
Middlesex HA9 0NG
tel 081 902 8880

Roehampton Institute
Roehampton Lane,
London SW15 5PU
tel 081 878 8117

Romantic Novelists' Association
Hon Sec Marie Murray,
9 Hillside Road,
Southport,
Merseyside PR8 4QB
tel 0704 60945

Royal Academy of Dancing
48 Vicarage Crescent,
London SW11 3LT
tel 071 223 0091

Royal Academy of Music
Marylebone Road,
London NW1 5HT
tel 071 935 5461

Royal College of General Practitioners
14 Princes Gate,
London SW7 1PU
tel 071 581 3232

Royal College of Music
Prince Consort Road,
London SW7 2BS
tel 071 589 3643

Royal College of Nursing
20 Cavendish Square,
London W1M 9AB
tel 071 409 3333

Royal College of Veterinary Surgeons
32 Belgrave Square,
London SW1X 8QP
tel 071 235 4971

Royal Horticultural Society (RHS)
Horticultural Hall,
80 Vincent Square,
London SW1P 2PB
tel 071 834 4333

Royal Incorporation of Architects in Scotland
15 Rutland Square,
Edinburgh EH1 2BF
tel 031 229 7205

Royal Institute of British Architects (RIBA)
66 Portland Place,
London W1N 4AD
tel 071 580 5533

Royal Institution of Chartered Surveyors
Surveyor Court,
Westwood Way,
Conventry CV4 8JE
tel 0203 694757

Royal Life Saving Society
Mountbatten House,
Studley,
Warwickshire B80 7NN
tel 052 785 3943

Royal Northern College of Music
124 Oxford Road,
Manchester M13 9RD
tel 061 273 6283

Royal Pharmaceutical Society of Great Britain
1 Lambeth High Street,
London SE1 7JR
tel 071 735 9141

Royal Scottish Academy
100 Renfrew Street,
Glasgow G2 3DB
tel 041 332 4101

Royal Society of Arts (RSA)
Progress House,
Westwood Way,
Coventry CV4 8HS
tel 0203 470033

Royal Society of Medicine
1 Wimpole Street,
London W1M 7AA
tel 071 408 2119

Royal Society of Musicians
10 Stratford Place,
London W1N 9AE
tel 071 629 6137

Royal Society of Painter-Printmakers
Bankside Gallery,
48 Hopton Street,
London SE1 9JH
tel 071 928 7521

Royal Town Planning Institute
26 Portland Place,
London W1N 4BF
tel 071 636 9107

Royal Watercolour Society
Bankside Gallery,
48 Hopton Street,
London SE1 9JH
tel 071 928 7521

Royal Yachting Association (RYA)
RYA House,
Romsey Road,
Eastleigh,
Hants SO5 4YA
tel 0703 629962

RSPCA (Royal Society for the Prevention of Cruelty to Animals)
Headquarters,
Causeway,
Horsham,
West Sussex RH12 1HG
tel 0403 64181

Rural Development Commission
11 Cowley Street,
London SW1P 3NB
tel 071 276 6969

Rycotewood College
Priest End,
Thame,
Oxon OX9 2AF
tel 084 421 2501

Saddlers' Company
Saddlers' Hall,
40 Gutter Lane,
London EC2V 6BR
tel 071 726 8661

St Bartholomews Hospital
West Smithfield,
London EC1A 7BE
tel 071 601 8888

School Transfer Consultants
21 Whitfield Place,
London W1P 5SB
tel 071 388 8994

Science Reference Library
25 Southampton Buildings
London WC2A 1AW
tel 071 323 7494

Scottish Enterprise (previously Scottish Development Agency)
120 Bothwell Street,
Glasgow G2 7JP
tel 041 248 2700

Scottish Film Training Trust
74 Victoria Cresent Road,
Glasgow G12 9JN
tel 041 337 2526

Scottish Salmon Growers' Association
Strattaird Ltd,
Drummond House,
Scott Street,
Perth PH1 5EJ
tel 0738 35420

Scottish Smoked Salmon Association
163c Cargo Terminal,
Turntown Road,
Edinburgh EH12 0AL
tel 031 317 7329

Sea Fish Industry Authority
Seafish House,
St Andrews' Dock,
Hull HU3 4QE
tel 0482 27837

Securities Institute
Stock Exchange Building,
Old Broad Street,
London EC2N 1ES
tel 071 628 2272

Securities and Futures Authority (SFA)
Stock Exchange Building,
Old Broad Street,
London EC2N 1EQ
tel 071 256 9000

Securities and Investment Board (SIB)
2 Bunhill Row,
London EC1Y 8SR
tel 071 638 1240

Senate of the Inns of Court and the Bar
11 South Square,
London WC1
tel 071 242 0934

Shellfish Association of Great Britain
Fishmongers' Hall,
London Bridge,
London EC4R 9EL
tel 071 283 8305

Shetland Salmon Farmers' Association
18 Alexandra Buildings,
Lerwick,
Shetland ZE1 0LL
tel 0595 5579

Ski Club of Great Britain
118 Eaton Square,
London SW1W 9AF
tel 071 245 1033

Small Business Research Trust
3 Dean Trench Street,
London SW1P 3HB

Small Independent Brewers' Association
2 Balfour Road,
London N5
tel 071 359 8323

Snail Centre, The
Mr Roy Groves,
Plas Newydd,
90 Dinerth Road,
Colwyn Bay,
Clwyd LL28 4YH
tel 0492 548253

Society for the Promotion of New Music
1 West Heath Yard,
174 Mill Lane,
London NW6 1NT
tel 071 431 3752

Society of Analytical Psychology
1 Daleham Gardens,
London NW3 5BY
tel 071 435 7696

Society of Apothecaries
Apothecaries Hall,
14 Blackfriars Lane,
London EC4V 6EJ
tel 071 236 1189

Society of Authors
84 Drayton Gardens,
London SW10 9SB
tel 071 373 6642

Society of Chiropodists
53 Welbeck Street,
London W1M 7HE
tel 071 486 3381

Society of Designer-Craftsmen
24 Rivington Street,
London EC2A 3DU
tel 071 739 3663

Society of Freelance Editors and Proofreaders
Membership Secretary
Michele Clark,
Rosemary Cottage,
Fore Street,
Weston,
Hitchin,
Herts SG4 7AS
tel 0462 79577

Society of Graphical and Allied Trades (SOGAT)
see Graphical, Paper and Media Union

Society of Homeopaths
2 Artizan Road,
Northampton NN1 4HU
tel 0604 21400

Society of Indexers
25 Leyborne Park,
Kew Gardens,
Richmond,
Surrey TW9 3HB
tel 081 940 4771

Society of Licensed Conveyancers
55 Church Road,
Croydon,
Surrey CR9 1PF
tel 081 681 1001

Society of Master Saddlers
The Cottage,
Mary Street,
Bovey Tracey,
Devon TQ13 9JA
tel 0626 832725

Society of Pension Consultants
Ludgate House,
Ludgate Circus,
London EC4
tel 071 353 1688

Society of Picture Researchers and Editors (SPREd)
BM Box 259,
London WC1N 3XX
tel 071 404 5011

Society of Scribes and Illuminators
54 Boileau Road,
London SW13 9BL
tel 081 748 9951

Society of Teachers of Alexander Technique
20 London House,
266 Fulham Road,
London SW10 9EL
tel 071 351 0828

Solid Fuel Advisory Service
Hobart House,
Grosvenor Place,
London SW1X 7AE
tel 071 235 2020

Southfields College (of Further Education)
Aylestone Road,
Leicester LE2 7LW
tel 0533 541818

Spotlight
7 Leicester Place,
London WC2H 7BP
tel 071 437 7631

Stock Exchange
London EC2N 1HB
tel 071 588 2355

Surrey University
Guildford,
Surrey GU2 5XH
tel 0483 300800

Tavistock Institute of Human Relations
120 Belsize Lane,
London NW3 5BA
tel 071 300 800

Teachers Pay and General Branch Division A
Department of Education and Science,
Sanctuary Buildings,
Great Smith Street,
London SW1P 3BT
tel 071 925 5000

Teaching as a Second Career
Department of Education and Science,
Sanctuary Buildings,
Great Smith Street,
London SW1P 3BT
tel 071 925 5000

Thames Television
Thames Studios,
Broom Road,
Teddington Lock,
Teddington,
Middlesex TW11 9NT
tel 081 977 3252

Thatching Advisory Service Ltd
Rose Tree Farm,
29 Nine Mile Ride,
Finchampstead,
Wokingham,
Berkshire RG11 4QD
tel 0734 734203

Timeshare Council
23 Buckingham Gate,
London SW1E 6LB
tel 071 821 8845

Trinity College of Music
Mandeville Place,
London W1M 6AQ
tel 071 935 5773

UK Central Council for Nursing, Midwifery and Health Visiting
23 Portland Place,
London W1N 3AS
tel 071 637 7181

UK Institute for Conservation
37 Upper Addison Gardens
London W14 8AJ
tel 071 603 5643

UK Training College of Hypnotherapy and Counselling
10 Alexander Street,
London W2 5NT
tel 071 221 1796/071 727 0255

Unit Trust Association
65 Kingsway,
London WC2B 6TD
tel 071 831 0898

University of London, Department of Extramural Studies
26 Russell Square,
London WC1B 5DQ
tel 071 631 6633

University College Cardiff
PO Box 68
Cardiff CF1 3XA
tel 0222 874000

University of East Anglia
Norwich,
Norfolk NR4 7TJ
tel 0603 56161

Victoria and Albert Museum
Cromwell Road,
South Kensington,
London SW7 2RL
tel 071 938 8500

Victorian Society
1 Priory Gardens,
London W4 1TT
tel 081 994 1019

Watford College
Hempstead Road,
Watford,
Herts WD1 3EZ
tel 0923 57500

Welsh Development Agency
Pearl Assurance House,
Greyfriars Road,
Cardiff CF1 3XX
tel 0222 222666

Welsh Office, Agriculture Department
Station Road,
Ruthin,
Clwyd LL15 1BP
tel 08242 2611

West Dean (College of Arts)
West Dean,
Chichester,
West Sussex PO18 0QZ
tel 0243 63301

Westminster Central Reference Library
Business and Official Publications
Section,
St Martin's Street,
London WC2
tel 071 798 2034

Wine and Spirit Education Trust
Five Kings House,
1 Queen Street Place,
London EC4R 1QS
tel 071 236 3551

Women's Enterprise Network
77 Guardhouse Road,
Coventry CV6 3DU
tel 0203 591824

Working Mothers' Association
77 Holloway Road,
London N7 8JZ
tel 071 700 5771

Writers' Guild (of Great Britain)
430 Edgware Road,
London W2 1EH
tel 071 723 8074

Writtle College
Chelmsford,
Essex CM1 3RR
tel 0245 420705

Young Concert Artist Trust
14 Ogle Street,
London W1P 7LG
tel 071 637 8743

Young Farmers' Clubs (The National Federation of)
National Agricultural Centre,
Stoneleigh,
Kenilworth,
Warwickshire CV8 2LG
tel 0203 696544

Youth Exchange Centre
Seymour Mews House
Seymour Mews
London W1H 9PE
tel 071 486 5101

Zoological Society of London
Regent's Park,
London NW1 4RY
tel 071 722 3333

Bibliography

AA Guides
Automobile Association
(London)
Annually

About Solicitors
Law Society,
113 Chancery Lane,
London W2A 1PL

Accountancy
The Institute of Chartered Accountants in
England & Wales,
40 Bernard Street,
London WC1N 1LD
Monthly

Accountancy Age
VNU Business Publications,
32–34 Broadwick Street,
London W1A 2HG
Weekly

Action Checklist for Business
Department of Trade & Industry,
1–19 Victoria Street
London SW1H 0ET

Actor's Handbook
Barry Turner
Bloomsbury Publishing

ACU Handbook
Autocycle Union,
Corporation Street,
Rugby,
Warwickshire CV21 2DN
Mail order

Adoption and Fostering
British Agencies for Adoption and
Fostering,
11 Southwark Street,
London SE1 1RQ
Quarterly

Advanced Reflexology
R Dalamore
Cockatrice Press

Adventures in the Screen Trade
William Goldman
Futura (London) 1985

**A Guide to Working in a Europe
Without Frontiers**
HMSO

Agriculture, Horticulture and Forestry
DES
Elisabeth House,
London SE1

Airline World
Travel Weekly Publications Ltd,
23 Dering Street,
London W1R 9AA
Weekly

Alexander Principle
Wilfred Barlow
Arrow Books (London)

Alexander Technique
Chris Stevens
Macdonald Optima (London)

American Way of Death, The
Jessica Mitford
Penguin (Harmondsworth)

Anatomy of the Orchestra
Norman del Mar
Faber & Faber

Animations
The Puppet Centre
Battersea Arts Centre
Lavender Hill
London SW11

Annual Careers Guide
COIC,
Manpower Services Commission,
Moorfoot,
Sheffield S1 4PQ

Antique Collector
National Magazine Co Ltd,
72 Broadwick Street,
London W1V 2BP
Monthly

Antique Dealer and Collectors Guide
IPC Magazines Ltd,
Kings Reach Tower,
Stamford Street,
London SE1 9LS
Monthly

Antiques Trade Gazette
Metropress Ltd,
17 Whitcomb Street,
London WC2H 7PL
Weekly

Apollo
22 Davies Street,
London W1Y 1LH
Monthly

Argento!
e una pubblicazione Argo s.r.l.
Piazza Q. Tommasini,
16–00162 Rome,
Italy

Art & Artists (*see* **Artist**)

Art of Psychotherapy, The
Anthony Storr
Penguin (Harmondsworth)

Artist (formerly Art and Artists)
The Artist Publishing Co Ltd,
Caxton House,
63–65 High Street,
Tenterden,
Kent TN30 6BD
Monthly

Artists Newsletter
Artic Producers,
PO Box 23,
Sunderland,
Tyne and Wear SR1 1EJ
Monthly

Artscribe
41 North Road,
London N7 9DP
Bi-monthly

Arts Review
Star City Ltd,
69 Faroe Road,
London W14 0EL
Fortnightly

ASA Teaching and Coaching Certificates
ASA,
Harold Fern House,
Derby Square,
Loughborough LE11 0AL

Ashley Courtenay Guides
A Courtenay
Annual

Author
Society of Authors,
84 Drayton Gardens,
London SW10 9SB
Quarterly

Autotrade
Morgan-Grampian (Publishers) Ltd,
Morgan-Grampian House,
Calderwood Street,
London SE18 6QH
Monthly

Basic Facts About Patents for Inventions in the UK
Patent Office (Marketing & Publicity),
State House,
High Holborn,
London WC1R 4TP

BBC Index
BBC Publications,
35 Marylebone High Street,
London W1M 4AA

BBC Small Business Guide
Colin Barrow
BBC Publications (London) 1982

Becoming a Solicitor
Law Society,
113 Chancery Lane,
London WC2A 1PL

Beecraft
Beecraft Ltd,
15 West Way,
Copthorne Bank,
Crawley,
West Sussex RH10 3QS
Monthly

Beekeeper's Quarterly
Northern Bee Books

Be Your Own Boss at 16
A Watts
Kogan Page (London) 1986

Be Your Own Boss – Starter Kit
National Extension College,
18 Brooklands Avenue,
Cambridge CB2 2HN

Better Mousetrap
Peter Bissel
Woodbase Publications

Bit on the Side, A
Christine Brady
William Collins (London) 1983

Blueprint
26 Cramer Street,
London W1M 3HE

Blueprint Guide to Private Investigation
Norman Smith,
Law Agency,
60 Carshalton Park Road,
Carshalton,
Surrey SM5 3SS
Monthly

Bluff Your Way in Publishing
Anne Tauté
Bluffers' Guides, Ravette
(Horsham) 1987

Boards
Yachting Press Ltd,
196 Eastern Esplanade,
Southend-on-Sea,
Essex
Nine issues pa

Body Learning
Michael Gelb
Aurum Press

Bone and Joint Surgery (Journal of)
British Editorial Society of Bone & Joint
Surgery; ads to: Ad Medica,
Stevenson,
Haddington,
East Lothian EG41 4PU
Five times per year

Book Indexing
Cambridge University Press

Bookseller
J Whitaker & Sons Ltd,
12 Dyott Street,
London WC1A 1DF
Weekly

BRAD
British Rates and Data,
Maclean Hunter Limited,
Maclean Hunter House,
Chalk Lane,
Cockfosters Road,
Barnet,
Herts EN4 0BU
Monthly

Breakthrough
Andrew Ferguson
Duncan Publishing
Available from the author
The Breakthrough Centre,
7 Poplar Mews,
Uxbridge Road,
London W12 7JS

Brewer's Guardian
Hampton Publishing Ltd,
10 Belgrade Road,
Hampton,
Middlesex TW12 2AZ

Brewing and Distilling International
Brewery Traders Publications Ltd,
Peel House,
Lichfield St,
Burton upon Trent,
Staffs DE14 3RH

Brides
The Conde Nast Publications Ltd,
Vogue House,
Hanover Square,
London W1R 0AD
Alternate months

British Alternative Theatre Directory
Conway & McGillivray,
The Conway & McGillivray Publishing
House Ltd,
22a Birchington Road,
London NW6

British Association of Concert Agents' List of Artists
British Association of Concert Agents,
12 Penzance Place,
London W11 4TA

British Bee Journal
ex C Tousley,
46 Queen Street,
Geddington,
Nr Kettering,
Northants NN14 1AZ
Monthly

British Blacksmith
NAFB & AE,
Avenue R,
7th Street,
National Agricultural Centre,
Stoneleigh,
Kenilworth,
Warwickshire CV8 2LG

British Dental Journal
Professional & Scientific Publications,
BMA House,
Tavistock Square,
London WC1H 9JR
Twice monthly

British Derivatives Markets Handbook
Charles Letts & Co Ltd,
Diary House,
77 Borough Road,
London SE1 1DW

British Jeweller
Official Journal of the British Jewellery
and Giftware Federation,
St Dunstan's House,
Carey Lane,
London EC2V 8AA
Monthly

British Journal of Photography
Henry Greenwood & Co Ltd,
234 Temple Chambers,
Temple Avenue,
London EC4Y 0DT
Weekly

British Medical Journal
BMA House,
Tavistock Square,
London WC1H 9JR
Weekly

British Music Year Book
ed Marianne Barton
Rhinegold Publishing Ltd,
239–241 Shaftesbury Avenue,
London WC2H 8EH

British Performing Arts Yearbook
Rhinegold Publishers 1988

British Printer
Maclean Hunter Ltd,
Maclean Hunter House,
Chalk Lane,
Cockfosters Road,
Barnet,
Herts EN4 0BU
Monthly

British Toy and Hobby Briefing
British Toy and Hobby Manufacturers'
Association,
80 Camberwell Road,
London SE5 0EG

British Toy Industry Handbook
British Toy and Hobby Association,
80 Camberwell Road,
London SE5 0EG

Build Your Own Rainbow
Barrie Hopson and Mike Scally
Life Skills Associates, 1984

Burlington Magazine, The
The Burlington Magazine Publications
Ltd,
6 Bloomsbury Square,
London WC1A 2LP
Monthly

Business Europe
Morris Boehm Geller
Macmillan Press 1992

Cab Trade News
Cab Trade News Co-operative Society
Ltd,
203–209 North Gower Street,
London NW1
Monthly

Cabinetmakers' Notebook
James Krenov
Van Nostrand Reinhold, 1983

Campaign
Marketing Publications Ltd,
22 Lancaster Gate,
London W2 3LY
Weekly

Car and Accessory Trader
Haymarket Publishing Ltd,
38–42 Hampton Road,
Teddington,
Middlesex TW11 0JE
Monthly

Career Change
Ruth Lancashire and RF Holdsworth
Hobsons Press (Cambridge) 1976

Careers Encyclopaedia
ed Audrey Segal
Cassell (London) 1984

Careers in Journalism
Leaflet published free by National Union
of Journalists,
Acorn House,
314 Gray's Inn Road,
London WC1X 8DP

Careers with Music
Incorporated Society of Musicians,
10 Stratford Place,
London W1

Careers in Politics
George Cunningham
Kogan Page (London) 1984

Careers in Psychology
Kogan Page Ltd,
120 Pentonville Road,
London N1 9JN

Cascade
Paul and Gabi Keasc,
Aubastrasse 7,
D-6200 Kriesbadau,
Germany
Quarterly

Caterer and Hotel Keeper
Reed Business Publishing,
Quadrant House,
The Quadrant,
Sutton,
Surrey SM2 5AS
Weekly

Cats Magazine
5 James Leigh Street,
Manchester M1 6EX

Cat World
10 Western Road,
Shoreham by Sea,
West Sussex BN43 5ND

Ceramic Review
21 Carnaby Street,
London W1V 1PH
Alternate months

Certified Accountant
Chapter Three Publications Ltd,
8a Hythe Street,
Dartford,
Kent DA1 1BX
Monthly

Changing Your Job
Godfrey Golzen and Philip Plumbley
Kogan Page Ltd (London)

**Chartered Society of Physiotherapy
Careers Handbook**
14 Bedford Row,
London WC1

Check Your Own IQ
HJ Eysenk
Penguin (Harmondsworth)

Chemical Engineer, The
Institution of Chemical Engineers,
George E Davis Building,
165 Railway Terrace,
Rugby CV21 3HQ
Monthly

Chemist & Druggist
Benn Publications Ltd,
Sovereign Way,
Tonbridge,
Kent TN9 1RW
Weekly

Childright
Children's Legal Centre,
20 Compton Terrace,
London N1

Classical Music
241 Shaftesbury Avenue,
London WC2H 8EH
Fortnightly

Cleaning
RJ Dodd Publishing,
Fairway House,
Dartmouth Road,
Forest Hill,
London SE23 3HN
Monthly

Cleaning Business News
RJ Dodd Publishing,
Fairway House,
Dartmouth Road,
Forest Hill,
London SE23 3HN
Fortnightly

Composer's Guide to Music Publishing
Association of Professional Composers

**Clinical Biomechanics (formerly British
Osteopathic Journal)**
Butterworth Scientific Ltd,
PO Box 63,
Westbury House,
Bury Street,
Guildford GU2 5BH
Quarterly

Clothing Industry Yearbook
British Clothing Industry Association,
7 Swallow Place,
London W1R 7AA

Commercial Motor
Reed Business Publishing,
Quadrant House,
The Quadrant,
Sutton,
Surrey SM2 5AS
Weekly

Community Care
Reed Business Publishing Ltd,
Carew House,
Wallington,
Surrey SM6 0DX
Weekly

Community Pharmacy
Joint Marketing & Publishing Services
Ltd,
8th Floor,
Newcombe House,
45 Notting Hill Gate,
London W11 3LQ
Monthly except December

Complete Guide to Executive Manners
L Baldridge

Complete Guide to Total Fitness
Jan Percival, Lloyd Percival and Joe
Taylor
EP Publishing (London) 1982

Computer Users' Year Book
VNU Business Publications,
VNU House,
32–34 Broadwick Street,
London W1A 2HG

Computing
VNU Business Publications,
VNU House,
32–34 Broadwick Street,
London W1A 2HG

Conference Blue Book
Spectrum Communications Group,
16–18 Acton Park Estate,
Stanley Gardens,
London W3

**Contact (Journal of British
Chiropractic Association)**
ed Peter Dixon
207 London Road East,
Batheaston,
Bath,
Avon

Contacts
Available from The Spotlight Casting
Directory & Contacts,
42 Cranbourn Street,
London WC2

Controlling Interest Rate Risk
Platt
Wiley 1986

Copy-editing
Judith Butcher
Cambridge University Press,
The Edinburgh Building,
Shaftesbury Road
Cambridge CB2 2RU

Counsel
Butterworth Law Publishers Ltd,
9–12 Bell Yard,
Temple Bar,
London WC2A 2JR
Alternate months

Country Life
IPC Magazines Ltd,
Kings Reach Tower,
Stamford Street,
London SE1 9LS
Weekly

Crafts
Crafts Council
8 Waterloo Place,
London SW1Y 4AT
Alternate months

Craftsman's Directory
ed S and J Lance
S and J Lance 1987

Craftsman's Handbook
Cennini
Dover Publications
London

**Crawford's Directory (of City
Connections)**
Economist Publications (London)
Annual

Creating Your Own Work
Micheline Mason
Cresham Books (Henley-on-Thames)

Creative Handbook
British Media Publications (East
Grinstead)

Creative Review
Centaur Communications Ltd,
St Giles House,
50 Poland Street,
London W1V 4AX
Monthly

Crescendo International
Whitehall Press Ltd,
230 Vauxhall Bridge Road,
London SW1V 1AL
Monthly

Daily Telegraph
The Daily Telegraph plc,
Peterborough Court,
South Quay,
181 Marsh Wall,
London E14 9SR
Daily

Dalton's Weekly
CI Tower,
St George's Square,
New Malden,
Surrey KT3 4JA

Dance and Dancers
Plus Publications,
248 High Street,
Croydon,
Surrey CR0 1TN
Monthly

Dance News
Dance News Ltd,
Hamble House,
Meadrow,
Godalming,
Surrey GU7 3HJ
Weekly

Dance Theatre Journal
Laban Centre,
Laurie Grove,
New Cross,
London SE14
Quarterly

Dancing Times
Clerkenwell House,
45–47 Clerkenwell Green,
London EC1R 0BE
Monthly

Debrett's Correct Form
Debrett's Peerage Ltd,
73/77 Britannia Road,
London SW6

Decanter
Decanter Magazine Ltd,
St John's Chambers,
2–10 St John's Road,
London SW11 1PN
Monthly

Dental Practice
AE Morgan Publications Ltd,
Stanley House,
9 West Street,
Epsom,
Surrey KT18 7RL
Twice monthly

Dentist
Update-Siebert Publications,
Friary Court,
13–21 High Street,
Guildford,
Surrey GU1 3DX
Eleven times pa

Design
Design Magazine,
The Design Council,
28 Haymarket,
London SW1Y 4SU
Monthly

Design Courses in Britain
The Design Council,
28 Haymarket,
London SW1Y 4SU

Designer's Journal
The Architectural Press Ltd,
9 Queen Anne's Gate,
London SW1H 9BY
Ten issues pa

Design Week
Centaur Communications Ltd,
St Giles House,
50 Poland Street,
London W1V 4AX
Weekly

Design Review
29 Bedford Square,
London WC1B 3EG
Alternate months

DeskTop Publishing Today
Industrial Media Ltd,
184–188 High Street,
Tonbridge,
Kent TN9 1BQ
Monthly

Despatch Rider
PO Box 398,
London SE13 5RW

Direct Mail Handbook
Exley

Direct Mail Magazine
Ferrary Publications Ltd,
Ground Floor,
Boundary House,
91–93 Charterhouse Street,
London EC1N 6HR
Alternate months from Feb

Direction
Marketing Publications Ltd,
30 Lancaster Gate,
London W2 3LP
Monthly

**Directory of Property Developers,
Investors and Financiers**
Building Economics Bureau,
Carlton Chambers,
Station Road,
Shortlands,
Bromley,
Kent BR2 0EY

Directory of Professional Puppeteers
The Puppet Centre Trust,
Battersea Arts Centre,
Lavender Hill,
London SW11

Dirt Bike Rider
EMAP National Publications Ltd,
Bushfield House,
Orton Centre,
Peterborough PE28 0UW
Monthly

Disco International
Mountain Lion Productions Ltd,
410 St John Street,
London EC1V 4NJ
Monthly

Dispensing Optics
Association of British Dispensing
Opticians,
6 Hurlingham Business Park,
Sulivan Road,
London SW6 3DU

DOG
New Opportunity Press Ltd,
London

Dog Business
Douglas Appleton
Popular Dogs (London) 1960

Drapers Record
International Thomson Publishing Ltd,
100 Avenue Road,
London NW3
Weekly

Driving
Driving Instructors' Association,
Lion Green Road,
Coulsdon,
Surrey CR3 2NL
Alternate months

Driving Instructor's Manual
Kogan Page (London)

Economist
25 St James's Street,
London SW1A 1HG
Weekly

Editing and Design
Five-volume manual of English
typography and layout
Harold Evans
William Heinemann (London) 1972–76

**Education and Training of Entrants to
the Solicitors Profession**
Law Society,
113 Chancery Lane,
London W2A 1PL

Egon Ronay
Greencoat House,
Francis Street,
London SW1
Annual

EFL Gazette
10 Wrights Lane,
London W8 6JA
Monthly

Embalmer
British Institute of Embalmers,
21c Station Road,
Knowle,
Solihull,
West Midlands B93 0HL
Six times a year

Employing Jobsharers, Part-time and Temporary Staff
Michael Syrett, 1983
Institute of Personnel Management,
35 Camp Road,
London SW19

Employment for Disabled People
Mary Thompson
Kogan Page (London)

Equal Opportunities, A Career Guide (for Women and Men)
Ruth Miller and Anna Alston
Penguin (Harmondsworth) 1987

Equestrian Trade News (Journal of British Equestrian Industry)
Wothersome Grange,
Bramham,
Nr Wetherby,
Yorks LS23 6LY
Monthly

Essential Law for Journalists
Macrae
Butterworth 1988

Estate Agent
National Association of Estate Agents,
21 Jury Street,
Warwick

Estates Gazette
The Estates Gazette Ltd,
151 Wardour Street,
London W1V 4BN
Weekly

Euromoney
Euromoney (Publications) plc
(London)
Monthly

Euronews Construction
Department of the Environment,
2 Marsham Street,
London SW1

European, The
Orbit House,
5 New Fetter Lane,
London EC4A 1AP

European Communities: General Guidance for Doctors
BMA,
BMA House,
Tavistock Square,
London WC1H 9JP

European Community (3rd edn)
B Morris & K Boehm
Macmillan Press 1990

Europe Open for Professions
Department of Trade & Industry
1-19 Victoria Street,
London SW1H 0ET

Executive Post
available from Fitzwilliam House,
2 Fitzwilliam Gate,
Sheffield S1 4JH
Weekly

Exhibition Bulletin
The London Bureau,
266–272 Kirkdale,
Sydenham,
London SE26 4RZ

Export
Institute of Export,
64 Clifton Street,
London EC2A 4HB
Monthly

FAB Cattery Construction and Management Manual
Feline Advisory Bureau,
235 Upper Richmond Road,
London SW15 6SN

Farmers' Weekly
The Farmers Publishing Group,
Reed Business Publishing,
Carew House,
Wallington,
Surrey SM6 0DX
Weekly

Fashion Extras
Reflex Publishing Ltd,
86 Clarendon Road,
Croydon,
Surrey CR0 3SG
Monthly

Fashion Weekly
Minot Ltd,
172–174 Tottenham Court Road,
London W1P 9LG
Weekly

Film and Televison Training
British Film Institute

Financial Decisions
VNU Business Publications,
VNU House,
32–34 Broadwick Street,
London W1A 2HG
Monthly

Financial Times
The Financial Times Ltd,
Bracken House,
10 Cannon Street,
London EC4P 4BY
Daily

Fire and Design for Schools (Bulletin No.7)
DES (Department of Education and Science)

First Ten Years
Incorporated Society of Musicians,
10 Stratford Place,
London W1N 9AE

First Voice
Magazine of the National Federation of Self-Employed and Small Businesses Ltd,
YCG,
17a Monckton Road,
Wakefield,
West Yorkshire WF2 7AL
Alternate months

Fish Farmer
Amber Publications,
34 Amberley Drive,
Woodham,
Weybridge,
Surrey KT15 3SL
Alternate months

Fish Farming International
Heighway Publications Ltd,
81–89 Farringdon Road,
London EC1M 3LL
Monthly

Fishing News Books
Blackwell Scientific Publications,
Osney Mead,
Oxford OX2 0EL

Five Day Course in Thinking
Edward de Bono
Pelican (Harmondsworth)

Forge
Avenue R,
7th Street,
Agricultural Centre,
Stoneleigh,
Kenilworth,
Warwickshire CV8 2LG
Alternate months

Franchise International
Franchise Information Centre,
Castle House,
Norwich NR2 1PJ

Franchise Magazine
Franchise Development Services Ltd,
Castle House,
Castle Meadow,
Norwich,
Norfolk NR2 1PJ
Quarterly

Franchise World
James House,
37 Nottingham Road,
London SW17 7EA
Alternate months

Free House
Libor Publications Ltd,
65 Blandford Street,
London WIH 3AJ
Monthly

Freelance Alternative
Marianne Gray
Piatkus Books (London) 1987

Freelance Photographer's Market Handbook
ed John Tracy and Stewart Gibson
Bureau of Freelance Photographers,
Focus House,
Green Lanes,
London N13

Freight
Freight Transport Association,
Hermes House,
St John's Road,
Tunbridge Wells,
Kent TN4 9U2

Fundamentals of Advertising, The
John Wilmshurst
William Heinemann (London) 1985

Futures
Oster Inc,
219 Parkaid,
PO Box 6,
Ceddar Falls,
Iowa 50613,
USA

Futures and Options World
Metal Bulletin,
Park House,
3 Park Terrace,
Worcester Park,
Surrey KT4 7HY

Galleries
Barrington Publications
(London)
Monthly

Garage Equipment (Garage and Automotive Retailer)
AGB Hulton Ltd,
Warwick House,
Azalea Drive,
Swanley,
Kent BR8 8JF
Monthly

Garage and Transport (Group Selector)
AGB Hulton Ltd,
Warwick House,
Swanley,
Kent BR8 8JF
Quarterly

Garden
Journal of the Royal Horticultural
Society,
Home and Law Publishing Ltd,
Greater London House,
Hampstead Road,
London NW1 7QZ
Monthly

Garden Centre Manual
Grower Books

Gateway to Europe
NEDO

General Practice for the Single European Market
RICS
12 Great George Street,
Parliament Square,
London SW1P 3AD

Geriatric Medicine and Gerontology
Brockelhurst

Going For It! How to Succeed as an Entrepreneur
V Kiam
Fontana (London) 1986

GNI Guide to Traded Options
Macmillan Press,
London

Going Freelance
Godfrey Golzen
Riverside Books (London) 1985

Goldsmiths Gazette
Goldsmiths Company,
Goldsmiths Hall,
Foster Lane,
London EC2

Good Communications Guide
National ISIS,
56 Buckingham Gate,
London SW1E 6AG

Good Food Guide
Hodder and Stoughton
(Sevenoaks) London
Annual

Good Hotel Guide
Macmillan London Limited
Annual

Good Times, Bad Times
Harold Evans
Hodder & Stoughton 1984

Graduate Post
Newpoint Publishing Co Ltd,
Newpoint House,
St James's Lane,
London N10 3DF
Fortnightly

Grape Press
English Vineyards Association,
38 West Park,
London SE9 4RH
Quarterly

Greatest Little Business Book, The
Peter Hingston
Hingston

Grove's Dictionary of Music (New)
ed Stanley Sadie
Macmillan (London) 1980

Grower
50 Doughty Street,
London WC1N 2LP
Weekly

Guardian
119 Farringdon Road,
London EC1R 3ER
Daily

Guidelines for Inspection of Boarding Establishments
British Veterinary Association,
7 Mansfield Street,
London W1A 0AT

Guide to Courses and Careers in Art, Craft and Design
NSEAD,
7a High Street,
Corsham,
Wiltshire SN13 0ES

GZ European Jeweller
GKC,
Heathfield Sandy Lane,
Dereham,
Norfolk NR19 2QA

Hairdressers' Journal International
Reed Business Publishing,
Quadrant House,
The Quadrant,
Sutton,
Surrey SM2 5AS
Weekly

Handbook Royal College of General Practitioners
14 Princes Gate,
London SW7

Hansard
HMSO,
St Crispins,
Duke Street,
Norwich NR3 1PD

Hart's Rules for Compositors and Readers
Oxford University Press,
Walton Street,
Oxford OX2 6DP
39th edition 1989

Here's Health
Argus Health Publications Ltd,
Victory House,
Leicester Place,
London WC2H 7NB
Monthly

Hi-Fi Choice
Dennis Publishing,
14 Rathbone Place,
London W1P 1DE
Monthly

Hi-Fi News and Record Review
Link House Magazines Ltd,
Dingwall Avenue,
Croydon CR9 2TA
Monthly

Hireman
Hireman Publishing Ltd,
174 Park Road,
Peterborough PE1 2UF
Monthly

Hire News
Response Publishing Ltd,
Wentworth House,
Wentworth Street,
Peterborough PE1 1DS
Monthly

Hollis (Press and PR Annual)
Contact House,
Sunbury-on-Thames,
Middlesex TW16 5HG

Home and Studio Recording
Music Maker Publications,
Alexander House,
Forehill,
Ely,
Cambridgeshire CB7 4AF
Monthly

Homeopathy; Medicine for the 21st century
Ullman
North Atlantic Books 1987

Honourable Member
Richard Needham
Patrick Stephens
(Wellingborough) 1983

Horse and Hounds
IPC Magazines Ltd,
Kings Reach Tower,
Stamford Street,
London SE1 9LS
Weekly

Horticulture Week
Haymarket Publishing,
38–42 Hampton Road,
Teddington,
Middx TW11 0JE
Weekly

House Magazine
Parliamentary Communications Ltd,
12–13 Clerkenwell Green,
London EC1R 0DP
Weekly

How Parliament Works
Paul Silk
Longman (London) 1987

How to Build a Successful Multi-level Marketing Organisation
Don Failla
Multi-level Marketing International Inc,
PO Box 889,
Gig Harbour,
WA 98335,
USA

How to Choose Business Premises
Kogan Page

How to Evaluate a Franchise
Martin Mendelsohn
Available from Franchise World,
James House,
37 Nottingham Road,
London SW17 7EA

How to Get Control of Your Time and Your LIfe
Alan Laikein
Signe, 1973

How to Start and Run Your Own Business
M Mogano
Graham and Trotman (London) 1985

How to Win Customers
Heinz Goldman
Pan (London)

Hypnosis
Ursula Markham
Macdonald Optima (London) 1987

Hypnosis: A Gateway to Better Health
Dr Brian Roet
Weidenfeld & Nicolson (London)

Hypnosis: Guide for Patients and Practitioners
David Waxman
Unwin (London)

Ideas for Self-Employment and Part-Time Work
T Crawley
Careers Consultants (Richmond) 1983

In Europe: Social Work Education and 1992
In Europe: Links and Exchanges
Central Council for Education and
Training in Social Work,
Derbyshire House,
St Chad's Street,
London WC1H 8AD

Incorporated Society of Musicians' Arts Festival Book
Incorporated Society of Musicians,
10 Stratford Place,
London W1

Independent
Newspaper Publishing plc,
40 City Road,
London EC1Y 2DB
Daily

Indexing, The Art:
A guide to the indexing of books and
periodicals.
G. Norman Knight
Allen & Unwin
Available only from the Society of
Indexers

Individual Therapy in Britain
Windy Dryden
Harper and Row (London) 1984

Initiative
PO Box 85,
50 Gray's Inn Road,
London WC1X 8XU
Monthly

Inside Book Publishing: A Career Builder's Guide
Giles N Clark
Blueprint Publishing Ltd/Book House
Training Centre

**Inside the Technical Consultancy
Business**
H Kaye
John Wiley (Chichester) 1986

Instrumental Orchestration
Alfred Blatter
Longman

Insurance
RICS Insurance Services Ltd,
Plantation House,
31–35 Fenchurch Street,
London EC3M 3DX

Insurance Journal
Chartered Insurance Institute,
20 Aldermanbury,
London EC2V 7HY

International Broker
Risk and Insurance Research Group

**International Newsletter of Music
Therapy**
AAMT (USA)

International Zoo News
73 Molesworth Street,
Wadelridge,
Cornwall PL27 7D8

International Zoo Yearbook
The Zoological Society of London,
Regent's Park,
London NW1 4RY

**Introducing Patents: A Guide for
Inventors**
Patent Office (Marketing & Publicity),
State House,
High Holborn,
London WC1R 4TP

Investigator's Library
Norman Smith
60 Carshalton Park Road,
Carshalton,
Surrey SM5 3SS

Investors' Chronicle
Financial Times Business Information
Ltd,
Greystoke Place,
Fetter Lane,
London EC4A 1ND
Weekly

Jazz Directory
from Jazz Services
5 Dryden Street,
London WC2E 9NW

Jazz Express
29 Romilly Road,
London W1V 6HP

Jazz Journal International
Jazz Journal Ltd,
35 Great Russell Street,
London WC1B 3PP
Monthly

Jazz Newspapers
26 The Balcony,
Castle Arcade,
Cardiff CF1 2BY

Job Ideas
COIC (Careers and Occupational
Information Centre),
Manpower Services Commission,
Moorfoot,
Sheffield S1 4PQ

Job Sharing
Atkinson
Institute of Manpower Studies,
Mansell Building,
University of Sussex,
Falmer,
Brighton,
Sussex

Jocks
Spotlight Publications Ltd,
Greater London House,
Hampstead Road,
London NW1 7QZ
Monthly

**Journal of Alternative and
Complementary Medicine**
Argus Health Publications Ltd,
Victory House,
Leicester Place,
London WC2H 7NB
Monthly

Journal of British Podiatric Medicine
Society of Chiropodists
53 Welbeck Street,
London W1M 7HE
Monthly

Journal of Osteopathic Education
General Council and Register of
Osteopaths,
56 London Street,
Reading,
Berkshire RG1 4SQ
Three times yearly, by subscription

Kennel and Cattery Management
Gladeside-Ardent Ltd,
PO Box 45,
Dorking,
Surrey RH5 5YZ

Know Your Own IQ
HJ Eysenk
Penguin (Harmondsworth)

Lady
39–40 Bedford Street,
London WC2E 9ER
Weekly

Laing's Review of Private Health Care
Laing and Buisson Ltd,
1 Perrin Street,
London NW5

Lancet
The Lancet Ltd,
46 Bedford Square,
London WC1B 3SL
Weekly

Landscape Design
5a West Street,
Reigate,
Surrey RH2 9BL
Alternate months from February

Law of Betting, Gaming and Lotteries
CM Smith and SP Monkcom
Butterworths

Law of Burial, Cremation and Exhumation
Mr Russell Davis
Shaw and Sons Ltd,
Shaway House,
Lower Sydenham,
London SE26 5AE

Legal 500
Jon Pritchard
Legalease 1989

Licensed Conveyancer
Journal of the Society of Licensed
Conveyancers,
35 Church Road,
Croydon CR9 1PF

Licensee
National Licensed Victuallers'
Association,
Boardman House,
2 Downing Street,
Farnham,
Surrey GU9 7NX
Monthly

Light on Pranayama
BKS Iyengar
George Allen & Unwin (London)

Light on Yoga
BKS Iyengar
George Allen & Unwin (London)

List 99
DES
London

Litho Week
Haymarket Publishing Ltd,
38–42 Hampton Road,
Teddington,
Middlesex TW11 0JE
Weekly

London Biker
Unit A,
183 Bow Road,
London E3

Look After Yourself
Health Education Council,
78 New Oxford Street,
London WC1A 1AH

Making Waves
ed David Butler
Artic Producers Publishing Company

Managing Negotiations
G Kennedy, J Benson and J McMillan
Business Books (London) 1986

Marketing
Marketing Publications Ltd
22 Lancaster Gate,
London W2 3LY
Weekly

Marketing
Eddie Martin
Mitchell Beazley

Marketing for the Small Firm
Rick Brown
Cassell (London)

Marketing Week
Centaur Communications Ltd,
St Giles House,
50 Poland Street,
London W1V 4AX
Weekly

Match Weekly
EMAP Pursuit Publishing Ltd,
Bretton Court,
Peterborough,
Cambs PE3 8DZ
Weekly

Media Week
Media Week Ltd,
20–22 Wellington Street,
London WC2E 7DD
Weekly

Megatrends
John Naisbitt
Futura (London)

Memoirs of a Tattooist
George Burchett

Michelin Guides
Michelin,
France

Micro Decision
VNU Business Publications,
VNU House,
32–34 Broadwick Street,
London W1A 2HG
Monthly

Microscope
Dennis Publishing,
14 Rathbone Place,
London W1P 2HB
Weekly

Miller's Professional Antique Price Guide
Miller's Publications (Cranbrook)
Annual

Money for Business
Bank of England

Money into Light
John Boorman
Faber (London) 1985

Money Magazine
Money Magazine Ltd,
Thames House,
18 Park Street,
London SE1 9ER

Money Management
Financial Times Business Information,
Greystoke Place,
Fetter Lane,
London EC4A 1ND
Monthly

Morning Advertiser
13–27 Brunswick Place,
London N1 6DX
Daily

Motor Cycle News
8 Herbal Hill,
London EC1R 5JB
Weekly

Motor Transport
Reed Business Publishing,
Quadrant House,
The Quadrant,
Sutton,
Surrey
Weekly

Musical Times
Novello & Co Ltd,
8 Lower James Street,
London W1R 4DN
Monthly

Music and Musicians
7–9 Greenland Place,
London NW1 0AP
Monthly

Music Journal
Incorporated Society of Musicians,
10 Stratford Place,
London W1N 9AE
Monthly

Music Teacher
Rhinegold Publishing Ltd,
241 Shaftesbury Avenue,
London WC2H 8EH
Monthly

Musician
Rhinegold Publishing Ltd,
241 Shaftesbury Avenue,
London WC2H 8EH
Quarterly

Musician's Handbook
Rhinegold Publishing Ltd,
239–241 Shaftesbury Avenue,
London WC2H 8EH

National Directory of Women's Business and Reference Guide 1990
Women in Enterprise,
St Gabriel's House,
24 Labernum Road,
Wakefield WF1 3QS

National Federation of Music Societies' Handbook
National Federation of Music Societies,
Francis House,
Francis Street,
London SW1

National Trust Magazine
The Publishing Consultancy Ltd,
15 Adeline Place,
London WC1B 3AJ
Tri-annually

Negotiator
FB Corporate Image Ltd,
Fotoscript House,
Jubilee Close,
Townsend Lane,
Kingsbury,
London NW9 8TR
Fortnightly

Neues Glas
Obtainable from Verlagsanstalt
Handwerk Gmbh,
AUFM Tetleberg 7,
4000 Dusseldorf 1,
Germany
or from Crafts Council Bookshop,
12 Waterloo Place,
London SW1Y 4AU

New English Vineyard
Joanna Smith
Sidgwick & Jackson Ltd (London) 1979

New Musical Express
Holborn Publishing Group,
IPC Magazines Ltd,
Room 330,
Commonwealth House,
1–19 New Oxford Street,
London WC1A 1NG
Weekly

Notes of Guidance for Proprietors on the Registration of Independent Schools
Registrar of Independent Schools,
Scottish Education Department,
New St Andrew's House,
Edinburgh EH1 3SY

Nursery World
Nursery World Ltd,
The Schoolhouse Workshop,
51 Calthorpe Street,
London WC1X 0HH
Fortnightly

Nurseryman and Garden Centre (N & GC)
Benn Business Magazines,
Monchelsea Farm,
Boughton Monchelsea,
Maidstone,
Kent ME17 4JD

Nursing Standard
Scutari Publications,
17–19 Peterborough Road,
Harrow-on-the-Hill,
Middlesex HA1 2AX
Weekly

Nursing: The European Dimension
Scutari

Nursing Times
Macmillan Magazines Ltd,
4 Little Essex Street,
London WC2R 3LF
Weekly

Occupation – Self-Employed
Rosemary Pettit
Wildwood House Ltd (Aldershot) 1981

Occupations
Careers and Occupational Centre
Annual (Sheffield)

Offensive Marketing
Hugh Davidson
Penguin (Harmondsworth)

Ogilvy on Advertising
David Ogilvy
Pan (London)

Old Bike Mart
PO Box 7,
Poynton,
Stockport,
Cheshire

On Being a Counsellor
E Kennedy
Macmillan (London)

On Board Windsurfing Magazine
The DRG Building,
Longmoor Lane,
Breaston,
Derby DE7 3BQ
Monthly

One Minute Manager, The
Kenneth Blanchard and Spencer Johnson
Fontana (London)

One Minute Sales Person
Spencer Johnson
Fontana (London)

Optician
Reed Business Publishing Ltd,
Quadrant House,
The Quadrant,
Sutton,
Surrey SM2 5AS
Weekly

Optometry Today
Bridge House,
233–4 Blackfriars Road,
London SE1 8NW

Orchestration
Cecil Forsyth
Dover (London) 1986

l'orafo, italiano
Via Nervesa, 2,
20139 Milan,
Italy

Osteopathy
Stephen Sandler
Pan (London) 1987

Oxford Writers' Dictionary
Oxford University Press 1981

Paint Magic
Jocasta Innes
Windward and Berger Paints (Leicester)

Panel News
Irchin,
23a Hawthorn Drive,
Heswall,
Wirral,
Merseyside L61 6UP
Quarterly

Parliament and the Public
Edmund Marshall
Macmillan (London) 1982

Parliament in the 1980s
Philip Norton
Basil Blackwell (Oxford) 1985

Pathfinders: How to achieve happiness by conquering life's crises
Gail Sheehy
Sidgwick and Jackson

PC User
EMAP Business and Computer
Publications,
155 Farringdon Road,
London EC1R 3AD
Fortnightly

PC Week
VNU Business Publications,
VNU House,
32–34 Broadwick Street,
London W1A 2HG
Weekly

PC Yearbook
VNU Business Publications,
VNU House,
32–34 Broadwick Street,
London W1A 2HG
Annual

Penguin Guide to the Law
Penguin (Harmondsworth)

Personnel Managers Yearbook
AP Information Services Ltd,
33 Ashbourne Avenue,
London NW11 0DU

Pharmaceutical Journal
The Pharmaceutical Society of Great
Britain,
1 Lambeth High Street,
London SE1 7JN
Weekly

Photographer
Penblade Publishers Ltd,
1 Gayford Road,
London W12 9BY
Monthly

Photo Journalism
Arthur Rothstein
American Photographic Book Publishing
Co

Physiotherapy
Journal of the Chartered Society of
Physiotherapy,
14 Bedford Row,
London WC1R 4ED
Monthly

Picture Researchers Handbook
Van Nostrand (UK)

Pictures on a Page; Photojournalism, Graphics and Picture Editing
Harold Evans
Heinemann Professional Publishing (London)

Picture Sources UK
Ed Rosemary Eakins
Macdonald

Pierced Hearts and True Love
Hans Ebensen

PIMS Media Directory
PIMS (London) Ltd,
4 St John's Place,
London EC1
Monthly

Please Follow Me
Don Cross,
Available from Wessexplore,
20 Coldharbour Lane,
Salisbury,
Wilts SP2 8BY

Practical Boat Owner
IPC Magazines Ltd,
Westover House,
West Quay Road,
Poole,
Dorset BH15 1JG
Monthly

Practical Guide to Making at Home, A
Olga Franklin
Macdonald (London) 1981

Practical Upholstering and the Cutting of Loose Covers
Frederick Palmer

Practical Woodworking
IPC Magazines Ltd,
Kings Reach Tower,
Stamford Street,
London SE1 9LS
Monthly

Precision Marketing
Centaur Communications Ltd
St Giles House
49–50 Poland Street
London W1V 4AX

Pricing Your Work for Profit
Norman Smith Law Agency
60 Carshalton Park Road,
Carshalton,
Surrey SM5 3SS

Principles and Practice of Embalming
Strub and Frederick
Lawrence G Frederick,
1827 Maryvale Drive,
Dallas,
Texas 75208,
USA

Printing World
Benn Publications Ltd,
Sovereign Way,
Tonbridge,
Kent TN9 1RW
Weekly

Private Eye
Presdram Limited,
6 Carlisle Street,
London W1
Fortnightly

Professional Conduct of Solicitors
ed Peter Camp
Law Society 1987

Professional Partnerships – Facing the Future
Spicer and Pegler,
65 Crutched Friars,
London EC3N 2NI

Profitable Garden Centre Manegement
Reston Publications

Pro Sound News
Link House,
Dingwall Avenue,
Croydon CR9 2TA
Monthly

PR Week
Rangenine Ltd,
100 Fleet Street,
London EC4Y 1DE
Weekly

Psychologist
British Psychological Society,
St Andrew's House,
48 Princes Road East,
Leicester LE1 7DR

Psychology of Interpersonal Behaviour
M Argyle
Penguin (Harmondsworth) 1984

Pub Caterer
Reed Business Publishing,
Quadrant House,
The Quadrant,
Sutton,
Surrey SM2 5AS
Ten times a year

Publican
Maclaren Publishers Ltd,
PO Box 109,
Maclaren House,
Scarbrook Road,
Croydon CR9 1QH
Twice monthly

Publisher (The)
Macro Publishing Ltd,
Conbar House,
Mead Lane,
Hertford,
Herts SG13 7AS
Monthly

Publishers' Freelance Directory
Elvendon Press,
The Old Surgery,
High Street,
Goring-on-Thames,
Reading,
Berks RG8 9AW

Publishing News
Tradegate Ltd,
43 Museum Street,
London WC1A 1LY
Weekly

RAC Guides
RAC Publications (London)
Annual

Racing Post
120 Coombes Lane,
Rayners Park,
London SW20 0BA
Daily

Ratel
Association of British Wild Animal
Keepers,
12 Tackley Road,
Eastville,
Bristol BS5 6UQ

Record Mirror
Punch Publications Ltd,
Ludgate House,
245 Blackfriars Road,
London SE1 9UZ

Reflexology
T Unwin and JM Foulkes
Cockatrice Press

Retail Jeweller
International Thomson Business
Publishing,
100 Avenue Road,
Swiss Cottage,
London NW3 3TP
Fortnightly

Road Racer
Road Racer Ltd,
Myatt McFarlane Publishing,
PO Box 28,
Altrincham,
Cheshire WA15 8SH
Alternate months

**ROGET (Register of Graduate
Employment and Training)**
AGCAS,
Central Services Unit,
Crawford House,
Precinct Centre,
Oxford Road,
Manchester M13 9EP

Roget's Thesaurus
Longman (London)

Roset
Law Society

Royal Doulton Figures
Desmond Eyles, Richard Dennis, Louise
Irving
Royal Doulton and Richard Dennis

Running Your Own Boarding Kennels
Sheila Zabawa
Kogan Page (London)

Running Your Own Catering Business
Kogan Page (London)

Running Your Own Driving School
Kogan Page (London)

Savoy Cocktail Book
Muller, Blond & White Ltd,
55–57 Great Ormond Street,
London WC1N 3HZ

Schools Book
Papermac (London)

Science of Homeopathy
George Vithoukas
Dawson Publications

Scottish Farmer
Holmes McDougall (Magazine Division),
The Plaza Tower,
The Plaza,
East Kilbride,
Glasgow G74 1LW
Weekly

Scottish Fish Farmer
PO Box 1,
Oban,
Argyll PA34 5PY
Monthly

**Scribe: Journal of the Society of
Scribes and Illuminators**
54 Boileau Road,
London SW13 9BL

Seafood International
AGB Heighway Ltd,
Cloister Court,
22–26 Farringdon Lane,
London EC1R 3AU
Monthly

**Secret Self, A Comprehensive Guide to
Handwriting Analysis**
Anna Koren
Adama Books

Selection
Institute of Management Consultants

Self-Sufficiency 16–25
R Bourne and J Gould
Kogan Page (London) 1983

Setting Up in Practice
Leaflet from RICS Publications
Department,
Norden House,
Basing View,
Basingstoke RG21 2HN

Shoe and Leather News
84–88 Great Eastern Street,
London EC2A 3ED
Weekly

Shoe Trade Directory
84–88 Great Eastern Street,
London EC2A 3ED
Annual

Shoot
IPC Magazines Ltd,
Berkshire House,
168–173 High Holborn,
London WC1 7AU
Weekly

Single Market: The Facts
DTI
1-19 Victoria Street,
London SW1H 0ET

Single Market News
DTI
1-19 Victoria Street,
London SW1H 0ET

Skills of Negotiating
B Scott
Gower (Aldershot) 1981

Ski Survey
The Ski Club of Great Britain 118 Eaton
Square,
London SW1W 9AF
*Five times a year (September, October,
November, December, February)*

Small Business Guide
Colin Barrow
BBC

Social Work Today
Macmillan Magazines Ltd,
4 Little Essex Street,
London WC2R 3LF
Weekly

Sound Recording Practice
Association of Professional Recording
Services,
2 Windsor Square,
Silver Street,
Reading,
Berkshire RG1 2TH

Spare-Time Income
Peter Farrell
Kogan Page (London)

Special Needs Drama Directory
ILEA Cockpit Theatre and Arts
Workshop

Spending Advertising Money
Simon Broadbent
Business Books Ltd (London) 1975

Spotlight (Casting Directory)
42 Cranbourn Street,
London WC2

Stage
Carson & Comerford Ltd,
47 Bermondsey Street,
London SE1 3XT
Weekly

Standard Handbook of Consulting Engineering Practice
Hicks and Mueller
McGraw-Hill (Maidenhead) 1985

Starting up in Practice
Susan Hay
Royal Institute of British Architects,
66 Portland Place,
London W1N 4AD

Starting Your Own Business
Consumers' Association (London)

Stress Check
Cary Cooper
Prentice Hall International,
66 Wood Lane End,
Hemel Hempstead,
Herts, 1975

Student Book, The
Klaus Boehm and Jenny Lees-Spalding
Annual

Student Handbook
(Higher Education in the European Community)
Kogan Page

Studio Sound
Link House Magazines Ltd,
Link House,
Dingwall Avenue,
Croydon CR9 2TA
Monthly

Sunday Times
Times Newspapers,
PO Box 496,
Virginia Street,
London E1 9XJ
Weekly

Swimming Teaching and Coaching to Level 1
ASA,
Harold Fern House,
Derby Square,
Loughborough LE11 0AL

Swimming Times
Amateur Swimming Association
Monthly

Symmetric System of Big Game Head Mounting
Fred Crandall
Available from Crowcraft,
Orchard Farm,
Escrick Road,
Wheldrake,
York YO4 6BQ

Systems International
Reed Business Publishing,
Quadrant House,
The Quadrant,
Sutton,
Surry SM2 5AS
Monthly

Taking Stock
Charles Handy
BBC Publications (London) 1983

Taxidermy
J Metcalf
Duckworth 1981

Tax Intelligence
Simmons
Butterworth (London)

Taxi
Licensed Taxi Drivers' Association,
9–11 Woodfield Road,
London W9 2BA
Fortnightly

Teach Yourself Bookkeeping
AT Piper
Hodder and Stoughton

Teaching Your Child to Swim
Usbourne Publishing

Technique of Radio Production
Robert MacLeish
Focal Press 1978

Thatch
Bob West
David and Charles (London) 1987

Thatch (Newsmagazine)
Thatching Advisory Service Ltd,
Rose Tree Farm,
29 Nine Mile Ride,
Finchampstead,
Wokingham,
Berks RG11 4QD

Thatcher's Craft
Rural Development Commission,
11 Cowley Street,
London SW1P 3NA

Think and Grow Rich
Napoleon Hill
Wiltshire

Third Wave
Alvin Toffler
Pan (London)

Thomson Local Directories
Thomson Directories,
Thomson House,
296 Farnborough Road,
Farnborough,
Hants GU14 7NU

Tiles and Tiling
Hyperion Publishing Company Ltd,
Vale House,
32 Vale Road,
Bushey,
Watford,
Herts
Eight times a year

Time Magazine
Time-Life International BV,
5 Ottho Heldingstraat,
1066 AZ,
Amsterdam,
The Netherlands (UK Office: Time &
Life Building, New Bond Street, London
W1)
Weekly

Times
Times Newspapers Ltd,
PO Box 496,
Virginia Street,
London E1 9XJ
Daily

Times Educational Supplement, The
Priory House,
St John's Lane,
London EC1M 4BX
Weekly

Towards the End of the Morning
Michael Frayn
Collins 1967

Trading in Oil Futures
Clubley
Woodhead-Faulkner 1980

Tradition of English Wine, A
Hugh Barty-King
Oxford Illustrated Press (Oxford) 1977

Travel News
ABC Travel Publications Ltd,
242 Vauxhall Bridge Road,
London SW1V 1AU
Weekly

Travel Trade Gazette
Morgan Grampian House,
30 Calderwood Street,
London SE18 6QH
Weekly

Truth About Publishing
Sir Stanley Unwin
Penguin (Harmondsworth)

TV Today
47 Bermondsey Street,
London SE1

UK Franchise Directory
Franchise Information Centre,
Castle House,
Norwich NR2 1PJ

UK Press Gazette
Bouverie Publishing Co Ltd,
Rooms 244–249 Temple Chambers,
Temple Avenue,
London EC4Y 0DT
Weekly

Unashamed Accompanist
Gerald Moore
Methuen (London) 1943

Understand Your Accounts
H Price
Kogan Page (London)

Upholstery
Desmond Gaston
William Collins (London) 1982

Use of The Self
FM Alexander
Gollancz (London)

Veterinary Record
British Veterinary Association,
7 Mansfield Street,
London W1M 0AT
Weekly

Vinegrowing in Britain
Gillian Pearkes
JM Dent (London) 1982

Vineyards of England, The
Stephen Skelton
SP & L Skelton 1989

Way to Write Radio Drama, The
Bill Ash
Elmtree Books

Westminster Blues
Julian Critchley
Hamish Hamilton (London) 1985

Westminster Man: A Tribal Anthropology of the Commons People
Austin Mitchell
Methuen (London) 1982

What Colour is your Parachute?
Richard Bolles
Ten Speed Press, 1983

What Hi-Fi?
Haymarket Publishing Ltd
London
Monthly

What to do When Someone Dies
Consumers' Association,
14 Buckingham Street,
London WC2

What's Brewing
The Campaign for Real Ale (CAMRA),
34 Alma Road,
St Albans,
Herts AL1 3BW
Monthly

Where to Ride
British Horse Society,
British Equestrian Centre,
Stoneleigh,
Kenilworth,
Warwickshire CV8 2LR

Where to Study
Compiled by Edward Martin
BIPP,
Henry Greenwood & Co Ltd,
20 Great James Street,
London WC1N 3HL

Willings Press Guide
British Media Publications 1989

Windsurf
Ocean Publications,
34 Buckingham Palace Road,
London SW1W 0QP
Nine issues a year

Windsurf Magazine
Arkwinds Ltd,
The Coach House,
Medcroft Road,
Tackley,
Oxfordshire OX5 3AH

Wine
The EVRO Publishing Co Ltd,
5–6 Church Street,
Twickenham,
Middlesex TW1 3NJ
Monthly

Woman in your own Right, A
Anne Dickson
Quartet Books (London) 1982

Woman's Wear Resources
Woman's Wear Resources Ltd,
25–26 Poland Street,
London W1V 3DB
Monthly

Woodworker
Argus Specialist Publications Ltd,
1 Golden Square,
London W1R 3AB
Monthly

Work for Yourself
Paddy Hall
National Extension College,
18 Brooklands Avenue,
Cambridge CB2 2HN

Working Abroad
Employment Service,
Overseas Placing Unit (OPS 5),
c/o Moorfoot,
Sheffield S1 4PQ

Working in the European Communities
AJ Raban

World Soccer
Websters Publications Ltd,
Onslow House,
60–66 Saffron Hill,
London EC1N 8AY
Monthly

Working for Yourself
Godfrey Golzen
Kogan Page (London)

Working Mother – A Practical Handbook
Litvinoff and M Velmans
Corgi Books (London)

Writers' and Artists' Yearbook
A & C Black Ltd (London)
Annual

Writer's Handbook
Barry Turner
Macmillan (London) 1988

Writing for Television
Gerald Kelsay
A & C Black

Yachting (Monthly)
IPC Magazines Ltd,
Room 2215,
Kings Reach Tower,
Stamford Street,
London SE1 9LS
Monthly

Yachts and Yachting
Yachting Press Ltd,
196 Eastern Esplanade,
Southend-on-Sea
Fortnightly

Yellow Pages
British Telecom

Yoga – A Gem for Women
Geeta S Iyengar
Allied Publishers Private Ltd

Yoga Journal – The Magazine for Conscious Living
PO Box 6076,
Syracuse,
NY 13217,
USA

Yoga and Health
Surgery Advertising,
64 High Street,
Lewes,
East Sussex BN7 1XG

Index